BUSINESS ECONOMICS AND MANAGERIAL DECISION MAKING

BUSINESS ECONOMICS AND MANAGERIAL DECISION MAKING

Trefor Jones

Manchester School of Management
UMIST

JOHN WILEY & SONS, LTD

Other Wiley Editorial Offices

John Wiley & Sons, Inc., 111 River Street, Hoboken, NJ 07030, USA

Jossey-Bass, 989 Market Street, San Francisco, CA 94103-1741, USA

Wiley-VCH Verlag GmbH, Boschstr. 12, D-69469 Weinheim, Germany

John Wiley & Sons Australia Ltd, 33 Park Road, Milton, Queensland 4064, Australia

John Wiley & Sons (Asia) Pte Ltd, 2 Clementi Loop #02-01, Jin Xing Distripark, Singapore 129809

John Wiley & Sons Canada Ltd, 22 Worcester Road, Etobicoke, Ontario, Canada M9W 1L1

Wiley also publishes its books in a variety of electronic formats. Some content that appears
in print may not be available in electronic books.

Library of Congress Cataloging-in-Publication Data

Jones, T.T. (Trefor T.)
  Business economics and managerial decision making / Trefor Jones.
    p. cm.
  Includes bibliographical references and index.
  ISBN 0-471-48674-4 (pbk. : alk. paper)
  1. Industrial management.   2. Industrial management – Decision making.
  3. Managerial economics.   I. Title.
  HD31.J629 2004
  658.4′03 – dc22   2004000657

British Library Cataloguing in Publication Data

A catalogue record for this book is available from the British Library

ISBN 0-471-48674-4

In memory of my parents

CONTENTS

PREFACE

The central concern of this book is decision making in privately owned firms; these come in a variety of sizes and adopt differing governance structures and objectives which are dependent on who owns and who controls the individual enterprises. Although there are other types of firms in the economy, such as publicly, mutually and co-operatively owned enterprises, of these only public enterprises are examined.

In the firm the owner or controller contracts to hire or buy resources to undertake production of goods or services. Therefore, there needs to be a planning system for the organization of production and distribution of goods and services. In smaller private firms, managers and owners are usually the same people and operate the firm in their own interest. In larger firms, managers are employed by owners to operate the business on their behalf and for the benefit of shareholders. In a state-owned enterprise, managers are employed by the government to operate the business on their behalf and in the public interest.

In private firms where ownership is dispersed and there are no significant share-holders, managers may control the enterprise and pursue objectives and policies that are in their interest rather than those of the shareholders. They may also determine the activities the firm undertakes and its boundaries. Some firms produce a single product while others a multiplicity, some produce many of their own inputs while others buy them from other enterprises. Some pursue growth through internal expansion while others do so through mergers and acquisition. These are important managerial decisions, which help determine the success of the firm as much, if not more so, than decisions about costs and prices.

OBJECTIVE

This book is primarily aimed at a second-year undergraduate business and management students who wish to understand more about the economics of the firm and managerial decision making. It presumes that students have completed an introductory course in microeconomic principles. It will be of use for courses in managerial or business economics which desire to extend their content beyond the traditional microeconomic tools approach and include material on the growth and development of the firm.

STYLE

The book is analytical in its approach, presenting traditional neoclassical analysis together with behavioural theories and new institutional analysis. It also aims to illustrate theories with reference to particular managerial problems. Theories are explained largely by the use of graphs, but there is a limited use of mathematics and statistical analysis to aid the application and testing of the analysis. Case studies are used to illustrate the measurement of economic relationships and the application of theories. Each chapter has a brief introduction to the topics to be studied, a brief summary of the main issues and a set of questions which will help the student understand the material presented, enhance their analytical skills and the relevance of the analysis to business decisions.

COURSE USE

The book is designed to provide material for a two-semester course in managerial or business economics. It could also be used for two single-semester courses with the first course in microeconomic decision making relating to production, pricing, advertising and investment, and the second in strategic decision making and the creation, growth and development of the firm.

CONTENT

The first four parts of the book discuss ownership and control and then analyse the decisions that firms have to make to achieve their goals, including the examination of consumer behaviour, the goods and services to be produced and their pricing and promotion. Subjects discussed include:

- Consideration of individual consumer choice in order to gain an insight into both individual and market demand decisions.
- Utilization of analytical tools to examine the choice of production techniques, measures of productivity and efficiency.
- Cost structures and the relevance of economies of scale, scope and learning to the competitiveness of the enterprise.
- How changes in the objectives of the firm or in the strategic direction taken by it affect its behaviour and the behaviour of its rivals.
- Economic principles underlying pricing and advertising which enable the firm to sell its products or services.

The fifth part of the book analyses the institutional and strategic decisions of the firm which determine its boundaries, growth and development. These latter aspects are considered particularly important in the context of management and business studies degrees, where a great deal of emphasis is placed on the strategic development of the firm. Aspects of economic analysis of importance to business strategists and decision makers as the firm strives to grow and gain a competitive advantage over its rivals are discussed. It explores:

- Transaction cost theories for the existence of firms.
- Entrepreneurship and the establishment of firms.
- Theories of the growth of the firm.
- The boundaries of the firm, diversification and vertical integration.
- Mergers as a major tool for achieving growth and altering the boundaries of the firm.
- The limits to the growth and size of firms because of organizational structure problems and principal agent problems.

The final part of the book (Part VI) examines the regulatory impact of government on private firms, the advantages and disadvantages of public enterprises and the difficulties they face in operating in supplying unpriced goods and services.

The book also has a glossary of terms; these are highlighted in the text the first time they are used.

FEATURES

The distinctive features of this book are that it:

- Examines the nature and structure of firms.
- Develops the economic principles underlying major business and strategic decisions.
- Uses graphical rather than mathematical techniques to illuminate economic theory.
- Uses examples and the results of research studies to illustrate the practical implications of the economic theories discussed.
- Includes a major case study of a single enterprise to illustrate various aspects of the material presented.

The book:

- Examines managers' responsibilities to owners and/or stakeholders.
- Covers the decision making of the firm in relation to the market.
- Examines why firms exist and how they determine their boundaries.
- Explores the economies of growth, diversification and vertical integration of the firm.
- Explores decision making by private firms in government-regulated industries.
- Examines the reasons for the existence of public sector organizations and the differences in objectives and decision making.

ACKNOWLEDGEMENTS

In writing this book, I owe a debt to many colleagues past and present who have helped my understanding of economics. I would particularly like to thank my colleague Stuart Eliot, with whom I shared the teaching of courses in managerial economics for many years, and without whose encouragement and willingness to read successive drafts of the chapters this book would never have been completed. Finally, I would like to thank my family for their support and for reading various chapters and correcting the text. All remaining errors are, however, my responsibility.

PART I

CORPORATE GOVERNANCE AND BUSINESS OBJECTIVES

1

OWNERSHIP CONTROL AND CORPORATE GOVERNANCE

CHAPTER OUTLINE

CHAPTER OBJECTIVES

This chapter aims to discuss the governance structures of large firms and the constraints on management by owners and corporate governance reforms. At the end of the chapter you should be able to:

◆ Distinguish between ownership and control.

◆ Outline and explain criteria for classifying firms as either owner or managerially controlled enterprises.

◆ Classify corporate governance systems as either insider or outsider systems.

◆ Identify and analyse the main internal and external constraints on managerial discretion.

◆ Outline the codes of practice that influence corporate governance structures and practices.

INTRODUCTION

Firms are major economic institutions in market economies. They come in all shapes and sizes, but have the following common characteristics:

- Owners.
- Managers.
- Objectives.
- A pool of resources (labour, physical capital, financial capital and learned skills and competences) to be allocated roles by managers.
- Administrative or organizational structures through which production is organized.
- Performance assessment by owners, managers and other stakeholders.

Whatever its size, a firm is owned by someone or some group of individuals or organizations.

These are termed **shareholders** and they are able to determine the objectives and activities of the firm. They also appoint the senior managers who will make day-to-day decisions. The owners bear the risks associated with operating the firm and have the right to receive the residual income or profits. Where **ownership** rights are dispersed, **control** of the firm may not lie with the shareholders but with senior managers. This divorce between ownership and control and its implication for the operation and performance of the firm is at the centre of many of the issues dealt with in this book.

OWNERSHIP STRUCTURES

The dominant model of the firm in Western economies is the limited liability company owned by shareholders, but the form varies significantly between countries. In some countries the control rights of the owners are limited by powers given to stakeholders who may share in the appointment and supervision of managers and in the determination of the enterprise's objectives. In Germany, for example, large companies recognize the role of workers and other groups by giving them half the positions on the supervisory board that oversees the management board (Douma 1997). There are also firms owned by members and operated as **co-operative** or **mutual** enterprises and some owned by national and local government.

The notion that privately owned enterprises should be run in the interests of shareholders is not a characteristic of companies in all advanced economies. Yoshimori (1995) proposed that shareholder companies can be classified as follows:

- **Monistic** – where the company serves a single interest group, normally shareholders. These types of companies are commonly found in the UK and the USA.
- **Dualistic** – where the company serves two interest groups. Shareholders are the

primary group but employees' interests are also served. These types of companies are commonly found in France and Germany.

■ **Pluralistic** – where the company serves the interests of stakeholders in the company and not just shareholders. Employee and supplier interests may be paramount. Such companies are found in Japan.

Since Yoshimori's study some commentators have argued that there has been some degree of convergence between European and Anglo-American forms of corporate organizations because of greater international competition between enterprises. Likewise, commercial and economic forces in Japan have put significant pressure on companies to reduce the emphasis on the long-term employment of staff and place greater emphasis on profitability.

PATTERNS OF SHAREHOLDING

The pattern of share ownership varies between countries and with time. In the UK and the USA, ownership is more widely dispersed than in continental Europe and Japan where it is more concentrated.

UK share ownership

Table 1.1 presents data on share ownership in the UK from 1963 to 2001.

Table 1.1 Shareholding in the UK

Owners	1963 (%)	1975 (%)	1989 (%)	1994 (%)	1997 (%)	2001 (%)
Individuals	54.0	37.5	20.6	20.3	16.5	14.8
Institutions	30.3	48.0	58.5	60.2	56.3	50.0
Of which:						
Pension funds	6.4	16.8	30.6	27.8	22.1	16.1
Insurance companies	10.0	15.9	18.6	21.9	23.6	20.0
Companies	5.1	3.0	3.8	1.1	1.2	1.0
Overseas	7.0	5.6	12.8	16.3	24.0	31.9
Others	3.6	5.9	4.3	3.1	2.0	2.3
Total	100.0	100.0	100.0	100.0	100.0	100.0

Source Compiled by author using data from:
CSO (1993) Share register survey 1993, Economic Trends, No 480, London, HMSO
CSO (1995) Share Ownership, London, HMSO
CSO (1999) Share ownership, Economic Trends, No 543, London, HMSO
National Statistics (2002) Share Ownership 2001, http://www.statistics.gov.uk

Table 1.2   Structure of share ownership in Europe 2000

Type of investor	France (%)	Germany (%)	Italy (%)	Spain (%)	UK (%)
Individuals	8	16	25	30	16
Private financial enterprises	29	18	20	14	48
Private non-financial organizations	21	40	25	20	3
Public sector	6	6	15	0	0
Foreign investors	36	20	15	36	32
Unidentified					1
Total	100	100	100	100	100

Source   Compiled by author using data from FESE (2002) Share Ownership Structure in Europe 2002, Brussels, http://www.fese.be

The key features are:

■ The largest group of domestic owners of company shares are financial institutions.
■ Financial institutions' share of ownership increased between 1963 and 1997, but fell to 50% in 2001.
■ Individual ownership of shares has been in long-term decline and fell to 14.8% in 2001.
■ Overseas ownership of UK companies has increased and stood at 31.9% in 2001. This trend reflects the growing internationalisation of the asset portfolios held by financial institutions.

Shareholding in Europe

Comparative data for the ownership of shares in France, Germany, Italy, Spain and the UK for the year 2000 are presented in Table 1.2. It shows that in each country the structures are different in broad terms compared with the UK:

■ Holdings by financial institutions are lower.
■ Holdings by non-financial companies are more important, particularly in Germany.
■ Individual ownership is more important in Italy and Spain, but less so in France.
■ Foreign owners are more important in France and Spain, but less significant in Germany and Italy.

CLASSIFYING FIRMS AS OWNER OR MANAGEMENT CONTROLLED

The pattern of share ownership at company level varies widely. In the UK, quoted companies ownership is generally described as being widely dispersed among large numbers of shareholders. The largest shareholder often owns 5% or less of the stock and a significant proportion is owned by non-bank financial institutions. The board of directors typically own a tiny proportion of the shares, often much less than 0.5%. Thus, managers rather than owners control many medium and large-sized companies and set the firm's objectives. In France and Germany shareholding tends to be more concentrated with greater blocks of shares held by companies and banks. According to Denis and McConnell (2003) concentrated ownership structures are more likely to be found in most countries in contrast to the dispersed ownership patterns that are typical only of the UK and the USA.

How then can companies be classified as owner or managerially controlled? If a single shareholder holds more than 50% of the stock, assuming one vote per share, then they can outvote the remaining shareholders and control the company. If the largest shareholder owns slightly less than 50% of the equity then they can be outvoted if the other shareholders formed a united front. If the majority of shareholders do not form a united front or do not vote, then an active shareholder with a holding of substantially less than 50% could control the company.

Berle and Means (1932), who first identified the divorce between ownership and control, argued that a stake of more than 20% would be sufficient for that shareholder to control a company but less than 20% would be insufficient and the company would be management-controlled. Radice (1971) used a largest shareholding of 15% to classify a firm as owner-controlled; and a largest shareholder owning less than 5% to classify a firm as managerially controlled. Nyman and Silberston (1978) severely criticized the "cut-off" or threshold method of assessing control and argued that the distribution and ownership of holdings should be examined more closely. They emphasized that there was a need to recognize coalitions of interests, particularly of families, that do not emerge from the crude data.

Cubbin and Leech (1983) also criticized the simple cut-off points for classifying firms. They argued that control was a continuous variable that measures the discretion with which the controlling group is able to pursue its own objectives without being outvoted by other shareholders. Management controllers, they argued, would be expected to exhibit a higher degree of control for any given level of shareholding than would external shareholders.

They then developed a probabilistic voting model in which the degree of control is defined as the probability of the controlling shareholder(s) securing majority support in a contested vote. Control is defined as an arbitrary 95% chance of winning a vote. This ability depends on the dispersion of shareholdings, the proportion of shareholders voting and the probability of voting shareholders supporting the controlling group. The likelihood of the controlling group winning increases as the proportion voting falls and the more widely held are the shares. Applying their analysis to a sample of 85 companies, they concluded that with a 10% shareholder turnout, in 73 companies less than a 10% holding was necessary for control and in 37 companies with a 5% turnout, less than a 5% holding was necessary for control.

Control of a company is therefore a function of the following factors:

■ The size of the largest holding.
■ The size and distribution of the remaining shares.
■ The willingness of other shareholders to form a voting block.

■   the willingness of other shareholders to be active and to vote against the controlling group.

Case Study 1.1   Manchester United – owner or managerially controlled?

Manchester United epitomizes the conflicts between commercialization and the influence of supporters. The club's origins lie in the formation of a football team by the workers of the Yorkshire and Lancashire Railway Company. It joined the Football League in 1892 in its fourth year of existence. The club finished bottom in their first two seasons and became founder members of the second division. However, since returning to the first division in 1906 and winning the title in 1909, they have played only 10 seasons in a lower division.

Until the early 1960s, no shareholder had overall control of the club. In 1958, Louis Edwards, a Manchester businessman was elected to the board at the behest of the then manager Matt Busby. This was at the end of the most successful period in the club's history having been League champions in 1952, 1956 and 1957. In 1962 he was elected chairman owning only 17 of the 4,132 issued shares. By 1964, he had acquired a majority and controlling interest in the club. In 1981 his son Martin became chief executive of the club. In 1989, Martin tried to sell his complete interest in the club to Michael Knighton for £20m, but the deal fell through. In 1991 the club was floated on the stock exchange. This led to the most successful period in the club's playing history. It won the first Premier League title in 1993, five more in the next seven years and the European Cup in 1999 – the latter a feat they had previously achieved in 1968.

The changing nature of football and the dangers of flotation were highlighted by the £635m takeover bid made for the club in 1998 by BSkyB. The satellite television station, 40% owned by Rupert Murdoch's media empire News International, shows live Premiership football on subscription channels. Payments from television companies are a significant source of income for the club. The bid was not motivated by the failure of the club's management, but by the strategy of BSkyB. It was agreed to by the board of directors, but was vetoed by the government after a reference to the Monopolies and Mergers Commission. The bidder was forced to reduce its stake in the company to below 10%. This left BSkyB owning 9.99% of the share capital and still being the largest shareholder in the company.

Since flotation, Martin Edwards has gradually reduced his stake in the club to 14% in 1998 and to 0.7% in 2002. The club's shares are now more widely dispersed with some 20,000 small shareholders owning 3.5% and the directors around 3%. The largest holdings in September 2002 were:

	%
BSkyB	9.99
Cubic Expression	8.65
Mountbarrow Investment	6.54
Landsdowne Partners	3.11
E.M. Watkins	2.31
C.M. Edwards	0.70
Other directors	0.10

In September and early October 2003 there was significant trading, giving the following estimated structure:

	%	
Cubic Expression Ltd	23.2	(J.P. McManus and John Magnier, Irish businessmen)
Malcolm Glazer	8.9	(Tampa Bay Buccaneers, USA owner)
Mountbarrow Investment	6.5	(Harry Dobson, Canadian-based Scottish businessman)
UBS	5.9	(Financial institution)
Talpa Capital	4.1	(John de Moi, Dutch television tycoon)
Landsdowne Partners	3.7	(Financial institution)
Legal and General	3.3	(Financial institution)
E.M. Watkins	2.3	(United director)
Amvesscap	1.8	(Financial institution)
Dermot Desmond	1.6	(Glasgow Celtic, dominant shareholder)
Shareholders United	1.0	(Activist group)
Other investment companies	16.8	
Ordinary United fans	15.0	
Others	5.9	

To determine whether the club is owner or managerially controlled, we would need to consider the size of the largest stake, the distribution and size of other holdings including the directors' holdings, the motivation for holding the shares and the propensity to vote. The club was owner-controlled when Martin Edwards was chief executive and the largest shareholder. There appeared to be a period when the company was managerially controlled when the board of directors controlled a small proportion of the shares and the largest shareholders were said to be investors rather than active owners. However, that position appears to have changed with the emergence of dominant shareholders who may wish to control the company.

SYSTEMS OF CORPORATE CONTROL

The differences between countries in shareholder ownership patterns influence the nature of their **corporate governance** systems. According to Franks and Meyer (1992), there are fundamental differences between the corporate control systems of the UK and the USA and France, Germany and Japan. The former they describe as outsider systems and the latter as insider systems. The characteristics that distinguish the systems are listed in Table 1.3.

Insider systems

Insider systems are characterized by relatively few quoted companies, concentrated ownership, dominance of corporate and/or institutional shareholders and reciprocal shareholding. Shares are infrequently traded, but when they are they often involve large blocks. Takeover activity is largely absent, and where mergers take place they are largely done by agreement. However, Vodafone did acquire Mannesmann

Table 1.3   Characteristics of insider and outsider systems

Characteristics	UK and USA	Europe and Japan
Listed companies	Many	Few
Trading ownership	Frequent; liquid capital market	Infrequent; illiquid capital market
Inter-company holdings	Few	Many
Shares	Widely held	Large holdings
	Dispersed individuals	Concentrated companies
	Financial institutions	
Concentration of ownership	Low	High

Source Author

following a hostile bid. These characteristics, it is argued, lead to more active owner participation. Owners and other stakeholders are represented on the boards of companies, and there is active investor participation in controlling the company; this minimizes external influences in the control of the company. Ownership lies within the corporate sector rather than with a multiplicity of individual shareholders. Directors are representatives of other companies and interest groups, while a two-tier board structure allows a wider group of stakeholders to offer the company a broader spectrum of advice tending to reinforce longer term goals and stability for the company. Information about the firm's problems and performance is available more readily to corporate or institutional shareholders than to individual shareholders; this enables them be better informed about the firm's performance because they have inside information.

Germany

Germany is an example of an insider system. It has according to Franks and Meyer (2001) around 800 quoted companies compared with nearly 3,000 in the UK. Ownership is much more concentrated with 85% of the largest quoted companies having a single shareholder owning more than 25% of the voting shares. Large ownership stakes tend to rest in the hands of families or companies with inter-connected holdings. Where shares are more widely dispersed then the influence of banks is stronger: for example, the largest shareholder in BMW is the Quandt family which owns 46% of the voting equity. Stefan Quandt is one of four deputy chairmen, and his sister Susanne is a member of the supervisory board. Head of the family is Joanna Quandt, who is the majority owner of Altana, a pharmaceutical manufacturer; this makes them the controllers of two of Germany's top 30 companies (*Financial Times* 16 August 2002). The supervisory board appoints the management board. When the company's acquisition of British Leyland was deemed unsuccessful the chairman of the management board and two other directors were quickly dismissed in early 1999 by insider action.

Outsider systems

Outsider systems are characterized by dispersed share ownership, with the dominant owners being nonbank financial institutions and private individuals. Owners and other stakeholders are not represented on the boards of companies. Shareholders are seen as passive investors who only rarely question the way in which a company is being operated. Shares are easily sold and tend to be held for investment purposes, as part of a diversified portfolio, rather than for control purposes; this discourages active participation in company affairs since shares are easily traded. Thus, dissatisfaction with the performance of a company leads the shareholder to sell shares, rather than initiate moves to change the management or even company policies.

Dispersed ownership is assumed to mean managerial control; this is particularly true when financial institutions hold numerous small stakes. While such institutional investors may have information advantages, they do not use this to influence management directly but to maintain the value of their investment portfolios on behalf of clients. The monitoring of managers is said to be superior in insider systems, with deteriorating performance more quickly acted on. In the outsider system, changing management and policies is a slower process and may involve the takeover of the failing business by other enterprises.

CONSTRAINTS ON MANAGERIAL DISCRETION

The degree of discretion that senior executive managers have in setting objectives is limited by both external and internal constraints. External constraints arise from the active market in company shares while internal constraints arise from the role of non-executive board members and stakeholders, trying to align the managers' and the owners' interests by the rules shaping corporate governance.

External constraints

There are five sources of external constraint on managerial behaviour in any system of corporate control. Those who potentially hold this power are:

- Holders of large blocks of shares who use or threaten to use their voting power to change management or their policies if they become dissatisfied.
- Acquirers of blocks of shares sold by existing shareholders unhappy with the performance of management.
- Bidders in the takeover process who promise to buy all the voting shares of the enterprise.
- Debtors/Investors, particularly in times of financial distress, who act to protect their interests in the company.
- External regulators and auditors.

In outsider systems, external control is exercised mainly through the workings of the stock market rather than voting. In the stock market, shares are continuously traded and the price reflects the relative numbers of buyers and sellers and their willingness to buy or sell. The influence of the workings of the stock market on managerial discretion assumes that a fall in the share price will make management more vulnerable to shareholder activism either in selling shares or in voting at shareholder meetings.

In outsider systems, shareholders are inclined to sell underperforming shares to maintain a balance in their diversified share portfolios. In insider systems the selling of shares is more difficult and, therefore, shareholders are more likely to use their voting power to influence management. In outsider systems the working of the stock market makes it feasible to acquire blocks of shares by purchase and to make a bid for all the equity of a company, thereby threatening the tenure of the existing management.

Other external constraints on managerial behaviour are the need to comply with company law, independent auditing of accounts and the lodging of company accounts with the regulators. The annual accounts of a company are designed to present a reasonable picture of the company's activities and its financial health in terms of profit and debt levels to actual and potential shareholders. On occasions, audited accounts have been found to have presented an inaccurate picture, in that a company has gone bankrupt after the accounts appeared to show a healthy financial situation. The bankruptcy of Enron in the USA in 2001 was a notable example.

Internal constraints

Within the organizational structure of the company, there are groups who may be able to influence management to change policies. The first of these are the non-executive directors, who are appointed to the boards of UK companies to oversee the behaviour of the executive directors. However, they are normally appointed by the executive managers and, therefore, may not be independent in their actions or effective in constraining executive directors. They are often few in number and can be outvoted by executive directors. One of the objectives of corporate governance reform in the UK is to make non-executives more effective. In the German system the supervisory board plays this role by influencing the management board, but its membership is more wide-ranging.

The second of these groups are the owners or shareholders, who can exercise their authority at meetings of the company or informally with management. Directors are elected at the annual general meeting of the company. Dissatisfied shareholders can vote against the re-election of existing executive directors or seek to get nominees elected. They can also vote against resolutions proposed by the executive of the company, such as those relating to executive remuneration. In the past this has rarely happened as shareholders have been passive rather than active in company affairs and sell underperforming shares. However, in the UK institutional shareholders have become more active in organizing coalitions to either influence management behind the scenes or forcing votes at annual general meetings.

A third group that can influence executive managers are the stakeholders within the company. These include employees of the firm as well as customers, suppliers, lenders and the local community. They may do this by expressing their criticisms/concerns either directly to the executives or indirectly by informing shareholders, the media and outside experts or commentators. Investment banks and stockbrokers offer advice to shareholders on the potential future earnings of the company, and such comments may help to influence attitudes toward incumbent managers.

Aligning the interests of managers and shareholders

It has been argued that the discretion executive managers exercise can be limited by the development of incentive mechanisms to ensure that the interests of managers and owners are more closely aligned. If we assume that shareholders wish to maximize profits, then managers may be encouraged to do so by the payment of profit-related bonuses in addition to their basic salary and/or by rewarding successful performance with share options in the company.

Critics of such schemes argue that senior managers may be motivated by non-monetary rewards and that it is difficult to devise incentive schemes that only reward superior performance. A survey by Gregg et al. (1993) explored the relationship between the direct remuneration (pay plus bonuses) of the highest paid director and the performance of around 300 companies in the 1980s and early 1990s. They found that almost all large UK companies had bonus schemes for top executives but that rewards were weakly linked to corporate performance on the stock market. The authors concluded that the results called into question the current system of determining rewards and that the incentive schemes did not successfully align managerial interests with those of the shareholders. (This aspect is further discussed as a principal agent problem in Chapter 20.) To achieve the desired alignment between owners and managers there have been many changes in the UK to corporate governance rules to prevent the misuse of managerial discretion.

IMPROVING CORPORATE GOVERNANCE IN THE UK

The final sources of constraint on the behaviour of executive directors are the rules that determine the governance structures and procedures of companies. The meaning of the term **corporate governance** has been much discussed. The Cadbury Committee, which was set up in 1991 to investigate corporate governance in the UK, defined it as "the system by which companies are directed and controlled." This definition implies two aspects to the problem: one relating to the direction of the company and a second relating to how the company is controlled by shareholders and society. Critics would narrow the concept by ensuring that corporate actions are directed toward achieving the objectives of a company's shareholders. Critics of the narrow definition argue that corporate governance relates not only to management's responsibilities to shareholders but also to stakeholders and the wider community. From a government point of view, corporate governance is about ensuring accountability in the exercise of power and financial responsibility, while not discouraging firms from being enterprising and **risk** taking.

Across the world, many countries have developed voluntary codes of practice to encourage good corporate practice. The website of the European Corporate Governance Network in August 2000 listed codes for 19 countries together with those agreed by the OECD (Organization for Economic Cooperation and Development) and various non-governmental organizations (**http://www.ecgn.ulb.ac.be**). All of the codes listed have been published since 1994, indicating the growing concern for corporate governance to be more effective.

In the UK the major concern has been the perception that directors of a company are only weakly accountable to shareholders. Such concerns include:

- The collapse of companies whose annual reports indicated they were profitable.
- The lack of transparency of a company's activities to shareholders.
- The competence of directors.
- The adequacy of board structures and processes.
- The growth of business fraud.
- Payments to directors and senior managers unrelated to performance.
- The short-term nature of corporate performance measures.

Three successive committees of inquiry appointed by the London Stock Exchange have examined these issues. The first was the Cadbury Committee (1992) which devised a voluntary code of practice to improve corporate governance. This was reviewed by the Greenbury (1995) and Hampel (1998) Committees. The end result was the Combined Code (CCG 1998) which requires each company to have:

- A non-executive chairman and chief executive with a clear division of responsibilities between them.
- Each board to have at least:
  - Three non-executive directors independent of management.
  - An audit committee including at least three non-executive directors.
  - A remuneration committee made up mainly of non-executive directors to determine the reward of directors.
  - A nomination committee composed wholly of non-executive directors to appoint new directors.

In addition the annual report to shareholders should include:

- A narrative account of how they apply the broad principles of the Code, explain their governance policies and justify departures from recommended practice.
- Payments to the chief executive and highest paid UK director to be disclosed in the annual report.

- Directors should receive appropriate training to carry out their duties.
- The majority of non-executive directors should be independent, and boards should disclose in their annual report which of the non-executive directors are considered to be independent
- The roles of chairman and chief executive should normally be separated, and companies should justify a decision to combine the roles.
- The names of directors submitted for re-election should be accompanied by biographical details, and directors who resign before the expiry of their term should give an explanation.

A fourth report (known as the Higgs Report) was commissioned by the Department of Trade and Industry and published in 2003. It proposed a fundamental restructuring of company boards by proposing that at least half the members should be independent non-executive directors and that the part-time non-executive chairman should also be independent of the company. One of the non-executive directors should be responsible for liaising with shareholders and raising issues of concern at board level. Non-executives should normally serve no more than two three-year terms and meet by themselves at least once per year. In addition, no one individual should chair more than one major company. These proposals have proved to be extremely controversial. Critics do not accept the notion that boards having a majority of non-executives will solve the problems associated with managerial discretion and misuse of power. The executive directors will still be the main source of information about the performance of the company and the non-executives will find it difficult to obtain information from other sources. In addition, there are doubts expressed as to where the numbers of independent non-executive directors will be found. The Higgs Committee recognized this problem and argued that the pool from which individuals are drawn should be widened and training offered. When agreed, these proposals will be incorporated in a new combined code.

Although voluntary, compliance with the Code is one of the requirements for listing on the London Stock Exchange and non-compliance requires an explanation in the annual company report. The Code, however, does not guarantee good conduct on the part of executives and compliance with the Code does not necessarily improve the company's profitability. In fact, in some circumstances it may adversely affect the declared profits of the company by ensuring that costs incurred by the company are fully declared to owners. Likewise, apparent compliance with the Code may not prevent fraudulent behaviour on the part of senior executives if that information is hidden from the non-executive directors on whom a heavy burden for compliance is placed.

Although companies conform to the letter of the corporate governance codes, it is questionable whether they fully comply with their spirit and whether such compliance would prevent fraudulent behaviour. The independence of non-executive directors is questioned since the vast majority of them are also directors of other companies. Also, their ability to fulfil the expectations of the Code and operate the necessary scrutiny of executive directors is again questionable.

Case Study 1.2   Ownership and governance structures in UK retailing

The ideal board would under the various codes (pre-Higgs) have the following composition and duties:

- A **part-time chairman** who is not involved in the day-to-day running of the business, thinks strategically, ensures directors are aware of their obligations to share-holders and makes sure non-executive directors are properly briefed.
- **Executive directors** who manage the company on a day-to-day basis whose contracts should not exceed three years without shareholder approval, whose pay is subject to recommendations of a remuneration committee and who may receive share options.
- **Part-time non-executive directors** who bring independent judgements to bear on issues of strategy, performance and appointments, who ensure the appropriate information is disclosed in the directors' reports and whose reward reflects the time devoted to their activities.
- A **chief executive** who is the top manager of the company and strives to meet the objectives set by the board. It is a role separate from that of the chairman to ensure that no one individual has unfettered power over decisions.

Table 1.4 shows for nine leading UK retailers the shareholdings of the largest shareholder and the mix of executive/non-executive directors on the boards of the companies. In terms of largest shareholders, Tesco has no shareholder owning more than 3%, but all the other companies have at least one shareholder owning more than 3%. In Sainsbury the largest shareholder controls 29% and seven non-institutional shareholders own 52.3% of the total equity. In Morrison the largest shareholder, who is also executive chairman, owns 17.76%

Table 1.4   Board structures and shareholding of leading retailers August 2000

	Board of directors		Largest share-holder (%)	Board share-holders (%)	Turnover[4] (£m)	Pre-tax profit[4] (£m)	Return on capital employed (%)
	Executive	Non-executive					
Boots	6	7	4.06	0.04	5,187	562	25.2
Debenhams	6	5	13.0[6]	0.13	1,379	139	20.1
Kingfisher	7	6	3.95	0.10	10,885	726	19.3
Marks & Spencer	6[1]	5	7.45	0.06	8,224	418	8.1
Wm Morrison	7[1]	0	17.76[5]	17.85	2,970	189	18.0
J Sainsbury	5	4	29.00[2]	0.01	16,271	509	11.1
Somerfield	7[1]	4	17.93[3]	0.14	5,898	209	24.5
Safeway	5[1]	4	13.02	0.07	7,659	236	9.24
Tesco	8	5	None	0.10	18,796	933	15.5

Notes   1 Includes executive chairman
2 Seven non-institutional shareholders have stakes in excess of 3% totalling 53.2% of equity
3 Six shareholders have stakes in excess of 3% totalling 48.64%
4 Financial year ending March/April 2000 except for Somerfield which is for 1999
5 Four individual shareholders have stakes in excess of 3% totalling 39.79%
6 Four institutional shareholders have stakes in excess of 3% totalling 32.26%
Source Author's analysis of annual reports

who with another three individuals own 39.7%. In both these companies the largest share-holders are members of the Morrison and Sainsbury families. Somerfield, Debenhams and Safeway have a significant single institutional shareholder owning more than 12% of all shares, while the first two companies have a small group of significant shareholders controlling more than 30% of the total. Marks & Spencer, Kingfisher and Boots also have institutional shareholders as their largest single shareholder, but their stakes are relatively small, less than 5% in the case of Kingfisher and Boots. The boards of directors, with the exception of Morrison, all own less than 0.2% of the total equity.

On balance Sainsbury and Morrison are family or owner-controlled; Tesco, Boots, Kingfisher and possibly Marks & Spencer are management-controlled; and the other three companies have significant institutional holdings which probably means they are management-controlled. However, poor performance can lead to significant changes in management. At Marks & Spencer a new chairman and chief executive were appointed in 1999, while Somerfield, which performed poorly after its merger with Kwik Save, came under significant shareholder pressure to improve performance.

All boards, except for Boots, have a majority of executive directors. Contrary to the codes of practice, Marks & Spencer, Morrison, Safeway and Somerfield have executive rather than non-executive chairmen. One firm, Morrison, in contravention of the codes, has no non-executive directors while all the others have three or more non-executive directors.

Case Study 1.3 Corporate governance in English football

The issues raised in this chapter concerned with ownership and control can be illustrated in relation to professional football. Professional football clubs were traditionally private limited companies. These were owned and run either by a single or a small group of individuals. The clubs developed a relationship with the local community and, particularly, their supporters who pay to watch matches. The objective of football clubs was not to make profits but to achieve the best league result possible, given the income of the club from football and the money contributed by the owners. Owners were expected to put funds into their clubs with little expectation of a commercial return.

Few clubs made profits on any consistent basis, and the majority made persistent losses. Of 40 League clubs listed by Szymanski and Kuypers (1999) in the period 1978 to 1997 only six were profitable, on average, for the whole period. These were Liverpool, Manchester United, Arsenal, Tottenham, Aston Villa, Oldham and Barnsley. The majority of clubs were perceived to be poorly managed and to have failed to keep up with changing social trends. Since the clubs were non-quoted companies there was no market in corporate control. While many clubs were bankrupt in the technical sense, they staggered on with the support of a changing cast of money providers, but better management and profitability were rarely the result.

The stakeholders in the clubs – the fans, the players, the staff and the local community – played no part in the running of the club. The fans who paid to watch their teams play were generally taken for granted by the clubs, facilities were limited and attendance declined, as football became one choice among a range of leisure options, was associated with violence of various kinds and offered poor value for money. The various stakeholders in a football club also have conflicting objectives. For example:

- Owners of Stock Exchange-quoted clubs might be interested in maximizing profits, football success and charging fans high admission prices.

- Owners of private clubs might be interested in minimizing losses, relative football success (e.g., avoiding relegation) and keeping fans happy.
- In a mutual, or fan-controlled, club the controllers/owners might seek to avoid losses, relative football success and low admission prices.
- Manager and players, given their abilities, are also interested in maximizing their earnings and football success, though their commitment to any one club might be for a short period only.
- Fans are interested in football success, a reasonable quality stadium and low admission prices.
- The community might be interested in football success, minimizing community disruption and encouraging the club to get involved in community projects.

(see Michie and Ramalinghan 1999 for further discussion). The turning point in making football in England a commercial activity came with the publication of the Taylor Report in 1990 into the Hillsborough Stadium disaster of 1989. It recommended that all First and Second Division club grounds should become all-seater stadiums. This was quickly followed by the formation of the elite Premier League as a separate entity from the Football League. These two changes have led to:

- Increasing crowds despite higher prices.
- Increased exposure of football on television, further widening the revenue base,
- The growth of wider commercial activity such as the selling of football kits.
- The non-sharing of home match receipts with visiting teams, enabling the larger clubs to increase their revenues.

As a result of increased revenue and the social acceptance of Premiership football, a small number of clubs become Stock Exchange-listed companies. Tottenham Hotspur became listed in 1983, but no other club followed until Manchester United did so in 1993. Now the majority of Premier League clubs are listed companies, leading to a greater emphasis on profitability and good stewardship, which at times conflicts with the need to be successful on the field of play.

Traditional supporters have been critical of these changes because they argue that, without their support, the football club would be of little value to the shareholders. The inelasticity of demand to watch the top teams and the limited capacity of grounds have given clubs significant **market power** to raise prices and revenue and to put shareholder value ahead of football success. Some have argued that the fans should be represented on the board of directors, while others have argued the football clubs should adopt co-operative or mutual structures to ensure they maintain their traditional role as a sports club rather than a purely commercial enterprise: for example, Barcelona, one of the most successful football teams in Europe, is still a club with real links with its community and supporter base.

Stock market flotation has widened the range of shareholders to include financial institutions and in more recent times, media companies particularly those involved in satellite and cable television. The bid by BSkyB Television for Manchester United brought many of these issues into the public arena. The prohibition of the merger by the Monopolies and Mergers Commission (MMC) has not ended the involvement of media companies, which changed their strategy from owning a single club to owning minority stakes in a number of clubs. The decision also ended the bid by NTL, a cable television company, for Newcastle United. The motivation for media companies seeking ownership stakes in major football clubs is to be able to influence negotiations about media rights, to advise on media development and to be involved in the development of club-based pay-per-view television services.

CHAPTER SUMMARY

In this chapter we explored issues relating to the ownership and control of the firm. To do this we analysed:

■ The ownership structures of firms and the pattern of shareholdings in different countries.
■ The divorce between ownership and control led to the distinction between owner controlled and managerially controlled enterprises.
■ The nature of control in different countries was examined. In the UK and the USA, where share ownership is widely dispersed, there are outsider systems of control using market mechanisms. In continental Europe and Japan, where share ownership is more concentrated, there are insider control systems. In whose interests firms are operated was also examined.
■ The major constraints on managerial discretion come through either external mechanisms, essentially through the Stock Exchange, or internal constraints where shareholders and stakeholders use their power of control within the formal and informal structures of the firm.

REVIEW QUESTIONS

Exercise 1 Share ownership

Using a sample of company annual reports extract information on the following:

a The distribution of shares by size of holding.
b The category of shareholders (e.g., banks, individuals, etc.) which are the main owners.
c The largest shareholder.
d Whether there is a coherent group of shareholders.
e The shareholdings of directors.

Based on the information collected, would you describe each company as either management or owner-controlled?

Exercise 2 Corporate governance compliance

Using a sample of company reports examine the corporate governance report:

a Does the report give evidence of compliance with latest code of practice?
b Do any of the firms fail to comply with the latest code. If yes, in what respect do they fail to do so and what justification did the company give for its actions?

Discussion questions

1   What is understood by the terms ownership and control?

2   What do you understand by the term "divorce between ownership and control"?

3   What size of ownership stake makes for control? How do we divide companies into managerial or owner-controlled? Is the use of a simple percentage cut-off rule too simplistic?

4   How does the growth of institutional shareholdings influence the way managers run a company? Would we expect them to adopt a passive or active role in monitoring a company?

5   Distinguish between "insider" and "outsider" systems of corporate control? What are the advantages and disadvantages of both systems?

6   How does the pattern of ownership and control vary between the UK and Germany?

7   Compare and contrast the degree of managerial discretion of a chief executive of a large company in an insider and outsider system of corporate control.

8   What are the main guidelines in the UK's corporate governance codes? Have they improved corporate governance in the UK?

9   Is football different? Is the listed company an appropriate organizational form or should they remain members' clubs?

10 Companies A, B and C have the following share ownership structure:

   – Firm A: the largest shareholder is an individual owning 10% of the equity, a further five members of the family own 25%, with the remaining shares owned by financial institutions and with no one institution owning more than 3%. The board of directors does not include the largest shareholder but does control 10% of the equity.

   – Firm B: the largest shareholder is an institution owning 3% of the equity. The remaining shares are owned by 20,000 individual and institutional shareholders.

   – Firm C: the largest shareholder is an individual owning 40% of the equity. A single bank owns 20% and three companies the remaining 40%.

   Classify each firm according to whether it is owner or managerially controlled and whether it is likely to be part of an insider or outsider system of corporate governance.

REFERENCES AND FURTHER READING

Berle, A.A and G. Means (1932) *The Modern Corporation and Private Property*. Macmillan, New York.

Cadbury, A. (1992) *The Financial Aspects of Corporate Governance*. London Stock Exchange.

CCG (1998) *The Combined Code*. Committee on Corporate Governance, London Stock Exchange/ Gee & Co., London.

Conyon, M., P. Gregg and S. Machin (1995) Taking care of executive compensation in the UK. *Economic Journal*, **105**(2), 704–714.

Cubbin, J. and D. Leach (1983) The effect of shareholding dispersion on the degree of control in British companies: Theory and measurement. *Economic Journal*, **93**, 351–369.

Denis, D.K. and J.J. McConnell (2003) International corporate governance. *Journal of Financial and Qualitative Analysis*, **38**(1), 1–36

Douma, S (1997) The two-tier system of corporate governance. *Long Range Planning*, **30**(4), 612–614.

Franks, J. and C. Meyer (1990) Corporate ownership and corporate control: A study of France, Germany and the UK. *Economic Policy*, **100**, 189–232.

Franks, J. and C. Meyer (1992) *Corporate Control: A Synthesis of the International Experience* (Working paper). London Business School.

Franks, J. and C. Meyer (2001) Ownership and control of German corporations. *Review of Financial Studies*, **14**(4), 943–977.

Greenbury, R. (1995) *Study Group on Directors Remuneration*. London Stock Exchange.

Gregg, P.S., S. Machin and S. Szymanski (1993) The disappearing relationship between directors pay and corporate performance. *British Journal of Industrial Relations*, **31**(1), 1–10.

Hamil, S., J. Michie and C. Oughton (1999) *A Game of Two Halves? The Business of Football*. Mainstream, London.

Hampel, R. (1998) *Committee on Corporate Governance* (Final report). London Stock Exchange.

Higgs, D. (2003) *Review of the Role and Effectiveness of non-executive Directors*. Department of Trade & Industry, London.

Jenkinson, T. and C. Meyer (1992) Corporate governance and corporate control. *Oxford Review of Economic Policy*, **8**(3), 110.

LSE (1998) *The Combined Code*. London Stock Exchange/Gee & Co., London.

Michie, J. and S. Ramalingham (1999) From Barnsley to Green Bay Packers – Local and fan ownership. Available at **http://www.imusa.org.uk/library/greenbay.htm**

Michie, J. and A. Walsh (1999) Ownership and governance options for football clubs. Paper given at *The Corporate Governance of Professional Football*. Available at **http://www.imusa.org.uk/library/owngov.htm**

Nyman, S. and A. Silberston (1978) The ownership and control of industry. *Oxford Economic Papers*, **30**, 74–101. Reprinted in L. Wagner (ed.) (1981) *Readings in Applied Microeconomics* (2nd edn). Oxford University Press, Oxford, UK.

Radice, H. (1971) Control type, profitability and growth in large firms: An empirical study. *Economic Journal*, **81**, 547–562.

Short, H (1994) Ownership, control, financial structure and the performance of firms. *Journal of Economic Surveys*, **8**(1), 205–249

Szymanski, S. and T. Kuypers (1999) *Winners and Losers*. Viking, Harmondsworth, UK.

Yoshimori, M. (1995) Whose company is it? The concept of the corporation in Japan and the West. *Long Range Planning*, **28**(4), 33–44.

2 BUSINESS OBJECTIVES AND THEORIES OF THE FIRM

CHAPTER OBJECTIVES

This chapter aims to discuss the alternative objectives of the firm by using models of the firm developed by economists. At the end of this chapter you should be able to:

◆ Understand the assumptions of the profit-maximizing model of the firm and explain the implications for price and output.

◆ Explain the sales revenue maximization model of the firm and analyse the implications for price and output.

◆ Outline the managerial utility model of the firm and explain the implications for resource allocation.

◆ Outline the main criticisms of neoclassical and managerial models.

◆ Explain the behavioural model of the firm and its advantages and disadvantages for economic analysis of the firm.

◆ Discuss the arguments for firms adopting wider social obligations.

INTRODUCTION

The objective of this chapter is to explore how economists have developed models of the firm based on control by owners and managers. Traditionally, it has been assumed that owners set the goal of profit maximization and that managers make decisions in pursuit of that goal. However, the divorce between ownership and control has led to the development of theories that emphasize the maximization of managerial objectives. The chapter also explores the notion that firms pursue multiple objectives and aim to satisfice rather than maximize an individual objective. The notion of incorporating wider social goals into the objectives of the firm is also examined.

PROFIT MAXIMIZATION

The traditional objective of the owner-managed firm is assumed to be short-run profit maximization. This presumption of **profit maximization** is the building block of neoclassical economics, not only for the theory of the firm but also for the theories of price and competitive markets. For firms where there is a divorce between ownership and control the assumption is that managers still maximize profits on behalf of the owners. Thus, the firm's owners and managers have a single objective.

The rules of profit maximization

Where profit maximization is the goal of the firm, economists have developed a set of rules to guide decision makers to achieve it. Assuming the firm produces and sells a single product, then, given the associated revenue and cost functions, profit (π) is the difference between **total revenue** (TR) and **total cost** (TC). These three functions are shown in Figure 2.1. The profit function shows a range of outputs at which the firm makes positive or super-normal profits. The profit-maximizing output is Q_π. The slopes of the total revenue and cost curves are equal at points A and B, which means that the addition to total cost or marginal cost is equal to the addition to total revenue or marginal revenue at output Q_π. The decision maker must, if he wishes to maximize profits, have information about the firm's revenue and cost functions and, more particularly, its marginal revenue and marginal cost curves. (These relationships are explained mathematically in Chapter 5.)

Similar information is presented in Figure 2.2, but using average and marginal revenue and cost curves. The firm maximizes profit where marginal revenue (MR) is equal to marginal cost (MC) at output Q_π. The price the firm charges is P_π and total profit is given by the area $P_\pi ABP_s$, which is equal to total profit (AB) in Figure 2.1.

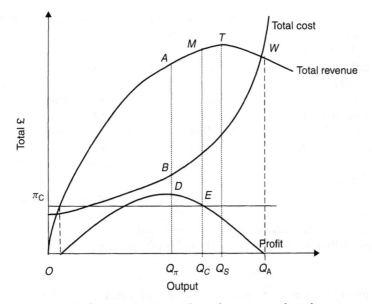

Figure 2.1   Profit maximization with total revenue and total cost curves

Criticisms of profit maximization

Criticisms of profit maximization as capturing the essence of a firm's objectives have come from empirical and theoretical perspectives.

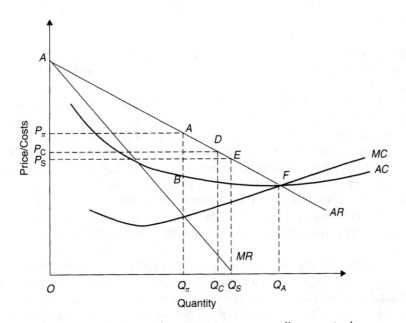

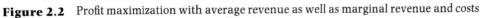

Figure 2.2   Profit maximization with average revenue as well as marginal revenue and costs

Empirical studies of the motives of firms, often associated with studies of pricing, tend to suggest that firms do not maximize profits. Two such studies of the UK are by Shipley (1981) and Hornby (1995). Shipley (1981) studied a sample of 728 UK firms using a questionnaire. He found that 47.7% of respondents said they tried to maximize profits and the remainder to make satisfactory profits. In response to a second question about the relative importance of profit maximization compared with other objectives, only 26.1% said it was of overriding importance. Further analysis led Shipley to conclude that only 15.9% of responding firms were "true" profit maximizers. This conclusion was reached by considering only those who said that they tried to maximize profit and that profit was of overriding importance. Hornby (1995) found on the basis of a sample of 74 Scottish companies that 24.7% of respondents could be regarded as "true" profit maximizers. These studies also showed that firms tend to have a range of goals rather than a single goal. Profit, therefore, is an important objective but not to the exclusion of other objectives.

The main criticisms of the assumption of profit maximization from empirical studies are:

- Profit maximization is a poor description of what many firms actually try to achieve.
- Other objectives may be more important, such as increasing sales in the short run.
- No single objective may be maximized.
- Marginalism is a poor description of the processes used by businesses to decide output and price.
- Profit is a residual and its outcome is uncertain.

Theoretical criticisms

Perfect information and rational decision makers are the cornerstone of the neoclassical analysis of profit maximization. The world is characterized by imperfect and uncertain information; this makes the calculation of marginal revenue and marginal cost quite difficult, even for a rational individual. Collecting information in an uncertain world is also difficult and expensive making for partial and imperfect information for decision making Rational decision makers capable of making perfectly rational decisions and precise economic calculations are not depictions of decision makers of typical businesses. Instead, they are boundedly rational in that they are only partially aware of the information available and are not able to fully analyse it.

Profit as a concept is related to time. Economists usually make a distinction between maximizing **short-run** and **long-run** profits. In practice, a firm may trade off lower profits in the short run for greater long-run profits, which is in the long-term interests of the firm.

The theory of profit maximization does not recognize the complexity of the modern organization. Although the presumption is made that owners or chief executives control their firms, in practice they are run by committees – and committees tend to make compromises so that the firm may adopt a mixture of goals and not necessarily maximize any single goal.

Defence of profit maximization

Machlup (1967) has argued that profit maximization is not a hypothesis that can be tested, but a paradigm that is not itself testable; yet, the paradigm allows a set of possible hypotheses to be defined for subsequent validation. He argues that firms do not need accurate knowledge to maximize profits. Marginal revenue and marginal cost are subjective concepts, and their use by managers is not deliberate but done in an automatic way. It has been likened to overtaking when driving a car or hitting a cricket or tennis ball. Scientifically, each decision requires significant amounts of information that have to be analysed in a very short time. Yet, most people overtake successfully and can hit a cricket or tennis ball reasonably well with a bit of practice, knowing nothing of the physics or the method of calculation.

An individual firm is also constrained in its choice of objectives by the actions of its rivals. If there is a significant degree of competition, then profit maximization may be the only goal the firm can adopt for it to survive and maintain its presence in the market. Likewise, pressure from shareholders will force the management of a firm to match the performance of their competitors if they are not to sell their shares. Further, unless the firm is earning a minimum acceptable level of profit it may find raising further capital difficult. However, while a certain level of profits are necessary to keep shareholders happy and to raise future capital, it does not necessarily mean maximizing profit, but it does suggest, in line with empirical studies, that profit is an important goal for the firm. Nevertheless, profit maximization remains an important assumption in economic analysis partly because it allows precise and predictive analysis of decisions and because surveys show it remains an important objective.

SALES REVENUE MAXIMIZATION

An alternative model recognizing the importance of profit, but assuming that managers set the goals of the firm, is that of sales maximization. This model was developed by Baumol (1959) who argued that managers have discretion in setting goals and that sales revenue maximization was a more likely short-run objective than profit maximization in firms operating in oligopolistic markets. The reasons are as follows:

- Sales revenue is a more useful short-term goal for the firm than profit. Sales are measurable and can be used as a specific target to motivate staff, whereas profits, which are a residual, are not so easily used in this way. Specific sales targets are thought to be clearly understood by all within the firm.
- Rewards for senior managers are often tied to sales revenue rather than profit, as they are for lower levels of staff.
- It is assumed that an increase in revenue will more than offset any associated increases in costs, so that additional sales will increase profit; therefore, increasing the size of the firm as measured by sales revenue or turnover is seen by shareholders as a good proxy for short-run profit increases.

■ Increasing sales and, hence, the size of the firm makes it easier to manage, because it creates an environment in which everyone believes the firm is successful. A firm facing falling sales will be seen as failing and lead to calls for managers to reappraise their policies.

The static single-period sales maximization model

The static model assumes that:

■ The firm produces a single product and has non-linear total cost and revenue functions.
■ The firm makes its price/output decision without taking account of the actions of other firms.
■ The firm's objective is to choose a level of sales or output that maximizes sales revenue (TR) subject to a minimum profit constraint set by shareholders (π_C).

The impact of the model can be observed in Figure 2.1. The total revenue curve (TR), the total cost curve (TC) and the profit function are shown. Sales revenue is maximized at output level OQ_S at the highest point of the TR curve where marginal revenue is zero and becomes negative for any further increases in sales. For output Q_S marginal cost is positive and marginal revenue zero. In fact, all units sold between Q_π and Q_S are sold at a loss because marginal cost exceeds marginal revenue. This effect can be seen in the fall in the profit curve after sales level OQ_π.

The profit constraint that reflects the preferences of shareholders (π_C) is shown as the absolute amount of profit that the firm has to earn on a given amount of capital employed (i.e., to give a guaranteed rate of return on capital). This profit constraint is set at a level below that of maximum profits. The profit constraint for each firm is determined after taking into consideration:

■ The normal profit levels/rate of returns in the sector taking into account cyclical/long-term trends.
■ The level of return that will satisfy shareholders with the firm's performance, so that they continue to hold or buy shares rather than sell.
■ If profits fall below expected levels, then the share price will fall and encourage further sales of shares and encourage takeover bids.
■ A level of profits that will discourage hostile takeover bids would also satisfy the management's desire to retain control of the firm.

In Figure 2.2 the information in Figure 2.1 is presented in terms of average and marginal revenue and cost. The firm would maximize profits at output level OQ_π and maximize sales revenue at OS_S. The constrained sales revenue maximization output level will be at OQ_C, which is somewhere between the profit and sales-maximizing outputs. Equally, the price set by the constrained sales revenue maximizer OP_C will be lower than that set by the profit maximizer OP_π, because the model assumes a downward-sloping demand curve. Therefore, where the constrained sales revenue-

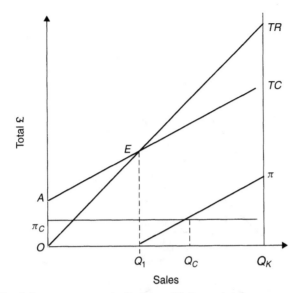

Figure 2.3   Sales revenue maximization with linear total revenue and cost curves

maximizing output is greater than the profit-maximizing output, the firm will always charge a lower price (i.e., OP_C will be less than OP_π).

In the short run, if the firm assumes it faces linear total cost and total revenue curves, then sales revenue maximization implies selling all the output the firm can produce. In Figure 2.3 the firm will break even, where total cost is equal to total revenue at point E selling output OQ_1. The firm will meet its profit constraint $(O\pi_C)$ selling output OQ_C, but will maximize sales revenue and profits at output OQ_K, the capacity output of the firm. Thus, in this case sales revenue and profit maximization lead to the same outcome.

Advertising and the static model

The sales revenue-maximizing firm is in a stronger position than the profit maximizer to increase market share, which business strategists see as an important objective. Baumol envisages enterprises moving to new and higher total revenue curves by advertising. Advertising is used to give information to consumers and to persuade them to buy the product. Baumol assumes that the marginal revenue of advertising is always positive and that the market price of the goods remains unchanged. Thus, additional advertising will always increase sales but do so with decreasing effectiveness.

In Figure 2.4, advertising replaces quantity on the horizontal axis with revenue measured on the vertical axis. Advertising is shown as a cost per unit, with total expenditure increasing linearly. Production costs are assumed to be independent of advertising expenditure, but are added to advertising costs, to give a linear total cost curve (TC). The total revenue curve (TR) is drawn showing revenue always increasing as advertising increases. There is no maximum point to the total revenue

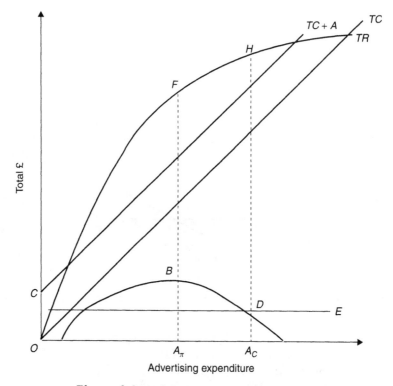

Figure 2.4 Sales maximization and advertising

compared with the curve in Figure 2.1. The level of advertising expenditure that maximizes profit is OA_π while the level of advertising that maximizes sales revenue subject to a profit constraint is OA_C. The sales maximizer will therefore spend more on advertising than a profit maximizer. The price charged by a sales-maximizing firm is again lower than that charged by a profit maximizing enterprise.

The relationships as postulated by Baumol between sales revenue and advertising, on the one hand, and advertising and production costs, on the other, have been criticized. The notion that no advertising campaign ever fails is clearly unrealistic. The impacts of advertising expenditure and price reductions are analysed independently, but can in practice be used in combination to increase sales revenue. The model also assumes that price reductions allow the consumer to move along an existing demand curve, whereas advertising is assumed to shift the demand curve, therefore allowing the firm to move beyond the constraint of a single downward-sloping demand curve.

The assumption that all costs other than advertising are fixed and do not vary with output has also been criticized. This simplifying assumption can be changed and traditional cost curves incorporated into the analysis, as was done by Sandmeyer (1964). The impact of both price and advertising on sales revenue can be explained with the aid of Figure 2.5; this is done by:

■ Treating the minimum profit constraint as a fixed cost that must be earned by the firm.

■ Assuming advertising expenditure is increased in discrete steps.
■ Assuming each level of advertising generates a unique sales revenue curve (and demand curve) that recognizes that revenue eventually decreases as prices fall.

The minimum profit constraint and advertising expenditure are measured on the vertical axis and output or sales on the horizontal axis. The lines $AC_1 + \pi$ represent the combined levels of the minimum profit constraint and advertising expenditure associated with total revenue curve R_1A_1. Thus, as expenditure on advertising increases from $AC_1 + \pi_C$ to $BC_2 + \pi X$ to $DC_3 + \pi_C$, the sales revenue curve moves from R_1A_1 to R_2A_2 to R_3A_3. The firm will continue expanding output from Q_1 to Q_2 to Q_3 and total revenue from Q_1T_1 to Q_2T_2 to Q_3T_3, since advertising consistently increases sales.

Analysis of cost changes

The static model also enables predictions to be made about the impact of changes in costs, taxes and demand on price and output combinations. An increase in fixed costs (or the imposition of a lump sum tax) will lead to a reduction in output. This contrasts with a profit maximizer which would keep output unchanged. In Figure 2.6(a) the impact of an increase in fixed costs is to move the profit function uniformly downward from π_2 to π_1. The profit-maximizing output remains unchanged at Q_1, while the profit constraint of the sales maximizer $C\pi_C$ induces a reduction in output from Q_2 to

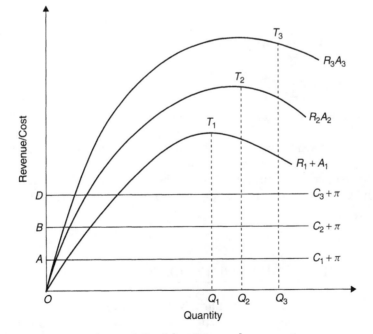

Figure 2.5 Advertising and revenue

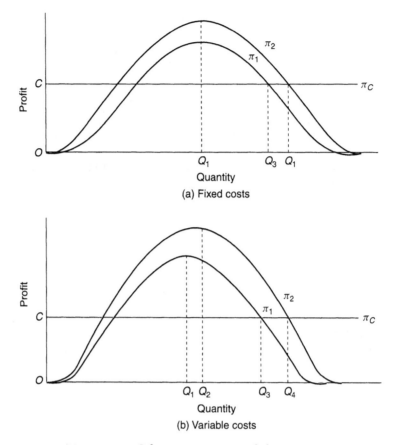

Figure 2.6   Sales maximization and changes in costs

Q_3 and an increase in price. This helps to explain price increases, following increases in fixed costs or lump sum taxes, such as tobacco duty, which are observed in the real world.

An increase in **variable costs** (or a sales tax), which shifts the profit curve to the left as well as downward (from π_1 to π_2), leads both the profit maximizer and the sales maximizer to reduce their output. This can be observed in Figure 2.6(b) where the profit maximizer reduces output from Q_2 to Q_1 and the sales maximizer from Q_4 to Q_3.

WILLIAMSON'S MANAGERIAL UTILITY MODEL

Williamson (1963) sought to explain firm behaviour by assuming senior management seeks to maximize its own utility function rather than that of the owners. Managers find satisfaction in receiving a salary, knowing they hold a secure job, that they are important, have power to make decisions and receive professional and public recognition. Of these, only salary is directly measurable in monetary terms, but the other non-pecuniary benefits are related to expenditures on:

- Staff (S), the more staff employed the more important the manager.
- Managerial emoluments or fringe benefits (M) are rewards over and above those necessary to secure the managers services and are received in the form of free cars, expense accounts, luxurious offices, etc. and are paid for by the firm.
- Discretionary investments (I_D), which allow managers to pursue their own favoured projects.

Together these three elements comprise discretionary expenditure or managerial slack. Expenditure on these three elements increases costs and reduces the firm's profits. Thus, these expenditures can only be pursued providing actual profits (π_1) are greater than the minimum profit that is necessary to keep shareholders happy and willing to hold their stock (π_M). The difference between π_A and π_M is π_D or discretionary profits that managers are able to utilize to increase their benefits. The proportion of discretionary profits not used in discretionary spending is added to minimum profits to give reported profits. The reported profits of a profit-maximizing firm would be $\pi_M + \pi_D$ since there is no discretionary spending, while the reported profits of a Williamson-type firm will be $\pi_M + \pi_D$ less discretionary spending.

The choices facing a manager can be illustrated graphically using Figure 2.7. On the axes are discretionary expenditure and discretionary profits. The manager's preferences are shown by a set of indifference curves, each one showing the levels of staff expenditure and discretionary profit, which give the same level of satisfaction or utility. It is also assumed that a manager will prefer to be on higher indifference curves. The relationship between discretionary expenditure and discretionary profit is shown by a profit curve. Initially, discretionary profit and staff expenditure have a positive relationship, but after point D further discretionary expenditure reduces discretionary profits and, eventually, they fall to zero.

The manager will maximize utility at point E, which represents a point of tangency between the highest achievable indifference curve and the discretionary profit curve. Managers, therefore, do not maximize utility where discretionary profits are maximized but at lower levels of discretionary profit and higher levels of discretionary expenditure.

Reactions to changes in economic variables can be analysed. A profit-maximizing firm has no managerial slack since costs are minimized and profits maximized. A managerial utility-maximizing firm will respond to changes by increasing or decreasing discretionary expenditure. Thus, an increase in demand not only creates opportunities to increase actual profits but also to increase discretionary expenditure. A reduction in demand will reduce actual profits but may not reduce reported profits to the same extent because discretionary expenditure is reduced particularly if reported profits fall below the minimum profit required to keep shareholders happy.

Using case studies, Williamson (1964) found that firms were able to make cost reductions in times of declining profit opportunities without hindering the operations of the firm.

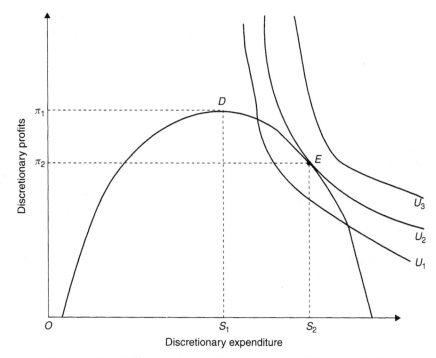

Figure 2.7   Williamson's model of managerial utility maximization

BEHAVIOURAL MODELS

Behavioural theories of the firm, while based on the divorce between ownership and control, also postulate that the internal structures of a firm and how various groups interact could influence a firm's objectives. Behavioural theories set out to analyse the process by which firms decide on their objectives, which are assumed to be multiple rather than singular in nature. The complexity of large modern enterprises means that the firm is made up of a number of separate groups, each responsible for a particular aspect of the firm's activities and each with its own objectives: for example, the marketing director and the finance director may have different priorities in terms of using the firm's resources. The overall strategy of the firm is based on the conflicting objectives of these groups and the processes used to achieve an agreed position. To achieve this, conflicts have to be resolved and compromises have to be made. Consequently, the firm tends to have a multiplicity of objectives rather than a single one and to have a hierarchy of goals, so that some are achieved sooner than others.

Simon (1959), a Nobel Prize winner for economics, argued that:

■ The firm is not a well-defined "individual entity" with its own set of goals.
■ Decisions are arrived at through interaction between the various interest groups or managerial departments of the firm.
■ Studying these interactions in terms of agreement/conflicts will indicate whether the firm will have any clearly articulated long-run objective.

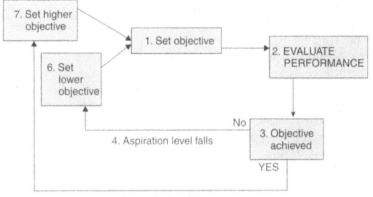

Figure 2.8   Decision-making process

He argues that the overriding objective of the firm is survival rather than the maximization of profit or sales. Survival is achieved if the performance of the firm is satisfactory and satisfies the various interest groups in the firm, including the owners. Galbraith (1974, p. 175) argued that "for any organisation, as for any organism, the goal or objective that has a natural assumption of pre-eminence is the organisation's own survival." Simon argued that a firm's goal is unlikely to be profit-maximizing and more likely to be about achieving a satisfactory rate of profit.

Simon termed such behaviour as **satisficing**, implying that the firm aims at outcomes that are satisfactory or acceptable, rather than optimal. He also articulated a process by which the firm arrives at a set of objectives through an iterative process of learning, as a result of either achieving or failing to achieve its set targets. In the long run this may lead to a performance that is close to the profit-maximizing position, but this is only achieved through revision of achieved targets rather than as the prime objective of the firm. In Figure 2.8 the process by which limited initial goals may lead to higher levels of achievement is illustrated:

- Initially, managers set an objective and, then, the firm or part of the firm tries to achieve it (box 1).
- The next stage is an evaluation of performance against the goals (box 2).
- If the objective has not been achieved and the managers accept that it was set at too high a level, then they might lower their expectations or aspirations and set a revised lower objective in the next period (box 6).
- If the objective has been achieved, then the managerial team will raise their expectations or aspirations and, as a consequence, raise the objective set in the next period (box 7).

Cyert and March model

Although satisficing generates a realistic learning process, the objectives associated with outcomes are rather vague compared with the precise objectives of profit and sales maximization. This would appear to make the construction of a predictive behavioural theory rather difficult. Nevertheless, Cyert and March (1963) developed such a model. They identify the various groups or coalitions which exist within the firm, defining a coalition as any group that shares a consensus on the goals to be pursued. The firm is seen as a collection of interest groups or stakeholders, each of which may be able to influence the set of objectives eventually agreed. The agreed goals for the firm are the outcome of bargaining and, to some degree, satisfy everyone.

It is assumed that salaried managers have both personal objectives and others that derive from membership of a group within the firm. The varying personal motivation of individual managers and their desire to see their own section succeed creates conflicts with other managers and with other groups which have to be resolved. Cyert and March (1963) identify areas of activity within the firm where objectives have to be set. These might include specific goals to cover production, stocks, sales and market share. These specific objectives then guide decision making in the individual sections of the firm as follows:

- Production goal: the production division is largely concerned with decisions about output and employment. They want the latest equipment, to be able to utilize it fully and to have long production runs. If sales fall, the production division would tend to favour an increase in stocks rather than a reduction in output.
- Stock goal: the warehouse division holds stocks of raw materials and finished products. Sufficient stocks are held to keep both production and sales divisions happy, but too many stocks cost money and will therefore be regarded by the finance department as unprofitable.
- Sales goal: the marketing division will be interested in increasing sales that could be set in terms of revenue or in terms of output. Clearly, if sales were pushed too far this might lead to conflict with the finance department seeking to maximize profits.
- Market share goal: the marketing division might prefer to see their goal set in terms of a market share goal rather than just a sales objective. Raising market share might be seen to raise managerial utility because the firm becomes more important. However, such a goal might conflict with the concerns of the finance department.
- Profit goal: the objective is a satisfactory profit that enables the firm to keep its shareholders happy and to satisfy the needs of divisions for further funds. The goal is not set as a profit maximization goal because managers are always willing to trade off profits to fulfil other goals.

To achieve an agreed set of goals for each of the above categories requires the various groups to resolve any disagreements about appropriate specifications. Differences can be resolved so that a consensus is agreed by:

- The payment of money (or additional allocation of resources) to groups or individuals to make them content with the course chosen by the firm.
- And the making of side payments or policy commitments to keep groups or

individuals happy with any agreement. These are not paid directly to individuals but enhance the work or importance of the group.

Once goals are agreed, the problem is then to set the level of prices, advertising and so on so that the goals can be achieved. Generally, rules of thumb are used to guide such decisions.

COMPARISON OF BEHAVIOURAL AND TRADITIONAL THEORIES

The behavioural model has been extensively criticized by economists. A summary of the assumptions of the model and those of profit-maximizing are presented in Table 2.1. The behavioural model makes use of a more realistic decision-making process for a large enterprise where the power of decision making is not in the hands of a single individual and helps to build a picture of the firm as an actual organization. It points to the way real organizations might operate and make decisions through the use of aspirational goals. However, it does adopt a rather short-term vision of what the firm is trying to achieve. The theory does not explain the behaviour of firms nor does it predict how actual firms will react to any given change in the external environment, because these will depend on the individual enterprise's rules of thumb. It also takes no account of the behaviour of other firms.

CORPORATE SOCIAL RESPONSIBILITY

Where firms have a degree of discretion over their objectives, there has been considerable debate as to the extent to which firms should behave in ethically responsible ways and be concerned with the social consequences of the pursuit of their objectives. In the market economy the pursuit of self-interest is presumed to be in the general interest of

Table 2.1 Comparison of traditional theory with behaviourism

Profit maximizing	Behavioural theory
Firm is synonymous with entrepreneur	Firm is made up of a coalition of groups
No conflict between members	Conflict between members settled by discussion/debate
Single goal to maximize profit	Multiple goals to achieve a satisfactory outcome
Entrepreneur has perfect information	Managers have imperfect information
Global rationality	Bounded rationality
Marginalism	Rules of thumb, search, learning
Factors paid in line with marginal product	Factors paid in excess of marginal product
No conflict	Conflict resolved by side-payments
Predictions of price/output made	No predictions – every case unique

Source Author

all. Contrary to this view, Matthews (1981) argued that the "the main-spring of the system appears to be a standard of behaviour, which, in a non-economic context would be regarded as deplorable." Self-interest in both business and social contexts is not always in the interest of the wider community.

Economics identifies various market failures that make the community worse off (see Chapter 23). It also identifies various actions by firms which have adverse external impacts on others and on the welfare of the community. Economic models of the market assume that private and social costs and benefits coincide. Where they diverge they are termed "externalities". The pursuit of self-interest in the presence of externalities is not necessarily in the interest of the community or of the firm, so it may therefore wish to modify its pursuit of profits, and incorporate other goals into its utility function. For example, the major commercial banks in the UK have closed numerous rural branches leaving many small market towns without a branch of any bank or building society. Although such a policy may be in the private interest of the bank, it imposes significant costs on rural communities and helps to destroy their development prospects. Such branch closures may also harm the image of the bank in the customer's mind and lead to a further loss of customers at non-rural branches.

The notion of corporate social responsibility can be defined as the extent to which individual firms serve social needs other than those of the owners and managers, even if this conflicts with the maximization of profits (Moir 2001). This means that the firm might:

- Internalize social goals.
- Represent concerns of groups other than owners and managers.
- Undertake voluntary action beyond that required by law.
- Recognize the social consequences of economic activity.

Examples of expenditures on social responsibility might include:

- Charitable giving.
- Seconding staff to help with the management of community projects.
- Sponsorship of arts and sports, though at some point such expenditure might be regarded as advertising.
- And behaving in an environmentally responsible way by not polluting rivers, etc.

Firms that serve any interest other than that of the shareholders have been criticized by some economists, such as Friedman. They argue that managers should not make ethical decisions that rightly belong to society or use profits for social ends that rightly belong to the shareholders.

Various arguments have been put forward for the firm explicitly recognizing externalities and the wider social context in which it operates. The theories of the firm considered in this chapter limit the objectives of the firm to those established by either the owners or the managers. There is little recognition of stakeholders within the firm, such as labour, or outside the firm such as customers and suppliers, or the wider community.

Some, such as Cyert and March, see the firm as part of a wider negotiated environment in which managers, who negotiate between themselves, are at the centre of affairs but need to keep various stakeholders happy. The managerial group in some firms will take into account the role of stakeholders in formulating their objectives, because, individually, they might have a significant impact on whether the firm is successful or not: for example, employees and customers are important to the success of the firm. Unhappy customers or workers can adversely affect the sales and costs of the firm.

Arguments in favour of firms explicitly incorporating social concerns into their objectives include:

- Long-run self-interest of the firm: socially responsible behaviour generates additional revenue and profits in the long run compared with firms that are less socially responsible; this has been termed "winning by integrity".
- Stakeholders: it is beneficial to the firm to keep in line with ethical, social and cultural norms, because this keeps workers, customers and suppliers happy and minimizes the risks to the reputation and profitability of the firm.
- Regulation: bad corporate behaviour may lead to the imposition of an expensive and inflexible regulatory regime to curb antisocial behaviour, while good corporate behaviour may lead to the avoidance of government regulation and be a more beneficial outcome for the firm. In many industries, such as advertising, governments have preferred self-regulation by the industry rather than government-imposed regulation.

The potential relationship between expenditure on social responsibility and profit can be viewed in two ways. first, profits and social expenditure can be regarded as substitutes or, second, as complements. The first relationship is illustrated in Figure 2.9(a), where on the vertical axis we have profits paid to shareholders and on the horizontal axis resources allocated to social concerns. The frontier assumes decreasing returns to social spending. Where the firm chooses to be on the curve will be a function of the preferences of management and are summed into a set of indifference curves. The firm chooses to be at point E where the two functions are tangential. The firm could have chosen a different point including point A where no social spending takes place or point$B$ where all discretionary profits are spent on social concerns.

The second relationship is illustrated in Figure 2.9(b), where profits and social expenditures are both complements and substitutes. The line AB represents profits that would be earned if the firm did not engage in social expenditure. Initially profit is reduced below AB when the firm starts social expenditures, but after point E social expenditure raises profitability to higher levels.

Profits and social responsibility

In the USA a number of researchers have tried to test statistically whether socially responsible firms earn higher or lower profits than companies who spend less. The difficulty lies in identifying and quantifying social corporate responsible behaviour (SCR): this not only involves expenditure but also good behaviour. Aupperle et al.

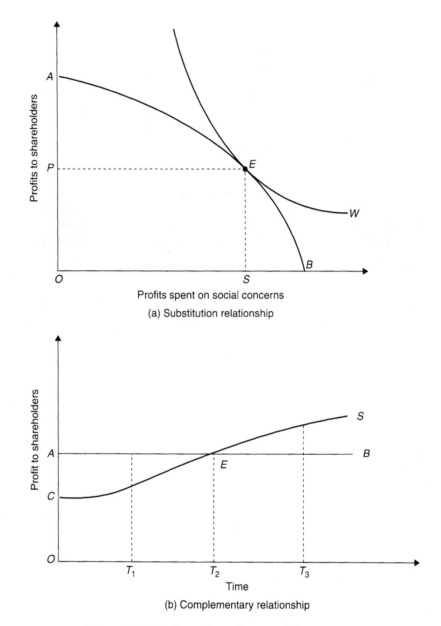

Figure 2.9   Profits and social responsibility

(1985) correlated SCR and share price, where SCR was measured by asking a sample of businessmen to rank companies according to their perceptions of their performance. They found no statistically significant relationships between a strong orientation to social responsibility and financial performance (Aupperle et al. 1985, p. 459). They concluded that it was, "neither beneficial or harmful for a firm to fulfil a social contract." Another study by McGuire et al. (1988) found a significant positive correlation between SCR and return on assets ($R^2 = 0.47$) but no significant correlation between social spending and stock market prices.

The pressure on companies to modify their goals beyond those that maximize or make satisfactory returns to shareholders and managers varies at different times and from country to country. In the 1980s and 1990s the "right of management to manage", irrespective of the social consequences, was reasserted. However, the impact of business decisions in pursuit of shareholder value has led to various pressure groups questioning the unfettered right of managers to decide: for example, Shell was forced to abandon dumping an old oil platform at sea because of criticism by environmental groups, which led to harming the image and the profitability of the company.

OWNERS, MANAGERS AND PERFORMANCE

Some studies have attempted to measure the performance of firms depending on whether owners or managers were able to set the objectives of the firm. Short (1994) surveying 26 studies finds that the majority give some support to the proposition that owner-controlled firms earn higher profits than managerially controlled firms. The results, however, are not always statistically significant (Short 1994, p. 206).

In studies of the UK, Radice (1971) found owner-controlled firms to be not only more profitable but also to have greater variability in profits than managerially controlled firms. Holl (1975) found no significant difference between owner-controlled and managerially controlled firms when the industries in which they operated were taken into account. Steer and Cable (1978) found owner-controlled firms outperformed managerially controlled firms, as did Leach and Leahy (1991). These results do not necessarily imply owner-controlled firms maximize profits but merely that owner-controlled firms achieve higher profits, confirming the comparative static outcomes of profit and sales revenue-maximizing models.

Case Study 2.1 Objectives in company annual reports

A visit to a company's website or a reading of its annual report will usually give some indication of the firm's objectives. A few examples follow:

- Stagecoach states in its Annual Report for 2000: "Stagecoach aims to provide long-term shareholder value by creating a global transport business, focussed on innovation and quality, which benefits both our customers and employees. Our strategy remains focussed on our core bus and rail operations where we believe there remains significant opportunities to generate shareholder value."
- BT in its annual report for 2002 states: "BT's strategy is to create value for the shareholders through being the best provider of communication services and solutions for everybody in the UK, and for corporate customers in Europe, achieving global reach through partnership."
- The National Express Company in its annual report for 1999 states: "We manage each of our businesses for growth – by investing in all aspects of our services, by working in partnership with our customers and by integrating our services with the wider public transport network. An important element of our business philosophy is

to attract more people on to our services – and to maximize the use of public transport systems to bring about environmental and social benefits to the communities we serve. Our 30,000 employees are dedicated to improving continuously the quality, value for money and, above all our services for our passengers."

- The Skansa Group of Sweden in its 1998 annual report states that its goal is to be a world leader, and that it aims to achieve an annual growth of net sales of 12%, while its profit target is to provide an average annual return on shareholders equity of 15%. It also states that, "growth is important, both to the shareholders' need for a return on their investment and to enable employees to hone their skills. However, growth must not be generated at the expense of lower profitability" (p. 3).
- NCC, another Swedish company, stated in 1998 its objective as, "increasing value growth in NCC shares. It recognises that profits are too low to provide a satisfactory return to shareholder and that to increase its profit margin it will be necessary to cut costs and increase growth."

The statements in annual reports tend to give a broad indication of the firm's objectives. Rarely does one find a simple objective such as shareholder value without additional objectives such as growth and internationalization. Some companies do stress growth ahead of shareholder value but tend to see this as a means to increasing profitability and long-run shareholder value. Some also mention satisfactory levels of profit to meet shareholder expectations. This might be more important in countries where share trading is more limited.

CHAPTER SUMMARY

In this chapter we explored the theoretically possible objectives pursued by the firm. To do this we analysed:

- How the chosen objective influences the decision-making process of the firm.
- How, despite a single objective leading to clarity of analysis, in practice firms are likely to pursue a multiplicity of objectives.
- The main models: which were profit-maximizing reflecting the preferences of managers, on the one hand, and sales and utility maximization reflecting the preferences of managers and behavioural theory, on the other. In practice, an individual firm may well have multiple objectives and satisfice rather than maximize.

REVIEW QUESTIONS

Exercise   Objectives of firms

Select a small number of annual reports and try to:

a   Identify the primary objectives of the firm.
b   Decide whether the firm has single or multiple objectives.

c   Decide whether it is trying to maximize profits or not.
d   Identify whether the firm has reported any social responsibility concerns and the extent of them.

Discussion Questions

1 What rules must a firm follow to maximize profits?
2 What are the main criticisms of the profit maximization hypothesis? Can it be defended as a reasonable description of the behaviour of firms?
3 What are the main assumptions about objectives in the managerial theory of Baumol?
4 How does the price–output combination differ between a sales and profit-maximizing firm?
5 Will the profit-maximizing output ever coincide with the sales-maximizing output?
6 What factors determine the profit constraint placed on managers in the managerial theories of the firm?
7 What are the main assumptions about the objectives of the firm in the Cyert and March behavioural model?
8 How will managers react to the following changes if they are profit maximizers, on the one hand, and sales maximizers, on the other:
    – An increase in demand?
    – A fall in demand?
    – An increase in fixed costs?
    – An increase in variable costs?
9 How would the objectives of a large firm differ for:
    – A small owner-managed firm?
    – A members-owned mutual?
    – A consumer co-operative?
10 What does the term "corporate social responsibility" mean? Why should firms expend resources on such concerns.

REFERENCES AND FURTHER READING

Aupperle, K.E., A.B. Carroll and J.D. Hatfield (1985) An empirical investigation of the relationship between corporate social responsibility and profitability. *Academy of Management Journal*, **28**(3), 446–463.

Baumol, W.J. (1959) *Business Behaviour, Value and Growth*. Macmillan, London.

Cyert, R.M and J.G. March (1963) *A Behavioural Theory of the Firm*. Prentice Hall, Englewood Cliffs, NJ.

Galbraith, J.K. (1974) *The New Industrial State*. Penguin, Harmondsworth, UK.

Griffiths, A. and S. Wall (1995) Firm objectives and firm behaviour. *Applied Economics* (Chapter 3). Longman, London.

Griffiths, A. and S. Wall (1996) Firm objectives and firm behaviour. *Intermediate Microeconomics* (Chapter 5). Longman, London,

Holl, P. (1975) Effects of control type on the performance of the firm in the UK. *Journal of Industrial Economics*, **23**(4), 257–271.

Hornby, W. (1995) The theory of the firm revisited: A Scottish perspective. *Management Decision*, **33**(1), 33–41.

Jones, T.T. and J.F. Pickering (1984) The firm and its social environment. In: J.F. Pickering and T.A.C. Cockerill (eds), *The Economic Management of the Firm*. Philip Allan, Deddington, UK.

Leach, D. and J. Leahy (1991) Ownership, structure, control type, classification and the performance of large British companies. *Economic Journal*, **81**(3), 541–562.

Koutsoyannis, A. (1970) *Modern Microeconomics* (2nd edn, Chapters 16–18). Macmillan, London.

Leibenstein, H. (1966) Allocative efficiency v X-efficiency. *American Economic Review*, **56**, 392–415.

Machlup, F. (1967) Theories of the firm: marginalist, managerialist, behavioral. *American Economic Review*, **57**, 1–33.

Matthews, R.C.O. (1981) Morality, competition and efficiency. *Manchester School of Economic and Social Studies*, **49**(4), 289–309.

McGuire, J.B., A. Sundamen and T. Schineeweis (1988) Corporate social responsibility and firm financial performance. *Academy of Management Journal*, **31**(4), 854–872

Moir, L. (2001) What do we mean by corporate social responsibility. *Corporate Governance*,**1**(2), 16–22.

Radice, H. (1971) Control type, profitability, and growth in large firms: An empirical study. *Economy Journal*, **81**(3), 547–562.

Sandmayer, R.L. (1964) Baumol's sales maximization model. *American Economic Review*, **54**, 1073–1081.

Shipley, D. (1981) Primary objectives in British manufacturing industry. *Journal of Industrial Economics*, **36**(4), 429–444.

Short, H. (1994) Ownership, control, financial structure and performance of firms. *Journal of Economic Surveys*, **8**(3), 203–249.

Simon, H. (1959) Theories of decision making in economics and behavioural sciences. *American Economic Review*, **49**, 253–283.

Simon, H. (1962) New developments in the theory of the firm. *American Economic Review*, **52**(2), 1–15 (Papers and proceedings).

Steer, P. and J. Cable (1978) Internal organization and profit: An empirical analysis of larger UK companies. *Journal of Industrial Economics*, **37**, 13–30.

Thompson, A.A. (1993) *Economics of the Firm: Theory and Practice* (5th edn). Prentice Hall International, London.

Wildsmith, J.R. (1973) *Managerial Theories of the Firm*. Martin Robertson, London.

Williamson, O.E. (1963) Managerial discretion and business behaviour. *American Economic Review*, **53**(5), 1032–1058.

Williamson, O.E (1964) *The Economics of Discretionary Behaviour*. Prentice Hall, Englewood Cliffs, NJ,

Williamson, O.E. (1970) *Corporate Control and Business Behaviour*. Prentice Hall, Englewood Cliffs, NJ,

3 RISK AND UNCERTAINTY

CHAPTER OUTLINE

CHAPTER OBJECTIVES

This chapter aims to help you understand the difference between risk and uncertainty, on the one hand, and how businesses adjust cost and revenue streams when faced with uncertain outcomes, on the other. At the end of the chapter you should be able to:

◆ Understand the difference between risk and uncertainty.

◆ Calculate expected values and measures of risk and uncertainty.

◆ Distinguish between risk-averse, risk-neutral and risk-loving individuals.

◆ Explain maxi-min, maxi-max and mini-max regret decision criteria.

◆ Identify techniques to limit the impact of risk and uncertainty on the firm.

INTRODUCTION

The models of the theory of the firm discussed in Chapter 2 have tended to assume certainty of information, and no attempt was made to include time or uncertainty in the analysis. In this chapter we explore ways in which economists have incorporated risk, uncertainty and the time value of money into decision making and objective setting. To do this, it is necessary to think in terms of the expected values of variables – expected in the sense that uncertainty may alter the certain outcome.

RISK VERSUS UNCERTAINTY

Economics, following Knight (1921), distinguishes between risk and uncertainty. **Risk** refers to outcomes where the range of potential future outcomes is known from past experience. Future values and objective probabilities can therefore be attached to all possible outcomes. The values of possible alternative outcomes are known and so too are the likelihoods of the given outcomes occurring: for example, the failure of machinery and the keeping of spares can be based on past experience.

Uncertainty refers to outcomes where estimates have been made but no probabilities can be attached to the expected outcomes; this is because there is no experience to guide decision makers about possible outcomes. Therefore, no objective probabilities can be assigned to outcomes, though **subjective likelihood** or confidence levels can be ascribed on statistically unverifiable grounds. The source of expected probabilities are the decision maker's guesses and hunches about future patterns of events (e.g., future movements in interest rates).

Situations also arise which might be described as pure uncertainty, where there is no information available about the future states of the world to help a decision maker. Consequently, the decision maker is in a position of complete ignorance. Introducing a completely innovative product has to be based on positive expectations of how the product might or might not sell: for example, the introduction of the home computer was successful, though many firms tried but failed to sell sufficient machines and make a profit. Similarly, the next major **innovations** in terms of new products or new technology which might adversely affect the sales or costs of existing products may, at present, be completely unknown.

SOURCES OF UNCERTAINTY

In assessing future outcomes there are a number of sources of uncertainty which might influence an individual decision maker's view of the future.

1 Changing market demand

The nature of demand can change as consumer tastes and incomes evolve. Some of these changes may be predictable, while others may be unforeseen and take suppliers by surprise. An individual enterprise, for example, can misunderstand the changes taking place. For example, a company might introduce a new, larger, more luxurious car in the expectation that, as consumers become better off, their tastes will change in that direction. In practice, they may find that, when the new model is introduced, consumers favour smaller, more fuel-efficient models, and the new model will not sell in the number expected when the decision was taken to introduce it.

2 Changing supply conditions

In production a firm may face unforeseen increases or decreases in the price of raw materials, or shortages or gluts of important components. Such changes could either adversely or favourably affect the forecast cost levels on which a decision was taken. Another source of uncertainty on the supply side lies in decisions made by competitors or new entrants about investment in new capacity. Decisions by either could lead to excess capacity and falling prices, on the one hand, or capacity shortages and increasing prices, on the other.

3 Invention and innovation

Invention and innovation are important sources of uncertainty. Firms undertake such activity in the belief that it will increase their long-run profitability. For other firms, invention and innovation means their products and production systems become outdated and make them less competitive. Firms can be leaders or followers in product and process development. Some choose to be leaders and spend significantly on research and development to produce new products and technological advances. The outcome of such a strategy is uncertain because the outputs and usefulness of the innovations are unknown. However, if they are successful, then the innovative firm will benefit from being first in marketing products or from using new process technology. Being first is not necessarily a guarantee of a highly profitable outcome; some new products may disappoint the consumer, while new process technology may face a number of teething problems. The alternative is for the firm to become a follower rather than a leader. It may be able to avoid the problems of being first, and benefit from waiting until market prospects become clearer and the use of the new technology is clearly beneficial. However, the firm might find that it is prevented from selling new products or using new technology if licences cannot be obtained from the innovative enterprise.

4   Macroeconomic risks

Macroeconomic risks are linked not to changes in the market but to the economy as a whole. Economic activity at the aggregate level tends to be cyclical with periods of growth followed by periods of decline. Timing the launch of a new product to take place in a slump will be harmful for sales, while launching in a boom will be beneficial.

5   Political change

Uncertainty may be associated with political change. Changes of government, even by democratic means, may lead to adverse conditions for business in general or some businesses in particular: for example, the election of a Green government would make the future extremely uncertain for resource-depleting, pollution-causing enterprises. Changes of government by non-democratic means, by military takeover or revolution, may change the business environment adversely and threaten foreign ownership of domestic enterprises.

INCORPORATING TIME AND UNCERTAINTY INTO DECISION MAKING

If the firm wishes to compare a number of investment projects or sales levels with uncertain future profit pay-offs, then it can measure the expected **net present value** for each project. To take account of risk or uncertainty, corporate planners will assign to each pay-off a probability or likelihood of occurrence; this is then used in calculating the expected value and statistical indicators of the comparative uncertainty associated with each project.

Expected value

The **expected value** (EV) is the outcome anticipated when the range of pay-offs have attached to them some estimate of objective probability or subjective likelihood of potential outcome. For example, depending on market and macroeconomic conditions, the sales of the firm may vary in ways the planning department believes can be quantified. In Table 3.1 we assume that there are three potential choices or decisions to be made and that the outcomes depend on the state of the economy which is classified as slump, normal and boom. The estimated profits depending on economic conditions are shown in column 2, while the estimated likelihood of each condition prevailing is to be found in column 3.

The expected value for decision A in a single period is measured by multiplying or weighting the expected profit (π) by the likelihood (p) and, then, summing the outcomes to measure the expected value or weighted average. Thus, the expected value for decision A can be expressed as:

$$EV_A = (p_S * \pi_S) + (p_N * \pi_N) + (p_B * \pi_B)$$

Table 3.1 Measuring expected value

		1	2	3	4
		State of the economy	Profit (π)	Likelihood (P)	Expected value (EV)
Decision A		Slump	4,000	0.1	400
		Normal	5,000	0.8	4,000
		Boom	6,000	0.1	600
				1.0	5,000
Decision B		Slump	1,000	0.1	100
		Normal	5,000	0.8	4,000
		Boom	9,000	0.1	900
				1.0	5,000
Decision C		Slump	101,000	0.1	10,100
		Normal	105,000	0.8	84,000
		Boom	109,000	0.1	10,900
				1.0	105,000

Source Author

where S = slump, N = normal and B = boom:

$$EV_A = (4,000 * 0.1) + (5,000 * 0.8) + (6,000 * 0.1) = 5,000$$

Thus the expected value of decision A is 5,000, decision B is 5,000 and decision C is 105,000.

Coefficient of variation

Although decisions A and B have the same expected profits, we cannot ascertain which of the projects is the more uncertain. To measure the degree of uncertainty or risk associated with each decision, it is usual to measure **variance**, **standard deviation** and the coefficient of variation. The process of calculation is illustrated in Table 3.2, using the same information for the three decisions in Table 3.1.

In Table 3.2, column 1 gives the expected profit and column 2 the expected value for each decision calculated in Table 3.1. Column 3 is the profit in column 1 minus the expected value in column 2 to give the deviations of each occurrence from the expected value. This deviation or difference is squared and shown in column 4, which is then multiplied by the likelihood (column 5) and shown in column 6; these are then summed to give variance, the square root of which gives the standard deviation for each decision. Thus, for decision A the standard deviation is 447, for decision B it is 1789 and for decision C it is 1,789; these are shown in column 7. In column 8 the

Table 3.2 Assessing uncertainty and risk

	1	2	3	4	5	6	7	8
	Profit	Expected value	Deviation		Likeli-hood	Variance	Standard deviation	Coefficient of variation
	(π)	(EV)	$D = \pi - EV$	D^2	(p)	$D^2 * p$		
Decision A	4,000	5,000	−1,000	1,000,000	0.1	100,000		
	5,000	5,000	0	0	0.8	0		
	6,000	5,000	1,000	1,000,000	0.1	100,000		
						200,000	447	0.089
Decision B	1,000	5,000	−4,000	16,000,000	0.1	1,600,000		
	5,000	5,000	0	0	0.8	0		
	9,000	5,000	4,000	16,000,000	0.1	1,600,000		
						3,200,000	1,789	0.358
Decision C	101,000	105,000	−4,000	16,000,000	0.1	1,600,000		
	105,000	105,000	0	0	0.8	0		
	109,000	105,000	4,000	16,000,000	0.1	1,600,000		
						3,200,000	1,789	0.017

Note   Column 7: standard deviation is the square root of variance
Column 8: coefficient of variation is the standard deviation divided by the expected value
Source   Author

coefficient of variation is calculated: that is, the standard deviation divided by the expected value, or column 7, divided by column 2.

The standard deviation and the coefficient of variation calculated in columns 7 and 8 can be used by decision makers to obtain an indication of the dispersion of the likely outcomes for each project given the risks. If the standard deviation is used, then the decision with the lowest standard deviation is considered the least risky of the three, because any outcome is likely to be closer to the expected value. Decisions B and C are in this instance indistinguishable, with the same standard deviation. However, the expected value of decision C is greater than that for decision B.

To distinguish further between the three decisions it is suggested that the **coefficient of variation** be used. It combines both the expected value and the standard deviation. It is a relative measure, rather than an absolute measure, of the risk or uncertainty associated with each project. The coefficient of variation has a value between 0 and 1: for project A it is 0.089; for project B 0.358; and project C 0.017. Thus, project C has the lowest coefficient of variation and all the projects can be distinguished. Whereas using the standard deviation projects B and C could not be distinguished, they are now clearly differentiated and the lower the value the less risky the project is considered to be. This is because the worse outcome is relatively closer to the expected value and the majority of outcomes will also be closer to the expected value for a project with a lower rather than a higher coefficient of variation.

Time and discounting

Time is accounted for in economics by discounting future benefits by an appropriate discount rate (see Chapter 12 on investment appraisal) to measure the net present value. The logic of this process is that:

- Money earned in future time periods has different values in the current period.
- £1 now is worth $£1 + r$ in one year's time, or £1.10, if r is 10% (or 0.10 in decimal terms).
- £1 in one year's time is worth $£1/(1 + r)$, or £0.91 now, if r is 10%.
- £1 in two years' time is worth $£11/(1 + r)^2$, or £0.826 now, if r is 10%.
- Future earnings have to be discounted by the interest rate they could have earned had they been held today.

Thus, in a world of certainty, future streams of profits, sales or cost should be discounted to measure the net present value. If future streams are uncertain, then for each year being considered the expected value should be calculated using the subjective likelihoods of occurrences in that year. Thus, with uncertainty the present value of a future stream of profits lasting n years can be expressed as follows:

$$\text{Present } EV \quad \rightarrow \quad \sum_{i=1}^{n} \frac{\pi_t}{(1+r)^t} \quad \text{or} \quad \text{the sum of} \quad \frac{E\pi_1}{(1+r)} + \frac{E\pi_2}{(1+r)^2} + \cdots + \frac{E\pi_n}{(1+r)^n}$$

where E_π = the expected value of profit and r = the discount rate or cost of borrowing. Thus, the objective of the firm is to maximize the net present value of expected future profits calculated to allow for uncertainty.

DECISION TREES

Business decisions are made in far more complex situations than those illustrated so far. Typically, choices are not made between a limited number of independent projects but between a series of interacting and interdependent outcomes. Decisions have to be made in sequence. The sequence of choices can be shown using a decision tree in which decisions are seen as branching out from one another. Each choice is assigned a potential profit and a probability, or likelihood, of occurring. The aggregated net present values of profits, weighted by their appropriate probabilities, may then be compared to indicate the most appropriate route to choose.

Figure 3.1 illustrates a simplified decision tree. A firm may have to make a decision to cut, hold or raise its price. The consequences depend on the reaction of rivals not only in terms of price changes but also in terms of changes in advertising expenditure and product specifications. If we restrict potential outcomes purely in terms of price, then a simple tree can be constructed: for example, if the firm increases its price then its rivals can increase, hold or cut their price.

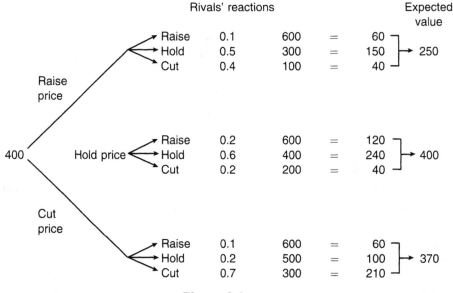

Figure 3.1 Decision tree

Let us assume the firm currently makes profits of £400. It reviews its prices and has to decide whether to increase, hold or decrease its price. The outcome of either policy depends on the reaction of rivals. Therefore, the firm has to estimate the likelihood of rivals holding or altering their prices. If there is a 50% chance that they will hold their prices, a 40% chance that they will cut their price and a 10% chance that they will increase their prices, then the expected value of an increased price can be calculated. This, given the expectations, results in an expected value of £250. Holding prices results in an expected value of £400 and cutting prices in £370. Given the assumptions, it would appear that the firm should hold its prices.

ATTITUDES TO RISK AND UNCERTAINTY

Different decision makers may have different attitudes toward risk and uncertainty. Some individuals are willing to pursue high-risk options, while others will prefer to avoid risk. These various attitudes to risk can be summarised as **risk-averse, risk-neutral** or **risk-seeking**. Decision makers and managers in large enterprises may be risk-averse, trying to avoid serious errors to keep their positions, while entrepreneurs may be **risk-loving** and seek out high-risk opportunities.

These notions can be explained by use of the marginal utility of income or money. The **marginal utility of money** refers to the additional utility or benefit an individual receives from, say, an additional £1 of income received. If the value of utility received from the additional unit is less than the previous one, then there is diminishing marginal utility of money. If the value of utility gained from an additional unit is the

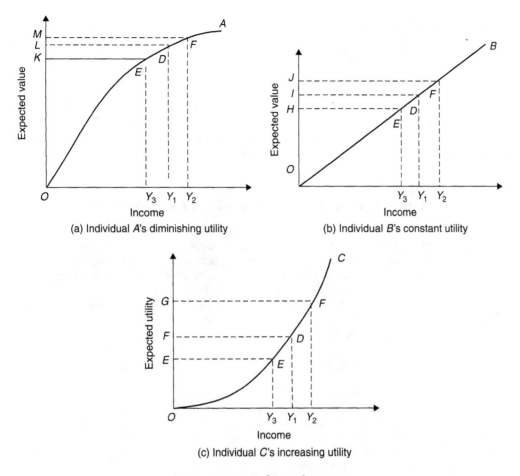

Figure 3.2 Utility and income

same as the previous one then there is constant marginal utility of money, while if the value of the additional unit is greater than the previous one then there is increasing marginal utility of money.

These relationships are illustrated in Figure 3.2. Utility is measured on the vertical axis and money income on the horizontal axis. The marginal utility of income for individual A decreases with additional increments; such individuals are described as risk averse. The marginal utility of money is constant for individual B; such individuals are described as risk-neutral. The marginal utility of money is increasing for individual C; such individuals are described as risk-loving or risk-seeking.

The rationale for these statements can be explained by referring to Figure 3.2. Each individual is assumed to have an income of Y_1 and each is given the opportunity of accepting a 50/50 probability of either increasing their income by Y_1Y_2 or decreasing their income by Y_1Y_3. In money terms each individual stands to gain or lose the same amount of money, but in terms of utility the picture is rather different. The individual with a diminishing marginal utility function will gain less utility (LM) from winning than from losing (*KL*). Such an individual will tend to be risk-averse because the gain in utility will decrease as income increases. An individual with a utility function exhibiting increasing marginal utility of income will gain more utility (*FG*) from winning than from losing (*EF*). Such individuals will be risk-loving because increments of income will bring increasing increments of utility. An individual with a utility function exhibiting constant returns to income will be indifferent between an increase or decrease in income because the gain in utility will be exactly equal to the loss of utility. Thus, the attitude of an individual to risk and uncertainty will depend on the nature of the utility of money income function.

Case Study 3.1   UK Lottery and risk-loving behaviour

A lottery is a game of chance that in the UK, and many other countries of the world, attracts a high proportion of the population to play on a regular basis. On a typical Saturday between 40 and 50 million lottery tickets are sold to the UK's population of around 60 million.

The UK lottery involves buying tickets for £1 each. The buyer selects six numbers from the 49 available. Twice a week a televised draw takes place and six numbers (plus a bonus number) are drawn. The winners of the jackpot are those ticket holders whose chosen six numbers match those drawn.

The UK National Lottery allocates the revenue earned as follows:

Allocation of Ticket Money	Percentage (%)
Prizes	45
Carry-over for special events	5
Good causes	28
Lottery tax	13
Retailer commission	5
Costs of lottery operator	3
Profit	1

Thus, only 45% of revenues are allocated to the weekly prize fund with 5% being retained to fund super-jackpots held to boost interest from time to time. The allocation of the prize fund to winners is shown in Table 3.3. Those getting three numbers correct receive £10. The remaining funds are then allocated by a predetermined ratio to the other prize winning categories. The odds of winning the jackpot prize are approximately one in 14 million and of winning £10 are one in 57.

The expected value of participating in the lottery can be calculated as previously explained. The calculation is shown in Table 3.4. The odds of winning are converted into probabilities in column 3, allowing the expected value of the average prize to be calculated as 45.7 pence. The measured variance is 20.7 pence and the standard deviation 81.5 pence. Thus, for every £1 ticket bought the buyer can expect to receive only 45.7 pence in prizes.

Why then do people buy lottery tickets given the low expected value and the approximately 1 in 14 million odds of winning the jackpot prize? The reason it may appear irrational is that we are assuming that the monetary rewards reflect the utility gained and that buyers exhibit constant utility of income. However, buyers appear to be risk loving because the

Table 3.3 UK National Lottery characteristics

Prize money split	Allocation	Odds	Average payout per winning ticket* (£)
For matching three numbers	£10	1 in 57	10
For matching four numbers	22% or remainder	1 in 1,033	62
For matching five numbers	10% of remainder	1 in 55,492	1,530
For matching five numbers plus bonus number	16% of remainder	1 in 2,330,636	102,000
For matching six numbers	52% of remainder (+ rollover)	1 in 13,983.816	2,100,000

*   Saturday payout
Source   National Lottery press release

expected utility from winning the lottery is greater than implied by the simple expected value.

The willingness to buy a lottery ticket despite the unlikely chance of winning the jackpot prize reflects the lack of opportunities the vast majority of the population have to acquire such large single sums of money. For them the prize of more than £2 million, is more than their lifetime earnings.

Therefore, buyers of lottery tickets value them more highly than the implied expected value assuming constant utility. Thus, lotteries appeal to many people because of the large prize relative to their income and the small amount of money required to buy a ticket. Thus, normally risk-averse individuals exhibit risk loving behaviour in relation to the lottery or they are motivated by altruistic concerns because of the proportion of revenue going to good causes.

Table 3.4 UK Lottery: calculating the expected value

1	2	3	4	5	6	7	8	9
Numbers matched	Chances	Probabilities	Average prize (£)	Expected value (£)	Difference	Squared difference	Variance	Standard deviation
0	2.3	0.43478261	0	0	−0.45714	0.20898	0.09086067	0.30143
1	2.4	0.41666667	0	0	−0.45714	0.20898	0.08707480	0.29508
2	7.5	0.13333333	0	0	−0.45714	0.20898	0.02786394	0.16692
3	57	0.01754386	10	0.17544	−0.28170	0.07936	0.00139223	0.03731
4	1,030	0.00097087	62	0.06019	−0.39695	0.15757	0.00015298	0.01237
5	55,492	0.00001802	1,530	0.02757	−0.42957	0.18453	0.00000333	0.00182
5 + Bonus	2,330,636	0.00000043	102,000	0.04376	−0.41338	0.17088	0.00000007	0.00027
6	13,983,816	0.00000007	2,100,000	0.15017	−0.30697	0.09423	0.00000001	0.00008
Total		1.00331586		0.45714			0.20734802	0.81530

Source   Calculation by author based on published odds

INDIFFERENCE CURVE ANALYSIS OF RISK AND RETURN

The choice between expected returns can be analysed using indifference curves. In Figure 3.3, riskiness is measured on the horizontal axis and expected return on the vertical axis. Thus, any point within the diagram shows the level of expected return and the risk attached.

We have argued that different individuals have different attitudes to risk and uncertainty. These attitudes can be represented by indifference curves. They show the different combinations of risk and return that give an individual an equal level of satisfaction or utility. In Figure 3.3, we show indifference curves for individuals who are risk-averse, risk-neutral and risk-loving.

In Figure 3.3(a) we have a **risk-averse** individual and show three indifference curves. Each curve slopes upward from left to right, the starting point is D because OD is the risk-free rate of return. Other points on the indifference curve I_1 will give equal satisfaction or utility, so that points D, A, B and C are equivalent in terms of utility, but each successive point is associated with a higher degree of risk. Thus, a risk-averse individual requires a higher rate of return to offset the additional risk. The more risk-averse the individual the steeper will be the slope of the indifference curves.

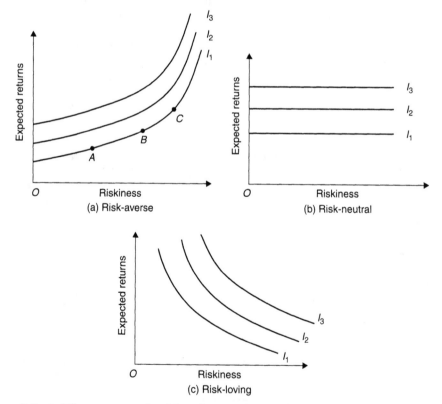

Figure 3.3 Indifference curves for risk and return. Note: riskiness is measured by the coefficient of variation

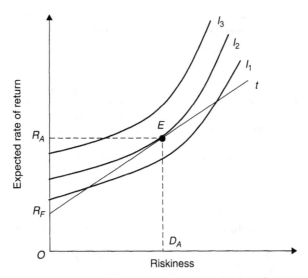

Figure 3.4 Equilibrium combination of risk and return

Further, indifference curve I_2 represents a superior position to curve I_1, so that higher returns for any given level of risk will be preferred to lower rates. For any given level of return a less risky position will be preferred to a riskier one.

Risk-neutral individuals would have horizontal indifference curves because risk or uncertainty do not influence their choices. Such a set is shown in Figure 3.3(a). Higher expected returns are preferred irrespective of the associated risks.

Risk-loving individuals view risk as a source of utility in a similar way to any other good. They prefer to give up expected returns for a greater amount of risk, so that their indifference curves slope downward from left to right as shown in Figure 3.3(c). They also prefer combinations of higher returns and higher risks to those less risky with lower returns (Douglas 1992, pp. 40–42).

The choice of an equilibrium position will depend on the nature of the asset or project to be undertaken and the trade-off between risk and return. A risk-free asset or project is one where future income streams are known with certainty. A risky asset or project is one where future income streams are uncertain. In Figure 3.4 the line $R_F T$ represents the trade-off between returns and uncertainty. The individual is assumed to be risk-averse, so that the individual maximizes utility at point E. The slope of the line $R_F T$ can be viewed as the price of risk, because it shows how much extra return is required for an individual to accept extra risk. If OR_F represents the risk-free rate of return and OR_A the actual rate of return, then the difference between the two $R_F R_A$ represents the additional return required for an individual to accept risk level OD_A.

DECISION MAKING AND ATTITUDES TO RISK

Different attitudes to risk can be summed into decision rules that reflect different attitudes toward risk bearing. To discuss these decision criteria, use will be made of

Table 3.5   Project pay-offs in differing economic conditions (£)

Project	State of the Economy			Minimum outcome	Maximum outcome
	Recession	Existing	Boom		
A	12,000	16,000	20,000	12,000	20,000
B	13,000	14,000	15,000	13,000	15,000
C	11,000	16,000	21,000	11,000	21,000

Source Author

Table 3.5. This presents returns for three projects depending on the state of the economy. The final two columns show the minimum and the maximum return for each project.

Maxi-min decision criterion

The first of these is the maxi-min criterion; this is a risk-averse test, because the individual identifies the worst possible outcome for each course of action being considered. He then selects the project with the highest value from the list of least values. By choosing the best of the worst, the decision maker avoids pursuing courses of action that will lead to significant losses. This is illustrated by reference to Table 3.5. The decision maker chooses the best of the worst outcomes. The worst outcome for each of the projects is associated with recession. The highest value of the worst outcomes is £13,000 for project B. This project is chosen by a risk-averse decision maker.

Maxi-max decision criterion

The second of these is the maxi-max criterion; this is a risk-loving test, because the individual identifies the best possible outcome for each course of action being considered. He then selects the project with the highest value from the list of the best values. By choosing the best of the highest outcomes, the decision maker seeks to achieve the highest return irrespective of the chance of making losses; this is illustrated in Table 3.5. The best outcome for each of the projects is associated with boom. The highest value of the best outcomes is £21,000 for project C. This project is chosen by a risk-loving individual.

Mini-max regret decision criterion

The third of these decision criteria is the mini-max regret decision; this makes use of the opportunity cost, or regret, of an incorrect decision and allows the decision maker to

Table 3.6 Mini-max regret decision pay-off matrix (£)

| Project | State of the economy | | | |
	Recession	Existing	Boom	Maximum regret
A	1,000	0	1,000	1,000
B	0	2,000	6,000	6,000
C	2,000	0	0	2,000

Source Author

analyse the gains and losses associated with a correct or incorrect decision. A regret matrix may be devised for the projects in Table 3.5 as follows. If we consider project A, then assuming recession prevails it would earn £12,000 compared with the best outcome, which is £13,000. The regret of having chosen the wrong project is therefore £1,000. The regret for each project can be calculated for each state of the world and is shown in the final column of Table 3.6. If project A had been chosen, then the maximum regret is £1,000. If project B had been chosen, then the maximum regret is £6,000. If project C had been chosen, then the maximum regret is £2,000. Thus, using the risk-averse mini-max regret rule the chosen project would be A, because it has the lowest regret; this contrasts with the choice of C using the maxi-max and B using the maxi-min test. Thus, depending on attitudes to risk and uncertainty, different individuals will choose different courses of action.

Bayes' (Laplace) decision criterion

The Bayes' (Laplace) criterion assumes that there is no information about the probabilities of future events occurring and that the decision maker should assume the equal probability of the unknown. This means that each outcome would be assigned the same probability and a weighted average calculated; this is illustrated in Table 3.7. The firm would choose the alternative with the highest expected weighted average or in this case either project A or project C.

Table 3.7 Bayes (Laplace) criterion (£)

| Project | Risk * Outturn | | | |
	Recession	Existing	Boom	Weighted average
A	1/3 * 12,000	1/3 * 16,000	1/3 * 20,000	16,000
B	1/3 * 13,000	1/3 * 14,000	1/3 * 15,000	14,000
C	1/3 * 11,000	1/3 * 16,000	1/3 * 21,000	16,000

Source Author

Hurwicz's alpha decision criterion

The Hurwicz alpha decision test is used to select the project with the highest weighted average, where the average is made up of the maximum and minimum outcomes; this is illustrated by reference to Table 3.8, where the maximum outcome is given a likelihood outcome value of 0.7 and the minimum outcomes at 0.3. The results show that project C would be chosen. The assignment of likelihood or expected probability values could reflect expectations about how the economy might perform or the attitudes of decision makers.

Table 3.8   Hurwicz's alpha decision rule (£)

Project	Min	Max	Min * 0.3	Max * 0.7	Weighted average
A	12,000	20,000	3,600	14,000	17,600
B	13,000	15,000	3,900	10,500	14,400
C	11,000	21,000	3,300	14,700	18,000

Source Author

LIMITING THE IMPACT OF UNCERTAINTY

Economics has traditionally assumed when building models that decision makers possess clear objectives, **perfect knowledge** and perfect foresight; as a consequence, rational and fully informed decision-makers never make mistakes. In practice, the future is uncertain and decision makers are boundedly rational. As a consequence, decision makers are unable to make firm estimates of future outcomes because of their limited ability to process all the available information for all the imagined states of the world which might occur. Consequently, firms take steps to limit the impact of uncertainty on them.

One way to cope with uncertainty is to develop routines to deal with unforeseen events. Instead of optimizing, decision makers have to satisfice. Instead of being able to identify the single optimal action, solutions are arrived at through a process of searching through possible alternative courses of action, using past experience and rules of thumb as guidelines; these routines and methods, developed within a company, bring together individuals who collect information, who process it and who try to interpret its significance. The information then has to be communicated to those making the strategic decisions who may or may not understand the significance of the information.

If such routines were expensive to devise, then risk-averse individuals should concentrate on devising routines to deal with those events that will have the greatest impact on the firm and the greatest probability of occurring. Airlines, for example, have routines in place to cope with sudden changes in demand because of localized wars, military takeovers of government, etc. However, none was able to design routines to cope with the aftermath of the attacks on the World Trade Center on 11 September 2001.

When a firm faces uncertainty in some aspect of its market and industry, it may seek to gain some degree of control over the source of the uncertainty. For example, a firm facing uncertainty over the supply of components might attempt to eliminate some part of the uncertainty by buying a supplier and bringing the activity within the enterprise. Alternatively, the firm might seek to sign a heavily specified "just-in-time" contract ensuring guaranteed delivery or the receipt of significant compensation or it might hold large stocks of components to ensure supplies are always available (see Chapter 16 on vertical integration). However, the negotiation of contracts in conditions of uncertainty can lead to transaction, management and enforcement costs because contracts are incompletely specified, as not all outcomes are foreseen at the time they are signed. In such circumstances one party may take advantage of the other (these issues are discussed in Chapter 14).

Another source of uncertainty for the firm is the behaviour of consumers. Between planning production and the product arriving in the market, consumers may have changed their tastes and preferences. To understand the market and the consumer better, the firm can undertake market and consumer research; this will help the firm understand the nature of the demand function and the factors likely to change consumer behaviour. In addition, a firm requires some understanding of the role of prices and advertising in influencing the consumer to buy the firm's product. However, consumers do not always behave in the way anticipated, so market intelligence is crucial to identifying key turning points (see Chapter 6 on demand). To overcome the uncertainty associated with selling a single product to a single market the firm may attempt to diversify its product base. If the firm could sell two products following inversely related product cycles, then it could even out its pattern of sales (see Chapter 17).

Case Study 3.2 Uncertainty and business decisions: buses and pharmaceuticals

Companies face uncertainty in their day-to-day operations and in making long-run decisions. The operations of daily bus services are seen to have low risk attached to them because passengers use them daily to make journeys to work. However, other types of bus activities, such as tours and excursions, are higher risk because they are associated with tourist activity which may rise and fall with economic prosperity, the weather and war and terrorist activity.

In the pharmaceutical industry, market success and profitability depend on bringing to the market innovative new products that are significantly more efficacious than current treatments. The chances of finding that new drug are very low because new drugs can be eliminated at different stages of the process:

■ At the experimental stage when promising compounds do not deliver expected benefits.
■ Rivals might reach the point of patenting a similar drug first.
■ Medical trials may prove unsuccessful.

- After licensing for use the drug may produce unexpected side effects and have its licence withdrawn.

To bring a new drug successfully to market is estimated to take 8–12 years – taking up many of the maximum number of years offered by patent protection. The profit record of pharmaceutical companies therefore exhibits a high expected return and a high coefficient of variation compared with the less innovative and stable sector.

Companies seeking to increase the size of the firm may have a number of alternatives available, which may include:

- Expanding in the domestic market.
- Expanding into new markets overseas.

The expected rates of return and risk profiles of these two different strategies are essentially as follows:

Strategy	Expected return	Uncertainty
Domestic expansion	Low	Low coefficient of variation
Overseas expansion	High	Higher coefficient of variation

The choice facing a company is one of potentially safe but low rewards at home compared with high but risky rewards overseas.

UK companies have looked overseas for expansion because:

- The home market is in decline or at best slow growing.
- Future mergers are unlikely to be sanctioned by the competition authorities.

They have looked to markets with some or all of the following characteristics:

- Highly fragmented market structures giving opportunities for acquisition and gaining market share.
- Demand growth.

Companies that have pursued unsuccessful overseas expansion in the past decade include British Telecom, Marks & Spencer and Stagecoach. In the first two instances, overseas acquisitions were disposed of when the companies' profits slumped or debt levels rose in the late 1990s. In the case of Stagecoach the acquisition of Coach USA proved unsuccessful and led to significant write-offs in 2002 and 2003 (see Chapter 21). The reasons for the lack of success include overestimating the expected profits and a failure to recognize the greater uncertainty and ,therefore, dispersion of returns in the new ventures.

Pharmaceutical companies have diversified into other health-related products and into toiletries and perfumes. There have been a significant number of international mergers as companies have sought to increase their size. Both moves have been motivated by the need to offset the uncertainty associated with developing new products, the falling proportion of products developed that overcome regulatory hurdles and reach the market, and the increasing cost of financing R and D. The pursuit of size and serving of international markets that has led to a number of mergers that have been successful including GlaxoSmithKline, a UK–US merger, and Astra Zeneca, a Swedish–UK merger.

CHAPTER SUMMARY

In this chapter we examined briefly some of the techniques for coping with uncertainty in decision making. To do this we analysed:

■ Mainly the techniques for weighting outcomes in line with subjective likelihoods of outcomes. The decision maker can then behave in a rational way and choose between projects with different degrees of uncertainty attached.
■ The choice of project, which depends on the attitude of the decision maker to risk and uncertainty.
■ Various formal rules.
■ Firms that try to limit the extent of uncertainty by adopting various strategies to understand and avoid using markets.

REVIEW QUESTIONS

Exercise

By looking at recent newspaper stories:

a   Identify business situations where risk is involved and whether insurance could be purchased to meet the consequences of an adverse outcome occurring?
b   Identify business situations where uncertainty is involved. Is insurance available in these situations?
c   Identify industries where the level of uncertainty is high and those where it is low. What are the main sources of uncertainty in these industries?
d   Identify firms that face high levels of uncertainty and those that face low levels of uncertainty in the business environment. Give reasons for your classification.

Discussion questions

1   Distinguish between risk and uncertainty. Identify two situations of risk and two of uncertainty and identify the characteristics that led to your choice.
2   Explain the difference in attitude toward risk and uncertainty of individuals who are described as risk-averse, risk-neutral and risk-loving.
3   Draw a diagram illustrating the shape of a set of indifference curves for a risk-averse and a risk-loving individual. Explain why the indifference curves take the shape you have drawn.
4   Using the following data calculate the expected value, the standard deviation and the coefficient of variation for each of the projects. Which project is the least risky and which is the most risky? Which project would a risk-averse individual and a risk-loving individual choose?

Project	Outcome	Probability
A	200	0.2
	400	0.6
	200	0.2
B	−200	0.3
	600	0.5
	1,200	0.2
C	100	0.1
	500	0.7
	1,000	0.2

5   Distinguish between and explain the differences between maxi-min, maxi-max and mini-max regret decision criteria. Using the following information identify which project a decision maker using each of these criteria would select:

State of the economy

Project	Low demand	Existing demand	High demand
A	8,000	12,000	2,0000
B	10,000	17,000	2,3000
C	4,000	16,000	2,5000

6   The pharmaceutical industry is said to have a high average rate of return and a high coefficient of variation. The electricity industry is said to have a low average rate of return and a low coefficient of variation. In which industry are returns more uncertain and explore some of the reasons why?

7   Explain the concept of a decision tree. How might it be used to clarify problems of uncertainty in decision making?

8   What routines might management develop to cope with uncertainty?

9   Why are managers in large organizations risk-averse and entrepreneurs risk-loving?

10   Why do normally risk-averse individuals play the National Lottery?

REFERENCES AND FURTHER READING

Besanko, D. and R. Breautingham (2002) Risk and information. *Microeconomics: An Integrated Approach* (Chapter 15). John Wiley & Sons, New York.

Cockerill, T.A.J and H. Kinloch (1984) Managing risk and uncertainty. In: T.A.J Cockerill and J.F. Pickering (eds), *The Economic Management of the Firm*. Philip Allan, Oxford, UK.

Davies, H. (1991) The importance of risk and uncertainty. *Managerial Economics* (Chapter 4). Pitman, London.

Douglas, E.J. (1992) Business decisions under risk and uncertainty. *Managerial Economics* (Chapter 2). Prentice-Hall International, London.

Griffiths, A. and S. Wall (1996) Risk, uncertainty and choice. *Intermediate Microeconomics* (Chapter 3). Longman, London.

Hirchey, M. (2003) Risk analysis. *Managerial Economics* (10th edn, Chapter 14). South-Western, Mason, OH.

Knight, F. (1921) *Risk, Uncertainty and Profit*. Houghton-Mifflin, Boston.

PART II

KNOWING THE MARKET

4

CONSUMER BEHAVIOUR

CHAPTER OUTLINE

CHAPTER OBJECTIVES

This chapter aims to explore the nature of consumer choice and use different economic models to explore how consumers make choices. At the end of the chapter you should be able to:

- Understand the concept of indifference curves and explain how they are used to represent consumer preferences.

- Analyse and explain how using indifference curves consumer choice is influenced by price and income changes.

- Understand the characteristic approach to consumer behaviour.

- Explain and analyse how consumers make choices between similar products with different characteristics and prices.

- Explain the notion behind the use of hedonic prices and their measurement.

- Understand the behavioural approach to consumer behaviour and describe the use of routines by consumers in making choices between products.

INTRODUCTION

Firms undertake the production of goods and services in anticipation of consumers wishing to purchase them in sufficient quantity for the firm to make a profit. This chapter focuses on the managerial problem of identifying the characteristics of consumer behaviour and the possibility of reshaping or altering products to align them more closely with the preferences of consumers. Understanding consumer behaviour is an important task for the business enterprise. Economists assume that consumers determine their preferences in a rational way, after engaging in search and evaluation of the products available. They also make rational choices to maximize utility or satisfaction. In practice, many decisions by consumers are shaped entirely by previous behaviour, while others are instant responses, without thought, to special offers of goods and services.

INDIFFERENCE CURVE ANALYSIS

Indifference curves are used to represent the preferences of consumers and enable economists to analyse potential consumer reactions to price, income and product changes. Indifference curves are used throughout this book on the presumption that readers are already familiar with the concept. Here we will briefly review the major characteristics of indifference curve analysis as applied to consumer choice.

To simplify the problem, the consumer is assumed to have preferences relating to two goods that are substitutes for each other and to prefer more of both goods rather than less. The goods themselves are consumed instantly and do not have any durable characteristics allowing consumption in more than one period.

The consumer's preferences and choice set are represented by indifference curves. A set of three are illustrated in Figure 4.1, where the quantities of each good, X and Y, are measured on the axis. A single indifference curve represents a level of utility that the consumer can obtain from buying varying bundles of the two goods. A set of curves are ranked in order of preference so that those to the right of an existing curve represent higher levels of utility and, therefore, preferred positions, while those to the left represent lower levels of utility and less preferred positions. Thus, indifference curves I_0, I_1 and I_2, each represent higher levels of satisfaction, so that point C is preferred to points B, D and E, which in turn are preferred to point A, so that any combination of goods on a higher indifference curve is preferred to one on a lower curve.

Shape and slope

The indifference curves in Figure 4.1 are drawn to be convex to the origin, to slope downward from left to right and not to intersect, because the same bundles of goods on both curves would have different utility levels attached to them. The changing

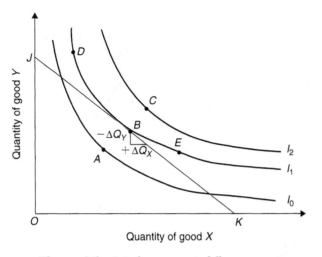

Figure 4.1   Set of consumer indifference curves

slope of the indifference curve depends on the willingness of the consumer to substitute one good for the other. When the consumer moves down an indifference curve (e.g., from D to E on indifference curve I_1) the number of units of X in each bundle increases, while the number of Y decreases. Conversely, if a consumer moves left up an indifference curve, each bundle contains more of Y and less of X. Indifference curves are therefore said to exhibit a **diminishing marginal rate of substitution** between the two goods. Thus, the consumer, in a downward move from B, is willing to give up some Y $(-\Delta Q_Y)$ to obtain more X $(+\Delta Q_X)$. The value of Y measured in terms of X is therefore $-\Delta Q_Y / + \Delta Q_X$. This relationship is termed the marginal rate of substitution between Y and X (MRS_{YX}) and for a small change is measured by the slope of the indifference curve. At point B on indifference curve I_1 it is measured by the slope of the line JK that is tangential to the indifference curve.

When a small amount of Y is given up to purchase an additional amount of X, the loss of utility from Y (MU_Y) is exactly equal to the marginal utility gained from the additional units of X (MU_X), because the indifference curve represents a given level of utility. Thus, we can derive the following relationship:

$$-\Delta Q_Y / \Delta Q_X = MRS_{YX} = -MU_X / - MU_Y$$

because:

$$-\Delta Q_Y = MU_Y * -\Delta Q_Y \qquad \text{and} \qquad +\Delta Q_X = MU_X * \Delta Q_X$$

Thus:

$$MU_Y * -\Delta Q_Y = MU_X * \Delta Q_X$$

Rearranging gives:

$$-\Delta Q_Y / \Delta Q_X = MU_X / - MU_Y$$

Budget line

Given the consumer's preferences, the constraints on which bundle of X and Y the consumer will choose are income and the prices of the two goods. Assuming a given level of money income (M) and known prices of X (P_X) and Y (P_Y), the budget line can be determined. If all income is spent on good Y, then the consumer will be able to buy M/P_Y units of the good (or Q_Y). However, if all income is spent on X, then the consumer will buy M/P_X units of the good (or Q_X). These points are represented by points J and K in Figure 4.1. The line JK is the budget constraint, and the consumer is able to purchase any of these bundles of goods on or within the line. However, any point beyond the line JK is not achievable, because the consumer does not have sufficient income to buy such comb)nations.

The budget constraint can be expressed as:

$$M = P_X Q_X + P_Y Q_Y$$

Rearranging gives:

$$P_Y Q_Y = M - P_X Q_X$$

and

$$Q_Y = M/P_Y - (P_X/P_Y)Q_X \qquad \text{or} \qquad Q_X = M/P_X - (P_Y/P_X)Q_Y \qquad (4.1)$$

For example, if $M = 50$, $P_Y = 2$ and $P_X = 5$, then equation (4.1 becomes:

$$Q_X = (50/2) - (5/2)Q_Y$$

Therefore, if $Q_X = 0$, then $Q_Y = 25$ and if $Q_Y = 0$, then $Q_X = 10$. If the price of X or Y changes, then the slope of the budget line changes.

Given a set of preferences and a budget constraint, a rational consumer will choose a point on the highest indifference curve achievable because that will represent the highest level of utility.

In Figure 4.1 the consumer prefers combinations on indifference curve I_2, but the available budget line KJ constrains the consumer to bundles of X and Y on or within budget line JK; this allows the consumer to choose positions on indifference curve I_0 or one point on indifference curve I_1. Since positions on I_1 are preferred to positions on I_0, to maximize utility the consumer should choose point B, because the indifference curve I_1 is tangential to the budget line JK.

The slope of the budget line JK is $-(OJ)/(OK)$, which is the ratio of the price of X to the price of Y or $-P_X/P_Y$. The slope of the indifference curve is the marginal rate of substitution between X and Y, or the ratio of the marginal utilities, or $MY_X/-MU_Y$. Thus, at the equilibrium point there is an equality between the relative prices of the two goods and the relative value of the marginal unit purchased by the consumer.

Price and Income Effects

Indifference curve analysis of consumer behaviour enables the economist to analyse the impact of changes in prices, income and tastes on the bundles of goods purchased by an individual consumer. In Figure 4.2, the initial budget line is JK. If the price of Y remains constant but the price of X falls, then the budget line shifts from JK to JL.

A fall in the price of one good has two effects: first, it will encourage the consumer to buy more of the cheaper good, because of the shape of the indifference curve; and, second, the consumer's real income increases, because less money is required to

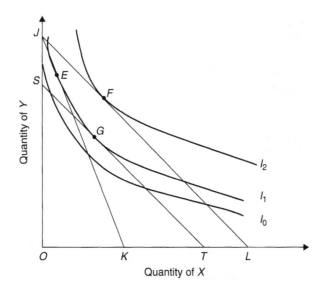

Figure 4.2 Price changes: income and substitution effects

purchase the original bundle of goods, thus allowing the consumer to purchase more of both goods, if that increases satisfaction.

The reaction of a rational consumer to a price change is illustrated in Figure 4.2. The consumer is initially at point E on indifference curve I_1 and budget line JK. If the price of X falls, then the new budget constraint in the line JL allows the consumer to move to point F on the preferred indifference curve I_2. The move from E to F has two components: the substitution and the income effect. If the relative prices at F had been in operation when the consumer was on I_1, then the relevant budget line would have been ST. The consumer would have chosen to move from E to G on the same indifference curve because good X is now cheaper; this is termed the substitution effect (i.e., the effect on consumption of one product being cheaper). However, because of the fall in the price of X the consumer's real income has increased, and this allows the consumer to move from G to F; this is termed the income effect.

Criticisms of indifference curve analysis

First, the theory says nothing about the process by which preferences are set or how preferences are changed. In practice, consumers may follow ingrained patterns of consumption based on experience and learning.

Second, the theory is static and, although it compares one position with another, the theory does not determine the path of change nor does it analyse how the consumer adjusts purchases in line with the new prices or income.

Third, the rules of rational behaviour do not represent the process by which individuals actually make decisions about consuming more or less of a particular good. Others argue that they are a reasonable approximation. Although consumers do not make marginal calculations explicitly in practice, they make such estimates in making such decisions.

Fourth, consumers are not sufficiently well informed to be able to make reasonable estimates of the benefits they expect to receive from a purchase nor to make rational choices between products.

Fifth, the ordering of preferences by individuals is a purely utility-driven process and takes no account of moral preferences or the notion of a hierarchy of needs with some being more important than others.

Sixth, consumers are assumed to behave independently of other consumers. In practice utility functions may not be independent and one consumer's utility may be influenced by the actions of another.

Seventh, the model deals only with private goods that are consumed instantly. It does not recognize goods that provide benefits over a period of time or where there are external effects nor does it recognize disappointing goods where the consumer's expectations of the benefit of consumption are not fulfilled.

CHARACTERISTICS APPROACH TO CONSUMER BEHAVIOUR

Characteristics versus goods

Lancaster's (1966) approach to consumer behaviour developed indifference curve analysis. He argued that consumers not only make choices between quantities of distinct goods but also between similar goods with different combinations of characteristics. Motor cars all have four wheels but many different body shapes and other features, giving the consumer a wider range of choice. The consumer, therefore, has the choice between many similar but different models – a long way from Henry Ford's philosophy of consumer choice which has been handed down as "any colour as long as it is black", a position strongly desired by production managers but not by consumers.

Lancaster argued that consumers do not want goods for their own sakes but for their inherent characteristics; this is supported by the work of Pickering et al. (1983) who found that consumers saw products grouped according to their characteristics. A characteristic is defined as a property of a good that generates utility for its purchaser. Market goods are transformed into characteristics through what is termed "consumption technology": for example, various cheeses have characteristics that can be identified by mildness, crumbliness and taste, whereas for clothing the important characteristics may be style, cut, colour and comfort.

Lancaster postulates that the utility an individual consumer obtains from the consumption of a good is a function of the characteristics that the good encompasses and seeks to maximize utility. A consumer's ability to buy a good with the most desirable set of characteristics is a function of income and the price of characteristics. The analysis assumes that:

Table 4.1 Characteristics of five brands

1	2	3	4	5	6	7	8
Brand	Texture (T)	Maturity (M)	Ratio of T/M	Price (£)	Ratio of T/price	Ratio of M/price	Point
I	90	360	1 : 4	0.90	10	40	a
II	400	100	4 : 1	1.00	40	10	b
III	240	480	1 : 2	2.40	10	20	c
IV	450	450	1 : 1	1.50	30	30	d
V	300	150	2 : 1	1.00	30	15	e

Source Author

- Each product will have more than one characteristic.
- Each product will have a mix of characteristics that will vary by brand.
- Characteristics are measurable objectively.
- Products are divisible and do not have to be purchased in whole units.
- Products (or brands) are substitutes for each other despite containing differing combinations of characteristics.

The nature of the choice process can be illustrated with a simple arithmetic and graphical example. Suppose the desirable characteristics of cheeses are texture (T) and maturity (M) in varying proportions. Each brand can be decomposed into the quantities of characteristics contained within them; these are indicated in Table 4.1 where columns 2 to 4 indicate the consumption technology, columns 2 and 3 show the total characteristics of T and M per brand and column 4 the proportion of T and M in each brand.

The budget constraint is expressed in terms of how many units of each characteristic the consumer can purchase. Assume product A is priced at £0.90 and product B at £1.00. A price per unit of each characteristic in each brand can then be calculated by dividing the number of characteristics in each product by the price. Thus, in Table 4.1:

- Column 5 shows the product price.
- Column 6 shows the price of characteristic T (i.e., the quantity of T divided by price per unit of quantity).
- Column 7 shows the price of characteristic M.

Initially, we assume that only brands I and II are available for the consumer to buy. The number of units of characteristics T and M which can be purchased for £1 is shown in Figure 4.3. Points A^I and A^{II} show how many characteristics each brand provides. A ray from the origin through points A^I and A^{II} represents the constant proportions of T versus M for the two brands. At any point on the ray for brand I the ratio of T to M is 1 : 4 and for brand II the ratio is 4 : 1.

The brand preferred by an individual consumer will depend on tastes and preferences. A consumer preferring texture over maturity would get better value from

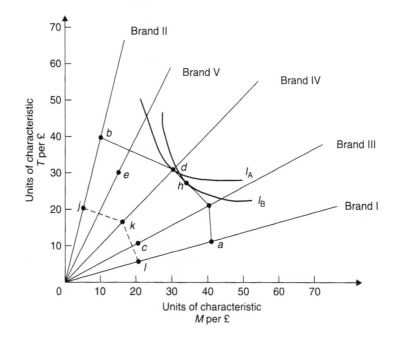

Figure 4.3   Characteristics of brands I and II

product II, while a consumer preferring maturity over texture would get better value from product I. A consumer who might prefer better texture and maturity in the same product is not satisfied by either of the existing products. However, given that cheese is a divisible product, the consumer could buy varying quantities of the two brands to obtain the desired combination of characteristics. If we join points A^I and A^{II}, then we can derive the efficiency frontier that represents the choices available and is the counterpart of the budget constraint in indifference curve analysis. At point A^I the consumer obtains 10 units of T and 40 units of M, while at point A^{II} the consumer obtains 40 units of T and 10 units of M. If the consumer was to spend £0.50 on each product, then he could obtain 25 units of T and 25 units of M at point B.

With a set of indifference curves representing the consumer's preferences between the two characteristics, an optimal position can be chosen; this in Figure 4.3 is at point B, where the slope of the indifference curve is equal to the slope of the efficiency frontier.

If product divisibility is not feasible, as is the case for consumer durables, then this option may not be available. Instead, producers may introduce new products offering differing combinations of the two characteristics to satisfy the demands of consumers. Brands III, IV and V might be introduced to fill the characteristics space between the existing products, giving the consumer a wider choice of cheeses. Information about products III, IV and V is also to be found in Table 4.1, and the information for all five brands is plotted in Figure 4.4. The units of each characteristic that can be purchased per £ for each brand are indicated by points a, b, c, d and e. The outermost points a, d and b are joined to form the efficiency frontier. Product III (point c) and product V

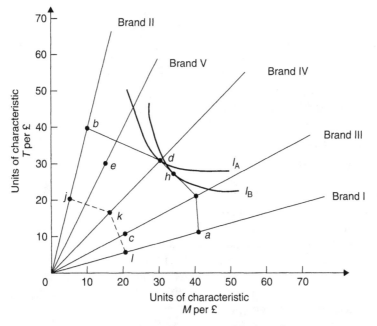

Figure 4.4 Characteristics per £ for brands I to V

(point *e*) are revealed to be inside the frontier and, therefore, are poor buys because £1 buys fewer units of characteristics than in the other three brands.

Consumer 1 with a set of indifference curves, of which I_A is representative, would choose to be at point *d*, purchasing brand IV. Consumer 2 with a set of indifference curves, of which I_B is representative, would prefer to be at a point *h* between brands III and IV.

Price changes will shift the frontier. For example, if the price of all brands were to double then the quantities of each characteristic that could be purchased per £ would be halved; this would move the frontier inward to points *j*, *k* and *l*. If the price of all brands were to decrease by 50%, then the frontier would move outward to the right, allowing the consumer to purchase more characteristics. Differential price changes between brands will alter the shape of the frontier and may make one brand more attractive than another. For example, if brand III were to be reduced in price to £1.20, the *T* : price ratio increases to 2 and the *M* : price ratio increases to 4. The impact of this change in price is to alter the shape of the efficiency frontier. Whether the price change alters consumption depends on the shape and location of the indifference curves. Income effects have similar consequences to changes in price. An increase in income will allow more units of characteristics to be purchased, while a fall in income will reduce the quantities of characteristics that can be purchased.

The characteristic approach leads to the determination of optimal consumption bundles in terms of characteristics and helps to explain the proliferation of brands, each of which aims to garner a group of consumers who prefer the bundle of characteristics offered. When only brands I and II are available, the consumer has to choose between two products with sharply differing combinations of characteristics. The introduction of brands II, IV and V fills the gap between the two initial products and would satisfy consumers wanting a product with a more equal balance of the two characteristics. Thus, if producers can identify such gaps, then they may find it worthwhile to differentiate their product in terms of the relative proportions of characteristics that the product contains. Consumers will only switch to the new product if it is priced in such a way that it either appears on the existing efficiency frontier between existing products or reshapes the frontier in its favour.

Criticisms of the Lancaster model

The main criticisms of Lancaster's model are that not all characteristics can be measured objectively. Different consumers may see the same product or brand as representing the same characteristics but in different proportions. The notion of substitution between similar but different products becomes more complex, because the consumer is expected to view them as essentially different products. While such a notion is relevant to consumer durables, it may be less applicable to goods where differentiation is more difficult. However, it is not beyond the ability of marketing departments to differentiate between homogeneous products.

Case Study 4.1 The characteristics approach and the provision of airline services

Deregulation of airlines in the USA and Europe has seen the entry of new airlines and the development of new products. The most important of these has been the low-cost, no-frills service developed by South West Air in the USA and Ryanair and easyJet in Europe. This product has encouraged existing consumers to substitute these new-style offerings for older style packages of services and has attracted many new customers to use air services for the first time.

The traditional, full-service airlines offered in a single aeroplane a variety of services that differed in terms of the quality of the facilities and services and in the absence of restrictions on the use of a given ticket. A comparison of the characteristics of the two models is presented in Table 4.2.

In summary, the major characteristics that might be identified are quality of service and ticket restrictions together with price differences. Traditional airlines have offered a range of fare deals depending on class of travel and restrictions on the choice of outward and return flights: for example, a weekend stay has been charged a lower price than the daily charge to people travelling out and back between Monday and Friday.

In Figure 4.5 the restrictions on the use of tickets are measured on the vertical axis and service quality is on the horizontal axis. Initially, two products are offered: first-class travel with few restrictions and high-quality service and tourist class with more restrictions on use and lower quality service, particularly higher seat density.

The new, no-frills airlines offer products to the left of tourist class rather than between the two existing products, offering only one combination of service and ticket restrictions. In practice, for some airlines there are a number of combinations in terms of price with a given quality, because flights purchased early have a lower price than those bought closer to departure.

Table 4.2 Characteristics of traditional and no-frills air services

Product feature	Traditional	Low cost
Fares	High-price, complex structure	Low-price, simple structure
Fares	Fares fall closer to flight time	Prices rise closer to flight time
Restrictions	Few on use	Restricted to one flight
Network	Hub and spoke – links to long-distance flights	Point to point – no link to long-distance flights
Distribution	Travel agents who are paid commission – tickets	Direct sales only – ticketless
Inflight service	Multi-class	Single class
	Seating density varies with class	High-density seating
	Seats are allocated	No seat allocations
	Meals and drinks provided	No meals
	No payment	Payment for drinks and snacks
Airports	Major airports	Secondary, non-congested airports/new locations

---

Source   Author

The no-frills airlines also offer lower prices than traditional carriers. The impact of the introduction of new products at lower prices is shown by changes in the efficiency frontier. Initially, the consumer is limited to choices on efficiency frontier *EF*. With the introduction of the low-fare, no-frills alternative the efficiency frontier moves from *EF* to *HF*, with point *E* becoming an inefficient point. The consumer with the preference function shown in the figure will move from *E* to *F*, which is on a higher indifference curve. Other consumers may still prefer traditional services, because of the higher quality associated with the major carriers.

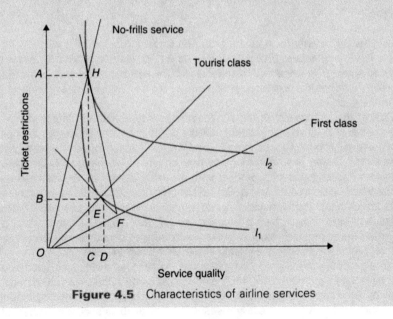

Figure 4.5   Characteristics of airline services

HEDONIC PRICES

The characteristics approach has been used to estimate hedonic (or pleasure) prices. If we assume that there are many brands available of the same product (e.g., toothpaste or cars) which can be purchased at different prices, then the hedonic price approach measures the implied price for each characteristic in each product available.

The hedonic prices approach postulates that price differences between brands reflect differences in the benefits or value to the consumer of the various characteristics in each brand. Thus, where characteristics can be measured, **regression analysis** can be used to estimate the implicit or hedonic prices paid for each characteristic. The equation to be estimated is as follows:

$$P_i = a + \beta_i C_{1i} + \beta_2 C_{2i} + \cdots + \beta_n C_{ni}$$

where P_i = the actual price of brand i, C_n = the units or number of individual characteristics contained within the product and the estimated β_i's = the regression-derived weights, or prices, of the characteristics. The estimated value of the sum of the coefficient $\beta_i \cdots \beta_n$ is the estimated value of the characteristics placed on the product by the consumer.

Case Study 4.2 Estimating and using hedonic prices: cars and wine

Regression analysis has been used to estimate the prices of motor cars in the USA and the UK. A study by Agarwal and Ratchford (1980) estimated the following equation:

$$P = 6.5970 + 0.0349ED + 0.0334LV + 0.2674RL + 0.0664(1/PT) + 0.1492H + 0.2391R,$$
$$R^2 = 0.684$$

where P, the price paid for a car, is assumed to be a function of the following physical characteristics: engine size (ED), luggage volume (LV), rear leg room (RL), passing time or overtaking speed (PT), handling (H) and ride (R). The estimated equation is in log form, and each coefficient has the expected positive sign: for example, increasing engine size (ED) adds to the price of a car.

Each of the coefficients in the above equation represents the effect of a percentage change in the respective independent variable on the percentage change in price, while a 1% increase in ED brings about an estimated 3.49% increase in the price of an automobile.

Another use that has been made by economists of the hedonic price approach is to compare the actual price of a product with its value, based on the estimated prices of characteristics. Hall and Lloyd (1985) used the UK Consumer Association's *Which?* reports to calculate good buys. A good buy was when the estimated value of the product was higher than the actual price, and a poor buy when the actual price was higher than the estimated value. A similar exercise was conducted by Geroski and Toker (1992) on telephone handsets available in the UK market in 1989.

More recently, more advanced estimation techniques have been used and hedonic prices have been estimated for such products as wine (Oczkowski 2001) and classical recordings (Harchaoui and Hamdad 2000). Wine is a highly differentiated product where assessment of quality is less easily measured than variables such as engine size; others, such as the vineyard and vintage year, are more precisely measured. In studies where the price of wine is a function of quality, reputation and objective characteristics the researchers have found all to be important, but reputation to be economically more important than quality (Landon and Smith 1997, 1998).

Oczkowski has used the notion of hedonic price to develop the Australian Wine Price Calculator (available at **http://athene.riv.csu.edu.au/~eoczkows/winestart.htm**). The potential buyer enters information about quality, reputation, vintage, grape variety, the region where the grapes are grown and the shop price. The calculator then estimates the implicit value of the wine and compares it with the shop price. The difference indicates whether the shop price is higher or lower than the measured values. If it is lower, then the buyer has a bargain.

BEHAVIOURAL APPROACH TO CONSUMER BEHAVIOUR

An alternative approach to understanding consumer behaviour is provided by behavioural economics theory, the starting point of which is dissatisfaction with neo-classical analysis, based on rational behaviour that is divorced from the way consumers actually make decisions. Consumers are not perfect or fully rational decision makers, able to efficiently process the information available. Instead, they utilize rules of thumb and decision routines to help them overcome their limited abilities and the partial information available to them.

Consumer decisions can be about routine purchases, such as eggs or cheese, or about large or infrequent purchases, such as motor cars, or overseas holidays, which requires the collection of significant information and processing before a decision is reached.

When making choices about which cheese to buy consumers will be conditioned by their previous experience and the position the purchase of cheese has in their overall budget. Many cheeses will not be considered because they are disliked, and the choice as to whether to buy a particular type may be a function of the type purchased last week, the availability of other types of cheeses in the shop and whether used for eating or cooking. Price may or may not influence the decision as to which cheese to buy, though a special offer on an untried cheese may encourage consumers to change their anticipated choice or a price higher than anticipated for the usual cheese might discourage its purchase. Thus, many of these routine decisions are made without a great deal of preparatory collection of data or any formal decision mechanisms.

Big decisions may involve much more deliberation. The purchase of a new motor car may involve many stages and visits to showrooms before a decision is made. In the UK in January 2001 there were more than 200 models of motor car available, without taking into account further variations within any one model. Initial decisions may be made to narrow the choice by deciding on the type of car required (e.g., a small city car or an estate car) and the price range that can be afforded. These decisions may reduce the range of models to 5 or 10 which are then compared in greater detail regarding engine size, design, fittings, fuel economy, etc. It is this process that behavioural theory attempts to model (i.e., to explore the decision-making routines that enable consumers to make decisions).

Behavioural theories tend to be inductive in nature in that they study and observe the decision making processes used by consumers and deduce the decision rules used. The consumer is viewed as following a process that involves collecting information, processing information, comparing and eliminating products and finally making a choice. Of particular interest are the rules and routines used in processing information as well as in eliminating and selecting products for further consideration. For example, a general rule used by consumers and businessmen is to obtain three quotes and choose the cheapest service. As a consequence the consumer has satisficed because he does not know whether a fourth or fifth or twentieth quote might have produced a cheaper and better specified option. In such circumstances a decision maker is said to satisfice rather than maximize satisfaction.

Decision-making cycle

Choice is therefore seen as a process of problem solving that involves the decision maker going through a decision cycle. A decision might involve some of the following stages that involve gathering and processing information in a number of stages (see Earl 1995, chap. 2):

- *Recognition* of the need to make a choice.
- *Search* for possible solutions to the problem.
- *Evaluation* of rival alternative courses of action.
- *Choice* by ranking alternatives in order of preference.
- *Implementation* of a chosen course of action.
- *Hindsight* by examining the outcome to see whether outcome matched perception.

To cope with these, decision makers develop "rules of thumb" or "decision heuristics", which continue to be used as long as they produce satisfactory results. Olshavsky and Granbois argue that consumers tend to use simple procedures for making choices not only in routine situations but also in more complex ones. They also found that, "for many purchases a decision process never occurs, not even on the first purchase" (Olshavsky and Granbois 1979, pp. 98–99)

Procedures for Making Choices

Information-processing tasks can be viewed as constructing a choice matrix with rival products on one axis and relevant characteristics on the other. Magazines, such as *Which?* provide the consumer with comparative information on many consumer durables and services. The rules used by consumers to evaluate the information have been codified by behavioural theorists and are listed in Table 4.3; these rules are grouped under two headings: compensatory rules that compare positive and negative features and non-compensatory procedures that eliminate products on a single criterion or absolute level of performance.

Table 4.3 Decision-making rules

		Choice of Product
Compensatory procedures		
Weighted averaging	Weight some characteristics as more important and choose product with highest score	D
Unweighted average	Average scores and select product with highest average score	C
Additive differences	Select a pair of products and assign values to the differences. Winner is then compared with other products until one product emerges as the dominant choice	C
Polymorphous test	Set target scores for each characteristic which must be exceeded and then rank products according to the number of tests passed	B or C
Non-compensatory procedures		
Disjunctive rule	Choose product that scores best in one characteristic	A
Conjunctive rule	Set targets for each characteristic and reject those that fail to meet the standard	Uncertain
Elimination by aspects rule	Eliminate those that fall below the target, one aspect at a time; aspects chosen in random order	Uncertain
Naive lexicographic rule	Rank characteristics in order of priority and then choose product with highest score on that aspect	A
Characteristic filtering rule	Sets target scores for characteristics; products eliminated in order of priority of characteristic	Uncertain

Source Compiled by author, based on discussion in Earl (1995).

The application of the rules is demonstrated with the use of the simple arithmetic example found in Table 4.4. The consumer is assumed to have narrowed the choice of products to four on the basis of a preferred price range and to have assessed each of the products for four key characteristics labelled CA, CB, CC and CD, each of which are marked out of ten. In addition, the final row shows the weight attached to each characteristic.

Table 4.4 Product matrix

| Product | Characteristics | | | | | Outcomes | | |
	Price	CA	CB	CC	CD	Total	Weighted average	Simple average
A	65	5/10	8/10	6/10	6/10	25	6.2	6.25
B	60	6/10	6/10	8/10	7/10	27	6.3	6.75
C	70	6/10	6/10	7/10	9/10	28	6.5	7.00
D	75	9/10	7/10	5/10	3/10	24	7.0	6.00
Weights		0.4	0.3	0.2	0.1			

Source Author

The choice of product using the different rules is shown in the final column of Table 4.3. The weighted and unweighted average scores lead to the choice of product C and D, respectively. The additive differences rule examines pairs of products and compares scores allocated for each characteristic: the one with the biggest difference is selected and compared with other products until one emerges as the best buy. If we compare products A and B, then A scores better for characteristic A only, while product B scores better for the other three characteristics: its overall net score is +4. If B is compared with C, then the latter emerges victorious with a score of +1, being equal for two characteristics but scoring more strongly for characteristic D. Finally, if product C is compared with product D, then C wins with a score of +5. The consumer's preferred option is therefore C. The polymorphous test sets a number of required scores and chooses the products with most scores in excess of, say, 6. On this basis, products B and C have four characteristics with scores of 6 or better, which produces an indeterminate result. The indeterminacy would only be removed if the test score was raised to 9 or better, with C emerging as the dominant product.

The disjunctive rule selects one characteristic as being important and chooses the product with the best score. If characteristic A were selected, then product D would be chosen. If another characteristic is selected, then the choice will change. The conjunctive rule sets target scores for each characteristic considered. If characteristics B and D are considered important and the test level is 9, then product C emerges as the chosen product. Following the naive lexicographic rule involves ranking the characteristics in order of importance and choosing the product that scores best for that feature. In this example product B is chosen since that has been given the greatest weight. The characteristic filtering rule selects a characteristic, and a test level. If more than one product emerges, then they are tested against the second most important characteristic, until one product emerges as the dominant choice.

The behavioural approach concludes, therefore, that consumers are not perfectly rational and fully informed individuals who make choices to maximize utility but are boundedly rational and not fully informed and therefore make choices that satisfies their preferences.

CHAPTER SUMMARY

In this chapter we examined three economic approaches to consumer behaviour. To do this we analysed:

- The traditional neoclassical approach, in which the consumer maximizes utility.
- The characteristics approach, which recognizes the proliferation of similar but different goods.
- The behavioural approach, in which consumers make use of rules of thumb and routines to help them make decisions in a world of imperfect information.

Each adds something to our understanding of the analysis of consumer behaviour.

REVIEW QUESTIONS

Exercise

Visit the websites of a number of airlines, including low cost and full service ones, which fly a similar route between Britain and continental Europe. Find for a given service on the same day:

a   The fare.
b   The restrictions on ticket use.
c   The cabin services provided.
d   The distance of the airport from the city centre.

Can the services offered by the different airlines be distinguished in terms of their characteristics? If they can, then plot the products in characteristic space, using two dimensions, explaining the reasons for your choice. Why might different types of consumers prefer one combination of fare and characteristics to another.

Questions

1   Explain the concept of an indifference curve for an individual consumer choosing between two goods. What is the marginal rate of substitution?
2   Explain the concept of the budget constraint and the role of relative prices and income in determining its position and slope.
3   What conditions are necessary for the consumer to maximize utility? Why must the slope of the indifference curve and the budget line be equal for the consumer to maximize utility?
4   Using indifference curve analysis analyse the impact on consumption of both goods of a fall in the price of one good. Identify the income and the substitution effect.
5   Using Lancaster's theory distinguish between a characteristic and a market good and explain the concept of consumption technology?
6   Given the data below on the characteristics of shirt brands construct a diagram in characteristic space showing:

    – The choice facing the consumer in terms of brands.
    – The efficiency frontier.
    – Which brands are inefficient and which efficient?

Brand	Style	Comfort	$S:Cm$	Price	S/P	Cm/P
A	9	36	1:4	9	1	4
B	24	48	1:2	24	1	2
C	45	45	1:1	15	3	3
D	30	15	2:1	10	3	1.5
E	40	10	4:1	10	4	1

Note S = style, Cm = comfort, $S:Cm$ = the ratio of the characteristics in each brand, P = price; S/P and Cm/P are the characteristic units purchased per unit of price.

- What additional information is required to determine an optimal position for a consumer?
- Given the data above, suppose P_A rises to £12. What happens to the efficiency frontier?
- What are the similarities and differences between traditional and characteristic models in the optimal position of a consumer?
- A new brand of shirt (F) is introduced. If the shirt possesses 40 units of S and 30 units of Cm and is priced at £10, what happens to the efficiency frontier?

7 What advantage does the characteristic model have over the traditional model for someone writing advertisements?

8 What is a hedonic price? How are they estimated? How might they be used by consumers to decide whether they are obtaining value for money?

9 What are the assumptions of the behavioural approach to consumer behaviour? What are the main implications?

10 How do consumers react to changes in price according to indifference curve analysis, Lancaster's analysis and behavioural analysis.

REFERENCES AND FURTHER READING

Agarwal, M.K. and B.T. Ratchford (1980) Estimating demand functions for product characteristics: The case of automobiles. *Journal of Consumer Research*, **8**, 249–262.

Cubbin, J. (1975) Quality change and pricing behaviour in the UK car industry 1956–69. *Economica*, **42**, 43–58.

Douglas, E.J. (1987) *Managerial Economics* (4th edn, pp. 86–101). Prentice Hall International, Englewood Cliffs, NJ.

Eastwood, D.B. (1985) *The Economics of Consumer Behaviour* Allyn & Bacon, Boston.

Earl, P.E. (1995) *Microeconomics for Business and Marketing*. Edward Elgar, Cheltenham, UK.

Geroski, P. and S. Toker (1992) What is a good buy? *Economic Review*, **9**(4), April.

Hall, G. and T. Lloyd (1985) The usefulness of hedonic prices to the Consumers' Association. *Applied Economics*, **17**, 191–203.

Harchaoui, T.M. and M. Handad (2000) The prices of classical recorded music: A hedonic approach. *International Journal of Industrial Organisation*, **18**, 497–514.

Lancaster, K. (1966) A new approach to consumer theory. *Journal of Political Economy*, **74**, 32–57.

Lancaster, K. (1971) *Consumer Demand: A New Approach*. Columbia University Press, New York.

Landon, S. and C.E. Smith (1997) The use of quality and reputation indicators by consumers: The case of Bordeaux wine. *Journal of Consumer Policy*, **20**, 289–323.

Landon, S. and C.E. Smith (1998) Quality expectations, reputation and price. *Southern Economic Journal*, **64**, 628–647.

Olshavsky, R.W. and D.H. Granbois (1979) Consumer decision making – Fact or fiction? *Journal of Consumer Research*, **6**, 93–100.

Pickering, J.F., J.A. Harrison, B.C. Isherwood, J.J. Hebden and C.D. Cohen (1973) Are goods goods? Some empirical evidence. *Applied Economics*, **5**, 1–18.

Unwin, T. (1999) Hedonic price indexes and the qualities of wines. *Journal of Wine Research*, **10**, 95–104.

5

DEMAND ANALYSIS

CHAPTER OUTLINE

CHAPTER OBJECTIVES

This chapter aims to explore the nature and characteristics of demand functions for individual products. At the end of the chapter you should be able to:

◆ Identify the main components of demand and explain their influence on demand.
◆ Identify the properties of a linear demand curve and explain the derivation of the marginal revenue curve.
◆ Measure own price point elasticity on a linear demand curve.
◆ Explain the relationship between own price elasticity and marginal revenue.
◆ Elucidate factors influencing the value of own price elasticities.
◆ Explain the income elasticity and advertising elasticities of demand.
◆ Explain the importance to a firm of knowing its demand curve and relevant elasticities.

INTRODUCTION

The decision by a firm to produce any particular good or service is based up the existence of adequate demand for that product. In this chapter we are interested in combining all the individual demand curves obtained from individual preference functions to derive an aggregate or market demand curve: this is a function that every enterprise needs to know and understand, usually before engaging in production. It is important because it sums together all the individual demand curves of all consumers interested in purchasing a particular product. The firm will therefore need to identify:

- The characteristics of the market demand curve.
- The determinants or conditions of demand for the product.
- Those features of demand that can be altered in the interest of the firm.

THE DEMAND FUNCTION

Demand refers to the expected number of goods consumers will buy, given the price of the good, the price of other goods, incomes and tastes. The demand function attempts to specify those factors influencing demand and the way in which they influence the quantity demanded. A demand function for an individual product may be expressed as follows:

$$Q_X = f[P_X, P_Y, A_X, Y, T, O]$$

where Q_X = quantity demanded of good X, P_X = price of good X, P_Y = price of another good Y, A = advertising expenditure on good X, Y = real disposable income of consumers in the market, T = consumer tastes and O = other factors.

A change in size of any of these variables is presumed to influence the level of demand for good X. For example, the demand for hats may increase if tastes or fashions change in their favour or decrease if going hatless becomes more fashionable, all other factors being held constant. Likewise, if the price of hats were to fall, then, with all other factors held constant, demand would increase, whereas if the price were to increase fewer hats would be purchased. Initially, we will concentrate on the relationship between price and quantity demanded, but later the possible relationships between the quantity demanded and each of the other variables identified as well as how they might be measured will be examined in more detail.

THE DEMAND CURVE

Demand is the desire of a consumer to purchase a good or service, backed by the ability to pay and the willingness to part with purchasing power to make the desire effective. The demand curve is a graphic representation of the path along which the consumer would choose to purchase quantities of the good or service at various prices, other things being constant. The shape of the individual demand curve is based on the propositions that:

- The marginal utility gained from the purchase of additional quantities of a good will diminish, so that the consumer will pay a lower price for each additional unit bought.
- The substitution effect of a fall in price is positive, which means a consumer will switch to purchase more of a cheaper good compared with more expensive substitutes.
- The income effect of a fall in price makes the consumer better off and enables the consumer to purchase more of everything.
- The price effect, which combines the substitution and income effects, is normally positive, so that the demand curve slopes downward from left to right.

MARKET DEMAND

The market demand curve is the summation of individual demand curves and shows the quantities of a product that would be purchased by a group of consumers over a range of possible prices. The market demand curve would include all consumers who are "in the market", but it may be more narrowly defined to include only those who are likely to purchase a product from a particular seller. The market demand curve is derived by adding horizontally all individual demand curves that are, at any given price, adding the quantity demanded by each consumer.

The functional notation representation of the demand curve may be given by:

$$Q_X = f(P_X)$$

where Q_X = the quantity demanded of good X and P_X = the price of the good X. This function shows that the quantity demanded of good X is determined by the price of good X. All other possible influences on demand are ignored and the general presumption is that all other determinants of demand remain unchanged. The functional form (f) is presumed to be inverse for the relationship between quantity demanded and price (i.e., as price increases the quantity demanded will fall and as price falls the quantity demanded increases).

The equation for such a linear demand curve is given by:

$$Q_X = a + b(P_X)$$

where a = the quantity–axis intercept and b = the normally negative slope of the demand curve. The linearity of this demand curve is assumed only for purposes of simplicity. In reality, a demand curve may exhibit any degree of curvature and may slope upward rather than downward in special circumstances.

If the demand relationship is estimated to be:

$$Q_X = 20 - 2P_X \tag{5.1}$$

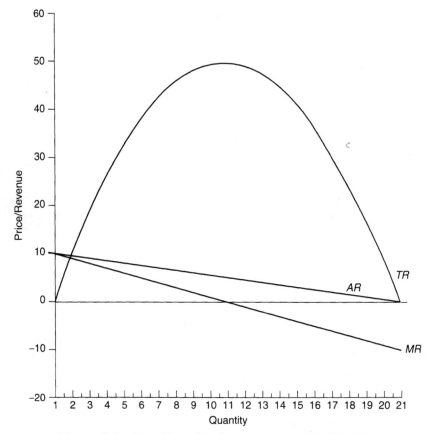

Figure 5.1   Price demand and revenue where $Q = 20 - 2P_X$

It can also be expressed by rearrangement as a price equation:

$$P_X = 10 - 2Q_X \qquad (5.2)$$

Then, using equation (5.2) the major co-ordinates of the demand or average revenue curve (*AR*) are derived as follows:

- The vertical intercept, or maximum price, is found where $Q_X = 0$ and $P_X = a$ or 10.
- The horizontal intercept, or maximum quantity, is given where $P_X = 0$ and $Q_X = 20$ or $a * 1/b$.
- The slope of the demand curve is given by the change in quantity for each unit change in price $(\Delta Q_X / \Delta P_X)$ or $-b$ or 2.

DEMAND AND REVENUE

The demand curve can also be used to calculate total and marginal revenue. The price of the product is the average revenue earned per unit sold by the firm. Thus:

■ Total revenue ($P_X Q_X$) is calculated by multiplying the output sold by the price obtained.
■ Average revenue (P_X) is calculated by dividing total revenue by the quantity sold.
■ Marginal revenue (MR_X) is the addition to total revenue by selling an additional unit of output.

Using the example above, where the estimated relationship is:

$$P_X = 10 - \tfrac{1}{2}Q_X$$

Total revenue can be obtained by multiplying equation (5.1) by Q to give:

$$P_X Q_X = aQ_X - bQ^2 \quad \text{or} \quad P_X Q_X = 10Q_X - \tfrac{1}{2}Q_X^2 \qquad (5.3)$$

The total revenue curve (*TR*) for this function is plotted in Figure 5.1.

Marginal revenue (*MR*) is the first derivative of the total revenue function (*TR*) with respect to a small change in quantity. Thus, the change in total revenue ΔTR is related to the change in quantity ΔQ_X. From equation (5.3), following the rules of differentiation, we obtain:

$$MR = \Delta TR / \Delta Q = 10 - Q_X$$

This compares with the relationship for average revenue of $P_X = 10 - \tfrac{1}{2}Q_X$.

Thus, in Figure 5.1 when $Q = 0$ the vertical intercept of the marginal revenue curve is 10 and when $MR = 0$ the horizontal intercept is also 10. Thus, we have the following relationships between average revenue (the demand curve) and marginal revenue:

■ A linear demand curve implies a linear marginal revenue curve.
■ A linear demand curve implies a marginal revenue curve whose slope is twice that of the demand curve.
■ Total revenue is maximized where marginal revenue is 0; thus, when $MR = 0$, $P = 5$, $Q = 10$ and total revenue is 50.

The relationships described above provide useful managerial insights, which we have already utilized in Chapter 2 when discussing the sales-maximizing theory of the firm. If the objective of the firm is to produce a quantity of a product and sell it at a price that yields the maximum possible revenue, then it can do so by finding the quantity for which marginal revenue is zero. Marginal revenue is also an important concept in the context of profit-maximizing along with marginal cost.

ELASTICITY AND REVENUE

An important piece of information for the management of a firm is knowledge of the shape of its demand curve for its product and the responsiveness, or elasticity, of the quantity demanded to changes in key economic determinants of demand, such as price or income. The slope of the demand curve $\Delta Q_X / \Delta P_X$, for example, tells managers how many extra units the firm will sell in response to any change in the price of the good. If the firm is interested in nothing more than predicting the number of additional units that can be sold by changing price, then the slope of the demand curve $\Delta Q_X/\Delta P_X$ will suffice. However, if the firm is concerned about the additional revenue generated by lowering the price, then the slope of the demand curve alone is an inadequate indicator; this is because the slope of a linear demand curve never changes and is always constant. However, as can be observed in Figure 5.1, total revenue varies from one point to another along the demand curve. Even if the slope of the demand curve does change, because it is non-linear, the simple slope still fails to convey information about how the revenue of the firm changes, consequent to a price change.

OWN PRICE ELASTICITY

The own **price elasticity of demand**, which measures the responsiveness of the quantity demanded to a given change in its price, can also be used to indicate expected changes in revenue. Own price elasticity is calculated by measuring the ratio of the percentage change in quantity demanded to the percentage change in the price that caused the quantity change; this relationship can be expressed symbolically as:

$$\text{Own price elasticity of demand} = (\Delta Q_X/Q_X)/(\Delta P_X/P_X)$$

By rearranging we obtain:

$$\text{Own price elasticity of demand} = (\Delta Q_X/Q_X) * (P_X/\Delta P_X)$$

By further rearranging we obtain:

$$\text{Own price elasticity of demand} = (P_X/Q_X) * (\Delta Q_X/\Delta P_X)$$

In this relationship the element $(\Delta Q_X/\Delta P_X)$ is the reciprocal of the slope of the demand curve, which is a constant term when the demand curve is linear; while the ratio (P_X/Q_X) is the ratio of the initial price and quantity; this measure is known as the point elasticity of demand.

Thus, using the equation $Q_X = 20 - 2P_X$, own price elasticity with initial prices of £8, £5 and £2 are calculated as below:

P_X	Q_X	$\Delta P_X/\Delta Q_X$	Own price elasticity $Q_X/Q_X * -\Delta P_X/\Delta Q_X$
8	4	$-2/1 = 2$	$(8/\ 4) * 2 = -4$
5	10	$-2/1 = 2$	$(5/10) * 2 = -1$
2	16	$-2/1 = 2$	$(2/16) * 2 = 1/4 = -0.25$

Thus, when price is £8 the own price elasticity is −4, when price is £5 it is −1 and at a price of £2 it is −0.25.

The linear demand curve can thus be divided into ranges as indicated in Figure 5.2:

■   The upper portion of the demand curve, from price OA to OP (10 to 5), is termed the elastic range. It is associated with positive marginal revenue and own price elastici-

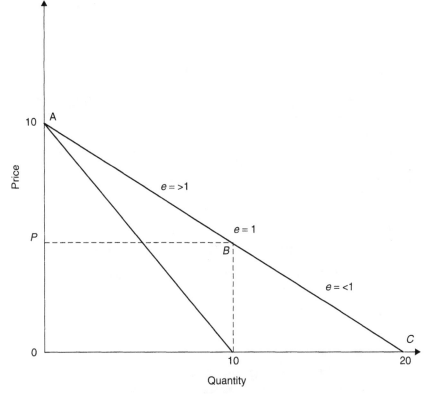

Figure 5.2 Linear demand and marginal revenue curve

ties greater than 1 (by convention in economics the minus signs are usually ignored when discussing own price elasticity, thus an elasticity of -4 is described as being greater than −1).

■ The lower portion of the demand curve, from price *OP* to *O* (5 to 0), is the inelastic range. It is associated with negative marginal revenues and an own price elasticity less than 1.

■ At the midpoint on the linear demand curve at price *OP* (5), elasticity is 1 and marginal revenue is 0.

In the elastic range of the demand curve any particular percentage decrease in price will result in a larger percentage increase in the quantity demanded. Thus, what is lost to revenue by cutting price is more than made up for by the increased quantity sold, so that total revenue increases.

OWN PRICE ELASTICITY AND MARGINAL REVENUE

The relationship between own price elasticity and marginal revenue can be clarified mathematically. Consider the linear demand curve $Q_X = a - bP_X$. The coefficient b is the reciprocal of the slope of the demand curve: that is, $1/(\Delta Q_X/\Delta P_X)$. Thus:

$$Q_X = a - (\Delta Q_X/\Delta P_X)P_X$$

Let own price elasticity of demand be termed e, then:

$$e = (P_X/Q_X) * (\Delta Q_X/\Delta P_X)$$

By rearranging we obtain:

$$Q_X = a - eQ_X$$

Dividing both sides by Q_X we obtain:

$$1 = a/Q_X - e \qquad \text{or} \qquad e = (Q_X - a)/Q \tag{5.4}$$

By substituting in equation (5.4) for quantity we obtain:

$$e = (a/2 - a)a/2$$

Using the equation $Q_X = 20 - 2P_X$ we then get:

$$e = ((20/2) - 20))/(20/2) = -10/10 = -1$$

Thus, at an output of 10, the midpoint output, own price elasticity of demand is -1. In addition, marginal revenue can be defined as $P(1 - (1/e))$; this relationship can be derived as follows where:

$$e = -(P_X/Q_X)(\Delta Q_X/\Delta P_X)$$

By rearranging we obtain:

$$-e(Q_X/P_X) = (\Delta Q_X/\Delta P_X)$$

By further rearranging we obtain:

$$-(P_X/eQ_X) = (\Delta P_X/\Delta Q_X) \tag{5.5}$$

Marginal revenue is given by:

$$\Delta TR_X/\Delta Q_X = P_X(\Delta Q_X/\Delta Q_X + Q_X(\Delta P_X/\Delta Q_X)$$

By rearranging we obtain:

$$MR = P + Q(\Delta P_X/\Delta Q_X) \tag{5.6}$$

Substitute (5) into (6) gives:

$$MR = P_X - Q_X(P_X/eQ_X)$$

By rearranging:

$$MR = P - (P/eP) \qquad \text{or} \qquad MR = P(1 - 1/e) \tag{5.7}$$

Again, using our demand equation for a price of 5 and an own price elasticity of demand of -1, we obtain using equation (5.7):

$$MR = 5(1 - 1/1) = 0$$

Thus, when own price elasticity of demand is -1, marginal revenue is 0.

The relationships between price changes, price elasticity, marginal revenue and total revenue are summarized in Table 5.1. Thus, a firm operating on the portion of its demand curve where price is inelastic (i.e., marginal revenue is negative) would

Table 5.1   Elasticity, price changes and total revenue

Demand is price	Marginal revenue	Impact on total revenue	
		Price rise	Price fall
Inelastic <1	Negative	Increase	Decrease
Elastic <1	Positive	Decrease	Increase

Source Author

increase total revenue by raising its price. If it were operating on the portion of the demand curve where price elasticity is greater than 1 (i.e., marginal revenue is positive), then it would increase its total revenue by lowering its price.

Case Study 5.1   Own price elasticity and rail travel pricing

Economists have measured the price elasticities of demand for railway journeys and found that for peak travel they are less than 1 and for off-peak travel they are greater than 1 (see Oum et al, 1992 and ORR 2001). Train-operating companies would be able to raise total revenue by increasing peak and lowering off-peak fares. The ability to raise fares successfully at peak will depend on any alternative forms of transport which travellers could use to avoid paying the higher price. Where the alternatives are impractical the passenger will continue to travel and pay the higher fare. However, in such circumstances the ability of the company to set fares to maximize revenue may be limited by regulatory action.

To maximize revenue from each market segment, train-operating companies offer a range of prices, charging the highest prices to those consumers operating on the least elastic portions of their demand curves and the lowest prices to those consumers operating on the most elastic portions of their demand curves. In spring 2002, Virgin Trains offered at least eight fares for any journey from London to Manchester depending, in part, on the time of departure and the class of travel. The fares ranged from £252 for a travel-any-time, first-class ticket to £20 for a 14-day-advanced-booking value ticket where travel both ways is by specified trains. Generally, the earlier a ticket is booked and the more restrictions imposed the lower the price; this is also a strategy adopted by low-cost airlines, such as easyJet and Ryanair – the nearer the date of departure a flight is purchased the more expensive it is likely to be. Whether prices relate to elasticities of demand or an ability to plan ahead is a matter of debate. However, the laws of supply and demand come into play as the fewer the number of seats available relative to demand the higher the price, and only those willing to pay the higher price are able to travel at short notice (price discrimination is discussed further in Chapter 9).

FACTORS AFFECTING THE OWN PRICE ELASTICITY OF DEMAND

The shape of the demand curve which determines the own price elasticity of demand depends in turn on the shape of the price consumption curve and its two components: the substitution and the income effect, which again depend on consumer preferences.

The substitution effect depends on the availability of substitutes, so that the demand for a commodity is more elastic if there are close substitutes available. The degree of substitutability for any product will vary from consumer to consumer, depending on the nature of the need satisfied by the good, with necessities tending to have inelastic demands because of a lack of substitutes, while non-necessity goods are more price-elastic.

The time period is also important. Demand tends to be more price-elastic in the long run, because it may take time for consumers to adjust their consumption behaviour. When prices of products, such as oil, increase a reduction in consumption may depend on changing a complementary product, such as a less fuel-efficient car for a more fuel-efficient car or an oil-fired central heating boiler for a gas-fired one. All this takes time and expenditure.

The income effect of a fall in the price of a good depends on the proportion of income spent on the commodity. When a small proportion of income is spent on a product, the demand for a good might be inelastic, because price changes would not call for an adjustment to the consumer's spending pattern.

Elastic and inelastic demand curves

A set of linear demand curves with the same vertical intercept will have the same own price elasticity at the same price level. Thus, if we have two goods X and Y with demand functions $Q_X = 20 - 2P_X$ and $Q_Y = 40 - 4P_Y$, then the price intercepts of both equations are 10 but the quantity intercepts are 20 and 40, respectively. The own price elasticities for good Y at prices 8, 5 and 2 are -4, -1 and -0.25, respectively – the same as those calculated earlier for good X.

Linear demand curves with different vertical intercepts will have differing own price elasticities at the same prices. If the demand curve for good X shifts to the right, so that it now takes the form $Q_X = 40 - 2P_X$ or $P = 20 - 1/2Q_X$, then the price intercept is now 20 and the quantity intercept is now 40. For prices 8, 5 and 2, own price elasticities are now -0.66, -0.33 and -0.13, lower than the values for the previous demand curve for good X.

Demand curves are not normally expected to be linear in shape over their entire length. Non-linear, downward-sloping demand curves create very few problems for the measurement of elasticity, except that the slope of the demand curve is different at every point. In one sense it is a non-issue, since only one price, the current price, is relevant at any decision-making time. It is at this price or point on the demand curve that an estimate of the slope of the demand curve for a very small change in price has to be estimated. Thus, the formulas presented so far to estimate price elasticity are still relevant. Graphically, when the demand curve is non-linear, the question of whether demand is elastic or inelastic can be discerned by observing the slope of a tangent drawn to the demand curve at any particular point.

Demand curves are often described as either elastic or inelastic. Since all downward-sloping demand curves have elastic and inelastic ranges, it would be more accurate to calculate elasticity for the relevant price range being considered by the firm. Sometimes the terms "elastic" and "inelastic" are used to describe demand curves. However, we have observed that for any given price change the responsiveness in quantity demanded will be greater for an elastic than an inelastic demand curve (i.e., the percentage increase in sales for a given price fall will always be greater for one demand curve than another). In practice, when firms wish to equate marginal cost with marginal revenue, they will confine themselves to operate where the marginal revenue curve is positive and the relevant portion of the demand curve has an own price elasticity of greater than 1.

Arc elasticity

Point elasticity is calculated with information from a single point on a known demand curve. If nothing is known other than the existing price and sales quantity, or a quantity change for a large change in price, then an approximation to point elasticity, known as "arc elasticity", can be measured. To do this information must be available for two distinct combinations of price and quantity. The formula for **arc price elasticity** is defined as:

$$\frac{\text{Change in quantity demanded/The average quantity demanded}}{\text{Change in price/The average price}}$$

or symbolically:

$$\frac{\Delta Q/((Q_1 + Q_2)/2)}{\Delta P/((P_1 + P_2)/2)}$$

or:

$$\Delta Q/\Delta P((P_1 + P_2)/(Q_1 + Q_2)) \qquad \text{or} \qquad ((Q_1 - Q_2)/(P_1 - P_2))((P_1 + P_2)/(Q_1 + Q_2))$$

where the subscripts refer to the two points identified as points 1 and 2.

In using arc elasticity, it must be recognized that it is only an approximation to the true elasticity at either known point or any point on the arc between the known points. Depending on the shape (i.e., concavity) of the demand curve, the average arc elasticity measured may be an overestimate or underestimate of true point elasticity.

INCOME ELASTICITY

Income elasticity of demand measures the relationship between changes in consumption of a good following an increase or decrease in income. Income elasticity of demand is defined as the ratio of the percentage change in quantity demanded and the percentage change in income.

Income elasticity of demand can be either positive or negative. For a normal good the income elasticity of demand is expected to be positive, while for an inferior good it is expected to be negative:

■ Positive income elasticities of greater than 1 imply that the demand for the product will increase at a rate faster than that of the increase in income.

- Positive income elasticities of less than 1 imply that as income increases the demand for the product will increase at a slower rate.
- Negative income elasticities of less than 1 imply that the demand for the product will decline at a lower rate than the increase in income.
- Negative income elasticities of greater than 1 imply that the demand for the product will decline at a faster than the increase in income.

The firm would prefer to produce goods with positive income elasticities, as it can then look forward to a growth in demand for its output, even if it performs relatively poorly compared with its rivals. In such circumstances, falling market share is compatible with increased sales. For goods with positive income elasticities of less than 1 or negative income elasticities, it will be difficult for a firm to increase sales, as this will require winning market share from other firms; this may only be possible if the firm's product has a competitive advantage or the firm is the lowest cost competitor.

The income elasticity of demand for a particular good will depend on the income level of the consumer. For poor people, income increases their discretionary income and enables them to widen the range of goods they purchase; this may lead to decreases in consumption of goods already purchased, which are replaced by additional spending on goods already bought or goods not previously purchased. Thus, for some goods, income elasticity will be negative and for others positive and significant. For the very rich, income changes may have no impact on their spending, with the result that income elasticity is very low or zero.

A second factor may be the status of the good. Some goods are necessities whose consumption increases with income until a saturation level is reached, after which consumption does not increase even with further increments in income. Such a good might be electricity whose consumption increases rapidly with increasing income, as individuals begin to acquire consumer durables. However, the rate of increase slowly decreases as individuals become richer and they have all the electricity-using consumer durables they can use. In such a country as the UK significant increases in electricity consumption would be dependent on significant new uses for electricity being developed, such as electric-driven cars or air conditioning.

A third factor may be the age of the product. Some products have distinct life cycles: significantly positive income elasticities in the early years, decline sets in at some point and eventually they may become negative. For example, many consumer durables, such as video recorders, follow this pattern. Initially, demand grows slowly, then very rapidly and then slows when virtually every household has one and/or more technologically advanced new products become available.

ADVERTISING ELASTICITY OF DEMAND

One way a firm can try to influence the demand for its product is to spend on advertising and promotion. It will do so in the hope that the advertising will generate a more than proportionate increase in demand compared with the expenditure. An indicator of the size of such an effect is the **advertising elasticity of demand**. This is defined as the ratio of the percentage change in quantity demanded (Q_X) to the percentage increase in advertising expenditure (A_X), or symbolically as:

$$(\Delta Q_X/Q_X)/(\Delta A_X/A_X) \qquad \text{or} \qquad (Q_X/A_X)(\Delta A_X/\Delta Q_X)$$

The resulting value for the elasticity of advertising can be either positive or negative, close to 1 or much larger or smaller. The impact of advertising on consumer spending will depend on its nature and the susceptibility of the consumer to respond. Advertising may provide consumers with information that they find useful and may influence a decision to buy the product. Alternatively, the advertising may be of a more persuasive nature encouraging additional consumption of the product. However, in some circumstances additional advertising may have no effect on quantity demanded or may even lead to a decline, if the campaign were found to be in some sense offensive. From the viewpoint of the firm an advertising elasticity of demand of more than 1 would encourage the firm to spend more on advertising (see Chapter 11 for a more detailed analysis of advertising).

CROSS ELASTICITY OF DEMAND

The final elasticity of demand to be discussed is one that relates changes in the quantity of demand for good X to changes in the price of another good Y; this is termed cross elasticity of demand. It is defined as the ratio of the percentage change in the quantity of demand for good X to the percentage change in the price of good Y. Symbolically, it is defined as:

$$(\Delta Q_X/Q_X)/(\Delta P_Y/P_Y)$$

The measured result of cross elasticity of demand can be either positive or negative. A positive cross elasticity indicates that the two goods are substitutes for each other. Thus, an increase in the price of good Y will lead to a decline in the quantity purchased of good Y but an increase in the quantity demanded of good X, as consumers replace the more expensive Y with additional quantities of the relatively less expensive X. Conversely, a fall in the price of good Y, will lead to a fall in the quantity demanded of good X. If the value of cross elasticity is negative, then it indicates that the two goods are complementary products. A rise in the price of good Y will lead to a fall in the quantity demanded of X, since both goods are consumed together. If the price of good Y were to fall the quantity demand of good X would increase.

The importance of cross elasticity of demand is that it enables a firm to identify those products that consumers see as substitutes for its own products. In the UK quality daily newspaper market, there are four competing newspapers. One of the papers, *The Times*, owned by News International, has from time to time engaged in price cuts. While the cross elasticities of demand between the four newspapers are all positive they are all less than 1, indicating that a 10% cut in the price of *The Times* reduced the sales of the other papers by less than 10%. In fact, the effect on *The Guardian* was less than a 1% fall in sales, indicating that *The Times* is not a very good substitute in the eyes of readers of *The Guardian* but a better substitute for readers of *The Independent*.

Case Study 5.2   Estimating elasticities for petrol

Estimates of elasticities of demand are generally derived from modelling demand using regression analysis. These methods are discussed in Chapter 6, but an example of the outcomes for such studies is given below using petrol as its subject.

Companies make estimates of own price elasticities of demand for their products. Likewise, academic economists undertake similar studies and many have been undertaken for products, such as alcoholic drinks, petrol and tobacco products, which governments in many countries tax heavily, in expectation that demand is inelastic. Goodwin (1992) surveyed a number of studies of the elasticity of demand for petrol. He found that in the short run – a period of less than 1 year – the average elasticity of demand estimated using **time series data** was −0.27 and cross-section data −0.28. In the long run – a period of 5 or more years – the elasticities were higher but still less than 1. Using time series data the estimate was −0.71 and using cross-section data −0.84. The results confirm that, overall, the price elasticity of demand for petrol is less than 1 and can be described as inelastic.

However, although the overall elasticity for the market as a whole is less than 1, the own price elasticities for individual companies might be expected to be higher. A price advantage for one petrol station in a neighbourhood may significantly increase the quantity demanded at that outlet by attracting customers who might normally go to another station if the prices were the same. Petrol is a homogeneous product bought partly on the basis of price and partly on the basis of convenience in terms of petrol stations passed. A small price differential may only work if the consumer finds it convenient to stop at the cheaper one. To encourage people to visit the same petrol station irrespective of price, oil companies engage in promotional activities to promote brand loyalty.

DEMAND ELASTICITIES AND BUSINESS

Knowledge of the demand curve and the associated elasticities of demand are important for decision making in a number of business areas. These include decisions about setting and changing prices and making decisions about which products to produce and which to cease producing. Managers may not explicitly calculate elasticity ratios or understand the concept of own price elasticity of demand, but they may employ an elasticity-type thought process and by trial and error grasp its significance. A company may increase or decrease its price and find that changes in demand do generate more revenue. By trial and error the firm may adjust prices until it finds itself on a portion of the demand curve with the appropriate value for elasticity.

CHAPTER SUMMARY

In this chapter we examined the nature of the demand function for the products of a firm. In doing this we analysed:

- The demand curve and its associated marginal revenue curve.
- Various elasticity concepts, including own price elasticity, income, advertising and cross-price elasticities of demand; these are important to the firm because they influence the pricing and advertising strategies of the firm.

In the next chapter the empirical estimation of demand functions will be explored.

REVIEW QUESTIONS

Exercise 1

A firm's demand curve in period 1 is $Q = 25 - P$. Fixed costs are 20 and marginal costs per unit are 5.

a   Derive equations for total revenue and marginal revenue.
b   At what output will marginal revenue be zero?
c   At what price will total revenue be maximized?
d   At what price and output will profit be maximized?

Calculate the maximum profits the firm makes.

The firm engages in an advertising campaign that increases fixed costs by 5 and shifts the demand curve for period 2 to $P = 35 - Q$:

a   What is the new profit-maximizing price and output combination?
b   Calculate the point price elasticity of demand at the price that maximizes profit in period 1 and at the same price in period 2. Has price elasticity increased or decreased?
c   What are the profits made in period 2?
d   What criteria would you use to decide whether the advertising campaign was successful or not?
e   Was the advertising campaign worthwhile?

Exercise 2

A firm markets watches in the UK, importing them at a cost of £6 each. (Assume that marginal cost is constant at £6.) Sales last year were 12,000 units at a price of £24 each. Analysis of recent market research returns suggests that the relationship between sales volume measured in thousands of units (Q) and price (P) is given by the equation $Q = 60 - 2P$:

a   Draw a diagram showing how average revenue and marginal cost vary with quantity. Plot the given price and quantity data on the diagram.

b   Suppose that the firm wished to maximize sales revenue. Can we say without doing any calculations whether price would need to be higher or lower than the profit-maximizing price. Why?

c   Derive equations for total revenue and marginal revenue and determine the revenue maximizing price and quantity. Draw the marginal revenue line on your earlier diagram.

d   Explain the significance for managerial decision making of the concept of price elasticity of demand. What is the point price elasticity of demand for the firm when $P = 24$ and when $Q = 30$? What is the relationship between MR and price elasticity when $MR = 0$?

e   What could the firm deduce if it knows its price elasticity was less than unity? Write an equation for the firm's marginal costs. What price should be charged in order to maximize total profits and what would be the sales volume?

Discussion questions

1 Identify the main factors that should be included in a demand function for seaside holidays in a hot climate.

2 What is the significance for decision making of the slope of the demand curve and the own price elasticity of demand?

3 Describe the elasticity ranges of the linear own price demand curve and discuss the significance of this information for price setting.

4 Explain the relationship between marginal revenue and elasticity of demand. Why it is relevant to managerial decision making?

5 If management's objective is to maximize revenue, how should price be changed if:
   – The firm is currently charging a price in the elastic portion of the demand curve?
   – The firm is currently charging a price in the inelastic portion of the demand curve?

6 How can the elasticity of demand at a point on a non-linear demand curve be measured?

7 Explain the concept of income elasticity. Explain the significance to a firm of:
   – A good with a positive income elasticity of more than 1.
   – A good with a positive income elasticity between 0 and 1.
   – A good with a negative income elasticity.

8 Explain the concept of cross elasticity of demand. What does a positive cross elasticity of demand and a negative cross elasticity of demand tell us about the nature of a good? What are the managerial implications of {substitute/complementary} relationships

9 Explain why the price elasticity of demand will be greater for luxury motor cars than for a pint of milk?

10 Would you expect the income elasticity of demand for electricity in a rich country to be greater or less than for digital (DAB) radios?

11 The estimated own price elasticities for rail travel are as follows:

First class	-0.5
Commuting	-0.4
Business	-0.2
Personal	-1.0
Leisure	-1.4

- Suggest reasons why elasticities for business travel are lower than those for commuting and leisure travel.
- Which of the existing prices are at levels set either to maximize profit or sales revenue? Which prices should be increased and which lowered to maximize revenue?

REFERENCES AND FURTHER READING

Baumol, W.J. (1961) Theory of demand. *Economic Theory and Operational Research* (Chapter 9). Prentice-Hall, Englewood Cliffs, NJ.

Douglas, E.W. (1992) *Managerial Economics: Analysis and Strategy*. Prentice Hall, Englewood Cliffs, NJ.

Goodwin, P. (1992) A review of new demand elasticities with special reference to short- and long-run effects of price changes. *Journal of Transport Economics and Policy*, **26**(2), 155–170.

Griffiths, A. and S. Wall (1996) Market demand. *Intermediate Microeconomics: Theory and Applications* (Chapter 2). Longman, London.

Koutsoyannis, A. (1979) Theory of demand. *Modern Microeconomics* (2nd edn, Chapter 2). Macmillan, London.

Oum, Tae Hoon, W.G. Waters and Jong Say Yong (1992) Concepts of price elasticities of transport demand and recent empirical estimates. *Journal of Transport Economics and Policy*, **26**, 139–154.

ORR (2001) *Analysing Allegedly Excessive Prices Charged by Train Operating Co's* (Report prepared by NERA, Appendix B). Office of the Rail Regulator, London.

6

ESTIMATION OF DEMAND FUNCTIONS

CHAPTER OBJECTIVES

This chapter aims to explore the empirical estimation of demand functions. At the end of the chapter you should have an understanding of the main empirical techniques to gain information about consumer behaviour and should be able to:

◆ Describe the main methods of data collection.
◆ Discuss the advantages and disadvantages of using survey and question-naire techniques.
◆ Understand the nature of regression analysis.
◆ Distinguish between rime series and cross-sectional data.
◆ Interpret the statistical coefficients and explain their economic significance.
◆ Understand the main statistical tests used to verify the significance of estimated regression.
◆ Explain the advantages and disadvantages of regression analysis.

INTRODUCTION

Knowledge of the market demand function and of the key factors influencing future changes in demand is important for the management of the firm, not only for setting prices but also for planning production capacity and the choice of goods or services to produce. The purpose of this chapter is to discuss aspects of the empirical estimation of demand functions including:

- Methods of data collection.
- Interview and survey analysis.
- Regression methods for analysing the data and obtaining demand functions.
- Statistical verification of resulting functions.
- Case study of alcoholic drinks.

ESTIMATING DEMAND FUNCTIONS

The task of estimating a formal statistical demand function for a single product is sufficiently arduous and costly for few firms to be willing to devote the necessary resources to the task when demands for more than a few items must be estimated. Many firms rely on traditional behavioural rules of thumb to gain some insights into the shape of their demand curves. Such rules are based on past experience, data collection and experiments and generally work well when the conditions of demand are relatively constant. Managers may make educated guesses based on a summing up of the situation when compared with experience of similar situations in the past or they can engage in more formal statistical methods. The hunch, or educated guess, method is what managers do most of the time. From this process an implicit demand curve or function is postulated and a guess is made of the likely quantity demanded for a narrow range of prices. Such an informal approach may be the only feasible method for many firms for both existing and new products. The latter present a particular problem because the hunch has to be made without any current or historical data being available.

Many firms, however, prefer to be better informed about the nature of their demand function, so that they can answer the "what if" questions that many businessmen ponder. The usual "what if" questions relate to the consequences of altering one of the variables thought to be important in influencing demand: the response of consumers to changes in prices, advertising or in the case of consumer durables credit terms. To do this, more formal statistical modelling of the demand function is required. This process requires choices to be made about:

- The key variables to be included in the demand function.
- The likely mathematical relationship between dependent and independent variables.
- The method of collecting information for each of the independent variables.

This chapter will now examine, in a non-technical manner, survey and statistical methods to estimate demand functions.

INTERVIEWS AND SURVEY METHODS

The most obvious way to try to identify the relationships important in a demand function is simply to ask actual or potential buyers. Thus, you could ask a group of buyers how they might react to price changes, product re-specification and cheaper credit. Collating the results of the study should then give some indication to the firm of the likely consequences of changing one or more of the key variables. This kind of information can be collected by:

- Selecting a sample of existing buyers and asking each person a series of questions.
- Selecting a random sample of people and asking each person a series of questions.
- Gathering together a group of buyers (nowadays known as a focus group) for discussion and questioning.

In all of these approaches the sample of people to be asked is important. On some occasions it may be appropriate to have a random sample of the population as a whole, on others a random sample of existing buyers might be appropriate. Yet again, it may be that only a subgroup of buyers is required: for example, a firm may be interested in the leisure drinking habits of 18 to 25-year-olds, while another might be interested in the holidaying preferences of the over-65s.

The use of questionnaires and interviews is a common procedure administered on behalf of firms by specialist market research companies. In many high streets on any day of the week shoppers and passers-by are asked for their responses to a given set of questions. The results are then used to offer information and advice to managers to enable them to make more informed decisions. However, for whatever purpose a survey is used, its validity is always questioned on a number of grounds.

Shortcomings

1   The first relates to the group of people questioned and whether they were appropriate for the purpose. Clearly, those participating should represent the target group as a whole. If they do not, then the sample is biased and the results may not be meaningful.

2   A second problem relates to the response rate. A questionnaire sent to a randomly selected group of buyers may not be so random when the returns are received. A low response rate may mean that the data collected are not representative of the group as a whole: for example, a postal survey may bring responses from people who either have the time for or enjoy filling in questionnaires.

3   The third relates to the answers given by respondents. At the time of the question-naire the respondent may or may not tell the truth. Even if they think they might

respond to a price cut at the time of the survey, they may not do so at the time of the actual price change. In a similar way, consumers asked to classify themselves into income or social groups may either overestimate or underestimate their actual income or social class.

4   A fourth relates to face-to-face interview, as the answers may be influenced by the interviewer. The attitude and personality of the interviewer may influence the answers of respondents who may be unwilling to give answers which may be truthful but which they perceive the interviewer does not wish to receive or which might make them feel uncomfortable.

5   A fifth problem may relate to the questions asked. If the questions are not simple and precise they may be open to misunderstanding and misinterpretation by respondents.

6   A sixth problem relates to respondents who may be asked about aspects of a product or market that they do not have sufficient knowledge to be able to answer.

Baumol (1965, p. 212) describes interviews as a, "dangerous and unreliable procedure. People just have not thought out in advance what they would do in these hypothetical situations, and their snap judgements thrown up at the request of an interviewer cannot inspire a great deal of confidence."

QUESTIONNAIRES

Much work has been done by statisticians and practitioners to overcome many of these problems and to make surveys and interviews an efficient method of collecting information. Questionnaires must be constructed carefully to encourage respondents to give truthful answers and for answers to be checked one against another to ensure consistency. Problems may arise with words having multiple meanings, with questions that can be misinterpreted, with multiple answers that do not allow the respondent to reflect fully their opinions or preferences and with the order of questions which may guide the respondent to particular answers.

The derivation of a demand curve using hypothetical data is illustrated in Table 6.1. Assume that 1,000 people are asked whether they would purchase a new product at a variety of prices: each is asked to assess their willingness using a 5-point scale ranging from 1, "no", to 5, "definitely yes". The 5-point scale is as follows:

1   100% chance of saying no, 0% chance of saying yes.
2   75% chance of saying no, 25% chance of saying yes.
3   50% chance of saying no, 50% chance of saying yes.
4   25% chance of saying no, 75% chance of saying yes.
5   100% chance of saying yes.

From the data in Table 6.1 we can find the anticipated quantity demanded at each price

Table 6.1 Responses to survey question

Price (£)	Chance of a number of people buying the product					Quantity demanded	Percentage of sample buying
	0%	25%	50%	75%	100%		
10	425	225	175	125	50	287.5	28.75
9	375	175	200	125	125	362.5	36.25
8	250	150	250	150	200	475	47.5
7	150	100	250	225	275	593.75	59.37
6	75	25	275	275	350	700	70.0
5	25	0	200	325	450	793.75	79.37

Source Author

level. At a price of £10, for example, the quantity demanded (D_Q) is the sum of the anticipated volume of sales to each group of respondents given their responses, or:

$$D_Q = (425 * 0.0) + 225 * 0.25 + 175 * 0.5 + 125 * 0.75 + 50 * 1.0 = 287.5$$

The anticipated values for the other prices can be calculated in a similar way. The results show that demand increases as the price falls. This information can be plotted in a price quantity diagram to form an anticipated demand curve for the samples shown in Figure 6.1. If the sample is random and typical of a larger group of customers, a demand curve for the larger group can be inferred. The information could also be plotted as a buyer response curve with the proportion buying on one axis and price on the other, as shown in Figure 6.2. The six data points shown in Figure

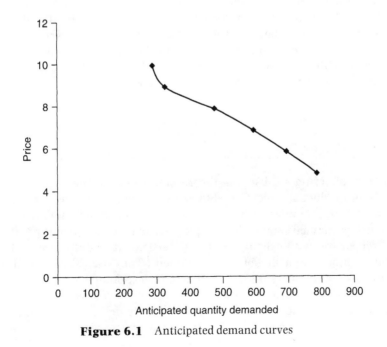

Figure 6.1 Anticipated demand curves

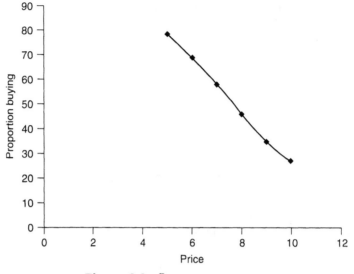

Figure 6.2   Buyer response curve

6.1 indicate an inverse relationship between price and quantity demanded. A simple regression line can be estimated between quantity demanded and price. The result obtained is as follows:

$$Q = 1315.7 - \underset{(-31.5)}{103.9}P \qquad R^2 = 0.995$$

where the t statistic is in parentheses. This linear regression would give a quantity intercept of 1,315.7 and a price intercept of 12.6. The estimation of linear regression relationships is discussed later in this chapter. The equation can be used to predict demand at any price. For example, at a price of £5 the predicted quantity demanded is 796 compared with the survey estimate of 783.75. For a price of £3, not included in the original survey, the model predicts that the quantity demanded would be 1,004.

CONSUMER EXPERIMENTS

Another way of trying to discover the response of consumers to changes in price, advertising or product specification is to invite a group of people to a consumer clinic, or laboratory, and simulate situations in which their behaviour can be observed. Different groups may be shown varying price structures or different product configurations in comparison with existing products. Participants may, for example, be asked to spend "play" money in a shopping environment. They are asked to visit the shop and make purchases with different sets of prices in operation at each visit.

The results of such artificial experiments have to be assessed carefully because they may not reflect what the respondent would actually do in a real situation. They may just play the game, providing the organizers with the answers they are expecting, rather than their own true views. Nevertheless, they may provide useful information, particularly about product characteristics and the combinations of characteristics that consumers prefer.

The Gabor–Granger Test is used to test the potential of new products by comparing a new product with an existing one: Half the group are shown the new product and asked whether they would buy it at various prices on a random price list. They are then shown the existing product. The other half are shown the original product, first, and the new product, second. The objective is not only to gain some idea of the acceptance of the product by consumers but also to eliminate bias by showing the products to the two groups in a different order.

MARKET STUDIES

Market studies involve testing real products in real markets with real people. For example, a firm might select a region of the UK with its own regional or local commercial radio and television station to test-market a new chocolate bar or washing powder. If the new product sells sufficiently well against a competitor's and is seen as indicating consumer acceptance and satisfaction, the producer may then decide to launch the product in other regions or to go nationwide. An existing product might be promoted in one area at a lower price, backed by advertising to again check consumer reactions.

STATISTICAL ANALYSIS

The traditional economic approach to estimating a demand function is for the firm to use statistical methods, using data collected either by the firm or other outside sources, such as industry associations or government agencies. Historic data can be of two types: first, time series data for sales and other variables over a period of time measured for a discrete time interval, such as monthly, quarterly or yearly; second, **cross-sectional data**, such as expenditure by different income groups on a product at the same point in time. Statistical procedures are applied to these data to look for meaningful relationships, the most commonly used methodology being linear regression analysis.

When modelling the relationship between quantity demanded and independent variables, the analysis we undertook in Chapter 5 enables us to hypothesize what the expected sign of the coefficient for each independent variable should be: for example, the sign of the coefficient for the product's own price should normally be negative; for a substitute product and income the coefficients should normally be positive. Assuming data have been collected for the key independent variables, the task then is to obtain from the available data the best fit, or statistically most acceptable, equation that explains the quantity demanded.

The typical form of such a linear demand equation for cars using more than one independent variable would be:

$$Q_c = a + b_1 P_c + b_2 P_y + b_3 Y + b_4 A + b_n X_n$$

where $Q_c =$ quantity demanded, $P_c =$ price of the product, $P_y =$ the price of other products, $Y =$ income, $A =$ advertising expenditure and $X_n =$ all the other variables that might be included in the model.

If the equation for the demand for cars is recast logarithmically, then we have:

$$\log Q_c = a + b_i \log P_c + b_2 \log P_y + b_3 \log Y + b_4 \log A + b_n \log X_n$$

The advantage of this procedure is that the estimated coefficients of the demand function are the various elasticities of demand: that is, $b_1 =$ the own price elasticity of demand, $b_2 =$ the cross price elasticity of demand, $b_3 =$ the income elasticity of demand, $b_4 =$ the elasticity of advertising and $b_n =$ the elasticity with respect to that variable. To estimate a demand function using regression analysis, data have first to be collected for each of the variables to be included in the model: that is, for quantity demanded, prices, income, advertising and any other variable considered worthy of inclusion.

The simplest estimating procedure is linear regression analysis. Linear regressions can be estimated using various computer software programs including spreadsheets and specific statistical packages for economists and social scientists, such as SPSS (see Judge 2000; Whigham 2001). The resulting output is an equation together with statistical inference statistics, which provides the means for assessing the statistical significance of the estimated coefficients of the included variables. A simple example of this procedure is illustrated in Chapter 21, where a demand function is estimated for the UK bus market using time series data. The case study of alcoholic drinks in this chapter estimates demand functions for beer, wine and spirits.

PITFALLS USING REGRESSION ANALYSIS

Specification errors

A specification error arises when one or more important determinants of demand are omitted from the model or when the wrong functional form was specified to estimate the function: for example, if a linear rather than a non-linear relationship is specified. The results of mis-specification show in a low value for R^2, while the omission of important variables leads to variables not having the expected signs.

Identification problems

The identification problem occurs because of the simultaneous change between one variable included in the model and one not included: for example, there may a simul-

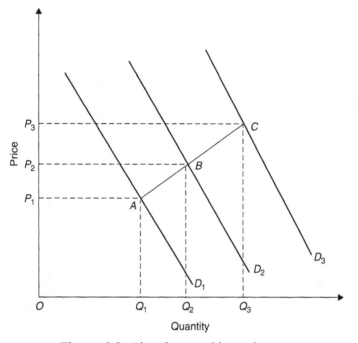

Figure 6.3 Identification of demand curves

taneous relationship between quantity demanded and consumer income, which was not included in the model.

The problem is illustrated in Figure 6.3, where cross-sectional data collection yields the three combinations of quantity and price, labelled A to C representing price–quantity combinations P_1Q_1, P_2Q_2 and P_3Q_3. These points joined together show that a fall in price leads to an increase in the quantity demanded. This relationship suggests an upward rather than a downward-sloping demand curve, which is not normally expected. The problem may arise because points A, B and C do not lie on a single demand curve but on separate demand curves D_1, D_2, D_3, each demand curve being associated with different levels of income and/or preferences. The true position of each demand curve cannot be identified. The identification problem occurs, therefore, because of the simultaneous change between price, included as an explanatory variable, and income, which is not included. If an upward-sloping demand curve is estimated from the data collected but the identification problem is not identified, then the measured price elasticity would have a positive rather than a negative sign, indicating specification problems.

THE ECONOMIC VERIFICATION OF REGRESSION MODELS

Statistics are known to generate apparent strong but spurious statistical relationships. The first things an economist should check when looking at the output of a regression calculation are the signs and magnitudes of the estimated variables. Economic analysis suggests that for a normal good the own price elasticity of demand should have a negative sign, the cross-price elasticity of demand should have a negative sign and the income elasticity of demand should be positive. While contrary signs are not necessarily wrong they indicate that one should proceed with caution. Likewise, if the magnitude of the estimated variables is outside the expected range, then again one should proceed with caution. In Table 6.2 there are a number of results contrary to expectations: for example, the own price elasticity for beer has a positive sign. Significance tests show this coefficient to be significant at the 5% level. The coefficient for the price of other goods is also negative, contrary to expectations, but significance tests show that its value is not significantly different from zero.

STATISTICAL VERIFICATION OF REGRESSION MODELS

The second stage is to examine the statistical indicators as measured by the estimating procedure to see whether the model is statistically significant and successfully explains variations in the dependent variable or quantity demanded. These tests deal with the overall explanatory power of the model, as well as the role of each independent variable.

Correlation coefficient

The overall explanatory power of a regression model is measured by R^2 or adjusted R^2. R^2 measures the goodness of fit, or the amount of variation explained by the independent variables included in the model. The adjusted R^2 takes into account degrees of freedom, because otherwise the value of R^2 can be improved by adding more independent variables. Thus, an R^2 of 0.9 indicates that independent variables account for 90% of the variation, or changes, in the dependent variable. It also indicates that 10% of variation is unaccounted for – explained by missing variables. As a general rule the closer the value of R^2 is to 1 the better the fit, while the closer it is to 0 the poorer the fit. A good overall fit, or high R^2, is not the end of testing, because it may be the result of problems with independent variables. The degrees of freedom are measured by deducting the number of independent variables from the number of observations: for example, if there are 25 observations and 4 variables, then the degrees of freedom would be 21. In Table 6.2 the adjusted R^2's are all highly significant for all three products, showing that, initially, the model has been successfully constructed.

F-test

The F-test also assesses the overall validity of the regression model. It is used to see whether there is a significant relationship between the dependent variable and the group of independent variables. The test itself is based either on accepting or rejecting the null hypothesis that there is no significant statistical relationship between the dependent and independent variables as a group. The test proceeds by comparing the F-value estimated when measuring the regression relationship and the benchmark value obtained from F distribution statistical tables. The benchmark values are a function of the degrees of freedom of the denominator, the degrees of freedom for the numerator and the probability of being wrong. Thus, a 5% probability combined with 20 degrees of freedom for the denominator and 20 degrees of freedom for the numerator gives a benchmark value for F of 2.12; whereas with 120 degrees of freedom for both denominator and numerator a 5% probability gives a benchmark value of 1.35.

If the estimated F-value is greater than the benchmark value, then the null hypothesis can be rejected and, obversely, it can be claimed that there is a significant relationship between the two variables.

The degree of freedom for the numerator is the number of independent variables (excluding the constant term), while the degrees of freedom for the denominator is given by the total number of independent variables including the constant and subtracting them from the number of observations. Thus, a regression function with 3 independent variables and 28 observations would have 3 degrees of freedom for the denominator and 24 degrees of freedom for the numerator, giving a benchmark value for F of 8.64.

t-test

The t-test is used to establish whether there is a significant statistical relationship between an independent and a dependent variable. It is based on the hypothesis that there is no significant statistical relationship between the dependent and the independent variable; this is known as the null hypothesis. The t-test tries to show that the null hypothesis can be proved incorrect and that there is a significant relationship between the dependent and independent variables.

The test proceeds by comparing the t-value estimated when measuring the regression relationship and the benchmark value obtained from statistical tables. The benchmark values are a function of the degrees of freedom and the probability of being wrong. Thus, a 5% probability combined with 20 degrees of freedom produces a benchmark value for t of 1.81. If the estimated t-value is greater than the benchmark value, then the null hypothesis can be rejected and, obversely, it can be claimed that there is a significant relationship between the two variables. Thus, as a general rule the benchmark value for t is taken to be around 2, and if the estimated t-value is greater than 2, then that independent variable is assumed to play a significant role in the model.

In Table 6.2 the significant t-tests that indicate that the null hypothesis can be rejected are marked by a superscript "a"; these show that the real price and real income are significant explanatory variables for all three products. The price of other goods is significant for spirits and wine, while advertising is only significant for beer.

Standard error of estimate

The standard error of estimate is used to check whether the relationship between an independent and dependent variable is significant. It measures the degree of dispersion of the data around the estimated value for the variable. It can then be used to indicate the degree of confidence that the value of the variable will fall within the measured limits. The general rules for using the standard error are that there is:

- A 68% probability that actual values will fall within plus or minus one standard errors of its estimated value.
- A 95% probability that actual values will fall within plus or minus two standard errors of its estimated value.
- A 99.7% probability that actual values will fall within plus or minus three standard errors of its estimated value.

ECONOMETRIC VERIFICATION OF THE REGRESSION ESTIMATES

Initially, it was suggested that the first step in checking the overall validity of a regression model was to look at the value of R^2. However, economic modelling is beset with difficulties that can inflate the value of R^2, because of problems associated with relationships between the independent variables, as well as a particular problem associated with the use of time series known as autocorrelation.

Multi-collinearity

Multi-collinearity is said to exist when the independent variables within an estimated model are correlated to each other. Problems arise when two independent variables present the same information in a different way: for example, if social class and income are included in a demand model for different types of alcoholic drink, then social class may duplicate the information provided by the income variable, in so far as social class is associated with income levels. High levels of multi-collinearity will have an effect on the estimated coefficients.

Detecting multi-collinearity is usually achieved by investigating the pattern of correlation coefficients between the independent variables and by examining the R^2 and t-statistics: for example, the model may achieve a high R^2, but the t-statistics may indicate that a number of variables, expected to be significant, are in fact insignificant. If multi-collinearity is identified as a problem, then the solution may be to drop the less significant of the highly correlated variables or to introduce time lags for some of the variables and to re-estimate the model.

Autocorrelation

Autocorrelation may be found where the error terms within a regression are serially correlated. It is a problem because it can lead to either overestimating or underestimating the unexplained variation in the dependent variable. The consequences may be to accept a model as a good fit when the result is dependent on autocorrelation. The test for autocorrelation relies on a comparison between the Durbin–Watson Statistic and an upper and lower value derived from statistical tables. The Durbin–Watson Test checks to see whether null hypothesis holds and that there is no autocorrelation present in the model. For the 5% level of significance with 25 data observations and 3 independent variables, the lower limit is 1.12 and the upper limit is 1.66. If the estimated Durbin–Watson Statistic is less than 1.12, then the null hypothesis is rejected; while if the estimate Durbin–Watson Statistic is greater than 1.66, then the null hypothesis that there is no autocorrelation present in the model is accepted.

Duffy (1983) uses the Durbin–Watson Statistic to demonstrate that serial correlation is not a problem and that the overall model works well (see Table 6.2).

Thus, if the estimated model passes the various statistical tests outlined, then the estimated model may be regarded statistically as a model that fits the data in a statistically acceptable way. The economic value of the model depends on whether the correct explanatory variables have been included.

Case Study 6.1 The demand for beer, wine and spirits

To illustrate the use made of regression analysis by economists to estimate demand functions, reference will be made of studies that have estimated demand functions for alcoholic drinks. Duffy (1983) estimated demand functions for beer, spirits and wine using quarterly data for the years 1963 to 1978. His aim was "to obtain reasonably reliable estimates of the quantitative importance of the various factors which influence the demand for alcoholic drink" (pp. 126–127). The demand equations were derived using different methods, but here only the log-linear results using ordinary least squares which were found to have the greatest explanatory power are reported: these are found in Table 6.2.

Table 6.2 Estimates of log-linear demand functions for alcoholic drink in the UK

Variable	Beer	Spirits	Wine
Constant	−3.1418 (11.2225)[a]	−2.2399 (4.9596)[a]	−2.6390 (4.3719)[a]
Real price of good	0.2376 (1.7141)[a]	−1.1802 (4.8437)[a]	−0.6385 (1.7227)[a]
Real price of all other goods	−0.1530 (1.0896)	0.9827 (5.3567)[a]	0.6714 (2.1715)[a]
Real income	0.8018 (6.7752)[a]	1.6677 (8.9648)[a]	2.5045 (11.6745)[a]
Real per capita advertising	0.0742 (2.6327)[a]	−0.0142 (0.3770)	−0.0865 (1.3869)
Adjusted R^2	0.950	0.975	0.963
Durbin–Watson Statistic	1.716	2.048	2.109
Standard error ($\times 10^3$)	0.5068	0.4376	0.3070

Note   t-ratios in parentheses
        [a] Statistically significant at the 5% level
Source Parts of table 1 from Duffy (1983).

In Table 6.2 the following information is reported for the log-linear demand functions for each product:

- Constant term.
- Real price of the good.
- Real price of all other goods.
- Real income.
- The coefficient of determination, or adjusted R^2.
- Coefficients for each independent variable.
- *t*-ratios for each variable.
- The Durbin–Watson Statistic.

The significant results found by Duffy (1983) include the following:

- Changes in real income are significant for all three products and measured income elasticities are positive: for beer it is less than 1 (0.8), for spirits (1.6) and wine (2.8) it is greater than 1.
- Own price elasticities are negative for wines and spirits (the expected sign), but less than 1 for wine (−0.6) and greater than 1 for spirits (−1.18); for beer price elasticity is positive rather than negative though the measured elasticity of (0.2) is not significantly different from 0.
- The elasticity for advertising is positive and significant, but small for beer (0.07) and negative and insignificant for wine (0.01) and spirits (0.08). The results show that advertising has a very small impact on the total sales of beer, wine and spirits.
- Statistically, the adjusted R^2 indicates that the models have significant explanatory power, while the Durbin-Watson Statistic indicates there were no problems with autocorrelation as explained above.

The studies by Duffy and others (see Brewster 1997, pp. 153–154) show that beer tends to have a very low price elasticity, a low cross elasticity of demand and a low but positive income elasticity of demand.

More sophisticated models have been developed using demand systems to estimate the elasticities: Duffy (1987) found the own price estimate of the elasticity of demand for beer, using data from 1975 to 1983, to be −0.36, for income to be +0.71 and for advertising +0.05.

CHAPTER SUMMARY

In this chapter we briefly reviewed the methods used to obtain information about the characteristics of the demand function for a firm's products. In doing this we analysed:

- Surveys and questionnaires.
- Consumer and market experiments.
- Regression.

None of the methods is entirely satisfactory: survey methods have drawbacks relating to the questions asked and the veracity of the answers and statistical methods also suffer from information, estimation and interpretation problems. Despite the shortcomings identified, it is imperative for the firm to discover the nature of the demand functions for its products and the variables influencing demand.

Knowing the size of the elasticities for price, income and advertising can shape not only the pricing and sales strategies of firms but also the long-term growth of sales.

REVIEW QUESTIONS

1   In what circumstances should a company employ survey methods to obtain more information on the demand for its product and the relative merits of its product compared with those of rivals?
2   What are the advantages and disadvantages to a company of using surveys and questionnaires to estimate demand functions?
3   What are the advantages and disadvantages of using regression analysis to estimate a demand function?
4   What is the identification problem?
5   The estimated log-linear regression, where P_X = the price of the product, P_O = the price of another product and Y = real income, is as follows:

$$Q_X = 450 - 1.53P_X + 0.87P_O + 2.36Y \qquad R^2 = 0.91$$

where the t-ratios are in parentheses.

  – Explain the meaning and significance of the coefficients for each variable. Are the signs in line with economic theory?
  – If the initial values of the variables are P_X = £100, P_O = £120 and Y = £1,000, then calculate the quantity demanded.
  – Calculate the impact on sales of a plus or minus change of 10 in the value of each of the independent variables on the quantity demanded.

5   What are the difficulties that a firm faces in making estimates of the potential demand for a new product? What methods might it use to gauge potential consumer reaction?
6   If you were to estimate demand functions for beer, wine and spirits now, in what ways would you expect the results to be different from those of Duffy (1983). In your answer consider the own price elasticity of demand, the income elasticity of demand and cross-price elasticity.
7   You are asked to estimate a demand function for electricity. What information would you need to collect to estimate such a function?

REFERENCES AND FURTHER READING

Baumol, W.J. (1965) On empirical determination of demand relationships. *Economic Theory and Operations Analysis* (2nd edn, Chapter 10). Prentice Hall, Englewood Cliffs, NJ.

Brewster, D. (1997) Demand and revenue analysis. *Business Economics* (Chapter 7). Dryden Press, London.

Duffy, M. (1983) The demand for alcoholic drink in the UK, 1963–78. *Applied Economics*, **15**, 125–140.

Duffy, M. (1987) Advertising and the inter-product distribution of demand: A Rotterdam model approach. *European Economic Review*, **31**, 1051–1070.

Green, P.E. and D.S. Tull (1988) *Research for Marketing Decisions* (5th edn). Prentice Hall, Englewood Cliffs, NJ.

Griffiths, A. and S. Wall (1996) Market demand. *Intermediate Micro-economics* (Chapter 2). Longman, London.

Hill, S. (1989) Demand theory and estimation. *Managerial Economics* (Chapter 5). Macmillan, Basingstoke, UK.

Judge, G. (2000) *Computing Skills for Economists*. John Wiley & Sons, Chichester, UK.

Luck, D.J., H.G. Wales and D.A. Taylor (1987) *Marketing Research* (7th edn, Chapters 9 and 10). Prentice Hall, Englewood Cliffs, NJ.

Whigham, D. (2001) Demand analysis. *Managerial Economics Using Excel* (Chapter 5). Thompson Learning, London.

PART III

UNDERSTANDING PRODUCTION AND COSTS

7

PRODUCTION AND EFFICIENCY

CHAPTER OUTLINE

CHAPTER OBJECTIVES

This chapter aims to explore the nature of the production function and the measurement of productive efficiency. After studying this chapter you should be able to:

◆ Outline the properties and characteristics of isoquants.
◆ Explain the necessary conditions to select an optimal combination of factors.
◆ Elucidate the laws of production and construct product curves.
◆ Outline the concepts of labour, capital and total factor productivity.
◆ Explain and apply Farrell's Methodology for measuring relative performance.
◆ Discuss the shortcomings of using labour productivity as an indicator of improved performance.
◆ Explain how productivity differs between plants, firms and countries.

INTRODUCTION

The production of goods and services is one of the key activities of any firm. The technology chosen to produce its goods and services helps determine the capital and labour to be employed, the efficiency of the firm and the costs incurred. In this chapter we will examine:

■ The nature of the production function.
■ Isoquant analysis.
■ Technical progress.
■ Measurement of efficiency and productivity.
■ The use of productivity as a performance indicator.

PRODUCTION FUNCTIONS

Production is concerned with the transformation of inputs into more desirable outputs (e.g., crude oil into petrol and other useful petroleum products) that are either used by consumers or by industry to produce further useful products. These relationships can be made precise in the form of the production function, which specifies the technical possibilities open to producers, given the current state of technological knowledge. It is from this menu of possibilities that the firm chooses the most efficient combination of factors that best serve its requirements.

Assume the firm produces a single homogeneous product (Q), using three factors of production – labour (L), capital (K) and entrepreneurship (E). Then, the production function can be written as: $Q = f(K, L, E)$ where $f(\ ) =$ the form of the production function; this may take various mathematical forms, the simplest of which are additive and multiplicative.

If the function takes the following form:

$$Q = aK + bL + cE$$

then it would be described as an additive function. If we assume $a = 3$, $b = 2$ and $c = 1.5$, then the production relationship would be fully specified and, for any given quantity of the factors K, L and E, the quantity of Q produced can be calculated. If K, L and E were equal to 20, then the value of Q would be 115, whereas if the quantity of each factor employed were doubled, then output would increase to 230; this would be described as a state of **constant returns to scale**, when doubling inputs leads to a doubling of output.

If the function takes the form:

$$Q = aK^b L^c E^d$$

then the function is described as multiplicative. If the values of the powers b, c and d and the constant term are specified, then the production relationship would be fully

Table 7.1 Multiplicative production function

Period 1			Period 2		
Factor	Power	Output Q_1	Factor	Power	Output Q_2
(1) *Constant returns to scale*					
$K = 20$	0.6	6.034 176	$K = 40$	0.6	9.146 101
$L = 10$	0.3	1.995 262	$L = 20$	0.3	2.456 456
$E = 5$	0.1	1.174 618	$E = 10$	0.1	1.258 925
Total	*1.0*	42.426 4	*Total*	*1.0*	84.852 8
(2) *Increasing returns to scale*					
$K = 20$	0.7	8.141 810	$K = 40$	0.7	13.226 41
$L = 10$	0.3	1.995 262	$L = 20$	0.3	2.456 456
$E = 5$	0.1	1.174 618	$E = 10$	0.1	1.258 925
Total	*1.0*	57.245 22	*Total*	*1.0*	122.707 8
(3) *Decreasing returns to scale*					
$K = 20$	0.5	4.472 135	$K = 40$	0.5	6.324 555
$L = 10$	0.3	1.995 262	$L = 20$	0.3	2.456 456
$E = 5$	0.1	1.174 618	$E = 10$	0.1	1.258 925
Total					
1.0					

specified and, for any given quantity of the factors K, L and E, the total output of Q could be calculated. Three possible situations are illustrated in Table 7.1:

■ **Constant returns to scale** are illustrated in Table 7.1(1). The sum of the powers $(b + c + d)$ adds to 1 and gives an initial output of 42.426. If the volume of factors is doubled, then output also doubles to 84.852 The ratio of Q_2 to Q_1 is 2.

■ **Increasing returns to scale** are illustrated in Table 7.1(2). The sum of the exponents $(b + c + d)$ adds to 1.1 (or more than 1) and gives an initial output of 57.25. If the volume of factor inputs is doubled, then output more than doubles to 122.71. The ratio of Q_2 to Q_1 is 2.14.

■ **Decreasing returns to scale** are illustrated in Table 7.1(3). The sum of the exponents $(b + c + d)$ adds to 0.9 (or less than 1) and gives an initial output of 31.44. If the volume of factor inputs is doubled, then output less than doubles to 58.7659. The ratio of Q_2 to Q_1 is 1.866.

ISOQUANT ANALYSIS

The production function can be illustrated diagrammatically, using isoquant analysis. An isoquant is similar in conception to an indifference curve. It shows how different combinations of two factors can be combined to produce a given level of output. Each

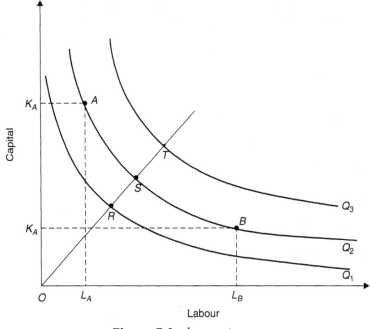

Figure 7.1 Isoquant map

level of output will be represented by a separate isoquant. If we assume that there are two factors of production – capital (*K*) and Labour (*L*) – then Figure 7.1 shows an isoquant map for three levels of output: namely, Q_1, Q_2 and Q_3. A move along the ray *OT* sees output increase, because *OT* represents a greater output than *OS* and *OS* represents a greater output than *OR*.

Each isoquant is drawn convex to the origin, reflecting the diminishing effectiveness of substituting one factor for the other in the production process. Each isoquant also shows the various combinations of factors that can be used to produce each level of output. Thus, output Q_2 can be produced using differing combinations of labour and capital. For example, at point *A* on isoquant Q_2, output Q_2 is produced by combining OK_A of capital with OL_A of labour and at point *B* output Q_2 is produced by combining OK_B of capital with OL_B of labour. At point *A* the ratio of capital to labour is higher than at point *B*, so that production at *A* is described as being more capital-intensive than at point *B*. Conversely, since the ratio of labour to capital is greater at point *B* than at point *A*, production at *B* is described as being more labour-intensive than at *A*.

The shape and position of an isoquant will depend on the state of technical knowledge and the degree of substitution between factors. The slope is a measure of the degree of substitution between the two factors; this is given by dividing the change in input factor *K* by the change in the input of labour. Thus, employing one less unit of capital requires more labour to be employed to maintain output or, put another way, one more unit of labour implies reducing capital by a number of units. This relationship is termed the **marginal rate of technical substitution** (or MRTS) between capital and labour and is defined at any point on an isoquant as the change in capital divided by the change in labour, or $\Delta K/\Delta L$. At any point on the isoquant the MRTS is given by the slope of a line drawn tangential to the isoquant.

A reduction in the use of capital as a consequence of a move along an isoquant involves a reduction in output. To remain on the same isoquant this loss of output is compensated for by employing more labour. Thus, the reduction in capital multiplied by the marginal product of capital $(-\Delta K * MP_K)$ is compensated by an increase in labour multiplied by the **marginal product of labour** $(\Delta L * MP_L)$. Thus:

$$\Delta Q = -\Delta K * MP_K + \Delta L * MP_L = 0$$

and transposing gives:

$$\frac{-\Delta K}{\Delta L} = \frac{MP_L}{MP_K}$$

or the slope of the isoquant; this means that the MRTS of capital for labour is equal to the ratio of the marginal product of labour and the **marginal product of capital**.

If the slope of the isoquant is $\frac{1}{2}$, then 1 unit of capital would be substituted for by 2 units of labour; this also implies that the marginal productivity of capital is twice that of the marginal product of labour.

OPTIMAL CHOICE OF FACTORS

A firm wishing to maximize profits will also seek to minimize the costs of production of a given output. Profit can be defined as total revenue minus total costs, where total costs are the sum of payments to labour and capital. Thus:

$$\pi = TR - TC = Q \cdot p - (rK + wL)$$

where $\pi =$ profit, $TR =$ total revenue, $TC =$ total cost which is quantity sold (Q) multiplied by price (p), $K =$ quantity of capital employed, $r =$ payment to a unit of capital, $L =$ quantity of labour employed and $w =$ payment to a unit of labour.

In Figure 7.2 the firm wishes to produce output Q: therefore, it has to choose a position on isoquant Q_1. This choice depends on the relative prices of labour and capital (r/w) and the isocost curve.

The **isocost curve**, or **budget curve** in consumer analysis, is a line representing in factor space all combinations of two factors that can be purchased for a certain sum of money, given the prevailing factor prices. Its slope represents the relative prices of the two factors and its position determines the isoquant the firm can reach. It can be defined as follows, where $X =$ total expenditure on the two factors:

$$X = wL + rK$$

Rearranging gives:

$$rK = X - wL$$

By dividing by r, we obtain:

$$K = X/r - (w/r)L$$

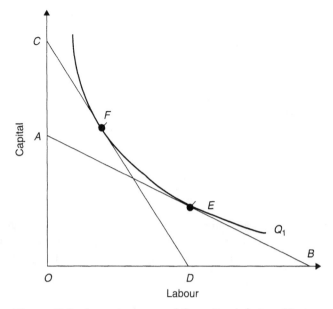

Figure 7.2   Isocost curves and the optimal choice of factors

Alternatively, we can obtain an expression for L:

$$X = wL + rK$$

$$wL = X - rK$$

$$L = X/w - (r/w)K$$

The K intercept in Figure 7.2, assuming $L = 0$, is given by X/r and the L intercept, assuming $K = 0$, is given by X/w. The slope of the isocost curve $\Delta K/\Delta L$ is equal to $(-w/r)$ or the relative prices of the factors. Thus, an initial isocost curve for the firm might be the line AB in Figure 7.2. A higher level of expenditure or total cost incurred will move the isocost curve to the right of the isocost curve AB, while a change in the relative prices of the two factors will alter the slope of the isocost curve and move it to a position like CD.

A simple arithmetical example will make the relationships clear. If we assume $X = 100$, $r = 10$ and $w = 5$, then X/r (100/10) or 10 will give intercept A on the capital axis, while X/w (100/5) or 20 will give intercept B on the labour axis. The ratio $-w/r$ (5/10) or the ratio OA/OB (10/20) or 1/2 gives the slope of the isocost curve. If the price of labour becomes 10 and the cost of capital 5, then a new isocost curve CD could be derived in a similar way.

To minimize the costs of production the firm will choose that point on an isoquant that is tangential to the lowest **isocost line**. With isocost curve AB, this point on isoquant Q_1 is at point E, where, the slope of the isocost line $(-w/r)$ is equal to the slope of the isoquant $(-\Delta K/\Delta L$ or $-MP_L/MP_K)$. Thus, $-w/r = -MP_L/MP_K$: that is, the ratio of the factor prices is equal to the ratio of the marginal products of the factors.

If the relevant isocost curve were CD then the firm would choose point F and move from E to F, substituting capital for labour, because capital is now relatively cheaper than labour. Changes in the relative prices of the factors will lead the firm to choose a different labour capital mix to produce output Q_1.

TECHNICAL PROGRESS AND THE SHAPE OF ISOQUANTS

Technical progress in the production process is important for the firm in that it enables fewer factors to be used and cost savings to be made. Technical progress results in either more output being produced by the same quantities of factors or the same output being produced by fewer factor inputs. In terms of isoquant analysis, technical progress utilizes the second approach and results in the movement of an isoquant toward the origin.

The exact position of the new isoquant depends on the nature of technical progress. Three types of technical progress are identified depending on which factor's use is reduced the most:

1   **Neutral technical progress** occurs when the use of both factors is reduced at the same rate. As a result the isoquant maintains its shape but is located closer to the origin. Thus, the relative marginal products of both factors reflected in the marginal rate of technical substitution remain the same but the absolute levels of productivity increase; this is demonstrated in Figure 7.3(a). The initial isoquant is labelled Q_t, representing how the output can be produced in the first time period. The second isoquant labelled Q_{t+1}, represents the same output produced in a second time period, after technical progress has occurred. The shape of both isoquants is such that along any ray from the origin, such as OB, the capital–labour ratio is constant:
    – The slope of the isoquants (MRTS) at A and B (OK/OL) are the same.
    – The ratio of the marginal products of labour and capital are the same at A and B.
2   **Capital-deepening** or **labour-saving technical progress** favours the greater use of capital and decreases the use of labour. The isoquant shape changes between the two periods with the upper part moving closer to the capital axis. As a result the marginal product of capital increases faster than that of labour; this is illustrated in Figure 7.3(b). A move from B to E along the ray OB holds the capital–labour ratio constant. At E the slope of the isoquant becomes less steep than at B, so that the MRTS falls and:
    – The marginal product of capital relative to labour increases.
    – Capital is substituted for labour with production becoming more capital-intensive: for example, a move from B to E.
3   **Labour-deepening** or **capital-saving technical progress** favours the greater use of labour and decreases the use of capital. The isoquant shape changes as the lower part moves closer toward the labour axis. As a result, the marginal product of labour increases faster than that of capital; this is illustrated in Figure 7.3(c). A

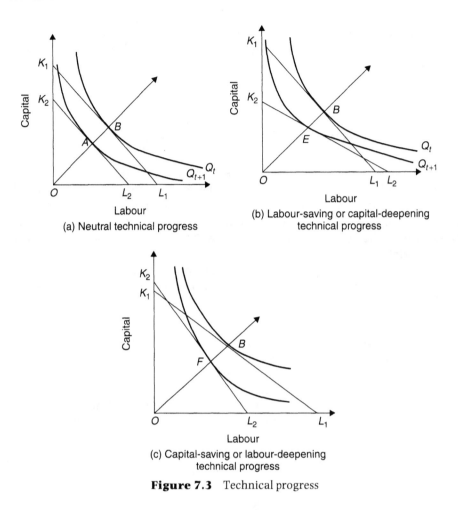

Figure 7.3   Technical progress

move from *B* to *F* along a ray *OB* holds the capital–labour ratio constant. At *F* the slope of the isoquant become steeper, so that the MRTS increases and:

- The marginal product of labour relative to capital increases.
- Labour is substituted for capital with production becoming more labour-intensive: for example, a move from *B* to *F*.

LAWS OF PRODUCTION

So far, we have concentrated largely on either one or two isoquants. We now need to pay attention to the complete set of production possibilities open to the firm. A fuller picture is presented in Figure 7.4, where a set of isoquants are mapped and are presumed to present a complete picture of the options open to a firm in the long run.

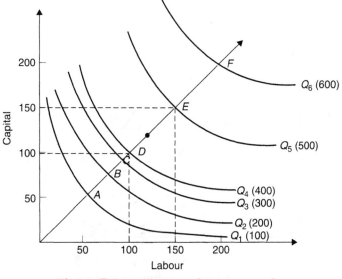

Figure 7.4 Isoquants and returns to scale

The firm could choose any point within the map, depending on the output it wishes to produce and the relative prices of labour and capital.

The isoquant map also shows that the production possibilities initially exhibit increasing returns to scale and then decreasing returns to scale. Changes in scale result from movements from one isoquant to another rather than from movements along a particular isoquant. If the firm moves from isoquant Q_1 to isoquant Q_4, then the firm is able to increase output from 100 to 400, while increasing capital employed from 50 to 100 and labour employed from 50 to 100. Thus, output increases fourfold, while inputs increase twofold. The firm can therefore benefit from increasing returns by operating on isoquant Q_4. From isoquant Q_4 to isoquant Q_5 output increases by 25%, but the factors employed increase by 50%. Thus, by moving to a higher isoquant the firm incurs decreasing returns to scale.

If a firm decides to install a plant to produce 400 units of output with the labour and capital combination at point D, then it is assumed in the short run that the firm cannot vary its capital but can vary its labour input. The short-run situation is illustrated in Figure 7.5, where the firm is constrained to operate along the horizontal line KT. Thus, if the firm is producing 400 units, then it can increase production by employing more labour but cannot vary the fixed factor capital.

TOTAL, AVERAGE AND MARGINAL PRODUCT CURVES

Product curves relate output to factors used and allow information from the production function to be presented in two or, sometimes, three dimensions. The information in Figure 7.5 along the line KT can be plotted in a diagram like Figure 7.6, where output

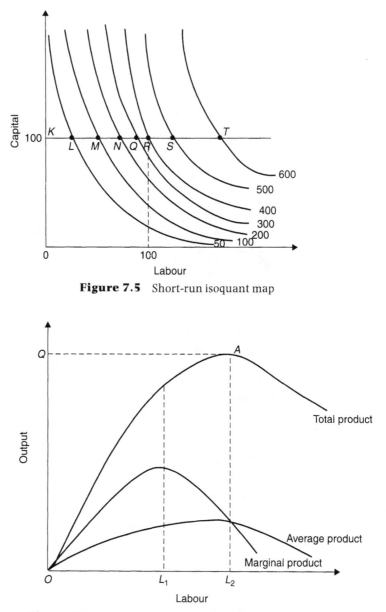

Figure 7.5 Short-run isoquant map

Figure 7.6 Total, average and marginal product curves

is measured on the vertical axis and the variable factor labour on the horizontal axis. The total product curve plots the output produced on each isoquant, together with the units of labour used. The total product curve in the figure is drawn so that total output declines after a certain quantity of labour has been used. The total product curve shows initially increasing returns to labour with output peaking at output level OQ, utilizing labour input OL_2 with a given fixed quantity of capital. The average product curve is total output divided by the units of labour employed, and the marginal product curve measures the change in output resulting from the employment of an extra unit of labour.

Given the production function the total product curve for either one or more variable factors represents the maximum output that can be obtained. Points beyond the total product curve are not attainable, while those on or below the curve are. Points inside the frontier are inefficient in that the firm is not utilizing best practice techniques. The distance a firm is from the frontier is a measure of the inefficiency of the firm.

EMPIRICAL PRODUCTION FUNCTIONS

Economists try to measure production functions by fitting statistical functions to data on outputs and inputs. A widely used production function in empirical research is the **Cobb–Douglas Function**. The form of the relationship is specified as follows:

$$Q = AL^a K^{1-a} \qquad \text{or generalized to} \qquad Q = AL^a K^b$$

The function is linear in logarithms and can be written as:

$$\log Q = \log A + a \log L + b \log K$$

which is also the form in which it is estimated.

The function has a useful property that derives from the fact that for any change in $\log Q$, $\delta \log Q$ is equal to $\delta Q/Q$. Similarly, $\delta \log L$ and $\delta \log K$ correspond to $\delta L/L$ and $\delta K/K$. Moreover, $\delta \log Q = a(\delta \log L) + b(\delta \log K)$.

Taking each term in turn reveals that $\delta Q/Q * L/\delta L$ is equal to the exponent a and $\delta Q/Q * K/\delta K$ is equal to exponent b. These relationships measure the elasticity of output with respect to inputs. The elasticity of output in relation to labour is a, and the elasticity of output with respect to capital is b; thus, a 1% increase in labour yields an a% increase in output, and a 1% increase in labour and capital yields an $(a + b)$% increase in output.

Case Study 7.1   Production function for a retail chain

An example of the use of the Cobb–Douglas Function can be shown by estimating the data for a chain of 77 shops. The problem the retailer was trying to address was whether smaller shops should be closed or whether larger stores should be built. The question was whether there were economies of scale in retailing. The dependent variable is turnover and the two independent variables are the size of shop (representing capital) and labour (measured in full-time-equivalent staff). The result was as follows:

	Estimated coefficient	t-statistic
Sales area	0.202	1.915
Labour	0.838	10.356
Constant	3.731	5.709
R^2	0.930	
F	503.85	

The result shows that labour was the dominant factor and that the sum of the labour and capital (sales area) coefficients adds to 1.04, which indicates very weak increasing returns to scale; this meant that small shops were not at a significant disadvantage compared with larger shops. However, the results were derived from the existing stock of stores, and observation showed that other chains operated larger units, indicating that the consensus in the industry favoured larger units.

MEASURING PRODUCTIVITY

Productivity measures are one of the main performance indicators used by firms, industries and countries to measure both absolute and relative performance. We have already indicated that the slope of an isoquant measures the relative productivity of the two factors. In practice, absolute measures of productivity are needed, and the indicators generally used are labour productivity capital productivity, and total factor productivity. The first two relate output to a single factor, ignoring the contribution of the other factor, while total factor productivity attempts to relate output to a combined measure of both inputs. The measurement of each of the indicators is illustrated in Figure 7.7.

The firm is initially on the best practice isoquant to produce output Q_1 in period t and has chosen to be at point G, utilizing OK_G units of capital and OL_G units of labour. The various measures of productivity for point G can be defined as follows:

■ Labour productivity is output Q_1 divided by the amount of labour employed OL_G.
■ Capital productivity is output Q_1 divided by the amount of capital employed OK_G.

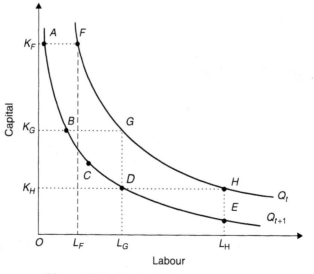

Figure 7.7   Productivity measurement

■ Total factor productivity is output Q_1 divided by the amount of both capital and labour employed: that is, OK_G plus OL_G.

Partial or single-factor measures of productivity give different results for each point on an isoquant. On isoquant Q_t labour productivity is greater at F than at G and greater at G than at H. Capital productivity has a reverse order, so that at H capital productivity is greater than at G and greater at G than at F. Total factor productivity avoids these problems, because output is divided by the total quantities of factors used. The difficulty with this measure is finding an appropriate methodology of adding capital and labour together when they are measured in different units and each unit is of varying quality.

If there is technical progress and the firm moves to isoquant Q_{t+1}, then it produces the same output as on Q_t. In terms of total factor productivity all points on Q_{t+1} are superior to all points on Q_t, because fewer factors in total are used. Single-factor measures of productivity will only give an unambiguous indicator of improved performance if the firm moves from G to points on the new isoquant between B and D. At point B, labour productivity will have increased, but capital productivity will be unchanged. The reverse is true at point D, where labour productivity is unchanged and capital productivity has increased. Only at such points as C will both labour and capital productivity have increased.

A move from G to point A, a more capital-intensive production position, will result in a fall in capital productivity and an increase in labour productivity. A move from G to point E, a more labour-intensive production position, will result in a fall in labour productivity and an increase in capital productivity.

Single-factor measures of productivity such as labour productivity, have to be used cautiously. Only if capital is fixed and fully utilized when labour productivity is measured in two time periods can all the improvement in performance be attributed to the greater effort of labour. If capital utilization increases, then capital is contributing to improved labour productivity.

RELATIVE MEASURES OF EFFICIENCY

A second approach to measuring the relative performance of a single enterprise *vis-à-vis* the current best practice frontier isoquant is to use the measures of relative efficiency proposed by Farrell (1957). The best practice isoquant represents the minimum quantity of inputs required to produce a given output. A firm producing on the best practice isoquant is therefore **technically efficient**. To be economically (or allocatively) efficient the firm has to choose a point on the isoquant where the marginal rate of technical substitution between the two factors is equal to the ratio of the factor prices.

The best practice isoquant may be derived:

■ Through knowledge, common to those in an industry, about the technical features of the latest technology being used.
■ Or, statistically, from the population of existing plants.

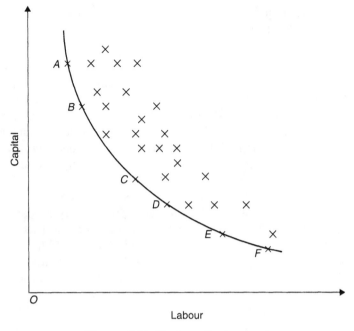

Figure 7.8 Best practice isoquant

This second technique is illustrated in Figure 7.8, where the labour and capital requirements per unit of output of existing plants are plotted. A best practice isoquant is fitted using the innermost points available and passes through points A, B, C, D and E, representing the most efficient plants. Finding the best practice frontier can be done using data envelopment analysis which utilizes linear programming techniques.

In Figure 7.9 the best practice production isoquant for the industry (Q_{BD}) is drawn in capital–labour space. One firm finds itself at point A, some way from the frontier, while others are at points B and D on the best practice frontier. The relative performance of firm A, according to Farrell (1957), can be measured as follows. If a ray is drawn from the origin to point A, then it establishes the capital–labour ratio prevailing at A. The ray OA cuts the best practice frontier at point B, so that both firm A and B have the same capital–labour ratio. However, firm A uses more capital and labour than firm B to produce the same output. Firm B is technically efficient, but firm A is not. Comparing the quantity of factors used at A and B provides a basis for comparing efficiency. The ratio OB/OA is a measure of the relative technical inefficiency of firm A. If the ratio has a value of 0.75, then firm A is using 25% more inputs to produce a unit of output than if it were in the position of firm B. The closer firm A is to firm B the nearer the ratio will be to 1.

A second source of inefficiency arises when the firm is not economically efficient. Firm D is both technically and economically efficient when the relative prices of capital and labour are represented by the isocost curve PR. Being economically efficient ensures that firm D minimizes the costs of production. Firms A and B are not cost minimizers. Therefore, in not being economically efficient, firms A and B incur higher

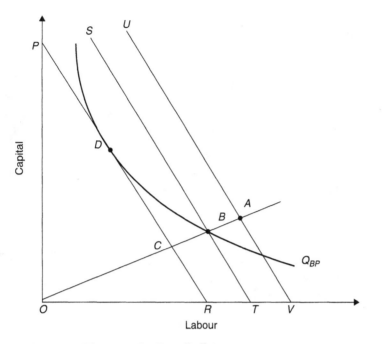

Figure 7.9 Farrell efficiency measures

costs of production than the most efficient firm D. The degree of cost-inefficiency incurred by firm A is measured by the ratio OC/OB. The cost level at C is the same as at D. Firm B is on a higher isocost line ST and firm A is on an even higher isocost line UV, making both higher cost producers than firm D. If firm A was to become technically efficient by moving to B, it would still be cost-inefficient because it is not using the optimal capital–labour ratio, given current factor prices.

These two measures of inefficiency – technical efficiency and cost-efficiency – can be combined to give a single measure of economic inefficiency; this is measured as follows with reference to firm A in Figure 7.6:

■ Technical efficiency is measured by OB/OA.
■ Cost-efficiency is measured by OC/OB.
■ Economic efficiency is measured by multiplying the two measures together to give OC/OA.

To reach the efficiency frontier firm A could:

■ Make more efficient use of its existing resources (i.e., obtain more output from the existing resources).
■ Make use of fewer units of labour and capital to produce a given output.
■ Improve the quality of labour by providing vocational training.
■ Invest in new capital, utilizing the latest technology and allowing the optimal capital–output ratio to be used.

Case Study 7.2 Measuring relative efficiency

Farrell's Efficiency concepts have been widely used by economists to measure the extent of inefficiency in various industrial sectors. Todd (1985) used the technique to measure efficiency in UK and German industry, while Forsund and Hjalmarsson (1979) used it to explore efficiency in the Swedish dairy industry. Pickering (1983) applied the technique to a department store group. The two key factors identified by Pickering were capital (in terms of retail selling space measured in square feet) and labour (in terms of full-time-equivalent employees). Output was measured in terms of the volume of sales in constant price terms for two years, 1975 and 1980, to enable productivity trends to be measured for each store in the group. It also enabled the factor–output combinations for each store to be measured and efficiency isoquants to be constructed. The relative efficiency of stores could then be measured against best practice.

Cubbin et al. (1987) employed data envelopment analysis (DEA), developed by Charnes et al. (1978), which utilizes linear programming to estimate the frontier isoquant. They were able to identify more clearly the sources of inefficiency, compared with regression techniques where comparisons are made against a central or average tendency rather than the extreme or best performers. Oum et al. (1999) reviewed studies made of the railway industry using DEA analysis.

PRODUCTIVITY DIFFERENCES

A firm may wish to compare its performance over time and make comparisons with competitor enterprises both at home and overseas. To do this it can make use of productivity measures. Productivity differences between plants, firms, industries and countries have been much explored by economists, starting with Salter (1966) who tried to explain differences in productivity between the USA and the UK.

Explaining productivity differences at whatever level of aggregation is fraught with difficulties. The major problems include:

- Methods used to measure productivity.
- Measuring inputs.
- Valuing outputs.
- Whether similar or identical activities are being compared.
- Using exchange rates to value outputs and inputs between countries.

Comparisons at plant level

Many of the problems of comparing productivity might be avoided if two or more plants in the same industry are compared. Nevertheless, a number of difficulties still have to be faced if the explanation is to be full and clear; these include:

- The nature of the product: products may be more or less homogeneous; where they are significantly different or more complex to manufacture comparisons may be difficult.

- Labour inputs: theory assumes that all units of labour are homogeneous both in terms of ability and effort supplied. However, workers will not have identical skill and application levels, but accounting for the homogeneity of labour units may be extremely difficult in practice. Workers may also work different lengths of time in a week, so that comparisons should be made per similar time period, such as per hour. Work practices, training and many other factors might also account for one group of workers being more efficient than another.
- Capital inputs: the theory assumes that the capital employed comes in homogeneous units. The capital employed in two different plants can vary significantly in terms of age or vintage, degree of sophistication, intensity of use and maintenance practices. In general terms, plants operating with the latest technology incorporated into the newest machinery will be expected to have higher levels of efficiency and productivity.
- Quality of management and supervision: this may vary between plants. Work within one plant may be less well co-ordinated than in another, and workers may not be motivated or be unable to produce the scheduled output for such reasons as the lack of raw material or inadequate maintenance. Such difficulties might account for productivity differences between plants.

In a survey of productivity in the UK, HM Treasury (2000) found a wide distribution among labour productivity in manufacturing. Productivity of labour, measured in terms of gross value added per worker, at a couple of sample points of the distribution was as follows: 10th percentile £8,180 and 90th percentile £45,200 with a mean value of £28,000. The report suggests that the factors driving productivity differences and rates of change, based on a survey of small and medium-sized enterprises, were as follows:

- Increasing competition.
- Market growth, skilled labour and management skills.
- Availability and cost of finance for expansion and availability and cost of overdraft finance.
- Acquisition of technology.
- Difficulties in implementing new technology.
- Availability of appropriate premises or site.
- Access to overseas markets.

The report suggested a number of ways of increasing productivity at the firm level; these were to:

- Improve the access of firms to capital and incorporate the latest technology.
- Improve the productive potential of the workforce by greater education and training.
- Encourage firms to undertake their own R and D to reduce the delay in adopting best practice techniques.
- And promote greater competition between rivals so that firms and plants with low productivity will be unable to survive (HM Treasury 2000, chap. 3).

Case Study 7.3　Explaining productivity differences in the biscuit industry

One way of accounting for productivity differences between plants and countries is to undertake detailed studies of individual industries, using matched samples of plants; one such study has been of the biscuit industry: first, in Europe and, then, between Europe and the USA (Mason et al., 1994; Mason and Finegold, 1997).

The study estimated productivity per hour, with output measured by the tonnage of biscuits produced; tonnage was adjusted to allow for the complexity of the types of biscuits manufactured. Plain digestive biscuits, for example, require fewer processing stages than chocolate-covered digestive biscuits.

Table 7.2 reports the measured productivity per person hour relative to performance in the USA. In terms of tonnage the USA advantage over UK bakeries is around 30% and over German bakeries 45%. If output is adjusted for the complexity of the production process the difference is narrowed for all European countries, except the UK. Germany in particular, as a result of this adjustment, moves within 10% of the performance of the USA.

The researchers then set about seeking explanations of the observed differences in measured productivity. The first factor considered is economies of scale; these give productivity and cost advantages to larger plants over smaller plants (see Chapter 8). Using regression analysis they found that in larger plants a doubling of weekly output requires only 72% more labour, thereby increasing labour and productivity by 16%. Average plant sizes are recorded in Figure 7.2. The UK had the largest plants, so that the UK should have a productivity advantage over its US and European neighbours.

The second factor considered was the quality of capital employed; this was not found to account for productivity differences, except in the case of the Netherlands. Generally, the quality of capital available to workers was similar across all countries, except for US workers who had more capital than in other countries.

The third factor considered was machinery maintenance. In the UK and the USA plants were used more intensively, as a result of multiple shift working; this was found to hinder maintenance in the UK but not in the USA. In the UK 10% of planned production time was lost because of plant breakdowns compared with only 4% in other countries, thus reducing productivity.

The fourth factor considered was variations in human capital endowments; these were found to be an important explanation of differences in productivity (see Tables 7.3 and 7.4). The most significant differences in shop floor skill levels were found in the process

Table 7.2　Productivity levels: tonnes per person hour

	USA	UK	Netherlands	Germany	France
Output[1]	100	70	80	55	70
Adjusted output[2]	100	65	85	90	75
Plant size[3]	550	1,170	280	350	380

Note　[1] Tons per person hour
　　　　[2] "Quality adjusted" output per person hour
　　　　[3] Employment

Source　Mason and Finegold (1997, pp. 85–98, parts of table 1, p. 86 and Table 3, p. 87)

Table 7.3 Qualifications and training of process workers

	USA	UK	Netherlands	Germany	France
Vocational qualification	None	None	40%	90%	10%
Initial on-the-job training	2 months, single task	2 months, single task	7 months, full range	4 months, full range	12 months, full range

Source   Mason and Finegold (1997, pp. 85–88, modified extract of Table 7, p. 92).

Table 7.4 Qualifications of supervisors and maintenance workers

	USA	UK	Netherlands	Germany	France
Production supervisors	10–15% graduate + semi-skilled	15% graduate +semi-skilled	66% vocational qualification	75% vocational qualification	40% vocational qualification
Maintenance	2% graduates 60% craft 38% semi-skilled	80% craft 20% semi-skilled	50% technicians 50% craft	100%craft	10% technician 75% craft 15% semi-skilled

Source   Mason and Finegold (1997, modified extract of table 7, p. 92)

departments. The process and engineering skills of UK and US process workers were deemed to be at a semi-skilled level, with no externally validated vocational training. In contrast, in continental Europe a highly significant proportion of workers possessed vocational qualifications. Many were trained as craft bakers and had greater formal qualifications and on-the-job training. In the UK on-the-job training was limited to a few months and was given in a single task only. The result was a lack of flexibility between workers trained in different tasks, so that UK plants required more workers per machine than in other countries.

There was a similar story for maintenance workers and supervisors: a higher proportion of workers had vocational qualifications in continental Europe compared with the UK and the USA. However, one significant factor in the USA explaining productivity differences was the employment of graduates as supervisors, giving higher quality and more flexible supervision.

In conclusion, Mason et al. deduce that:

1   US productivity leadership depends on greater opportunities for scale economies of production.
2   Differences in the age and sophistication of machinery contribute only partially and weakly to the explanation of productivity differences between countries.
3   The USA benefits from higher levels of physical capital per worker.
4   The USA devotes more time and thought to adapting and improving machinery, facilitated by the employment of graduates as supervisors.
5   In the USA graduate substitution at the supervisory level has led to more efficient working practices.

COUNTRY DIFFERENCES IN PRODUCTIVITY

There have been a number of studies of productivity differences between countries, which usually put the USA at the top of the table and the UK at or near the bottom of the group of countries compared. One such study was that by the McKinsey Global Institute (1998). Table 7.5 summarizes the results of a comparison between the UK, France, West Germany and the USA, using labour, capital and total factor productivity. In terms of labour productivity the UK is not only 37 percentage points behind the USA at the top it is also bottom of the table. In terms of capital productivity, the USA leads the UK, which in turn performs better than France and Germany. Overall, in terms of total factor productivity the USA outperformed the UK by 10 percentage points and the UK outperformed Germany and France. While the US outperforms the other countries, the UK's position depends on the measure used: it performs better in terms of capital productivity and less well in terms of labour productivity.

The report argues that UK management often fails to adopt global best practices, even when they are readily understandable and achievable, that the UK has relatively low capital intensity, but raising investment per worker would not necessarily raise output. The report also compares relative productivity by sector with productivity in the best practice country. The results are to be found in Table 7.6. In only one sector, food retailing, was the UK a benchmark country, but even then labour productivity was lower than capital productivity. In all the other identified sectors, except motor cars, the USA was the sector leader. The results for the UK are generally attributed to

Table 7.5   Productivity differences between countries

	Total factor productivity	Labour productivity	Capital productivity
UK	100	100	100
France	113	126	92
Germany	114	126	93
USA	126	137	110

Source Compiled by author from data extracted from Mckinsey Global Institute (1998, exhibit 2)

Table 7.6   Productivity by Sector: UK versus benchmark country

Sector	Relative labour productivity	Relative total factor productivity	Benchmark country
Motor cars	50	55	Japan
Food process	75	80	USA
Food retail	75	100	UK, France
Telecommunications	50	60	USA
Software	70	NA	USA
Weighted average	67	NA	USA
All sectors	73	79	USA

Source Compiled by author from data extracted from McKinsey Global Institute (1998, exhibit 9)

lower labour productivity, a lack of investment in training labour and poor management. This report differs from conventional wisdom in that capital investment, although a contributory factor, was not identified as a primary cause of poor performance.

CHAPTER SUMMARY

In this chapter we explored the economics of production by primarily using isoquant analysis. In doing this we analysed:

■ The relative performance of plants and firms.
■ Productivity to measure relative performance.
■ The shortcomings of using a single-factor measure of productivity to ascertain the changing performance of the firm.
■ Various factors that might explain poor performance.

The concepts developed in this chapter are important for an individual firm in at least two respects: first, the selection of optimal production to produce a good or service and, second, the measurement of performance to make either internal or external comparisons.

REVIEW QUESTIONS

1 What factors determine the shape of an isoquant? What shapes might isoquants take?

2 Define the marginal rate of technical substitution (MRTS)? What is the relationship between the MRTS and the marginal products of the factors?

3 Why would a firm seek to equate the marginal rate of technical substitution to the ratio of factor prices? What are the consequences of a failure to achieve such an equality?

4 What is technical progress? Distinguish between different types of technical progress. What impact do these different notions of technical progress have on:
   – The position of the isoquant?
   – The shape of the isoquant?

5 Are firms more likely to engage in capital-using or labour-using technical progress?

6 Does technical progress inevitably mean the production process becomes more capital-intensive?

7 Demonstrate, using isoquants, how labour productivity, capital productivity and total factor productivity are measured?

8 The following are estimates of increases in inputs and total productivity for manufacturing and service industries in the UK for 1981–1989:

	Services (%)	Manufacturing (%)
Labour	2.2	−2.1
Capital	5.5	1.3
Total inputs	3.1	−1.5
Output	4.1	3.7
Total factor productivity	1.0	5.2
Capital productivity	−1.4	5.2
Labour productivity	1.9	5.6

- Do these changes represent unequivocal increases in efficiency in both manufacturing and services?
- Is production becoming more or less capital-intensive?
- Are firms using capital efficiently?
- Demonstrate the relative changes in the two sectors using isoquant analysis.

9 Historically, the UK has a poor comparative record in terms of productivity. What factors might account for the poor UK performance? What policies might the government adopt to increase productivity?

10 Define Farrell Efficiency and distinguish between technical efficiency and cost (or price) efficiency. Using the following data (input requirements per 1,00 tonnes of product) construct a best practice isoquant and estimate the degree of productive inefficiency of the least efficient company and identify the most efficient company?

Company	Units of labour	Units of capital	Company	Units of labour	Units of capital
1	9	360	7	2	305
2	7	280	8	8	360
3	10	240	9	11	400
4	10	245	10	4	430
5	6	240	11	12	200
6	5	330	12	9	183

11 Discuss the meaning of the production function. What is the short run? What is the long run? How does the short-run production function differ from the long-run production function?

12 Describe what is meant by increasing returns to scale, decreasing returns to scale and constant returns to scale. Discuss the factors that might be responsible for increasing and decreasing returns.

13 A firm claims that it has the following production function:

$$Q = 3 + 4L + 2P$$

where Q = output, L = labour and P = paper.

- Does this production function include all relevant inputs? Explain.
- Does this production function seem reasonable, if applied to all possible values of L and P? Explain.
- Does this production function exhibit increasing or decreasing marginal returns?

14 The following function was estimated for the bus industry:

$$Q = \underset{(-2.4)}{-1.80} + \underset{(2.0)}{0.21B} + \underset{(3.3)}{0.41F} + \underset{(3.2)}{0.37L} \qquad \text{adjusted } R^2 = 0.97$$

Explain the role and function of the exponents in the multiplicative production function. Does the estimated production function indicate that there are economies of scale?

REFERENCES AND FURTHER READING

Charnes, A., W.W. Cooper and E. Rhodes (1978) Measuring the efficiency of decision making units. *European Journal of Operations Research*, **2**, 429–444.

Cubbin, J., S. Domberger and S. Meadowcraft (1987) Competitive tendering and refuse collection: Identifying the sources of efficiency gains. *Fiscal Studies*, **8**(3), 49–58.

Douglas, E.J. (1992) *Managerial Economics* (4th edn, Chapters 6–8). Prentice Hall, Englewood Cliffs, NJ.

Farrell, M.J. (1957) The measurement of productive efficiency. *Journal of the Royal Statistical Society (General Series)*, **120**, 253–290.

Field, K. (1990) Production efficiency of British building societies. *Applied Economics*, **22**, 415–426.

Forsund, F.R. and L. Hjalmarsson (1979) Generalised Farrell measures of efficiency: An application to milk processing in Swedish dairy plants, *Economic Journal*, **89**. 294–315.

Heathfield, D.F. and Wibe, S. (1987) *An Introduction to Cost and Production Functions*. Macmillan, Basingstoke, UK.

HM Treasury (2000) *Productivity in the UK: The Evidence and the Government's Approach*. HM Treasury, London.

Mason, G. and D. Finegold (1997) Productivity, machinery and skills in the US and Western Europe. *National Institute Economic Review*, **162**, 85–88.

Mason, G., B. van Ark and K. Wagner (1994) Productivity, product quality and workforce skills: Food processing in four European countries. *National Institute Economic Review*, **147**, 62–83.

McKinsey Global Institute (1998) *Driving Productivity and Growth in the UK Economy*. McKinsey, Washington, D.C.

Oum, T.H., W.G. Waters II and C. Yu (1999) A survey of productivity and efficiency measurement in rail transport. *Journal of Transport Economics and Policy*, **33**(1), 9–42.

Pickering, J.F. (1983) Efficiency in a department store. *Omega*, **11**(3), 231–237.

Schefczyk, M. (1993) Operational performance of airlines: An extension of traditional measurement paradigms. *Strategic Management Journal*, **14**, 301–307.

Salter, W.E.G. (1996) *Productivity and Technical Change* (2nd edn). Cambridge University Press, Cambridge, UK.

Todd, D. (1984) Productive performance in the firm: The economic approach. In: J.F. Pickering and T.A.J. Cockerill (eds), *The Economic Management of the Firm*. Philip Allan, Deddington, UK.

Todd, D. (1985) Productive performance in West German manufacturing industry 1970–1980: A Farrell frontier characterisation. *Journal of Industrial Economics*, **33**, 295–316.

8

COSTS

CHAPTER OUTLINE

CHAPTER OBJECTIVES

The aim of this chapter is to examine the economic analysis of costs and demonstrate how the successful management of costs can gain competitive advantage for a firm over its rivals. At the end of this chapter you should be able to:

◆ Distinguish between fixed and variable costs and long and short-run costs.

◆ Analyse the relationship between short and long-run costs.

◆ Understand the cost allocation problems in a multi-product firm.

◆ Explain the differences between economic and accounting concepts of costs.

◆ Identify procedures to estimate cost functions.

◆ Understand the concepts of economies of scope, scale and learning and explain how they may be utilized to give a firm competitive advantage.

INTRODUCTION

The objective of this chapter is to explore the nature of costs, their importance in decision making and in gaining a competitive advantage. The main topics covered in the chapter include:

- Economic concepts of costs in the short and long run.
- Cost concepts used by managers.
- Empirical procedures for estimating cost functions.
- Economies of scale, economies of scope and economies of learning.
- Costs and competitive advantage.

SHORT-RUN COST CURVES

In the short run, economic analysis assumes that one factor of production, usually capital, is fixed. The firm (as shown in Figure 7.5) is constrained to choose points on the line KT; this allows both a total product curve to be derived and a total cost curve by calculating the total cost at each production point, using isocost curves for given prices of labour and capital. These relationships are plotted in Figure 8.1.

The short-run total cost curve has two elements:

- **Fixed costs**: these are the costs of buying the necessary capital before production can begin. These costs do not vary with output and more generally can include any cost that must be met before production commences.
- **Variable costs**: these vary with output and are incurred in employing labour to work with the capital to produce output. More generally, they include all costs (e.g., raw materials) that vary with output.

The sum of **total fixed costs** (TFCs) and **total variable costs** (TVCs) gives the total costs of the firm. In Figure 8.1(b), total fixed costs are shown as a horizontal line, because they do not vary with output, while the total variable cost curve is shown as upward-sloping. Its shape will depend on the relationship between inputs used, costs incurred and output.

From the total cost curve, short-run average and marginal costs can be derived. The main concepts that are used in decision making include:

- **Average fixed costs** (AFCs), or total fixed costs divided by output: this gives a curve that slopes downward from right to left as output increases (see Figure 8.2).
- **Average variable costs** (AVCs), or total variable costs divided by output. The shape of the average variable cost curve depends on the shape of the total variable cost curve. A linear relationship will give the horizontal variable cost curve, or AVC_1, in Figure 8.2(a), and a non-linear relationship will produce a U-shaped curve like AVC_2 in Figure 8.2(b).
- **Average total costs** (ATCs): these are the sum of average fixed and average variable costs. In Figure 8.2(a), ATC_1 slopes downward from right to left, approaching but

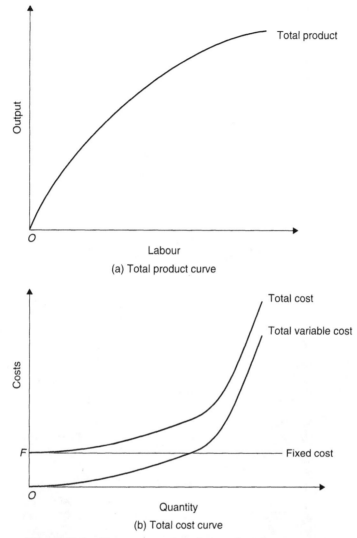

Figure 8.1 Short-run total product and total cost curves

never touching the average fixed cost curve, while in Figure 8.2(b), ATC_2 slopes initially downward and then upward, being described as U-shaped.

■ **Marginal costs** (MCs): these are the addition to total costs by producing an additional unit of output. Since fixed costs do not vary with output, the marginal cost curve is the increment in total variable costs, as a result of producing an extra unit of output. In Figure 8.2(a), average variable costs and marginal costs are identical, but in Figure 8.2(b) the marginal cost curve initially slopes downward and then upward, cutting the average total cost curve and average variable cost curve at their lowest point.

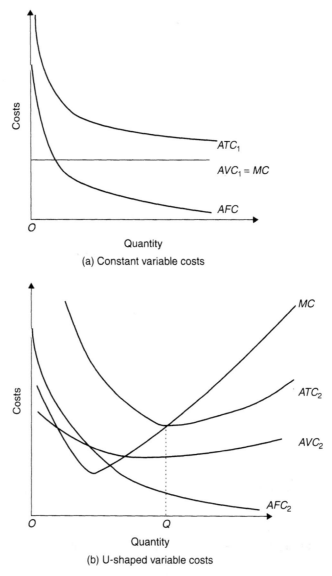

Figure 8.2 Average and marginal cost curves

Mathematically, the relationships can be expressed using a cost function. If Q is the quantity produced, then the cost function can take the quadratic form:

$$\text{Total cost} = a + bQ + cQ^2$$

$$\text{Average variable cost} = b + cQ$$

$$\text{Average total cost} = a/Q + b + cQ \qquad \text{or} \qquad AFC + AVC$$

$$\text{Marginal cost} = \delta TC/\delta Q \qquad \text{or} \qquad \delta TVC/\delta Q = b + 2cQ$$

The marginal cost curve will rise as a constant function of output, where the cost function takes the cubic form:

$$\text{Total cost} = a + bQ + cQ^2 + dQ^3$$

$$\text{Average variable cost} = b + cQ + dQ^2$$

$$\text{Average total cost} = a/Q + b + cQ + dQ^2 \quad \text{or} \quad AFC + AVC$$

$$\text{Marginal cost} = \delta TC/\delta Q \quad \text{or} \quad \delta TVC/\delta Q = b + 2cQ + 3dQ^2$$

The average total cost and marginal cost curves will be U-shaped with the marginal cost curve intersecting the average total cost and average variable cost curves at their lowest point and from below, as in Figure 8.2(b).

Determinants of short-run costs

Short-run costs are essentially a function of:

■ The technology used to determine the capital–labour ratio. The more capital-intensive is production the more important will be fixed costs relative to variable costs.
■ The technology used to determine the labour–output ratio. With given capital this changes as output increases. The more labour intensive is production the more important will be variable costs to fixed costs The changing labour–output ratio initially favours lower costs, but eventually increases costs when capital is over-utilized.
■ To produce more output the firm may employ additional labour units to meet orders or get existing workers to work overtime. The latter will receive premium payments and the former may have to be paid higher wages to secure their services.
■ Managerial abilities. Costs may vary between firms depending on the abilities of their managers to organize production and motivate their employees effectively. Efficient management may achieve higher productivity and lower unit cost levels than inefficient management.

Economists tend to assume that the short-run cost curve is U-shaped. The downward portion is explained by the more efficient use of fixed or indivisible factors. Many resources are to some degree indivisible and can only be fully utilized at greater levels of output. The upward portion is explained by overuse of the fixed factors, which makes them less efficient, so that unit costs increase. Increasing prices for inputs as output moves beyond the planned output will reinforce this effect.

LONG-RUN COST CURVES

In the long run all factors are variable. Therefore, the firm can choose the most efficient size of plant to fulfil production plans in the most cost-effective way. In the long run the firm can choose the plant that best fulfils its plans from a series of plant sizes.

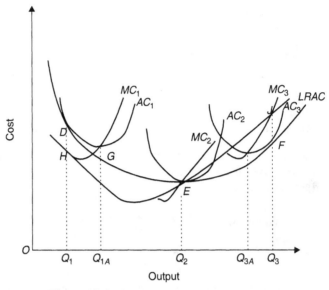

Figure 8.3 Long-run average cost curve

A small selection of three potential plant sizes is shown in Figure 8.3, but keep in mind that theoretically there is an almost infinite number of plants, all of slightly different sizes. Each individual plant is characterized by a U-shaped short-run average cost curve. Joining the outer points of successive short-run cost curves (e.g., D, E and F) gives the **long-run average cost curve** (LRAC). Such a curve is shown in Figure 8.3 and is described as an envelope curve enclosing the myriad of **short-run average cost curves**. Every point on the curve shows the lowest average cost to produce any given output in the long run. It should be noted that to produce output Q_1 on average cost curve AC_1, necessitates carrying excess capacity, because the lowest average cost for that curve is achieved at output Q_{1A}. However, output Q_{1A}, could be produced more cheaply at point G on another short-run average cost curve (not shown).

The long-run marginal cost curve joins the points on the short-run marginal cost curves associated with the short-run average costs at each output on the long-run average cost curve. Thus, in Figure 8.3 at output Q_1 the relevant marginal cost is Q_1H. The long-run marginal cost curve joins points H, E and J. The optimum-sized plant is AC_2, assuming sufficient demand, and the optimal output is OQ_2, where long and short-run marginal and average costs are all equal.

Elasticity of cost relative to output

The relationship between cost and output can be measured using cost–output elasticity, which is defined as the percentage change in total cost divided by the percentage change in output. Symbolically, cost elasticity (E_{CQ}) is given by:

$$E_{CQ} = (\Delta TC/TC)/\Delta Q/Q)$$

which can be rearranged to give:

$$E_{CQ} = (\Delta TC/\Delta Q)/(TC/Q)$$

or marginal cost divided by average cost, or MC/AC. From this final ratio we have the following relationships:

1   If E_{CQ} is less than 1, then the marginal cost is less than average cost and, therefore, the cost function exhibits economies of scale.
2   If E_{CQ} is greater than 1, then the marginal cost is greater than average cost and, therefore, the cost function exhibits **diseconomies of scale**.
3   If E_{CQ} is equal to 1, then the marginal cost is equal to average cost and, therefore, the cost function exhibits constant costs.

Short and long-run costs and investment decisions

The relationship between short and long-run marginal costs can be used to ascertain whether a firm should build a larger or a smaller plant. The rules are:

■   If the short-run marginal cost of producing the current output is greater than the long-run marginal cost, then the firm should build a larger plant.
■   If the short-run marginal cost of producing the current output is less than the long-run marginal cost, then the firm should consider operating a smaller plant.

In Figure 8.3 short-run marginal cost exceeds long-run marginal cost at output Q_{1A}; consequently, the firm should build a larger plant, because it can produce the same output more cheaply. Likewise, if the firm were producing output Q_{3A}, then long-run marginal cost exceeds short-run marginal cost, indicating that the output could be produced more cheaply with a smaller plant.

COSTS AND THE MULTI-PRODUCT FIRM

The discussion so far has assumed that the firm produces only a single product. In the real world most firms produce a number of products. When moving from a single to a multi-product firm, some of the cost concepts so far developed have to be modified or even abandoned.

To illustrate some of the differences, assume that a firm produces two products, product 1 and product 2, using the same capital equipment. Total costs (TC) will then be the sum of fixed costs (F) and the variable costs associated with producing both products (c_1 and c_2) multiplied by the output of both products (Q_1 and Q_2). Thus, total cost would be given by:

$$TC = F + c_1Q_1 + c_2Q_2$$

The average cost of production of each product can only be calculated if there is agreement on how fixed costs should be allocated between the two products. Typical methods of allocating fixed costs are:

■ To allocate all fixed costs to one product, because it is regarded as the main product of the firm.
■ To allocate fixed costs between the two products on the relative use made of the fixed factors by both products, measured by time used or output produced.
■ To allocate fixed costs on an arbitrary basis.

Weighted average cost

An average cost of production for the firm as a whole also requires some agreement about the nature of the unit of output. If the two products are produced in fixed proportions, then the concept of weighted average cost can be used. However, for every proportion in which output might be produced there would be a separate average cost.

The weighted average cost (AC_w) is calculated in the following way:

$$AC_w(Q) = \frac{F + c_1(X_1 Q) + c_2(X_2 Q)}{Q}$$

where X_1 and X_2 are the proportions in which products 1 and 2 are produced, or the weights used in calculating average costs, and $Q =$ the total output. If the two products are initially produced in equal numbers, then if the variable cost for product 1 is $2Q_1$, for product 2 it is $3Q_2$, fixed costs are 200, output is 100 and the **total cost function** is given by:

$$TC = 200 + 2(0.5 * Q) + 3 * (0.5 * Q)$$

Total cost for an output of 100 is given by:

$$TC = 200 + 2(0.5 * 100) + 3 * (0.5 * 100) = 450$$

with a weighted average cost equal to 4.5. The total cost for an output of 200 with the same proportions of products would be 700, and the weighted average cost would be 3.5.

If the proportions of the two products were to change to 0.3 for product 1 and 0.7 for product 2, then the total cost function for an output of 100 would be:

$$TC = 200 + 2(0.3 * 100) + 3 * (0.7 * 100) = 470$$

with average cost equal to 4.7. If output were 200, then total cost would be 760 and average cost 3.8.

Marginal cost

The concept of marginal cost only has meaning for an individual product if the output of the other product is held fixed. Thus, if the output of product 1 is held constant, then any cost incurred by increasing the output of product 2 can be attributed to product 2 and be regarded as the marginal cost of that product.

ECONOMICS VERSUS ACCOUNTING COST CONCEPTS

The economist's concepts of costs do not necessarily coincide with the cost concepts used by businesses or accountants: for accounting, costs are only incurred where a ledger entry is required because money has been spent; and for economists, the main concept is that of opportunity cost. The cost of any input in the production of any good or service is the alternative it could have produced if used elsewhere, whether valued in monetary terms or not: for example, if financial resources can earn 5% in a bank account, then this is a measure of the opportunity cost of using the funds for some other purpose. However, the alternative use is not always easily identifiable or translatable into monetary values. It may also be difficult to attribute alternative values to two inputs that are used together to produce a single product. The simple solution is to use market prices; but, they only fully reflect opportunity costs if all resources are scarce and price is equal to marginal cost. If resources have no alternative use, then their opportunity costs are zero (see Chapter 23).

Explicit and implicit costs

Another difference between the two approaches is the distinction between explicit and implicit costs. **Explicit costs** involve expenditure, whereas **implicit costs** do not. For example, if a retail firm operates two shops, one of which it rents the other it owns, then in terms of costs incurred, rent is paid to the owner of the premises for shop 1, but no rent is paid to itself as owner of shop 2. To make a fair comparison of the cost incurred by the two shops, the implicit cost of the shop owned by the firm should be quantified and imputed into the accounts to reflect alternative uses of the premises. In this case, rental values for other premises in the same street would indicate the implicit value of the resource.

Direct and indirect costs

If costs can be attributed to a particular activity, then they are termed direct costs; if they cannot easily be attributed to a particular activity, then they are termed indirect costs or overhead costs. The test for allocation of costs is whether costs are separable and attributable, whereas the economic distinction between fixed and variable costs is whether they vary with output.

Replacement and historic costs

Another distinction is made between replacement and historic costs. Historic costs are those paid at the time of purchase, while current or replacement costs reflect the current price or cost of buying or replacing the input now, which, better reflects the opportunity cost of employing equipment or other resources that may have been in stock for some time.

Sunk and non-sunk costs

Sunk costs are those incurred in buying assets, such as plant or machinery, or spending on advertising that cannot subsequently be retrieved by selling the resource or deploying it in another use. Generally, these costs have been incurred in making a previous decision and are not relevant to a decision being currently made. For example, a decision to enter the airline industry will involve buying aeroplanes, setting up support services and advertising new routes. If the venture is unsuccessful, then the aeroplanes can be sold and a substantial part of the initial costs recovered, making only a small portion sunk; but, many of the set-up costs are sunk in that they cannot be retrieved because they were specific to that particular venture. Generally, the more specific the asset is to a particular use (i.e., the fewer alternative uses it has) the greater the element of sunk costs.

Incremental cost

Marginal costs, discussed earlier on p. 147, are those costs incurred by producing an extra unit of output. A related concept used in business is incremental cost, defined as the additional cost relating to any change, not just a unit change, in output: for example, the incremental costs to the firm of introducing a new product would include both capacity and variable costs. Incremental costs are those that will be incurred as the result of a decision and can be thought of as the long-run marginal costs of the decision.

Costs and profits

Costs and profits are also a source of confusion. The concept of profit to an economist differs from that of the accountant. Both consider it to be the difference between revenue and costs, but they regard costs differently. **Normal profits** are earned in economic analysis when total revenue equals total cost, because total costs are calculated to reflect the opportunity costs of all services provided, including that of the entrepreneur; this is just enough to keep the firm in the industry (i.e., more profit cannot be earned elsewhere). Pure profit is that which arises from the excess of revenue over opportunity costs. Accounting profit has to be adjusted for owned resources, while normal profit needs to be modified to account for the varying degrees of risk involved in different activities.

EMPIRICAL COST ANALYSIS

Identifying the shape and nature of the cost function is important for many decisions. Economists view short-run cost curves as being U-shaped, while accountants see the relevant costs as being constant per unit. The two views are reconciled in the short run by proposing a bath-shaped cost curve (see Figure 8.4), with a significant horizontal section to it before diseconomies set in; this is because firms build their plants with flexibility in mind. The plant will have a capacity larger than the "expected" level of sales to meet variations in demand and to accommodate growth. The horizontal portion of the average cost curve has been supported by statistical cost analysis. For long-run costs, the view has emerged that it is more likely to be L-shaped, with average costs declining initially to a point described as the **minimum efficient scale** (MES); this is the first plant size that minimizes long-run average costs. Thereafter, long-run average costs remain constant, so that there is no relevant point at which diseconomies of scale become operative; this is illustrated in Figure 8.5.

Statistical estimation of short-run cost functions

Cost functions can be estimated by statistical cost analysis if there are sufficient observations. There are a number of models, linear and non-linear, available to fit to

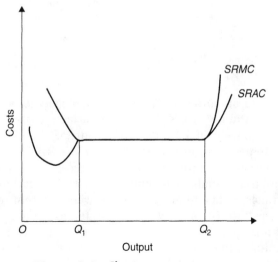

Figure 8.4 Short-run cost curve

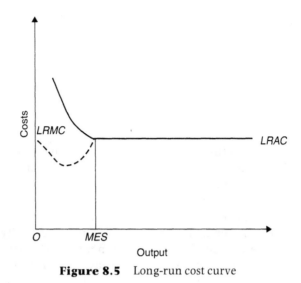

Figure 8.5 Long-run cost curve

the data. Generally, several different models are fitted to the data to see which is statistically the more appropriate.

Time series regression is the most popular method for estimating the short-run variable cost function. The model to be estimated, as long as the relationship is assumed to be linear, is $TVC = a + bQ$, where a and b are the parameters to be estimated. The intercept may have little meaning as it lies well outside the range of observations. The parameter b measures the variable cost function within the data range that relates cost changes to changes in output. More complex models are used in empirical work; these include the translog cost function that allows for the possibility of U-shaped long-run cost curves (see "Appendix: statistical cost functions" on p. 165).

An example of the output of such a study is the following equation; this was estimated using ordinary least squares regression and was derived from the 30 weeks of data found in Table 8.1:

$$TVC = \underset{(8.316)}{901.983} + \underset{(52.145)}{0.701Q} \qquad \text{adjusted } R^2 = 0.989, F = 2715.165$$

The t-statistics are in parentheses. The equation appears to be a good fit and explains over 98% of the variation in costs. Average variable costs are given by $(901.983/Q) + 0.701$. For an output of 10,000 tonnes (outside the sample range) the average variable cost per tonne is £0.09 + 0.70, or £0.79.

Much of the early work estimating short-run cost curves was undertaken by Dean (1941). He found that variable cost and output were linearly related and that short-run average variable costs and marginal costs were constant over the observed range of output. Johnson (1960) reported 31 separate case studies and found the results supported the view that marginal cost was constant over a wide range of output within the operating range of the firm. In some cases a curvilinear cost function was found to be statistically more significant, but there was little loss of explanatory power

Table 8.1 Cost data for product X

Week	Output units	TVC (£)	Week	Output units	TVC (£)
1	7,200	5,890	16	9,500	7,580
2	7,500	6,120	17	9,100	7,230
3	8,300	6,640	18	8,500	6,890
4	6,500	5,450	19	8,300	6,880
5	6,500	5,500	20	8,200	6,790
6	7,200	5,910	21	7,500	6,250
7	8,500	6,850	22	7,200	5,950
8	9,400	7,450	23	7,000	5,870
9	9,500	7,550	24	6,800	5,780
10	9,500	7,570	25	6,700	5,740
11	9,400	7,500	26	6,500	5,520
12	9,350	7,520	27	6,700	5,640
13	9,200	7,340	28	6,800	5,520
14	9,200	7,360	29	7,000	5,670
15	9,300	7,430	30	7,100	5,710

Source Author

by using the linear model. Koot and Walker (1970) estimate cost functions for a plastic container manufacturer and found evidence of linear average variable costs. Recent studies of hospitals find that short-run variable costs of hospitals are constant (Aletras 1999). The empirical evidence tends to suggest that short-run average variable costs are constant over the range of outputs the firm is most likely to produce.

Long-run statistical cost estimation

In the long run, all inputs are variable and the problem is to determine the least cost production curve for plants of different size. Cross-sectional data are used in preference to time series, because they are better able to give cost data for a wide range of plants of different sizes. However, there are data problems, because plants are of different technology vintages, are at different locations and may face different factor and input prices.

The great majority of empirically estimated long-run cost functions in manufacturing and utilities exhibit sharply falling average costs at low output levels, but the extent of these scale economies declines as output increases and constant costs appear to hold over a wide range of output. Very few studies have found evidence of decreasing returns to scale. The long-run average cost curve has therefore been described as L-shaped, as illustrated in Figure 8.5. Wiles (1956), who studied 44 sets of data, Johnson (1960) and Walters (1963) all support this contention. No diminishing returns are found in the long run, partly because such plants may not have been built. These results have been confirmed in some service sectors, such as building societies and hospitals (see Case Study 8.1).

Engineering approach

Because of the difficulties with statistical studies, economists have sometimes used an engineering approach. The technique consists of developing the physical production function, or isoquant map, that exists between inputs and output and, then, attaching cost values to obtain a total cost function for producing a different output level: for example, in producing ethylene or cars, in plants of different sizes, the capital costs can be estimated by calculating the size and type of equipment needed to build a plant from scratch at the time of the study and, then, postulating an idealized relationship between inputs and outputs.

The engineering technique comes closest to reflecting the timeless nature of theoretical cost functions. It is based on currently available technology and avoids problems of improper data observations. The problems with the technique involve trying to extend the engineering functions beyond the range of current systems, particularly if experience is only with pilot-sized plants.

The method was used by Pratten (1971) who made estimates for a number of UK industries. More recent estimates have been made by the EU, mainly for manufacturing industries (Schwalbach 1988). A classic study by Cookenboo (1955) applied the engineering technique, made use of isoquant analysis and estimated long-run cost curves for oil pipelines. He built an engineering-based production function, taking into account three main factors: pipe diameter, the horsepower of pumps and the number of pumping stations. By converting input quantities into costs, total cost functions and average costs were estimated.

Case Study 8.1 Estimating cost functions for hospitals

Hospitals tend in many parts of the world be to not-for-profit organizations. However, they are interested in minimizing costs, because it makes best use of funding whether via government grants or insurance payments.

Hospitals provide many medical procedures for patients with the objective of improving their health. Besides treating patients to restore them to health, hospitals also provide treatment to ease pain suffered by terminally ill patients. They may also provide cosmetic surgery and other treatments that, though medically unnecessary, restore the patients' social esteem. They also provide services to inpatients and outpatients.

Hospitals, therefore, are multi-product enterprises. To avoid the problems inherent in combining heterogeneous outputs, resort is made to measuring throughputs or intermediate outputs; these include such measures as the number of cases treated, treatment episodes and patient care days for both inpatients and outpatients.

Aletras (1999), using Greek data, estimates both short run and long-run cost functions using translog and Cobb–Douglas cost functions. The dependent variables were total variable costs for the short-run model and total costs for the long-run model. The independent variables were inpatient and outpatient cases. Two shift variables, teaching and case mix, were included; these shift the cost function but do not alter its basic shape.

The short-run model found costs increased by 9.86% when output increased by 10%; this was not statistically significant and could not support either increasing or decreasing costs.

The long-run model found costs increased by 8.28% when output increases by 10%; this was a statistically significant result and indicates that there are economies of scale available to Greek hospitals.

Economies of scale for general hospitals have been examined extensively. Studies have found that economies of scale are fully exploited in hospitals that have roughly 200 beds and that larger hospitals with 400 or more beds are at best no more efficient than smaller units; this suggests that long-run costs are constant. However, these results are contradicted by Aletras's study.

COST CONCEPTS AND STRATEGIC ADVANTAGE

Lower costs per unit of output may give a firm a competitive advantage over its rivals. A firm may strive to be the least cost operator in an industry, so that it can either charge lower prices than its rivals and still make positive profits or, at the same price, it will achieve a higher profit margin. In this section three sources of advantage will be examined: namely, economies of scope, economies of scale and economies of learning (Grundy 1996).

Economies of scope

Economies of scope occur when products share common inputs and **diversification** leads to cost savings. A manufacturing firm may be able to utilize machinery more efficiently by producing a range of goods that are complementary in production. The potential for doing so can affect the profitability of the firm significantly. For example, in the operation of bus services, firms operating a single bus on a single route may not be disadvantaged in terms of operating costs. However, a bus company operating a network of routes may be able to reduce its unit costs by attracting a higher number of passengers through operating connecting services and through ticketing. Network operation may also allow lower unit costs for marketing and providing timetable information. Knowledge may be a common input bringing together two separate but often linked production processes. Production techniques may have a number of common features that a single firm can make better use of than if the products were produced separately.

The extent to which scope economies exist for a firm with three activities can be measured by estimating a scope index S. Thus:

$$S = [c^1 + c^2 + c^3 - c^{1+2+3}]/[C^1 + C^2 + C^3]$$

where $C^1 + C^2 + C^3 =$ the cost of the three activities carried out separately and $C^{1+2+3} =$ the cost when carried out together. If S is negative, then the three activities are better carried out separately. If S is positive, then the three activities are better carried out together in the same plant. The problem with estimating economies of scope is that it may be difficult to identify the nature of the cost function where common inputs are used to produce multiple products. The implications for the firm are that it is more efficient to produce a number of products within the same plant. The source of economies of scope may not only be found in manufacturing but also in such areas as marketing: for example, it may be cheaper to market different financial services from the same premises, a strategy adopted by banks, building societies and insurance companies.

Case Study 8.2   Economies of scope in car production

In a multi-product industry, such as motor cars, a firm can gain cost advantages from both economies of scope and economies of scale. Friedlander et al. (1983) investigated economies of scope and product specific economies of scale in the US motor industry. They estimated a multi-product cost function for each of the four US car manufacturers. It was also found that General Motors, besides benefiting from scale economies, also achieved substantial benefits from combining the production of large cars with small cars, plus trucks. The estimated scope measure was 25%. No economies of scope arise from producing trucks together with small and large cars; it appears that truck production could occur in a separate firm with no loss of efficiency. As a result GM's strategy, which stressed the production of a large number of different products, brought economies of scope, whereas Ford, which concentrated on large-scale production of a standard vehicle at the time, did not obtain such benefit.

Economies of scale

Economies of scale are a long-run phenomenon by which increasingly larger plants exhibit lower average costs of production. The scale at which lowest unit costs are first reached is termed the **minimum efficient scale** of production. Plants intended to operate at maximum efficiency, or at lowest cost, must be at least of this size. Firms operating below minimum efficient scale will suffer cost penalties, the extent of which depends on the slope of the long-run average cost curve to the point of minimum efficient scale.

Economies of scale, or lower costs, can be achieved through savings in resources used as the size of plant increases or because the firm can obtain inputs at lower prices as it gets larger. The former are termed real economies of scale, while the latter are termed pecuniary economies of scale. Real economies of scale are to be found in various activities of the plant, or firm, and are associated with savings in capital, labour, marketing, transport, storage and managerial economies as the size of plant or firm increases.

Lower long-run costs can arise from the division of labour as workers specialize in a small part of the whole process and become familiar with the tasks performed. Labour economies also arise from automation or workers operating with greater capital inputs. Thus, as output doubles, labour requirements will increase by, say, 80%, leading to lower costs.

Lower costs can arise from technical economies that are associated with specialization of capital, lower set-up costs, lower reserve requirements and size or volume relationships. Doubling the volume of a cube or cylinder does not double the surface area and, therefore, the material required to make it. Because volume increases by r^3 and area or costs by r^2 in process industries, such as oil refining, this has led to the adoption of the 0.6 rule: a general rule of thumb that says doubling the size of a plant raises capital costs by only 60%. Haldi and Whitcomb (1967) estimated scale coefficients for 687 types of basic equipment. Fitting the function $C = aQ^b$, where C = costs, Q = output capacity and a, b = constants, they found in 90% of cases that there were increasing returns and in process plant industries the size of plant raised capital costs by a value of 0.73 rather than 0.6.

Unit selling, or marketing costs, may also decline with increasing output. Expenditures on advertising are assumed not to vary directly with output. To some extent the costs have to be incurred before the product is sold, because consumers have to be made aware of its existence and perhaps be persuaded to buy. Advertising costs per unit of output therefore decline as output increases (see Chapter 11).

Managerial economies may also arise. As firms grow, the responsibilities of management tend to become more specialized; this enables the managerial function to grow and for management to become less costly per unit of output, allowing firms to achieve managerial economies as they grow (see Chapters 15 and 20).

Research and development is a vital activity for some firms in producing new products (e.g., in the pharmaceutical industry) or for improving product reliability and quality (e.g., electrical household goods). If R and D budgets have to be of a large minimum size before they can become effective, then they may be affordable only by firms of a certain size. In addition, if R and D is treated as a fixed cost, then the cost per unit sold will fall the larger the size of the firm.

Financial economies may also arise. Large firms may be able to raise finance more cheaply than small companies; this may be attributed to the previous track record of large companies in repaying loans and their success, so that they are less of a risk than smaller, newer companies. Larger companies may also be more diversified than smaller companies; so, the failure of one element of the company is less of a threat to its financial viability than for small companies. Large companies may also have access to cheaper sources of finance, not easily available to smaller companies (e.g., access to the new equity market). Even if access is gained, larger share issues are cheaper than smaller share issues.

Case Study 8.3 Economies of scale in building societies and insurance companies

Hardwick (1990) investigated economies of scale in building societies. He measured what he termed "augmented economies of scale" which allow for the growth in the number of building society branches as output increases. He found that economies of scale existed for small societies with a cost elasticity of 0.91 to 0.94 (i.e., a 10% increase in size would lead to a 9.1% increase in costs). However, building societies with assets in excess of £5.5bn incurred diseconomies. If growth could have been achieved without more branches, then the cost elasticity would have been 0.72.

A study by Drake and Simper (1992) of building societies, using a more sophisticated cost function, found that estimated elasticity of scale economies were 0.907. The authors describe this as a highly significant result, suggesting that the UK industry is characterized by substantial economies of scale, particularly for larger societies. The results are similar to Hardwick's estimates for smaller societies, but not for larger societies.

Hardwick (1993) undertook a survey of managers of life insurance companies to discover the sources of economies of scale. Respondents considered the main sources of economies of scale, in terms of the number of respondents agreeing:

■ More efficient use of computers 75%.
■ Name awareness 68%.
■ More cost-effective advertising 64%.
■ Office equipment and vehicles at discount prices 61%.

Diseconomies of scale were considered to be:

■ Rising cost of monitoring and control 81%.
■ Development/Adjustment cost of diversification 61% (9% disagree).

Learning curve

It has been observed in particular production processes that the average costs per unit tend to decline over time as the factors of production, such as labour and management, learn the production process and become more efficient; this process is termed learning by doing. The learning curve shows how manufacturing costs fall as volume rises. It also shows the relationship between the costs per unit of output and cumulative output since production began. The experience curve traces the decline in the total costs of a product over extended periods of time as volume grows. Typically, it includes a broader range of costs than does the learning curve.

Hypothetical learning curves are shown in Figure 8.6 based on the data given in Table 8.2. Unit cost is measured on the vertical axis and cumulative output on the horizontal axis. Thus, curve 1 shows unit costs starting at £500 for 10 units, with costs at 90% of their previous level for every doubling of output; such a curve is described as a 90% learning curve. Curve 2 shows an 80% curve where unit costs are 80% of their previous level for every doubling of output. The steeper the slope of the learning curve the greater the cost savings by doubling output. If it is assumed that there is a constant rate of learning, then the leaning curve is linear when transformed into logs.

The effects of learning are to lower unit costs. According to Abernethy and Wayne (1974) the sources of lower costs include:

■ Greater familiarity of workers and managers with the production process.
■ Reduction of overheads over a greater volume of output.
■ Reduction of stocks as production becomes more rational.
■ Process improvements leading to lower unit labour costs.
■ Division and specialization of labour leading to more effective work and lower costs.

Empirical studies have shown that costs per unit in many manufacturing processes exhibit a downward trend in real terms over time: the cost gain is greatest when

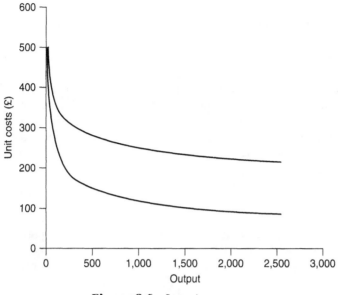

Figure 8.6 Learning curves

Table 8.2 Learning curves

Output	Curve 1 (90%)	Curve 2 (80%)
10	500	500
20	450	400
40	405	320
80	365	256
160	328	205
320	295	164
640	266	131
1,280	239	105
2,560	215	84

Source Author

output increases at the outset and then eventually diminishes and becomes insignificant. In practice, separating learning effects from other causes of cost reductions, such as economies of scale, may be difficult and make empirical estimation harder.

Many efforts have been made to measure the learning curve (see Baden-Fuller 1983). An early example identified by Abernethy and Wayne (1974) was the Model T Ford. Over a period of 16 years the price of the car fell from $4,500 to $950 as output increased from 15,000 to 9,000,000. Reinhart (1973) estimated the learning curve for the Lockheed Tristar aeroplane to be 77.4%.

Learning effects are thought to be most significant in activities using advanced technology and where capital input dominates the production function. However, learning effects are not confined to assembly operations and can occur in any part of the business where repetition gives rise to knowledge-based effects. Knowledge of the learning curve is important to managers in assessing their cost advantages over rivals. It gives early starters a cost advantage that later entrants cannot match for some time. It also enables a firm to build volume and market share and to protect a profitable position (Baden Fuller 1983).

Manufacturers who enter an industry early gain a first-mover advantage in terms of unit costs over late entrant competitors because of their greater production experience. The advantage of the first-mover can be negated if subsequent entrants start with large output rates, avoid the mistakes of older firms and learn faster. In consequence, new firms may not only catch up with the existing leader but may also overtake it without having to replicate its experience. Disadvantages suggested by Abernethy and Wayne (1974), as a result of following this strategy single-mindedly, are a loss of flexibility and a loss of innovative capability.

MANAGEMENT OF COSTS

Managing a business to ensure costs are minimized is a major task. In practice, ensuring costs are minimized is difficult, and concern with cost levels may only arise if the firm's price–cost margin is squeezed or managers become aware that competitors are achieving lower costs and higher profits; such awareness can be gained by benchmarking the firm against rivals to be able to identify sources of inefficiency, to identify better practices and whether what is done better elsewhere can or cannot be adopted.

Sources of costs being higher than best practice might include:

- *Raw materials*: excessive use of materials, paying higher prices and maintaining excessive stocks relative to production levels.
- *Labour*: excessive labour may be employed, it may be used inefficiently and may be rewarded with higher than average wage rates.
- *Quality of inputs*: workers employed may be less skilled than those employed elsewhere and lack training, capital may be of an older vintage and more prone to breakdown.
- *Volume*: average costs are a function of volume of production, and too low (or too high) an output can lead to higher costs of production. Similarly, a lack of cumulative volume can also result in higher unit costs.
- *Overheads*: excessive levels of management, buildings and machinery can also be a source of higher unit costs.
- *Outsourcing*: some activities undertaken within the firm may not be justified on cost grounds. If they can be purchased from other producers more cheaply, then production should cease.

Simplistic, across-the-board cost cutting, however, should be avoided, because of the knock-on effect on other costs and revenue: for example, ceasing the production of one product may have adverse effects on the costs of another because of economies of scope. The price–cost margin may not be restored if revenue is adversely affected by cost cutting: for example, if the quality of the product or after-sales service is reduced, consumers may switch to alternative suppliers. Likewise, cutting the advertising or sales promotion budget may adversely affect sales and the ability to charge a higher price. Cost cutting must be done when the main sources of excessive costs have been identified.

CHAPTER SUMMARY

In this chapter we examined aspects of the analysis costs relevant to firm decision making. To do this we analysed:

■ The nature of short-run cost functions and cost curves when one factor of production is fixed, and the relationship between average and marginal costs.
■ The nature of the cost function in a multi-product firm and the difficulty of identifying the costs to be borne by an individual product.
■ The differences between economic and accounting cost concepts.
■ Estimation of cost functions, using regression analysis.
■ Long-run cost functions and economies of scale, scope and learning.
■ The management of costs and first-mover advantage.

APPENDIX: STATISTICAL COST FUNCTIONS

1 Translog cost function

The translog cost function postulates a quadratic relationship between the log of total cost and the logs of input prices and output. The equation of the translog function is:

$$\log TC = b_0 + b_1 \log Q + b_2 \log w + b_3 \log r + b_4 (\log Q)^2 + b_5 (\log w)^2 b_6 (\log r)^2$$
$$+ b_7 (\log w)(\log r) + b_8 (\log w)(\log Q) + b_9 (\log r)(\log Q)$$

If b_4 to b_9 are all equal to 0, then the translog function becomes a constant elasticity cost function.

2 Constant elasticity cost function

This specifies a multiplicative relationship, as with the Cobb–Douglas production function, between total cost, output and input prices. With two factors the cost function is specified as follows:

$$TC = aQ^b w^c r^d$$

where a, b, c, d = are positive constants; this converts into a linear relationship in logs:

$$\log TC = \log a + b \log Q + c \log w + d \log r$$

The constant b is the output elasticity of total cost, while c and d are the positive elasticities of long-run total cost in relation to the prices of inputs. An increase in price will increase total cost.

REVIEW QUESTIONS

1 Distinguish between fixed and variable costs. Comment on which potential cost sources are truly variable and those that are wholly or partially fixed.

2 Distinguish between short and long-run cost curves. Demonstrate how the long-run average cost curve is derived from a series of short-run cost curves.

3 Why do economists argue that cost curves are U-shaped? Why do diseconomies occur in the short run?

4 The short run cost function of the firm is of the form:

$$TC = 300 + 50Q - 10Q^2 + Q^3$$

   – What is the value of fixed costs?
   – Write expressions for average total costs, total variable costs, average variable costs and marginal cost.
   – Calculate the output at which average total costs are minimized?

5 What are the differences between economists' and accountants' views of costs?

6 What are the differences between explicit and implicit costs? Why do economists concern themselves with implicit costs?

7 According to Dean's classic study of a hosiery mill, total cost = $2,936 + 1.998Q$. How does marginal cost behave? How does average cost behave? What factor would account for Dean's findings on the shape of the marginal cost curve?

8 According to many empirical studies of long-run average cost in various industries, the long-run average cost curve tends to be L-shaped. Does this mean that there are constant returns to scale at all levels of output?

9 What do you understand by the term "economies of scale?" What are the main sources of economies of scale? How might economies of scale be measured?

10 What are economies of scope? If economies of scope are significant, then what are the implications for the strategy of the firm?

11 What are economies of learning. Distinguish between the learning curve and the experience curve. Distinguish between a 90% and a 70% learning curve. What are the sources of lower unit costs? What are the limits to learning effects? Does the first firm to produce have an advantage over later entrants?

REFERENCES AND FURTHER READING

Abernethy, W.J. and K. Wayne (1974) Limits of the learning curve. *Harvard Business Review*, September/October, **52**, 109–119.

Aletras, V.H. (1999) A comparison of hospital scale effects in short-run and long-run cost functions. *Health Economics*, **8**, 521–530.

Baden-Fuller, C. (1983) The implications of the learning curve for firm strategy and public policy. *Applied Economics*, **15**, 541–551.

Bailey, E.E. and A. D. Friedlander (1982) Market structure and multiproduct industries, *Journal of Economic Literature*, **20**, 1024–1048.

Cookenboo, L. (1955) Costs of operation of crude oil trunk lines. *Crude Oil Pipelines and Competition in the Oil Industry* (pp. 8–32). Cambridge University Press, Cambridge, MA. Reprinted in H. Townsend (1971) *Price Theory: Selected Readings*. Penguin, Harmondsworth, UK.

Dean, J. (1941) Statistical cost functions of a hosiery mill. *Journal of Business*. Reprinted in E. Mansfield (1979) *Microeconomics: Selected Readings* (3rd edn). W.W. Norton, New York.

Douglas, E.J. (1992) Cost concepts for decision making. *Managerial Economics: Analysis and Strategy* (Chapter 7). Prentice Hall, Englewood Cliffs, NJ.

Drake, L. (1992) Economies of scale and scope in UK building societies: An application of the tanslog multiproduct cost function. *Applied Financial Economics*, **2**, 211–219.

Drake, L. and R. Simper (2000) *Economies of Scale in UK Building Societies: A Re-appraisal* (Economics Paper No. ERP 00-08). Loughborough University, UK.

Ferguson, P.R., G.J. Ferguson and R. Rothschild (1993) *Business Economics* (Chapters 4–6), Macmillan, Basingstoke, UK.

Friedlander, A.F., C.Winston and Kung Wang (1983) Costs, technology and productivity in the US automobile industry. *Bell Journal of Economics*, **14**, 1–20.

Grundy, T. (1996) Cost is a strategic issue. *Long Range Planning*, **29**(1), 58–68.

Haldi, J. and D. Whitcomb (1967) Economics of scale in industrial plants. *Journal of Political Economy*, **75**, 373–385.

Hardwick, P. (1989) Economies of scale in building societies. *Applied Economics*, **21**(10), 1291–1304.

Hardwick, P. (1990) Multi-product cost attributes: A study of UK building societies. *Oxford Economic Papers*, **42**, 446–461.

Hardwick, P. (1993) Cost economies in the life insurance industry. *Service Industries Journal*, **13**(4), 240–251.

Johnson, J. (1960) *Statistical Cost Analysis*. McGraw-Hill, London.

Koot, R.S. and S.A. Walker (1970) Short-run cost functions of a multi-product firm. *Journal of Industrial Economics*, **18**(2), 118–128.

Pappas, J.L., E.F. Brigham and B. Shipley (1983) Empirical cost analysis. *Managerial Economics* (UK edn, Chapter 10). Holt, Rinehart & Winston, London.

Pratten, C. (1971) *Economies of Scale in Manufacturing Industry*. Cambridge University Press, Cambridge.

Reinhart (1973) Break-even analysis for Lockheed's Tri-Star. *Journal of Finance*, **28**(4), 821–838.

Rhys, D.G. (1977) European mass producing car makers and minimum efficient scale (A note). *Journal of Industrial Economics*, **25**(4), 313–320.

Rhys, D.G. (1993) Competition in the car industry. *Development in Economics* (Vol. 9). Causeway Press, Ormskirk, UK.

Schwalbach, J. (1988) *Economies of Scale and Intra-community Trade* (Economic Paper No. 68). European Commission, Brussels.

Walters, A.A. (1963) Production and cost functions. *Econometrica*, **31**, 1–66.

Wiles, P.D. (1956) *Price, Cost and Output*. Basil Blackwell, Oxford, UK.

PART **IV**

PRICING, PROMOTIONAL AND INVESTMENT POLICIES

PRICING AND MARKET STRUCTURE: THEORETICAL CONSIDERATIONS

CHAPTER OBJECTIVES

This chapter aims to explore the various theoretical market structures developed by economists, which are used to explain the varying constraints that market structure places on the ability of a firm to make its own prices. At the end of the chapter you should be able to:

♦ Identify the main characteristics of perfect competition, **monopolistic competition** and the implications for the pricing behaviour of individual firms.

♦ Understand the nature of interdependence of firms in oligopolistic markets and the use of reaction curves.

♦ Explain the insights of the kinked demand curve model and the concept of price stickiness.

♦ Analyse the equilibrium outcomes of the Bertrand and Cournot models and the incentives to cheat and collude.

♦ Explain tacit methods of co-ordination, including price leadership.

♦ Outline the conditions necessary for firms to operate a profit-making cartel.

INTRODUCTION

A major decision for the firm is setting the price of its goods and services. The price set determines sales, and the resultant revenue less costs determines profits. The objective of this chapter is to examine price setting in a theoretical context. The following aspects will be explored:

■ Price setting in perfect and monopolistically competitive markets.
■ Price setting in oligopolistic markets where there is recognition that in setting a price a firm must recognize the potential reaction of rivals.

Oligopolistic markets will be explored extensively and various models will be examined; these include:

■ The kinked demand model.
■ The Cournot and Bertrand models, using both reaction curves and game theory.
■ The final section will examine collusive and non-collusive strategies to co-ordinate the actions of oligopolists.

PERFECT COMPETITION

The essential assumptions for a market to be described as perfectly competitive are:

■ A large number of small firms and large numbers of consumers, with none able to influence the price by individual action.
■ All firms produce a homogeneous product.

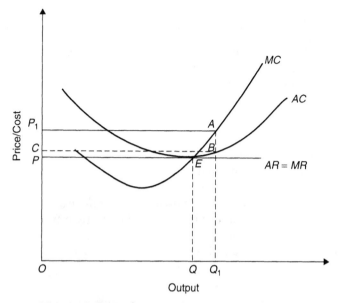

Figure 9.1 Perfect competition: price and output

- Firms can enter and leave the market freely.
- Firms are owned and managed by individual entrepreneurs.
- Decision makers are unboundedly rational and perfectly informed.
- Owners seek to maximize profits.
- Consumers seek to maximize utility.

As a result the market price is determined by the interplay of rivalry between suppliers and consumers. Given the market price, all controllers select an output for their firm that will maximize profits; this is illustrated in Figure 9.1. The demand curve for a single firm's product is the horizontal average revenue curve (AR). This curve is also the firm's marginal revenue curve (MR). The production possibilities of the firm are shown in terms of the average and marginal cost curves. These cost curves are assumed to include a normal profit, which is defined as that level of profit necessary to keep the firm in the market. If profits are less than normal in the long run the firm will leave the market and use its resources elsewhere. The firm maximizes profit where marginal revenue is equal to marginal cost. Given a price of OP the firm produces output OQ and makes only normal profits. If the price is OP_1, then the firm produces output OQ_1 and makes supernormal profits of P_1ABC, because the market price is greater than the firm's average cost. Thus, in a perfectly competitive market the firm works with a price beyond its control and in no sense does it make or set its own prices. Such firms have no market power and accept the market price.

MONOPOLISTIC COMPETITION

Chamberlain (1933) and Robinson (1933) developed models of monopolistic and imperfect competition, respectively, in which the firm has some degree of market power. The key assumptions for a market to be described as monopolistically competitive include:

- Large numbers of small firms and consumers.
- Each firm produces a differentiated product.
- Firms can freely enter and leave the market.
- Firms are owned and managed by an owner entrepreneur.
- Decision makers are unboundedly rational and perfectly informed.
- Owners seek to maximize profits.
- Consumers seek to maximize utility.

The key difference between perfect and monopolistic markets is the production of **differentiated products**. As a consequence, consumers do not regard any two products as perfect substitutes and, as a result, the firm faces a downward-sloping demand curve as an increase in the price of its differentiated product will not lead to all consumers deserting the firm and buying cheaper similar but different products. The slope of the average revenue curve is dependent on how successful the firm is in differentiating its product from those of its rivals. The smaller the number of consumers who cease to buy the product for a given price rise the more inelastic is the demand curve.

The production possibilities of the firm are presented graphically in Figure 9.2. In part (a) the firm sets a price of P_1 and produces output OQ_1. In the short run the firm makes supernormal profits of P_1CDB. In the long run the earning of supernormal profits will encourage new firms to enter the market and take sales from existing producers. In part (b) the firm loses some demand to new entrants, so that it ends up in a position where the average revenue curve is tangential to the average cost curve. The firm charges price P_2, produces output OQ_2 and earns a normal profit: that is, average cost is equal to average revenue. Both price and output are lower in the long run than in the short run. In this market structure the firm can set its own price in the short run but that power may be limited in the long run, as new competitors emerge.

OLIGOPOLY

The key elements of oligopolistic industries are the small number of firms, the recognition of the interdependence of their actions and the nature of the product.

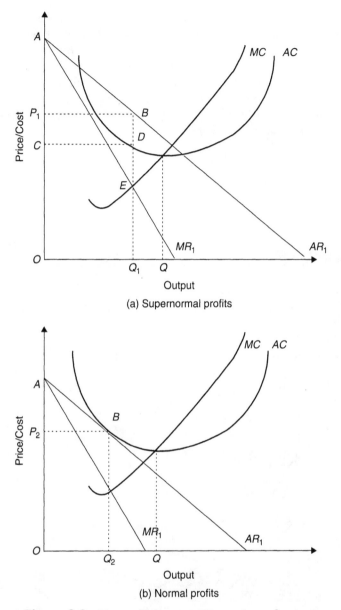

Figure 9.2 Monopolistic competition: price and output

Interdependence

Oligopolists are significant players in a market. Any action they take to alter price or output will have some impact on their competitors. In deciding what price to charge the firm must consider the potential reaction of other firms in the market. For example, if firm 1 were to lower its price how would firm 2 react? If its product is strongly differentiated from that of its rival, then it may ignore the price cuts and continue charging the same price. If its product is weakly differentiated, then its consumers may purchase the cheaper alternative. To discourage them, firm 2 may lower its price and match the price cut of firm 1.

By varying supply to a market an oligopolist can also influence price. Thus, in the international oil industry the withdrawal of supply by the larger producers, such as Saudi Arabia, can significantly influence the market price. Dominant oligopolists have market power but must also be aware of the reactions of their smaller rivals. Since conjecture about how other firms might or might not respond to a particular action can vary, it opens up the possibilities of developing various oligopoly models with different consequences for pricing behaviour.

KINKED DEMAND CURVE MODEL

The kinked demand curve model is based on a price conjecture and differentiated products. The price conjecture assesses the reactions of rivals to a fall and an increase in price.

Price reduction: if firm 1 lowers its price, then all other firms producing similar products will either maintain or lower their prices. In this model the firm assumes its rivals will reduce price because they fear losing sales to their cheaper rival. In Figure 9.3 the firm is initially at point B on demand curve AR_2, charging price OP and

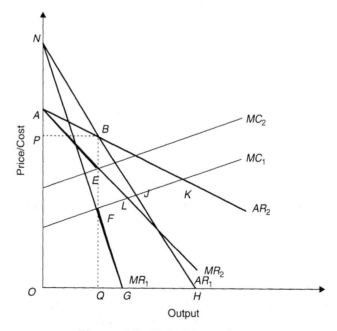

Figure 9.3 Kinked demand curve

selling OQ units of output. If firm 1 considers reducing price to sell more products, then it must be aware of the reaction of its rivals. If no other firm follows its move, then firm 1 will expect to move along the demand curve AR_2 from B toward point K, significantly increasing its market share. If rivals lower their prices in response to the price cut, then firm 1 will expect to move along demand curve BH from B toward J.

Price increase: if firm 1 were to increase its price, then all other firms producing similar products could maintain or increase their prices. If firm 1 in Figure 9.3 increases its price above OP and its rivals also increase their prices, firm 1 will move from B toward N on demand curve AR_1. If rivals maintain their price, then firm 1 will expect to move along demand curve AR_2, from B toward A.

If the managers of firm 1 combine the price conjectures, then its anticipated demand curve will be ABH with a kink at B. Above the kink (point B) the demand curve is relatively more elastic than below the kink, where it is relatively more inelastic. If firm 1 accepts this conjecture, then it may be unwilling to move its price, either up or down, from OP unless it expects its rivals to follow.

The resulting kinked demand curve also has implications for the shape of the marginal revenue curve. For prices above OP the relevant demand curve is ABK and the related marginal revenue curve is AEL. For prices below P the relevant demand curve is NBH and the related marginal revenue curve NFG. Thus, the marginal revenue curve associated with the kinked demand curve ABH is $AEFG$. The AE element in the marginal revenue curve is associated with the demand curve ABK, while the FG portion relates to demand curve NBH. The element EF represents a discontinuity in the marginal revenue curve, because the price elasticity of demand at B on demand curve ABK is higher than for the same point B on demand curve NBH.

A profit-maximizing oligopolist would equate marginal revenue and marginal cost. With marginal cost curve MC_1 the profit-maximizing price would be OP, as it would also be with marginal cost curve MC_2. In the range EF, discontinuity in the marginal revenue curve means price will not change even if marginal costs increase from MC_1 and MC_2. This feature of the model tends to reinforce the unwillingness of the firm to move its price from OP unless there are compelling reasons to do so and these also apply to competitors.

The kinked demand curve model helps explain why prices are sticky in oligopolist markets and why a firm will resort to non-price competition (discussed in Chapter 11) to help influence demand. The model does not explain how price was established but does help to explain why it does not change.

Evidence on the existence of the kinked demand curve

Diamantopoulos and Matthews (1993) asked product managers to indicate how they would respond to price cuts or rises ranging from 5 to 50%. The research covered 900 products consolidated into 21 groups in the UK medical supplies industry. From the responses, they identified that for most products there appeared to be a price interval around the current price, where small price changes have little or no effect on volume because rivals do not react. In 15 out of 21 products there appeared to be a double kink in the demand curve. In general, for price changes in excess of 20% or more,

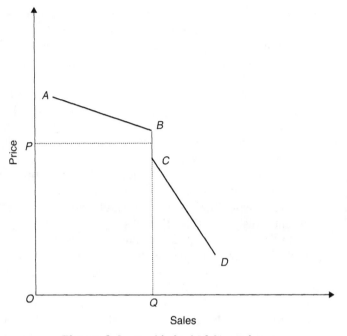

Figure 9.4 Double-kinked demand curve

demand elasticity was found to be greater for upward than for downward price movements, in line with the conjectures of kinked demand theory. This double-kinked demand curve is illustrated in Figure 9.4, with kinks at B and C. The reasons for the lack of initial response to a price change may be consumer loyalty to the product, the search costs of identifying alternatives, the costs of switching to a new supplier and the lack of reaction from rivals because of the costs of changing price.

BERTRAND OLIGOPOLY

The Bertrand model examines the setting of price in a **duopoly**. Bertrand's conjecture is that firm 1 will set its own price on the assumption that the other firm will hold its price constant.

The logic of the Bertrand model can be explained by assuming: homogeneous products, both firms have the same constant level of marginal cost, sufficient capacity to serve the whole market, the market demand curve is linear and consumers are indifferent between the products of either supplier and will buy whichever product is cheaper. Thus:

■   If firm 1 has a slightly lower price than firm 2, then it supplies the whole market with firm 2 supplying nothing.

■ If firm 2 has the lower price, then it captures the whole market and firm 1 supplies nothing.

■ If both firms set the same price, then they are assumed to each supply half the market.

The optimal price for firm 1 depends on its conjectures about what firm 1 will do. If firm 1 expects firm 2 to set the **monopoly** price, then by slightly undercutting this price firm 2 would capture the entire market and make profits close to the monopoly or maximum level, while firm 1 would sell nothing. Firm 1's optimal strategy is always to price just below firm 2's expected price and firm 2's optimal strategy is to price just below firm 1's.

The firm that sells nothing will set a price below that of its rival with its rival responding in the same way. This process ends, logically, when neither can lower its price any further and still make a profit. Thus, the process ends theoretically when profits are zero (i.e., where price is equal to marginal cost). Neither firm would choose to lower its price below marginal cost because they would then make losses, and neither would want to raise its price independently above marginal cost because the first-mover would sell nothing.

These optimal choices can be shown in a **reaction function** or best response curve; these are drawn for both firms in Figure 9.5, with the price of each firm measured on each axis and the 45° line showing points of equal price. If firm 2 is expected to set the monopoly price P_2^M at point A on the 45° line, then firm 1 will set a price at point D just below the monopoly price P_1^M. Since firm 2 behaves in a similar way the reaction curves are symmetrical, starting from the level of marginal cost. Equilibrium will occur where the two reaction curves intersect (i.e., where both firms set price equal to marginal cost). Therefore, the Bertrand model predicts that the two firms serving the

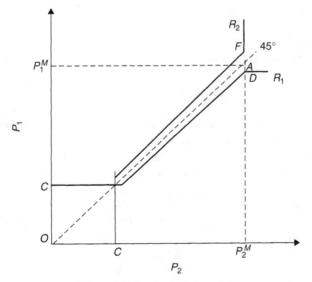

Figure 9.5 Bertrand model

market will set those prices equal to marginal cost that would prevail in a competitive market.

If the market demand curve is given by $P = 100 - Q$ and marginal cost is 10, then the monopoly price and output would be 55 and 45, respectively, and the competitive price and output would be 10 and 90, respectively. To be able to meet all the demand generated, each firm would require a capacity of 90. Thus, if firm 1 were to charge the monopoly price of 55, then firm 2 could supply the whole market by pricing at 54. This process of undercutting continues until the competitive price is established. As a result, profits fall from the monopoly level of £2,025 to 0.

In real world markets served by few firms, prices normally appear to be greater than marginal costs and firms earn supernormal profits. The reasons the prediction of the Bertrand model are rarely observed include:

- *Capacity constraints*: individual enterprises may not have the capacity to supply the whole market. Thus, the higher priced firm will still meet any portion of market demand not met by the lower priced firm. Firms can also set prices above marginal cost, providing capacity is less than the competitive level of supply.
- *Product differentiation*: if the two firms sell differentiated products, then the higher priced product will not lose all its sales to the lower priced products.
- *Long-run competition*: the notion that each firm will retaliate in successive periods in a continual price war may not be realistic because firms learn that they can co-exist at a price level that ensures both make supernormal profits.
- *Other competitive weapons*: if an acceptable price is established, then firms may compete by using advertising or emphasizing quality and characteristic differences.

COURNOT OLIGOPOLY

An alternative model of oligopoly uses quantity setting rather than price as the competitive weapon. Cournot assumes that if firm 1 has already determined its output/sales, then firm 2 will make its choice of output on the assumption that firm 1 will not change its output in any given period. The total output of the two firms will then determine market price.

We initially explain the model by the use of Figure 9.6. The market demand curve is AD, the marginal revenue curve is AM and the marginal cost curve, assuming constant costs, is CE. In part (a) firm 1 initially acts as a monopolist and sets the monopoly price OP_1 and quantity OQ_1. Firm 2 conjectures that firm 1 will continue to sell OQ_1, leaving it with the residual demand curve FED and the marginal revenue curve FN. Firm 2 maximizes profit and sells Q_1Q_2. Total sales are now OQ_2.

In the next round, firm 1 assumes that firm 2 will continue to sell Q_1Q_2. Firm 1's residual demand curve now has an intercept on the horizontal axis which is derived by deducting Q_1Q_2 from AD, with the same slope as the original demand curve; this is shown as the demand curve ST in part (b) of Figure 9.6. Firm 1 chooses its profit-maximizing output OQ_3. The residual demand curve for firm 2 then becomes UT and it selects output Q_3Q_4. This process continues until each firm faces identical demand curves; these are shown in part (c), where firm 1 sells OQ_5 and firm 2 produces OQ_6.

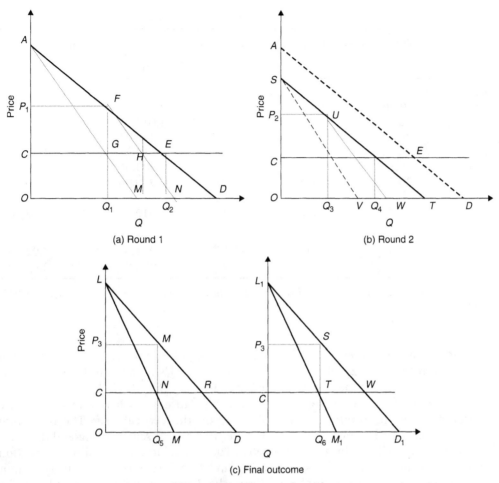

Figure 9.6 Cournot duopoly

Both firms charge price OP_3, and total supply to the market is two-thirds the competitive level of sales.

Assuming a market demand curve of $P = 100 - Q$ and a constant marginal cost of 10, the competitive output will be 90 and the monopoly output 45. In a Cournot oligopoly, convergence of the sales of both firms is shown in Table 9.1, for five rounds. Firm 1 initially sets the monopoly price and makes profits of £2,025. The sales of firm 1 reduce from the monopoly output of 45 toward 30, and the sales of firm 2 increase from 22.5 toward 30. Eventually, both firms have a residual demand curve of $P = 70 - Q$, both selling 30 with a market price of £40.

Cournot equilibrium and reaction functions

An alternative approach to explaining equilibrium in Cournot oligopoly is to construct reaction curves for both firms in a duopoly. A reaction curve, or best response

Table 9.1 Cournot duopoly, collusion and cheating (£)

Period	Firm 1's sales	Firm 2's sales	Market sales	Market price	Profits		
					Firm 1	Firm 2	Industry
Cournot duopoly							
1	45.00	0.00	45.0	55.0	2,025.0	0.0	2,025.00
2	45.00	22.5	67.5	32.5	1,012.5	506.25	1,518.00
3	33.75	28.125	61.875	38.125	949.21	791.02	1,740.23
4	30.94	29.53	60.47	39.53	913.65	872.02	1,785.67
5	30.24	29.88	60.12	39.88	903.57	892.81	1,796.38
Final	30.00	30.00	60.00	40.00	900.00	900.00	1,800.00
Collusion	22.5	22.5	45.0	55.0	1,012.5	1,012.5	2,025.0
Cheating							
Firm 1	23.5	22.5	46.0	54.0	1,034.0	990.0	2,024.0
Firm 2	22.5	23.5	46.0	54.0	990.0	1,034.0	2,024.0

Note Assumes market demand is given by $P = 100 - Q$, marginal revenue by $100 - 2Q$ and marginal cost is equal to 10.

Source Author

function, for firm 1 defines the profit-maximizing output for firm 1, given the output of firm 2. Given that firm 2 sells Q_2 units of output, firm 1's output can be expressed as $Q_1 = R_1(Q_2)$. For firm 2 the reaction function is given by $Q_2 = R_2(Q_1)$.

Reaction functions for a duopoly are shown in Figure 9.7, where firm 1's sales are measured on the horizontal axis and firm 2's on the vertical axis. The horizontal intercept of firm 1's reaction curve Q_1^M assumes that firm 2 sells nothing and that firm 1 behaves as a profit-maximizing monopolist. The vertical intercept of firm 1's reaction curve Q_2^C assumes that firm 1 sells nothing and firm 2 sells the competitive output where price is equal to marginal cost. Using the demand equation $P = 100 - Q$, the horizontal intercept would be at sales of 45 and the vertical intercept at sales of 90. Firm 2's reaction curve is derived in a similar way, with the vertical intercept Q_2^M having a value of 45 and the horizontal intercept Q_1^C a value of 90.

If firm 1 initially behaves as a monopolist, then it will sell output OQ_1^M on reaction curve R_1. Firm 2 will respond by choosing point A on its reaction curve (R_2), selling output OQ_2^1. Firm 1 reacts by moving to point B on its reaction curve, producing OQ_1^2. Firm 2 will respond by moving to point C on its reaction curve, producing output OQ_2^2. The process continues until Cournot equilibrium is reached at point E, where firm 1 sells OQ_1^3 and firm 2 sells OQ_2^3; this is a position from which neither firm would want to move, given the other firm's output.

Reaction functions can also be derived algebraically. To maximize profits, firm 1 must set marginal revenue equal to marginal cost for any given level of firm 2's output. Therefore, when $P = 100 - Q$:

$$\text{Total revenue } (IR) = Q_1 P = Q_1(100 - Q_1 - Q_2) \quad \text{or} \quad R = 100Q_1 - Q_1^2 - Q_1 Q_2$$

$$\text{Marginal revenue } (MR) = \delta TR_1 / \delta Q_1 = 100 - 2Q_1 - Q_2$$

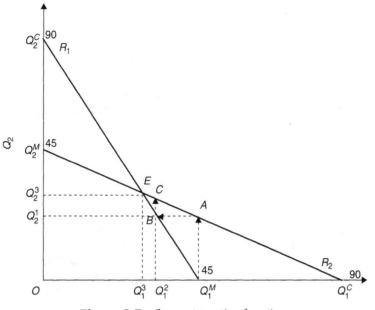

Figure 9.7 Cournot reaction functions

Since marginal cost is equal to 10, marginal revenue equal to marginal cost can be expressed as:

$$100 - 2Q_1 - Q_2 = 10$$

or

$$Q_1 = f(Q_2) = [(90 - Q_2)/2] = 45 - \tfrac{1}{2}Q_2$$

$$Q_2 = f(Q_1) = [(90 - Q_1)/2] = 45 - \tfrac{1}{2}Q_1$$

If firm 2 sells 40 units, then firm 1 would choose to produce $[(90 - 40)/2]$, or 25. If firm 2 produces 30, then firm 1 would produce $[(90 - 30)/2]$, or 30. The equilibrium output is to be found at point E in Figure 9.6. At this point, both firms make profits of £900, which is derived by deducting marginal cost from price multiplied by output or $(40 - 10) * 30$.

COLLUSION AND CHEATING

In a market dominated by only a few firms, there may be an incentive for firms to collude either implicitly or explicitly. In a duopoly, there is a superior position for both firms and that is sharing the monopoly output. As can be observed in Table 9.1, both firms can increase their profits from £900 to £1,012.5 by colluding and producing the same output.

However, when both firms achieve profit maximization output, each firm has an incentive to cheat. It would be in the interest of firm 1 to produce a little more output.

Likewise, firm 2 has the same incentive to cheat: if firm 1 increases its output by 1 to 23.5 while firm 2 continues to produce 22.5, then firm 1 can increase its profits by £21.5 to £1,034 at the expense of firm 2, whose profits are reduced by £22.5 to £990. Overall, joint industry profits fall by £1 to £2,024. Firm 2's incentive to cheat is exactly the same as that for firm 1; these outcomes are found in Table 9.1. Thus, Cournot equilibrium may or may not be a stable position, depending on whether the two firms are able to co-ordinate their activities to reach a joint profit-maximizing position.

GAME THEORY

Game theory is the study of how interdependent decision makers make choices. A game must include players, strategies and decisions. Each firm tries to identify the possible moves of its rivals in response to any move it might itself make. For ease of explanation only games involving two firms will be considered. Key concepts include:

- Strategy: a specific course of action taken by one of the firms or players.
- Policy variables: these include price, product differentiation and advertising.
- Counter-strategies: these are adopted by rivals to counter moves made by their competitors.
- Pay-off matrix: this records the net gains for each set of strategies and counter-strategies adopted by rivals.
- Dominant strategy: this is a strategy that outperforms any other, no matter what strategy a rival chooses.
- Zero sum game: a game in which gains by one firm are exactly offset by the losses of other firms.
- Positive sum game: a game in which every participant can gain.
- Information: this can be perfect or imperfect, complete or incomplete.
- **Nash equilibrium**: a position from which it is not possible to move without someone being worse off, given the choice of a rival. It occurs when each firm chooses the strategy that maximizes profit, given the strategies of the other firm in the game.

NON-ZERO SUM GAME

In a non-zero sum game the total pay-off varies according to each firm's chosen strategies. In any market the profits earned by individual firms and by the industry as a whole will depend on industry output and the price set by each firm. The pay-offs in a two-firm game are shown in Table 9.2. It is assumed that both firms set either a high or low price with the profits depending on the quantity sold.

The game is one of imperfect information because players select strategies and move simultaneously. If both firms select high price as their chosen strategy, then they each

Table 9.2 A non-zero sum game (£)

Firm 1	Firm 2			
	High price		Low price	
	Low quantity		High quantity	
High price Low quantity	120	120	20	150
Low price High quantity	150	20	80	80

Source Author

make profits of £120, and combined industry profits are £240. If both select a strategy of low price, then they each make profits of £80 and combined industry profits are £160. If one firm chooses a high-price strategy and the other a low-price strategy, then the low-price firm makes £150 and the high price firm makes £20, indicating a degree of product differentiation because sales of the higher priced product do not fall to zero.

The strategic options facing firm 2, which are dependent on the choices of firm 1, are as follows:

■ If firm 1 sets a high price, then firm 2 could price low and earn £150 or price high and earn £120.
■ If firm 1 sets a low price, then firm 2 could set a low price and earn £80 or price high and earn £20.

Whichever strategy firm 1 selects, firm 2 should always set a low price because it earns either £150 or £80, compared with the high-price strategy outcomes of £20 and £120. Thus, setting a low price is a dominant strategy for firm 2, since its only move would be to set a high price that would see its profits drop to £20. Since the pay-off matrix is perfectly symmetric, firm 1's dominant strategy is also low price. Both firms should therefore set low prices and earn £80. However, both firms could move to a preferred position if they both set high prices and earn £120. However, even if they collude to set high prices, there is always an incentive for one or other firm to lower their price to earn £150. This basic form of the game is also known as the **prisoner's dilemma** because it demonstrates the conflict between joint and independent action.

PRICE STICKINESS

Price stickiness is a characteristic of oligopolies that has been much commented on; this means that prices are altered infrequently even if cost and market conditions appear to justify either a price increase or a price fall. The explanation for this behaviour is to be found both in theoretical models considered in this chapter and in practical considerations.

Theoretical explanation of price stickiness can be found in the kinked demand model and in game theory. The behavioural conjectures in the kinked demand curve model (i.e., that rivals will match price cuts but not price increases) reinforces the stick-ability of the existing price. The danger in price cutting is that rivals may overreact, not just matching price cuts but imposing bigger cuts leading to a damaging price war. The price stickiness effect may also be reinforced by uncertainty about how a rival might react to a change in price: for example, they may respond by increasing advertising in an attempt to increase the degree of product differentiation to protect their product and make the price cutter worse off. The kink demand curve model also explains the limited impact of cost changes. Other theoretical explanations can be found in the game theory approach, where firms are unwilling to move from a Nash equilibrium.

Practical reasons are also suggested to explain unwillingness on the part of firms to change their prices frequently; these considerations include the costs involved in changing prices, issuing new price lists, or catalogues, informing customers, the loss of customer goodwill and the pricing methodology used by individual firms. For example, price reviews may only be carried out quarterly or even annually, so that prices by custom and practice are changed only infrequently, even if changing conditions might suggest some adjustment.

Evidence on price stickiness

Blinder (1991) studied price changes in the USA with the aim of establishing the degree of price stickiness and reasons for not changing prices. A similar exercise was carried out by Hall et al. (1997) for the Bank of England. This study asked a sample of 1,100 companies about their pricing behaviour and found that:

- 79% of firms review their prices at a specific interval.
- 37% of firms change their price annually, 26% twice per year and 6% more than 12 times per year. The median firm changed its prices twice per year;
- this compared with once per year in Blinder's 1991 US survey.
- Large firms review their prices more frequently than small firms.
- Firms in more competitive industries review and change their prices more frequently than in those in less competitive industries.
- Firms with a greater percentage of long-run contracts review and change their prices less frequently than other firms.

The survey also asked about the reasons behind price stickiness. Respondents were asked to assess the importance of various factors in explaining its behaviour and how it influenced the changing of prices. The results, to be found in Table 9.3, rank the factors in order of importance according to the Bank's survey, along with Blinder's US findings. The top three factors explaining **price rigidity** in the UK were explicit contracts, cost-based pricing and co-ordination failure. In the USA they were non-price elements, co-ordination failure and cost-based pricing. Prices set by explicit agreement can only be changed at the end of a contract or by mutual consent. With

Table 9.3 The recognition and importance of different pricing theories

Explanations	Bank of England survey (rank)	Blinder's survey (rank)
Explicit contracts	1	5
Cost-based pricing	2	3
Co-ordination failure	3	2
Pricing thresholds	4	8
Implicit contracts	5	4
Constant marginal cost	6	10
Stock adjustment	7	9
Non-price elements	8	1
Pro-cyclical elasticity	9	7
Price means quality	10	11
Physical menu costs		6

Source Compiled by author using data extracted from Hall et al. (1997).

cost-based pricing, price changes only occur when there are significant moves in prices, wages and/or raw materials (see Chapter 10). Co-ordination failure refers to the unwillingness of a firm to be first to change its prices, while non-price elements refer to rigid prices accompanied by quality or quantity changes. In these circumstances a firm may prefer to reduce the number of biscuits in a pack rather than raise the price.

COLLUSIVE OLIGOPOLY

The theory of oligopoly stresses the difficulty that individual enterprises have in co-ordinating their strategic moves. Wrong moves or misinterpreted moves may lead to aggressive competitive moves by rivals, such as a price war. Oligopolists may seek ways of avoiding low-price outcomes by devising behavioural rules or communications channels to promote co-ordinated behaviour. The potential channels of communications can be classified as either informal (or tacit) or formal. Informal, or tacit, rules include rules of thumb for price changes and/or **price leadership**. Formal arrangements involve the creation of **cartels**. The ability of oligopolistic firms to co-ordinate their activities depends on a number of market characteristics; these are listed in Table 9.4.

The number and size of firms will influence the ability of firms to co-ordinate their activities. The smaller the number of firms serving a market and the more equal their size the simpler will be co-ordination. The larger the number of firms and the more unequal they are in size the more difficult it will be. If a large firm dominates the market, then small firms may resent its position and seek to undermine it, while an agreement between 20 firms is more difficult to police than an agreement between 2.

The nature of the product will also influence the ability of firms to co-ordinate their activities. A high degree of product differentiation gives individual enterprises a greater degree of independence from their rivals in terms of price setting. The more

Table 9.4   Factors influencing the ability of firms to co-ordinate their activities

Favouring co-ordination or collusion	Hindering co-ordination
Small number of sellers	Large number of sellers
More equal and larger the sellers	More unequal in size the sellers
Product homogeneity	Product differentiation
Frequent small orders	Infrequent lumpy orders
Low proportion of fixed costs to total costs	High proportion of fixed costs to total costs
Slow rate of technical progress	Rapid rate of technical change
Openness between partners	Secrecy and unauthorized discounts

Source Author

homogeneous the product the smaller the room for independent action. Frequent small orders tend to facilitate co-ordination, whereas infrequent large orders will tend to lead firms to compete vigorously. Where fixed costs are a high proportion of total costs, an individual firm will strive to maintain the maximum level of output to keep average fixed costs to a minimum. A fall in demand tends to an increase in the degree of competition. **Price fixing** is also easier in an industry where there is little technical change. Rapid technical change leading to lower costs or new products will encourage the technological leader to compete more openly. Finally, there is the degree of trust and openness between the parties. If the firms trust each other and are willing to share information, then co-ordination will be more successful than if they distrust each other.

CARTELS

A cartel is a formal agreement among producers. The cartel is designed to overcome uncertainty of actions by rivals and to maximize joint profits for the industry. It achieves this by controlling or restricting output and operating as a multi-plant monopolist. A cartel can establish a joint profit-maximizing position by selling the monopoly output and charging the monopoly price; this would result in a lower output and higher price, compared with the Cournot position.

To determine the optimal output for a cartel, we assume that there are two firms with differing operational efficiencies. To maximize joint profits, the cartel allocates more output to the most efficient firms. It does this by summing horizontally the marginal costs of each member and equating them with the market marginal revenue curve. The monopoly price can then be established. Individual firms in the cartel are asked to contribute to industry output by producing an output quota according to their marginal costs.

The process is illustrated in Figure 9.8(a, b), which show the average and marginal cost curves, respectively, for firm 1 and firm 2. Firm 1 is more efficient than firm 2 in that it has a lower average cost curve. In part (c) the market demand, marginal revenue and marginal cost curves are shown. The marginal cost curve for the market is derived by adding horizontally the marginal cost curves of firms 1 and 2. At any

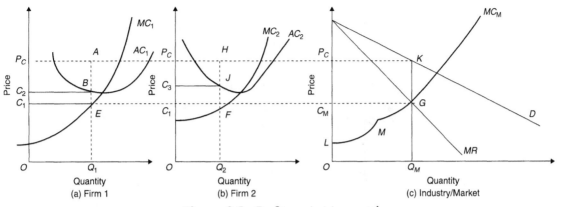

Figure 9.8 Profit-maximizing cartel

level of marginal cost the output of both firms is summed. Thus, at marginal cost OC_1, firm 1's output C_1E plus firm 2's output of C_1F gives the industry output C_MG and a point on the market's marginal cost curve. The portion of the market marginal cost curve LM is made up only of the initial portion of firm 1's marginal cost curve. Above point M its position is determined by the marginal cost curves of both firms.

The cartel's total output is determined where the industry marginal cost is equal to industry marginal revenue at G, as in Figure 9.8(c). The output OQ_M determines the cartel's price P_C. Each cartel member produces the output given by the market equilibrium level of marginal cost OC_M. Thus, firm 1 produces OQ_1, and sells at P_C, and firm 2 produces OQ_2 and sells at P_C. The sum of the output of both firms is equal to the total output of the cartel.

Each firm makes profits: firm 1 makes P_CABC_2 and firm 2 makes P_CHJC_3. However, the low-cost firm (1) makes more profits than the high-cost firm (2), unless there is some scheme to share joint profits, to ensure neither firm is worse off than before the cartel was formed. If firm 2 is dissatisfied with the outcome, then firm 1 could transfer a share of its profits to firm 2 to compensate it for forming the cartel. However, if the firms do not seek to minimize costs and maximize profits, alternative allocation rules might be used to determine the output quota of each firm.

Instability of cartels

It is argued that cartels are inherently unstable, because the members will have inevitably conflicting interests. Finding an agreement on sharing output that is acceptable to all members may prove difficult to achieve in practice and, once agreed, may be difficult to enforce. Firms have an incentive to cheat on their fellow members. Since the price the cartel establishes (OP_C) is in excess of the marginal cost of each participating firm, each member has an incentive to increase output by small quantities to increase its profits. If the firm that cheats assumes that its increase in output will have no impact on price, either because its increase is small or because other members will sell slightly less, then we can demonstrate the potential profit gain. If the firm in

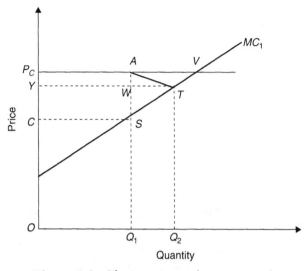

Figure 9.9 The incentive to cheat in a cartel

Figure 9.9 is selling its cartel-determined output OQ_1 at the cartel's set price OP_C, then it will be making profits of P_CASC. If the firm increases its output to the point where marginal cost is equal to the cartel-set price, then it would make additional profits equal to the triangle AVS by producing output OQ_2: hence, the incentive to increase output.

However, if an increase in output by one firm reduces the price below that set by the cartel, then the impact on profits depends on the elasticity of demand. Figure 9.9 shows that if firm 1 increases its output while all other members of the cartel maintain their agreed outputs, then the market price will fall along the curve AT. If price OY is established, then firm 1 will be able to increase its profits by the triangle AST less the area P_CATWY. The size of this latter area will depend on the fall in price and the extra output produced by the firm that cheats.

To prevent cheating, the cartel has to have an effective policing and enforcement department able to identify firms that cheat and encourage them to produce the agreed quota. If quotas are allocated on the basis of marginal costs, then an individual firm may have an incentive not to identify its costs correctly; this may be exacerbated if firms have widely differing levels of costs, if costs of individual firms cannot be clearly identified or if costs of production are constantly changing, because of changes in input prices affecting firms differently. Likewise, if economies of scale are important or if fixed costs are a high proportion of total costs, then members will also have an incentive to increase output, to reduce average fixed costs and increase profits.

Cartels are difficult to police, as is the enforcement of their rules. Cheating has to be detected before action can be taken against a recalcitrant member. Punishment threats have to be meaningful to deter firms from leaving a cartel that they joined voluntarily. For cartels that are illegal, it is difficult to enforce the rules through legal means; so, the other members have to ensure that rule breakers lose any gains they might have made; this is best achieved by the other members threatening to increase their own output and so ensure a greater fall in price than expected by the cheating firm that increases output.

Case Study 9.1   The vitamin cartel and the EU

In both the EC and the UK all cartels are illegal, and firms participating in them are subject to fines of up to 10% of their turnover in the appropriate market. Each year a number of cartels are identified. One of the most significant in recent years was a "vitamin cartel" of 13 companies that engaged in a series of agreements to distort the market. Participants were fined a total of €855.22m in June 2001. The cartel had earlier been identified in the USA, and executives received fines and jail sentences. The leading companies involved were Hoffmann-La Roche and BASF. The companies' collusive behaviour enabled them to charge higher prices than if the full forces of competition had been at play, damaging consumers and allowing the companies to make greater profits.

The participants in each of the cartels fixed the prices for different vitamin products, allocated sales quotas, agreed on and implemented price increases and issued price announcements in accordance with their agreements. They also set up machinery to monitor and enforce their agreements and participated in regular meetings to implement their plans.

The EC estimated that European revenues from sales of vitamin C slumped from €250m in the last year that cartel arrangements were in place (1995) to less than half – €120m – three years later (1998). The EC found Hoffmann-La Roche and BASF to be the joint leaders and instigators of the collusive arrangements, and they were more heavily fined than the other participants. Eight companies were fined as follows:

	(€m)
■ Hoffmann-La Roche AG (Switzerland)	462
■ BASF AG (Germany)	296.16
■ Aventis SA (France)	5.04
■ Solvay Pharmaceuticals BV (Netherlands)	9.10
■ Merck AG (Germany)	9.24
■ Daiichi Pharmaceutical Co. Ltd (Japan	23.4
■ Eisai Co. Ltd (Japan)	13.23
■ Takeda Chemical Industries Ltd (Japan)	37.05

Five companies were not fined, because they co-operated with the competition authorities (source: http://www.useu.be/ISSUES/vita0406.html).

TACIT COLLUSION

The alternative to formal collusion is to organize the co-ordination of oligopolists through informal or tacit understandings. The most common examples of tacit collusion involve some form of price leadership. Prices of individual companies, therefore, move in parallel, often with a slight lag. When one firm, the price leader, moves its price it expects all its rivals in the market will follow. There are a number of commonly identified forms of price leadership including dominant-firm price leadership and barometric price leadership.

Evidence of price co-ordination in the UK was found by Domberger and Fiebig (1993). They studied 80 industries between 1974 and 1985 and found that the more oligopolistic an industry the more symmetrical were price changes: that is, they tended to be in the same direction, to be of similar size and to occur in a relatively short period of time.

Dominant-firm price leadership

Dominant-firm price leadership involves members of an oligopolistic market accepting the price changes made by the largest firm in the market. Suppose that an industry consists of a dominant firm that controls a significant percentage of the sales in the market, with the remainder supplied by a small number of fringe producers. In such a market it makes sense for the dominant firm to set the industry price and for the fringe firms to accept it. Thus, fringe firms act as **price takers** and maximize their profits by equating price to marginal cost.

In Figure 9.10, DD_I is the industry demand curve. The dominant firm's supply curve is given by its marginal cost curve MC_D, which is at a lower level than the supply curve of the fringe suppliers, the marginal cost curve MC_F. The dominant firm is assumed to set its price and to leave the fringe to act as the residual supplier.

The dominant firm's demand curve is the industry demand curve less the fringe's

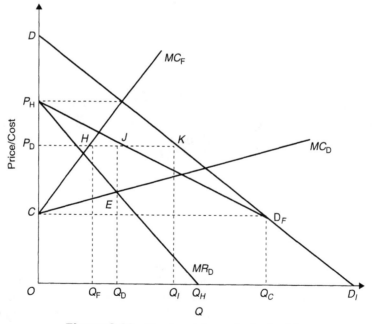

Figure 9.10 Dominant-firm price leadership

supply at any price set by the dominant firm. If the dominant firm sets a price of OC, then the fringe will supply nothing because the market price is equal to its marginal cost. Thus, he dominant firm supplies the whole market. If the dominant firm sets a price at P_H, then at this point the fringe's marginal cost curve cuts the industry demand curve, with the result that the fringe would, theoretically at least, supply the entire industry output. The residual demand curve for the dominant firm is thus $P_H D_F D_I$. The marginal revenue curve for the dominant firm is $P_H Q_H$.

The profit-maximizing output for the dominant firm is determined where the residual marginal revenue curve intersects the dominant firm's marginal cost curve (at point E). Therefore, it produces OQ_D and charges a price of OP_D. Once the dominant firm has set its price, the fringe, acting as a price taker, will supply the quantity where the marginal cost of the fringe is equal to the price set by the dominant firm, or output $Q_D Q_I$, or OQ_F.

Who will be the leader?

In dominant-firm price leadership the largest firm in terms of market share is expected to take the lead in changing its price either in response to changing economic conditions or because prices are adjusted annually. Being the largest firm it is able to exert its influence over the other enterprises because they may fear some form of retaliation if they do not follow.

If the dominant firm loses its position and there exists a small group of similarly sized large firms that co-ordinate the industry, then such a situation is referred to as collusive price leadership. The key is not the identity of the leader but that the others follow whoever makes the first move. The leader may not necessarily be the firm with the largest market share: it could be the one with the lowest costs or one that has historically led the market; firms might even take turns.

Another form of co-ordination is termed **barometric price leadership**. Here, industry is assumed to respond to a price move by a non-dominant price leader that changes its price because of cost changes that affect all the firms in the industry. Although the barometric leader makes the first move in the expectation that the larger and more important firms will follow, unless the leader's timing is accepted by those firms they may not in fact follow and co-ordination may break down. Both collusive price leadership and barometric price leadership are weaker forms of co-ordinating a market and ensuring all firms follow the leader. The difference is that a dominant leader can discipline the market by its moves, while smaller leaders cannot.

Case Study 9.2　Price leadership in the salt industry

Examples of price leadership are to be found in many industries. Examples of dominant-firm price leadership can be found in Shaw and Sutton (1976) and of barometric price leadership in Waldman and Jensen (1998, chap. 9). Rees (1993a) analysed the price co-ordination found in the UK salt industry, following a report by the Monopolies and Mergers Commission (MMC): there were two producers whose co-ordination was facilitated by barriers to entry and significant fixed costs. The MMC investigated 17 price changes between January 1974 and January 1984, which were initiated by either firm and always followed more or less exactly by the other. The leader would normally inform the follower of its planned price change four weeks before it was to be implemented. The follower would consider the proposals and make identical changes within that period. One of the reasons firms co-ordinate their activities is the fear of the consequences of being out of line and being caught in a low-price market and, thus, of losing market share to the lower price firm.

Case Study 9.3   UK digital television

An example of an industry in which the incumbent has acted aggressively is the UK digital television market. The UK government took the decision to convert the country from analogue to digital television, with the aim of switching off the analogue supply between 2006 and 2010. Signals were to be delivered via three platforms:

- Digital satellite where customers receive the signal via a satellite dish. The existing analogue supplier BSkyB, approximately 35% owned by News International, needed to encourage its existing customers to switch to the new service, which required a new dish and set-top digital box, and to entice new customers by offering up to 200 channels compared with the 5 analogue channels available to the majority of the population.
- Cable television where customers receive the signal via a cable connection. Cable companies offer both television and telephone services. They have been building networks in cities for a considerable time but have a small customer base. The change to digital television also involved them in upgrading their equipment and providing customers with digital set-top boxes.
- Digital terrestrial where customers receive the signal through existing television aerials and by means of digital set-top boxes; this new service was offered by ON Digital, a company jointly owned by Granada and Carlton – existing commercial television providers – and offered up to 50 channels, far less than the other platforms.

When ON Digital (later renamed ITV Digital) entered the market the decision was made on the basis that customers would purchase their own set-top box to convert digital pictures for viewing on analogue television and pay a subscription for the channels. However, BSkyB decided to offer customers free set-top boxes. Since these boxes initially retailed at around £200 this was an aggressive threat to the new network. After some consideration of the options, other entrants decided to match the offer and offer their potential customers free set-top boxes. The result was to increase the set-up losses faced by ON Digital in any given year and to increase the period required for the enterprise to break even; this put significant commercial and stock exchange pressure on the owners of ON Digital, with critics questioning whether the enterprise would ever be profitable. In 2002 the company went bankrupt and closed its operation. Since then BSkyB have continued to offer free boxes and special installation packages to continue winning new customers. The digital terrestrial system has been relaunched as Freeview by a BBC-led consortium, a free service with up to 30 television channels plus digital radio stations. Customers still have to buy a digital converter at a price of £100 or less.

CHAPTER SUMMARY

In this chapter we examined the influence of market structure on the price-setting behaviour of firms. In doing this we analysed:

■ Oligopolistic market structures in which firms have a degree of independence in setting prices and need to be aware of moves by their rivals. In oligopolistic markets, firms co-ordinate their activities by using specific or tacit collusion.

■ The dominant firm, which has more control over price than its smaller rivals, obliging them to be price followers.

■ How a small number of firms, which are more equal in size, seek to co-ordinate the market either through tacit or explicit collusion.

REVIEW QUESTIONS

Exercise

Use the media to identify one or more of the following situations:

a   Price leadership in industries, such as cars, petrol, etc. Try to identify the price leader and the price followers.
b   Sectors where competition is mainly by non-price methods. Explain the nature of the competition.
c   A cartel identified by the competition authorities. Try to identify the reasons that collusion was possible and how the cartel was discovered.

Discussion questions

1   In what ways does a firm acquire market power in a monopolistic market?
2   Compare and contrast the pricing outcomes in perfect and monopolistic competition.
3   What do you understand by the term "strategic interaction".
4   What assumption does the kinked demand model make about strategic interaction? Why are prices sticky? Does the empirical evidence support the notion of price stickiness?
5   Compare and contrast the assumptions a firm makes about the behaviour of its rivals in the kinked demand, Bertrand and Cournot models.
6   Explain how reaction curves and isoprofit curves are derived in the Cournot oligopoly. Using diagrams show and explain how equilibrium is reached?
7   Using reaction curves and isoprofit curves, explain the incentive for firms in a duopoly to move from a Cournot equilibrium position.
8   Explain the following terms: Nash equilibrium, dominated strategy, zero sum game and positive sum game.

9 Consider the usefulness of the "prisoner's dilemma" model in explaining the dilemma of firms trying to decide whether they should collude or act independently.

10 What factors facilitate the formation of cartels and, once formed, what factors make them unstable?

11 What do you understand by the term "price stickiness"? Why are prices sticky in oligopolistic industries?

12 Why do duopoly markets not result in prices being set at competitive lewels.

REFERENCES AND FURTHER READING

Baye, M.R. (1997) *Managerial Economics and Business Strategy* (2nd edn, Chapters 9 and 10). Richard D. Irwin, Chicago.

Blinder, A. (1991) Why are prices sticky? Preliminary results from an interview study. *American Economic Review*, **81**(2), 89–100.

Chamberlain, E.H. (1933) *The Theory of Monopolistic Competition*. Harvard University Press, Cambridge, MA.

Diamantopoulos, A. and B.P. Matthews (1993) Managerial perceptions of the demand curve. *European Journal of Marketing*, **27**(9), 5–18.

Dixit, A. and B. Nalebuff (1991) *Thinking Strategically*. W.W. Norton, New York.

Domberger, S. and D. Fiebig (1993) The distribution of price changes in oligopoly. *Journal of Industrial Economics*, **41**(3), 295–313.

Hall, S., M. Walsh and A. Yates (1997) *How do UK companies set prices?* Bank of England, London.

MMC (1986) *The UK Market for White Salt Monopolies and Mergers Commission* (Cmnd 9778). HMSO, London.

OFT (1991) *Cartels: Detection and Remedies*. Office of Fair Trading, London.

Rees, R. (1993a) Collusive equilibrium in the great salt duopoly. *Economic Journal*, **103**, 833–848.

Rees, R. (1993b) Tacit collusion. *Oxford Review of Economic Policy*, **9**(2), 27–40.

Robinson, J. (1933) *Economics of Imperfect Competition*. Macmillan, London.

Shaw, R.W and C.J. Sutton (1976) *Industry and Competition*. Macmillan, London.

Waldman, D.E. and E.J. Jensen (1998) *Industrial Organization: Theory and Practice* (Part II). Addison-Wesley, Reading, MA.

10

PRICING IN PRACTICE

CHAPTER OBJECTIVES

This chapter aims to discuss the various pricing practices adopted by firms. At the end of the chapter you should be able to:

◆ Understand the various dimensions of price.
◆ Distinguish between different discriminatory pricing practices.
◆ Understand the methodology to maximize profits when practising third-degree price discrimination.
◆ Understand the appropriate use of peak load pricing.
◆ Distinguish between cost plus, full cost and mark-up pricing.
◆ Be aware of other factors that might influence the price charged.

INTRODUCTION

Setting a price is one of the major decisions that a firm has to take. In most market structures the firm has the ability to make prices, though it may be severely limited by the structure of the market it operates in. In the most competitive markets, firms will have to accept the market price and be price takers. In setting a price a firm will have to consider both demand factors and costs. In some circumstances, demand factors will be the dominant influence in setting a price; in others, costs may be more influential. In this chapter we will examine ways in which firms make or set prices in imperfectly competitive markets. It will explore:

- The nature of price.
- Pricing practices in monopolies, such as price discrimination.
- Cost plus pricing.
- Pricing practices to gain strategic advantages.

THE NATURE OF PRICE

A price is a charge made by a producer to a consumer for the right to be supplied with a good or service. Fares, tariffs, charges, premiums and interest rates are prices in the appropriate context. In many instances the price will be the same for all supplies of a particular product, but in other circumstances there may be a variety of prices even for the same product. For example, branded chocolate bars may be on sale in a sweet shop at £1 per bar and in other outlets close by at either a lower or a higher price. However, provided that the price is clearly displayed, the consumer will be able to see the price and decide whether to purchase.

Other prices may not be so simple. For example, the prices of railway journeys is extremely complex, with the price per journey depending on day of travel, the time of day, the class of travel and how far in advance the ticket is booked. In addition, the purchase of a railway pass for a given sum of money allows the passenger to have a further discount on some fares. This kind of structure creates a two-part pricing structure: a fixed fee and a lower price when journeys are made.

Some prices are quoted according to the quantity of an item purchased. The more units purchased at the same time the lower the unit price. Such practices are known as quantity discounts. Further distinctions in pricing may be between the list price and the actual price paid. New motor cars have list or recommended prices, but the consumer would not necessarily pay the list price; instead, he would expect to receive a discount. In other instances there may be distinctions between trade and retail prices, on the one hand, and retail and wholesale prices, on the other. The term "price" can therefore cover a wide range of concepts, depending on the particular product or situation being discussed.

Alfred (1972) argued that the nature and complexity of pricing structures will vary with the type of competition or market structure, the age of the product, whether the buyers are consumers or industrial users, whether products are singly or jointly produced and the age and utilization of productive capacity.

DOMINANT-FIRM PRICING AND CONSUMER SURPLUS

A dominant firm acting as a monopolist, aiming to maximize profits and using a single price will equate marginal revenue to marginal cost and set the appropriate price for that output. The firm will be able to earn supernormal profits in the long run, since it faces no competition. In Figure 10.1 the firm faces a downward-sloping demand curve and a conventional marginal cost curve. A profit-maximizing firm will charge price OP_M, sell quantity OQ_M, and earn profits of $P_M BEL$. However, all the buyers of the intra-marginal units of the product purchased would have been prepared to pay a higher price for them than they actually did. The buyer of the initial unit would have been prepared to pay OA, but in practice is only charged OP_M. The difference AP_M is termed **consumer surplus** for the unit purchased. For all units sold the sum total of consumers' surplus is the difference between the demand curve and the price line, or ABP_M. If the total value to consumers of OQ_M units is the area $OABQ_M$, then the monopolist who only captures $OP_M BQ_M$ will devise strategies to acquire the remaining consumer surplus. Such strategies involve price discrimination.

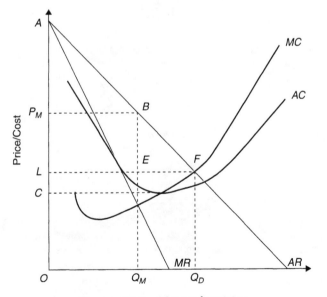

Figure 10.1 Monopoly pricing

PRICE DISCRIMINATION

Price discrimination involves exploiting demand characteristics that allow the same product to be sold at various prices unrelated to the cost of supply. In practice a single consumer may be charged different prices for different units of a good bought or different consumers may be charged different prices for the same product or service.

Economists distinguish between three types of price discrimination.

1 First degree price discrimination

First-degree price discrimination occurs where a firm charges a different price for each unit sold. Thus, the price paid is the marginal revenue to the firm of each extra unit sold. For monopoly-level output OQ_M in Figure 10.1 the firm is able to charge a different price for every unit of output sold and to capture as revenue and profit the previous area of consumer surplus ABP_M; this raises profit from P_MBEL to $ABEL$. However, if the firm now equates its new marginal revenue curve to marginal cost, then its new equilibrium position is at F and it expands output to OQ_D, the competitive output; this increases profit to AFL. All available consumers' surplus is now translated into monopoly profit, to the benefit of the seller. The mechanisms to achieve this end are difficult to find. The usual examples of perfect price discrimination relate to the supply of personal services, where the supplier is able to charge each customer according to his willingness or ability to pay. Other examples relate to the use of auctions.

Case Study 10.1 Licence auction: third-generation mobile phones

In 1999 the UK government decided to auction licences for five blocks of radio spectrum for the delivery of 3G services. The largest block was reserved for a new entrant to the UK mobile telephone market, while the other four were open to any bidders, including those four companies already holding licences to operate their own networks. The reserve price for the five licences was set at £500m.

The auction process was a modified version of that used by the US Federal Communications Commission. Bidding for the licences took place in a sequence of rounds, with participants bidding simultaneously by fax for any one of the five licences. The auction proceeded as follows:

■ In round 1 all participants put in bids simultaneously, with the highest bids for each licence becoming the current holder of the licence. At the end of each round all bidders are advised of the value of all the bids made.

■ In round 2, current holders of the licence are not allowed to bid and cannot do so again until displaced as the highest bidder by another participant. All others may bid, and holders of one licence may bid, for any of the other licences they are eligible to hold.

■ The auction ends when there are no further bids against current holders of licences.

There were 13 bidders that took part in the auction, which lasted 150 rounds before only 5 bidders were left – each holding a licence. By round 106, 5 companies had withdrawn. In the final round, only one company NTL was eligible to bid against the existing highest bidders, but chose not to do so and withdrew. The winners of the licences after 150 rounds are shown in Table 10.1. The newcomer's licence went to TIW of Canada, who subsequently sold its licence to Hutchinson Communications, after they had sold Orange to Mannesman. The other four licences went to the existing operators. The total sum bid was £22.477bn compared with the £500m reserve price; this amounts to approximately £430 per man, woman and child in the UK.

Table 10.1 Winners of the UK 3G mobile phone auction

Licence	Bidder	Price (£)	Winning round
A	TIW	4,384,700.000	131
B	Vodafone	5,964,000,000	143
C	BT3G	4,030.100,000	149
D	One2One	4,003,600,000	146
E	Orange	4,095,000,000	148
Total		22,477,400,000	

Source   Compiled from data found at http://spectrumauctions.gov. uk.auction/ auction_index.htlm

The auction system encouraged individual participants to bid up to their estimated value of the excess profits they expected to earn. The incumbents were also driven to keep bidding by the fear of losing and not being able to offer the next generation of mobile phones. Subsequent events appear to indicate that companies overbid in such an auction and that successful bidders have been struck by what has been termed the "winner's curse".

2   Second-degree price discrimination

Second-degree price discrimination occurs where the monopolist charges different prices for different quantities, or blocks, of the same product. In Figure 10.2 the first block of units are sold at price OP_1 and successive blocks at lower prices giving a stepped marginal revenue curve $P_1BHCJDKELF$. If the firm maximizes profit and equates marginal revenue to marginal cost, then total output is OQ_5, which is greater than the output (Q_M) when a single monopoly price is charged. The consumer benefits from larger output and retains some consumer surplus. Examples of block tariffs are to be found in the utility industries, such as gas and electricity. The consumer is charged a price that varies with consumption in which initial units incur a higher price than later units; this is a similar practice to quantity discounts where the more one buys the cheaper the product becomes.

3   Third-degree price discrimination

Third-degree price discrimination occurs where the monopolist is able to separate the market demand into two or more groups of customers and then charge each group a

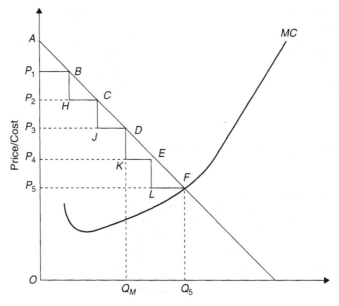

Figure 10.2   Second-degree price discrimination

different price for the same product. To be able to achieve such market separation, there must exist some barriers to prevent consumers moving from the expensive to the cheaper market, as well as to prevent customers in the cheaper market selling to consumers in the more expensive one. In addition, the price elasticity of demand must be different for each group of customers, so that market separation is profitable.

In Figure 10.3 the monopolist is able to split demand into two separate markets by differences in price elasticity. The customers in market 1 are those with relatively inelastic demands and the customers in market 2 are those with more elastic demands. There is also a single marginal cost curve for all output since the goods are produced together. The marginal revenue curves from market 1 and 2 are summed horizontally to give the combined marginal revenue curve ($\Sigma\,MR$). Thus, the first portion of the combined marginal revenue curve GH is the portion AE of MR_1, while the portion HZ combines portions of MR_1 and of MR_2, so that TU plus VL is equal to RZ.

In the combined market the firm equates the combined marginal revenue with marginal cost and produces the output OQ_M. This output is allocated between the two markets, where the marginal cost of producing the total market is equal to the marginal revenue in the individual markets; this gives:

- In market 1 a supply of OQ_1 and a price of OP_1.
- In market 2 a supply of OQ_2 and a price of OP_2.

No other combination of output would maximize profits. If another unit of output were produced, then marginal cost would exceed marginal revenue, thereby incurring a loss on that unit. Likewise, selling another unit in either market would mean marginal cost exceeding marginal revenue.

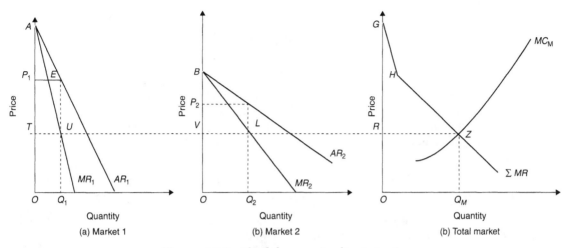

Figure 10.3 Third-degree price discrimination

The implication of third-degree price discrimination is a higher price in the market with less elastic demand and a lower price in the market with more elastic demand. We know that $MR = P(1 + 1/e)$, where P = price, MR = marginal revenue and e = price elasticity of demand (see Chapter 5). Profit maximization requires the equality of marginal revenue in both markets with combined marginal cost. Thus, we can equate $P_1(1 + 1/e_1) = P_2(1 + 1/e_2)$. If e is lower in market 1 than market 2, then $1/e$ is higher in market 1 than market 2 and $(1 + 1/e)$ is lower in market 1 than market 2. Therefore, price must be higher in market 1 than market 2. Thus, if marginal revenue in both markets is 10, price elasticity in market 1 is -2 and market 2 is -4, then the prices charged in market 1 would be 20 and in market 2 would be 13.3.

Arithmetical examples of relationships in third-degree price discrimination

These relationships can be explained by making use of two simple quantitative examples.

Example 1   Assume two market demand curves:

$$P = 30 - Q_1, P = 40 - Q_2 \quad \text{and} \quad MC = 10$$

The objective is to find the profit-maximizing price and quantity in both markets. To do this we need to equate marginal revenue in market 1 (MR_1) with marginal revenue in market 2 (MR_2) with marginal cost (MC). Thus, marginal revenue – the first derivative of the demand equation – is $MR_1 = 30 - 2Q_1$ for market 1 and $MR_2 = 40 - 2Q_2$ for market 2. Thus, equating marginal revenue in each market with marginal cost gives:

$$30 - 2Q_1 = 10 \quad \text{and} \quad 40 - 2Q_2 = 10$$

Solving these equations gives the following values for quantity and price in each market:

$$\text{Market 1} \quad Q_1 = 10 \quad \text{and} \quad P_1 = 20$$
$$\text{Market 2} \quad Q_2 = 15 \quad \text{and} \quad P_2 = 25$$

We can also calculate the price elasticity of demand for both P_1 and P_2. The formula for point elasticity is $(P/Q) * (\Delta Q / \Delta P)$, so that the price elasticity for P_1 is given by $[(20/10) * -1]$, or -2. Price elasticity for P_2 is given by $[(25/15) * -1)$, or -1.66.

We can also verify the relationship between marginal revenue, price and price elasticity of demand. We also know that $MR = P(1 + 1/e)$, where e (price elasticity) is negative:

- In market 1, $10 = P_1(1 + 1/ - 2) = P(1/2)$. Thus, P_1 is equal to $(10/0.5)$, or 20.
- In market 2, $10 = P_2(1 + 1/ - 1.66)$. Thus, P_2 is equal to $(10/0.4)$, or 25.

Example 2   This example repeats the process in example 1 but with a more complex marginal cost curve. Assume two market demand curves:

$$P = 30 - Q_1, MR = 30 - 2Q_1; P = 40 - Q_2, MR = 40 - 2Q_2 \quad \text{and} \quad MC = Q_1 + Q_2$$

The objective again is to find the profit-maximizing price and quantity in both markets. To do this we need to equate MR_1 with MR_2 and marginal cost. Thus:

$$30 - 2Q_1 = 40 - 2Q_2 = Q_1 + Q_2$$

To solve this set of relationships with two unknowns we can proceed as follows. We take the equations for MR_1 and MR_2 to form one equation and the equations for MR_2 and MC to form a second equation. Thus, we have:

Stage	$MR_1 = MR_2$		$MR_2 = MC$	
1	$30 - 2Q_1 = 40 - 2Q_2$ $-2Q_1 + 2Q_2 = 10$	(10.1)	$40 - 2Q_2 = Q_1 + Q_2$ $Q_1 + 2Q_2 + Q_2 = 40$ $Q_1 + 3Q_2 = 40$	(10.2)
2			Multiplying (10.2) by 2 we obtain: $2Q_1 + 6Q_2 = 80$	(10.3)
3	Now add (10.1) and (10.3): $-2Q_1 + 2Q_2 = 10$ $2Q_1 + 6Q_2 = 80$ to obtain: $8Q_2 = 90$ or $Q_2 = 90/8 = 11.25$	(10.1) (10.3)		
4	Inserting the value of Q_2 in (10.1), we obtain the value for Q_1 of 6.25			
5	Thus we can obtain the price in market 1: $P_1 = 30 - Q_1 = 30 - 6.25 = 23.75$ and market 2: $P_2 = 40 - Q_2 = 40 - 11.25 = 28.75$			

The value of marginal revenue and marginal cost is calculated as follows:

$$MR_1 = 30 - 2Q_1 \qquad MR_2 = 40 - 2Q_2$$
$$MR_1 = 30 - 2(6.25) \qquad MR_2 = 40 - 2(11.25)$$

$$MR_1 = 30 - 12.5 \qquad MR_2 = 40 - 22.5$$
$$MR_1 = 17.5 \qquad MR_2 = 17.5$$

Since marginal revenue is equal to marginal cost, it must be equal to 17.5, or $Q_1 + Q_2$, which is equal to $11.25 + 6.25$, or 17.5.

We can also calculate the price elasticity of demand for both P_1 and P_2. The formula for price elasticity is $(P/Q) * (\Delta Q/\Delta P)$, so that price elasticity for P_1 is given by $[(23.75/6.25) * -1$, or -3.8, and for P_2 is given by $[(28.75/11.25) * -1]$, or -2.6.

We can also verify the relationship between marginal revenue, price and price elasticity of demand. We also know that $MR = (1 + 1/e)$, where e (price elasticity) is negative. In market 1 this is given by $17.5 = P_1(1 - 1/ - 3.8)$, which gives a value for P_1 of 23.75. In market 2 this is given by $17.5 = P_2(1 + 1/ - 2.55)$, which gives a value for P_2 of 28.75.

Practical examples   Third-degree price discrimination tends to be found in many industries, but particularly transport. Railway companies offer a variety of prices for a given journey in terms of class of travel, day of travel, season of travel, time of travel and how many weeks in advance the journey was booked. Low-cost airlines also offer low prices for journeys booked in advance with prices increasing the closer the date of the actual journey and the proportion of seats unfilled. Those wanting to travel closer to the time of the journey are willing to pay higher prices and their elasticity of demand is lower.

TWO-PART TARIFFS

An alternative strategy much used by monopolists is to adopt a variation of second-degree price discrimination and use a two-part tariff, or pricing structure, which combines a fixed charge and a variable rate. Such pricing is sometimes referred to as non-linear pricing. Variations on such pricing structures are not only widely used in the telephone, electricity and gas markets but also by sports clubs who charge a membership fee and a charge per session: for example, TXU Energi offered electricity (in January 2002) to domestic consumers at a fixed charge of 8.04p per day, or £6.43 per 80-day period, plus 5.860p per kWh, while British Gas offered a fixed charge of 7p per day, plus 1.295p per kWh. There is also a practice of offering consumers of telephone services varying combinations of fixed charges and prices per unit. A higher fixed charge means that the consumer pays a lower unit price. This structure is intended to encourage additional consumption, as the marginal cost of additional calls is lower than under a single-price tariff. An extreme version of this strategy is a fixed charge and the zero consumption charge used, for example, by Internet providers.

A simple two-part tariff is illustrated in Figure 10.4. The consumer pays a fixed or entry charge of *OF*, whether or not any product is consumed. If all units purchased are sold at a fixed price, then the total expenditure function is the upward-sloping linear line *FE* in Figure 10.4. The average price paid by the consumer declines continually and is shown by the line *FP*. Thus, for the electricity example quoted above, no purchase per quarter costs £6.43 and the first unit purchased costs £6.48 plus 5.860p. The average price of 10 units purchased is 70.6p, 100 units purchased is 12.016p and 1,000 units purchased is 6.503.

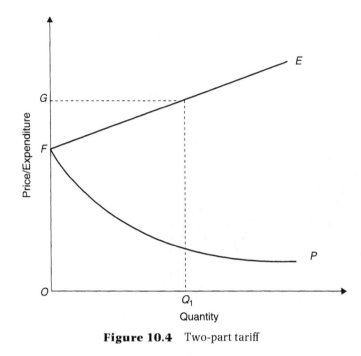

Figure 10.4   Two-part tariff

A two-part tariff pricing strategy has been employed in utility industries where the fixed charge is designed to recover fixed costs and the variable element is intended to reflect more closely the marginal cost of consumption; this encourages additional consumption, particularly in industries with high fixed cost, declining average costs and excess capacity. However, while the marginal price might more closely reflect the marginal cost of supply, the method has adverse distributional consequences for those who consume small quantities, especially if these consumers are the poorest members of the community.

PEAK LOAD PRICING

When demand varies significantly by time of the day, the week or the year and costs of supply vary with the level of demand, then price structures may be constructed to reflect the variations in costs or to limit investment in capacity. For example, a hair-dresser's salon may find that demand for its services are significantly higher on Friday and Saturday, so that demand exceeds the capacity of the establishment, whereas on other days of the week demand is much less than capacity. One way for the hairdresser to bring demand into line with available capacity is to lower prices on Mondays to Thursdays and to increase prices on Friday and Saturday. If demand exceeds capacity sufficiently, then it may be in the interests of the firm at some point to invest in new capacity, to employ more hairdressers and to meet a higher level of demand. In this instance the variation in price at peak is intended to limit demand, so

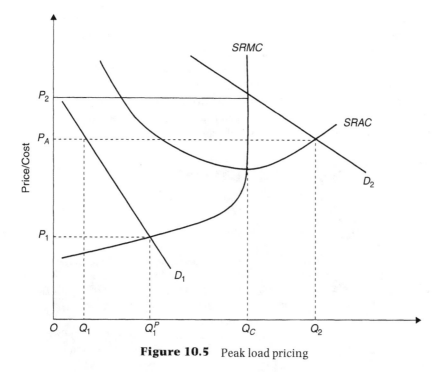

Figure 10.5 Peak load pricing

that the peak price is not explicitly related to costs. The hairdresser is also exploiting differences in the willingness of individual consumers to pay higher prices on peak days.

Assume a firm has two separate and independent demand curves for its services, separated by time of the week. Its short-run marginal cost curve increases with the quantity sold to capacity, at which point it rises vertically. The short-run average cost curve is shown as falling to capacity output Q_C and then increasing; this situation is illustrated in Figure 10.5.

If a hairdresser charges a single price OP_A in both periods, then demand for its services will be OQ_1 in off-peak periods and OQ_2 in the peak period. The firm can meet demand in the off-peak period and still have excess capacity, while demand OQ_2 exceeds the capacity of OQ_C in the peak period. To limit demand to capacity at peak the firm will institute a rationing system, such as dealing only with regular customers or only those who had booked in advance.

To make better use of capacity the firm could set prices equal to short-run marginal cost. This would mean charging price OP_1 to off-peak customers and supplying OQ_1^P, a price less than short-run average cost. It would also mean charging price OP_2 to peak customers to bring demand into line with capacity. While the off-peak price clearly reflects short-run marginal cost, the peak price can be seen as restricting demand to capacity. This practice can therefore be seen as either setting price equal to short-run marginal cost or charging what the market will bear (i.e., extracting consumer surplus from those willing to pay higher prices for the service in the peak period). The ability of one hairdresser to institute such a price structure may depend on the loyalty of customers and their unwillingness to use alternative salons.

Time-of-day pricing in electricity at both peak and off-peak can be justified by cost variations because electricity is produced by power stations whose costs are higher at peak than at off-peak. Railway pricing tends to be similar to that of the hairdresser, with higher prices at morning peak to restrict demand and lower prices off-peak to encourage greater usage of unused capacity. In the electricity industry, price differences are justified by cost differences and are not regarded as price discrimination, whereas on the railways differential pricing is regarded as price discrimination because prices do not closely reflect cost differences.

Case Study 10.2   BT's Pricing Structure

British Telecom's pricing structure exhibits a number of features including two-part tariffs, a choice of fixed charges, multiple part tariffs and peak load, or time-of-day pricing. In addition, some price differences are justified by costing differences, while others are demand-related.

The structure for charges to domestic users for January 1999 is set out in Table 10.2. The basic structure is a two-part tariff: a fixed monthly rental charge and a variable call rate, with charges made on a per minute basis. The call rate also varies by time of day, time of week and distance. In addition, there are a host of premium rate services that charge a higher call rate and a number of free services used by some firms for calls made to them. Calls to mobile telephones also have a separate charging regime. In addition, BT offers customers various discount services, such as Friends and Family, if they pay a higher rental charge.

Table 10.2   British Telecom residential prices (January 1999)

Type of charge				
Fixed charge or rental	£26.27 per quarter			
Variable charges (pence per minute[a])	Local	Regional	National	To mobile[b]
Day-time: Monday to Friday, 8 a.m to 6 p.m.	3.95	7.91	7.91	30.0
Evenings and night-time: Monday to Friday: 6 p.m to 8 a.m.	1.49	3.95	4.18	20.0
Weekend: midnight Friday to midnight Sunday	1.00	2.95	2.95	10.0
Residential discounts				
Family and Friends	10% for 10 numbers; 20% best friend; free to join			
Premier line	15% plus £24 per year fixed charge; breakeven £70 of direct dialled calls per quarter			
Option 15	11% plus £3.20 per quarter; breakeven £31 of direct dialled calls per quarter			
Light user scheme	If the call bill is less than £10.81 per quarter, then rental is reduced by 12.72p for every 10p the bill is less than £10.81.			

Note   [a] Minimum charge 5p.
              [b] To Cellnet.
Source   Compiled by author using data then available to customers.

PRICING IN IMPERFECT MARKETS

In imperfect markets where there are a small number of competitors producing differentiated products the firm has a degree of flexibility to make its own prices, tempered by concern for the pricing behaviour of rivals. Economics suggests two competing methodologies for price setting. First, a firm can relate prices to costs of production. At its simplest this represents a desire on the part of a firm to ensure that revenues cover costs and allow the firm to make a profit. Such practices are described as cost-plus pricing. At its most sophisticated, it implies that a firm that seeks to maximize profits should strive to equate marginal revenue to marginal cost. Second, it can relate price to the conditions of demand and the position and slope of the demand curve. It is the downward slope of the demand curve that gives the firm the ability to set its own prices and the inelasticity of demand its ability to raise prices above marginal cost. Thus, the manager in setting prices should be aware of the cost structure of producing an individual product, its demand curve, the product's degree of uniqueness and the number of rivals.

STUDIES OF PRICING

Economists have from time to time tried to discover how managers set prices and whether they follow the prescriptions of marginalism. The methods that have been used include investigative interviews, case studies and questionnaires. Studies tend to be old and widely quoted. Among them are Hall and Hitch (1939), Andrews (1949), Andrews et al (1975), Barback (1964), Skinner (1970), Hague (1971), Atkin and Skinner (1975) and Dorward (1987) – the latter surveyed the post-war literature. These studies tend to find support for cost-plus pricing using a standard mark-up and full cost pricing. Demand only weakly influenced price setting. Firms tended to use time-honoured rules of thumb in determining the mark-up. These findings were partly confirmed by Hall et al. (1997), who also found an increasing recognition of the role of demand.

Hall et al. (1977) undertook a survey of the price-setting behaviour of 654 UK firms. They found, "cost-based rather than market-led pricing was widespread and the overwhelming majority of companies indicated that they would be more likely to increase overtime (working) and capacity than change their price in response to a boom in demand" (p. 5). Firms were asked to choose their preferred method or the most influential factors in their price formation. Respondents were able to choose more than one response as their first preference, so that total first preferences exceed 100%. The results are summarized below in order of preference:

1 Prices are set at the highest level the market would bear (39%).
2 Prices are set in relation to their competitors (25%).
3 Prices are set equal to direct cost per unit plus a variable percentage mark-up (20%).

4   Prices are set equal to direct costs plus a fixed percentage mark-up (17%).
5   Prices are set by customers or buyers (5%).
6   Prices are set by regulators (2%).

The survey showed that 64% of first preferences said they used the market-based process in setting their prices compared with 37% that used cost-plus pricing procedures. Cost-plus mark-up pricing tended to be more important for small companies than for medium and large ones. The report suggests that the cost mark-up rule of thumb is more suitable for small companies that cannot afford expensive market research. The overall conclusions from these studies are that businesses still use cost-plus pricing as their basic approach, but that that there is a growing recognition of the role of market forces in modifying those prices obtained by cost-plus methods (i.e., by modifying the mark-up).

ANALYTICS OF AVERAGE COST PRICING

The empirical evidence suggests that there are two main methods of calculating price based on average variable costs. The first, the full cost method, involves estimating the average variable (or average direct) costs for a chosen or normal output and then adding average fixed or (average indirect) costs and an average profit margin. Managers as a matter of experience know the average profit margin that is appropriate to any sector. Such a price should yield a "fair" return on capital, so that the firm is in a position to borrow or acquire the necessary capital to fund investment, given the risks particular to the industry. All three elements are treated as costs in the sense that they have to be covered by the price charged. The second method involves estimating the average variable or (average direct) costs for a chosen or normal output and then adding a costing margin to cover indirect costs and deliver the desired profit margin.

Crucial to both methods is the nature of the cost function and, more particularly, the average variable cost curve. In Chapter 8 the empirical evidence suggested that the short-run average variable cost function was constant in the relevant range of output. Thus, in Figure 10.6 the short run average variable cost is saucer-shaped with a significant horizontal section. Short-run marginal cost coincides with short-run average variable cost when they are both constant. Average total cost is made up of average variable costs plus average fixed costs.

If the firm produces a single product, then average fixed costs or overhead costs are simply calculated. If the firm is multi-product-based, then some arbitrary decision has to be made to allocate overheads to individual products; this is usually achieved on the basis of rules of thumb, such as the relative production of two or more products jointly produced. If there is no agreed procedure to allocate fixed costs between products, then average total costs cannot be calculated for individual products. Therefore, it is simpler for a firm to measure average variable cost and add a costing margin to cover the fixed costs of the firm in total from the sales of all the products; this sometimes

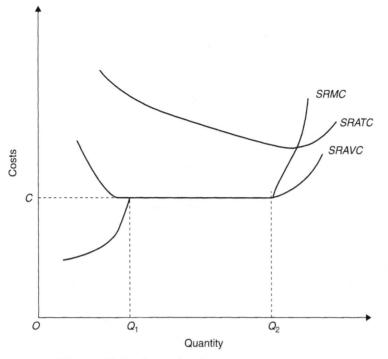

Figure 10.6 Cost curves for average cost pricing

leads to a contribution approach, in that products are given a share of fixed costs and profits they are expected to contribute.

In Figure 10.7 the full cost price maker chooses a normal output Q_N and then adds average variable costs, average fixed costs and profit to obtain the full cost price of OP_F. If sales were less than Q_1, then the firm would start making losses because average total cost exceeds average revenue OP_F.

In Figure 10.8, a firm, using mark-up pricing, estimates average variable costs and adds a margin to cover total costs and profit. Thus, for normal output OQ_N average variable costs are $Q_N B$, to which is added the mark-up equivalent to AB to give the price of OP_N. The margin reflects a number of different influences. It can reflect experience and tradition in a particular sector of what is required to make the product's contribution to overheads and generate a normal profit. Alternatively, it can reflect the firm's estimate of the slope of its own demand curve and its ability to raise price above average variable costs. Products with low price elasticities would be expected to have higher margins than products with higher price elasticities.

If the mark-up is related to the price elasticity of demand, then it can be calculated as follows. We know that $MR = P(1 + 1/e)$ and that $AVC = MC = MR = P(1 + 1/e)$. Expressed in terms of price we obtain:

$$P = AVC(e/(e + 1))$$

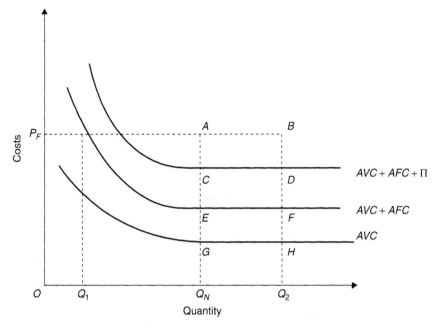

Figure 10.7　Full cost pricing

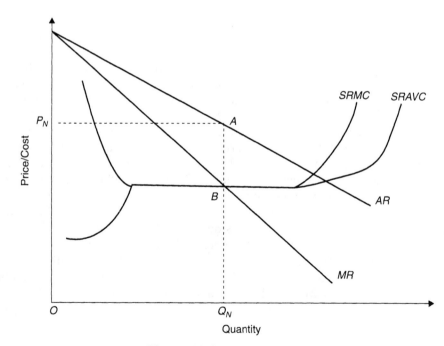

Figure 10.8　Mark-up pricing

this can be rearranged as:

$$P = AVC + (-1/(e + 1))AVC$$

where the second term represents the mark-up on average variable costs (see Douglas 1992, pp. 425–426). Thus, if the price elasticity of demand is -3 and $AVC = 10$, then the mark-up can be calculated as follows:

$$P = 10 + (-1/(-3 + 1)) * 10$$
$$P = 10 + (1/2) * 10$$
$$P = 10 + 5 = 15$$

a mark-up of 50%. A price elasticity of -2 would give a mark-up of 100%, a price elasticity of -4 would give a mark-up of 33.3% and a price elasticity of -5 would give a mark-up of 25%. If the correct mark-up is chosen, then the firm would also be maximizing profits, since marginal revenue is assumed to be equal to average variable cost, which is also equal to marginal cost. If firms are willing to adjust their mark-ups in the light of market conditions, then by a process of trial and error they may approach the optimal mark-up despite a lack of knowledge about the positioning of the demand curve. Cyert et al. (1962) were able to predict retail prices quite accurately on the basis of wholesale costs and a percentage mark-up rule.

Cost-plus pricing: responses to cost, demand and tax changes

A firm using cost-plus pricing procedures would not immediately alter price if there were only small changes in variable costs. These would be absorbed by the firm in the short run but would lead to a change in price at the next review. If costs increase significantly and are incurred by all firms in the industry, then the change could lead to an immediate price change by all firms in the sector. Increases in taxes, such as value-added and sales taxes, would be considered as a cost increase affecting all firms and, therefore, lead to immediate price increases because average variable costs would have increased. If the cost increase affected only one firm, then mechanical application of the rules would lead to a price change at the next price review.

Short-run increases in demand will not influence price. If the firm cannot increase output to meet an increase in demand, then it will adopt a rationing or queuing system to allocate output. If demand exceeds supply in the short run, then the price is maintained until the next review and the products (e.g., cars) are allocated to customers in order of joining the queue. Such a response may be justified by the belief that a fair price has been set and the demand change may only be temporary. In the longer run, prices may be adjusted upward if the firm is sensitive to market conditions, the normal output of the firm is revised and increases average variable costs. If a firm is a strict cost pricer, then, unless average variable costs change, price will not be adjusted. If demand were to fall, then the firm would not lower its price. At the next price review a cost-plus firm would be inclined to increase its price if it had reduced its normal output, because average variable and average total costs would have increased. Such behaviour has been noted in the UK, particularly in capital-intensive industries, such as brick making and cement, when price changes were monitored and regulated in the 1970s.

Reconciling cost-plus pricing and marginalism

When investigating pricing behaviour, economists have looked for evidence that managers make use of the marginalist framework. Instead, they find that price makers make use of rules of thumb to guide them in their making of prices rather than equating marginal revenue with marginal cost. Rules of thumb are important because managers are not unboundedly rational decision makers, do not have perfect information and cannot predict the reaction of rivals to their own pricing decisions. They make much use of the most certain information available: average variable costs of production in the current period, information about past sales and profit margins. In setting prices for the next period, managers make use of expected output and expected average variable costs as the starting point for price fixing. Full cost pricing appears to leave little space for demand in determining or even adjusting price, though expected sales or past sales clearly influence the choice of normal output. Those who use mark-up pricing recognize demand influences by adjusting the mark-up either to increase profit or to ensure prices are in line with competitors' prices, depending on market conditions.

The full cost price will only coincide with the profit-maximizing price if the selected normal output coincides with the profit-maximizing output and the mark-up rule gives the same price. Such a position is illustrated in Figure 10.8, where the short-run average variable cost is saucer-shaped. For normal output (Q_N) a mark-up price of P_N is set, the mark-up being designed to cover fixed costs and provide the desired profit margin. For the mark-up price to equal the profit-maximizing price the normal output and the profit-maximizing output would have to coincide and the mark-up would have to be equal to the difference between marginal revenue and the demand curve, or AB; this would occur if a firm is willing to adjust its mark-up in the light of sales and profit information to get closer to the profit-maximizing price by trial and error.

OTHER CONSIDERATIONS IN SETTING PRICE

Pricing intervals

The notions of pricing so far pursued have emphasized the role of costs in determining price. The reverse may also be true where price determines costs. Many prices are set at convenient intervals (i.e., particular points like £9.99). Where such practices apply, a firm would not set its price at £10.03 even if the full cost or mark-up pricing rule suggested it. Market convention would be recognized and the price set at £9.99. Where products are intended to be sold at predetermined prices, firms will adjust the direct costs of the product to ensure the fixed costs and the profit margin are met.

Typical examples include biscuit manufacturers that may adjust the number of biscuits in a packet or make each biscuit smaller. Clearly, such adjustments are not possible in all circumstances, and the firm may have to accept a cut in its profit margin.

Relative pricing

Firms may attempt to position the price of their product relative to a similar but different product. If the product has a number of characteristics that consumers find attractive, then the firm may be able to establish a higher price than the benchmark for the product. If the characteristic mix of the product was less desirable, then a lower price might be appropriate. Thus, with many consumer-durable products, such as vacuum cleaners or washing machines, some are perceived to have more desirable characteristics and are able to charge a premium price, compared with products with less desirable features.

Product line pricing

Where a producer offers a range of products (e.g., motor cars in different market segments), then the firm is not only concerned with the pricing of a single product but of the whole range. The firm has to take account of the interrelationships between the individual brands, as some of the products may be regarded as substitutes for each other. A change in the price of one product may affect sales of both its own and other firms' products. Where products are complements, firms may have to decide on a pricing structure and whether to sell the goods separately or to bundle them together. A classic example is the sale of model railways. Initially, the track and the rolling stock are bundled together to encourage consumers to buy the product. However, product and track are also sold separately, so that those buyers of bundled sets can buy more of either component. Unit prices of the unbundled products tend to be higher because demand is more inelastic for a particularly desirable accessory than for the original sets.

New products

Setting prices for new products presents greater difficulties, as there is no previous experience of the costs of production or of the likely level of demand. Producers may have two strategies. The first is to set what is termed a **skimming price**, which is a high initial price that yields high revenues from the limited number of customers placing a high value on the product. As demand increases and unit costs fall, the price is allowed to fall to attract new customers into the market. The second strategy is to set what is termed a **penetration price**. A low initial price is set with the objective of winning as many customers as possible to the product. Sometimes the initial price may be set below the costs of production to promote sales in the expectation that, once purchased, consumers will repeat the exercise even at higher prices. Larger sales may also lead to cost advantages as plants are more fully utilized.

Predatory pricing

In certain circumstances a firm may set a price below that of its rival to win increasing market share with the added strategic motive of driving a rival from the market. The aggressive price cutter will probably argue that its costs are lower and reflect lower costs of production. However, if prices are set at less than average variable cost, where the firm neither covers its direct cost nor makes a contribution to fixed costs, then the firm is considered to be practising predatory prices. In the UK bus industry following deregulation, a number of price wars were fought in which aggressive newcomers flooded towns with additional buses and cut prices with the objective of either driving the incumbent from the market or preventing a new firm from entering. Stagecoach adopted such tactics in Darlington where they were the entrant and in Hastings where they were the incumbent. When the competitor leaves the market or an accommodation is reached, prices are increased to cover fixed and variable costs and service frequency is reduced.

CHAPTER SUMMARY

In this chapter we examined how prices are set in practice. Prices are set for many purposes and by many methods. In doing this we examined:

- Firms charging prices that relate to variations in the elasticity of demand or quantity demanded by time of day, week or season.
- Firms setting prices by using a set of conventions that include mark-ups on average variable costs.
- Firms working their way toward prices that approximate to a profit-maximizing price.
- Firms setting prices to maintain market share, stabilizing or increasing their profit margin or meeting the prices of competitors.
- In setting prices firms must be aware that if prices are set too low, then profit-making opportunities may be lost; likewise, setting prices too high may have a similar consequence. Setting price at the appropriate level is crucial to the success of the firm. Thus, establishing criteria to determine whether price is too high or too low may be important for the firm.

REVIEW QUESTIONS

Exercise

1   Visit the websites of a number of airlines, choose a flight and obtain a price for:

  - Flights at different times of the day.
  - Flights on different days of the week.
  - Flights one week, one month and three months ahead.

  What pricing patterns emerge?
  How does the economics of pricing help to explain your observations?
2   Observe the pricing of petrol on your route to college:

  - What pricing patterns emerge?
  - Do they all charge the same price?
  - If the price of petrol increases, do all the stations move their price together or does one take the lead?
  - Which economic models help to explain what you observe?

Discussion questions

1   Explain the terms "first, second and third-degree price discrimination". Give examples of the use of such practices.
2   Explain the concept of consumer surplus. In what ways might firms expropriate consumer surplus by charging different prices to different buyers?
3   Suppose a firm can identify two separate markets for its product, with demand curves $P_1 = 60 - 0.5Q_1$ and $P_2 = 110 - 3Q_2$ and a marginal cost of $MC = 9 + 0.2Q$, where $Q = Q_1 + Q_2$:

  - What quantity should the firm supply in each market in order to maximize profit?
  - What price should be charged in each market?
  - What market conditions must be satisfied for the firm to be able to practise profitable price discrimination?

4   Explain the concept of full cost pricing. Why do firms adopt such a method of determining prices?
5   Explain the term mark-up pricing. What factors might determine the mark-up?
6   Can cost-plus pricing be reconciled with profit-maximizing pricing?
7   What does the empirical evidence tell us about how firms determine prices? Do more recent studies (e.g., Hall et al., 1997) indicate a greater influence of demand factors and competitor behaviour in determining prices?
8   In what circumstances will a firm adopt cost-plus pricing?
9   How would a firm recognize that it has set its price at too high a level compared with its competitors?

REFERENCES AND FURTHER READING

Alfred, A.M. (1972) Company pricing policy. *Journal of Industrial Economics*, **21**, 1–16.

Andrews, P.W.S. (1949) *Manufacturing Business*. Macmillan, London.

Andrews, P.W.S. and E. Brunner (1975) *Studies in Pricing*. Manufacturing Business, Oxford, UK.

Atkin, B. and R. Skinner (1975) *How British Industry Prices*. Industrial Market Research, London.

Atkinson, B., F. Livesey and B. Millward (1998) *Applied Economics*. Macmillan, Basingstoke, UK.

Barback, R.H. (1964) *The Pricing of Manufacturers*. Macmillan, London.

Cyert, R.M., J.G. March and C.G. Moore (1962) A model of retail ordering and pricing by a department store. In: R.E. Frank, A.A. Kuehn and W.F. Massy (eds), *Quantitative Techniques in Marketing Analysis*. Richard D. Irwin, Homewood, IL.

Dorward, N. (1987) *The Pricing Decision* (Chapters 8 and 9). Harper & Row, London.

Douglas, E.J. (1992) Pricing decisions in practice. *Managerial Economics* (Chapter 10). Prentice Hall, Englewood Cliffs, NJ.

Eugester, C.C., J.N. Kakkor and E.V. Roegner (2000) Bringing discipline to pricing. *The McKinsey Quarterly*, **1**, 132–139.

Hague, D.C. (1971) *Pricing in Business*. George Allen & Unwin, London.

Hall, R.H. and C.J. Hitch (1939) Price theory and business behaviour. *Oxford Economic Papers*, **2**, 12–45.

Hall, S., M. Walsh, and A. Yates (1997) *How Do UK Companies Set Prices?* (Working Paper No. 67). Bank of England, London.

Hay, D.A. and D.J. Morris (1991) Pricing in practice. *Industrial Economics* (2nd edn, Chapter 7). Oxford University Press, Oxford, UK.

Kamshad, K.M. (1996) A price for every customer. *Financial Times*, 9 March (Mastering management series).

Koutsoyannis, A. (1979) A representative model of average cost pricing. *Modern Microeconomics* (2nd edn, Chapter 12). Macmillan, Basingstoke, UK.

Livesey, F. (1998) How firms decide prices? In: B. Atkinson, F. Livesey and B. Millward (eds), *Applied Economics*. Macmillan, Basingstoke, UK.

Silberston, A. (1970) Surveys of applied economics: Price behaviour of firms. *Economic Journal*, **80**, 512–582.

Skinner, R.C. (1970) The determination of selling prices. *Journal of Industrial Economics*, **18**, 201–217.

Smyth, R. (1967) A price-minus theory of cost. *Scottish Journal of Political Economy*, **14**, 110–117.

ADVERTISING

CHAPTER OUTLINE

CHAPTER OBJECTIVES

This chapter aims to examine issues surrounding the level of advertising a firm should choose for any product. At the end of the chapter you should be able to:

- Identify the main roles and motives for advertising.
- Analyse the expected impact of advertising expenditure on demand and costs.
- Identify and explain how various factors, such as the elasticity of demand, the nature of the good, the degree of rivalry between competitors and the information available to consumers, influence the level of advertising in any market.

INTRODUCTION

The term "advertising" is generally taken to mean expenditure undertaken by a firm to promote the sales of its products or services. The most visible form of advertising is paid-for space in print, radio or television media. Advertising also includes promotional activity for a product, such as special displays, offers in shops or at commercial shows. Advertising is intended to influence consumer choice in favour of the advertiser's product or service. In this chapter we will explore:

- The nature of advertising.
- The role of advertising in changing consumer preferences.
- The impact of advertising on demand and costs.
- The optimal level of advertising.
- The impact of advertising on costs.
- The products most advertised.

ROLES OF ADVERTISING

Economists distinguish two roles for advertising. The first is the provision of factual information to consumers about the characteristics of a product, its price and its availability. Such advertising helps consumers overcome information deficiencies. The second is the persuasion of consumers to buy a particular product or visit a particular shop or restaurant, by emphasizing the qualities of the product or associating the product with a particular life style or celebrity. Such advertising is sometimes comparative in nature, with one producer comparing its product with those of others, with the intention of making the advertised firm's product look superior. The implicit assumption is that **informative advertising** is good for the consumer, while **persuasive advertising** is not; though in practice it may be hard to distinguish between the two. In the UK, print advertisements are governed by a voluntary code of practice, which requires advertisements to be legal, decent and honest. The code requires specific, factual claims to be verifiable but less specific claims are also allowed. Therefore, consumers should have confidence in such information as a car having a 1,500-cc engine, but less confidence in less verifiable claims about quality of ride and the comfort of the driving position.

Firms engage in advertising for a number of reasons. First, they try to change consumer preferences by persuading consumers of the superior quality of their product by providing information about it and by promoting brand loyalty. As a consequence, the firm promotes extra sales or is able to sell its product at a higher price. In addition, the firm may be able to lower average costs of production by producing and selling more output, thereby increasing profits.

ADVERTISING AND CHANGING CONSUMER PREFERENCES

Advertising is designed to alter the consumer's preferences in favour of advertised products and against non-advertised products. In Figure 11.1 a consumer's preference between two goods A and B is shown in the form of an indifference curve map. The pre-advertising indifference curve is labelled IC_1. With budget line DE, the consumer is in equilibrium at point K on indifference curve IC_1. The consumer buys OA_1 of good A and OB_1 of good B. In equilibrium, the marginal rate of substitution between the two goods is equal to the ratio of the two prices and the inverse ratio of the product's marginal utility, so that:

$$MRS_{AB} = P_A/P_B = MU_B/MU_A$$

(see Chapter 4). The producer of good A decides to advertise and successfully persuades the consumer that its product is superior to B. A unit of good A will now generate more utility than previously. It also means that, for a given price ratio between the two products, more A will be purchased than previously. The consumer is willing to sacrifice additional quantities of B to acquire an extra unit of A. The indifference curve IC_1, initially tangential to the price line at K, will swivel to reflect the change in consumer preferences between A and B, giving a new indifference curve IC_1^A. A similar change will take place to other indifference curves in the preference set. A new equilibrium is established at point L, on a higher indifference curve IC_2^A, with the consumer buying more of $A(A_1A_2)$ and less of $B(B_1B_2)$. The more effective the

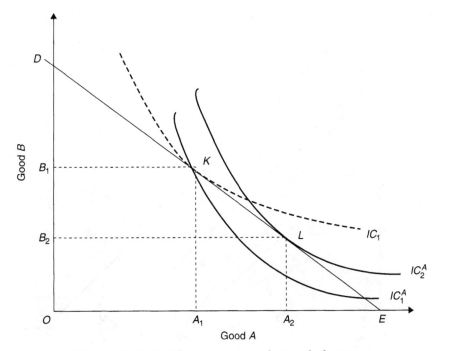

Figure 11.1 Indifference curve analysis and advertising

advertising campaign the greater the increase in the marginal rate of substitution between *A* and *B*.

ADVERTISING: PRICE AND DEMAND

Advertising is often the principal method employed by firms to increase perceived differences between products among consumers and to create brand loyalty. Therefore, advertising is a major competitive tool, especially when used in combination with other competitive weapons, such as price. In some oligopolistic markets, such as washing powders in the UK, variations in advertising expenditure is thought to be more important than price in trying to sell more of a product.

Advertising is undertaken to stimulate demand and, thereby, lower the price elasticity of demand for the product. If consumers are persuaded to buy more of a good at every price, so that the demand curve shifts outward to the right, then consumers will buy more at the current price; but, the price elasticity of demand on a linear demand curve will have fallen. Alternatively, the firm can charge a higher price for the same level of output (see Chapter 5). In Figure 11.2 the firm's initial demand curve is DD_1. The firm then engages in a successful advertising campaign that generates a

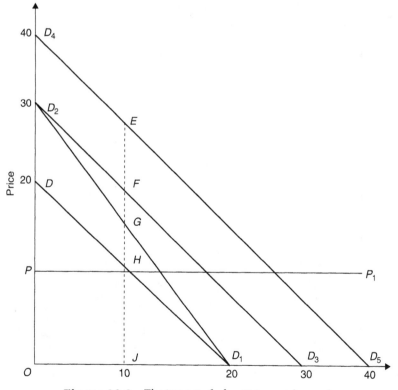

Figure 11.2   The impact of advertising on demand

Table 11.1 The impact of advertising on sales and the price elasticity of demand

Demand equations	DD_1 $P = 20 - Q$	D_2D_3 $P = 30 - Q$	D_2D_1 $P = 30 - 1.5Q$	D_5D_4 $P = 35 - Q$
Model 1 where P = 12				
P = 12	Q = 8	Q = 18	Q = 12	Q = 23
Price elasticity	(12/8) * 1	(12/18) * 1	(12/12) * (2/3)	(12/23) * 1
$(P/Q) * (\Delta Q / \Delta P)$	e = −1.5	e = −0.67	e = −0.67	e = −0.52
Model 2 where Q = 8				
Q = 8	P = 12	P = 22	P = 18	P = 27
Price elasticity	(12/8) * 1	(22/8) * 1	(18/8) * (2/3)	(27/8) * 1
$(P/Q) * (\Delta Q / \Delta P)$	e = −1.5	e = −2.75	e = −1.5	e = −3.375
Model 3: sales revenue-maximizing quantity and price				
Price	P = 10	P = 15	P = 15	P = 17.5
Quantity	Q = 10	Q = 15	Q = 10	Q = 17.5
Revenue	R = 100	R = 225	R = 150	R = 306.25

Source Author

new demand curve D_2D_3, which is to the right of the existing demand curve, so that at every price the quantity demanded has increased. Alternatively, a new demand curve D_2D_1 may be generated with a higher price intercept and the same quantity intercept.

In Table 11.1 these demand curves are expressed in quantitative terms and the impact of advertising on quantities and price elasticity is calculated. If the existing price of the product is 12, then the firm will sell 8 units when the relevant demand curve is DD_1, 18 when it is D_2D_3 and 12 when it is D_2D_1. The price elasticity of demand at price 12 remains the same if the demand curve shifts from D_2D_1 to D_2D_3, both with the same vertical intercept. If the new demand curve is completely outside the original demand curve (DD_1), such as D_2D_3 or D_4D_5, then price elasticity will decline from −1.5 to −0.67 and then to −0.52; this is also true for demand curve D_2D_1, which has the same horizontal intercept.

The shift in the demand curve also allows the firm to charge a higher price for the initial quantity of 8, if it so chooses. With demand curve D_2D_3 the price charged would be 22, with demand curve D_2D_1 it would be 18 and with demand curve D_4D_5 the price charged would be 27. The revenue-maximizing price and quantity are also shown in Table 11.1.

ADVERTISING AND COSTS

Another motive for advertising is to lower average production costs as a consequence of selling more output. A firm with a short-run, U-shaped cost curve will face lower costs if it sells more, providing it is operating on the downward-sloping element of the average cost curve. For example, in Figure 11.3 the short-run average production costs (AC_P) for the firm is shown. A firm that is able to increase output from OQ_1 to

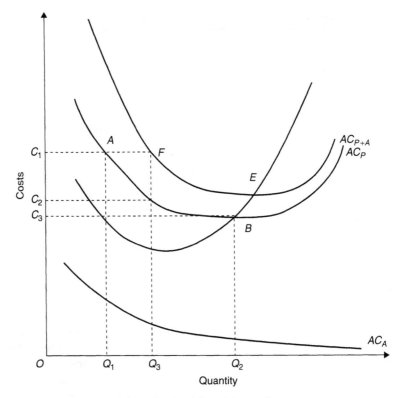

Figure 11.3   Advertising and costs

OQ_2, will experience a fall in average production costs from OC_1 to OC_3. If the firm is also on the downward portion of its long-run average cost curve, then significant increases in sales could lead to larger production facilities being constructed and further falls in average production costs.

Advertising is also an expense, and the average unit expenditure on advertising may more than offset the reductions in production costs achieved by selling more. If the costs of an advertising campaign are treated as fixed, then in Figure 11.3 average advertising costs (AC_A) decline per unit of output; this shifts the average total cost curve from AC_P to AC_{P+A}. Nevertheless, if an advertising campaign could increase output by at least Q_1Q_3, then average total costs would be lower than at output OQ_1.

SALES AND ADVERTISING

The relationship between sales and advertising expenditure can be expressed as a ratio. The average ratio would be measured by S/A, where S is total sales revenue and A is total advertising expenditure. The marginal relationship between sales and advertising expenditure is given by $\Delta S/\Delta A$. Baumol (1959) in his sales maximization model, discussed in Chapter 2, assumed that the marginal-sales-to-advertising ratio was always positive and greater than 1; this assumption means that all advertising campaigns are successful. In practice, advertising campaigns can be unsuccessful; this is indicated in two ways: first, a positive advertising-to-sales ratio of less than 1 would indicate that sales revenue had increased by less than the increase in advertising expenditure; and, second, a negative sales-to-advertising ratio would indicate that an increase in advertising expenditure had led to a decline in sales.

It is expected that advertising initially generates a $\Delta S / \Delta A$ ratio of substantially greater than 1, but that the ratio declines with successive increments in spending. The declining responsiveness of demand to a change in advertising expenditure may be linked to:

- The life cycle of the product and its falling growth rate as consumers, satiated with the product, cease buying for the first time and buy only for replacement reasons.
- The perceived requirement of competitors to spend heavily on advertising to maintain or increase their market share in a declining market, because of the unwillingness of consumers as a result of brand loyalty to switch from one brand to another.

OPTIMAL LEVEL OF ADVERTISING

In imperfectly competitive markets, competition between firms is based on using a combination of advertising, price and product characteristics. If the firm can adjust both price and advertising expenditure, then the firm is able to use a combination of both to compete with its rivals. To maximize profits a firm will equate marginal revenue to marginal cost whether it advertises or not. In Figure 11.4 the curve AC_A shows the average cost of advertising; this increases average total cost from AC_P to AC_{P+A}, but does not alter the marginal cost curve since advertising expenditure is treated as a fixed cost. This level of advertising generates a demand curve (AR) and allows the firm to maximize profits by selling OQ products and charging price OP. The average cost of advertising is QG or EF. For every level of advertising expenditure, the profit-maximizing position can be determined and the price, quantity and average advertising cost can be determined.

In Figure 11.5 the combinations of price and quantity that maximize profit for each level of advertising expenditure are plotted as the AAR curve. On this curve two combinations, P_1 and Q_1 and P_2 and Q_2, are identified at points E and F. For each price–quantity outcome there is an associated average cost of advertising. These points are plotted as the AAC curve. On this curve the average cost of advertising for output Q_1 is $Q_1 G$ and for output Q_2 it is $Q_2 H$. The general shape of these new curves reflects the underlying presence of diminishing returns to advertising expenditure and the increasing average cost of advertising as it becomes less effective. Since both represent average functions, it is necessary to derive their respective marginal functions. Parts of these curves are shown in Figure 11.5 as the AMC and AMR curves. The optimal level of advertising expenditure for the firm is determined where

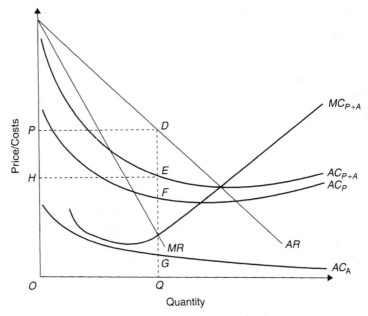

Figure 11.4   Profit maximizing with advertising

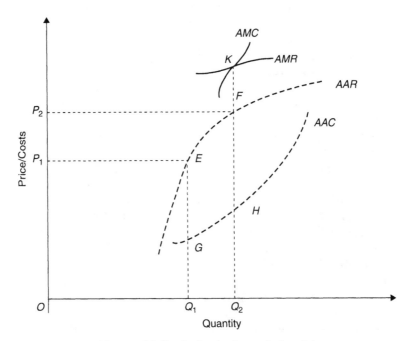

Figure 11.5   Optimal price and advertising

the marginal increase in costs of advertising are equal to the marginal increase in revenue; this is achieved at point K where the firm charges price OP_2, sells quantity OQ_2 and incurs average advertising costs of Q_2H.

This approach to optimal advertising has certain advantages and limitations. It allows the myriad individual combinations of advertising and price outcomes to be combined into the AAR and AMR curves to demonstrate the incremental or marginal nature of the process. Its shortcomings are related to the assumption that the firm will know with certainty the nature of the cost and revenue functions required to determine the optimal level of advertising. In practice, however, this is rarely possible due to the lack of detailed disaggregated data and the cost of obtaining such information. In addition, the firm in the models outlined is able to reach decisions without taking into account the possible reactions of its rivals (see Douglas 1992, chap. 13).

Optimal advertising in monopolies

Dorfman and Steiner (1954) formulated a model using price and advertising elasticities to explain variations in advertising sales ratios between products for monopolists. They show that for a monopolist the advertising-to-sales ratio (A/PQ) is equal to the ratio between the advertising elasticity of demand and the price elasticity of demand, or:

$$\frac{A}{PQ} = \frac{\text{Advertising elasticity of demand } (e_A)}{\text{Price elasticity of demand } (e_D)}$$

or

$$A/PQ = e_A/e_D = [(P - MC)/P]e_A$$

where $1/e_D = (P - MC)/P$. Thus, if (as in perfect competition) price is equal to marginal cost, then $((P - MC)/P)$ is equal to zero and no advertising will take place. If price is greater than marginal cost, then $((P - MC)/P)$ is positive and advertising will take place. The ratio of advertising to sales, A/PQ, is therefore:

■ Directly related to the price–cost margin $(P - MC)/P$.
■ Inversely related to the price elasticity of demand (e_D).
■ And directly related to the advertising elasticity of demand (e_A).

(See Clarke 1985, pp. 121–123 or Waldman and Jensen 1998, p. 320 for the mathematical derivation of this result.)

WHICH PRODUCTS DO FIRMS ADVERTISE?

The theoretical analysis of advertising suggests that a firm should vary expenditure from product to product, depending on the elasticity of demand. Products with low price elasticities would be expected to have a higher advertising-to-sales ratio than products with higher price elasticities. However, it has to be remembered that one of

Table 11.2   Number of products and differing levels of advertising

Advertising/Sales Ratio	Number of products
More than 20%	4
15–20%	1
10–15%	7
5–10%	27
4–5%	7
3–4%	13
2–3%	13
1–2%	34
0.5–1%	24
0.1.1 to 0.5%	48
0 to 0.1	12
Total number of products	190

Source Author analysis of data extracted from Advertising Association (1998)

the objectives of advertising is to reduce the elasticity of demand for a product and to promote brand loyalty. Cause and effect are therefore intertwined.

Advertising-to-sales ratios in the UK

Data on advertising-to-sales ratios for 190 selected products in the UK for 1997 can be found in Table 11.2. Of these, 84 products have ratios of less than 1%, 12 products have ratios in excess of 10% and only 4 have ratios in excess of 20%; these 4 were vitamins, hair colourants, indigestion remedies and shampoos. Products with advertising-to-sales ratios of less than 0.5% include shampoos, light bulbs, carpets and shaving cream.

Industrial goods and advertising

Industrial goods generally have very low advertising-to-sales ratios. The reasons lie in the nature of industrial goods and their buyers. The products are generally intermediate goods bought with the specific purpose of making another good. They are purchased by a small number of people who are well informed about the alternatives available. In such situations, advertising and sales promotion are narrowly focused on trade journals and personal contact.

In contrast, most consumer goods are sold to large numbers of consumers who are not necessarily so well informed. To inform consumers of their products or services, producers have to advertise more widely to reach all potential customers.

Consumer goods and advertising

The level of advertising intensity may vary by type of consumer product or service being sold.

Durable/Non-durable goods Durable goods, such as washing machines and refrigerators, generally have lower advertising-to-sales ratios than non-durable goods, such as chocolate bars. Given the high price of durable products, it is argued that consumers will undertake more detailed searches of the products available and the characteristics and attributes of each using the behavioural search and decision procedures discussed in Chapter 4. For example, when purchasing a video recorder or hi-fi system consumers may choose to consult specialist magazines to obtain unbiased information, rather than rely on the seller's advertising, which besides being informative also has a persuasive purpose.

For goods that are relatively cheap, consumers are unlikely to undertake significant search activities. The opportunity cost of a mistake is so small that consumers will try the product and then decide whether to buy it again. Doyle (1968) argued that such goods, which are more likely to be subject to persuasive advertising, are those that are purchased frequently. He argued that persuasive advertising is needed in such circumstances to keep people buying the product. If consumers continually enter and leave markets or switch products because they are inexpensive, then there is a high rate of turnover, or "churn", of consumers. In such circumstances, advertising expenditure on a product would be expected to be greater than for a product with a lower level of "churn". If the "churn" is lowered, advertising expenditure may fall.

Search and experience goods Consumer goods are divided into those with search characteristics and those with experience characteristics (Nelson, 1974). Goods with search qualities, like style, size, colour and weight, can be evaluated before purchase. Goods with experience qualities, like taste, feel and effectiveness for consumers to benefit from their purchase, cannot be ascertained before consuming the product: it is only with the experience of consumption that consumers will know whether the good fulfils or fails to meet their expectations or perceptions. **Experience goods** include toiletries, food and drink. Experience goods, it is argued, are more likely to have a higher degree of advertising intensity because consumers have no source of factual information about the product, the experience is personal and sellers are trying to persuade consumers that their product has the necessary qualities. Search products, on the other hand, have measurable characteristics and sellers are more likely to use **informative advertising**. Buyers may also be more responsive to price changes than is the case for experience goods, which are more likely to be heavily advertised.

Experience goods may be characterized by a high degree of product differentiation, so that a consumer will not perceive other similar products as close substitutes for the product they buy. Therefore, if a firm is going to attract buyers away from other goods, it may have to spend heavily on advertising because of the reluctance of consumers to try other, similar products. Another aspect of product differentiation is the branding of products; this likewise generates a barrier against consumers switching to alternative brands because they become associated with lifestyles and demonstrate acceptance of that particular lifestyle.

Evidence to support the notion that experience goods will be more heavily advertised than **search goods** is found in a study by Davis et al. (1991). In ascending order of advertising-to-sales ratios for 1989 they found that:

1 Search goods had the lowest ratio of 0.4%.
2 Goods where experience is of little value had the second lowest ratio of 1.8%.
3 Short-term experience goods had an average ratio of 3.6%.
4 Long-term experience goods had the highest ratio of 5.0%.

They also found:

- The highest advertising-to-sales ratios were for products bought less than once a month and more than once every six months.
- There existed a positive relationship between the advertising-to-sales ratio and product quality for long-term experience goods whose characteristics cannot easily be observed.
- Advertising-to-sales ratios were also high for products where innovation and changing specifications were important.

New products

Firms may have to spend heavily on advertising for new products in order to make consumers aware of the product's existence, characteristics and, if relevant, superiority over existing ones. If the new product creates a new market, then advertising will initially be both informative and persuasive; but, as the market develops and rivalry between sellers increases, the nature of the advertising will be expected to become increasingly persuasive. If the new product is sold in an existing market, then advertising may be mainly of a persuasive nature as consumers are encouraged to switch from rival products.

ADVERTISING AND MARKET STRUCTURE

Another factor determining the level of a firm's advertising expenditure is the size and number of competitors in the market. If the firm sells a homogeneous product in a perfectly competitive market, then advertising would appear to be unnecessary. However, if consumers are not perfectly informed, then industry-wide advertising would make sense to overcome this deficiency. At the other extreme, a monopolist would likewise hardly need to advertise because consumers would have no other source of the product. In practice, a monopolist may advertise to encourage consumers to buy more of its products in particular, rather than on other products in general. Therefore, the market structures in which advertising might be expected to be

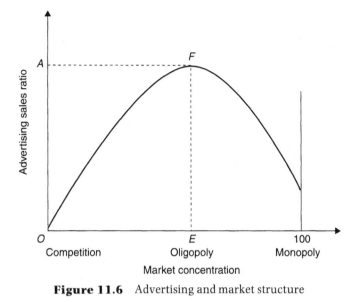

Figure 11.6 Advertising and market structure

a significant competitive weapon will be those ranging from monopolistic competition to duopoly where products are differentiated and there are relatively few competitors.

In monopolistically competitive markets, products are differentiated; this means that, although there are large numbers of competitors, each firm's product is not a perfect substitute for the products of other suppliers. The demand for each firm's product tends to be more price-inelastic than in more competitive markets and, following the analysis of Dorfman and Steiner, the advertising-to-sales ratio would be higher. In oligopolistic markets with differentiated products, similar considerations apply. Therefore, the expectation is that advertising-to-sales ratios will be low in competitive markets and monopoly, but higher in imperfectly competitive markets where products are differentiated. This relationship is illustrated in Figure 11.6, where market concentration is measured on the horizontal axis and the advertising-to-sales ratio on the vertical axis.

Interdependence and rivalry

In Chapter 9 the kinked demand curve model of oligopoly was discussed. The main implication of the model, supported by empirical evidence, was that prices would be sticky because of the anticipated responses of rivals to price changes. If a firm is unwilling to use price as a competitive weapon, then it is more likely to engage in advertising to promote the sales of its product. If a firm should cut its price, then its rivals can respond quickly. In contrast, it is not to easy to respond to an advertising campaign by a competitor because of the time it takes to plan and implement a

Table 11.3   A profit pay-off matrix in a duopoly with given advertising expenditures

Firm I's advertising expenditure (£m per year)	Firm II's advertising expenditure (£m per year)					
	4		6		8	
4	12	12	10	17	5	18
6	17	10	16	16	14	15
8	18	5	15	14	13	13

Source Author

campaign. Similar advantages may be gained by changing the specifications of a product in ways that cannot easily be copied by rivals.

The smaller the number of firms competing with each other the greater the incentive for an individual firm to pursue policies that will take sales from its rivals. In oligopolies there is both an incentive to compete and an incentive to collude either explicitly or implicitly. The incentive to advertise is to gain market share, while the disincentive is the cost of an advertising campaign, the uncertainty of outcome and the desire to peacefully coexist with rivals to the mutual benefit of all.

The interdependence between two duopolists is explained with the help of Table 11.3. Both firms are able to choose three levels of advertising expenditure £4m, £6m and £8m per year. The level of profit expected from any given expenditure depends on the level of advertising chosen by rivals. Thus, if firm I chooses an advertising level of £4m, then its profit will be £12m if firm II also spends £4m: £10m if firm II spends £6m and only £5m if firm II spends £8m. Firm I's profits and, by implication, market share fall as firm II increases its advertising spend relative to that of firm I and vice versa for firm II. Firm I maximizes its profits if it spends £8m and it rival only £4m, while firm II maximizes its profits when it spends £8m on advertising and its rival only £4m.

What level of spending should each firm choose, given the conjectures presented in Table 11.3? If both firms were risk-averse they would each spend £6m. For firm I this guarantees profits of £17m, £16m and £14 no matter what level of spending firm II selects. Thus, the worse outcome for firm I following this strategy is £14m; this is the mini-max or "best of the worst" strategy (see Chapter 3 for an explanation).

If firm I wanted an opportunity of making the maximum profit possible, it would choose to spend £8m because there is an opportunity of making a profit of £18m. However, depending on the choice of firm II, it could also make profits of £15m and £13m; this choice of strategy is described as the maxi-max or "best of the best" strategy which a seeker after risk would be prepared to pursue.

Advertising and barriers to entry

If a firm gains an increased market share in a rapidly expanding market by advertising, then it will experience growth. It will also gain market power and be expected to have a higher price–cost margin. Thus, larger firms will have higher profit rates than smaller firms. Having achieved higher profits through increasing its advertising-to-sales ratio, the firm may continue to increase its ratio because it makes life difficult for its less successful rivals to maintain their position. High advertising-to-sales ratios, which are difficult for smaller rivals to match, may also deter potential entrants to the market; this creates a barrier to entry against potential entrants.

ADVERTISING AS INVESTMENT

Advertising expenditure may have an impact on consumer preferences and sales in more than one period. Some consumers may react instantly to the message of the campaign, others may react more slowly and may only remember the advertising content when they consider purchasing the product sometime in the future. For example, infrequently purchased items may only be replaced when they cease working or fashions change. Few households replace fireplaces or baths frequently, but when they come to do so they may remember the advertisement for "the largest showroom in the north". Advertising in one period, therefore, can have an impact on sales in future periods because advertising builds continued awareness of the product or firm among consumers. By capturing the delayed response on the part of consumers from each campaign, a cumulative effect on sales may be observed.

The conditions for optimal advertising outlined earlier were based on the assumption that all effects occurred in one time period. Clearly, the greater the impact of advertising within one period the more relevant the analysis, but the greater the impact of the advertising in subsequent periods the less relevant the analysis. Giving consideration to future impacts would justify higher levels of advertising in the initial period than the single period model might suggest.

BRANDING

A brand name is a title, or label, given to a single or group of products in order to identify it more closely in the mind's eye of the consumer. It is usual to distinguish between products and brands, although the two terms are often used interchangeably. For example, "Persil" is both a brand name and a range of products for washing clothes. The brand, owned by Unilever, has a long history of acceptance by consumers and of continued product development in terms of quality improvements and alternative formats to suit particular situations. Virgin, on the other hand, is both the name of the company and of a diverse range of products from airlines and trains to financial services and mobile telephones.

Doyle (1989) identified four factors that can determine brand performance: quality, innovation, superior service and differentiation. Each of these factors is interrelated. For example, quality embodies features like reputation, performance and durability and is itself a function of process and product innovation as well as pre and after-sales service activity. Effective branding is an element in the differentiation of products and is a way of capturing the loyalty of consumers and providing protection against rival products that lack such protection. Branding should therefore make buyers less price-sensitive.

Advertising is an important ingredient in the marketing mix in developing and nurturing the image of a brand, establishing and maintaining a desired product image and the reputation for quality. Once customers have become accustomed to purchasing a particular brand (and hence have been captured), they often remain loyal and are willing to pay more for the branded items than for similar unbranded goods, leading to increased sales and profits. Brands are often associated with higher levels of quality, whether perceived or real. However, if one product in the brand range fails to meet the perceived quality standards, it may damage the other products within the brand.

Evidence of the importance for a firm in gaining and maintaining a successful brand is shown by the fact that, in a number of acquisitions, significant brands have been purchased at well above their current estimated value. For example, when Nestlé bought Rowntree for £2.4bn, it paid over five times its book value to purchase a well-known chocolate brand – KitKat. Once established, brands often remain popular for many years. For instance, in the USA the main brand in 19 out of 22 product categories in the early 1990s had also been the brand leader in 1925 (*The Economist* 1991).

Case Study 11.1   Tobacco advertising

Tobacco advertising has been at the centre of public policy debate for some time. The established link between tobacco and health problems has led to calls for bans on advertising tobacco products. In the UK, advertisements for cigarettes were banned on television in 1965 and in the print media in 2003. Tobacco products also carry a government health warning that takes up a significant portion of the front of a cigarette packet.

The cigarette market in the UK and many Western countries has been in long-term decline. Evidence collected by the DoH (2000) shows (Table 11.4):

■ The percentage of adults smoking cigarettes in England has declined from 40% in 1978 to 27% in 1998.
■ Average weekly household expenditure on cigarettes has declined in real terms from £7.00 in 1978 to £5.30 in 1998.
■ 69% of smokers in 1998 wished to give up.
■ 9% of 11–15-year-olds smoked regularly.

In addition:

■ The demand for cigarettes is price-inelastic and less than 1 (Stewart 1993).
■ The income elasticity of demand is positive but less than 1 (Duffy 1994).

Table 11.4   Cigarette statistics

Year	Percentage of adult smokers			Average weekly expenditure[1] (£)	Consumer expenditure[2] (£m)	Real price index	Number smoked per week (men)
	All	Men	Women				
1978	40	44	36	7.00	16,415		125
1988	31	32	30	5.90	12,220	100	119
1998	27	28	26	5.30	8,022	158	100

Notes [1] Average weekly expenditure 1998/9 prices
[2] Consumer expenditure at 1985 prices
Source Based on data extracted from DOH (2000)

In a declining market, tobacco companies might be expected to advertise to:

■ Encourage non-smokers to become smokers and, in particular, to encourage young people to try tobacco and become regular consumers.
■ Encourage existing smokers to increase consumption.
■ Discourage smokers from reducing their consumption or ceasing altogether, by creating an environment in which smoking is seen as a normal and acceptable activity, so that health warnings are not taken seriously or are undermined.
■ Encourage smokers to switch to advertised brands.
■ Counter anti-smoking campaigns.

Tobacco companies argue that they do not advertise to increase market size; instead, in a mature market, advertising is about competing for market share. Advertising is designed to influence consumer choice and brand preference, because a significant proportion of UK smokers change brands each year. In addition, winning an additional 1% market share increases volume and profitability.

Expenditure on direct tobacco advertising in the UK was estimated to be around £25m in the year ending September 2002. The advertising-to-sales ratio for cigarettes was estimated to be 0.1% in 1999 (Advertising Association, 2001). Tobacco companies also spend money on sports sponsorship; this has been estimated to amount to £70m per year on Formula One racing and £8m on other sports. They have also engaged in brand stretching, which has led to the appearance of tobacco brand logos on fashion clothing and accessories (ASH 2002).

Tobacco companies have argued against a ban on tobacco advertising because:

■ There is no proven evidence that banning advertising discourages consumption.
■ It is used to alter the preferences of smokers.
■ Adults are aware of the risks and should be allowed to obtain the benefits of smoking.
■ Smoking is a legal activity and companies should be allowed to advertise.
■ Self-regulatory measures have worked effectively in the UK.

Cigarettes are not considered to be a normal good because consumption has a number of negative effects that appear to go unrecognized, by many consumers. Where they are recognised, the addictive nature of the product makes it harder for the consumer to stop smoking.

The main argument for banning the advertising of cigarettes is that it is injurious to the health of smokers and non-smokers. Cigarette smoking is a recognized cause of lung cancer and of respiratory and heart diseases. In 1995, 120,000 deaths were attributed to smoking-related cancer and respiratory diseases. Health concerns also apply to the effects on children of smoking during pregnancy. Passive smokers are also likely to be affected by smoky environments.

The main measures to discourage smoking in the UK have been tax increases ensuring cigarette prices increase in real terms and health promotion. In addition, the growing concern of non-smokers who become passive smokers has led to smoking bans in the workplace and public places of entertainment. While these have been effective in reducing the number of smokers, critics have called for further action and, in particular, the banning of advertising.

Those in favour of banning advertising have the support of a number of econometric studies. They find that increased expenditure on tobacco advertising increases demand for cigarettes, while banning advertising leads to a reduction in tobacco consumption (Andrews and Franke 2000). A review by the DOH's Chief Economic Adviser of cigarette consumption in countries before and after an advertising ban found that there was a drop in tobacco consumption of between 4% and 16% countries that had implemented a tobacco advertising ban (Smee et al. 1992).

Saffer and Chaloupka (2000) examined the evidence on the effect of tobacco advertising in 22 OECD (Organization for Economic Cooperation and Development) countries. The main conclusion was that advertising bans must be comprehensive in order to reduce tobacco consumption. In countries where partial bans or voluntary agreements have operated, falls in consumption have been negligible because tobacco companies have switched their advertising budgets from the banned media to non-banned, undermining the effectiveness of the limited advertising restrictions.

Stewart (1993) found a contrary result. He examined tobacco consumption in 22 OECD countries from 1964 to 1990. By 1990, 6 of the 22 countries had implemented a ban on all forms of tobacco advertising. The research showed that the average effect on per capita tobacco consumption of advertising bans had been a small increase in the number of smokers. This increase was not however statistically significant; but, clearly, it does not support the contention that advertising bans will appreciably reduce consumption. Duffy (1994) found advertising effects to be negative. As a result of his investigations he concluded, "that there is nothing in the present results to indicate that a complete ban on cigarette advertising *per se* would produce a reduction in total consumption (p. 28).

A critical view of the evidence is also found in High (1999). He argues that most cross-sectional studies of the tobacco–advertising relationship which purport to find a positive relationship are fatally flawed and that studies using better data and/or more sophisticated econometric techniques typically find little or no relationship between tobacco advertising and total tobacco consumption. Likewise, country-by-country studies that purport to find an advertising/total consumption relationship typically suffer from similar errors and do not provide evidence that advertising restrictions will curb tobacco consumption.

In the UK cigarette advertising was banned from UK television in 1965. All other forms of advertising and promotion were controlled by two voluntary agreements between the tobacco industry and the government: one agreement covered advertising and the other governed tobacco sponsorship of sport. Critics argue that these agreements were ineffective in reducing cigarette consumption. As a result, the Tobacco Advertising and Promotion Act 2002 was passed, which banned tobacco advertising and promotion in all forms of media from 2003. In due course, regulations banning sports sponsorship, brand sharing (indirect advertising) and point-of-sale advertising will also be implemented.

Thus, the tobacco industry has lost the argument on being able to continue advertising. Whether cigarette consumption will decline as a result will only became clear in the coming years.

CHAPTER SUMMARY

In this chapter we explored the nature and role of advertising as a means of competing with rivals. In doing this we showed how:

- Advertising can be used to change consumer preferences so as to increase demand and make demand less price-sensitive.
- Expenditure on advertising is a cost incurred to increase sales. The relationship between incremental advertising expenditure and incremental sales is important in determining the optimal level of advertising expenditure.
- Advertising expenditure also varies with the nature of the product or service the firm is selling. Search and experience goods have greater levels of advertising spending than other types of goods.
- The level of advertising is also influenced by the type of market in which the firm operates and the type of competitive activity adopted by competitors.

REVIEW QUESTIONS

Exercise

1 Read a copy of a local newspaper and look closely at the advertising:
   - Classify the advertisements according to whether they are informative or persuasive or a mixture of both.
   - Classify the products advertised into durable/non-durable, search/experience and branded/non-branded.
   - Assuming the size of the advertisement reflects costs, which type of product appears to have most spent on its promotion.

Discussion questions

1 The firm's initial demand curve is $P = 25 - Q$, fixed costs are 20 and marginal costs per unit are 5. Calculate the profit-maximizing-price, output and point elasticity of demand and the profits of the firm. The firm engages in an advertising campaign that increases fixed costs by 5. The campaign shifts the demand curve to $P = 35 - Q$:
   - Calculate the new profit-maximizing price and output position for the firm and the profits made.
   - Calculate price elasticity of demand in the second period at the price prevailing in the first period and the average cost of advertising per unit sold.
   - Compare the increase in profits with the cost of advertising.
   - Was the campaign worth while undertaking.

2   What are the Dorfman–Steiner conditions for optimal advertising? If the advertising-to-sales ratio is currently 1/10, the elasticity of advertising 0.2 and price elasticity −2.0, what are the consequences for the advertising-to-sales ratio if the price elasticity of demand is 1?

3   Using diagrams explain the derivation of the *LAAC* and *LAR* curves and explain the relationship between sales and advertising. Where will the equilibrium level of advertising be?

4   Compare and contrast the relative advantages of price and non-price competition.

5   The advertising-to-sales ratio for product *X* is 20% and for product *Y* is 1%. How might these differences be explained? What does this tell us about the nature of the two products?

6   A firm estimates its sales advertising function as follows:

$$Q = 20,000 + 600A - 0.6A^2$$

Calculate the impact on the quantity sold of increasing the advertising spend from 100 to 200 and 400.

7   Why do firms advertise?

8   What is the role of branding in helping the firm to sell its products?

9   Discuss the view that all advertising is informative in nature.

10   Why should the advertising of cigarettes be banned?

11   For what types of products should advertising be banned?

12   Is it possible to distinguish between the informative and persuasive elements of advertisements? Do they help customers overcome information deficiencies?

REFERENCES AND FURTHER READING

Advertising Association (1998) *Advertising Statistics Yearbook*. Advertising Association, London.

Andrews, R.L. and G.R. Franke (2000) The determinants of cigarette consumption: A meta-analysis. *Journal of Public Policy and Marketing*, **10**, 81–100.

ASH (2002) Tobacco advertising and promotion (Fact Sheet). Action on Smoking and Health, London (http://www.ash.org.uk/html/factsheets/html/fact19.html/).

Baumol, W.J. (1959) *Business Behavior, Value and Growth*. Macmillan, New York.

Brewster, D. (1997) Advertising and branding decisions. *Business Economics: Decision Making and the Firm* (Chapter 11). Dryden Press, London.

Clarke, R. (1985) Advertising. *Industrial Economics* (Chapter 6). Basil Blackwell, Oxford.

DOH (2000) *Statistics on Smoking in England since 1978* (Bulletin No. 2000/17). Department of Health, London.

Dorfman, R. and P.O. Steiner (1954) Optimal advertising and optimal quality. *American Economic Review*, **44**, 826–836.

Davis, E.H., J. Kay and J. Starr (1991) Is advertising rational? *Business Strategy Review*, **2**(3), 1–23.

Douglas, E.J. (1992) *Managerial Economics: Analysis and Strategy* (4th edn). Prentice-Hall, Englewood Cliffs, NJ.

Doyle, P. (1968) Economic aspects of advertising: A survey. *Economic Journal*, **77**(3), 570–602.

Doyle, P. (1989) Building successful brands: The strategic options. *Journal of Marketing Management*, **5**(1), 77–95.

Duffy, M. (1994) *Advertising and Cigarette Demand in the UK*. UMIST School of Management, Manchester.

High, H. (1999) *Does Advertising Increase Smoking?* Institute of Economic Affairs, London.

Nelson, P. (1974) Advertising as information. *Journal of Political Economy*, **82**(4), 729–754.

Porter, M. (1980) *Competitive Strategy: Techniques for Analysing Industries and Competitors*. Free Press, New York.

Smee, C., M. Parsonage, R. Anderson and S. Duckworth (1992) *Effect of Tobacco Advertising on Tobacco Consumption* (A discussion document reviewing the evidence). Economics and Operational Research Division, Department of Health, London.

Saffer, H. and Chaloupka, F. (2000) The effect of tobacco advertising bans on tobacco consumption. *Journal of Health Economics*, **19**, 1117–1137.

Stewart, M.J. (1993) The effect of advertising bans on tobacco consumption in OECD countries. *International Journal of Advertising*. **12**, 155–180.

The Economist (1991) Managing the brands (7 September).

Waldman, D.E. and E.J. Jensen (1998) Product differentiation and advertising. *Industrial Organization: Theory and Practice* (Chapter 13). Addison-Wesley, Reading, MA.

INVESTMENT APPRAISAL

CHAPTER OBJECTIVES

This chapter aims to examine issues surrounding decisions on investment. At the end of the chapter you should be able to:

◆ Outline the basic steps in investment appraisal.

◆ Distinguish between the main methods of investment appraisal.

◆ Explain the advantages and disadvantages of discounting procedures and other methods of appraisal.

◆ Elucidate the advantages and disadvantages of the procedures available for coping with uncertainty.

◆ Explain the difficulties encountered in measuring the cost of capital of a firm.

INTRODUCTION

Investment is undertaken by every firm. Without investment in capital the firm's production facilities will slowly become outdated, depreciate and eventually cease to function. To be competitive in terms of costs and quality of product, the firm must from time to time spend money on new plant and equipment, either to replace existing equipment or add to the firm's stock of capital. In economics, investment is defined as the setting aside of current resources to produce a stream of goods in the future. While the cost of the investment programme is known with a fair degree of certainty, the benefits are uncertain because future market conditions are not precisely known.

BASIC STEPS IN INVESTMENT APPRAISAL

Investment appraisal involves some or all of the following steps.

Defining the objectives

The objective of the firm is to make profits and/or to satisfy the preferences of its management and or owners. Investments have the same objectives. However, just as the firm has to decide what product to produce, so it has to decide the type of investment projects that will support the goal of making a profit. Projects might be classified as follows:

- Replacement investment: where equipment has to be replaced if production is to continue. Old equipment might not be replaced by similar equipment, but by more up-to-date machinery, enabling the firm to increase efficiency and reduce unit production costs.
- Expansionary investment: where the firm expands its capacity to meet growing demand for its existing products or wishes to produce new products or enter new markets.
- Other investments: such as those required for health and safety or environmental reasons.

Identifying options

Once the objective of an investment programme has been set, the firm or organization can then consider the various ways in which the objective might be met. If the investment is of a simple replacement type, then the range of options may be limited to replacing like with like; otherwise, the rest of the equipment may not work. If the old equipment is to be replaced by more up-to-date equipment, then there may be a broader range of options.

Identifying the costs, benefits, timing and uncertainties of each option

Once each option has been identified, it is necessary to quantify the timing and size of the streams of costs, as well as the revenues accruing as a consequence of the project. For each year of the project, a schedule should be constructed showing the expenditure and expected income. The initial costs of the project may be known with certainty, but the net revenue stream will depend on future economic conditions. It may be necessary either to estimate different streams of revenues depending on projected market conditions or to estimate the likelihood of different conditions prevailing. The prices to be used to value sales have also to be assessed and allowance made for real changes. It is also necessary to identify the length of time during which the project is expected to operate.

Choosing the method of appraisal

Theoretically (as will be shown), the soundest method of appraising a proposed project is by discounted cash flow techniques. However, the data requirements for such analysis may lead managers to use other methods, such as **payback** or the rate of return.

Choosing the cost of capital

The cost of capital is a crucial variable in evaluating projects. The choice of value to represent the opportunity cost of the resources to be used is important as too high or too low a value will distort choice.

Test of viability

When all the information is gathered, projects should be assessed to see whether they are individually worth while and ranked in order of merit. "Worthwhileness" is taken to mean that the expected revenues exceed the expected costs of each project, given the cost of capital.

Presenting the results

The present value of each of the projects should be presented to the decision makers in a form that allows them to rank them in order of desirability to the firm. Information regarding uncertainties in the estimates or crucial assumptions should also be identified.

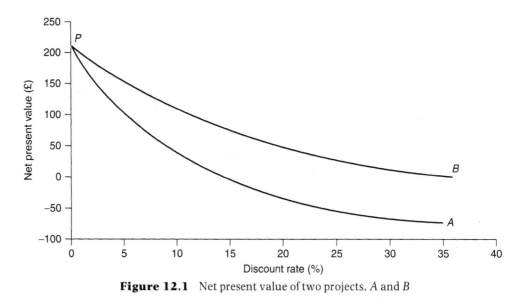

Figure 12.1   Net present value of two projects, *A* and *B*

ESTIMATING CASH FLOWS

For example, if an electricity supplier has decided to build a new power station to meet an expected growth in demand, then the steps outlined above could be implemented as follows. Initially, the alternative technologies available should be considered for similar sized increments in capacity. The costs of undertaking each alternative plan should then be estimated. Once operational, the variable costs of producing electricity including fuel, labour, and management should be estimated based on the expected output together with expected revenues over the anticipated life of the project. For a power station this might be 25 years or more. At the end of its life, there may be significant costs in closing the power station, particularly if it is of the nuclear type. The four key elements in estimating the cash flows of a project are capital costs, operating costs, revenues and decommissioning costs.

Hypothetical data for two projects are presented in Figure 12.1 and Table 12.1. For each project it is assumed that there are capital costs in year 0, followed by expenditures and revenue in the following 10 years of operation and, then, a final expenditure to terminate the project, which in these examples is classified as capital expenditure. The total net cash flow for both projects is £210m, but the timing of the revenue and cost flows is different.

TIME AND THE VALUE OF MONEY

Money is a resource that has value at a particular point in time. Money put aside in a risk-free account in a building society may have an interest rate attached of 10% per annum. In one year a sum of £100 will have increased to £110 (i.e., £100 deposited

Table 12.1 Net cash flows for project *A* and project *B*

Year	Capital cost (£m)	Operating costs (£m)	Revenue (£m)	Net cash flow (£m)
Project A				
0	−150			−150
1		120	100	−20
2		120	120	0
3		125	160	35
4		130	180	50
5		135	185	50
6		130	185	55
7		130	190	60
8		125	190	65
9		115	180	65
10		115	175	60
11	−60			−60
Total	−210	1,245	1,665	210
NPV at 10%				41.04
Project B				
0	−150			−150
1		115	175	60
2		115	180	65
3		125	190	65
4		130	190	60
5		130	185	55
6		135	185	50
7		130	180	50
8		125	160	35
9		120	120	0
10		120	100	−20
11	−60			−60
Total	−210	1,245	1,665	210
NPV at 10%				112.46

Source Author

plus £10 of interest). If the money is kept in the account, then at the end of year 2 the sum would have increased to £121 (i.e., the £110 plus another £11 of interest payments). This kind of accumulation is termed compound interest. It can be expressed as follows:

■ At the start of year 0 a deposit D of £100 is made.
■ After 1 year the terminal value T will be $T = 100 * (1 + 0.1)$ or $T = D(1 + r)$, where the interest rate r is expressed as a decimal.
■ After 2 years the terminal value would be $100 * (1 + r) * (1 + r)$ or $100 * (1 + r)^2 = T = D(1 + r)^2$.
■ After n years the formula to calculate the terminal value would be $T = D(1 + r)^n$.

Therefore, money has a time value with an exchange rate between money now and money in the future. Thus, in our simple example, money now is worth £121 in two years' time or, alternatively, £121 in two years' time is worth £100 now. If a firm is considering borrowing to finance an investment, then it can obtain money now by paying an interest rate of $r\%$ per annum and paying it back out of future earnings. At the end of year 1 the borrower would have to pay back the sum borrowed plus the interest owed. Thus, after one year on a borrowing B of £100 at an interest rate of 10%, £110 would be owed, or, symbolically, $B(1 + r)$. By being willing to pay interest, the rate of exchange between money now and money in the future is established. Thus, in both cases, £100 now is worth £110 one year on. The price of money, whether borrowed or deposited, is the interest rate.

DISCOUNTING AND PRESENT VALUE

Future revenues or costs accruing to the firm as a result of an investment should be adjusted to allow for the value of the time cost of money. This process is known as discounting. To make all sums of money comparable, it is necessary to discount all future inflows and outflows back to the present and calculate what is termed the present value of all the cash flows.

The two projects presented in Table 12.1 have expenditure in year 0, or now, and net cash flows for the next 11 years, which should be expressed in terms of current money. To find the present value of a series of net cash flows, the return for each year is discounted by a factor reflecting the cost of capital and the year in which receipts or costs are recorded. Thus, the net present value of a project in year 0 can be expressed algebraically as follows:

$$\text{NPV} = -K_0 + (S_1 - C_1)/(1 + r) + (S_2 - C_2)/(1 + r)^2$$
$$+ (S_3 - C_3)/(1 + r)^3 + \cdots + (S_n - C_n)/(1 + r)^n - K_n/(1 + r)^n$$

or as:

$$\text{NPV} = \sum_{t=1}^{n}(S_t - C_t)/(1 + r)^t - K_0 - K_n/(1 + r)^n$$

where S_n = sales revenue in year n, C_n = current costs in year n, K = capital cost and r = the discount rate. Assuming r is the firm's cost of capital for all the funds required to finance a project, then it should be undertaken if its net present value is positive (i.e., it adds to the present value of the firm). This rule can be extended to any project the firm is considering; if they all have positive net present values, then they should all be undertaken. Projects having a negative net present value should be rejected because they reduce the future value of the firm.

This process can be illustrated by comparing the two projects in Table 12.1. Both have the same total net cash flows of £210m. On that basis the projects are equally desirable. However, their cash flow time patterns are different. If the two net income streams are discounted at the cost of capital to the firm of 10%, then project A has a net present value of £41.04m and project *B* of £112.46m. Thus, project *B* has a higher net present value than project *A* and is therefore a more highly rated project.

The present value of the two projects will vary with the discount rate used; this is illustrated in Figure 12.1, where the discount rate is plotted on the horizontal axis and the net present value on the vertical axis. Line *PA* shows the net present value of project *A* at a range of discount rates from 0 to 36%. At discount rates up to 15% the project has a positive net present value, but for discount rates in excess of 15% it has negative net present values. Line *PB* shows similar information for project *B*: it has positive net present values for discount rates up to 35% and negative ones thereafter. The line *PB* is after year 0 always above line *PA*, meaning that project *B* has a higher net present value than project *A* whatever the discount rate.

It might not always be the case that one project is superior to another whatever discount rate is used. Figure 12.2 plots the net present value of projects *C* and *D* (lines *PC* and *RD*) whose cash flows are given in Table 12.2. At discount rates up to 9% project *C* is preferred, while at discount rates greater than 9% project *D* is preferred. Thus, at a discount rate of 5% the net present value of projects *C* and *D* is £368.02m and £314.98m, respectively, with project *C* being preferred. At a discount rate of 15% the net present values of projects *C* and *D* is £205.19m and £251.18m respectively, with project *D* being preferred. This comparison demonstrates the importance of the choice of discount rates and the time pattern of the net income stream in determining which project will have the higher net present value. The differences in net present value are accounted for by the time pattern of flows. Project *C* has significant negative returns at the beginning and higher positive returns in later years, so that discounting at higher interest rates has a more significant effect on later returns and on the net present value. Project *D* has lower overall cash returns, but they occur in the early

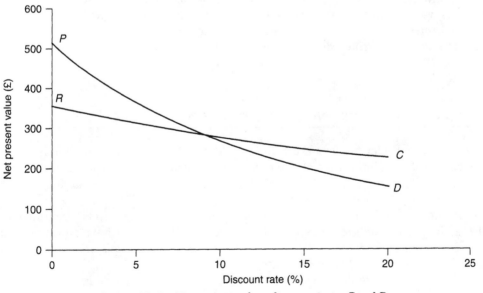

Figure 12.2 Net present value of two projects, *C* and *D*

Table 12.2   Net cash flows of project C and project D

Year	Project C's net cash flow (£m)	Project D's net cash flow (£m)
1	−100	60
2	−100	150
3	80	50
4	70	30
5	60	30
6	50	30
7	50	30
8	50	30
9	50	5
10	50	−60
Total cash flow	510.00	355.00
NPV at 5%	368.02	314.98
NPV at 15%	205.19	251.18

Source Author

years of the project's life and, consequently, become more important the higher the rate of discount used.

Internal rate of return (IRR)

An alternative discounting procedure is to use the internal rate of return; this is the rate of discount that makes the net present value of the cash flow of a project equal to zero. Projects with higher internal rates of return are preferred to projects with lower internal rates of return. Thus, the internal rate of return for project A is 15% and for project B it is 35%. Project B is therefore preferred.

RANKING OF PROJECTS AND THE CAPITAL-SPENDING PLAN

If a large number of projects are being considered, then the decision rule is to rank projects in descending order of their net present value to the firm. Projects with a positive net present value should all be undertaken if there are unlimited funds available at the firm's cost of capital.

If the internal rate of return criterion is used, then projects are ranked in descending order and the firm should undertake all projects that have an internal rate of return greater than the firm's cost of capital. If unlimited funds are available, then all these projects should be implemented.

However, the two criteria do not necessarily rank the projects in the same order because different discount rates are being used, which affects the discounted value of

Table 12.3 Two projects ranked by various criteria

Cash flows	Project E	Project F
Year 0: capital expenditure (£m)	−9,000	−9,000
Year 1: net cash flow (£m)	3,000	6,000
Year 2: net cash flow (£m)	5,000	4,000
Year 3: net cash flow (£m)	6,000	3,000
Net cash flow: years 1 to 3 (£m)	*14,000*	*13,000*
Net present value at 10% (£m)	2,367	2,014
Internal rate of return (%)	22.5	24
Payback (years)	3	2
Accounting annual rate of return (%)	51.9	48.1

Source Author

individual projects; this is illustrated in Table 12.3 when comparing project E with project F. Using the internal rate of return, project F is preferred to project E; but, using the net present value, project E is preferred to project F.

A second problem with the internal rate of return is that certain cash flow streams generate two values; this may occur where the flows are initially negative, then positive and then negative again. Thus, the preferred method for ranking projects is the net present value procedure using the firm's cost of capital as the discount rate.

In practice, the objections to using discounted cash flow methods to evaluate investment projects lie in their comprehensive nature, enormous data requirements and complex calculations. The method requires the project to be defined in its entirety with estimates of the cash flows for each year; this may give an impression of spurious accuracy, whereas the resulting value is only as good as the assumptions and data used. These problems can be overcome by the use of sensitivity analysis (see p. 252), but such arguments tend to lead managers to reject discounted cash flow procedures and to use alternative methods.

NON-DISCOUNTING METHODS OF INVESTMENT APPRAISAL

Two methods are often used by businesses, in practice: the payback method and the accounting rate of return. Neither of these methods takes into account the timing of cash flows or the time value of resources. Both methods can be explained by reference to Table 12.3.

The payback method calculates the time in years or months that projects have to run before they cover their original capital outlay. Thus, in Table 12.3 project E has a payback of 3 years: that is, it takes 3 years to accumulate £9,000 of net income to meet the capital costs. For project 2 the payback period is only 2 years to cover the original outlay. The decision rule is to prefer projects having the shorter payback period. Alternatively, the firm may have a cut-off payback period so that all projects with a payback period less than the norm will be accepted, while projects with a payback period longer than the norm are rejected.

The main criticisms of the payback method are that it ignores all benefits beyond the payback period and does not discount the cash flows. If the payback period is very short, such as 2 years, discounting may have little effect on the discounted cash values and cause very few changes in decisions. The more serious criticism is that it ignores all returns after the payback period. Thus, projects with significant benefits in later years will never be undertaken. It leads firms to adopt very short-time horizons for projects and to consider only those that repay their capital expenditure very quickly. Significant and worthwhile projects for the firm may be rejected because they take more than a few years to return benefits.

The second method is the accounting rate of return; this is calculated by adding total net cash returns and dividing by the initial capital outlay and the number of years. In Table 12.3 the total net cash flow for project E is £14,000 or £4,666 per annum, giving an annual accounting rate of return of 51.9%. For project F the accounting rate of return is 48.1%; therefore, project E is preferred to project F. In terms of the capital programme the firm should undertake all projects that have a rate of return greater than the firm's cost of capital. This method takes into account all the cash flows but ignores their time pattern. It is also said to utilize a rate of return that businessmen understand more easily than discounted net cash flow or even the payback method.

CAPITAL RATIONING AND THE CAPITAL-SPENDING PLAN

So far, we have assumed that the firm will undertake all projects that have a positive net present value at the firm's cost of capital. The relative size of projects has not been considered, as all projects should in theory be undertaken. However, many firms restrict their capital budget to a given sum of money. If this is the case, then all projects cannot be undertaken and some criterion is required to rank them, so that the most desirable are undertaken first. The recommended rule is that projects should be ranked by the ratio of net cash flow to initial capital expenditure to take account of the relative size of the projects under consideration.

In Table 12.4, there are three projects that are initially ranked by their net present

Table 12.4 Ranking of projects by various criteria

Project	Capital expenditure per unit of capital (£m)	Net present value (£m)	Rank of net present value	Net present value per unit of capital	Rank of net present value per unit of capital
G	120	70	2	0.58	2
H	80	60	3	0.75	1
J	200	90	1	0.45	3

Source Author

value; this would rank the projects in the order *J*, *G* and *H*. To undertake all these projects would require a total expenditure of £400m. With a budget restricted to £200m, all three projects could not be undertaken. The recommended procedure is to rank projects in order of net present value divided by capital outlay; this gives a ranking of *H*, *G* and *J*. The firm then proceeds down the new rankings until the budget is exhausted. Thus, in Table 12.4 the firm undertakes projects *H* and *G* and then exhausts the budget; this gives the firm a total net present value of £160m, whereas if the £200m had been spent on project *J*, then the firm would have achieved a net present value of only £90m.

INCORPORATING RISK AND UNCERTAINTY

Investment decisions are about the future and thus are surrounded by uncertainty. Estimates of future costs and revenues are to a greater or lesser extent "guesstimates" about future outcomes. Even an umbrella manufacturer in the UK faces uncertainties: some years are less rainy than others and occasionally a drought occurs. There are also uncertainties about the reactions of rivals. It is not unknown for two firms working independently to make significant additions to capacity at the same time, both working on the assumption that they are the only enterprise making such a decision.

The main sources of uncertainty are changes in market conditions affecting revenue and cost streams; these may arise from:

- Changes in consumer tastes.
- The introduction of new products, making existing ones obsolete.
- Changing the relative prices of products and inputs.
- Oversupply of the market because of too much investment.
- Increase in the cost of hiring factors of production because of shortages in supply.
- New production technologies making the plant obsolete.
- The use of unsound data, misinterpretation of data and bias in their assessment.

A simple illustration of such effects can be shown in a simple matrix. The two factors considered are favourable or unfavourable market conditions and the acceptability of the firm's product *vis-à-vis* its rivals; this is illustrated in Table 12.5, where discounted net cash flows vary from £1,500 in the most favourable conditions to −£400 in the least favourable. The problem for the management of the firm is in deciding which of these outcomes is most likely to occur. If the management believes that its product is an excellent example of its kind, then it will consider the two positive options, £1,500 or £400. If the product proves to be less acceptable than the firm expects, then it will consider either a positive £200 or a negative −£400 outcome. Most managers would back its own products, though there are many industries, such as the motor industry, which have launched models with great hopes, only to find that consumers do not reciprocate management's enthusiasm.

Table 12.5 Discounted net cash flow under different business conditions (£m)

Product acceptability	Market conditions	
	Favourable	Unfavourable
High	1,500	400
Low	200	−400

Source Author

COPING WITH UNCERTAINTY

The impact of uncertainty on an investment project can be dealt with in two ways: adjusting the net benefits or the discount rate.

Adjusting net benefits or expected net present value

Although we are dealing with uncertainty the decision maker could decide which of the potential outcomes are most likely or least likely to occur; this calls for decision makers to attach not probabilities but estimates of likelihoods to future events; these are not objective, like probabilities which are derived from past events, but subjective, reflecting the knowledge or expectations of those making the decision. To some extent this calls for decision makers to back their judgement, for they will inevitably mark up those scenarios that reflect their commitment and belief in the project and mark down those that put the project in a bad light.

If likelihood values can be attached to outcomes, then calculations of expected values can be made. The net cash flows for each year are derived with a likelihood value attached. Each possible outcome is weighted according to the likelihood of it occurring and an average return derived by adding the individual sums together. In addition, the dispersion of returns can also be observed by measuring variance and standard deviation (see Chapter 3 for the method of calculation).

In Table 12.6 both projects L and M have the same expected value of £340. However, the dispersion of returns for both projects is significantly different. Project L has a narrow range of positive returns, whereas project M has a wider range of returns from negative to positive. Two measures of dispersion – variance and standard deviation – are calculated; These both show that project L is less uncertain or risky than M because these measures are lower for project L than M.

Sensitivity analysis

Another way of coping with uncertainty is to identify key variables and check the sensitivity of measured net benefits to changes in their values. Such variables might

Table 12.6 Estimating the impact of uncertainty (£)

Project L		Project M	
Possible outcomes	Likelihood of each outcome	Possible outcomes	Likelihood of each outcome
(O)	(L)	(O)	(L)
100	0.2	−400	0.2
200	0.2	200	0.2
400	0.4	400	0.4
600	0.2	1,100	0.2
Total	1.0	Total	1.0
Expected value	340		340
Variance	30,400		230,400
Standard deviation	174.4		480

Source Author

include price, sales, labour and raw material costs. For example, when oil prices are high there is increasing interest in the potential of alternative energy sources. The price of oil is a critical variable in assessing the value of energy from biomass. Low oil prices would threaten the viability of a biomass project, while high prices would enhance it. The solution is to identify a range of values for key variables and then calculate the outcomes for all combinations of inputs and outputs. Likelihood values could be attached to the various prices and cost levels chosen, so that a wide range of outcomes may be narrowed down for analytical purposes.

Should the project under consideration be concerned with converting straw or sugar cane into oil, then the sensitive variables might be the availability of straw or sugar cane, the cost of collecting and delivering it to plants and the price of oil. If straw and sugar cane are currently burnt in the fields, then it implies that they have no alternative uses and, therefore, no value. However, they may only be available seasonally and be expensive to collect and deliver to the plant. The viability of the plant would depend on the acceptability of the substitute product, its price and the price of the crude oil alternative. If the new product's price is greater than an oil price of, say, $35 a barrel, then the project generates positive net present values and negative ones when the price is less; clearly, the project is only likely to be viable if oil is greater than $35 a barrel.

The sensitivity of the net present value of the project to the price of oil is illustrated in Figure 12.3, where the oil price is measured on the vertical axis and net present value is on the horizontal axis. Decision makers would have to take a view about the price of crude oil. If they believe it will always be in excess of $35, then the project should be considered further; if the price is always expected to be below $35, then the project should be forgotten.

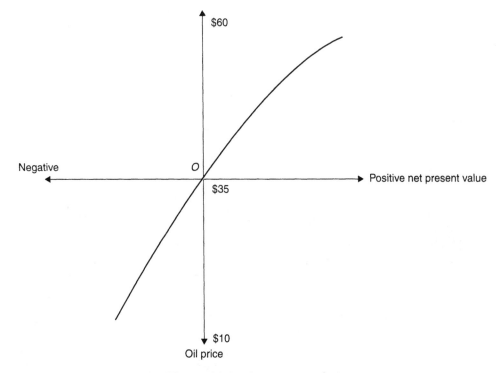

Figure 12.3   Sensitivity analysis

Simulation of returns

Simulation models attempt to assess the impact of changes in key variables. Combinations of price and cost are randomly made to produce net revenue data. With likelihoods attached to the possibility of each price or cost occurring, a distribution of possible outcomes is generated (Hertz 1964). These data can then be used to generate a range of potential cash flows with associated likelihoods. Expected values, variance and standard deviation can then be measured for any project. The result is that the decision maker is presented not with a single pay-off, but a variety of payoffs with the likelihoods of occurrence attached.

A simple example of generating an expected value curve for a single time period is demonstrated in Table 12.7. In Table 12.7(a) the matrix shows 4 prices and 4 costs, with the likelihood that each may occur independently. If we then combine each individual price and cost, there are 16 possible outcomes, with a likelihood of occurrence attached; these are shown in Table 12.7(b). We assume a simple demand price relationship, so that 150 units are sold at a price of £10, 120 units at a price of £20, 100 units at a price of £30 and 80 units at a price of £40. Profit/Losses per unit are shown in column 4 and total profits (sales × unit profit) are shown in the final column of Table 12.7(b). Some profit levels occur more than once. If we combine the individual likelihoods of each level of profit occurring, then we have the number of times each profit will occur (Table 12.7(c)). Thus, in 16 out of every 100 occasions,

Table 12.7 Simulation model of profitability

(a) *Matrix of price, cost, likelihoods and profit margins*

Cost	Price	10 0.1	20 0.4	30 0.4	40 0.1
			Profit margins		
10	0.1	0	10	20	30
15	0.4	−5	5	15	25
20	0.4	−10	0	10	20
25	0.1	−15	−5	5	15

(b) *Profit outcomes and likelihoods*

Likelihood	Price	Cost	Profit per unit	Sales	Total profit
0.01	10	10	0	150	0
0.04	10	15	−5	150	−750
0.04	10	20	−10	150	−1,500
0.01	10	25	−15	150	−2,250
0.04	20	10	10	120	1,200
0.16	20	15	5	120	600
0.16	20	20	0	120	0
0.04	20	25	−5	120	−600
0.04	30	10	20	100	2,000
0.16	30	15	15	100	1,500
0.16	30	20	10	100	1,000
0.04	30	25	5	100	500
0.01	40	10	30	80	2,400
0.04	40	15	25	80	2,000
0.04	40	20	20	80	1,600
0.01	40	25	15	80	1,200

(c) *Number of occurrences of profit level*

Occurrences	Profit
1	−2,250
4	−1,500
4	−750
4	−600
17	0
4	500
16	600
16	1,000
5	1,200
16	1,500
4	1,600
8	2,000
1	2,400
Expected value	687.5
Standard deviation	918.9

Source Author

profits of £1,000 are expected to occur. Overall losses will occur 13 times in 100 occasions, and positive profits will occur 70 times in every 100. The mean is £687.5 and the standard deviation is 918.9.

Adjusted discount rate

A third method posited to account for uncertainty is to adjust the discount rate. The greater the uncertainty the higher the discount rate. Higher discount rates discriminate against more distant cash flows and favour earlier cash flows, as they give greater weight to early returns, making them appear more certain to decision makers than later returns.

In financial markets the interest rate increases the more risky or uncertain are the projects or clients. However, this is not the kind of uncertainty involved with investment projects, as they revolve around cash flows and not around the cost of capital. The problem is how to determine an appropriate premium for each and every project.

Shortening the payback period

A final method to account for uncertainty is to shorten the payback period from, say, 4 to 2 years to cope with risk and uncertainty; this implies that net cash flows are reasonably certain in the first two years but are more uncertain thereafter.

THE COST OF CAPITAL

The investment appraisal techniques discussed in this chapter generally use the cost of capital to the firm as the test to see whether a project should be undertaken. Therefore, it is important that the cost of capital is measured appropriately. The use of a discount rate lower than the firm's true cost of capital would result in overinvestment, in the sense that the marginal benefits of marginal projects would be less than the marginal cost of undertaking them at the true cost of capital. The use of a discount rate higher than the firm's true cost of capital would lead to too few projects being undertaken because the marginal benefits of rejected projects is greater than their marginal costs at the true cost of capital.

Until now we have assumed a single cost of capital to the firm that reflects the marginal cost of borrowing any quantity of funds. In practice, the firm would face a rising cost of capital curve that increases the more money it wishes to borrow and a downward-sloping returns curve as more and more investments are undertaken. In Figure 12.4 the optimal level of investment is OD at a cost of capital OR (i.e., where the returns and cost of capital curves intersect at point E).

Sources of funds

In practice, the funds available to a firm to finance investment can come from either internal or external sources. Internal sources of funds include retained profits and

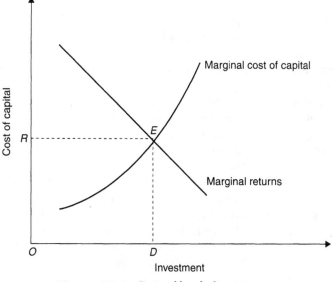

Figure 12.4   Optimal level of investment

funds set aside to meet depreciation charges. Such sources have no direct or accounting cost attached to them, but it is important that the opportunity cost of these sources should be estimated. External sources of funds include debt capital or bonds, equity or share capital and bank or other loans, such as from government agencies. External sources generally have an interest rate attached to their use, though this is not strictly true of equity capital where the payment of dividends depends on the profitability of the firm. Nevertheless, equity funds have an opportunity cost to the shareholder.

Cost of debt capital (R_D)

In order to obtain debt capital the firm has to pay an interest rate that will induce potential lenders to supply money to the firm. Given that there is a bond or securities market, the cost will be the market interest rate. If we allow for the variations in risks associated with individual firms, then the appropriate measure is the effective interest rate that the firm has to pay to secure its loans. The effective rate of interest for debt already issued is the coupon rate relative to the market price for the security. Thus, if a £100 bond is issued at 5%, then the effective interest rate is 10% if the current price is £50 (i.e., paying £50 earns £5 or 10%). If the price is £200, then the effective rate of interest would be 2.5%. This rate would indicate the minimum rate that the firm would have to pay to issue new debt. Whether it would have to pay a higher rate of interest would depend on the proportion of the firm's capital that is in the form of debt and the project for which the funds are to be used. If interest costs can be offset against tax, then the cost of borrowed money is $R_D = r(1 - t)$, where $R_D = $ is the cost of borrowing debt to the organization, $r = $ the interest rate paid and $t = $ the marginal tax rate.

Cost of equity (R_E)

If the firm raises funds through the issue of new equity capital, then the purchaser of the equity will expect to receive dividends equivalent to the risk-free rate of interest plus a **risk premium**. The current price of equity will reflect the discounted value of future dividends.

The risk-free rate of interest plus a risk premium is justified as follows. A lender requires a rate of return to compensate for the loss of consumption foregone by investing in equity (R_F). Since equities are risky investments a risk premium is also required (R_R). The required rate of return would be ($R_F + R_R$). The premium is paid because investing in a company's equity is riskier than government securities, as dividends can vary and there is always a chance of losing the sum invested if the company goes bankrupt. If a comparison is made with debt or bonds, then there is again greater risk because bond holders are more important creditors than the holders of equity. The firm has a legal duty to pay interest on bonds but has no duty to pay dividends. If the firm goes bankrupt, and bond holders are first in line for payment, equity holders last. Thus, if the risk-free interest rate is 5% and the equity premium is 8%, then the expected cost of equity would be 13%.

An alternative explanation for the cost of equity is the dividend evaluation model. Assuming the investor has full information, the value of a share is equal to the discounted value of future expected future dividends, or:

$$PV = \sum_{t=1}^{n} D_t/(1 + r_i)^t$$

where D_t = the dividend per share per year (assumed to be constant) and r_i = the investor's discount rate.

THE RISK PREMIUM AND THE DISCOUNT RATE FOR CAPITAL INVESTMENT

If a project is risk-free, then the appropriate discount rate is the risk-free rate of interest that is earned on UK government bonds, particularly Treasury bills. Capital investments are inevitably risky; therefore, a discount rate incorporating risk is one way a company can account for the uncertainty in a project (as suggested in the previous section). One explanation of the premium is contained in the Capital Asset Pricing Model (CAPM)

Capital Asset Pricing Model (CAPM)

The CAPM is used to include the risk of individual projects in the cost of capital (Sharpe 1962). The model suggests that the appropriate discount rate should consist of two components: the risk-free rate of interest and a premium based on the way the project's returns vary compared with those for the overall market.

If we assume an investor holds a portfolio of financial assets, then one consisting of one equity holding is riskier than one consisting of two equity holdings, as the volatility of returns to one share may be offset by the returns to another. An individual could lower company-specific risks by purchasing a diversified portfolio of shares, even though the overall equity market risk still exists.

The risk of holding equity can be broken into two elements of risk: company and market- related. Market-related risks cannot be avoided by investors, so they require a higher rate of return to compensate them for accepting it. Market risk is measured by the **beta coefficient**, which is measured as follows:

- When an individual firm's equity returns move in line with the returns on all shares in the market, the value of beta is equal to 1.
- When returns on the firm's equity vary more than the return on all shares in the market, the value of beta exceeds 1. A beta of 1.5 means a company's returns move up or down by 1.5% for each 1% move in the market.
- When the returns on the firm's equity vary less than the return on all shares, then the beta value is less than 1. A beta value of 0.5% means that the company's returns will move only 0.5% for every 1% move in the market.

The risk-adjusted discount rate is calculated as follows:

$$R_E = R_F + \beta(R_M - R_F)$$

where R_E = the risk-adjusted rate, R_F = the risk-free rate, R_M = the expected return on a portfolio of assets and β = the systematic risk (beta) for the specific project.

The resulting required rate of return is then used for discounting the net cash flows of any project.

The risk-adjusted discount rate shows how the expected return on equity is related to the riskiness of the assets. Thus, $(R_M - R_F)$ is the market risk premium or the risk premium on the average stock. Thus, if $R_M = 15\%$, $R_F = 10\%$ and $B = 0.5$, then the capital cost of equity (R_E) is given by:

$$K_E = 10 + 0.5(15 - 10) = 12.5\%$$

and if $B = 1.5$, then:

$$R_E = 10 + 1.5(15 - 10) = 17.5\%$$

The weighted cost of capital

Assuming a firm finances an investment using internal funds, debt and equity, it is argued that this cost should reflect the weighted average of both sources. Thus, the weighted cost (R_T) is given by:

$$R_T = W_I R_I + W_D R_D + W_E R_E$$

where R_T = the composite cost of capital for the firm, W_I = the proportion of finance represented by internal funds, R_I = the cost of internal funds, W_D = the proportion of finance represented by debt, R_D = the cost of debt, W_E = the proportion of finance represented by equity and R_E = the cost of equity.

Thus, if the ratio between internal funding, debt and equity is $20:20:60$ and the comparative cost of each source of capital is 8, 10 and 15%, then the weighted average cost of capital would be:

$$(0.08 * 0.2) + (0.10 * 0.20) + (0.15 * 0.6) = 0.126 \qquad \text{or} \qquad 12.6\%$$

The optimal choice of capital structure to fund an investment depends on market conditions and the degree of risk attached to the firm's activities. The firm should choose the combination of internal financing, debt financing and equity financing that minimizes the overall weighted average cost of capital. The advantage of internal funds and debt capital is that they are less costly than equity. A firm will use internal financing if that option is open to it. For debt, interest has to be paid as a prior charge on the firm's income. While equity is more expensive, its advantage is that dividends do not have to be paid if profits are not made. However, the cost of equity increases the higher the ratio of debt to equity in the firm's total funding.

CAPITAL BUDGETING IN LARGE BRITISH BUSINESSES

Surveys of the use of capital investment procedures in British firms have shown that they tend to use simpler techniques in preference to discounting methods. This was confirmed by Mills (1988) who found that the most widely used technique in British enterprises was the payback method and the second was the accounting rate of return. Where firms used discounted cash flow techniques, they preferred the internal rate of return method to the net present value method. He also found that great emphasis was laid on the importance of qualitative judgements by senior managers and that sophisticated methods for calculating the impact of risk and uncertainty were not widely used. Similarly, Pike (1982) reported that theoretically superior methods were not widely used and that only 17% of firms in the sample used net present value as their main method of appraisal, though 57% used discounted cash flow techniques. Only 54% of firms looked beyond 2 years in their analysis of investments, and only 37% of firms analysed risk and uncertainty systematically. The preference for simple techniques and qualitative or judgemental decision making is based on the uncertainty surrounding the data used in appraisal, which is a function of the future state of the product and input markets.

Case Study 12.1   Assessing the Concorde programme

The difficulties involved in making investment decisions can be illustrated using the Concorde supersonic passenger aeroplane programme; this had started as far back as 1956 and became an Anglo-French joint venture in November 1962. The first prototype flew in 1969. The first planes went into service on 21 January 1976, operated by Air France and British Airways, and were withdrawn from service in October 2003.

A conventional commercial investment appraisal requires the quantification of expected cost and revenue flows over the life of the project. Concorde was not a purely commercial proposition and had the support, financially and politically, of the British and French governments. In addition the major players were state-owned enterprises.

Costs

The development of a new aeroplane involves incurring research and development costs as well as production costs. Henderson (1977) estimated the expenditure on development between 1962 and 1976 to be £496m and production/launch costs between 1967 and 1976 to be £203m. With other costs of £54m this gave total expenditure of £699m.

The costs of making each Concorde were a function of the production run. A production run of 50 aircraft was estimated in 1974 to result in average production costs per plane of £15.5m and average total costs, including R and D, to be £34.9m. A production run of 300 would reduce these costs to £11.4m and £14.6m, respectively (OU, 1974, p. 19).

Revenue

The revenue side of the equation depended on how many aircraft would be sold. The case for buying the aircraft for use on longer routes was the shorter journey times and the potential for charging premium fares to those using the service. As a result, orders or options were placed for 74 aircraft from 16 airlines around the world (www.concorde sst.com). Long-term sales were expected to reach around 260 aircraft. Because of the great uncertainty surrounding sales, revenue flows were calculated on sales varying between say 100 and 300 planes; this was done in the Open University study where the planes were estimated to have a selling price of £13m (OU, 1974).

Net cash flows

On the basis of these assumptions, the net cash flows for the period 1972 to 1980 were estimated as follows:

Year	Sales of 100 (£m)	Sales of 200 (£m)	Sales of 300 (£m)
1972	−30	−30	−30
1973	−60	−60	−60
1974	−60	−80	−60
1975	−60	−40	−80
1976	−30	10	−20
1977	10	60	30
1978	10	90	80
1979			120
1980			70
NPV at 10%	−188	−135	−49

Source   Compiled by author using extracts from OU (1974, tables 3 and 4)

These data, which ignore earlier expenditure, suggest that the project would not be commercially viable even with the most optimistic sales figure. Henderson (1977) estimated the net present value of prospective returns between 1977 and 1981, discounted at 10%, to be −£138m.

Therefore, as a commercial project Concorde looked to be high-risk. It went ahead only because of the support of the French and British governments who envisaged wider benefits to their economies from the project (see Chapter 25 for a discussion of cost–benefit analysis and Woolley 1972).

Concorde in practice

The negative expectations when the decision to go ahead was taken were confirmed by later events. Although the aircraft was widely admired for its looks and gracefulness and was a success in the services operated, it had a number of limitations in terms of its flight range, heavy fuel consumption and operating costs estimated to be 70% greater than those for the Boeing 747. Opposition to the plane also came from communities because of sonic boom and environmental concerns. The decision by the US Congress to end funding of the US version, despite the opposition of President Nixon, also had adverse effects. While this made Concorde a monopoly supplier of supersonic passenger aircraft, it also helped to dissuade airlines from converting options to firm orders.

In the end only 20 Concordes were built, including prototypes. British Airways and Air France were the only airlines to purchase the aircraft, initially purchasing 5 and 4 respectively. The remainder of the aircraft later ended in the BA and Air France fleets and were purchased for £1/1 Franc each. Therefore, sales never reached the expected levels, making the project unsuccessful in commercial terms.

Concorde in service was apparently able to cover its operating costs and contribute to the profits of the two airlines. The planes continued operating transatlantic services until July 2000 when they were withdrawn following an accident in Paris in which 109 people died. Services were resumed in November 2001. However, passenger levels were lower than expected; this, combined with increasing maintenance costs of the ageing planes, led to the decision to withdraw them from service in October 2003.

CHAPTER SUMMARY

This chapter explored techniques for appraising investments, including discounting methods and payback. It also examined ways of incorporating uncertainty into the appraisal and factors influencing the determination of the cost of capital or discount rate. In doing this we analysed:

- Discounted cash flow methods, which are considered to be theoretically superior to such techniques as payback; however, in practice the latter are more often used. The reason lies in the nature of investment appraisal; this requires the comparison of the costs of undertaking the investment with forecasts of future revenues and costs. These latter estimates may be the result of qualitative judgements and market knowledge or more sophisticated methods of analysis.
- The key to successful investment appraisal, which may be the extent to which net cash flow estimates are realized, rather than the sophistication of the appraisal techniques used.
- The alternative view that superior methods should be used irrespective of the quality of the data, as the use of such methods will lead to better choices in any

given situation. In practice, it is important to use the correct method, to make the best estimates of future net cash flows and to be aware of the uncertainties attached to them.

REVIEW QUESTIONS

1 Explain the notion of the "time value" of money. Why does it lead to the discounting of future cash flows?
2 Explain the concepts of net present value and the internal rate of return of a series of net cash flows. Demonstrate their calculation. Which technique should be the preferred methodology for appraising investments?
3 What is the payback method of investment appraisal? How might the payback period be determined? What are its main shortcomings in appraising investment expenditure? Why is the payback method preferred by many firms to appraise investment proposals?
4 Why should discounted cash flow methods be used in preference to more traditional methods, such as payback and the accounting rate of return?
5 If the firm has access to unlimited funds at a given cost of capital, how should it rank projects using payback and net cash flow? If the firm faces a situation of capital rationing, how would the firm alter the ranking of projects?
6 Given the uncertainty in predicting future cash flows, why should a firm adopt anything other than a simplistic appraisal rule?
7 How should a firm measure its marginal cost of capital?
8 Explain the CAPM approach to measuring the cost of capital.
9 Evaluate the various approaches to dealing with the problem of uncertainty in appraising investment proposals.
10 Using the following data for project A and B:
   - Calculate the net present value for each project, assuming a cost of capital of 15%.
   - Calculate the internal rate of return for each project.
   - Which project should the firm choose based on using net present value and the internal rate of return?
   - If the cost of capital were to increase to 20%, would project A or B be preferred?

Year	Project A's net cash flow	Project B's net cash flow
0	−1,000	−1,000
1	500	100
2	450	100
3	400	100
4	300	150
5	200	250
6	150	350
7	150	450
8	150	500
9	100	500
10	100	−600

REFERENCES AND FURTHER READING

Allen, D. (1991) *Economic Evaluation of Projects* (3rd edn). Institution of Chemical Engineers, London.

Brewster, D. (1997) Investment and financing decisions. *Business Economics* (Chapter 12). Dryden Press, London.

Bromwich, M. (1976) *The Economics of Capital Budgeting*. Penguin, Harmondsworth, UK.

Dimson, E. (1995) The capital asset pricing model. *Financial Times*, Mastering Management Part 4, 7–8.

Douglas, E.J. (1992) Capital budgeting and investment decisions. *Managerial Economics* (4th edn, Chapter 15). Prentice Hall, Englewood Cliffs, NJ.

Farkas, A. (1995) Project approval: The key criteria. *Financial Times*, Mastering Management Part 2, 13–14.

Habib, M. (1995) The importance of capital structure. *Financial Times*, Mastering Management Part 4, 9–10.

Hawkins, C. and D.W. Pearce (1971) *Capital Investment Appraisal*. Macmillan, London.

Henderson, P.D. (1977) Two British errors: Their probable sizes and some possible lessons. *Oxford Economic Papers*, **20**(2), 159–205.

Hertz, D.B. (1964) Risk analysis in capital investment. *Harvard Business Review*, January/February, **42**(1), 95–105.

Hertz, D.B. (1968) Investment policies that pay off. *Harvard Business Review*, January/February, **46**(1), 96–108.

Hertz, D.B. (1979) Risk analysis in capital investment. *Harvard Business Review*, **57**, September/October, **57**(6), 161–181.

Mills, R.W. (1988) Capital budgeting – The state of the art. *Long Range Planning*, **21**(4), 76–81.

Modigliani, F. and F. Miller (1958) The cost of capital, corporation finance and the theory of investment. *American Economic Review*, **48**(2), 261–297.

OU (1974) *Microeconomics*, Vol. 6, *Case Studies*. Open University Press, Milton Keynes, UK.

Pike, R.H. (1982) *Capital Budgeting for the 1980s*. Chartered Institute of Management Accountants, London.

Pike, R.H. and M.B. Wolfe (1988) *Capital Budgeting for the 1990s*. Chartered Institute of Management Accountants, London.

Sharpe. W.F. (1962) A simplified model for portfolio analysis. *Management Science*, **9**, 277–293.

Whigham, D. (2001) Investment appraisal. *Managerial Economics Using Excel* (Chapter 10). Thomson Learning, London.

Woolley, P.K. (1972) A cost-benefit analysis of the Concorde project. *Journal of Transport Economics*, **6**(3), 225–239.

PART V

STRATEGIC DECISIONS: THE GROWTH AND DEVELOPMENT OF THE FIRM

THE ENTREPRENEUR AND THE DEVELOPMENT OF THE FIRM

CHAPTER OUTLINE

CHAPTER OBJECTIVES

This chapter aims to explore the nature and role of entrepreneurship within the firm. At the end of this chapter you should be able to:

◆ Identify the main characteristics of entrepreneurship.
◆ Explain the main roles played by entrepreneurs in a dynamic market economy and within the firm.
◆ Analyse the role of entrepreneurs in starting new enterprises.
◆ Explain the difficulties new firms face in surviving.

INTRODUCTION

Although the firm is the central focus of this book, little has been said of how firms are created, why they exist and what factors determine their boundaries. In the neoclassical economic theories of the firm, examined in earlier chapters, the firm is essentially conceived as a production system and the role of owner-controllers is to make decisions that maximize the owner's profits. In these models the decision maker of the firm is presumed also to be an entrepreneur in the sense that the firm is created as a result of his willingness to bear risk and his perception of profitable opportunities. In this chapter we concentrate on the nature and role of the entrepreneur in creating and re-shaping firms.

ENTREPRENEURSHIP

Entrepreneurship tends to refer to what entrepreneurs do. Entrepreneurs are initiators, not imitators, putting into place new production techniques, introducing new products, and starting new firms. They look for profitable opportunities, are willing to accept the risks involved in testing their ideas and shift resources in response to opportunities. Entrepreneurship is sometimes considered to be the fourth factor of production, after land, labour and capital. An economy requires an agent to bring together the other three factors in the production process (i.e., to undertake a co-ordination role, once a decision has been made as to which product or service to produce). Therefore, entrepreneurs are central actors in both firms and markets and at the same time they help the market economy to function by shifting resources to new uses that have higher productivity and potential profits in response to price signals. Many metaphors are used to describe entrepreneurship. Hyrsky (2000) identified 40 of them and of these he identified "five conceptual dimensions of entrepreneurship"; these were "work commitment and energy, economic values and results, innovativeness and risk taking, ambition and achievement and egotistic features" (Hyrsky 2000, p. 18). Of these dimensions, economists have tended to concentrate on the roles and functions of entrepreneurs as innovators and risk takers and neglected the nature and motivation of individuals who engage in entrepreneurship.

ECONOMIC DEVELOPMENTS

There is no simple definition in economics of the term "entrepreneur". It is translated from the French word *entreprendre* "to undertake", as in someone who undertakes or initiates a project. Thus, entrepreneurs are responsible for the creation of firms and seeing a project from its perception as an idea through to its creation, development and subsequent use. Entrepreneurs also engage in risk bearing, arbitrage and co-ordinating activities.

The study of entrepreneurship in the economy has been mainly the preserve of economists operating outside the main neoclassical school; this is explained partly by the fact that these traditional models assume certainty of information and rational decision making. In such static models, decision makers respond to freely available price signals and are sometimes described as being entrepreneurless because of the absence of uncertainty. Economists have identified and emphasized various aspects of the role of entrepreneurs in a market economy; together, these give a rounded picture of their roles and activities.

Schumpeter (1934) viewed "entrepreneurship" as the creation of new enterprises and entrepreneurs as the individuals who undertook such tasks. Schumpeter not only considered independent businessmen to be entrepreneurs, but any individual who fulfilled the role whether being an employee of a company or not. He does not include as entrepreneurs the heads of firms who merely operate an established business. He distinguishes between being enterprising and entrepreneurial, on the one hand, and being an administrator or manager, on the other. Entrepreneurs create new organizations to pursue new opportunities, while managers run and co-ordinate activities in existing businesses. Entrepreneurs can be found in existing firms, where they pursue new ideas, create new divisions and set new directions for the firm. Entrepreneurs are not necessarily inventors nor are they necessarily risk bearers, since inventors often see no economic role for their idea and risk can be borne by venture capitalists.

To Schumpeter the entrepreneur is an extraordinary and heroic person, an individual of great energy, a revolutionary and innovator, someone who overturns tried-and-tested conventions to produce novel solutions to problems. He was concerned to analyse economic processes in dynamic rather than static markets. The economy consists of growing and declining markets and firms, and it is in these conditions of disequilibrium that opportunities arise that attract the attention of entrepreneurs. Thus, entrepreneurs as a group help to bring about change and disequilibrium as a consequence of their actions, which include:

- Introducing new goods.
- Introducing new methods of production.
- Creating new markets.
- Identifying new sources of supply of raw materials and/or intermediate products.
- Forming new enterprises to compete with existing ones.

Knight (1921) emphasized the importance of uncertainty in the economy. It is in conditions of uncertainty that entrepreneurs have the ability to foresee favourable patterns of change that generate profitable opportunities for those who are able to see them and who have the resources available to exploit them. This Knight viewed entrepreneurs as bearers of uncertainty who are rewarded for having borne it.

In an uncertain world, choices are made between rival courses of action, none of which can be fully specified or actualized. Shackle (1984) argued that entrepreneurs have a creative imagination, so that they choose courses of action by comparing the imagined consequences of different actions. A path-breaking new product requires an entrepreneur to have a vision of the new market, including the number of potential customers and their willingness to buy at different prices. Entrepreneurs make decisions on the basis of their assumed conditions prevailing. If they do, then the decision is seen to be successful and profitable; if not then it is seen to be unsuccessful and possibly loss-making.

Casson (1982) introduced the concept of entrepreneurial judgement, "An entrepreneur is defined as someone who specialises in taking judgemental decisions about the allocation of scarce resources" (Casson 1982, p. 23). The essence of a judgemental decision is one, "where different individuals, sharing the same objectives and acting under similar circumstances, would make different decisions" (Casson 1982, p. 24). Two individuals with the same objectives and the same information about the future would likely arrive at different decisions because they have different perceptions of the information and the opportunities. Thus, one individual would see a profitable opportunity, while another would see an unprofitable opportunity not worth pursuing. For example, television in the UK was essentially provided "free" to the population until the advent of satellite and digital subscription television. With the availability of new technology requiring viewers to pay to watch, one individual might see this as an opportunity to establish subscription television, whereas another might dismiss the whole notion of consumers paying for television while "free" television continued to be provided. In the UK, Sky TV hired space on the Astra satellite owned by the country of Luxembourg to transmit programmes to the UK. By offering specialist sport and film channels, Sky has persuaded a growing proportion of households to install the necessary equipment and pay a subscription to watch these programmes. Being first in pay TV appears to have given Sky a significant advantage over later entrants.

Another role of the entrepreneur is to start new firms by making use of new production and technological innovations; this was recognized by Coase (1991) who argued that firms, "come into existence when the direction of resources is dependent on an entrepreneur" (p. 22). The creation of new firms is a significant activity of entrepreneurs and involves bringing together and co-ordinating all the necessary resources.

Kirzner (1973) placed less importance on uncertainty and more on the alertness of entrepreneurs to opportunities for making profit; this is the main motivating force for individuals to engage in entrepreneurship. To be alert to opportunities, the entrepreneur needs to acquire and process information and to be aware of its significance in terms of the opportunity to make profits. Entrepreneurs are also able to identify opportunities overlooked by others. They also engage in arbitrage, which arises when two or more prices exist in a market. This view envisages entrepreneurs facilitating the working of markets and making them work more effectively to make the best use of existing resources rather than as an initiator of significant change and the bearer of uncertainty.

Therefore, the entrepreneur possesses special skills that are crucial to the way a dynamic market economy works. Knight's entrepreneur is willing to make decisions when faced with uncertainty, Schumpeter's is ruthless and pursues change, Kirzner's is alert to profitable opportunities, Shackle's is endowed with a creative imagination and Casson's specialises in making judgemental decisions.

A BEHAVIOURAL EXPLANATION OF ENTREPRENEURSHIP

If we examine entrepreneurship in a sequential way, then the processes of decision making will consist of a series of successive activities with an individual having to decide at the end of each stage whether or not to continue to the next; this is dependent, as discussed in Chapter 2, on whether the goals set have been satisfactorily achieved. If they have been met, then the decision maker will proceed to the next stage; if not, then the activity may start again or be discontinued.

An outline of the behavioural linkages in the entrepreneurial process is shown in Figure 13.1. The process starts in box 1, when an individual starts to search for an opportunity to behave in an entrepreneurial way, with the objective of finding a

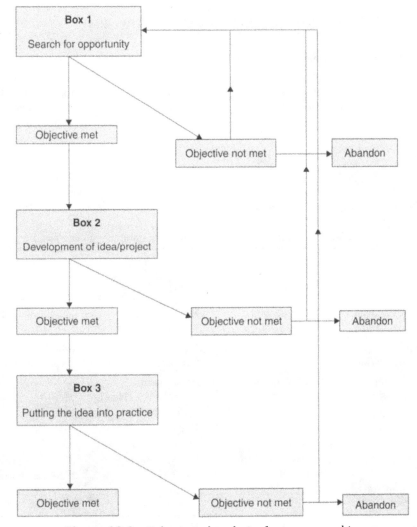

Figure 13.1   Behavioural analysis of entrepreneurship

potentially successful project. The outcome of the search process is either the production of an idea or a plan for future evaluation of the idea. If the objective is not met, then the potential entrepreneur either gives up or goes back to box 1 and starts the process again.

If the objective is met, then the individual proceeds to box 2, when the idea is developed to the point where it can be put into practice. If the objective is met, then the individual can proceed to box 3. If the objective is not met, then the individual either goes back to box 2 or even box 1 (if the idea is considered a total failure). In box 3 the idea is put into practice with the aim of developing a successful product or process. If the objective is met, then the project is successful with the full implementation of the idea. If the objective is not met, then the individual can return to box 1, box 2 or box 3.

ENTREPRENEURSHIP AND THE DEVELOPMENT OF THE FIRM

The behavioural approach enables us both to develop a sequential model of entre-preneurship and to develop self-sustaining enterprises; this requires the enterprise to develop general management functions as it moves from creating organizations to operating them. This process is illustrated in Table 13.1, where activities are classified in a four-stage development process extending the ideas contained in Figure 13.1.

Stage I

The potential entrepreneur seeks an opportunity and/or an idea. An idea or opportunity once identified has to be developed into a plan to be presented to potential financiers

Table 13.1   Entrepreneurship and the development of an enterprise

Entrepreneurship ←			→ Management
Stage I	Stage II	Stage III	Stage IV
Pre-entrepreneurial activity	Entrepreneurial activity	Developing an organization	Sustainable enterprise
Scanning for opportunities/ideas	New venture creation	Building new structures	Marketing and production
Concept development	Bringing resources together	Learning and developing efficient production	
	Prototype/Market testing	Production/Sales	
Success – move to stage II	Success – move to stage III	Success – move to stage IV	Success – profit Failure – withdraw
Failure – stop/start again	Failure – stop/start again	Failure – stop/start again	

Source Developed by author from various sources

and suppliers of other resources. If their support is to the entrepreneur's satisfaction, then a move can be made to stage II. If the entrepreneur fails to establish the viability of the project and to find the necessary funding, then the process ends or starts again.

Stage II

The entrepreneur creates a new organization to bring the innovation to fruition; this requires the co-ordination of the various factors required for manufacturing a product or providing a service, such as finance, specialist capital assets, skilled labour and management. If the entrepreneur has achieved the goals set at the end of this stage, then a fledgling organization should have been created and sufficient products produced to test the market. If the set objectives have not been achieved, then the entrepreneur will either recommence stage II again or abandon the project.

Stage III

The new firm starts to build an organization capable of producing a product in sufficient quantities to meet market requirements. In this stage, there is entrepreneurial activity to promote growth and development, as well as the day-to-day management of production, marketing, finance and accounting. At the end of stage III the entrepreneur's new organization will either have successfully met the entrepreneur's and financiers' goals or not. Achievement of targets enables the process to continue to stage IV. Non-achievement of the goals will either lead to a prolonging of stage III or abandonment of the project. Failure at this stage may be an inability to manufacture a product of sufficient quality to meet the expectations of consumers or to produce the product at a cost level that allows a profit to be made at the expected market price.

Stage IV

The venture aims to become a self-sustainable operation with revenue not only covering costs but also making an acceptable level of profit. At this stage the firm becomes a managerial rather than an entrepreneurial enterprise, since the bulk of management time will be concerned with production and marketing. Successful fulfilment of the set goals will see the new firm continue in existence. Failure to achieve the goals will lead to a reassessment of the project and to either a prolonging of the period before viability is achieved or closure of the enterprise. If the firm is successful and the founder is still in charge of the company, then the process may start over again with the development of a new division within the enterprise, rather than a completely new firm.

If the development of the firm is controlled by one individual, then entrepreneurial activity has to be replaced by managerial activity. The latter can be delegated through management specialists though the division of labour. However, within the firm the whole range of entrepreneurial activity does not have to be the preserve of one individual. Entrepreneurship may be subdivided into specialist activities. One individual may have ideas, while another may be better at evaluating them and yet another may bring them to fruition. It might also be easier for those not involved with the original ideas to abandon them. While usually considered an individual activity, entrepreneurship can therefore also be considered a team activity.

Entrepreneurship can also take place within existing firms. At this point the classical entrepreneur hands the firm to managers and starts the process again. Alternatively, the entrepreneur will look for new ideas within the firm and encourage staff to bring forth new ideas that may lead to new ventures. Salaried managers and other employees can undertake entrepreneurial activities which, with the support of the senior managers, can lead the firm into new activities and the creation of new business divisions rather than new firms.

THE BIRTH OF THE FIRM

The rate of birth of new firms is seen as an indicator of the dynamism of an economy and as a major source of new employment and competitive advantage. The birth of a new firm is the consequence of entrepreneurial activity and the willingness of the entrepreneur and financial supporters to bear the consequences of uncertain outcomes; these are borne in the view of economists because entrepreneurs' imagined outcomes have a good chance of making future profits, but in practice the individual may be motivated by less tangible goals, such as economic independence and being in control of one's own business. Thus, an individual or group of individuals will start a firm in pursuit of their personal objectives. In doing so they may be responding to changing economic conditions, such as market demand, exploiting cost-saving new technology and changing conditions favourable to new products.

These different influences on new-firm formation can be classified as "pull" and "push" factors. The push factors are those that make an individual want to start a new firm, including dissatisfaction with one's present position. Pull factors are those that entice an individual into starting a new firm and are essentially the perceived profit opportunities. The precise classification of any one cause as a push or pull factor may in practice be very difficult to make.

Pull factors

The founders of new firms must have sufficient belief in their ability to recognize an opportunity capable of being grasped. They are pulled toward responding to the opportunity because they believe they possess the necessary technical or managerial skills or they have access to new products or processes to give them a reasonable chance of successfully establishing a new enterprise.

Particular working environments may draw individuals into entrepreneurship. A seedbed theory for the development of entrepreneurs has been suggested: individuals are more likely to establish their own businesses if they have worked previously in smaller entrepreneurial firms and gained experience of a wider range of business roles. The opposite is true in larger organizations where individuals are confined to specialist functions. Such experience, together with the examples set by the owner managers of such enterprises, gives individuals the vision to want to be entrepreneurs. Such people display lower relative risk aversion against entrepreneurship than their counterparts in larger firms, since there is perceived to be a higher risk of losing one's job in a smaller firm.

Opportunities are another pull factor. Suitable opportunities can arise from changing industry conditions or market conditions, such as technical change, weakly competitive incumbents and new products. Technical change may favour efficient production in smaller quantities, thus lowering the entry costs and making it relatively easier for new entrants to overcome the risks of entry. For example, new printing technology and computerization have made it less costly to establish new magazines and newspapers. If existing firms are perceived to be weak in a particular area of activity, then a new, small firm, by having closer contact with customers, may be able to compete with larger, existing enterprises. If the new firm brings a superior product or service to the market, then it may be able to compete with existing products: for example, the Dyson Turbo vacuum cleaner, developed by entrepreneur James Dyson, utilized newly patented technology and design and won significant market share against established suppliers, such as Hoover and Electrolux, despite its premium price.

The changing strategies of existing firms may also create opportunities. Rationalization and divestment may cause firms to withdraw from markets, the former creating room for new entrants with the latter creating opportunities for existing businesses to be acquired.

Two other aspects of changing market conditions may be important: first, the rate of growth and, second, the changing structure of consumer demand. A rapidly growing market usually creates more entrepreneurial opportunities than a slow growing or declining market.

The changing structure of consumer demand may open the market to niche suppliers: for example, some consumers may want to buy a differentiated or superior product compared with that supplied to the mass market. If they can be identified, then there may be opportunities for entrepreneurs to take advantage of such omissions.

Governments may create schemes that make it easier for potential entrepreneurs to gain access to opportunities by lowering entry barriers and encouraging the financial system to become more willing to support riskier projects. Such policies include a range of support programmes to help individuals start up by offering free business consultancy advice, subsidised buildings and capital equipment.

Push factors

Founders of new firms may be found among those made redundant or dissatisfied with their existing role and/or remuneration. The redundancy of managers or other workers may lead them to consider starting their own business. A long-cherished ambition to implement a particular idea or economic necessity may push them toward forming a new firm. In this they may be helped by having a redundancy payment to partially or wholly finance their venture. In the UK many new trading enterprises start up as a single-person organization and may operate initially as labour-only contractors in industries, such as construction. Many of these "enterprises" never move beyond this stage, but some may develop into conventional firms employing capital and other employees.

Another push factor is brought about by individual enterprises reorganizing themselves. The decision may be made to dispose of certain activities no longer considered central to their business or to put activities currently undertaken in-house out to contract. Existing staff in these functions may be motivated to form a new enterprise to supply those requirements. A further example is when product or service divisions that supply external markets are put up for sale. Again, existing staff may be motivated to acquire such activities and start a new firm. Such a move by the existing management may require financial support from institutional investors as well as the selling firm. Such arrangements are known as management buyouts. In the 1980s and 1990s management buyouts were a significant activity in the UK as a result of the narrowing focus, or downsizing, of large companies and of the process of **privatization** and compulsory tendering in the public sector. When the National Bus Company was broken into some 70 individual enterprises, the existing management acquired many of the companies.

Inventors are another potential source of entrepreneurs. They may strive to get their invention manufactured and on to the market. If they cannot persuade existing companies to make the new product, then they may be motivated to set up their own enterprise. However, there is no close link between individuals who are inventors, those who are entrepreneurs or those who start up new firms.

Individuals attempting to start a new enterprise must, in addition to their creative and imaginative ideas, have the ability to obtain financial support, to organize resources and to gain customers if they are to be successful. Although potential entrepreneurs may be motivated by financial gain they may have to wait for their rewards. In the short run, they may have given up secure and well-paid employment in return for long working hours, modest salaries and the worry and concern about whether the enterprise will be successful – all for the promise of uncertain financial benefits in the long run.

Constraints

When establishing a new firm the founder has to overcome many constraints and difficulties; these include finance, premises, regulations and managerial skills.

Traditionally, finance has been a major constraint on starting a new firm. With no track record it is difficult for a potential founder to convince financial institutions that the project is worthy of support. Even if the necessary money can be found for the enterprise, financial problems do not disappear with the start-up. Having to wait for revenues to cover operating costs and finding the finance to meet the needs of a fledgling business is a continual problem. Lenders view such businesses with suspicion as they have insufficient security to guarantee the loans. Government has tried to overcome this aspect of market failure by offering financial support to encourage new-firm formation.

The finding of suitable and affordable premises is often a stumbling block; if the firm cannot be started in the garden shed or garage, then commercial premises are required. Another problem for small firms is the lack of managerial and/or technical skills of the founders. While they have the drive to create the firm, they may not actually have the skills to run the firm and prevent it from an early death. Help with both these aspects may be available from development and other agencies that have government support.

However, government regulation of firm behaviour, together with planning controls, is seen to be a major constraint on new-firm start-up. It is disproportionately more expensive for small firms to comply with regulations than large firms with specialist departments to deal with the issues.

Storey (1985) surveyed newly created firms in Cleveland in the UK between 1972 and 1979. He found that the main problems making life difficult for new firms were shortfalls in predicted demand, difficulties in obtaining key material supplies, high labour turnover, higher than expected wage costs and skill shortages.

CHARACTERISTICS OF NEW-FIRM FOUNDERS

There have been a number of studies of the source and characteristics of new-firm founders in the UK. Johnson and Cathcart (1968) found that new-firm founders were 14 times more likely to emerge from firms employing fewer than 10 people than firms employing more than 500. Cross (1981) found that 54% of firms in Scotland between 1968 and 1977 were founded by two or more partners, thereby sharing risk and pooling their expertise.

Storey and Strange (1993) identified the characteristics of new-firm founders as follows:

- 91% were aged between 21 and 50, with 37% between 31 and 40. Only 5% were older than 50.
- 75% were men.
- 65% had some formal or professional qualification, but only 5% had university degrees.
- 42% were time-served craftsmen.
- 62% of founders established firms in the same sector in which they had previously worked.
- 41% had previous managerial experience, 55% of these in firms employing less than 4 people and 28% in firms employing between 5 and 10.
- 28% had been previously self-employed.
- 44% were either unemployed or expected to become unemployed.

The main motives leading to the group establishing new firms were:

- Necessity (35%).
- Ambition (48%).
- Identification of a market gap (46%).
- Chance (10%).
- Family event (6%).
- Government enterprise allowance (2%).

THE FORMATION OF NEW FIRMS IN THE UK

Statistics on new-firm formation in the UK come from registrations for the payment of value-added tax (VAT), which is compulsory if turnover exceeds a minimum threshold (£51,000 in 1999). These data do not include firms below the threshold. Figure 13.2 shows the total numbers of firms registering and deregistering for VAT purposes for selected years between 1980 and 2000. New registrations are taken as an indicator of the birth of new firms and deregistration as an indicator of the death of firms. The stock is the total number of enterprises registered at the end of each year. The figure shows registrations exceeding deregistrations in the 1980s and late 1990s. The late 1980s and early 1990s saw deregistrations exceed registrations as the economy contracted. However, on average 18,000 new enterprises were added to the stock each year. Figure 13.3 shows similar information. It plots net addition to the stock as a proportion of the stock of firms at the end of each year.

In the UK there is also significant variation in the net creation of new firms between

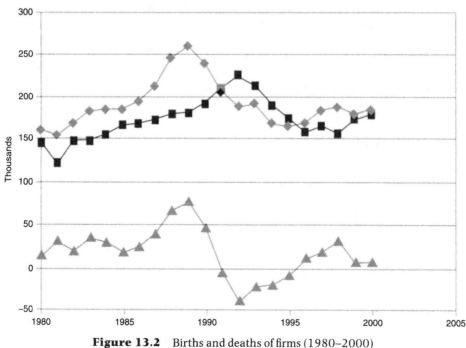

Figure 13.2 Births and deaths of firms (1980–2000)
Source DTI. Births (◆); deaths (■); net change (▲)

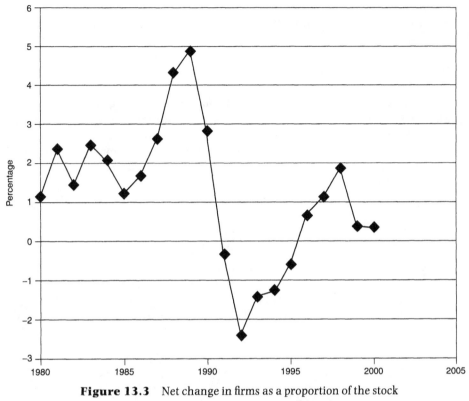

Figure 13.3   Net change in firms as a proportion of the stock
Source   DTI

regions. Generally, the further north and west a region is from London the lower are the rates of new-firm formation. Standardizing this for the population, in 2000 the rate of new-firm formation per 10,000 adults was: London 65, the east of England 43, Scotland 28 and the north-east of England 21 (Small Business Service 2001).

If these ratios are taken as being indicative of a region having a dynamic economy and a culture conducive to entrepreneurship, then generally the older heavy industrial areas of the north and west have less conducive economic and social conditions than the south-east. However, within any region there may also be significant variations in new-firm formation, with particular localities having higher rates. In Scotland, for example, Edinburgh has a higher rate of new-firm formation than the rest of Scotland, as does Cambridge in the east of England. Concentrations of new-firm formation in small areas, such as Cambridge, are usually linked to large numbers of small firms operating in a small number of industries, to networking between owners and researchers and external or agglomeration economies. For example, Athreye and Keeble (2000) found evidence that agglomeration economies, strong linkages between firms, public support for R and D and university spending led to higher rates of innovation and entrepreneurial activity.

The difficulties faced by new firms are illustrated by Hart and Oulton (1998), who examined a database of UK registered companies, identified the birth of a firm by the date of company incorporation and its death by withdrawal from the registration. The data show the death rate of companies in 1996 and the year in which they were incorporated. Thus, firms registered in 1994 which were 2 years old had a death rate of 26.8%, while firms registered in 1980 had a death rate of 8.6%. The death rate tends to decline as the firm gets older, and the third year is the most dangerous in a new firm's existence.

Holmes et al. (2000) estimated firm hazard functions using data on 931 firms established between 1973 and 1994 in Wearside in the north-east of England. Statistical models were estimated for enterprises employing fewer than 10 employees and those employing more than 10. Of the 931 firms in the sample, 442 (or 47.5%) survived. The hazard function shows that the chances of death increases for both types of firms up to 12 years and thereafter it declines.

Case Study 13.1   Sir Richard Branson and the Virgin Group

Sir Richard Branson has exhibited many different aspects of entrepreneurship in the development and growth of the Virgin Group of companies. He and his company have continually started new entrepreneurial ventures and disposed of the financially successful ones to help finance new ones. His first venture was selling records and magazines by mail order, while still at school; this became Virgin in 1970. He then developed a record label and record shops, which the company no longer owns. Currently, the company consists of 200 separate businesses and is best known for its airline, mobile phone, rail and financial services. He also operates joint ventures. Virgin Atlantic is 51% owned by Singapore Airlines and Virgin Railways is 49% owned by Stagecoach. The company changes its shape constantly, as new activities are started and old ones sold. In 1999 the company employed 25,000 staff and had a turnover of more than £3bn.

Branson is usually described as flamboyant and unconventional and not afraid to take risks. He has also been described as an agent of change, having challenged the conventional business model in the many markets he has entered; this has been rationalized as entering markets where the existing dominant firm is resting on its laurels, where competition barely exists and the consumer is not well served. In other words, he finds gaps in the market and produces things people need.

Virgin styles itself as a small company that takes on big businesses. Companies challenged by his strategy include British Airways, Coca-Cola, mobile phone operators, banks and financial service companies.

The group operates a flat organizational structure, with each operating unit kept small. For example, he does not operate a single, large airline but three smaller privately managed ones (at present) – Virgin Atlantic, Virgin Express and Virgin Blue; this not only makes the disposal of units and the start-up of new ones possible it also avoids disrupting the limited organizational structures of the group.

Virgin delivers its existing products and services in innovative ways and therefore, Sir Richard can be described as an entrepreneur because he is:

■ Alert to new opportunities to make profits.
■ Able to imagine profitable outcomes in an uncertain world.
■ Introduce new "old" goods.

- Introduce new methods of production.
- Create new markets and extend others by bringing in new consumers.
- Willing to bear risk and uncertainty.
- An agent for change.

CHAPTER SUMMARY

This chapter examined the concept of entrepreneurship. In doing this we analysed:

- The main characteristics of entrepreneurial activity; these include a willingness to take decisions in conditions of uncertainty and to start new ventures based on imagined future outcomes.
- A behavioural model of entrepreneurship showing both the sequential nature of the development of an idea into a successful product and, similarly, for the development of a new enterprise.
- Entrepreneurial activity that is found inside existing firms and the key entrepreneurial activity in starting up new firms. The number of people becoming entrepreneurs and willing to start new firms are influenced by what are termed "push" and "pull" factors.
- Some empirical evidence on the supply of entrepreneurs and the birth of new firms.

The chapter demonstrated the multifaceted nature of entrepreneurship and the role of entrepreneurs in starting up new firms. Entrepreneurs are also active in existing firms by changing the range of products produced and the boundaries of the firm. These aspects will be examined in the Chapter Summaries of subsequent chapters.

REVIEW QUESTIONS

Exercise

Read the business pages of newspapers and identify a story about:

a   An individual who has taken a decision that you would classify as entrepreneurial.
b   The start-up of new ventures by existing firms.
c   The start-up of new firms.

Explain your reasons for choosing these stories and what aspects of entrepreneurship they illustrate.

Discussion questions

1   What do you consider are the main functions of entrepreneurship?

2 Distinguish between management and the entrepreneurial functions within a firm.
3 Which of the following activities might be described as entrepreneurial and give your reasons?:

- Introducing a new product that meets previously unfulfilled demand (e.g., the first electronic calculator).
- Introducing a product similar to those already existing but with superior performance.
- Introducing a product similar to those already existing but with no advantages.
- Inventing a product.
- Reallocating resources in the firm to reflect the changing market prices of factors.
- Reallocating resources in the firm to reflect the relative rates of growth of different products.
- Buying products at a lower price at one location and selling them at a higher price at another location (e.g., buying branded pharmaceuticals or clothing in one market and selling in another at or below the existing market price).
- Introducing revolutionary technology to produce an existing product.
- Starting up a new firm.
- Starting up a new division within an existing firm.

4 Compare Shackle's notion of imagination with that of Casson's judgemental decision.
5 What difficulties face an individual in starting a new firm?
6 What are the main push and pull factors encouraging individuals to start up their own firm?
7 Identify some individuals you consider to be entrepreneurs. How does each one exhibit the characteristics of entrepreneurship identified by economics.

REFERENCES AND FURTHER READING

Athreye, S.S. and D. Keeble (2000) Sources of increasing returns and regional innovation in the UK. Paper given at *The Schumpeter 2000 Conference, Manchester, UK.*
Bower, T. (2001) *Branson.* Fourth Estate, London.
Bygrave, W.D. and C.W. Hofer (1991) Theorising about entrepreneurship. *Entrepreneurship Theory and Practice,* **16**(2), 13–22.
Carton, R.B, C.W. Hofer and M.D. Meeks (1998) The entrepreneur and entrepreneurship: Operational definitions of their role in society. University of Georgia Terry College of Business. Available at http://www.sbaer.uca.edu/Research/1998/ICSB/koo4.htm
Casson, M. (1982) *The Entrepreneur: An Economic Theory.* Martin Robertson, Oxford, UK.
Coase, R.H. (1991) The nature of the firm. In O.E. Williamson and S. Winters (eds), *The Nature of the Firm: Origins, Evolution and Development.* Oxford University Press, New York.
Cross, N. (1981) *New Firm Formation and Regional Development.* Gower, Aldershot, UK.
Greiner, L.E. (1972) Evolution and revolution as organizations grow. *Harvard Business Review,* July/August, 30–46.

Hart, P.E. and N. Oulton (1998) *Job Creation and Destruction in the Corporate Sector: The Relative Importance of Births, Deaths and Survivors* (NIESR Discussion Paper No. 134). National Institute of Economic and Social Research, London.

Holmes, P., I. Stone and P. Braidford (2000) *New Firm Survival: An Analysis of UK Firms Using a Hazard Function* (Working paper). University of Durham, UK.

Hyrsky, K. (2000) Entrepreneurial metaphors and concepts: An exploratory study. *International Small Business Journal*, **18**(1), 13–34.

Jackson, T. (1996) *Richard Branson: Virgin King – Inside Richard Branson's Business Empire*. Pima Lifestyles, London.

Johnson, P.S. and D.G. Cathcart (1968) The manufacturing firms and regional development: Some evidence from the Northern Region. *Regional Studies*, **13**, 1979.

Kirzner, I.M. (1973) *Competition and Entrepreneurship*. University of Chicago Press, Chicago.

Kirzner, I.M. (1997) How markets work. *The theory of entrepreneurial discovery* (Chapter 4). Institute of Economic Affairs, London.

Knight, F. (1921) *Risk, Uncertainty and Profit*. Houghton-Mifflin, Boston.

Moscheandreas, M. (1994) Entrepreneurship and profit. *Business Economics* (Chapter 5). Routledge, London.

Ricketts, M. (1994) The entrepreneur. *The Economics of the Business Enterprise* (2nd edn, Chapter 3). Harvester-Wheatsheaf, London.

Schumpeter, J. (1934) *The Theory of Economic Development*. Oxford University Press, New York.

Shackle, G.L.S. (1984) To cope with time. In: F: Stephen (ed.), *Firms Organisation and Labour*. Macmillan, London.

Small Business Service (2001) *Business Start-ups and Closures: VAT Registrations and Deregistrations in 2000* (Press release, 23 November). Department of Trade and Industry, London.

Storey, D.J. (1985) The problems facing new firms. *Journal of Management Studies*, **22**(3), 327–345.

Storey, D.J. (1992) *Entrepreneurship and the New Firm*. Croom Helm, London.

Storey, D.J. and A. Strange (1993) *Entrepreneurship in Cleveland 1979–1989* (Research Series No. 3). Department of Employment, London.

THE BOUNDARIES OF
THE FIRM

CHAPTER OBJECTIVES

This chapter aims to explore the reasons why firms exist. At the end of the
chapter you should be able to:

◆ Explain the nature and determinants of transaction costs.

◆ Analyse factors that influence transaction and management costs and
  the creation of firms.

◆ Distinguish between adverse selection, moral hazard and opportunistic
  behaviour.

◆ Explain the characteristics of knowledge.

◆ Elucidate the main characteristics of the team and contracts approach for
  the existence of firms.

INTRODUCTION

The purpose of this chapter is to explain the existence of firms and the boundaries they themselves put on their activities. Initial observations show that firms vary in terms of size, the number of products produced, the range of markets served, their ownership and organizational structures and management cultures. Whatever their current size, status and structure, at some point in the past all firms were created as a result of a decision by one or more individuals, with either a short or long history of development. Those currently operating are survivors of decisions made by their owners and managers, the influence of competitor actions and changes in the economic environment. Some firms appear to have found the secret of a long life, while others find survival difficult and disappear through financial failure or takeover.

To explain why firms exist and have certain boundaries, we will explore "new" theories of the firm, using the concepts of transaction costs and contracts. This chapter will examine the development of theories relating to:

- Transaction costs.
- Imperfect and asymmetric information.
- Knowledge.
- Property rights and contracts.

This material is largely theoretical but lays the foundations for Chapters 16–19, which look at strategies to change the boundaries of the firm.

TRANSACTION COST APPROACH

Coase's theory of the firm

Coase (1937) contrasted the resource allocation role of the market and the firm. He contended that the market influenced resource allocation by price signals, while within the firm it was assumed resources that were allocated or moved at the direction of an "entrepreneur co-ordinator" and the "distinguishing mark of the firm is the suppression of the price mechanism." Thus, "it is clear that these (the market and the firm) are alternative methods of co-ordinating production" (p. 42).

Coase further defined a firm as a "system of relationships which comes into existence when the direction of resources is dependent on an entrepreneur" (p. 45). The reasons entrepreneurs start firms is that they are a more efficient method of organizing production and because there is a cost attached to using the market. By organizing production within a firm where resource movements are directed by the entrepreneur-manager, such market or transaction costs can be avoided or reduced. Therefore, firms will come into existence when the costs of consciously co-ordinating resources (governance costs) within the firm are less than the transaction costs of using the market.

An entrepreneur wishing to organize the production of a product has a choice between co-ordinating its procurement in the market by contracting others to undertake the necessary tasks or to undertake some or all of these within a firm created to produce the final product. In making this decision for any given activity, the entrepreneur will compare the marginal costs of making market transactions with those of doing it within the firm. Thus, one activity may be undertaken in the market and others within the firm, depending on the balance of advantage. Some firms may hire an outside agency to plan and undertake their advertising, while another firm may undertake the activity within the firm. Thus, within any firm a decision has to be made as to those activities that will take place within the firm and those that will be organized through the market. According to Coase the key to the decision is to compare the marginal cost of a transaction conducted in the market with the marginal cost of the same transaction conducted within the firm. If the marginal transaction cost of the market is less than the marginal transaction cost within the firm, then the transaction will take place in the market; if the reverse holds, then the transaction will take place in the firm.

TRANSACTION COSTS

To analyse the boundaries of the firm it is necessary to examine in further detail the nature of transaction and **management costs**. Table 14.1 lists the various costs that a firm might incur.

A transaction is an agreement between two or more economic agents to exchange one thing for another. **Transaction costs** are those incurred when using the market.

Table 14.1   Economic costs

Concept	Costs of	Cause

Production and distribution costs	Making products of services:
	    Labour costs
	    Capital costs
	    Raw material costs
		Industrial arts
		Production function

Transaction costs	Using the market:
	    Discovering prices
	    Negotiating contracts
	    Monitoring contracts
		Bounded rationality
		Asset specificity

Management costs	Co-ordinating the actions of specialized agents:
	    Costs of obtaining information
	    Costs of co-ordinating inputs in production
	    Cost of measuring performance
		Bounded rationality

Motivation costs	Motivating agents to align their interests with managers or owners:
	    Costs of cheating or opportunistic behaviour
	    Agency costs of owners and managers
		Opportunism

Source Author

For example, workers agree to sell their labour in exchange for a payment, while consumers agree a payment in return for receiving a desirable commodity or service. For the producer, transaction costs include discovering the range of potential suppliers, the specifications of the products and their prices, negotiating contract terms, monitoring performance and enforcing the terms of the agreement. The costs arising from organizing the same transaction within the firm might be termed "firm transaction costs" or "management or governance costs". These costs derive from the organization and management of production within the firm. Demsetz (1988) suggests transaction costs are the costs of any activity undertaken to use the price system. In a similar way, management costs should include those of any activity undertaken to manage consciously the use of resources.

Transaction costs arise from decision makers initially having to discover potential suppliers and identify market prices. Such a process may seem simple, but even for the consumer it can be an expensive one. For example, a regular purchaser of chocolate bars will know the prices of competing brands, but an infrequent buyer will be unaware of current prices. The latter would need to spend time discovering prices before making a decision. Such research is especially needed when goods are expensive and infrequently purchased.

Firms can avoid or limit the costs of using the market by negotiating long-term contracts with their workers and suppliers. The fewer the number of contracts signed in a given period of time the lower will be some aspects of transaction costs. However, long-term contracts have certain disadvantages in that market conditions and production technology may change in ways not foreseen when the contracts were signed. These changes will advantage one or other of the parties. However, within the firm these problems can be overcome by the ability of the entrepreneur/owner to redirect employees to new areas of activity, retrain workers and alter wages. However, this ability may depend on the flexibility of the contracts signed. In the UK many industrial disputes have followed attempts to get workers to do work not previously part of their duties.

INFORMATION, IMPERFECT MARKETS AND TRANSACTION COSTS

Transaction costs are a result of imperfect markets. In a world of perfectly competitive markets both transaction and governance costs would be zero because the prices of all products and factors of production together with consumer preference and production functions would all be fully known to decision makers. The assumptions of perfect competition necessary for this conclusion to be reached are presented in Table 14.2. In imperfect markets, transaction costs exist because these assumptions do not hold.

Perfect markets are characterized by the assumption of unbounded rationality; this assumes that decision makers always make optimal transaction decisions because they have full knowledge of all the relevant information and have the ability to sift and process all this information. Consequently, mistakes are never made. Imperfect markets are characterized by **bounded rationality**; this means that decision makers

Table 14.2 Characteristics of perfect and imperfect markets

Characteristic	Perfect markets	Imperfect markets
Individual	Unbounded rationality	Bounded rationality
Information	Perfect Total Symmetrical	Imperfect Partial Asymmetrical
Motivation	Honesty	Opportunistic behaviour
Transactions costs	Zero	Positive

Source Author

may wish to act rationally but their ability to do so is limited because they have a limited ability to absorb and handle information.

In imperfect markets a decision maker may not be fully informed or may only have available part of the information required to make a decision. Unfortunately, the decision maker will not know the quality of the information he does have nor the importance of the information he does not have. In addition, some information may be difficult to acquire and be known to only a few people, who may be unwilling to sell or impart it to anyone else. All information about future prices or costs will be uncertain. Where information is unequally available to the parties trying to reach an agreement, this is described as a situation of asymmetric information.

Adverse selection

Situations of **adverse selection** arise where information is both asymmetric and hidden from one party to a potential agreement; this is described as *ex ante* **asymmetric information**. Akerlof (1970) illustrated the consequences by examining the market for used motor cars. He sought to explain the wide differences in price between new, and nearly new, or second-hand, cars. The answer he argued lay in the existence of asymmetric information (i.e., the seller knows more about the motor vehicle than the buyer).

Buyers lacking the full detailed history of the car may wonder why the seller wishes to dispose of it. The real answer may be that it is a "lemon", a poor quality and unreliable car. All prospective buyers are suspicious about the quality, and the result is that good cars are excluded from the market. The consequences can be illustrated as follows. First, assume that there are two types of used motor cars: good and bad. Second, assume that sellers know the difference but buyers do not. Buyers, therefore, have to decide what value to put on a second-hand car without knowing whether it is a good or bad one. As a result, high-quality cars are driven from the market as buyers are unwilling to pay high prices just in case the one they buy might be a lemon.

Let us assume that the seller of a low-quality motor vehicle is willing to sell for £500 and the seller of a high-quality car is willing to sell for £1,200 and that buyers are willing to pay £700 for a low-quality motor vehicle and £1,500 for a high-quality car. Buyers will have to estimate how much they are willing to offer for a second-hand car, without knowing which car is the good one and which is the bad one. If we assume that the probability of obtaining a high or low-quality car is equal, then the expected value of any car to a buyer is given by the weighted average of the two values multiplied by the probability ratio. Thus, the expected value is equal to $(0.5 * 700) + (0.5 * 1,500)$, or £1,100. If the buyer is only willing to offer £1,100, then the only sellers willing to sell their cars would be the owners of low-quality cars; this is because the selling price of low-quality cars is less than the buyer is offering, while the selling price of quality cars is greater than the offer price. The seller of the quality car wants £1,500, but the buyer is only willing to offer £1100. As a result, quality cars are withdrawn from the market, only low-quality cars would be offered for sale and buyers would expect to get low-quality cars. Market failure will occur because buyers' perception of the quality of all motor cars is adversely affected through the presence of asymmetric information.

Solutions to the problem involve trying to redress the inequality of information available to both parties. Sellers may try to develop a reputation for selling only high-quality products to give buyers confidence in the product they are buying. In a similar way, sellers may offer guarantees and warranties to signal the quality of the cars for sale. Buyers might try to improve their knowledge or hire experts to advise them.

Moral hazard

Moral hazard arises where parties to an agreement have different information about the actions of the other party and the outcomes; this is described as a situation of *ex post* asymmetric information. In such a situation one side to an agreement (the employer) cannot fully observe the actions and efforts of the other (the worker) and therefore cannot fully observe whether the worker has fully complied with the contract; this is also termed "hidden action". The results of moral hazard are an increased probability of undesired outcomes for one party after the transaction or agreement is signed. For example, motor insurance companies sell comprehensive policies more cheaply to 50-year-olds than 20-year-olds on the basis that the latter are less good drivers and more likely to be involved in accidents. However, some 50-year-olds may behave more recklessly because they have less expensive cover. The seller cannot observe this behaviour before reaching an agreement to supply the buyer.

Motivation and opportunistic behaviour

In making agreements it is presumed that all parties will behave truthfully and honestly and fulfil their part of any agreement. In a world of complete information and unbounded rationality, each party to an agreement will know whether the agreement has been kept or not. Where one side of an agreement cannot fully observe the behaviour of the other party, an opportunity arises to behave opportunistically. **Opportunism** has been defined as a lack of candour or honesty in agreements or transactions: in short, self-interested behaviour to deny the other party of the agreed benefits. Individuals may behave deceitfully and misrepresent the quality of a product. A firm may have contracted for the supply of first-grade coal, but actually be supplied with a lower grade; this might be difficult for the purchaser to observe. Such difficulties are less likely when input is purchased frequently, but is more likely when there is only one supplier, when swapping suppliers is more difficult and when there is uncertainty as to how quality is measured. The greater the possibility of opportunistic behaviour the more likely that purchasers will explore making or providing their own supply of the input concerned.

WILLIAMSON'S ANALYSIS

Williamson extended the analysis of transaction costs by identifying and exploring the impact of various factors on transaction costs and the boundaries of the firm. He distinguished between different governance structures, between firms and markets and analysed situations and characteristics that will tend to favour one institutional arrangement or governance structure rather than another. In particular, he stressed the avoidance of market transactions where the potential for opportunistic behaviour is greatest.

According to Williamson (1996), "transaction cost economics is a comparative approach to economic organisations, in which technology is de-emphasised in favour of organisation and the ability to economise resides in the details of transactions and the mechanisms of governance." These elements are combined to yield, "a predictive theory of economic organisations in which a large number of apparently dissimilar phenomena are shown to be variations on a few key transaction cost economising themes" (Williamson 1996, p. 136).

Transaction cost economics views firms and markets as alternative governance structures designed to manage transactions. The objective of the firm is to minimize transaction costs. To understand the various forces generating transaction costs and to see whether they are more efficiently undertaken in the market or within the firm, Williamson assumed that all decision makers are boundedly rational to ensure that the perfect contract, which foresees all possible future events, cannot be constructed. Consequently, he concentrated on analysing the *ex ante* (or potential) impact on transaction costs of the various phenomena listed in Table 14.3.

A   Economies of scale and scope

Economies of scale and scope were discussed in Chapter 8. Both are long-run phenomena that lead to lower average costs the greater the level of output. A firm that requires a plant of less than minimum efficient scale to meet its input requirements would incur higher production costs if the operation was organized within the firm rather than in the market. The market would therefore be the preferred option.

Table 14.3 Factors influencing the relative efficiency of market
and firms

Factor		Market	Firm
A	Economies of scale/scope	+	
B1	Large numbers of suppliers	+	
B2	Small numbers of suppliers		+
C	Management costs	+	
D	Opportunism		+
E	Asset specificity		+
F	Firm-specific knowledge		+
G	Uncertainty		+

Note + indicates a factor favouring the use of the market or the firm
Source Reprinted from Ferguson et al. (1993, p. 11) by permission of
Macmillan.

Economies of scope arise from producing two or more goods using common inputs.
Thus, if a firm requires a single input that benefits from joint production, then again
the firm would find the market the more efficient outcome. For example, supermarkets
that sell own brand products find the preferred method of sourcing these goods is by
using an outside supplier who benefits from both economies of scale and scope, rather
than making the goods themselves.

B Number of firms

Economists define market structures in terms of the number of firms that compete for
the patronage of customers. Where there is competition among a large numbers of
firms, theory suggests that prices will be close to the marginal and average costs of
production. Where there are few firms competing, such oligopolistic models as
Cournot's suggest that there will be a divergence between price and marginal cost,
with price being greater than average costs. Thus, with given cost levels, prices will be
lower where there are a large number of firms competing.

When there are small numbers of suppliers, then these firms will have a degree of
monopolistic power *vis-à-vis* the buyers of the input. These buyers may prefer to avoid
the market and produce their own goods rather than be in the power of a small
number of suppliers. An alternative strategy might be to form buyer groups to create a
degree of monopsonistic power to offset the market power of suppliers. In the presence
of large numbers of suppliers a firm will tend to favour market transactions whereas
small numbers of suppliers will lead to the avoidance of market transactions and
making their own.

C Management costs

Management or governance costs are those incurred by co-ordinating transactions
within the firm. They include the costs of organizing factors of production, of deciding

where within the enterprise these will operate and the costs of incentives to ensure the allotted tasks are carried out. Management costs are a function of the effectiveness of an organization in getting members of the firm to work together efficiently with the available capital. Thus, management costs will be greater:

- The higher the costs of incentives required to generate acceptable performance from staff.
- The higher the costs of sanctions required to discipline inappropriate staff behaviour.
- The greater the difficulty in controlling the opportunistic behaviour of staff.
- The larger and more complex the organization of the firm and the longer the chains of command.

However, these costs can be reduced by organizational changes that have the effect of making the organization more efficient. An example might be the delayering of the organization to remove bureaucratic procedures by shifting decision making closer to the point where the activity is taking place. These aspects will be discussed in Chapter 20.

D Opportunism

Opportunism occurs where one party is able to exploit differences in information that is only available to that party and thereby makes an agreement in its own interest. Williamson defines it as "a lack of candour or honesty in transactions, to include self-interest seeking with guile" (Williamson 1975, p. 9). The main source is asymmetric information. A firm may be poorly informed about the characteristics of products or services compared with their suppliers. For example, hotel owners might mislead a package tour holiday company about the quality and availability of the rooms they contract to provide. A tour operator might then include a hotel in its brochure that is not yet completed or poorly located based on the word of the owners. Only when holidaymakers arrive does the tour operator realize the information provided has been untruthful and misleading. Clearly, such problems can be overcome by regular inspection of such hotels (and those under construction). The presence of the potential for opportunistic behaviour will therefore encourage firms to undertake such transactions within the firm rather than rely on the market.

E Asset specificity

Asset specificity is defined as the degree to which resources, whether capital or labour, are committed to a specific task. As a consequence, such assets cannot be used to do other tasks without a significant fall in their value. For example, an oil refinery may be constructed to refine particular types of crude oil. While the refinery can be reconfigured to refine either heavy or light crude oils, it cannot be used for refining any other product. The most extreme type of asset specificity is where the only alternative use is as scrap.

Asset specificity is a key concept in organizational economics and can be applied to any form of asset, human or non-human, dedicated to fulfilling a particular transaction. Human asset specificity arises where individuals develop skills for a specific process or service. These skills are acquired by specialist training and on-the-job experience and are not easily transferable. Other forms of specificity include assets that are site-specific (i.e., specially designed for that particular piece of land) and those that are customer-specific (i.e., dedicated to meeting the needs of a particular contract).

Asset specificity is a major determinant of whether a transaction takes place in the market or the firm. The more committed an enterprise is to a particular contract or the greater the specificity of its assets the more it stands to lose if external conditions change. An enterprise providing a service that requires specific assets is vulnerable to changes in customer demand. Likewise, the buying firm may be in a weak position relative to the supplier if it wishes to increase its demand, for the firm with the specific assets would then be in a stronger position when coming to an agreement. Either party to a contract has the possibility of behaving opportunistically in given circumstances to increase their profits. Thus, asset specificity makes the parties to such agreements reluctant to commit themselves to such contracts. The greater the degree of asset specificity the more likely are firms to internalize the activity and avoid the market.

F   Firm-specific knowledge

If a firm has specialized knowledge relating to its product or service or to its production technology, then there is a tendency to favour retaining that knowledge within the firm to give a competitive advantage over rivals. For example, manufacturers of soft drinks, such as Coca-Cola, Vimto or Ir'n Brew, keep the recipe a secret. Although they may have contracts with other companies to manufacture and distribute the product, knowledge about the drink is not released. Similar considerations may apply to process technology, particularly in the early stages of its development.

G   Uncertainty about the future

In a certain world, using the market and entering into long-term contracts may be a simple and inexpensive process. In an uncertain world, a large number of contingencies would have to be considered and covered in the terms and conditions, making contracts more complex and expensive; this would make co-ordination within the firm more attractive.

Boundaries of the firm

According to the transactions cost viewpoint, the extent of a firm's activities will be determined where the cost of internalizing an external transaction is equal to the cost of organizing that transaction in a market or in another firm. However, the role of individual factors will lead different firms to adopt different attitudes to particular issues. In the UK bus industry, most companies own and operate their own vehicles. However, National Express, which operates a national network of long-distance coach services, hires all their vehicles from local suppliers. The difference in approach cannot be explained by the asset specificity of buses and coaches; it may have more to do with servicing and maintenance of vehicles in a widespread national network compared with the concentrated networks of the majority of bus companies.

KNOWLEDGE-BASED THEORY OF THE FIRM

Grant (1996) attempts to develop a knowledge-based theory of the firm. He argues that, "fundamental to a knowledge based theory of the firm is the assumption that the critical input in production and primary source of value is knowledge ... on the grounds that all human productivity is knowledge dependent, and machines are simple embodiments of knowledge" (Grant 1996, p. 112). The critical input in production and primary source of value is knowledge which is embodied in both machines and human capital.

Knowledge is a key resource and can be defined as "that which is known". A distinction is usually made between knowing about and knowing how. The former is termed "explicit knowledge" and the latter "implicit, or tacit, knowledge" that is only revealed when actually undertaking a task. The key characteristics of knowledge include:

- *Transferability*: knowledge can be transferred between individuals within a firm and between firms. Explicit or objective knowledge can be made known to others by means of communication, such as writing or video. Such knowledge has some characteristics of a **public good** in that, once available, it can be used by all without reducing the quantity available to others. Tacit knowledge is known only to the individual and is difficult to transfer to others because it is only revealed through application. Consequently, its transfer is slow, costly and uncertain.
- *Capacity for aggregation*: the stock of human knowledge is constantly being added to, but the ability of individuals to absorb and make use of new knowledge may be limited. For individuals to add to their stock of knowledge, it has to be available in a form that can be understood and absorbed. It is easier to absorb if it is available in a "common language", such as that of a discipline with which the reader is familiar.
- *Appropriability of knowledge*: appropriability is the ability of the owner of an input or factor to ensure payment for its use by another party. Selling explicit knowledge at a price is difficult because, once it is made public, the owner's stock of knowledge is not reduced and the buyer can easily pass it to another person without payment to the original seller. To ensure a full reward to the originator, owners may try to protect their rights through patents and copyrights. A second problem is deciding

the ownership of knowledge. If it is created within a firm does it belong to the firm or the individual or is there some type of joint ownership? This becomes a particular issue if an individual moves to another firm and takes significant tacit knowledge with them; this may give the firm that has acquired the individual access to information it did not previously have. The firm that sees the knowledge transferred will find it difficult to receive compensation.

■ *Specialization in knowledge acquisition*: because of bounded rationality, individuals do not have an unlimited capacity to acquire knowledge. Consequently, individuals have to specialize in the knowledge they acquire; this means that new knowledge tends to be created by specialists and that the firm has somehow to find a way to bring these specialist together, so that the firm as a whole can benefit.

Implications for the existence of the firm

The characteristics of knowledge as identified above help explain why it is necessary for a firm to exist. It is a, "response to a fundamental asymmetry in the economics of knowledge: knowledge acquisition requires greater specialisation than is needed for its utilisation" (Grant 1996, p. 112). Production requires the owner-managers of firms to bring together the efforts of individual possessors of different types of knowledge. Markets cannot do this because of the immobility of tacit knowledge, the in-appropriability of explicit knowledge and the fair chance it might be expropriated by others. According to this theory, the firm exists because it can create conditions that foster the bringing together of specialist holders of knowledge, while avoiding problems of opportunism. Therefore, a firm is "a knowledge integrating institution" (p. 112).

The boundary the firm has with the market will be determined by the relative efficiency of acquiring knowledge through market processes compared with obtaining and integrating it within the firm. Given the argument that markets transfer products more efficiently than knowledge, then the firm will acquire within its boundaries the necessary product-specific knowledge. Therefore, gaps will appear between firms, as they tend to specialize in particular products. If knowledge is not product-specific, then firms will tend to be multi-product producers and the knowledge domain of the firm will not coincide with a single product.

THE FIRM AS A TEAM

The firm is viewed by Coase as a hierarchical organization in which resources are directed or commanded by the owner-entrepreneur. In the Coasian firm, workers accept instructions and carry them out to the letter. This authoritarian justification for the existence of the firm is rejected by Alchian and Demsetz (1972), who believe that the position of controller of a firm is no different from someone contracting through the market. Instead, they develop their own theory to explain the existence of firms based on team production and monitoring.

Team production is defined as a way of organizing production requiring the simultaneous efforts of more than one individual. Identifying and measuring the effort of an individual working in a team, as opposed to the team as a whole, is difficult. Thus, an individual has an incentive to cheat, shirk or not to pull his weight. If the reduced effort of one member is not replaced by the greater efforts of others, then the effectiveness of the team as a whole is reduced and it can be assumed that the income or benefit the team receives as a whole (and to its individual members) is reduced. Therefore, Team production generates a moral hazard problem in that the actions of one team member are only imperfectly observable by other members.

One way of trying to ensure that all members make their full contribution is for the team to appoint a monitor to observe individual effort and to ensure all members make the required effort. If the monitor is used to working in the team, then he would have the necessary inside knowledge to know, albeit imperfectly, when shirking is taking place and to be effective. If the monitor receives the same reward as all the other team members, then he has the same incentive as other team members to disguise their efforts and may not supervise performance effectively. To provide the monitor with sufficient incentive to undertake the task effectively, it is necessary to give him a set or bundle of rights that are similar to those of the owner of a private company (Alchian and Demsetz, 1972). The firm is then defined as "team production in the service of the monitor". So, the monitor should be given rights:

- To the residual income of the firm.
- To be able to alter team membership.
- To be able to sell the rights to profits and control.

Therefore, the team will have to create a hierarchical type of organization to overcome the public good elements of team production which may weaken the incentives to maximize efficient operation. The contractual relationships established within the firm can be viewed as establishing property rights over the use and direction of the firm's resources as well as over ownership of the output produced. Therefore, firms and organizations exist not only to pool the talents of individual specialists and team members but also to use them efficiently. Thus, it is the need to establish property rights that brings the firm into existence.

THE FIRM AS A NEXUS OF CONTRACTS

It has been argued that trying to define the firm as a separate entity from the market is not helpful; this is because the main reasons for firms existing is contractual failure. Since contracts are used in the market and within the firm, they are subject to similar analysis: "There is, therefore, little point in trying to distinguish between transactions within a firm and those between firms. Rather both categories of transactions are part of a continuum of types of contractual relations with different types of organisations representing different points on this continuum" (Hart 1990 p. 10).

Contracts are the cornerstone of the "new" theories of the firm. In a world of perfect information and unbounded rationality, comprehensive contracts can be written to cover every eventuality since the future can be foreseen at the time of the agreement. In a world of imperfect information and bounded rationality, comprehensive contracts cannot be written. Such contracts are termed "incomplete" since they cannot cover every situation that may occur in their lifetime. Events may occur that will see one party wishing to revise the contract. In such circumstances, negotiations are likely to be opened and agreement may be reached. If agreement is not reached, then the parties might refer the decision to an arbitrator whose decision may or may not be binding on the parties.

Where there are incomplete contracts, whether markets or firms are used depends on who controls the residual rights to use an asset. Residual rights are defined as the ability to use an asset in any way not specified in a contract. This approach emphasizes the right to control the use of assets rather than ownership rights to residual profits.

Let us assume there are two firms, A and B, and that B produces a good or service that A requires – the potential relationships between A and B could be as independent firms or as divisions of a single enterprise. First, if they remain independent firms and A is to get B to agree to supply the desired input, then A will need to negotiate a contract with B, specifying price, quantity, quality and delivery. Suppose the two firms sign an incomplete contract to deliver fixed quantities of the input per time period, but with no arrangement to vary the number of units to be supplied. In this case if demand for A's product increases or decreases, then it would have to renegotiate the contract. Without a mechanism to vary supplies, A may find itself either short of or stockpiling the input. Since A will be forced to renegotiate the terms and conditions of the contract and B has to agree to any variation in the terms, it is B that possesses the residual rights of control. B also possesses the assets to make the product and, therefore, it is argued that the residual rights of control tend to be associated with the ownership of the assets required to make the input.

If the firms are merged, then the question of who possesses the residual rights will depend on which firm acquires the other. If A acquires B to obtain the desired input, then the manager-controller of firm A will be able to give orders to the division that was formerly firm B. If the order is given to increase output, then the managers of division B will increase production. If they do not co-operate, then they could be dismissed. Clearly, the position of the managers of the supply division is much weaker than when it was an independent company.

The implications for the boundary of the firm are that, in the absence of complementary assets and lock-in effects, "non-integration is always better than integration – it is optimal to do things through the market, for integration only increases the number of potential hold-ups without any compensating gains" (Hart 1990, p. 16). Thus, the firm should integrate activities only if there are compelling reasons to do so.

Case Study 14.1 The changing distribution of Coca-Cola and Pepsi: a transaction cost explanation

Muris et al. (1992) applied the transaction cost framework to the changing pattern of production and distribution adopted by the major cola producers in the USA. The dominant cola firms, Coca-Cola and Pepsi-Cola, moved the distribution of their drinks from a network of independent bottlers to captive bottling subsidiaries because of changes in the economic environment which had led to increasing transaction or co-ordination costs.

Traditionally, soft drinks were produced locally because of the low-cost bulk nature of the main ingredient – water, which is expensive to transport – and the small size of bottling plants. The emergence of branded soft drinks selling in wider areas presented a challenge for these companies: How could they manufacture and distribute the product to national and later on to international markets?

The solution for the cola companies was to become syrup concentrate manufacturers and to use independent bottlers, who were granted exclusive territories in perpetuity in local markets to manufacture, bottle and distribute the product to customers. Despite the asset specificity of the investments required by bottlers, this arrangement was preferred because:

- Local distributors knew the local market better than corporate headquarters and were more able to increase sales.
- The management costs of an owned local bottling and distribution system would be higher than the transaction costs in using contracts.
- The potential for managerial discretion in local bottle plant units was greater in owned rather than contracted bottlers.

The companies reversed this strategy by making the local bottlers and distributors wholly owned subsidiaries and bringing them within the boundary of the firm. According to Muris et al. (1992) these changes can be explained by those changes in the production and marketing characteristics of the industry that increased transaction costs. These changes included:

- Changes in bottling technology leading to significant economies of scale, thereby reducing the number of plants required.
- The tendency of larger independent bottlers to follow their own traditional marketing strategies in conflict with central campaigns.
- Mixed marketing messages where territories overlapped.
- The growth of larger national and regional buyers, such as supermarket chains, who wished to deal directly with headquarters.
- The growth of national marketing campaigns that required the co-operation of bottlers to be successful.

These pressures led to the need for greater co-ordination between headquarters and regional bottlers, so that national and local advertising were using the same tools and presenting the same message. These changes had led to increased transaction and co-ordination costs. To reduce these transaction costs the companies decided to alter the boundaries of the firm and to own the local bottlers and distributors. Although this increased management costs, these were considered to be less than the savings in transaction costs.

Muris et al. also carried out empirical studies to show that the change in strategy was driven by the need to reduce transaction costs. They compared the centralized distribution system of Coca-Cola and the local system of Pepsi-Cola to on-tap, or draught, users in the catering trade, where the product is distributed in glasses rather than bottles or cans. The results showed that the captive system had lower costs and thus supported the more general move to ownership of bottling and distribution plants in the USA.

CHAPTER SUMMARY

In this chapter we explored various reasons to explain the existence of firms in a market economy. The main reasons put forward were all concerned with the various aspects of imperfections in markets; these arise either because the assumptions of the perfect competition model do not hold or because there are advantages in not using the market. The models discussed were:

- *The transaction cost approach*, which compares the costs of using markets with the costs of co-ordination within the firm. The decision about which strategy to adopt is dependent on asset specificity, opportunistic behaviour, small numbers, firm-specific knowledge and uncertainty.
- *The knowledge and team approach*, which emphasizes the difficulty of appropriating the full benefits of knowledge and individual effort. These activities have some of the characteristics of public goods. The knowledge approach argues firms exist because it is the only efficient way of bringing together the various holders of tacit knowledge, which if used individually would not produce an efficient outcome. Team production emphasizes the need for a co-ordinator or monitor if the team is to produce effectively and the effort of individual members is not to fall below the desired level. The appointment of a co-ordinator or monitor is used to argue the importance of authority and property rights.
- *The contacts approach*, which emphasizes that the firm is a nexus of contracts – some with market contractors and others with internal suppliers. One of the problems with contracts in a world of imperfect knowledge is that they cannot be written to cover all eventualities. Where there are incomplete contracts, there may be advantages in bringing the contractor within the firm to achieve greater control over the supply and obtain a greater share of the benefits.

The relevance of these concepts will be developed in Chapters 16–19 when changing the boundaries of the firm will be discussed.

REVIEW QUESTIONS

1   What do you understand to be the transaction costs of using the market?
2   What do you understand by the term "management or firm transaction costs"?

3   Explain the concepts of bounded rationality and asymmetric information and their role in determining the boundary between the market and the firm.

4   What is the importance of asset specificity in encouraging the avoidance of the market?

5   Explain the concepts of adverse selection and moral hazard.

6   Many firms contract out services and offer their suppliers long-term contracts. What factors would encourage the firm to acquire its supplier?

7   In the analysis of incomplete contracts what advantages does ownership have over a market contract?

8   Can a "clear blue line" be drawn between the firm and the market, as argued by Coase?

9   What are the characteristics of knowledge and team production that make the market an inadequate governance structure?

REFERENCES AND FURTHER READING

Akerlof, G.A. (1970) The market for lemons: Quality, uncertainty and the market mechanism. *Quarterly Journal of Economics*, **89**(3), 345–364.

Alchian, A.A. and H. Demsetz (1972) Production, information costs and economic organization. *American Economic Review*, **62**, 772–795.

Clark, R. and T. McGuinness (1987) *The Economics of the Firm* (Chapters 1 and 3). Blackwell, Oxford.

Coase, R.H. (1937) The nature of the firm. *Economica*, **4**, 386–405. Reprinted in L. Putterman and R.S. Randall (1996) *The Economic Nature of the Firm* (Chapter 7). Cambridge University Press, Cambridge, UK; and P.J. Buckley and J. Michie (1996) *Firms Organisations and Contracts* (Chapter 2). Oxford University Press, Oxford, UK.

Demsetz, H. (1988) The firm in economic theory: A quiet revolution. *American Economic Review*, **87**(2), 426–429.

Dyer, J. (1994) Dedicated assets: Japan's manufacturing edge. *Harvard Business Review*, November/December, 174–178.

Ferguson, P.R., G.J. Ferguson and R. Rothschild (1993) Firms and markets: Identifying the optimal boundary. *Business Economics* (Chapter 2.4). Macmillan, Basingstoke.

Grant, R.M. (1996) Toward a knowledge based theory of the firm. *Strategic Management Journal*, **17**, 109–122 (Special Winter Issue).

Grossman, S. and O. Hart (1986) The costs and benefits of ownership: A theory of vertical and lateral integration. *Journal of Political Economy*, **94**, 691–791.

Hart, O. (1990) An economists perspective on the theory of the firm. In: D.J. Lamdin (ed.), *The Managerial Economics Reader*. Kolb, Miami, FL.

Hart, O. (1991) Incomplete contracts and the theory of the firm. In: O.E. Williamson and S.G. Winter (eds), *The Nature of the Firm*. Oxford University Press, New York.

Muris, T., D. Schafmar and P. Spiller (1992) Strategy and transaction costs: The organisation of distribution in the carbonated soft drink industry. *Journal of Economics and Management Strategy*, **1**, 83–128.

Williamson, O.E. (1975) *Markets and Hierarchies: Analysis and Anti-trust Implications*. Free Press, Glencoe, New York.

Williamson, O.E. (1996) Economics and organization: A primer. *California Management Review*, **38**(2), 131–146.

THE GROWTH OF THE FIRM

CHAPTER OBJECTIVES

This chapter aims to discuss various attempts to model the growth of the firm. At the end of this chapter you should be able to:

◆ Identify the main motives for growth.
◆ Explain the main components and analytics of the growth models of Baumol and Marris.
◆ Elucidate Penrose's endogenous growth model.
◆ Identify the main forces promoting and constraining the growth of the firm.
◆ Explain the contribution of the resources and competence approach to the growth of the firm.

INTRODUCTION

In Chapter 2 the objectives of the firm were analysed in terms of a single-period, or static, model. The main motives analysed were profit, sales and managerial utility maximization. The missing element in these models is the consideration of time; and how firms will behave when the future of the firm is considered. In the future the firm can grow or decline or stay the same, and become larger or smaller or static in terms of output, sales or assets. In this chapter we will examine:

■ The growth models of Baumol and Marris.
■ The endogenous growth model of Penrose.
■ Limits to the growth of the firm.
■ Resources and competences.

MOTIVES FOR GROWTH

Growth is seen as an important corporate objective because it is generally held that increasing output will be associated with:

■ Raising total profits.
■ Increasing efficiency through economies of scale, scope and learning.
■ Increasing market share and market power, allowing higher prices to be charged.
■ Reducing unit management costs, as governance structures are to some extent indivisible whatever the size of the firm.
■ Reducing transaction costs if key suppliers and sales outlets are acquired.
■ Reducing risk and uncertainty because greater size makes the firm more competitive, while diversifying into new products reduces the problems faced by falling demand in key markets.
■ Increasing managerial security against unwanted takeover bids.

A SIMPLE GROWTH MODEL

A growing firm will be concerned with the same variables as a static firm, but in a more dynamic way. Thus, the firm will be concerned with the growth of revenue, the growth of costs and the growth of profits. Since the firm wishes to consider flows of potential future earnings, the present value of each stream is used for comparative purposes (see Chapter 12).

Following Baumol (1962), we assume that the firm achieves a fixed percentage growth rate per annum and that input and output prices are fixed. The consequences for the growth of revenue are as follows. Let R = the initial net revenue of the firm, g = the growth rate and i = the cost of capital. Now, for a firm wanting to look ahead

t time periods, the revenues earned in years 0 to t can be considered. To convert the revenue stream to present values the annual revenue sums are discounted at the cost of capital of the firm. The discounted present value of revenue (PVR) would then be:

$$R = [R(1+g)/(1+i)] + [R(1+g)^2/(1+g)^2] + \cdots + [R(1+g)^t/(1+g)^t] \qquad \text{or}$$

$$PVR = \sum_{t=0}^{n} R(1+g)^t/(1+i)^t$$

The net present value of the stream of costs (PVC) is calculated in a similar fashion, giving:

$$PVC = \sum_{t=0}^{n} C(1+g)^t/(1+i)^t$$

The difference between the present value of revenue and the present value of costs will be the net present value of profits. The relative rates of growth of costs and revenue are crucial in determining the net present value of profits. If the rates of growth of revenue and costs are the same, then the net present value of profits will be positive as long as initial revenue exceeds initial costs. However, if the costs of the firm start to increase at a faster rate than revenue as the rate of growth increases, then the net present value of profits will start to decline, thus putting a constraint on the optimum growth rate for the firm.

BAUMOL'S DYNAMIC SALES GROWTH MODEL

Baumol also developed a dynamic version of his sales maximization model (discussed in Chapter 2). The model assumes that the objective of the firm is to maximize the rate of growth of sales revenue in the long run. Baumol assumes that the growth of sales is financed by profits dependent on the growth of sales revenue and costs. Unlike the static model where profit is a constraint determining optimal output, in the dynamic model profits are a means of financing growth. The model assumes that retained profits are used to finance growth and that the higher the proportion of profit retained the higher the rate of growth of sales revenue. Thus, the rate of growth of sales (g) is a function of profits (π) and current sales (R_t), or $g = f(\pi, R_t)$, while profit is a function of current sales, the rate of the growth of sales, capital costs and other costs.

In Figure 15.1 the rate of growth is measured on the vertical axis and sales revenue on the horizontal axis. With a given initial level of sales revenue, the growth function is a mirror image of the profit function. Thus, the highest rate of growth (G_M) will be achieved where profits are maximized at sales level R_M. Beyond this point the achievable growth rate declines as profits fall. The firm can choose any combination of g and R.

The preference function of the firm is to maximize the present value of sales and is represented in Figure 15.1 by a set of iso-present value curves (PV); these slope downwards from left to right and show the combinations of revenue and growth that give the same present value of sales, given the discount rate. Thus, they depict the

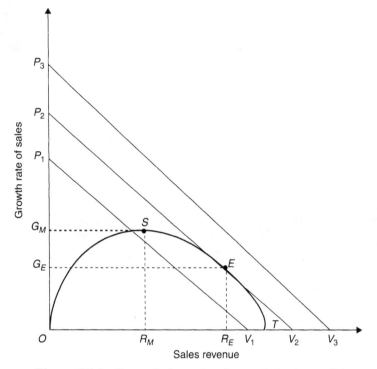

Figure 15.1 Baumol's dynamic sales-maximization model

trade-off between growth and revenue and the firm will choose to be on the highest feasible iso-present value curve; this is at point E, with G_E and R_E being the level of growth and sales revenue that maximizes the present value of future sales revenue.

MARRIS'S MODEL OF MANAGERIAL ENTERPRISE

Marris (1964) developed a managerial theory of the growth of the firm. It assumes that the owners and managers have different objectives: owners maximizing profit and managers growth. Purchasing a share, or ownership rights, in the firm grants the owner a right to receive future dividend payments. The share price is a function of the current dividend (D), the growth rate of dividends (g) and the share owners' discount rate (r), which reflects what they could earn in alternative investments. Thus, assuming a 3-year time horizon, the share price (SP) can be calculated as follows:

$$SP = \frac{D_1(1+g)}{(1+r)} + \frac{D_2(1+g)^2}{(1+r)^2} + \frac{D_3(1+g)^2}{(1+r)^3}$$

Managers are assumed to want to maximize the growth rate of the firm and are prepared to sacrifice profits now for higher future growth. Therefore, managers would prefer to retain profit within the firm, so that they can use the retained earnings to

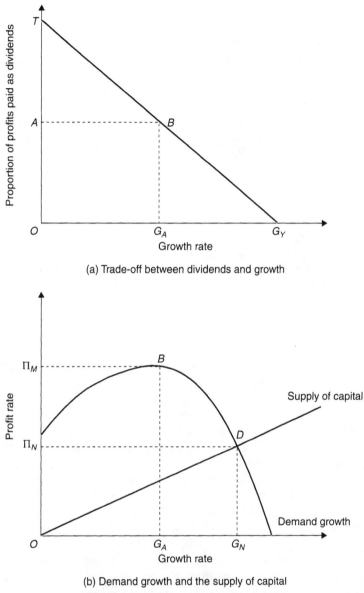

(a) Trade-off between dividends and growth

(b) Demand growth and the supply of capital

Figure 15.2   Marris's growth model

pursue growth opportunities. Thus, there is a trade-off between the retention or distribution of dividends and the growth rate that the firm can achieve; this is illustrated in Figure 15.2(a). On the vertical axis is measured the proportion of profit paid as dividends and on the horizontal axis the growth rate. Thus, if OA% of profits are paid as dividends, then proportion AT is retained by the firm to finance growth. Thus, with a distribution ratio of OA the achievable growth rate is G_A. If the proportion of profits paid out as dividends is greater than OA, then the achievable growth rate is lower;

while if the proportion of profits paid out as dividends is less than OA, the achievable growth rate is greater.

The managerial pursuit of growth is restricted by the need to pay dividends to shareholders, limiting the proportion of profits that can be retained to finance growth. If shareholders view the proportion of dividends retained adversely, they may seek to change the company's policy or sell their shares. Thus, managers can only pursue growth, as long as they keep shareholders happy, if they want to retain their positions! To consider this further we need to explore the relationship between growth and profitability via the demand growth curve and the supply of capital curve and the managerial security constraint.

Security constraint and sources of finance

The current stock market value of the firm is the number of issued shares multiplied by the share price; this will be maximized when the present value of expected returns to shareholders is also maximized (i.e., the share price is at its highest when the firm achieves a growth rate that maximizes profits). Both growth and future profits require a commitment to allocate a proportion of current profits in any one year to finance growth. However, the firm is not constrained to using internal finance only and can seek to raise funds via debt capital or new equity.

Debt borrowing requires the future repayment of the amount borrowed together with annual interest payments. These payments are a prior charge on the firm's profits and must be made before paying dividends to shareholders. Therefore, debt payments reduce the amount of profit available for distribution and will lead to a fall in the share price and in the market value of the firm if they reduce expected future dividend payments.

The other source of new finance is the issuing of new equity. The cost of equity is the future dividends new shareholders will receive along with the existing shareholders. To ensure that the new equity does not dilute the profits due to existing shareholders and, therefore, depress the share price, managers must ensure that the investment will be profitable enough to maintain or pay an increased dividend to all shareholders in line with expectations. Otherwise, shareholders may become discontented, sell their shares and the market value of the firm will be reduced.

The response of shareholders to the future prospects of the firm helps to constrain the managerial pursuit of growth without concern for the consequence for profits. If more shareholders start selling their shares relative to those who want to buy them, then the price will start to fall; this will reduce the stock market value of the firm relative to its assets and may encourage other companies to consider making a takeover bid for the company. If successful, this may end in existing senior managers losing their positions.

The stock market valuation of the firm represents the market's assessment of the current and future performance of the firm. The book value of the firm represents the value of the resources utilized by the firm and forms the capital, or asset value, of the firm. Marris named the ratio between market value and book value as the "valuation ratio". If the valuation ratio is less than 1, then the firm is in a weak position, because its market value is less than the value of the assets it is using. If the valuation ratio is greater than 1, then the market value is greater than the book value of the assets used. If the firm's valuation ratio is greater than a value thought by the market to be appropriate for that sector, then the firm is in a strong financial position and its management is considered to be doing a good job. If the firm's valuation ratio falls below the expected value for the sector, then the firm is in a relatively weak position and the management is perceived to be doing less well than its rivals in the sector. Therefore, from the viewpoint of management the valuation ratio is an indicator of how well they are doing. If they are to avoid their firm becoming a takeover target, then they must make good use of their assets and pursue policies on dividend retention or distribution and borrowing that keep the valuation ratio above the threshold that triggers a negative response from shareholders. The valuation ratio and growth rate relationship is plotted in Figure 15.3(b). Initially, its value rises with increases in the rate of growth of the firm, but eventually declines because growth is at the expense of current dividends and fails to deliver expected profits.

The model

Marris's model, showing the impact of the differing objectives of owners and managers, the financial constraints and the relationships between profit and growth, can be illustrated diagrammatically using a schema developed by Radice (1971). The two-way relationship between growth and profitability is captured by the demand growth curve and supply of capital curve. The demand growth curve shows the relationship between the growth rate of demand and the profit rate that the firm can earn. Initially, the higher the growth rate achieved the higher the rate of profit earned. Eventually, higher growth rates will only be achieved by lowering price, increasing expenditure on advertising or by developing and introducing new products. Thus, the curve initially increases and then declines as illustrated in Figure 15.2(b). The growth rate in demand that maximizes the profit rate is G_A, giving a maximum profit rate of Π_M.

The supply of capital curve in Figure 15.2(b) shows the relationship between the profit rate and growth in supply capacity. It is a function of the ability of the firm to raise capital to finance growth and varies with the level of profits earned. Thus, the higher the rate of profit the more easily will it be for the firm to raise capital, whereas the lower the rate of profit the more difficult will it be. If the firm is dependent on retained earnings, then the supply of capital curve is a function of the retention ratio shown in Figure 15.2(a). The supply of capital curve is represented as a linear function of growth and shows the maximum growth rate achievable by the firm to be G_N (given the supply constraints): that is, where the demand and supply growth curves intersect at D.

The growth and profit rate combination chosen by a firm will depend on the preferences of owners and managers. The preferences of owners are shown in the form of a set of indifference curves (O_1, O_2, etc.) in Figure 15.3(a). The curves show the levels of shareholder utility that are functions of the rate of profit (or dividends) and the rate of growth (or capital gains). Equilibrium is at point E_O, a point of tangency between indifference curve I_2 and the demand growth curve. The point E_O corresponds to point H in Figure 15.4(b), the highest point on the valuation curve.

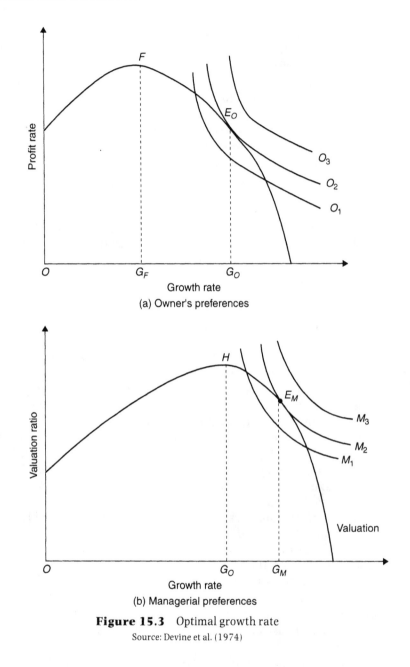

Figure 15.3 Optimal growth rate
Source: Devine et al. (1974)

The preferences of managers are represented in Figure 15.3(b) in the form of a set of indifference curves (M_1, M_2, etc.) which show preferences between the growth rate and the valuation ratio. Utility will be maximized at point E_M, the point of tangency between the managerial indifference curve M_2 and the valuation curve. Managers are presumed to favour a higher growth rate than owners, so that the preferred growth rates G_M and G_O do not coincide. However, they will do so if the only secure position for the managers is at the maximum point on the valuation curve.

DIVERSIFICATION AND THE GROWTH OF THE FIRM

The rate of growth of demand for existing products is a constraint on the growth of the firm. This constraint can be overcome if the firm diversifies into new products that are being sold in faster growing markets. Marris analysed the optimal or balanced growth position for a firm in terms of diversification, using the same concepts discussed in the previous section. Diversification is a risky strategy in that all new products do not necessarily succeed in winning profitable positions in markets. Whether they do so depends on the number of consumers who switch expenditure to the new products. The impact of a strategy of diversification on profits will depend on the number of diversification projects undertaken. Initial ones might earn higher rates of profit than later ones, because the most profitable projects are undertaken first.

In Figures 15.4 and 15.5 the growth rate of demand and supply is measured on the vertical axis and the rate of diversification on the horizontal axis. In Figure 15.4 the curves labelled $D\pi$ show the relationship between the growth in demand and diversification for different levels of profits. The curves slope upward to the right with a diminishing slope. Each demand growth curve shows the relationship for a given level of profit, with $D\pi_1$ being a lower level of profit than $D\pi_2$ and $D\pi_3$. Thus, for a given rate of growth of demand OG_2, increasing levels of diversification R_1, R_2 and R_3 are associated with higher levels of profit. For a given level of diversification OR_2, the growth rate of demand associated with curve $D\pi_3$ is OG_3, but with $D\pi_1$ it is OG_1. Profits are lower on $D\pi_3$, because of the additional costs involved in achieving a higher

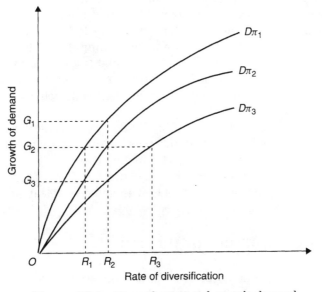

Figure 15.4 Diversification and growth: demand

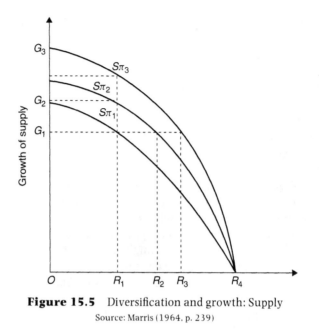

Figure 15.5   Diversification and growth: Supply
Source: Marris (1964. p. 239)

rate of growth of consumer demand. Thus, with a given rate of diversification and a given price of the product, the profit margin will be lower if the expenditure required to sell the new products is larger.

Figure 15.5 shows the growth of supply curves $S\pi$ that plot the relationship between the rate of diversification and the rate of growth of supply. The growth in the supply of resources in diversification projects is a function of the ratio of dividends retained or distributed. The higher the rate of retention the higher the rate of diversification achievable. If it is assumed in Figure 15.5 that there is a limit to the level of diversification achievable by the firm, then that point is OR_4. The growth in supply curves slope upward from right to left with a diminishing slope. Thus, for a given level of growth, say OG_1, higher levels of profit allow higher rates of diversification to be achieved (namely, R_1, R_2 and R_3). For a given rate of diversification, say R_1, the higher the level of profits the higher the rate of growth achievable. Thus, OG_3 is associated with $S\pi_3$ and OG_3 with $S\pi_1$.

By combining Figures 15.4 and 15.5 in Figure 15.6, the equilibrium position for each level of profits can be found at the point of intersection of the growth and demand curves for each given level of profit. Joining these equilibrium positions gives the "balanced growth" levels indicated by the dotted line LMN. Thus, for a given level of profit there is an optimal combination of growth and diversification.

ENDOGENOUS GROWTH THEORY OF THE FIRM

Penrose (1959) proposed that key determinants of the growth of the firm were internal processes that increased the capacity of production. Since the emphasis is on change

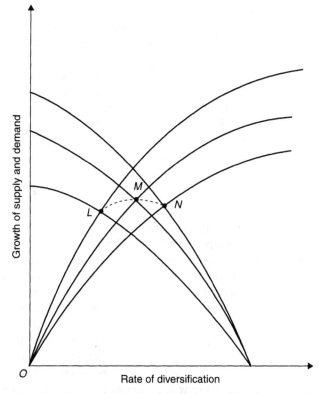

Figure 15.6 Diversification and growth: equilibrium outcome
Source: Marris (1964, p. 239)

within the firm, it is known as an endogenous growth theory. Firms consist of resources, and it is the growth and changing abilities of these that enables a firm to continually increase its productive capacity.

Tangible and intangible resources

The resources of the firm are both tangible and intangible. Tangible resources include physical assets, such as plant, equipment and physical labour, while intangible resources include skills and knowledge about productive and managerial processes. These resources are employed to supply a heterogeneous range of services to the managers of a firm, to be used in the various activities that the firm undertakes. Thus, the output that any given unit of a tangible resource can produce is not dependent just on the production function but also on the intangible resources embedded in the inputs. Knowledge enables the productive capacity of a resource to increase over time. Thus, the firm tends to generate unused productive resources that the firm's management tries to find uses for in the pursuit of increased rates of profit and growth.

Tangible assets can be purchased in the market, and more machines or workers can be hired at a price. However, intangible knowledge and skills reside within human capital and cannot be so easily purchased because they are acquired from training and experience within the firm and may only be valuable within its specific structures despite residing within individuals who can be hired or fired. Such considerations may apply to management resources, in particular. Managers plan and co-ordinate the operation of the firm using firm-specific structures and routines. Individual members of a management team are skilled in the ways of the firm as well as their specialist functions. The interaction between members of the team means that the sum of the parts is greater than that of the individuals alone because the effectiveness of one is dependent on the effectiveness of others.

Competences

The abilities of resources that combine tangible and intangible qualities have come to be termed "competences". A competence is the ability of the resources employed to perform a task or activity involving complex co-operation between people and other resources. Because of their knowledge and skills some resources are unique and can perform particular tasks more efficiently than others (see Foss and Knudsen 1996). Individual firms possess competences in unique combinations, are part of what Kay (1993a) terms the architecture of the firm and are particularly effective in given industries or markets. When these competences can be clearly identified as being at the heart of the firm and form the basis of its competitive advantage, they are termed **core competences** (Prahalad and Hamel 1990); these represent the collective learning of the organization: that is, the know-how needed to undertake the complex tasks of organizing a particular activity. Some firms may understand the oil industry better than their rivals, but their competences do not necessarily transfer to other business activities. If they do, then they can form the basis of a development pattern for the firm.

Growth

The Penrosian model concentrates on the growth process within the individual firm and identifies those forces that enable it to grow. As time passes there is an inherent tendency for the resources of the firm to accumulate knowledge and skills. In addition, the time and commitment required to undertake any given tasks is reduced as procedures become routines that are easily learned by others. Learning, experience and the routinization of managerial and production processes enables the firm to gradually expand its production capabilities; this implies the creation of unused resources that are available to the firm at zero marginal cost, to be used in new productive activities. It also implies increasing returns to the managerial function as the scale of the business increases.

Firms can grow at a given rate with a given managerial team for two reasons:

a   Indivisibilities in resource units means that as the firm grows these resources are more fully used.

b Managerial specialization and experience means an increase in their capacity and the emergence of unused resources that can be devoted to expansion.

Thus, underutilized managerial resources become available to the entrepreneurial function, which can use them in existing or new ventures to expand the firm.

LIMITS TO GROWTH

The Penrose effect or managerial constraint

Penrose (1959) and Richardson (1964) identify management as the main constraint on the growth of the firm. This constraint has been termed the "Penrose effect". Firms wishing to grow can always raise the necessary finance and find new markets, but they face difficulties in expanding the size of the managerial team without reducing its effectiveness. Thus, the limit to the size of the firm is the capacity of the existing team to manage an organization of a given size and complexity. Expansion of the management team may reduce its effectiveness, because new members have to be trained and assimilated and may not perform at the same level of efficiency as existing ones.

Reid (1994) sees this as a problem of adverse selection. To hire outsiders is to invest in an asset of uncertain yield. The willingness to recruit at higher levels may be limited by consideration of risk. Newcomers are at a disadvantage because they have a learning curve to overcome. This process can be explained with the aid of Figure 15.7.

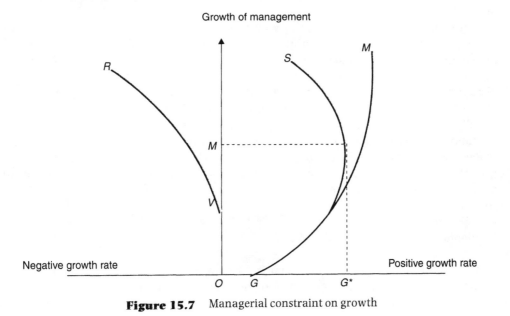

Figure 15.7 Managerial constraint on growth

On the horizontal axis is measured the growth rate of the firm and on the vertical axis the growth rate of the managerial team. Curve *GM* shows a positive relationship between the growth of the managerial team and the growth of the firm. The starting point of the curve on the horizontal axis is at *G* because *OG* is the rate of growth a firm can achieve with a stationary managerial team. The slope of the curve also reflects the diminishing returns to a higher growth of management, reflecting that expansion of the absolute size of the management team requires recruitment of new members who are less effective than existing staff. Curve *VR* shows a negative relationship between the rate of expansion of management and the rate of growth of the firm; this is because the management team has to spend increasing time on training and integration of new members, leaving less time to devote to the pursuit of expansion. Curve *GS* shows the overall effect on the growth of the firm by increasing the growth rate of management; this is the sum of two opposite effects illustrated by curves *VR* and *GM* and shows that a firm's growth rate can increase from *G* to G^* as the rate of managerial recruitment increases to OM^*. Any faster rate of expansion of the managerial team will have a negative impact on the growth of the firm. Thus, the maximum possible growth rate G^* is determined by the ease or difficulty with which management can expand itself (see Hay and Morris 1991, pp. 347–351).

The costs of growth

The costs of growth prevent firms from moving instantaneously to any desired size. Theoretically, a growing firm faces two sets of costs: first, those related to the operation of the current business and, second, those related to expanding or growing the business. If these costs are separable, then expanding the business has no impact on current operations because short-run marginal costs are unchanged and unaffected by growth (Slater 1980).

Costs may not be separable in this way and may be jointly incurred, so that growth adversely affects the costs of existing activities. The building of a new plant and the installation of new equipment to expand production capacity and potential output may require the redirection of other factors of production from their normal tasks, disrupting current production. For example, the time of key management and engineering staff may increasingly be directed to solving problems associated with installing and bringing on stream the new capacity, leading to the neglect of current operations and less efficient operation. Thus, the current cost levels of the firm are not independent of the growth strategy of the firm. The additional opportunity costs of growth may include higher current production costs because of less stringent supervision and/or the loss of current production.

Availability of non-managerial resources

It is not just the management team that is difficult to expand, it may also be difficult to expand other resources that are vital to the growth of the firm. A major constraint may be the availability of other key workers with particular skills. For example, train-operating companies in the UK were forced to cancel services in 2001 and limit growth because of a shortage of train drivers. Becoming a train driver requires training and the learning of routes and safety procedures, all of which takes time and assumes that sufficient people are willing to train at the going wage rate. If such problems can arise in traditional skill areas such as train driving, it is safe to assume they will arise in the new skill areas of computation and information technology. Similar concerns may arise over key physical inputs, particularly in the short run, when they are not readily available because of a shortage of capacity in supply industries.

Demand growth

The rate of growth of demand for a product within a geographical market is a function of the income elasticity of demand and changing tastes in favour of the product. The rate of growth is also a function of the age of the product in terms of its introduction to the market. The life cycle theory of a product envisages that it sells slowly initially, then at a faster rate, then slows down and then declines.

The growth of the firm is also limited by the growth of the markets it serves. If a market is growing at 2%, then the firm will grow at that rate to maintain its market share. If it is able to increase its market share, then it will be able to grow at a faster rate. If the firm is losing market share, then its growth rate will be less than the market rate.

If demand for the product is growing more quickly in a geographically separate market, then the firm may be able to increase its growth rate by selling in this new market, assuming it can gain a position in the market and achieve a faster rate of growth. However, entry into a new market incurs marketing and transport costs that are likely to be higher than those of existing firms; this will result in lower profits unless in time the new entrant can match the cost levels of the incumbents. An alternative strategy for the firm, one identified by Penrose and Marris, is for the firm to diversify. **Diversification** means that the firm produces new products for either new or existing markets. The incentive to diversify lies in the opportunities to use existing resources and to maintain or increase the growth rate.

Availability of finance

A major determinant as to whether the firm can achieve its plans for growth is the availability of finance. The main sources of finance are retained earnings, debt and equity. The ability to raise funds is a function of the profitability of the firm. Low profit rates will depress share prices and make it difficult for the firm to raise finance. A higher rate of profit and growth tends to make it easier for the firm to raise funds. However, firms in particular situations may find it difficult to find the finance needed. Various gaps have been identified in the finance market which affect small and medium-sized firms that find it difficult to obtain external funds at particular points in their growth.

Available opportunities

Economic models tend to assume that the management of an enterprise will have a host of projects to choose from in developing the firm. In practice, management may be unable to identify suitable opportunities that may be profitable for an enterprise, given its resources and competences; this may be reinforced by a cautious management who only see future difficulties rather than future opportunities.

LIMITS TO GROWTH: EMPIRICAL EVIDENCE

Richardson (1964) along with Leyland (1964) interviewed a group of 16 companies over 3 years, to explore the major factors limiting the growth of firms. Four major factors were considered: a lack of availability of labour or physical inputs, finance, lack of suitable investment opportunities and a lack of sufficient managerial capacity. Of these, they found that the group, "expressed the view without hesitation that the availability of suitable management had been, and was, the operative check on their expansion" (Richardson 1964, p. 10). Richardson then went on to examine the meaning of a managerial limit to the expansion of the firm. He emphasized the cost of organizational change within the growing firm, caused by the need to train and assimilate management recruits.

Richardson also argued that, "there is a functional relationship between organisational efficiency and its rate of growth, and that the former will decline after a point, as the latter rises" (p. 11). Further, "managerial difficulties associated with an unduly high rate of growth will show up not just in costs, but in all of the determinants of profits" (p. 14). In other words, Richardson argued that there is a growth–efficiency trade-off. Firms with superior core competences would be less subject to this trade-off, while expansion into new markets is more likely to reduce organizational efficiency than expansion within existing markets.

Reid (1994) set out to test Richardson's theory statistically by using a database of 73 small firms. The firms were classified into three types: sole proprietor, partnership and private companies. The importance of the growth–profit trade-off is confirmed by statistical and econometric evidence. The descriptive statistics in Table 15.1 indicate the mean values of average asset growth for the three organizational forms that typify organizational change associated with the growth of small businesses. It is clear that private companies have the highest growth rates and the lowest profit rates, while businesses run by a sole owner have the lowest average growth rate and the highest average profitability. The data suggest an inverse association between growth and profitability. However, within each type of organization, smaller firms tend to grow faster than larger firms. The growth–profitability trade-off confirms the presence of a Penrose effect and the importance of the valuation ratio.

Thus, the short-term performance of a firm is adversely affected by the growing complexity of its organizational structure. An increasing growth rate is related to falling short run profits, because a change of organizational form is costly as it

Table 15.1 Performance and business type 1985–1988

Business type	Performance			
	Asset growth		Profitability	
	Mean	SD	Mean	SD
Sole proprietor	22.75	52.1	31.74	49.9
Partnership	56.37	140.5	33.98	42.3
Private company	78.30	234.3	5.84	33.2

Note SD = standard deviation
Source Compiled by author using data from Reid (1994)

involves the creation of a new organizational architecture. Firms undertake change in the expectation that it will be more efficient in the long run (i.e., expected benefits exceed the costs) and that growth will lead to lower costs and improved business performance.

RESOURCES AND COMPETENCES

According to Kay (1993a) the main elements of the resource or competence-based theory of the firm are that:

- Firms are essentially collections of capabilities.
- The effectiveness of a firm depends on the match between these capabilities and the market the firm serves.
- The growth and appropriate boundaries of a firm are limited by its capabilities.
- Some capabilities can be purchased or created and are available to all firms.
- Others capabilities are irreproducible or reproducible only with substantial difficulty by other firms, and it is on these capabilities that the competitive advantage of the firm depends.
- Unique capabilities are generally irreproducible because they are a product of the history of the firm or their nature is not fully understood by the firm itself.

Resources include both products and inputs. Therefore, the firm may gain competitive advantage by possessing a product that is distinctive in the eyes of consumers; this enables the firm to gain market share at the expense of it competitors. If the firm does not have such an advantage and sells a product identical to that of its rivals, then the only way it can achieve a superior profit performance is to have competences that allow it to achieve lower costs. Alternatively, such superior profits can be seen as rents earned by factors for their superior performance or scarcity. The firm can attempt to identify resources or combinations of resources, to generate rents and, more importantly, to ensure the rents are long-lived (i.e., the competitive advantage is long-lasting).

The success of firms is generally based on the identification and exploitation of distinctive capabilities – factors that one company enjoys and other companies are unable to emulate, even after having recognized them. The ownership of distinctive capabilities is attributed to the ability of the firm to innovate to create new processes, products and managerial methods (Grant 1995).

Case Study 15.1   Stagecoach: core competences

Stagecoach (see Chapter 21), the UK bus company, grew very rapidly between its inception in 1980 and the late 1990s. It appeared to have found that its core competences lay in running short-distance, fare-stage bus routes. It also appeared to have an organizational structure that was able to incorporate acquisitions into the company quickly and then apply Stagecoach's unique method to reduce costs and improve price–cost margins. This successful formula was applied to acquisitions abroad and culminated in the expensive acquisition of Coach USA, a company specializing in coach hire and taxis, but not the day-to-day operation of timetabled bus services. The competences possessed by Stagecoach were applied successfully to internal growth and later to acquisitions. However, the success was not unique and long-lasting, in that in time other companies were able to emulate its success. Likewise, the key competences were not as successfully applied to new activities as the company grew and were not translated successfully to overseas acquisitions, particularly in the USA.

THE DEVELOPMENT OF THE FIRM

The economic models of the growth of the firm assume that a firm can diversify its operations when the growth in demand for its products slows or ceases and that the unused resources generated within the firm, particularly management, will be recognized and used in an effective way. Economic models tend to abstract from such issues as the quality of management and other resources available to the firm. These issues have been addressed by business strategists. They have developed theories of the firm to help explain why some firms achieve higher growth rates than others. The discipline has striven to develop a strategic theory of the firm, as reviewed by Phelan and Lewin (2000), who argued that the subject needs a strategic theory of the firm to inform decisions about the appropriate activities and boundaries of the firm.

Firms have a number of choices in terms of growth strategies, which can be characterized as follows:

1   Whether to choose a strategy of internal or external growth.
2   Whether to diversify the company by producing new products and serving new markets or entering new geographical markets (particularly, overseas).
3   In addition, the firm may move to extend into another part of a vertically linked production chain or it may move into completely unrelated activities.

Internal growth is where the company uses its existing capabilities, resources and finances to expand the business. The growth is entirely endogenous, but may be supported by external finance. The alternative external route is to grow by acquisition of existing companies. These issues will be discussed in the Chapters 16–19.

CHAPTER SUMMARY

In this chapter we reviewed various theories of growth including those of Baumol, Marris and Penrose. They all suggest that the key objective of firms is growth. The theories are more concerned with maximizing the growth rate of the firm than with maximizing profits, although profits are important in helping to finance growth. In our review we looked at:

■ The Penrose model, which is important in that it pays attention to the internal operation of the firm; this has been the starting point of theories more concerned with explaining successful strategies. It emphasizes the role of resources, capabilities and competences.
■ The Marris model, which combines the conflicting objectives of managers and owners and the rate of the stock market in determining the growth rate.
■ The Baumol model, which is an extension of the static sales maximization models and explains growth through the desire to maximize the rate of sales growth.
■ The factors limiting the growth of the firm, which include management, finance, demand and other resources.

The Penrose model, unlike the managerial models of Baumol and Marris, has no equilibrium solution since the growth outcome for any particular firm depends on the way in which individual enterprises make use of any underutilized resources and overcome the limits to growth.

REVIEW QUESTIONS

1 Explain Baumol's sales maximization model of growth.
2 How does Marris reconcile the conflicting interests of managers and shareholders?
3 Explain how a firm finds the optimal combination of growth and profits.
4 What factors encourage an endogenous growth process within a firm?
5 Explain Penrose's managerial constraint and explain why it limits the growth of the firm.
6 What are the factors that limit the growth aspirations of a firm?
7 What are the main characteristics of the resource-based view of the firm?
8 Identify a company and examine its growth record over the past 10 years. Try to identify factors that explain periods of fast and slow growth.

REFERENCES AND FURTHER READING

Baumol, W.J. (1958) *Business Behaviour, Value and Growth*. Macmillan, New York.

Baumol, W.J. (1962) On the theory of expansion of the firm. *American Economic Review*, **52**, 1078–1087.

Devine, P.J., R.M. Jones, N. Lee and W.J. Tyson (1974) Corporate growth. *An Introduction to Industrial Economics* (Chapter 4). Allen & Unwin, London.

Foss, N.J. and C. Knudsen (1996) *Towards a Competence Theory of the Firm* (Chapters 1 and 2). Routledge, London.

Grant, R.M. (1995) *Contemporary Strategic Analysis* (2nd edn). Blackwell, Oxford, UK.

Hay, D.A. and D.J. Morris (1991) The growth of firms. *Industrial Economics and Organisation* (2nd edn, Chapter 10). Oxford University Press, Oxford, UK.

Kay, J. (1993a) *The Foundations of Corporate Success*. Oxford University Press, Oxford, UK.

Kay, J. (1993b) The structure of strategy. *Business Strategy Review*, Summer. Reprinted in Kay, J. (1996) The business of economics. *The Business of Economics* (Chapter 6). Oxford University Press, Oxford.

Koutsoyannis, M. (1979) Marris's model of the managerial enterprise. *Modern Microeconomics* (2nd edn, Chapter 16). Macmillan, London.

Leyland, N.H. (1964) Growth and competition. *Oxford University Papers*, **16**(1), 3–8.

Marris, R. (1964) *The Economic Theory of Managerial Capitalism*. Macmillan, London.

Penrose, E.T. (1959) *The Theory of the Growth of the Firm*. Oxford University Press, Oxford, UK.

Phelan, S.E. and P. Lewin (2000) Towards a strategic theory of the firm. *International Journal of Management Reviews*, **2**(4), 305–323.

Prahalad, C.K. and G. Hamel (1990) The core competences of the corporation. *Harvard Business Review*, May/June, 79–91.

Radice, H. (1971) Control type, profitability and growth in large firms: An empirical study. *Economic Journal*, **81**, 547–562.

Reid, G.C. (1994) *Limits to a Firm's Rate of Growth: The Richardsonian View and Its Contemporary Empirical Significance* (CRIEFF Discussion Paper No. 9426). University of St Andrews, UK.

Richardson, G.B. (1964) The limits to a firm's rate of growth. *Oxford Economic Papers*, **16**(1), 9–23.

Slater, M. (1980) The managerial limits to the growth of the firm. *Economic Journal*, **90**, 520–528.

16

CHANGING THE BOUNDARIES OF THE FIRM: VERTICAL INTEGRATION

CHAPTER OUTLINE

CHAPTER OBJECTIVES

This chapter aims to explore and explain the economic motivation for a firm to engage in a strategy of vertical integration. At the end of this chapter you should be able to:

◆ Outline the meaning of the term "vertical integration".

◆ Explain the economic advantages and disadvantages of vertical integration for the firm.

◆ Elucidate the analysis of traditional economic explanations.

◆ Explain and analyse the transaction cost approach to explaining vertical integration.

◆ Outline the difficulties involved in implementing a strategy of vertical integration.

INTRODUCTION

Vertical integration involves joining together under common ownership a series of separate but linked production processes. Such a strategy is used by many enterprises to widen the boundaries of the firm and to enlarge its size. In this chapter we will examine:

■ The concept and dimensions of vertical integration.
■ The motivation for pursuing vertical integration.
■ Traditional economic explanations of the advantages of vertical integration.
■ Transaction cost explanations.

CONCEPT OF VERTICAL INTEGRATION

A decision by a firm to integrate vertically alters both the boundaries and the size of the firm. The production of goods and services involves a chain of linked activities from raw materials to final product. At each point the product of the previous stage is used as input for the next stage of production. Ultimately, all the various inputs are combined to meet the demands of final consumers. **Vertical integration** is the outcome of a make or buy decision. If the firm decides to make its own inputs, then it becomes vertically integrated. If it does not, then it remains vertically unintegrated. Vertical integration is often taken to mean that the firm will either supply all its requirements for a particular input or use all the output it produces. However, vertical integration does not necessarily imply that all the output of every stage is used only within the firm, nor that all inputs are produced within the firm. It may suit the firm to sell some output at some stages and to buy some inputs at other stages, resulting in partial integration.

Vertical integration in the business sense is the ownership by one firm of two or more vertically linked processes. The more stages owned and controlled by one firm the greater the degree of vertical integration and the fewer stages owned and controlled by one firm the lower the degree of vertical integration. Traditionally, the emphasis has been on ownership of successive stages and has generally been understood to be an all or nothing concept. However, some writers have placed the emphasis on control rather than ownership.

Blois (1972) coined the term "quasi-vertical integration" to describe a vertical relationship not linked by ownership but where effective control over a supplier or buyer is exercised by such means as long-term contracts. Harrigan (1985) followed a similar line. She argued that a firm may control vertically linked operations without full ownership and may enjoy the benefits of vertical integration without transferring all its output internally. A firm may also integrate many or few stages in the chain of linked processes. Where a firm relies on a mixture of its own and market supplies for its requirements or a mixture of owned and non-owned outlets for its sales, it is termed "tapered, or partial, vertical integration".

Case Study 16.1   Production linkages in the oil industry

The stages of the production process through which a firm may integrate depend very much on the technological and production functions of the industry concerned. Figure 16.1 presents a simplified vertical chain for the oil industry, from oil production/ extraction to the point where the product is sold to another user. For the retailing of petrol, the supply of heavy fuel oil for the generation of electricity and feedstocks for the chemical industry, there are up to eight vertically linked stages. Oil majors, such as Shell, Esso and BP, have traditionally striven to be fully integrated, producing and processing all the oil required to meet all their own demand in the final stages of the production chain. On the other hand, oil companies may not be fully integrated in that they may not use all the crude oil they produce (e.g., they may sell some to other firms for refining) or they may not produce sufficient crude oil to meet all their internal requirements.

The nationalization of oil-resources and production by some oil-producing countries altered the degree of vertical integration achieved by many oil companies and changed the strategic perspective of companies. Previously, oil majors had strived to be self-sufficient in terms of oil supply. After the enforced loss of ownership, but not necessarily of operational control of their oilfields, many companies began reappraising their commitment to a maximum degree of vertical integration. Many companies may not produce all the crude oil required to keep their refineries going and may have to purchase crude oil from other suppliers or they may not produce sufficient refined

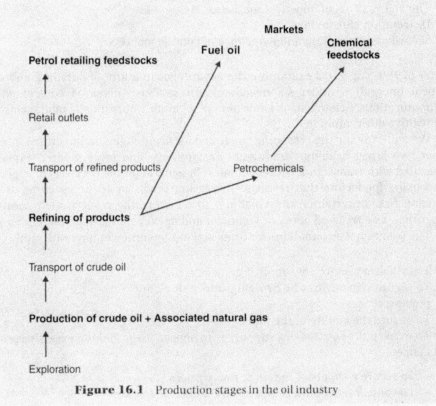

Figure 16.1   Production stages in the oil industry

products to meet all their needs. Thus, not all firms will necessarily be fully integrated: for example, a firm may only own crude oil and refineries and purchase transport, such as pipelines or tankers, to move its crude oil. Other firms may only own a refinery and a petrochemical plant thereby making a lateral move into another vertical chain. (For examples in the petrochemical industry see Burgess 1984). Firms may be fully involved at various stages and only partially involved at other stages. Firms "may adjust the dimensions of their vertical integration strategies to suit competitive or corporate needs; vertical integration need not be the same under all circumstances in order to be effective. Managers can fine tune their use of vertical integration in accordance with changes in the forces which shape the economic environment" (Harrigan 1985, p. 399).

MOTIVATION TO VERTICALLY INTEGRATE

Firms may decide on a strategy of vertical integration for a host of reasons that do not lend themselves to neat economic categorizations. Pickering (1974, p. 57) suggested that the various motivations can be categorized under four main headings:

- Efficiency gains in terms of technological joint economies.
- The ability to avoid imperfect markets.
- Distribution cost savings.
- Security and planning and avoidance of volatile markets.

Porter (1980) suggested examining the advantages to a firm of pursuing a strategy of vertical integration under six headings: cost savings, increased control, improved communications, changed organizational climate, operations management and competitive differentiation.

We will examine the reasoning suggested for firms engaging in vertical integration under two broad headings: traditional explanations and more modern explanations associated with transaction cost economics. In general terms, both sets of explanations are looking for factors that result in increasing profits or reducing costs, as well as reducing risk, uncertainty and volatility. In addition, the modern view sees vertical integration as a trade-off between technical and agency, or managerial, efficiency.

The traditional explanations for firms seeking to vertically integrate are:

- To establish a source of supply if none exists.
- To secure cost savings by bringing under single ownership technologically linked processes.
- To ensure the quality of the input.
- To weaken the position of a supplier who appears to be making excessive profits and hence:

  - To secure a supply of inputs at lower prices.
  - To control retail outlets and ensure market presence.
  - To strengthen monopoly power and raise barriers to entry.

TRADITIONAL EXPLANATIONS

Technical efficiency and production cost savings

In Chapter 7 the traditional concept of the production function was explored for a single product using two inputs in a single time period. The objective of the firm was to achieve minimum costs. A real firm would want to use or move toward least cost production methods. In the discussion of vertical integration the notion of the production function is more complex than the simple format presented earlier. Not only does it involve labour and capital but other key inputs or raw materials. While all these inputs can presumably be purchased in the market, the implication of vertical integration is that linking the production of an input and output through ownership produces a more cost-effective solution.

Thus, the traditional argument for a firm adopting a strategy of vertical integration is associated with the technological imperatives of the production process. In process industries, such as iron and steel, aluminium and petrochemicals, significant cost savings can be made by linking the production of a key input with a given product. Thus, smelting, rolling and fabricating of steel and aluminium, which could take place as independent processes, may be more effectively combined as a single chain of linked processes within one plant or complex; this gives significant savings on energy costs that would otherwise be required if the processes were separated and the metal required reheating. Similar arguments have been made in relation to motor car assembly: having car body plants close to the assembly plants saves on transport and storage costs and avoids delays in scheduling deliveries.

Production cost economies resulting from locating successive stages of production next to each other do not necessarily require single ownership of each stage: independent firms will locate such plants close to the source of the input if there are significant gains to be made. For example, chemical companies that make use of refinery outputs cluster around the refinery, so that the input can be piped over-the-wall, making savings on transport costs. In some instances, rather than being linked by a contract there is joint ownership of plants.

A disadvantage of vertical integration may be that the firm is committed to a technological set-up for the chain of linked activities. If there is a major technological advance at a single stage available to independent producers, it may not be usable by the integrated firm unless it updates its equipment; this may place the firm at a competitive disadvantage. However, if part of the process can be disengaged and supplies are available from independent producers, it would be cheaper to purchase supplies of the input through the market.

Management and co-ordination economies

Within an integrated firm the controller of a firm has the ability to direct resources between divisions and to vary output at different stages of the process. If the input is purchased from an independent supplier, then the firm seeking variation in supplies will have to renegotiate or enforce contractual terms. By avoiding the market, the integrated firm can avoid market transaction costs but does incur additional costs for managing a larger firm. Thus, the costs of the combined management functions required for the single enterprise are expected to be lower than for two independent enterprises linked by market transactions. On the other hand, the increased complexity of the firm may increase management costs compared with separately owned operations. However, even if management costs are higher they may be offset by production cost savings.

UNCERTAINTY AND SECURITY OF SUPPLY

Vertical integration may reduce the uncertainties faced by non-integrated firms. The controller of a firm is a boundedly rational individual making decisions with imperfect information in an uncertain environment. The controller may be called on to react to unexpected or unforeseen events. Vertical integration may be seen as a way of reducing information deficiencies and having to react to market or industry changes.

The sources of uncertainty in relation to supply include:

■ Unexpected unreliability of suppliers to deliver on time and the consequences for production scheduling of losing critical supplies.
■ Unexpected use of monopoly power by suppliers.
■ Variable quality of input that affects quality of output.

The sources of uncertainty in relation to selling the product include:

■ Fluctuating price movements and consequent changes in output leading to either cuts in output or increased storage of unsold output.
■ Unexpected changes in demand with similar consequences.
■ Greater certainty of access to sales outlets, particularly if the sector is dominated by powerful monopsonistic groups.

Vertical integration allows the firm to become more of a planning system. It enables management to overcome uncertainties relating to quality of product, uncertainty of supply and unexpected changes in prices for inputs. It does not, however, remove uncertainty relating to the market for final users in the production chain.

Vertical integration may give the firm two advantages in relation to information: first, the firm learns about the production issues relating to all aspects of linked activities compared with competitors who are not integrated and, second, the vertically integrated firm may also be able to hide information from competitors since all processing takes place in-house.

Market power

A traditional argument for vertical integration is to increase monopoly power. Market power enables the firm to raise prices above competitive levels in product markets. In some sense the vertical integration of two stages of production does nothing to alter the number of firms operating at each stage and, therefore, appears to have little impact on the degree of monopoly at each stage. However, it may change relationships between firms, in that a previously independent supplier may now be owned by a competitor. Thus, the competitor could stop supplying and disrupt production for its rival, thereby increasing opportunities to increase its market share. The competitor would then need to seek supplies from elsewhere. Therefore, the market structures at each stage of the production chain need to be analysed to see the potential for increasing the dominance of an integrating firm or for the integrating firm to become less efficient and for costs to increase.

Market power requires dominance at more than one stage of the chain. It enables a dominant firm to damage its non-integrated competitors by denying access to markets or to raw materials or by manipulating prices. If these conditions exist, then the integrated firm has a dual role, in that it may supply independent competitors with raw materials and then compete with them in a subsequent stage; this offers opportunities not available to single-stage producers to engage in both price and non-price discrimination. By narrowing the margin between the price at which it sells an input and the price at which it sells the output of stage II, the firm can limit the profits of independent competitors.

Let us examine two stages of a production chain in which there is one or more firms operating. On this basis we can show the potential relationships between them as set out in Table 16.1: in case 1 the seller stage and buyer stage are both competitive; in case 2 the seller stage is a monopoly and the buyer stage is competitive; in case 3 the buyer stage is competitive and the buyer stage a monopoly; and in case 4 both stages are monopolies.

Market structure 1: competitive sellers and buyers

If a sector is competitive, then we assume that price will be set equal to marginal cost and if it is a monopoly, then the price will be greater than marginal cost. Thus, if both

Table 16.1 Relationships between buyers and sellers in a vertical production chain

		Stage II: buyer	
	Structure	Competition	Monopoly
Stage I: seller	Competition	1. C/C	3. C/M
	Monopoly	2. M/C	4. M/M

Note   C = Competitive structure; M = Monopoly or dominant firm
Source Author

stages are competitive, then it will not be in the interest of either buyer or seller to integrate into the other stage because the buyer will not be able to achieve a lower price for the input with its own production facilities. Likewise, a seller could not achieve a higher price for the final product if there is effective competition. Therefore, there would be no incentive to alter the structure and to integrate the stages. Threats to withhold supplies would also not be relevant.

Market structure 2: monopoly seller and competitive buyers

If one firm dominates the seller stage and the buyer stage is competitive, then the monopoly seller will be able to charge a monopoly price to the buyer. If the buyer has to procure product I in fixed proportions with other inputs, then the buyer has little choice but to continue purchasing the input at a monopoly price, particularly if the seller benefits from economies of scale. Clearly, there may be some incentive for the buyer to integrate backward to reduce the monopoly power of the seller, but only if cost levels close to the incumbents could be achieved. If the buyer can vary the combination of inputs, then the buyer could substitute the lower priced input for the higher priced input supplied by the monopolist; this would place a limit on the market power of the seller. The seller might have an incentive to acquire control of the buyer to ensure that its input is purchased; this can be explained with the help of Figure 16.2, which presents the input options of a stage II firm to produce its output.

On the vertical axis is measured the quantity of input B and on the horizontal axis is measured the quantity of input A. Input A is produced by a monopolist and input B by competitive enterprises. The isoquant for a given output Q^* shows the possible input

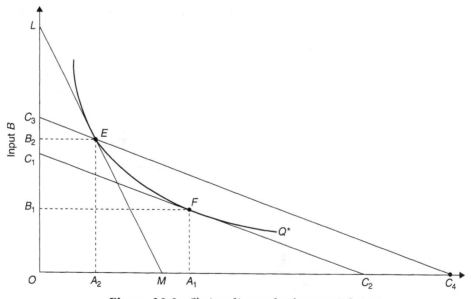

Figure 16.2 Choice of inputs for the stage II firm

combinations. The shape of the isoquant shows that inputs can be substituted in response to changes in relative prices of the inputs. The budget line that faces the buyer if both sectors are competitive is C_1C_2 and ML if sector A is a monopoly. Thus, if the buyer faces price line ML, then the monopoly price restricts the use of input A and the cost-minimizing equilibrium position is at point E compared with point F if competition prevailed in both sectors. Since the price lines are also cost ratios, point E is a more expensive position than point F because E is on the higher iso-cost curve C_3C_4 compared with F which is on the iso-cost curve C_1C_2.

If the dominant firm were to integrate forward and acquire an insignificant market share in stage II, so that it could not influence the market price, then there would appear little incentive to do so because it could not influence the selling price. It would also not be in its own interest to withhold supplies from competitors if it only had a small presence.

Market structure 3: competitive sellers and monopolistic buyers

If the seller stage is competitive and the buyer stage is a monopoly, then the buyer will have little incentive to integrate backward, because the firm would be unable to buy the input at any lower cost. The sellers of the input may have an incentive to integrate forward to control the monopoly buyer, to obtain a higher share of the monopoly profits or to establish a second stage II producer if entry conditions permit.

Market structure 4: monopsonistic seller and monopoly buyer

If both stages are monopolies, then both firms will be earning monopoly profits. Both firms have an incentive to acquire the other to obtain the total monopoly profit and remove any threat from the other of entering its stage of production. Whether entry is possible would depend on how easy or difficult it is to overcome the barriers to entry. The monopolist protected by the highest entry barriers will be in the stronger position.

These conclusions can be illustrated using the arithmetical example in Table 16.2. It is assumed that:

■ In stage I the marginal cost is 20, the competitive price is 20 and the monopoly price is 30 (i.e., a profit margin of 10).
■ In stage II the marginal cost is 40, the competitive price is 40 and the monopoly price is 60.
■ The final price is the sum of the two individual marginal costs plus any profit margin that market conditions allow.

We have the following final prices for stage II output:

■ *Market structure 1*: where both stages are competitive. The price is £60, which is the sum of the marginal costs in both sectors.

Table 16.2   Vertical integration and market structure

Structure	Stage 1			Stage II		
	Marginal cost (£)	Profit (£)	Final price (£)	Marginal cost (£)	Profit (£)	Final price (£)
1. CC	20	0	20	40	0	60
2. MC	20	10	30	40	0	70
3. CM	20	0	20	40	20	80
4. MM	20	10	30	40	20	90
5. Integrated	20	NA	NA	20	60	100

Source Author

- *Market structure 2*: where the seller is a monopolist and there are competitive buyers. The price of the stage II product is £70, which is the price of the input plus the marginal cost of stage II production, giving a monopoly profit in stage I and normal profit in stage II.
- *Market structure 3*: where the seller is competitive and the buyer is a monopolist. The price of the stage II product is £80; this is the sum of the marginal cost in stage I plus the monopoly price in stage II; a normal profit is earned in stage I and a monopoly profit in stage II.
- *Market structure 4*: where both stages are monopolized. The final price is now £90, the sum of the monopoly prices in both stages, with both firms earning monopoly profits.
- *Market Structure 5*: where two monopolists integrate. This allows the enterprise to make maximum profit. In this example it is assumed that the additional market power allows a price of £100 to be charged, allowing a profit margin of £60 to be earned per unit. Thus, the motivation for a monopolized vertically integrated enterprise is that the maximum profit is earned. Where there are two independent monopolies, they may reduce each other's profit by bargaining; this would not happen if they were unified under a single management.

A study of the UK petrochemical industry by Burgess (1984) concluded that vertical integration does not produce extra profitability and is likely in the long run to produce lower profitability. It did not make for more stable profitability because all production chains end in a final product market: if that is volatile, then upstream sectors will also be volatile. He also found that vertical integration put the downstream business at a disadvantage because of the removal of a commercial relationship between the two businesses.

ALTERNATIVE EXPLANATIONS OF VERTICAL INTEGRATION

The newer theories explaining the motivation for vertical integration make use of transaction cost economics. It is argued that vertical integration will result in:

- Savings in transaction costs by not using the market, whereas buying through the market involves: incurring costs in searching for suppliers, discovering prices; writing, agreeing and monitoring contracts. Contracting costs are avoided.
- Increasing management costs because internalized activities will require supervision and co-ordination.

Thus, the increase in management cost has to be less than the savings in transaction costs to justify vertical integration.

Integration also avoids problems associated with contracts. If incomplete, long-term contracts are signed, they can create problems when unforeseen changes take place in the business environment and the contract has to be revised; this gives the supplier the chance to engage in opportunistic behaviour, particularly if the buyer wishes to increase the quantity supplied. If suppliers have invested in highly specialized assets to produce the required input, then they may be able to exploit this to negotiate a higher price. Vertical integration allows the buyer to avoid opportunistic behaviour by the supplier.

Williamson's model

Williamson (1985) developed a model to determine the optimal level of vertical integration and the size of the firm. He distinguishes between:

- Technical efficiency, which indicates whether the firm is using least cost production techniques.
- And agency efficiency, which indicates the extent to which the firm minimizes co-ordination, agency and transaction costs.

He argues that the optimal vertically integrated firm minimizes the sum of production and transaction costs compared with the market alternative. The model assumes that the quantity of the good being exchanged is fixed. In Figure 16.3 the vertical axis measures differences between costs arising from internal organization and costs arising from market transactions. Positive values indicate that costs from internal organization exceed costs from market transactions. The horizontal axis measures asset specificity where higher values (or positions to the right) indicate a greater degree of asset specificity. Asset specificity is the extent to which assets can only be used to meet the requirements of one customer. If the asset has no alternative use other than its present use, then it has no value in any alternative use.

The curve ΔC measures the differences in technical efficiency: that is, the minimum cost of production under vertical integration (C_i) minus the minimum cost of production under market exchange (C_m). ΔC, or $(C_i - C_m)$, is positive for any level of asset specificity because outside suppliers can aggregate demands from other buyers and, thus, take advantage of economies of scale and scope to achieve lower production costs than firms that produce the inputs themselves. The cost difference declines with increasing asset specificity because greater asset specificity implies more specialized uses for the input and, thus, fewer outlets for the outside supplier. As a result, with

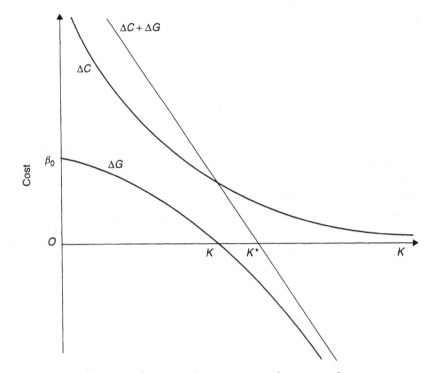

Figure 16.3   Vertical integration and asset specificity
Source: Reproduced from Williamson (1985, p. 93) by permission of The Free Press

greater asset specificity the scale and scope-based advantages of outside suppliers are likely to be weaker.

The curve ΔG reflects differences in agency efficiency. It measures differences in transaction costs when the item is produced internally (G_i) and when it is purchased from an outside supplier (G_m) in an arm's length transaction. When the item is purchased from an outside supplier, these costs comprise the direct costs of negotiating the transaction, the costs of writing and enforcing contracts, the costs associated with hold-ups and with underinvestment in relationship-specific assets. ΔG reflects the differences in agency efficiency between the two modes of organizing transactions. The curve is positive for low levels of asset specificity and negative for high levels of asset specificity. When asset specificity is low, hold-up is not a significant problem. In the absence of asset specificity, market exchange is more likely to be agency-efficient than vertical integration.

The curve $\Delta C + \Delta G$ is the vertical summation of ΔG and ΔC. It represents production and exchange costs under vertical integration minus production and exchange costs under market exchange. Therefore:

- If $\Delta C + \Delta G$ is positive, then arm's length market exchange is preferred to vertical integration. The firm will be located between O and K^*.
- If $\Delta C + \Delta G$ is negative, then vertical integration is preferred because the exchange

costs of using the market are more than offset by the production costs savings. The firm will be located to the right of point K^*.

Thus:

- Market exchange is preferred when asset specificity is low (i.e., K is less than K^*).
- Vertical integration is preferred when asset specificity is high (i.e., K is greater than K^*).

Vertical integration becomes increasingly attractive as economies of scale become more pronounced. The position of the ΔC curve reflects the ability of the independent producer to achieve scale economies in production by selling to other firms. Weaker economies of scale would shift ΔC to the right, reducing the range in which vertical integration dominates market transactions. Stronger economies of scale associated with large firms would shift ΔC to the left, increasing the relevant range that favours vertical integration.

The following conclusions can be drawn about the drivers of vertical integration:

1   If scale and scope economies are significant, then the firm gains less from integration the greater the ability of the external supplier to take advantage.
2   The larger the product market the more a firm will gain from vertical integration. The more the firm produces and the faster its growth the more likely it will be to vertically integrate.
3   The firm with multiple product lines and few inputs may benefit from vertical integration.
4   Where asset specificity is important the firm gains more from vertical integration. If asset specificity is significant enough, vertical integration will be more profitable than market transactions, even when production of the input is characterized by strong scale economies or when the firm's product market scale is small.

Incomplete contracts

The discussion in Chapter 14 of incomplete contracts is also relevant to the discussion of vertical integration. When two firms sign a contract that does not cover all potential states of the world, there may be an incentive for one of the partners to control the other enterprise; this would enable them to remove the opportunistic behaviour of one partner to hold up production of the other partner by withholding supplies. The partner that owns the asset has control over its use. All rights of control not specified by the contract remain with the owner of the asset. Thus, by owning the assets of the supplier firm the first enterprise will have a stronger bargaining position and the rights to any residual income.

Some of these issues together with asset specificity are illustrated by the well-documented case of General Motors and Fisher Body (see Case Study 16.3). A broader survey of transaction cost studies of vertical integration can be found in Shelanski and Klein (1995). They argued that, "Asset specificity and uncertainty appear to have significant effects on the vertical structure of production. This is especially remarkable when compared to the dearth of evidence on market power explanations for integration" (p. 344). Grossman and Hart (1986) focused their analysis on the importance of asset ownership and control.

Case Study 16.2   Kuwait National Oil Company

The traditional importance of vertical integration in the oil industry is illustrated by the strategies pursued by the state oil companies of the major oil producing companies. The Kuwait National Oil Company (KNOC) is one such example. It was first established in 1960 and became fully state-owned in 1975. Its task was responsibility for the country's oil-related assets including oil extraction, oil refining, pipelines and shipping. The company then proceeded to seek opportunities to integrate forward to acquire expertise in exploration, drilling and engineering and to find outlets for its crude oil and refined products. The country is a member of the oil producers' cartel OPEC (Organization of the Petroleum Exporting Countries) and a major producer of crude oil.

The prime objectives of vertical integration for KNOC were:

- To process within Kuwait as much crude oil as possible.
- To sell higher value products in international markets.
- To obtain international outlets for its oil.
- To gain greater security for long-term sales by shifting the emphasis from sales through markets to supply to owner-controlled facilities.

As a first step toward achieving these objectives, the company began acquiring refinery interests in the main oil markets of Western Europe and Japan. Supplying new markets with refined products from Kuwait-based refineries was seen to be high risk, given the market control of the oil majors and the possibility of retaliatory action against the company by other governments. The company acquired refineries and petrol stations in Western Europe: by 2000 it operated a wholly owned refinery in the Netherlands, a 50% share in one in Italy and 5,500 petrol stations. To obtain the necessary engineering and exploration skills, in 1981 it acquired Sante Fe, a Dallas-based oil engineering and drilling company.

The ultimate step in this direction came with the company building up a stake in British Petroleum; this started when the British Government sold a final tranche of shares in the company, following a stock market collapse (19 October 1987) in which 95% of the shares remained unsold with brokers. The shares were offered at 330p, but the market price fell to 75p before investors were prepared to commit themselves. The stake held by KNOC increased to 24%, significant in terms of control given the dispersion of other holdings. At this point the British Government became concerned that a key British-owned company would fall into the hands of a state-owned enterprise after the British Government had just sold its 51% stake to the private sector. The potential control that such a stake offered led to an investigation by the Monopolies and Mergers Commission (MMC). It recommended that KNOC should reduce its stake to 9.9% over a period of 12 months (MMC 1988). The issues of concern to the government also included BP being forced to buy oil from Kuwait, KNOC would have access to commercially sensitive information and would be less interested in developing high-cost North Sea fields.

Case Study 16.3   Fisher Body and General Motors

A case study that has been much studied by American economists was the relationship between Fisher Body and General Motors (GM) in the 1920s (Klein 1991). General Motors assembled motor cars and Fisher Body was geared up to manufacture pressed metal bodies to replace the traditional wood and metal bodies. In 1919, Fisher signed a long-term (10-year) exclusive contract with GM for the supply of car bodies. Fisher made the necessary investment in capital equipment, which was highly specific to meeting the model requirements of the assembler.

Each party to the contract tried to protect itself against the potential opportunistic behaviour of the other party. For example, Fisher could disrupt production at GM by holding up supplies or by supplying substandard bodies, while GM could threaten the existence of Fisher by reducing orders, terminating the contract or pushing for lower prices.

Fisher protected itself by signing an exclusive contract, so that GM could not seek supplies elsewhere. GM protected itself by agreeing to a pricing formula to ensure competitive prices. Prices were set on the basis of average variable costs plus a mark-up of 17.6% and could not be greater than those it charged to other companies.

The contract was incomplete in that it could not be written to take account of all changes in the economic environment. The unforeseen change was an increase in the demand for cars and, particularly, for those with closed metal bodies. This increase in demand created an opportunity for Fisher to behave opportunistically by holding up GM production and by increasing their share of the benefits (i.e., profits) at the expense of GM. The change in demand made Fisher a much more important and specialized input supplier to GM than previously. The new level of demand was outside the range envisaged in the original contract and made it profitable for Fisher to drag their feet on increasing output. The reason it was profitable for Fisher to hold up GM was the average variable cost plus pricing procedure that was based on production and transport costs: the mark-up was intended to cover the unspecified capital costs of the company. By using labour-intensive production process and refusing to locate plants close to those of GM, Fisher was able to opportunistically increase its profits; this was the case because the price paid was entirely a function of variable costs. Therefore, Fisher had no incentive to increase the capital intensity of the production process. The contract proved to be incomplete, illustrating the difficulty of writing a comprehensive contract to cover all eventualities.

By 1924 GM decided that the solution to the problem was to acquire Fisher on terms highly favourable to Fisher. The reasons for the move included stopping Fisher holding up production, avoiding contract problems and being able to plan the growth of capacity in line with the growth in demand.

Thus, when Fisher was an independent contractor, "it was necessary to write an explicit automobile body supply contract which ex post turned out to create significant hold-up problems. With vertical integration GM avoided these contractual difficulties by buying the machine (Fisher Corporation) and, in the sense of eliminating the need for an automobile body supply contract, eliminating the second transactor" (Klein 1991, p. 221).

VERTICAL INTEGRATION AND PROFITABILITY

After studying vertical integration in 15 large companies, Campbell (1995) suggested that the probability of successful vertical integration is low. The lessons of many vertically integrated mergers show that the key factor influencing success or failure is the corporate parent's influence on the acquired business. For this to be a positive influence:

1   The acquired business must have the potential to improve its performance independently of its relationships with other divisions or business units within the company.
2   The parent company must have the skills or resources necessary to help the business. In practice, they may not have the skills, and the methods chosen to integrate the company may cause more problems than they solve.
3   The parent company must understand the business well enough to avoid influencing it in ways that damage its performance (Campbell 1995, p. 126).

However, in many mergers these three conditions are rarely met because the parent company does not have the necessary skills or competences that can be applied to new areas of a chain. For example, when Sony acquired Columbia Pictures in 1994, critics argued that Sony had few skills that were applicable to the film industry and that the gain Sony would make from owning Columbia Pictures could have been achieved through alliances or contractual arrangements. Vertical integration should only be considered if there is a major obstacle to a voluntary arrangement. Voluntary arrangements are more likely to produce a better result because both groups will concentrate on what they do best, whereas acquisition may create more problems than they solve.

CHAPTER SUMMARY

In this chapter we examined the motives behind firms altering their boundaries through vertical integration. In doing this we analysed:

1   Costs savings in production and the advantages of not using the market – two of the major motives. Although the emphasis was on ownership of successive stages in the production chain, some of the advantages of vertical integration can be achieved in other ways.
2   How firms committing themselves to such a strategy should consider alternative means that might achieve the same objectives. Chief among these are long-term contracts of various kinds which tie firms together in exclusive relationships. However, such arrangements can lead to difficulties associated with incomplete contracts.
3   The circumstances in which vertical integration can be beneficial: where there are strong technological linkages, high transaction costs, problems relating to asset specificity and incomplete contracts.

REVIEW QUESTIONS

Exercise

Try to identify from your reading of current events an instance of a firm seeking to vertically integrate either by acquisition or by organic expansion. In addition, try to identify the motives and advantages claimed for such a development.

Discussion questions

1 What do you understand by the term "vertical integration"?
2 Explain and evaluate the saving of production costs argument for vertical integration.
3 How does vertical integration reduce costs?
4 Explain and evaluate Williamson's model of vertical integration.
5 If a competitor buys a supplier of a key input for your enterprise, what factors should your firm consider in deciding whether to copy the integration?
6 In what circumstances does a strategy of vertical integration increase the profits of the firm?
7 Consider the relationships between motor car manufacturers and motor dealerships and between brewers and pubs, identifying the nature of their vertical relationship.
8 What alternative arrangements can give the firm the advantages of vertical integration without the disadvantages of ownership?
9 In what ways does vertical integration increase the monopoly power of the firm?
10 Try to identify a recent merger or business venture that might be classified as vertical integration. In addition, try to identify the main advantages expected from such a strategy.

REFERENCES AND FURTHER READING

Besanko, D., D. Dranove and M. Shanley (2000) The vertical boundaries of the firm. *The Economics of Strategy* (Chapter 3). John Wiley & Sons, New York.

Blois, K. (1972) Vertical quasi-integration. *Journal of Industrial Economics*, **20**, 253–272.

Burgess, A.R. (1983) Vertical integration in petrochemicals: Parts 1 and 2. *Long Range Planning*, **16**(4), 55–60, **16**(6), 29–34.

Burgess, A.R. (1984) Vertical integration in petrochemicals: Part 3. *Long Range Planning*, **17**(1), 54–58.

Campbell, A. (1995) Vertical integration: Synergy or seduction? *Long Range Planning*, **28**(2), 126–128.

Grossman, S. and O. Hart (1986) The costs and benefits of ownership: A theory of vertical and lateral integration. *Journal of Political Economy*, **94**, 691–791.

Harrigan, K.R. (1985) Vertical integration and corporate strategy. *Academy of Management Journal*, **28**(2) 397–425.

Hart, O. (1991) Incomplete contracts and the theory of the firm. In: O.E. Williamson and S.G. Winter (eds), *The Nature of the Firm*. Oxford University Press, New York.

Klein, B. (1991) Vertical integration as organisational ownership: The Fisher Body–General Motors relationship revisited. In: O.E. Williamson and S.G. Winter (eds), *The Nature of the Firm: Origins, Evolution and Development.* Oxford University Press, New York.

Krickx, G. (1995) Vertical integration in the computer mainframe industry: A transaction cost interpretation. *Journal of Economic Behaviour and Organisation,* **26**, 75–91.

MMC (1988) *The Government of Kuwait and the British Petroleum Company plc* (Monopolies and Mergers Commission Cmnd 477). HMSO, London.

Pickering, J.F. (1974) Industrial Structure and Market Conduct, London, Martin Robertson.

Porter, M.E. (1980) *Competitive Strategy: Techniques for Analyzing Industries and Competitors.* Free Press, New York.

Shelanski, H.A. and P.G. Klein (1995) Empirical research in transaction cost economics: A review and assessment. *Journal of Law, Economics and Organisation,* **11**(2), 335–361.

Williamson, O.E. (1975) *Markets and Hierarchies: Analysis and Anti-trust Implications.* Free Press, New York.

Williamson, O.E. (1985) *The Economic Institutions of Capitalism.* Free Press, New York.

17

CHANGING THE BOUNDARIES OF THE FIRM: DIVERSIFICATION

CHAPTER OUTLINE

CHAPTER OBJECTIVES

This chapter aims to discuss the motivation and economic benefits that firms will obtain by pursuing a strategy of diversification. At the end of this chapter you should be able to:

◆ Identify the motives for diversification.

◆ Distinguish between related and unrelated diversification.

◆ Identify and analyse the main economic benefits from diversification.

◆ Elucidate and analyse the main costs and benefits of diversification.

◆ Explain the limits to diversification.

INTRODUCTION

The typical unit of analysis in microeconomic theory is a single-product, single-plant firm serving a single market. In practice, however, many firms produce a range of products and serve a number of markets. Such companies are described as diversified or as conglomerates. **Diversification** occurs when a single-product firm changes itself into a multi-product firm. Most diversification firms get involved in products that are related to their initial activity; this gives a diversified firm a degree of coherence and economic logic that may appear at first sight to be absent. However, where the firm diversifies into products that are unrelated, the economic benefits and logic are not so easily identified.

This chapter examines the economic and strategic motives for altering the boundaries of the firm through diversification. It examines:

■ The directions and types of diversification.
■ The firm as a portfolio of activities.
■ Economic advantages.
■ The performance of diversified firms.

DIRECTIONS OF DIVERSIFICATION

Diversification involves starting or acquiring new activities either related to or unrelated to a firm's existing activities. It can also be widened to include selling existing products in new, geographically distinct markets. Therefore, a firm can diversify in one of two directions: it can develop new products or enter new markets as illustrated in Table 17.1.

The firm is initially located in box 1 (its existing product market) and box 5 (its existing geographical market). The firm can achieve growth by sharing in the general growth of its existing market and by outperforming its competitors. It might achieve this by changing the product's characteristics and image, on the one hand, and by increasing promotional effort and advertising, on the other. When this market matures the growth of the undiversified firm ends unless it can take an increasing share of a stationary market.

Table 17.1 Directions of diversification

Product	Product markets		Geographical markets	
	Existing	New	Existing	New
Existing	1	2	5	6
New	3	4	7	8

Source Author

To overcome this constraint the firm can diversify. Diversification can take a number of directions. One form of diversification is moving from box 1 to box 4: that is, supplying new products or services to new product markets or to new geographical markets (box 8). However, existing products can be sold in new product markets (box 2) or new geographical markets (box 6). A good example of selling an existing product in a new market is the fizzy soft drink Ir'n Brew; this was marketed in Glasgow at the end of the 19th century. In Scotland it is still the market-leading fizzy drink and outsells colas. Geographical diversification was sought by selling the drink in the larger market of England and Wales, where it now has a 3% market share (Bruce-Gardyne, 2002).

The alternative strategy of producing new products to sell in existing geographical markets involves identifying an unfulfilled need and, of course, developing a new product to meet it. This strategy requires investment in both product and market development facilities and in research and development facilities. The benefits of R and D are uncertain and might not produce new products that are able to generate continuous growth for the firm. Sometimes, the firm whose product helps to create a new market does not necessarily survive the arrival of imitators offering superior products. In the UK home computing market, early innovator Sinclair with its Spectrum computers and later innovator Amstrad, which helped to popularize the PC, did not survive to be major players, both failing to keep up with the pace of technological change in the home PC market.

RELATED AND UNRELATED DIVERSIFICATION

Firms that diversify become conglomerate companies (i.e., they produce a range of products and serve a range of markets). These activities can be further broken down into related and unrelated diversification.

Related diversification

This occurs where a number of products jointly use some of the resources of the firm; this may mean using production machinery to make different products: for example, plastic moulding machinery may be used to make kitchen bowls and watering cans. Sometimes, the relationship is not through shared production technology and assets but through marketing and management. Fizzy soft drinks and chocolate use different production technology but they may have similar marketing and distribution requirements. The same managerial functions or assets may be able to service a multiplicity of products, generating economies of scope. Such links have justified the diversification of Cadbury's from chocolate into soft drinks to become Cadbury-Schweppes.

Unrelated diversification

This occurs when the new activities or products have little or no overlap in terms of their required managerial competences or asset requirements. Thus, a company making bricks and processing frozen chickens has neither markets nor production techniques that overlap, except in the very broadest sense. Companies engaged in unrelated diversification are further subdivided into:

- Managerial enterprises in which a managerial team provides general services to all the operating divisions within the company and decides which activities or products to add to or delete from the firm's portfolio.
- Financial or holding companies where the relationship between the core and the individual division is more or less purely financial, with little or no managerial input into the operation of divisions or subsidiary enterprises.

These two functions are combined in Williamson's M-form organization, or multi-divisional firm (discussed in Chapter 20), in which the central management offer both managerial and financial services to individual subsidiaries, which in turn return profits to the central management who reallocate funds to divisions.

THE FIRM'S PORTFOLIO OF ACTIVITIES

An undiversified firm produces one product, while a diversified firm produces at least two. Each of these products will have particular strengths and weaknesses and make varying contributions to the profitability of the firm. Strategy analysis suggests a diversified firm should analyse its portfolio of products using SWOT analysis (strengths, weaknesses, opportunities and threats) to determine whether they are making an appropriate contribution to the overall performance of the firm.

A SWOT analysis might involve the firm assessing:

- Existing products in terms of their attractiveness *vis-à-vis* competing products, particularly in terms of product characteristics.
- Existing markets in terms of demand, size and growth rate, the price and income elasticities of demand and the product's life cycle.
- Existing markets in terms of the structure of supply, the firm's relative size compared with its rivals and the availability of economies of scale.
- The competitive strengths of competitors in each market segment or for each product.

The firm can assess its position in each market relative to its rivals and record the results in a matrix, as shown in Table 17.2, which shows the potential growth rate for each market and the competitive strength of the company; this generates nine potential boxes in which activities can be categorized.

Activities or products in box 9 are those where the company's competitive strength is estimated to be strongest and where the market is growing fastest. At the other extreme is box 1, where the competitive strength of the company is judged to be weak and the market is growing slowly. The prescription for the firm is to concentrate

Table 17.2 Categorizing a firm's portfolio of activities or products

		Potential market growth		
		Low	Medium	High
Competitive strength of company	Weak	1	2	3
	Medium	4	5	6
	Strong	7	8	9

Source Author

resources in box 9 products and withdraw from box 1. Boxes 3 and 6 represent high-growth sectors where the firm is not strongly competitive. Decisions should be made as to whether a strongly competitive position can be attained and, if not, whether resources should be moved to alternative uses. In low-growth sectors represented by boxes 1, 4 and 7, the firm should consider its position in boxes 1 and 4, but stay in the low-growth market (box 7) where the firm is strongly competitive. In general, medium competitive positions call for appraisal to see whether the position can be improved, while a weak competitive position initially indicates withdrawal. The notion of removing resources from weakly competitive sectors may generate push factors to reutilize them either in the growing, medium to strong competitive sectors or to use them in new activities to replace weakly competitive activities.

Products or activities could be further classified in terms of their net contribution to profit (i.e., sale minus allocable costs). In a static context, one might expect products in box 9 to make a greater net profit contribution per unit sold than products in box 1. Likewise, activities in boxes 7 and 8 should make greater unit contributions than activities in boxes 1 to 6. In a static framework a firm should commit resources to the point where the marginal unit contribution from each product is the same; only then will each resource be allocated optimally. In a dynamic model where the company has to commit investment now for future benefits, the appropriate measure would be the net present value of future profit flows. If uncertainty is taken into account, then the firm should attempt to equalize the present expected value of the future flows from each product.

In a dynamic model it will be difficult to measure marginal returns in any given period, let alone equalize them: for example, activities like those in box 9 require investment of resources because of the high-growth rate of demand, while activities in box 7 where growth is low may require no investment and the firm's strong competitive position should produce above average returns. Surpluses generated in some activities can then be used to invest in those activities requiring investment.

ECONOMIC ARGUMENTS FOR DIVERSIFICATION

The starting point for diversification may occur when a firm's existing objectives *vis-à-vis* profit and growth cannot be met by its existing product. The threat to profitability is the spur to considering a diversification strategy. Thus, the adoption of a diversification strategy may be driven by a number of push factors arising from the current position of the firm. Push factors may include: the limited size of the existing market; the existence of underutilized assets that might be used to produce new products or manage new activities; and surplus investment resources that could be used to finance new activities.

There may also be a number of pull factors, or incentives, for firms to adopt diversification. Managers may also be pulled toward diversification where the potential rewards from investing in new market opportunities promise greater profitability than ploughing them back into existing activities. The greater the profit potential of new activities compared with its existing activity the stronger the pull. However, any diversification will have a higher degree of uncertainty attached compared with the more certain but limited returns in existing activity. Therefore, diversification may be a high-risk strategy because it involves new products, new markets and the commitment of financial and managerial resources for uncertain returns.

The pursuit of diversification may be tempered by the need to make sufficient profits to keep shareholders happy and to maintain the valuation ratio of the firm. If this cannot be achieved, then shareholders may prefer to see retained earnings returned in the form of dividends. A poor stock market performance may threaten the incumbency of the existing management, either as the result of shareholder dissatisfaction or by outside interests buying assets they consider to be undervalued. Therefore, managers must also consider the threats and risks posed to the firm as a consequence of diversification.

Synergy

Synergy is defined as the sum of the whole being greater than the sum of its parts and is often described as $2 + 2 = 5$. Thus, synergy serves to generate greater revenue or lower costs if two activities are carried out under a single management rather than separately. The source of these synergies is increased utilization of assets that are currently not fully used or the sharing of costs between a number of activities. Such assets could be: physical machinery, buildings and land; human capital like managerial and worker skills; and intangible assets like embedded knowledge, R and D skills and brand names. Such sources of synergy are sometimes termed "economies of scope". Larger firms may also benefit from economies of size, which may lower the costs of buying inputs, borrowing money or marketing products, that are unavailable to smaller firms.

Utilization of the firm's resources

Making better use of the firm's existing assets and competences could lower unit costs and increase labour and capital productivity. Greater use could be made of:

■ Indivisible plant and equipment by making new products alongside existing ones.

- The distribution and logistics system by distributing related goods to the same outlets.
- The marketing department to advertise and promote the new product using its accumulated knowledge and expertise of particular markets and customers.
- The brand name to sell new products using the goodwill built up for its existing branded products.
- Retained earnings that are not required to develop current activities can be used for investment in new activities rather than keeping them in the non-interest earning form of cash.
- Managerial talent, in general, and specific functions of the firm to extend its range of activities.

In her exogenous theory of the firm Penrose (1959) (see Chapter 15) demonstrated how the capacity of the managerial team increases as managers move down their experience curve and reduce initially complex procedures into simple and routine decision-making rules for subordinates. This surplus management capacity can then be deployed in managing new activities.

If a company has a particular managerial expertise it may be applied effectively in other markets. While some competences are industry-specific, others may be generic and can be applied with learning in a wide range of activities. If a firm possesses such competences, then it will look for sectors where its expertise might be applied when push factors encourage the firm to diversify. Such firm-specific resources may not be fully valued if used outside the context of the firm, because their firm-specific nature prevents their true value being revealed. When used within the firm these resources are likely to have a greater value than if used in isolation. The existence of unused resources raises the question of how long these resources can be used without further investment. While some resources, such as brand names and knowledge, might be used indefinitely without reducing their value and contribution, other resources, particularly those of a physical kind, may soon exhaust their capacity and require replacement and or expansion.

An important advantage of the diversified firm is that its corporate headquarters may have better access to information than that available to the market. The diversified enterprise may be more efficient in allocating its existing resources between product divisions and, more particularly, to new activities than the market. Acquiring capital from the market for new ventures is particularly difficult as external lenders do not have access to all the information collected by the firm. In a similar way, staff trained by the firm and steeped in its methods may be more easily transferred to new activities to form a project team because their qualities are well known. In contrast, assembling a team of completely new individuals is fraught with danger as their skills and ability to work together are completely unknown.

Economies of scope and size

Synergy may also be derived from economies of scope (see Chapter 8). Economies of scope are not about using existing resources more fully, but arise from the nature of the production function, so that two or more products or activities can be produced more cheaply together than separately. These benefits are not available to single-product firms.

The increase in size of the firm that comes with diversification may also produce economies of size. For example, an increase in size, might mean that larger firms may be able to use its buying power to obtain lower cost inputs. The extent to which this is possible may depend on the degree of relatedness between the various activities of the firm. Economies arising from buying power may only be achieved where common raw materials are used in several activities. Marketing benefits may only be achieved if the same methods are applicable to different activities.

Size may also allow the company to achieve lower management costs through organizational efficiency. Diversification may be a spur to a firm adopting more cost-effective organizational forms, such as the M-form organization identified by Williamson. This structure allows the firm to add new activities and new divisions with limited disruption to existing activities (see Chapter 20).

If synergy gains are either non-existent or very difficult to achieve in practice, a particular product from a diversified firm may have no advantages over the same product produced by a single-product, free-standing or specialist enterprise. Many specialist firms will claim advantages from lower production, marketing and governance costs without having to share in the many joint costs of the diversified enterprise.

Reducing the volatility of profits and risk spreading

A single-product, single-market firm is vulnerable to erratic and cyclical variations in demand and input costs, as well as to long-term decline in demand. Together, these two factors lead to cyclically fluctuating revenue and costs and hence profits, as well as to profits that are potentially in secular decline. Therefore, diversification is a way for the firm to reduce the dispersion and offset the decline in profits. Cyclical variations can be offset by the acquisition of products whose sales move counter-cyclically to its existing product, while secular decline can be offset by acquiring products exhibiting long-term growth. Such diversification strategies are intended to both stabilize and prevent the firm from making losses, because such diversification may be a strategy designed to avoid bankruptcy and the death of the enterprise.

Diversification enables a firm to spread risks by offering a degree of insurance against unexpected changes in any one market for any one product. A market shock affecting a single product will have greater impact on a specialist firm's profits than those of a diversified one. For example, the demand for air travel has been adversely affected by unexpected shocks, such as the invasion of Kuwait by Iraq in 1991 or the events of 9-11 in the USA. A given fall in sales may have a bigger proportionate impact on specialist airlines than a diversified company with an airline division, leading to losses, retrenchment and, ultimately, bankruptcy.

A diversified company with a portfolio of two products whose sales move counter-cyclically can achieve a more even flow of revenues. Counter-cyclical activities could involve products whose cycles are inversely related to existing products and products whose cycles lag behind other products and reach their peak at different times. Together, the difference between highs and lows in overall sales can be reduced.

Likewise, shifts toward new geographical markets may offset fluctuations in sales. If the economic cycle in one economy is out of step, then variations in sales will likewise be reduced. For example, it is argued that the economic cycle in the UK follows a different time path from that of continental European economies. Having a significant presence in both economies will not stop fluctuations in sales but will lessen their amplitude. Seasonal variation in sales in one market can also be overcome by combining products whose peak sales are in different seasons. Long-term product decline can also be overcome by having a portfolio of products at different stages of their life cycles. Therefore, the object of spreading risk is to ensure that a failure of one product or one market does not threaten the firm with bankruptcy.

Financial synergies

Diversification may limit profit variability and, hence, variations in dividend payments to shareholders; this may give the firm a cost of capital advantage compared with firms whose profits are more variable. The firm may find it can raise new equity capital and loans on advantageous terms that are unavailable to firms with greater profit variability. If the firm has a choice between equity and debt finance, as discussed in Chapter 12, then a more stable profit and dividend flow will allow the firm to increase the proportion of its finance raised through debt capital. The greater stability of earnings reduces the risk to debt holders of not receiving their interest payments. Debt capital may also offer tax advantages to the firm, since the interest payments are treated as a cost rather than an element of profit. Dividends in contrast are regarded as profits distributed to shareholders. Thus, if a firm wanted to raise an equal amount of capital using debt and equity, then the level of corporation tax payable would be higher if the equity route was chosen.

The risk of no-dividend payment to shareholders is also reduced. However, individual shareholders do not necessarily require the enterprise to reduce the risk associated with an individual shareholding because by acquiring a diversified portfolio of shares they are better equipped than the firm to spread or counteract risk. A diversified share portfolio enables them to stabilize their incomes. However, if investors are unable to acquire fully diversified portfolios, then the firm's efforts to do so may be welcomed.

A larger firm has the opportunity to utilize funds generated from one activity for investment in another. The use of internal funds negates the need for the firm to borrow from external sources. Such funds are always available at a price, but spending on diversifying to produce new products may be viewed as very risky by potential lenders. With their own resources the firm is better able to finance these strategies and to back their superior knowledge of the proposed change. This argument assumes that internal capital markets are more efficient than external capital markets. However, the firm must consider the opportunity cost of internal funds and whether retained earnings should be paid to shareholders or funds acquired through the market.

Shareholders and stock markets appear to have little confidence in the ability of diversified firms to use available resources effectively. A noted feature of diversified firms is that they trade at a lower price, given their earnings, than focused firms. This difference, which has been noted in the UK and the USA, is known as the "diversification discount".

Managerial risks and rewards

The senior managers of a company, unlike their shareholders, cannot diversify their employment risks. If the firm does badly, then they face being dismissed by shareholders or the company being acquired by another enterprise. As a result, it is in the interests of senior managers to diversify the activities of the firm to reduce the variability of overall profits, dividends and, hence, share price to reduce the risk of their own dismissal. If managerial rewards are also tied to the size of the firm, then growth by diversification satisfies both their need to protect security of employment and the desire to see the remuneration package increase in size. However, if managers take diversification too far in pursuit of managerial security, then it may eventually reduce profitability and bring managers into conflict with shareholders.

The pursuit of growth

Diversification may be pursued as part of the growth strategy of the firm. Diversification not only reduces risks but may also be a route to securing the growth of assets, sales and profits. Firms whose major objective is growth will wish to escape from the constraints of their existing slow-growing markets. This push factor will be stronger the greater the proportion of sales accounted for by slow-growing markets and the greater its market share, making it more difficult to increase sales and to acquire competitors. Companies may be pulled toward other geographical markets when a product is at a late stage of its life cycle in one market and at an early stage in another. If the firm does not have a portfolio of promising products, then the pursuit of growth will encourage the acquisition of other companies with portfolios of potentially successful new products.

For example, in the banking industry the Hong Kong Shanghai Bank, facing a politically uncertain future when the territory was handed back to China, sought to diversify into other geographical markets. In the UK they acquired Midland Bank, one of the big four English banks. It also has banking interests throughout the world, mainly through acquisition. Other financial services companies have diversified into new products. For example, the Prudential Insurance Company decided to move into banking by establishing Egg, an Internet-based bank.

Transaction costs

The transaction cost framework developed in Chapter 14 has been used to explain the boundaries of the firm. Efficiency-based arguments for diversification have to be compared with the alternative of using the market. Only if the gains from utilizing unused resources internally exceed the gains made by arranging to sell the use of the resources to third parties can the efficiency arguments for diversification hold. Grant (1995) argues that, "for diversification to yield competitive advantage requires not only the existence of economies of scope in common resources but also the presence of transaction costs that discourage them from selling or renting the use of the resource to other firms" (p. 381). Treece (1982) argues that it is not only efficiency gains but also the presence of transaction costs that discourage the firm from selling or renting the resources to other firms. He further argues that transaction costs are likely to be substantial when intangible assets, such as brand names and technical knowledge, are involved. Likewise, the more tacit the knowledge and the more unique it is to the firm the lower its value outside the firm.

If a firm jointly produces two products, then the efficiency argument is that the combined costs of making both goods are less than if they are made separately. The alternative to both products being produced by a single enterprise is for a contract to be agreed between the producer of product 1 and product 2 to jointly produce the two products. For example, spare printing capacity owned by a newspaper may be used to justify the launch of a new newspaper. The alternative is for the newspaper to sell its spare capacity to another company requiring printing facilities. An alternative arrangement is to have the relationship between newspaper firms and printing firms regulated by contract rather than ownership. A contractual arrangement might be more expensive or less expensive than joint production within the firm. Thus, if the production costs are the same for both arrangements, then the choice between the two alternatives requires a comparison of governance and transaction costs. If the transaction costs of writing and enforcing contracts are greater than the governance costs, then the firm may find diversification the preferred option. However, the alternative to using excess capacity to diversify is to rent the excess capacity to other potential users.

Therefore, the transaction cost approach calls for closer assessment to see whether the efficiency arguments for diversification are justified. The firm should always consider the alternative of seeking to sell spare resources to outside users and, therefore, identify the core activities of a diversified firm. The transactions cost approach also focuses attention on the potential failures of the market system to organize these resources.

Market power

Diversification does not add to the market power of the firm in the sense that its market share is increased in a single market. However, it does increase its ability to adopt other anti-competitive practices. The ability to do so comes from the strength of the company to finance activity in one market with support of profits made in another. The implication, according to Hill (1985), "is that diversified firms will thrive at the expense of non-diversified firms not because they are more efficient, but because they have access to what is termed conglomerate power ... which is derived from the sum of its market power in individual markets" (p. 828).

A diversified firm can engage in practices unavailable to single-product enterprises. It might engage in predatory pricing to make life difficult for competitors and possibly drive them from the market. A **predatory price** is generally perceived to be one that does not cover its variable costs in the short run and average variable and fixed costs in the long run; this may be difficult to prove since the allocation of joint overhead costs is generally based on arbitrary rules. Although price cutting may lead to a firm not covering its full costs in the short run, the intention is that it will attract additional customers and perhaps drive single-product rivals from the market in the long run. Such cross-subsidization in pursuit of a long-term goal may also apply to other forms of competition, such as advertising and product enhancement. These policies may not be in line with the resource allocation rules of the diversified enterprise and may be ignored in pursuit of other managerial goals.

The use of selective price cuts in the UK newspaper market by News International, a diversified media group, has been described as predatory pricing, particularly by its critics and specialist newspaper enterprises. However, despite complaints to the competition authorities in the UK such practices have not been found to be anti-competitive.

BENEFITS AND COSTS OF DIVERSIFICATION

The benefits of diversification give the firm cost advantages for given ranges of output and revenue possibilities: for example, using excess capacity to produce an additional product must have finite possibilities. Competences whose capacity expands with use would seem to have no limit to their exploitation. In practice, the firm has to combine cost advantages and cost disadvantages and determine the optimal degree of diversification that aids the maximization of profits or managerial utility functions.

Diversification that initially leads to cost savings may later lead to cost increases; this is more likely to happen the further the firm moves from its core activities and the larger the firm becomes. Increases in the number of products produced and markets served, particularly if they are unrelated to the core activities of the firm, may eventually lead to there being no synergy gains, while additional activities add more to the management costs of the enterprise.

The relationship between diversification and profitability can involve four scenarios: (1) profitability increases, (2) profitability decreases, (3) profitability increases initially and at some point starts to decline and (4) profitability decreases initially but at some point starts to increase.

Studies by Grant et al. (1988) and Markides (1985) conclude that cross-sectional studies show that scenario 3 (i.e., the U-shaped relationship between profit and diversification) is the appropriate one. Such a relationship is shown in Figure 17.1. Profit initially increases, but the more diversified the company becomes so the rate of profit declines. Thus, diversification taken too far eventually brings increasing costs and dwindling profitability; this is attributed to greater administrative and managerial costs the more diversified and complex the firm becomes, leading to information

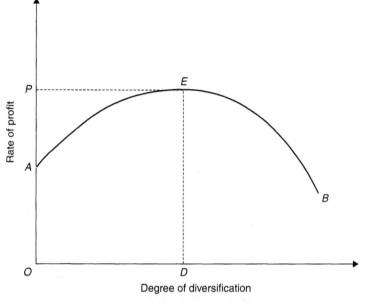

Figure 17.1 ■ Profit and diversification

distortion and control loss and is similar to the relationship postulated by Marris which we discussed in Chapter 15.

Managerial assets that can initially cope with diversification may be less able to do so the more diversified the firm becomes. The competences and skills of the managerial team may become less appropriate the farther away the new activities are from the original ones of the firm. For example, techniques appropriate to managing oil refineries may not be appropriate to managing supermarkets. Organizational structures may likewise become inappropriate for a larger and more diversified firm, leading to increases in management costs and less effective management as the span of control increases. The ending of synergy benefits will also contribute to increasing costs. Therefore, a position can be envisaged where the marginal benefits of increased diversification decrease and marginal costs increase; this is illustrated in Figure 17.2, with the optimal level of diversification at *OD* where marginal benefits equal the marginal costs of diversification. Thus, it would not be in the interests of the firm to diversify beyond *OD*, because the costs of doing so would exceed the benefits.

Another problem with increasing diversification is that shareholders and financial markets find it increasingly difficult to value the firm because of the wide range of activity, the disbelief in effective internal capital markets and the absence of appropriate valuation techniques for highly diversified firms; this leads to a decline in its valuation ratio as shareholders sell rather than buy shares. Thus, if shareholders believe, rightly or wrongly, that the enterprise may be more valuable broken into its component parts than as a single enterprise, then the management may be forced to yield to shareholder pressure and split its businesses: for example, in 2000, Kingfisher

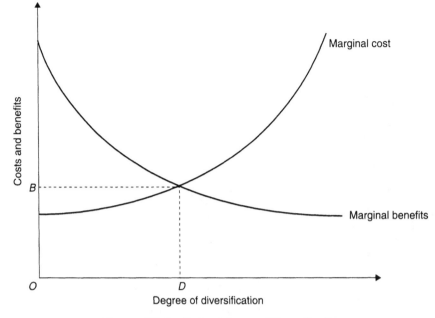

Figure 17.2 Optimal degree of diversification

split its Woolworth variety store business from its DIY and electrical businesses; and in 2001, British Telecom divested itself of its mobile phone operation.

THE PERFORMANCE OF DIVERSIFIED FIRMS

Our previous discussion suggests that if diversified firms are more effective at utilizing resources than single-product firms, then they might be expected to earn a higher rate of profitability. If they are not, then we might expect single-product firms to be more profitable. Studies of the impact of diversification on firm performance can proceed at two levels: first, case studies of individual enterprises charting the progress of diversification and profitability and, second, studies of samples of firms to measure the relative profitability of diversified and non-diversified firms.

The evidence from the second group of studies is deemed by reviewers of such studies to be inconclusive when either related or unrelated diversification is involved. One of the problems with statistical studies is that researchers use differing methods for measuring the degree of diversification. In addition, there are problems in obtaining appropriate samples of firms and obtaining financial data in a common format.

One of the first studies of the impact of diversification on performance was that by Rumelt (1974). He found that highly diversified firms performed less well than that more focused or less diversified enterprises, but that diversified firms grew faster than single-product firms. A second study by Luffman and Reed (1984), examining UK enterprises, came to a similar conclusion. Rumelt also found evidence that firms that diversified into related activities were more profitable than firms engaged in unrelated diversification.

Financial studies using stock market data have been more conclusive. Markides (1992) found that announcements of refocusing by diversified enterprises led to significant upward movements in share prices. Pandya and Rao (1998) suggested that, "while management and marketing disciplines favour related diversification, finance makes a strong case against" (p. 67). In a study of financial performance on a large sample of US firms, they found that, on average, diversified firms showed better performance than undiversified firms in terms of risk and returns and that the best performing undiversified firms had the best returns, but these were more variable.

A number of studies have been made into the diversification and performance of Australian enterprises. Bosworth et al. (1997) examined the performance of 942 companies for the period 1989–1994 and found more focused firms had higher profitability. Feeny and Rogers (1999) investigated the impact of diversification, market share and concentration on profitability, using a sample of 722 large Australian companies. The extent of diversification appeared to have little influence on profitability, although more focused firms appear to have higher profitability when loss-making firms are excluded from the analysis.

Jenna and Leslie (2000) reported on the strategic behaviour of European utilities freed by privatization and deregulation to pursue diversification. They concluded that shareholders should question how well the companies are using their resources and that some are in danger of losing their way. The evidence suggests that initial diversification into related activities generates increased profitability but that higher degrees of diversification lead to declining performance. The reasons appear to be that existing resources eventually become fully utilized and limit the profitability of further diversification when they are also used in related sectors.

Case Study 17.1 Virgin Group – Diversification and branding

The Virgin Group may be used to illustrate the use of underused competences or resources. The essence of the group might be said to be its brand name and it marketing ability. Led by the entrepreneurial Sir Richard Branson the company has a disparate range of activities from airlines to mobile phones to financial services to railways, which might be considered unrelated activities. However, the common factor linking all these ventures is the use of the Virgin brand name and the marketing skills of the company. Industry and product-specific skills where required are provided by partners through joint ventures or purchased through contracts. Sir Richard has commented that, "Virgin is not a one-product brand, like Nike or Coca-Cola. It is different and diverse, so there are opportunities to extend it across a wider range of marketing areas. I want to make Virgin the number one brand in the world, instead of around tenth, which is where it is now. There is great scope for this globally, but I think we've probably gone as far as we can in the UK" (Kane 2002). However, an unsuccessful venture that fails to deliver the benefits the consumer associates with the Virgin brand may damage the other products in its portfolio. For example, critics argue that the company's railway ventures in the UK are having that effect.

Case Study 17.2   US oil industry: related and unrelated diversification

A study by Ollinger (1994) of the US oil industry examined the success or failure of alternative strategies for changing the boundaries of 19 major oil firms and the limits to the transferability of firm-specific skills in the growth process.

The study evaluated the success of horizontal growth, vertical integration and related and unrelated diversification between 1930 and 1990.

First, oil companies grew by transferring skills from one industry to another (following Penrose 1959). In general, they initially expanded domestically and then internationally, then diversifying into the related petrochemicals sector and finally into unrelated activities after exhausting their sources of related growth.

Second, the number of complementary skills required determined the success of diversification. Oil companies initially profited from diversification into petrochemicals because the industry's research, input needs and production technology were complementary to the oil business. They were less successful in businesses in which fewer complementarities existed, such as coal, land development and road building. Diversification completely failed in businesses in which managers had no grasp of the final market and in which no commonalities with the oil business existed, such as retailing, computers and electronics.

Third, the multi-divisional form of organization provided an efficient structure for diversifying firms. It allowed top managers to consolidate operations and subordinate managers to take direct control and be accountable for well-defined markets.

Thus, the major oil firms were successful at diversifying as long as they made use of the core competences acquired in the oil industry but were unsuccessful in unrelated diversifications.

Case Study 17.3   Hanson Trust: its rise and dismemberment

The Hanson Company became a large conglomerate that evolved a successful organizational structure, allowing it to acquire and dispose of companies and to become a fast-growing and profitable diversified enterprise.

The men behind the success of Hanson were James Hanson and Gordon White, who started the business together in the late 1950s, importing comic greeting cards. In 1962 they took charge of a family-controlled lorry dealer called Tilloston. In 1964, Tilloston was bought by the Wiles Group and Hanson and White joined the board of directors. A year later Hanson and White took control of Wiles, with Hanson becoming chairman. The company also bought White's publishing firm Welbescon. The company then had a market capitalization of £300,000. By 1975, the company – renamed Hanson Trust – had become the 112th largest company in the UK, by 1985 it had risen to 33rd and by 1995 to 7th in *The Times 1000* list of largest UK companies.

The Hanson Company developed a decentralized management structure with the objective of growth through acquisition. In the process it became a highly diversified company with a wide range of products serving markets throughout the world. Companies were bought and reorganized, with parts retained and others sold.

The motives for acquiring firms were mainly financial, with the object of increasing shareholder value. Companies were identified as targets as a result of searching for inefficient companies that were asset-rich but undervalued by the stock market. Such companies were judged to be able to benefit from the Hanson treatment and release significant value to the acquirers, so that the purchase price was recovered by disposal of assets. The target companies were characterized as being in low-technology, low-risk, basic industries, with not much competition and little or no government interference. Essentially, Hanson purchased underperforming companies, sold their peripheral assets and focused on making the remaining assets as profitable as possible. The largest acquisitions were made in 1986 when Imperial, the UK-based tobacco and food group, and SCM, a US conglomerate, were acquired for £2.5bn and $930m, respectively. In 1995, after 30 years of development the company had many subsidiaries operating in chemicals, coal, building materials, cranes, forest products, tobacco and propane.

The company was extremely successful in its growth through acquisition strategy. In the period 1981–1985 the company achieved shareholder returns of 57%, outperforming the conglomerate index by 67% and the all share index by 128%. In the period 1986–1992 the company still outperformed the comparator indices but by a much lower margin. In the period 1990–1996 the company did less well than the market as a whole, underperforming the all share index by 35%. Declining shareholder returns led the company to revise its strategy of unrelated diversification.

To raise shareholder returns it was decided that the business should become more focused. In 1995 it was decided to concentrate on seven or eight areas and to dispose of subsidiaries that did not fit. The first disposal was a collection of 34 small US businesses that were floated as US industries (USIs). This successful move was followed in 1996 by the decision to break the company into four components:

1 Energy Group, including Eastern Electricity in the UK and Peabody, which mines coal in the USA and Australia.
2 Imperial Tobacco, the world's second largest maker of cigarettes.
3 Millennium Chemicals, including SCM and Quantum.
4 Hanson PLC, manufacturer of building materials and equipment.

The first three were floated on the stock exchange and the last continued as the rump of the original company.

The force pushing the company apart was the belief among shareholders that the company had lost its way and that this was reflected in its poor performance in the 1990s. It was becoming increasingly difficult to make the strategy work, because the size of acquisitions required to have the necessary financial impact on the group was becoming larger and larger combined with the difficulty of finding large underperforming companies. After 3 years the divestment strategy was judged to have been successful from the shareholders' viewpoint – the gain being estimated to be 35% in real terms.

CHAPTER SUMMARY

In this chapter we examined the reasons firms diversify. In doing this we analysed:

■ The notion of diversification, together with the firm as a portfolio of activities.
■ A number of advantages and disadvantages to diversification and the notion that there is an optimal degree of diversification.

■ Empirical studies, which are inconclusive in terms of determining whether diversification is always successful. The strongest conclusion for companies is summed up in the phrase "diversify with care".

REVIEW QUESTIONS

Exercise

a Select a company, read its annual report and determine its degree of diversification.
b From your reading of the business pages identify a company that has made a move to diversify either by organic change or by acquisition. Try to ascertain the motivation and expected economic benefits.

Discussion questions

1 What do you understand by the term "diversification"?
2 Distinguish between related and unrelated diversification. Why might the former be more successful than the latter?
3 Read a company's annual report and identify the firm's main activities in terms of turnover and profitability:

   – Assess the firm's degree of diversification.
   – Assess the relative contribution of each activity to profitability.
   – Which sectors are strong in terms of profitability and growth and which are weak?

4 Explore the main sources of economic gain a firm might expect from pursuing diversification.
5 Explore and explain the following rationales for diversification:

   – Unused resources.
   – Economies of scope and size.
   – Risk reduction for investors.
   – Managerial utility fulfilment.
   – Lower financial costs.

6 Scan the newspapers for recent reports on companies either proposing to diversify or to refocus their portfolio of activity. Try to explain the pressures that have brought about the change and the benefits identified by the firm.
7 Is it possible to define an optimal degree of diversification for a firm?
8 Why is diversification a popular strategy with management?

REFERENCES AND FURTHER READING

Bosworth, D., P. Dawkins, M. Harris and S. Kells (1997) *Diversification and the Performance of Australian Enterprises* (Working Paper No. 28/97). Melbourne Institute.

Bower, T. (2001) *Branson*. Fourth Estate, London.

Bruce-Gardyne, T. (2002) Och aye the Bru. *Financial Times Magazine*, 9 February, p. 23.

Feeny, S. and M. Rogers (1999) *Market Share, Concentration and Diversification in Firm Profitability* (Working Paper No. 29/99) Melbourne Institute.

Grant, R.M. (1995) Diversification strategy. *Contemporary Strategy Analysis*, (2nd edn, Chapter 14). Blackwell, Cambridge, MA.

Grant, R.M., A.P. Jammine and H. Thomas (1988) Diversity, diversification, and profitability among British manufacturing companies (1972–1984). *Academy of Management Journal*, **31**(4), 771–801.

Hill, C.W.L. (1985) Diversified growth and competition: The experience of 12 large UK companies. *Applied Economics*, **12**, 827–847.

Hill, C.W.L. and G.S. Hansen (1991) A longitudinal study of the cause and consequences of changes in diversification in the US pharmaceutical industry. *Strategic Journal of Management*, **12**, 187–199.

Hill, C.W.L and R.E. Hoskisson (1987) Strategy and structure in the multiproduct firm. *Academy of Management Review*, **12**(2) 331–341.

Jenna, J. and K. Leslie (2000) Diversify with care. *The McKinsey Quarterly*, **2**(Europe), 56–59.

Kane, F. (2002) A born again Virgin (interview with Sir Richard Branson). *The Observer Business Section*, p. 14, 17 March 2002.

Lamont, B.T. and A. Anderson (1985) A model of corporate diversification and economic performance. *Academy of Management Journal*, **28**, 926–934.

Lowes, B., C. Pass and S. Sanderson (1994) Conglomerate expansion. *Companies and Markets* (Chapter 4). Blackwell, Oxford, UK.

Luffman, G. and R. Reed, (1984) *The Strategy and Performance of British Industry*. Macmillan, Basingstoke, UK.

Markides, C.C. (1995) *Diversification Refocussing and Economic Performance and Economic Performance*, MIT Press, Cambridge, MA.

Ollinger, M. (1994) The limits of growth of the multidivisional firm: A case study of the US oil industry from 1930–90. *Strategic Management Journal*, **15**, 503–520.

Pandya, A.M. and N.V. Rao (1998) Diversification and firm performance: An empirical evaluation. *Journal of Financial and Strategic Decisions*, **11**(2), 67–81.

Penrose, E. (1959) *The Theory of the Growth of the Firm*. Blackwell, Oxford, UK.

Pickering, J.F. (1974) *Market Structure and Performance of Firms*. Martin Robinson, Oxford, UK.

Rajan, R., H. Servaes and L. Zingales (2000) The cost of diversity: The diversification discount and inefficient investment. *Journal of Finance*, **55**(1), 35–80.

Rumelt, R.P. (1974) *Strategy, Structure and Economic Performance*. Harvard Business School, Cambridge, MA.

The Times (1995) *The Times 1000*. Times Books, London.

Treece, D.T. (1982) Towards an economic theory of the multi-product firm. *Journal of Economic Behaviour and Organisation*, **3**, 39–63.

18

CHANGING THE BOUNDARIES OF THE FIRM: DIVESTMENT AND EXIT

CHAPTER OUTLINE

CHAPTER OBJECTIVES

This chapter aims to examine the issues surrounding decisions to make the firm smaller rather than larger and to close down activities rather than starting them up. At the end of this chapter you should be able to:

◆ Explain the nature and dimensions of the exit decision.
◆ Identify and analyse factors influencing the exit decisions of a firm.
◆ Explain the reasons unsuccessful firms stay in a market.
◆ Outline the main characteristics of bankruptcy procedures.

INTRODUCTION

So far in this book, we have analysed the growth and diversity of the firm. However, firms that grow can also decline, firms that diversify can refocus their activities on a narrower range of activities and firms that invest in growth can also divest themselves of activities in search of greater profitability. Thus, the withdrawal, or exit, from markets or ceasing to undertake an activity is as much part of the development of the firm as growth: put another way, the opposite of the creation of new firms is the death, or bankruptcy, of others. In a market economy a firm has to face making decisions involving exit from some activities or even the ultimate decision of closing the firm down. Therefore, this chapter explores three aspects of firm development associated with decline:

- Market exit.
- Divestment.
- Bankruptcy.

EXIT DECISIONS IN COMPETITIVE MARKETS

Economic analysis of the exit decision of the firm relates revenue to costs in both the short and long run. In the long run a single-product firm serving a single market will leave the industry when its revenue is unable to cover its variable costs and does not contribute toward fixed costs. This argument assumes that fixed costs are not relevant to current decisions but that variable costs are; this is illustrated in Figure 18.1. A price-taking firm faces a price of OP_1. With given average variable costs (AVC), average fixed costs (AFC) and average total costs (ATC), the profit-maximizing firm is able to cover its total costs and earn a normal profit producing OQ_1, where marginal cost (MC) is equal to price. This level of profitability is assumed to be sufficient to keep the firm in the market.

If a fall in demand reduces the market price to OP_2, then the loss-minimizing firm produces OQ_2, where marginal cost is equal to price, and is able to cover its variable costs but not all its fixed costs. In the short-run the firm is confined to adjusting output along its short-run marginal cost curve because it cannot adjust the size of the fixed factor employed. In the long run there is time to vary the size of the fixed capital employed or to retire it completely.

Thus, the firm is assumed to remain in the market in the short run because it is covering its current costs and is waiting to see what happens to prices in the next decision-making period or the longer run. Clearly, this position is not sustainable in the long run when the firm must cover all its accounting costs to survive.

If there is further decline in demand taking the market price to OP_3, then the loss-minimizing firm will produce OQ_3, but will be unable to cover its variable costs and make no contribution toward its fixed costs. Therefore, it should withdraw from the market. Thus, if the firm is unable to meet its variable costs at the current price, then

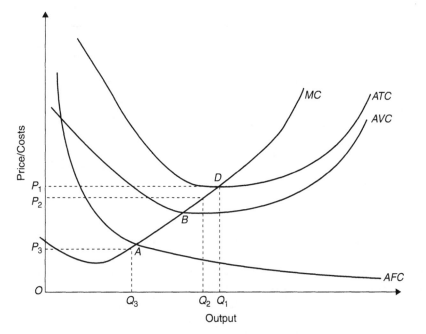

Figure 18.1   The exit decision in competitive markets.

it should exit the market as soon as possible. Firms making the greatest losses are expected to exit first. However, a firm – even one not covering its variable costs – may stay in the market if it is awaiting the decisions of other loss-making rivals. If sufficient capacity is retired by its competitors, then the firm may be able to return to a position of earning a normal profit as prices rise through the reduction in supply and the firm cuts its costs.

EXIT DECISIONS IN OLIGOPOLISTIC MARKETS

Firms serving any given market may differ in terms of the number of plants operated, the number of products sold, the degree of vertical integration and the degree of diversification. Thus, the notion that the most inefficient firm will be the first to leave the market is unlikely because there may be many reasons for it to stay. An individual firm may behave strategically and wait on the decision of other firms. The first to leave the market will make it easier for the remaining firms to survive, particularly if a significant amount of capacity is removed. However, the decision to do so will not be based on the level of losses alone. Large multi-product firms may be able to finance losses while they wait for improved market conditions because the activity may be crucial to some other part of the firm. Central to the question of how capacity is adjusted in a declining market is the behaviour and strategy of firms. If all firms believe that another firm will act first, then adjustment will be delayed. Likewise, if

Table 18.1 Pay-off matrix for exit game

		Firm B			
	Strategy	Stay		Exit	
Firm A	Stay	−100	−150	0	+200
	Exit	+300	0	0	0

Source Author

everyone expects demand to pick up in the near future, then adjustment will also be delayed.

These problems can be illustrated using game theory. Let us consider a duopoly with the pay-offs shown in Table 18.1. Here firm A is assumed to be more efficient than firm B and each firm has a choice of exiting or staying in the market. If both competitors remain in the industry, then they both lose money: firm A −£100 and firm B −£150. If both exit, then neither makes profits nor losses. If competitor A stays and B leaves the market, then firm A might expect profits of £300. If firm B stays and firm A leaves, then B might expect profits of £200. Thus, both firms find it more profitable to stay if the other quits. The problem may be solved by one firm leaving the market because of financial pressures or because it can deploy the resources elsewhere and earn greater returns. If neither is prepared to leave, then it may be solved by firm A paying firm B to leave the industry by paying £150 to cover its losses; this would still leave firm A with a net profit of £150. In a similar way, B could pay A to leave by covering its losses of £100 and still be better off. Another solution may be for the two firms to merge and for the new management to rationalize supply.

In practice, the size of a firm may affect its closure decision. Ghemawat and Nalebuff (1985, 1990) argued that larger firms may close plants or leave the industry before smaller firms. They suggested, "that survivability is inversely related to size: smaller firms, ceteris paribus, have lower incentives to reduce capacity in declining industries than do their larger competitors" (p. 184).

Smaller producers may suffer less from unit cost increases as output declines, can operate more profitably with smaller levels of output and their managements may have more to lose if they leave the industry. While a large firm may well be able to lose a plant or a division, the consequences for smaller firms are much more significant.

Baden-Fuller (1989) suggested that large diversified firms may encounter fewer management problems when evaluating plant closure decisions, making their plants more likely to exit than those of smaller, more specialized firms. Because of conflicts between owners, managers and creditors, the closure of unprofitable plants may be more difficult for an undiversified than a diversified firm. Qualitative and quantitative evidence on plant closures in the UK steel castings industry between 1979 and 1983 showed that the nature of the firm was more significant than the market in dictating the pattern of exit, with the result that closure patterns were inefficient in economic terms.

The author (Jones 1994) in a study of the adjustment process in the West European oil-refining industry between 1976 and 1992 found significant variation in the closure pattern in terms of firm size and plant size. In the period under study refining capacity was reduced by 53%. The breakdown was as follows:

- Of the three largest companies, BP closed 60%, Shell 57% and Esso 43% of their capacity.
- Chemical companies and state-owned companies generally closed at below the average rate because refining was integrated with chemical production.
- Firms operating only one refinery closed only 34% of capacity, though 13 of the 25 firms closed their operations.
- Only two firms increased capacity: Conoco +6% and Petrofina, a Belgium-based refiner, +17.9%. Conoco was the only multiple refinery operator not to close a refinery; this was attributed to greater efficiency.

Other strategies

If a multi-product firm has a normal expected profit rate for all its activities, then those activities that fall below the rate will have their existence questioned by central management. Clearly, while some of these activities may be returned to the expected level of profitability by restructuring and cost cutting, those with no expectation of increasing profitability might expect to be closed.

However, exit decisions may not be entirely driven by adverse market and industry conditions, on the one hand, and low levels of profitability, on the other. Instead, decisions may be taken in the competitive or strategic interests of the firm. In the search for competitiveness a firm may close old plants at undesirable locations and build new capacity elsewhere. This pursuit of rationalization is motivated by the desire to achieve lower unit costs by concentrating output on a more modern plant and by the pursuit of economies of scale.

In the search for profitability a firm may divest a whole division because it is unprofitable or loss-making and the existing management believe they cannot return it to profitability. A multi-product firm may wish to divest a business not seen as central to the overall objectives of the firm in order to release financial and managerial resources that could be more effectively employed in the firm's other divisions. Similar reasoning may cause a firm to concentrate on what are termed "core businesses" which utilize the firm's core competences; this is sometimes justified by a lack of focus in the firm's activities.

FACTORS ENCOURAGING EXIT

Entry into a market occurs as a response by entrepreneurs to their perceiving profitable opportunities in growing markets. To enter a market a firm has to invest in facilities, acquire a workforce and make a product or service to be offered to consumers. Once in the market the firm has then to compete with any rivals to persuade sufficient consumers to buy its offering rather than those offered by competitors.

Conversely a firm will be motivated to leave or exit a market where:

■ Demand is static or declining.
■ Enterprises are earning below-normal profits or making losses in the activity concerned.
■ Enterprises face cash flow problems and are unable to pay their debts.
■ Resources might be able to earn higher rates of return if deployed to new activities.
■ The firm is inefficient in terms of productivity and costs compared with its market rivals.
■ Enterprises are able to overcome barriers that discourage firms from leaving a market or from ceasing to make or offer a service.
■ The activity does not fit strategically with the current objectives of the firm.
■ The firm wishes to return to its core activities.

Demand

In many industries and markets the nature and level of demand changes over time. Demand may decline because of the introduction of substitutes that replace the existing product: for example, compact discs replacing vinyl records or a change in tastes, such as drinkers preferring lager to traditional British ale and bitter. Such changes in demand may be aided by demographic changes. If young people drink lager and older people bitter, then the market for bitter will decline as the number of elderly imbibers declines and the number of lager drinkers increases.

Demand in the long run may decline slowly or quickly, steadily or erratically. A slow and steady decline gives the firm more time to adjust capacity and to derive strategies to deal with the consequences. A rapid decline in demand or erratic shifts in demand may be more difficult to deal with, because the rapid downturn in demand may not be recognized as a turning point but merely as a short-run problem. The decline of a market may be masked where the pattern of demand change is erratic with any upturn in demand being taken as the resumption of growth.

When demand shifts from growing to long-term decline, rather than short-term decline, the turning point may be difficult for managers to recognize. For example, the European oil industry experienced rapid growth from the end of the Second World War for the next 30 years. In the 1970s oil companies were making plans to expand refinery capacity in line with previous experience. However, the trebling of the crude oil price in 1973–1974 had adverse short-run effects on demand; this was treated as a short-term downturn in response to the higher prices and recession that followed. No one at the time recognized this as a turning point. Most oil company managers envisaged that demand growth would resume in due course. In reality, the demand for oil entered a period of long-run decline masked by occasional upturns in demand – false heralds of resumed growth, which did not resume until the 1990s.

Uncertainty about the rate of decline in demand can also be important in influencing both the nature of competition and the timing of exit. When all companies are fairly confident about the rate at which demand will continue to fall, reductions in capacity are likely to be orderly; whereas, if some firms believe that demand growth will be resumed, then they may attempt to hold onto their positions, perpetuating over-capacity and intense competition.

Some industries are characterized by product differentiation: for example, while long-term demand is in decline, some products or brands may be able to beat the decline and increase their sales. Strong brand loyalty by consumers may lead to a slower rate of exit for firms with strong brands than those with weaker brands. In markets characterized by product differentiation, there is likely to be less price competition than in markets characterized by commodity-style products and companies with weak brands are more likely to leave the market than less efficient enterprises with strong brands.

Excess capacity

A consequence of declining demand and the lagging adjustment of capacity is the emergence of excess capacity, a symptom of the problems needing to be dealt with in declining industries. The prime cause for the emergence of excess capacity is the long-run decline in demand for a product at home and overseas. Other causes may include loss of home market share, with domestic supply being replaced by imports or overseas producers establishing more efficient plants in the domestic economy. In a similar way, exports may be lost to new domestic producers or increasing competition from more competitive international suppliers. Another source of excess capacity is over-investment in capacity by individual enterprises in anticipation of demand growth that is not realized and where two or more firms simultaneously decide to invest because their plans are not co-ordinated.

Implications of excess capacity

The initial implications of excess capacity within a firm are that unit costs will increase because output is less than that at which unit costs are minimized. The impact on unit costs will depend on the relative importance of fixed to variable costs. The more important are fixed costs to variable costs the greater the increase in unit costs for any given fall in output, while the more important are variable costs to fixed costs the smaller the rise in unit costs for any given fall in output.

Excess capacity may also be expected to squeeze profit margins. If the firm sets its prices using a cost-plus procedure, then at a given price higher actual unit costs will mean a lower price cost or profit margin if actual output is less than normal. If the firm is a price-taker, then excess capacity will reduce the market price as firms compete, which coupled with higher unit costs will reduce the price cost margin. Price competition is more likely to occur in industries where products are commodities and fixed costs are a high proportion of total costs; it is less likely in industries where variable costs are more important than fixed costs and products are differentiated. The combined effect of declining margins and falling output reduces profitability and may lead to losses being made.

Matching supply and demand within a firm is a key managerial function. However, some firms will find a declining market more hostile and less profitable than other firms who may find a declining market profitable, particularly if they can maintain sales and price competition is absent.

Excessive diversification

Another reason for divesting activities is that the firm believes that it has become so diversified that it cannot match the cost levels achieved by more specialist or more focused rivals. Voluntary divestment has become a commonplace strategy and has been associated with the decline in popularity of conglomerate-holding companies like Hanson Trust. In Chapter 17 it was postulated that the relationship between profitability and diversification is shaped like an inverse U. Profitability is initially an increasing function and then a decreasing function of the degree of diversification (Figure 17.2). The main reasons for increasing profitability with diversification were savings in transaction and management costs, economies of scope, risk avoidance and the increasing capacity of managerial and other factors as the firm grows.

The declining portion of the relationship between profitability and diversification is explained by various factors. One argument used is that the core competences of a firm may not be applicable to all business activities. The particular skills of a tobacco company may not be very useful in retailing. This lack of transferability of managerial skills is said to limit the breadth of diversification that is profitable. When this point is reached the argument is used that the firm should return to its core competences and, therefore, narrow its range of activities while increasing its profitability.

Penrose (1959) demonstrated that indivisibilities in factor supply, particularly management, eventually prevent further expansion and cause increases in management costs and the loss of control and effective transmission of information. Thus, organizational costs rise with increasing diversity because central management finds it more and more difficult to control their diverse empire. When the management constraint is reached it may prove difficult to recruit and assimilate new management and allocate tasks in a meaningful way.

Initially, diversification is justified by the fact that the firm is able to operate its own internal capital market. Funds controlled at the centre of a conglomerate are allocated to divisions or to new activities, such as acquisitions, by central management. At some point the internal capital market becomes less efficient as individual divisions fight harder to retain their own profits to finance their own projects. This case is strengthened when returns from mergers decline as less desirable targets are pursued, reducing the overall profitability of the enterprise. As a result the stock market has tended to downgrade the value of conglomerate enterprises and to put pressure on management to pursue divestment strategies that increase shareholder value.

Divestment has also been encouraged by the growth of management buyouts of unwanted divisions. This trend has been facilitated by the development of venture capitalists willing to finance management buyouts. A management buyout occurs where the existing management of an unwanted division believes that they can make the division more profitable than under the benign neglect of the parent company. For example, British Airways developed a low-cost, or budget, airline to compete with companies like Ryanair and easyJet in the European market. However, in 2001, BA decided to revise its strategy and to concentrate on those things it did best: providing high-quality air services to customers willing to pay higher prices. Consequently, in 2001, BA's budget airline Go was sold to its management for £100m, backed by the 3i venture capital company, and a year later the company merged with rival easyJet.

Haynes et al. (2000) investigated the determinants of divestment activity in the UK, over the period 1985–1989, by using a random sample of 141 UK firms selected from the 1985 *Financial Times* 500 list of largest enterprises. Altogether, a total of 1,149 voluntary divestments were identified, an average for each firm of 1.6 divestments per year, representing on average 4.4% of firms' assets in the previous year.

The results indicate that divestment was:

- Systematically related to leverage, corporate governance, strategy and; to a limited extent, market-structural characteristics.
- The value and extent of divestment activity was greatest in larger and more diversified firms.

The gains from divestment were found to be greatest for those firms experiencing control problems associated with size and diversity. However, the study failed to reveal any significant association between firm performance and divestment.

FACTORS KEEPING THE FIRM IN THE MARKET: EXIT BARRIERS

Exit barriers are obstacles to firms leaving an industry or market despite falling sales, narrowing profit margins and declining profitability. The concept was first developed by Porter (1976) and Caves and Porter (1976); it was further developed by Harrigan (1980). Porter suggested that these barriers could be classified as economic or strategic and can be identified by examining the structural characteristics of an industry and the strategies adopted by individual firms.

Economic exit barriers are those factors that result in the firm facing high opportunity costs if they leave the industry. The source of these exit barriers include the costs associated with closing and dismantling plant and equipment and the absence of markets in used capital equipment, allowing the firm to recover some of the initial costs. The significance of these barriers is a function of the capital intensity of the production process, asset specificity, the age of the assets and the reinvestment requirements of the firm.

Strategic exit barriers arise from the reluctance of the firm to sacrifice the cumulative benefits of intangible assets created by previous investments. The sources of strategic exit barriers include:

- A high-quality image created by previous expenditure on R and D, production and advertising.
- Facilities shared with other products that are profitable.
- Company recognition generated by previous advertising.
- Businesses that are of strategic importance to the firm.
- The potential damage in other markets of upset customers with significant buyer power.

Porter (1980) argued that a significant factor to come out of case studies was that exit for a single-product firm meant managers losing their jobs, while in a multi-product firm it may mean redundancy but could also lead to a sideways move or demotion. Thus, the cost of failure to an individual or group of managers is both financial and psychological. The visible sign of failure may be a blow to the self-confidence and pride of individual managers, while reducing their chances of obtaining another job. These adverse personal effects may be reinforced by the breaking of a long-standing commitment to an individual enterprise or industry. The attachment to an industry may explain why an individual firm stays in the market when more rational analysis suggests that exit should occur; this may be reinforced when the company's name is associated with a market or product. However, in a diversified firm, managers might find it easier to exit from one particular market since it has many others available and could minimize redundancies by redeploying managers and workers to other areas of the business. In the past such policies were pursued by large Japanese zaibatsu companies and Korean chaebol enterprises, guaranteeing jobs for life.

Harrigan (1980) identifies five potential exit barriers that help to keep the firm in the industry despite earning below-normal returns:

- *Future investment requirements*: if the firm is not required to make additional investments to remain competitive or to meet other requirements, such as health and safety regulation, then it may be inclined to stay in the market, providing the firm is covering its variable costs. If significant investment is required in the short run, then the firm may find it difficult to fund such investment, given its low returns, and may therefore decide to exit.
- *Age of assets*: if assets are old and fully depreciated, then total operating costs will be lower than if newer assets are being used and may encourage the firm to remain in the market despite low prices.
- *Asset specificity*: if the assets used by the firm are highly specific to the industry, then the opportunity cost of the assets may be very low. If the assets are less specific, then a market for second-hand equipment may exist and a significant proportion of the original costs may be recovered. Therefore, the more specific the assets the more likely is the firm to remain in the market because of the low second-hand value of its assets. If assets are hired or leased rather than purchased, then a firm can avoid the long-term commitment of buying capital; this facilitates exit from the market when the lease period ends.
- *Shared facilities*: if a firm produces two products, one profitable the other not, and they both rely on inputs produced by another shared facility, then the decision to withdraw from making the loss-making product would affect the costs of the

profitable product and the viability of the supply division. Therefore, the firm may decide to maintain production of the less profitable product, providing it covers its variable costs. However, it may be cheaper to close the component supply division and buy the inputs in the market. If the two products use the same facilities in their production this option may not be available.

■ *Vertical integration*: vertical linkages raise similar issues to those of shared facilities. It may be difficult to close a plant that is at a critical stage in a technologically linked production chain without having some impact on producing products downstream. However, the alternative is to seek long-term contracts to purchase the input; this may mean greater flexibility, once the vertical chain is broken.

■ *Breaking employment contracts*: closing a plant or ceasing to produce a product may involve the firm in making workers redundant and may involve the payment of redundancy payments, which can be significant; this would tend to keep the firm operating to avoid having to meet such costs.

■ *Access to financial markets*: exiting a market or closing a business may weaken the ability of a company to borrow in the future. A management associated with failure may not be trusted to generate future earnings, even if the exit decision is economically and financially justified. If the consequence is a fall in the company's valuation ratio, then it may become a target for acquirers.

■ *Government regulations and social costs*: in some countries, such as France and Italy, social contracts may make it difficult to close a plant and make workers redundant. In addition to redundancy costs, there may be rules requiring the firm to consult workers and even to stop workers being made redundant for a significant period of time. The loss of jobs and the depressing effects on the local area may mean that the government will incur significant costs in unemployment benefit, redundancy payments and support for the local economy. The costs incurred when firms fail lead governments to consider whether the necessary social expenditure that would be incurred could be used to support the retention and rejuvenation of the enterprise. For example, when Chrysler proposed closing its motor car assembly operations in the UK in 1975, it was estimated that the cost to the government of closure was £150m. In addition, there would be a loss of exports and a contract with Iran for the supply of kits for local assembly would be jeopardized. These negative effects were used to justify a rescue package of £162.5m. The rescue kept the company operating in the UK, but did not save the Scottish plants; however, it did preserve the Coventry operations, which continue to the present day under the ownership of Peugeot Citroen. Such rescues are now rarely attempted because they are judged to delay the process of adjustment and leave the government open to demands to rescue all failing enterprises. In some markets (e.g., banking) government regulation is intended to prevent firms leaving the market without fulfilling their obligations to existing customers.

BANKRUPTCY

Single product or multi-product firms may cease to exist if they become financially unviable. When this happens a firm is described as being bankrupt (i.e., it has insufficient assets to meet its debts). Many countries have bankruptcy procedures either to restructure financially distressed companies to prevent bankruptcy or, ultimately, to liquidate them.

Bankruptcy procedures are required when a firm cannot pay its debts to ensure fair treatment of all creditors by the bankrupt firm. In the absence of such procedures the first creditor who has a secured position to take legal action may receive payment but others might not. Rather than every individual creditor taking action, collective action or agreed procedures may provide a better solution. To receive recompense, creditors may try to restructure and revive the company under the present management, sell the company as a going concern or put the company into liquidation and sell the assets.

Bankruptcy law establishes an order of priority in which creditors receive payment. Secured creditors who have a direct call on assets come first and unsecured creditors come second. In terms of priority, shareholders come second to debt holders. In terms of debt holders, those who have lent against security of assets take priority over those who have lent money without security. Suppliers who have not been paid and customers who do not receive the goods they have paid for are both unsecured creditors and are lowly placed in the queue for compensation.

However, besides trying to ensure that creditors receive recompense, the bankruptcy procedure may want to place some emphasis on securing the future of the firm in terms of its managers, workers and customers. Therefore, between taking action to stop the firm trading or the creditors taking action to stop the firm operating and final liquidation, procedures may be in place to try to help the firm survive in one form or another. In the USA, Chapter 11 of the US Bankruptcy Code allows for such action with the firm run by its managers. Since 1986 in the UK an administrator, who is an insolvency practitioner, is allowed to run the firm during bankruptcy proceedings.

Rates of bankruptcy

Bankruptcy procedures differ significantly between countries, as does the relative numbers of firms that go bankrupt. Table 18.1 gives data on the average ratio of bankruptcies to the population of firms for various countries. The UK had a bankruptcy rate of 0.67% in the period 1992–1998. This rate is lower than that prevailing in Canada (2.96%) and the USA (3.65%), but higher than in Japan. In the EU, Spain (0.02%) and Italy (0.54%) have lower rates, while Germany (1.03%), the Netherlands (1.30%), France (1.89%) and Belgium (2.59%) have higher rates than the UK.

On the basis of the distinction between insider and outsider systems of corporate governance (see Chapter 1) it has been argued that insider systems will have lower rates of bankruptcy because of the presence of large insider shareholders who are able to protect their investments before losses become significant. In contrast, because of the dispersed nature of shareholdings and debt holding, on the one hand, and the

Table 18.2 Relative rates of bankruptcy: selected countries

Country	Period	Average bankruptcies as a percentage of number of firms
Belgium	1990–1999	2.59
Denmark	1990–1999	1.53
France	1998	1.89
Germany	1992–1998	1.03
Italy	1990–1996	0.54
Netherlands	1995–1999	1.30
Spain	1990–1999	0.02
Japan	1990–1999	0.22
Ireland	1990–1999	2.74
UK	1992–1998	0.67
Canada	1990–1998	2.96
USA	1990–1999	3.65
Australia	1994–1999	3.15
New Zealand	1993–1998	3.21

Source Data extracted from Klapper (2001, p. 15, table 2).

asymmetry of information between managers and outsiders, on the other, outsider systems will be less aware of an oncoming financial crisis.

Using the data in Table 18.2 we can compare the average rate of bankruptcy in English and non-English-speaking countries, which roughly coincides with the distinction between outsider and insider systems of corporate governance. It is higher in the USA, Canada, Ireland, Australia and New Zealand (3.15%) than in continental Europe and Japan (1.13%). However, the UK's rate was only 0.67%, which suggests that its experience is rather different to that of other countries with outsider systems; this might be explained by a low rate of new-firm formation and a greater willingness on the part of debtors to see young firms through periods of financial difficulty.

Chapter 11 Procedures

The US system of bankruptcy has been termed "manager-driven or manager-friendly", while the British system has been described as "creditor-friendly or manager-displacing". The particular feature of the US system that has led to it being given that description is Chapter 11 of the US Bankruptcy Code. This provision allows the managers of a firm in financial difficulty, but not necessarily insolvent, to seek protection against its creditors. The existing managers continue to run the business.

A freeze is put on creditors' claims, so that no creditor is able to seize or sell any of the firm's assets during the process, creditors are grouped into an order of precedence and the process is supervised by a judge. The latter oversees a process of bargaining between creditors and manages to determine a plan of action; this can proceed if it is determined by a majority of each claimant class or group. Once agreed a new plan cannot be put forward for at least 180 days.

Chapter 11 has been criticized for leaving the managers who have brought about the financial crisis in charge, of being too friendly to debtors, of being costly and time-consuming. Hart (2000) argues that there are two fundamental problems with Chapter 11 in that it is a structured bargaining process that: "tries to make two decisions at once: what to do with the firm, and who should get what in the event of a restructuring of claims" (p. 8). In addition those creditors that are fully protected may have more influence in the voting than those not protected. For example, debtors may push for liquidation because their claims may be able to be met in full, but shareholders who may receive nothing in such circumstances may wish to see the firm restructured with the hope of future returns.

The missing element in the UK system explaining the low rate of bankruptcy proceedings is attributed to the use of informal and secret procedures. The number of bankruptcies represents only a portion of companies in financial difficulties, many of which are solved through an informal arrangement termed "a manager-friendly substitute in place of formal bankruptcy proceedings". The process initially involves banks that have lent to a company agreeing not to take any actions against the company to recover their debts. The second stage is for the lead bank to negotiate with the company on behalf of all lenders to put in place arrangements to restore the company to financial health. Unlike Chapter 11 procedures that are initiated by company directors, this procedure is initiated by creditors.

Case Study 18.1   ITV Digital terrestrial service

The licence to broadcast digital services using terrestrial transmitters was granted in 1997 to British Digital Broadcasting, a consortium of Carlton, Granada, ITV regional companies and BSkyB. BSkyB was forced to withdraw by the EU competition authorities because it operated the satellite digital system in the UK; this had been started 8 years previously and already had 4 million subscribers when the new service was launched in November 1998.

The service was launched as a pay TV venture. Subscribers bought a digital box to receive programmes and paid a monthly subscription, which depended upon the number of channels being rented; these included sports and film channels from BSkyB. The business plan also envisaged breaking even with 2 million subscribers. The costs of the venture increased when BSkyB offered free set-top boxes, an offer matched by ON Digital.

In March 2002 the company, having been renamed ITV Digital, went into administration. The appointed administrators continued to run the company while trying to find potential buyers for the company. When these attempts proved unpromising they decided at the beginning of May 2002 to switch off its services and to go into liquidation. At the time of its failure the service had 1.3 million customers and debts were estimated to be £2bn owed to creditors and £1bn lost by Carlton and Granada, the owners of the venture.

Hindsight suggests that the company failed for some or all of the following reasons:

■ BskyB's first-mover advantage allowed it to build up a subscriber base of 4 million before ON Digital was launched. It also proved to be a powerful competitor in keeping viewers and attracting others because of the wider choice offered by digital services.

- The management of the new venture had no experience of pay TV and thought that their experience of operating terrestrial services could be transferred to the new format.
- The strategy of styling itself as a mini-Sky TV, but without the financial resources or the management. Sky TV was judged to have been successful because of its premium sports channels and, particularly, the showing of Premier League soccer. ON digital decided to launch a sports channels with the highlight being Football League matches (lower divisions). The company paid £315m for the rights to show live matches for three years, some 12 times that paid a year earlier for similar rights by Sky TV. Only a few lower league teams had substantial followings and very few people subscribed to the channel.
- Technical problems limited the service's availability in the UK: where the service was available reception was weak and expensive new aerials were required, set-top boxes kept crashing and piracy was thought to be widespread.
- The target of 2 million subscribers was not achieved partly because almost 25% of those who bought a prepaid subscription for 12 months did not renew. This high churn rate increased the costs of winning more customers as more expensive advertising was undertaken together with the relaunch of the service as ITV Digital.

CHAPTER SUMMARY

In this chapter we explored a number of aspects about firms that are either closing down, reshaping themselves by divestment or closing down activities that are either un-profitable or do not fit with the current strategy. In doing this we analysed:

- The various forces causing firms to either cease trading or to narrow the range of their activities.
- The institutional arrangements for dealing with financially distressed enterprises. The US system is considered to be manager-friendly because it gives the existing management an opportunity to restructure the enterprise while creditors are held at bay. In the UK, professional insolvency practitioners replace the managers of bankrupt companies. They generally focus on liquidating the company to repay debtors rather than attempting to resurrect the enterprise.

REVIEW QUESTIONS

Exercise

a Identify a firm that has decided to exit a market but not go out of business. Explain the reasons for the decision and the consequences for the firm.
b Identify a firm that has recently gone into liquidation. Explain the reasons for the decision and the consequences for the firm. Try to find out whether any attempts

were made to keep the firm operating or to sell it to new owners. Or did it just cease to exist?

Discussion questions

1 What factors might explain why a firm ceases to be viable?
2 Explain the concept of barriers to exit. How do they explain the reluctance of firms to leave industries or markets?
3 How might game theory help to explain the reluctance of firms to exit markets?
4 Can a firm overdiversify?
5 Explain the terms "manager-friendly" and "investor-friendly" used in bankruptcy proceedings.
6 Should the UK introduce a Chapter 11-type procedure to deal with companies in financial difficulties?
7 Identify a firm that has recently gone into administration or liquidation. Try to analyse the reasons for failure and the attempts made by administrators/ liquidators to keep the company operating and/or dispose of the assets.

REFERENCES AND FURTHER READINGS

Amour, J., B.R. Cheffins and D.A. Skeel (2002) *Corporate Ownership Structure and the Evolution of Bankruptcy Law in the US and UK* ESRC Centre for Business Research, University of Cambridge, Cambridge, UK (Working Paper No. 226).

Baden-Fuller, C.W.F. (1989) Exit from declining industries and the case of Steel Castings. *Economic Journal*, **99**, 949–961.

Baden-Fuller, C.W.F. (1999) *Managing Excess Capacity*. Blackwell, Oxford, UK.

Bhide, A. (1990) Reversing corporate diversification. *Journal of Applied Corporate Finance*, **3**(2), 70–81.

Caves, R.E. and M.E. Porter (1976) From entry barriers to mobility barriers: Conjectural decisions and continued deterence to new competition. *Quarterly Journal of Economics*, **91**, 241–262.

Ghemawat, P. and B. Nalebuff (1985) Exit. *Rand Journal of Economics*, **16**(2), 184–192.

Ghemawat, P. and B. Nalebuff (1990) The evolution of declining industries. *Quarterly Journal of Economics*, **105**(1), 167–186.

Hart, O. (2000) *Different Approaches to Bankruptcy* (Discussion Paper No. 1903), Harvard Institute of Economic Research, Cambridge, MA.

Haynes, M., S. Thompson and S. Wright (2000) *The Determinants of Corporate Divestment in the UK* (Discussion Paper in Economics No. 00/15) University of Nottingham, UK.

Harrigan, K.R. (1980) *Strategies for Declining Industries*, Lexington Books, Lexington, MA.

Harrigan, K.R. (1982) Exit decisions in mature industries. *Academy of Management Journal*, **25**(2), 707–732.

Harrigan, K.R. and M.E. Porter (1983) Endgame strategies for declining industries. *Harvard Business Review*, **61**(4), July/August, 111–120.

Ingham, H. and S. Thompson (1995) Deregulation, firm capabilities and diversifying entry decisions. *Review of Economics and Statistics*, **77**, 177–183.

Jones, T.T. (1979) Oil refining: An EEC and UK problem of excess capacity. *National Westminster Quarterly Review*, May, 34–42.

Jones, T.T. (1994) *Exit from the West European Oil Refining Industry*. School of Management, UMIST, Manchester.

Klapper, L. (2001) *Bankruptcy around the World* (Working paper for World Development Report). World Bank, Washington, DC.

Lowes, B., C. Pass and S. Sanderson (1994) Market entry and exit. *Companies and Markets* (Chapter 7). Blackwell, Oxford, UK.

Penrose, E. (1959) *The Theory of the Growth of the Firm*. Blackwell, Oxford, UK.

Pickering. J.F. and T.T. Jones (1981) *The Problem of Excess Capacity in British Industry* (Occasional Paper No. 8104). UMIST, Department of Management Sciences, Manchester.

Porter, M.E. (1976) Please note the location of the nearest exit: Exit barriers and organizational thinking. *California Management Review*, **19**(2), 21–33.

Porter, M.E. (1980) *Competitive Strategy: Techniques for Analysing Industries and Competitors*. Free Press, New York.

Shaw, R.W. and C.J. Sutton (1976) Price, competition and excess capacity. *Industry and Competition* (Chapter 3). Macmillan, London.

19

CHANGING THE BOUNDARIES OF THE FIRM: MERGERS

CHAPTER OUTLINE

CHAPTER OBJECTIVES

This chapter aims to discuss the use of mergers and acquisitions as a strategy to change the boundaries of the firm. After reading the chapter you should be able to:

◆ Identify different types of mergers.

◆ Explain the motives for merging and analyse their economic consequences.

◆ Outline the stages in the merger process.

◆ Explain and justify the choice of indicators to indicate the success or failure of mergers.

◆ Identify factors that head to mergers being successful or unsuccessful.

INTRODUCTION

In this chapter we will look at mergers as a strategy to grow and develop the firm. Mergers remain a frequent strategic choice of many firms. They involve the acquisition and incorporation of another enterprise into the acquiring firm; this may be motivated by reasons of market power, related or unrelated diversification or vertical integration. In this chapter we will examine:

■   The nature and process of merging.
■   The motivation for engaging in merger activities.
■   The costs and benefits of merging.
■   Measures of the success or failure of mergers

MERGERS, ACQUISITIONS AND TAKEOVERS

The words "merger" and "acquisition" are interchangeable. If the two terms are to be distinguished, then a merger occurs when two or more firms are voluntarily combined under common ownership, while an acquisition, or takeover, occurs when one firm acquires or buys the assets of another without the agreement of the controllers of the target company. Once a bid has been made, the controllers of the target company may or may not recommend the takeover to their shareholders. If they do not recommend the takeover and advise that it be rejected, then it becomes a contested bid. Another form of contest for the control of a company occurs when two or more companies try to acquire the target enterprise. To win control the bidder must receive the support of a majority of the shareholders of the target company.

A takeover requires one company to bid for each share of the target company. An offer price is made which is generally higher than the current market price. Payment may be made in cash, shares or a mixture of cash and shares. The rules for takeover bids in the UK are regulated by the Merger Code of the London Stock Exchange. In addition, mergers are regulated by the EU and by member states in the interests of maintaining competitive market structures.

TYPES OF MERGERS

Three types of merger – horizontal, vertical and conglomerate – are distinguished by economists:

■   **Horizontal mergers** occur when two firms in the same market are consolidated into a single enterprise; this means that the new enterprise will have increased its market share. This type of merger is designed to acquire market power.
■   **Vertical mergers** occur when two firms operating at different stages of a linked

production process merge. Vertical mergers are described as either bringing about backward or forward integration. Backward integration involves a firm moving closer to the raw material source and forward integration a firm moving closer to the market (see Chapter 16).

■ **Conglomerate mergers** occur when two firms producing independent products for different markets merge. Conglomerate mergers create larger diversified firms. Although these do not generate concerns about market dominance, there are concerns about their ability to compete unfairly against undiversified competitors because of their ability to cross-subsidize.

Types of mergers will vary according to the nature of the industry and the degree of fragmentation. In a sector like legal services, the vast majority of mergers will be horizontal because there are large numbers of small law practices that are currently consolidating. Some may be of a conglomerate nature in that firms in different industries may merge (e.g., legal and accountancy firms). In other industries that are more concentrated but have strong vertical linkages, mergers are less likely to be horizontal in nature and more likely to involve vertical integration.

In the UK the vast majority of mergers are horizontal in nature, as can be observed in Table 19.1. In contrast, in Japan nearly a third are categorized as conglomerate, but the majority of mergers are horizontal in nature.

NUMBERS OF MERGERS IN THE UK

In the UK the pattern of mergers is cyclical. Figure 19.1 shows the number of mergers between UK industrial and commercial companies between 1964 and 2001. The peak years of merger booms were 1965, 1972 and 1987. Figure 19.2 shows total expenditure on mergers and Figure 19.3 shows the average value of mergers (both figures at constant prices). In terms of total expenditure the peak years are 1989, 1995 and 2000 – the latter in terms of value is the most significant year of merger activity since records began. The average value of mergers peaked in 1976, 1995 and 2000 and, as can be clearly seen in the figures, the average value of mergers increased in the second half of the 1990s.

Companies also make acquisitions overseas. In 2000 there were 587 mergers made in the UK compared with 567 overseas involving UK companies, of which 123 were in

Table 19.1   Mergers by category: the UK and Japan (%)

	Horizontal	Vertical	Conglomerate
UK: 1990–1994	87	4	9
Japan: 1995–1997	56	14	30

Sources Compiled by author using data from Office of Fair Trading, annual reports, Fair Trade Commission and Komoto (1999)

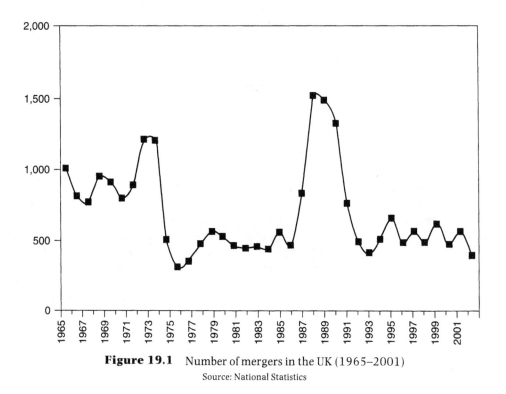

Figure 19.1   Number of mergers in the UK (1965–2001)

Source: National Statistics

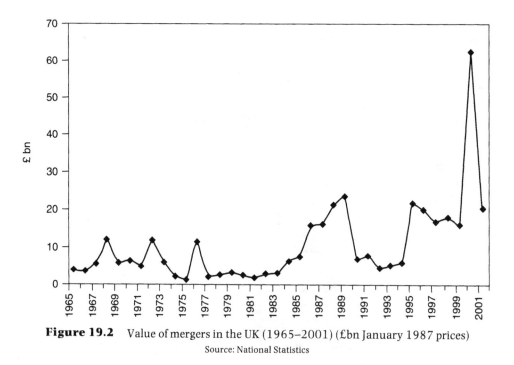

Figure 19.2   Value of mergers in the UK (1965–2001) (£bn January 1987 prices)

Source: National Statistics

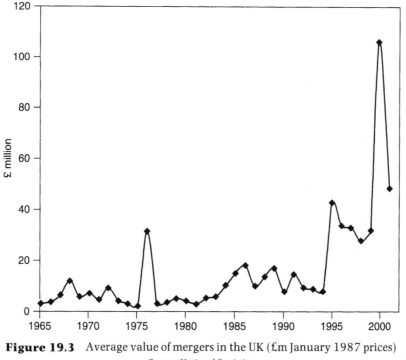

Figure 19.3   Average value of mergers in the UK (£m January 1987 prices)
Source: National Statistics

the EU, 114 in the USA, 52 in other developed countries and 59 in developing countries. In the same year 227 UK businesses were acquired by overseas enterprises.

MOTIVES FOR MERGING

The motives for merging are different in managerial and owner-controlled firms: the former may be more concerned with increasing the growth rate of the firm, while owners are presumed to be more concerned with increasing profits or shareholder value. The main sources of economic gain which enable firms to achieve higher growth and/or higher profitability through the pursuit of mergers are the same.

Mergers and growth

Marris (1964) in his analysis of growth envisaged the firm having to create opportunities for growth to satisfy managerial preferences. If the firm is limited in its growth opportunities in its existing activities, then the acquisition of other enterprises is one way of increasing its size and increasing its average growth rate as long as the acquired activity is in a faster growing sector. Acquisition is viewed as a more rapid way of achieving greater size and a higher growth rate than pursuing internal or organic growth.

Mergers and market power

Market power arises from a firm having a significant presence in a market. Greater market power can be achieved by increasing market share at the expense of rivals. Competing away the market share of rivals requires the firm be in a relatively stronger competitive position than its rivals; this may be achieved by having superior products, lower costs and better distribution systems. These advantages allow the firm to undercut its rivals' prices or to achieve a higher profit margin at any given price. As the competitive process evolves, some firms will gain market share at the expense of others and some firms may withdraw or be forced from the market; this will free up market share which existing competitors can strive to win.

The second way of achieving a higher market share is to acquire a rival; this eliminates a competitor and at the same time increases the market share of the acquiring firm. The firm can strive to maintain this increased market share against its remaining competitors. The larger the firm relative to its remaining competitors the greater its ability to raise prices above marginal cost; this allows the firm to increase revenue and its profits, as a consequence of restricting output.

The history of the brewing industry reflects the continued acquisition of rivals. The last 10 years or so have seen the number of large brewers in the UK reduced from 6 to 3: Interbrew, Scottish & Newcastle and Coors.

Mergers and diversification

Diversification, as argued in Chapter 17, can provide the firm with cost and revenue benefits and a less volatile profits profile. Diversification can be achieved by the firm by making use of its existing resources or by acquisition. Organic diversification requires the firm to develop new products or to engineer entry into new markets. Acquisition is a more rapid way to achieve diversification in that it allows the firm to acquire already existing products, assets and market presence.

Acquisition in contrast to organic development is often argued to be a less risky and more rapid way of achieving diversity and easy access to new markets. The problem for the acquirer is to ensure that the assets and products purchased by acquisition are appropriate to meet the firm's objectives. However, the purchase of another company is not free of risk. The acquired assets may not deliver the expected benefits, particularly if the existing management is dismissed and their expertise lost. On the other hand, the assets may have been acquired because they have not been managed effectively, thus making them attractive to another enterprise.

Case Study 19.1   Ford's acquisition of Kwik-Fit – a corporate error?

In 1999 the Ford Motor Company, the world's second largest maker of cars, acquired Kwik-Fit, a UK-based firm specializing in the fast replacement of car components, such as exhausts, shock absorbers and tyres. Three years later Ford sold it at a substantial loss.

Kwik-Fit was founded in Edinburgh by entrepreneur Sir Tom Farmer in 1971. His first tyre business was started in 1964, but was sold 4 years later. Returning from retirement he built the company from 1 to 1,900 outlets employing 9,500 staff. Ford offered 560p per share for Kwik-Fit – a 30% premium on the previous day's closure price. The cost of the acquisition to Ford was $1.6bn, or approximately £1,000m.

The reasons for the acquisition were:

- The desire to acquire the Kwik-Fit brand and its successful customer formula.
- This was in line with Ford's aim to broaden its activities beyond merely making and selling cars and becoming a complete consumer service provider.
- To acquire a successful management team.
- To bring back to Ford the repair business that its own dealerships had lost to firms like Kwik-Fit.

Kwik-Fit continued to operate as a separate company, maintaining its headquarters in Edinburgh and its existing management including Sir Tom Farmer as chairman. The deal was considered good for Kwik-Fit in that it enabled it to accelerate its European expansion and gave it greater buying power.

In 2001, following heavy losses of $5bn, Ford undertook a major reappraisal of all its activities with the objective of restoring profitability. The outcome was a decision to concentrate on using its core competences in motor assembly and to divest activities that did not come within this area of activity. Kwik-Fit was deemed not to be part of this new structure and the decision was taken to dispose of it.

Kwik-Fit was therefore disposed of as part of:

- A $1bn disposal target to help finance its core activities in car manufacturing.
- A change in strategy to sell its non-core operations in order to raise cash to finance its core activities.

When Kwik-Fit was initially put up for sale, the asking price was substantially greater. Eventually, it was sold to the CVC Capital equity group for $505.2m, or £330m, a loss of £670m. By this time Kwik-Fit had 2,500 service centres and 11,000 employees. The low price might be accounted for by the depressed state of financial markets, reported accounting irregularities that overstated profits and the desire of Ford to meet its sell-off target. Ford decided to retain a 19% stake in the company, but the existing board members resigned including the chairman. Thus, the 3-year ownership of Kwik-Fit proved to be an expensive error.

Acquiring competences

A firm may be motivated to acquire another because of the assets the target firm possesses. In particular, the concern is to acquire intangible assets or competences that cannot be purchased in the market. These assets, which were discussed in

Chapter 15, may include knowledge of a particular market, or of a particular technology, or a strong reputation for product quality. Such knowledge is embedded in individuals and the architecture of the firm; this means that these resources can be utilized within the firm at a constant or declining marginal cost and have high market transaction costs, so that the most profitable way to exploit them is within the firm and the only way to acquire them is through acquisition. It is these competences that make a firm potentially more profitable than its competitors, but it is also these competences that make the firm a potential target. The problem with acquiring a firm for its competences is that they reside in one or more individuals; so, if they leave after the acquisition, then the takeover may have been in vain. For example, Ernst and Vitt (2000) examined the behaviour of key inventors before and after their company was acquired. Identifying key inventors according to their patenting output, they found in a sample of 43 mergers that substantial numbers leave the company after the acquisition and that those who stay substantially reduce their patenting performance.

Mergers and cost savings

The majority of mergers are intended to produce cost savings from synergy between existing and acquired activities; these may arise from reorganizing the production, selling, distribution and management functions of the combined enterprises. The main source of these gains will be: economies of scale as production is concentrated at fewer facilities; from economies of scope as administrative functions are shared and purchases of raw materials are co-ordinated; and from economies of size, which allows larger firms to achieve lower costs than smaller ones. For example, motor car assemblers who merge their operations may be able to achieve benefits from all three sources. Whether the expected cost savings are achieved depends on the success or otherwise of the acquiring firm to integrate the new operation into its existing organizational and management structure and to pursue the necessary restructuring. If the costs of restructuring and setting up new management structures prove more expensive than anticipated, then the merger may not achieve its expected benefits.

Defensive and opportunistic reasons

The management of a firm may seek to merge for defensive reasons, such as to protect their own positions, to avoid bankruptcy or to avoid being taken over by an unwelcome bidder. Alternatively, an acquisition may be made because a company becomes available. If a firm fears that it will become the subject of a takeover bid, then it may itself launch a bid to increase its size and make the firm a more expensive target. An alternative approach to such a threat or to a launched bid is to seek another firm, or suitor, of the firm's own choosing to take the firm over in preference to the original bid. Opportunities to make acquisitions or seek mergers may present themselves from time to time. Two smaller firms in a market might merge to create a stronger firm to survive the challenge of a larger rival. There may be opportunities to deploy liquid assets (or a cash mountain) to acquire companies, which will improve the growth prospects of the firm and keep shareholders happy because of their dislike of excessive non-working assets.

Changes in the economy

Mergers are sometimes motivated by general changes in an industry, such as changes in demand and technology, and trends in the economy as a whole, such as globalization. For example, declining demand in the defence sector following the end of the cold war led to mergers of defence companies and consolidation of the industry.

The general state of the economy may also be conducive to mergers. For example, boom conditions with rising stock market prices may make takeovers financed by shares extremely attractive and encourage predatory firms to seek targets. Changes in particular economic policies may create opportunities for merger activity as previous restrictions on firm behaviour are removed. Deregulation in the US airline market created new opportunities for business experiment and consolidation. Deregulation and privatization, which have been a feature of economic development in many countries, created market structures that were designed by committee. The new firms that were created have often taken the opportunity to merge with each other or have themselves been taken over by others keen to enter the market. For example, the privatization and deregulation of the electricity industry in the UK created a market structure and pattern of firms that has since evolved, with very few of the organizations created in the early 1990s still in their original form or still in the same ownership.

Profit and efficiency benefits

The economic case for horizontal mergers is generally based on higher unit revenues from the use of market power and lower unit costs from efficiency savings; this is illustrated in Figure 19.4. If we assume that a market is supplied by two firms, both with identical average cost curves AC_1 and AC_2, that include a normal profit, then these two cost curves are drawn so that OQ_1 is equal to Q_1Q_2, and the average cost AC_2 is drawn with reference to a vertical axis rising from point Q_1, so that both cost curves are identical. Assuming that the nature of oligopolistic competition has led the firms to meet a given demand (DD_1) at prices that just cover average costs and that allow them to earn a normal profit, then each firm would supply the same quantity. Thus, at price OP_1, both firms operate at the minimum average cost, with firm 1 supplying OQ_1 and firm 2 supplying Q_1Q_2. If the two firms were to merge, then the new firm could use its market power to restrict output and raise prices. If price were increased from OP_1 to OP_3 then output would be reduced to OQ_3; this leaves the firm with excess capacity. The merged firm in the short run could produce this output using only one production unit at an average cost of OC, leaving the second unit idle, but it would still incur the fixed costs of unit 2. In the long run, rationalization of production and other functions might allow the average cost curve AC_3 to be achieved; this would allow the merged firm to charge higher prices and produce at lower average costs.

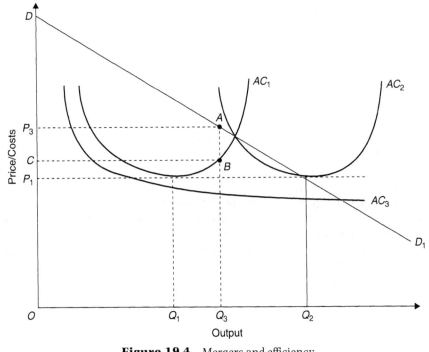

Figure 19.4   Mergers and efficiency

For vertical mergers there may be cost savings where two technologically linked stages of a production chain are joined together under common ownership. Such a link avoids recourse to market transactions and avoids transaction costs; however, these may be offset by increases in governance costs. For conglomerate mergers where the activities are unrelated, the cost savings may arise from more efficient management, from a lower cost of capital for market funding and from operating an internal capital market.

Expectation and stock market valuation

Mergers may be driven by the workings of the stock market and the market for corporate control. The firm's share price reflects its future earnings potential and, therefore, reflects the current expectations of shareholders. The firm's valuation ratio is given by the ratio of its market value and book value. The market value of the firm is given by the share price multiplied by the number of shares issued, while the book value of assets is the value recorded in the firm's balance sheet. The closer this ratio is to 1 the nearer is the market value of the assets to their book value. If the ratio falls below 1, then the market value of the assets is less than the book value; this means the assets can be purchased for less than their recorded value in the company's accounts. A low valuation ratio makes the firm a potential takeover target, particularly if potential buyers place a higher value on the assets of the target firm than the existing shareholders. A low valuation ratio should also encourage the existing management to take actions to restore the fortunes of the firm to raise the valuation ratio.

The market for corporate control, or the buying and selling of companies, operates on the basis that buyers who value companies more highly than the existing shareholders will try to acquire them. To encourage shareholders to sell their shares, potential buyers will offer a premium over the present share price. Clearly, the bidding company would prefer the price paid to be less than or no more than the value they put on the company.

The current state of the market for corporate control

The number and value of mergers taking place in any one year will vary according to business conditions and the expectations of managers. There are rises and falls in the number of mergers taking place. At the time of a merger boom, sometimes described as merger mania, it may be difficult for firms to remain aloof when all about them are making bids. Sometimes, the merger boom is not generalized but confined to one industry. If there is a recognized need for firms to be larger, then mergers may well be the solution. In the late 1990s, pharmaceutical companies decided they needed to be larger if they were to be able to afford research and development, bear the risks and uncertainty of getting new products clinically approved and to market and marketing the new products effectively. If a firm does not move early in such situations, then there may be no suitable targets left and the firm itself may become a target.

Evidence on reasons for merging

Some evidence on the reasons for mergers in Europe in 1985–1986 and 1991–1992 is presented in Table 19.2. In 1985–1986 the main motivation for merging was linked to rationalization, synergies and cost savings followed by diversification, growth and market power. In 1991–1992 the major motive was market power followed by

Table 19.2 Motives behind European mergers and acquisitions (%)

Motive	1985–1986	1991–1992
Growth and expansion	17.1	32.4
Diversification	17.6	2.1
Strengthening market position	10.6	44.4
Rationalization and synergies	46.5	16.2
R and D	2.4	0.0
Other	5.9	5.0

Source Compiled by author using data extracted from EC (1994)

growth, rationalization and synergies. Diversification was much less important and reflects the changing strategies of companies.

A questionnaire study by Ingham et al. (1992) asked managers to rank up to 10 motives that best described their company's merger policy. Based on 146 returns from the top 500 companies the average scores out of ten were:

Increased profitability	7.656
Pursuit of market power	6.708
Marketing economies of scale	3.568
Risk spreading	2.885
Acquisition of management	2.698
Cost reductions	2.521
Technical economies of scale	2.105

This shows increased profitability to be the most important motive – the first choice of 40% of respondents, second choice of 25% and third choice of 12.5%.

THE MERGER PROCESS

Once a company has decided on a target it has to decide on the best strategy to gain control, what price to pay and how to finance the acquisition. In terms of gaining control, the firm may try to win the support of the managers of the target company, so that they recommend the bid to their shareholders. If the bid is made with no support or meets opposition from management, then the aim of the bidder is to win support from the shareholders for the offer despite the opposition of managers. To support its acquisition strategy the bidder may build a stake in the company. The bidder is allowed under the UK Takeover Code to acquire 29.9% of the shares in a company before it has to bid for the remainder. If the remaining shareholders refuse, then the bidder will be left holding a substantial stake in a company it may not be able to control. The Takeover Code tries to ensure equal treatment for all shareholders and the adequate and timely disclosure of information, so that managers do not frustrate bids against the wishes of their shareholders.

The bid price

The bidding company is required to issue a bid document to the shareholders of the target company setting out the terms and conditions of the bid and a date by which they have to decide whether to accept the offer. The objective is to receive acceptances from a majority of shareholders, thus giving the bidder the right to acquire all shares in the company.

The bid per share may be in cash, which means the shareholder can easily compare the offer price with the current market price. If the current price is 100 pence and the bidder offers 110 pence, then the bidder is said to offer a 10% premium to encourage the shareholder to sell. Alternatively, the offer may be in terms of shares in the bidding firm; this makes valuing the offer more difficult because it is a function of the current and future share price of the bidder: for example, one share in the bidding company may be offered for two in the target company. In some instances the bid may be a combination of cash and shares.

Having decided on the nature of the offer the bidder has to decide the price to put on the company. The price will be a function of the value the bidder puts on the assets of the company and the expected profit stream that they will generate under new management. This calculation helps the bidder to decide the bid price. The bidder may also see value in assets that are not fully reflected in the current market price. The bidder may assume that disposal of unwanted assets may raise significant cash to offset the overall bid price. As a result of such calculations the bidder may decide to offer (or not) a premium, the size of which is determined by a number of factors including an estimate of the price at which existing sellers will be willing to sell their stake. For example, when Granada bid for Forte in 1995 the initial offer was either four shares plus £23.35 in cash for every 15 shares in Forte or a cash offer of 321.67 pence. The price at the time of the bid was 260 pence or a premium of 24%.

The initial offer may not be the final offer. Resistance by the existing management and the reluctance of shareholders to accept the offer may lead to either the withdrawal of the offer or to an increase in the offer price. The price may be driven higher if more than one company is interested in acquiring the target. For example, both the Royal Bank of Scotland and the Bank of Scotland bid for the National Westminster Bank, with the former eventually being successful. Such competition inevitably drives up the eventual price paid compared with an uncontested bid. In the case of Granada–Forte the final offer was raised in cash terms to 367.67 pence per share including a special dividend of 47 pence to be paid from Forte's reserves.

Defence strategies

The management of the target company may try to thwart the bid. They may try to make the company appear more desirable to its shareholders (i.e., more valuable than the current perception of the share price) by revaluing assets and emphasizing the anticipated future success of current strategies. The firm may attempt to question the ability of the bidder to manage the business, particularly if it has no experience of the sector and no understanding of how the industry works. The motivation and competences of new managers will also be questioned, and the existing managers may appeal to the loyalty of shareholders; such resistance may be successful or push up the eventual bid price. When Trafalgar House bid for Northern Electric, the privatized electricity supplier to the north-east of England, management were able to rely on the loyalty of large numbers of local shareholders, who had acquired their holding at privatization, to help defeat the bid.

INDICATORS OF THE SUCCESS OR FAILURE OF MERGERS

The merger as a strategy is intended to improve the performance of the bidding firm. When two firms merge the expectation is that the combined firm will be greater than the sum of its parts. The success or failure of mergers can be measured using some or all of the following criteria:

■ The profitability of the combined enterprise, which would be expected to have increased when measured absolutely or relative to capital employed.
■ Efficiency gains measured by reductions in costs or increases in productivity.
■ Returns to shareholders as measured by the share price.
■ Gains to other stakeholders, such as an increase in employment.
■ Subjective assessment of the benefits by management to ascertain whether corporate objectives have been achieved.

Distinguishing the impact of a merger from other influences affecting any of the performance measures may be difficult. If a merger takes place at the beginning of an upturn in the business cycle, then any observed subsequent increase in profits will be partly due to the state of business and partly to the merger; this makes it difficult to attribute the subsequent success or failure of the firm to the merger alone. There might also be more than one merger having an effect on an enterprise that is engaged in serial mergers; this will make disentangling the impact of each merger even more difficult.

The success of mergers

A survey of the evidence on post-merger performance by Pickering (1983) found that mergers, "on average do not have a favourable effect on the relative profitability of the merged company against either a control group or industry average ... Further, share price effects also tend to be considered unfavourable, with the shareholders in the target company more likely to benefit through the favourable terms on which they are bought out than the shareholders of the acquiring company" (p. 44).

In one of the first major studies of the effects of mergers in the UK, Meeks (1977) found that 60% of the acquirers were reporting declines in profitability in the years following a merger. The acquiring firms had been more profitable before the merger than the average for their industries, and the acquired enterprises generally earned average rates of return for their sectors.

These results were confirmed by Mueller (1980) who compared the consequences of mergers on company performance in seven countries. The success or failure of mergers was measured using three criteria: after-tax profit, the growth of sales and returns to shareholders.

In terms of profitability the results were mixed with the sample of mergers showing a slight improvement in four countries including the UK and a decline in the other three. The impact on the rate of growth was universally negative, while returns to shareholders improved in the period immediately after the merger, but this superior performance was not maintained beyond 3 years; this is not unexpected because if the merged firm becomes more competitive, then competitors can either lose market share or improve their own operation and become more efficient and competitive. The alternative explanation is that the stimulus of the merger to superior performance is lost with the passage of time.

Studies of the stock market effects of UK mergers agree that shareholders in target firms always gain in consummated mergers. However, empirical evidence regarding the long-run, post-merger benefits to shareholders of bidding firms has produced contrary results. An early study by Firth (1980) using a sample of 224 UK mergers between 1955 and 1975 found that on average the gains and losses were evenly balanced, that mergers were not value-creating and were more likely to be motivated by managers than owners. Later studies showed that the shareholders of bidding firms generally did not make gains (see Limmack 1991; Kennedy and Limmack 1996; Sudarsanam et al. 1996; Gregory 1997). However, other studies have reported gains to the shareholders of the bidding companies (see Parkinson and Dobbins 1993; Higson and Elliott 1998).

In the 1990s, when the effectiveness of diversified conglomerate companies like Hanson Trust were called into question, academic studies have been supported by management-consulting groups; these reinforced the conclusion that the majority of mergers were unsuccessful and that merging was a high-risk strategy. For example, Mercer Management Consulting (1997) found in the USA that 48% of mergers under-performed their industry average after 3 years. The conclusion applied whether the indicator of success was revenue growth, share price performance or the targets set when the acquisition took place. Another survey of 107 cross-border mergers conducted using telephone interviews in June 1999 found that 20% of mergers aimed to maximize shareholder value and 82% of respondents claimed they had been successful. However, less than half the mergers had been formally assessed to see whether they had been successful or not. Further analysis using comparative share price performance showed that only 17% had added to shareholder value, 30% had made no discernible difference and 53% had reduced shareholder value (KMPG 1999).

However, these generalized, negative conclusions for mergers as a whole still mean that some types of mergers are successful. Mercer explored 152 large transatlantic mergers between 1994 and 1999 and found that 82 (or 53%) of the acquisitions studied were successful. Success in this instance was measured by the ratio of growth in the stock market value of the company to corresponding growth in the industry index over the 24 months starting from one month before the announcement of the merger. To gain a greater understanding of the reasons for the higher rate of success than in previous studies senior executives were interviewed. The key to success was giving greater attention to implementing post-merger integration to ensure that regulatory and cultural barriers are overcome (Hill, 2002).

Abandoned mergers

Not all merger bids are successful. Pickering (1983) studied a sample of UK firms involved in abandoned mergers in the period 1965–1975 using questionnaires and identified three main factors explaining failure. First, when the target company put up a good defence; this requires the management of the target company to obtain the support of their shareholders and persuade them not to sell their shares. Management must demonstrate that their chosen strategy will be more beneficial to them than the alternative strategy of the acquirer. Second, when the bidding company makes mistakes in handling the bid or there are adverse movements in their own share price as a result of shareholders questioning the strategy (leading eventually to the withdrawal of the bid). Third, reference of the merger to the Competition Commission by the competition authorities, which automatically puts the merger on hold until the Commission decides whether the merger is in the public interest. Clearly, mergers that are against the public interest cannot proceed, but even bids that are cleared do not necessarily proceed (e.g., because of a change of mind by the acquirers).

Holl and Pickering (1988) compared 50 abandoned and 50 completed mergers, using profitability and growth as the criteria for success or failure. Overall, they found that mergers adversely affected profits and medium-term growth. Firms involved in abandoned mergers, both bidders and targets, performed better than the sample of successful acquirers. The authors concluded that a failed bid or the repulsing of a bid has a significant effect on the efficiency of firms that exhibit substantial growth in net assets. The improvement in growth rather than profitability suggests that abandoned mergers favour the interests of management.

Qualitative studies

While statistical studies of key indicators appear to throw doubt on the efficacy of mergers and the tendency for shareholders in the acquired company to be the main beneficiaries, managers continue to launch merger bids in the belief that mergers will be beneficial for their enterprises. An alternative approach is to ask senior managers whether they judge mergers to have been successful.

A study by Ingham et al. (1992) asked the chief executives of large UK companies about their merger activity between 1984 and 1988 and whether they could be regarded as successful. The results, based on 146 returns, contradicted statistical evidence and suggested that mergers had been successful. The analysis showed that in response to the question about whether profits had increased post-merger, 77% thought short-run profits had increased and 68% thought long-run profits had increased. Overall, 75% of senior managers thought that past mergers had been successful and 63% thought such success had influenced the decision to undertake further mergers. The results may be a function of the sample, which included several small takeovers, not just the mergers between large quoted companies which are normally the subject of statistical studies.

Failure of mergers

The failure of mergers is attributed to many factors. The general view is that too little attention is paid to the problems of integrating two organizations and disposing of particular activities in pursuit of rationalization. Rationalization requires the closure of plants, offices, etc. and the making of managers and workers redundant. Mergers, at best, create uncertainty for the staff of both companies and, at worst, discontent and declining productivity.

Cultural differences may be more significant if the merger is one of equals rather than a takeover. In a takeover the winner's culture is more likely to be imposed. Combining cultures in a merger of equals may be more problematic as to which one will predominate or whether a new one will be created; this will be more difficult if the partners come from different countries with significantly different corporate governance and management systems. Possibly because their corporate systems are similar, mergers between US and British companies are considered more likely to be successful than between continental European and US companies (KMPG 1999). The merger between Daimler of Germany and Chrysler of the USA was presented as a merger of equals. This agreement together with the different cultures compounded the difficulties of integration. In less than three years after the merger, escalating losses in the USA and changes of senior management led critics to declare the merger unsuccessful.

Beiker et al. (2001) argued that mergers fail because too much attention is paid to managing and cutting costs at the expense of encouraging revenue growth. They reported a study of 193 US mergers which showed that, compared with the industry average, only 36% of the merged companies maintained revenue growth in the first quarter and only 11% had avoided a slowdown in growth by the third quarter after the merger. This failure is attributed to uncertain customers who may look elsewhere for supplies and to staff distracted by the merger process. A further study by the authors of 160 companies in 1995–1996 showed that only 12% managed to accelerate their growth significantly over the next three years and, overall, the acquirers managed a growth rate that was four percentage points lower than the industry average.

Case Study 19.2 Granada–Forte takeover battle in 1995–1996

In December 1995, Granada, a television and leisure services company in the UK, bid for Forte, a hotel and catering company. Prior to the bid, Granada had made two significant acquisitions: Sutcliffe, a contract caterer bought from P&O in March 1993, and London Weekend Television, bought in February 1994 after a hostile bid. In the five years prior to the merger the company had seen its performance transformed from a pre-tax loss of more than £100m in the financial year ending in 1991 to a profit of £350m in 1995. During this period the share price had significantly outperformed the FT All Share index.

Forte, in contrast, had performed very poorly in the previous five years. Earnings per share had remained unchanged and the share price had underperformed the FT All Share index. It was estimated that £100 invested in Forte's shares 5 years earlier were now worth only £130, but a similar sum invested in Granada shares was now worth £544, a far superior performance.

Granada's motivation in bidding for Forte was to acquire its budget Travelodge hotels and the Happy Eater and Little Chef roadside restaurants. Forte's hotel chain was to be disposed of in due course. Granada argued that its management were superior and could make more effective use of the assets than the existing management.

The bid for Forte was launched on 22 November 1995 when its share price was 260p. The offer was 4 new shares plus £23.25 cash for every 15 Forte shares or a full cash offer of 321.67p; this valued Forte at £3.3bn which was described as hugely inadequate by Sir Rocco Forte who resolved to oppose the bid and maintain the independence of the company. Forte's management believed that they had started the turnround of the company and that they should be given the chance by shareholders to continue the company's recovery. They questioned Granada's management's knowledge and understanding of the hotel industry, claiming that its diversification was illogical and risky, especially when the spirit of times favoured more focused businesses. As part of its defence Forte agreed to sell its restaurant and Travellodge business to Whitbread for more than £1bn if the Granada bid did not succeed. It revalued its hotel assets, increased its dividend for the first time in 5 years, distributed shares in the Savoy Hotel to shareholders and made cost savings.

The outcome was that Granada won the support of a majority of Forte's shareholders. A key role was played by institutional shareholders, in particular MAM, a financial institution, which owned 14% of Granada and 12% of Forte. Forte finally decided to back Granada and gave Granada 66.68% of its shares. Forte's resistance had raised the final offer above the initial offer of 4 new shares plus £23.25 cash for every 15 Forte shares by adding a special dividend of 47p to be paid out of Forte reserves, giving a value of 371.67p or a cash offer of 362p; this valued Forte at £3.74bn compared with the initial bid of £3.3bn.

CHAPTER SUMMARY

In this chapter we examined mergers. In doing so we discovered that:

- Mergers are a major strategy for firms to increase their growth rates and profitability.
- Mergers are undertaken for a host of economic and strategic reasons to satisfy owners' desires to increase profitability and managers' desires to increase the size of the enterprise.
- The statistical evidence throws significant doubt on the efficacy of many mergers. While individual mergers are successful it would appear that acquiring other companies is a high-risk activity, with the chances of significant returns being rather low.

REVIEW QUESTIONS

Exercise

Identify a recent merger and follow it from the initial bid to acceptance by the target shareholders. Try to identify the objectives of the bidder, the reaction of the target, the anticipated benefits and the final price paid.

Discussion questions

1 Why should the management of a firm prefer:
   - Internal growth to external growth through mergers?
   - Growth through mergers to internal growth by organic expansion?
2 Distinguish between horizontal, vertical and conglomerate mergers and give examples of each.
3 For what reasons would a firm seek to be taken over?
4 What reasons motivate a firm to acquire another?
5 What are the anti-efficiency arguments against mergers?
6 What are the pro-efficiency arguments in favour of mergers?
7 Why do mergers fail to deliver anticipated benefits?
8 In the merger process:
   - What sort of firms become targets?
   - What sort of firms become acquirers?
9 How might the efficacy of mergers be measured?:
   - From the viewpoint of companies?
   - From the viewpoint of society?
10 Why do managers continue to believe in the effectiveness of mergers when the statistical evidence appears to point to the failure of most mergers?
11 Consider a recent merger proposal:
   - Identify the main motives of the acquirer.
   - Did the acquired company oppose the bid and, if so, why?
   - How success or failure might be measured?

REFERENCES AND FURTHER READING

Beiker, M.H., A.J. Bogardus and T. Oldham (2001) Why mergers fail. *The McKinsey Quarterly*, **4**.

DTI (1986) *Review of Merger Policy*. Department of Trade and Industry, London.

EC (1994) *Competition and Integration of the European Economy*. European Commission, Brussels.

Ernst, H. and J. Vitt (2000) The influence of corporate acquisitions on the behaviour of key inventors. *R and D Management*, **20**(2), 105–119.

Firth, M. (1980) Takeovers, shareholder returns and the theory of the firm. *Quarterly Journal of Economics*, **94**, 235–260.

Gregory, A. (1997) An examination of the long run performance of UK acquiring firms. *Journal of Business Finance and Accounting*, **24**(7–8), 971–1002.

Higson, C. and J. Elliott (1998) Post takeover returns – The UK evidence. *Journal of Empirical Finance*, **5**. 27–46.

Hill, A. (2002) Exposing the truth behind mergers. *Financial Times*, 25 March, p. 22.

Holl, P. and J.F. Pickering (1988) The determinants and effects of actual abandoned and contested mergers. *Managerial and Decision Economics*, **9**, 1–19.

Ingham, H., I. Kran and A. Lovestam (1992) Mergers and profitability: A managerial success story? *Journal of Management Studies*, **20**, 195–208.

Kennedy, V.A. and R.J. Limmack (1996) Takeover activity, CEO return and the market for corporate control. *Journal of Business Finance and Accounting*, **23**(2), 267–285.

KMPG (1999) Mergers and acquisitions: A global research report: Unlocking shareholder value: The keys to success. Available at http://www.kmpg.com

Knowles-Cutler, A. and R. Bradbury (2002) Why mergers are not for amateurs? *Financial Times* (12 February).

Komoto, K. (1999) *The Effect of Mergers on Corporate Performance and Stock Prices* (Paper 136). NLI Research Institute, Tokyo.

Limmack, R.J. (1991) Corporate mergers and shareholder wealth effects: 1977–1986. *Accounting and Business Research*, **21**, 230–251.

Marris, R. (1964) *The Economic Theory of Modern Capitalism*. Macmillan, London.

Meeks, G. (1977) *Disappointing Marriage: A Study of the Gains from Merger*. Cambridge University Press, Cambridge, UK.

Mercer Management Consulting (1997) *Post Merger Performance*. Mercer Management Consulting, Boston.

Mueller, D.M. (1980) *The Determinants and effects of Mergers*. Oelgeschlager, Gunn & Hain, Cambridge, MA.

National Statistics (2003) Mergers and acquisitions involving UK companies. Available at http://www.statistics.gov.uk

Parkinson, C. and R. Dobbins (1993) Returns to shareholders in successfully defended takeover bids: UK evidence 1975–1984. *Journal of Business Finance and Accounting*, **20**(4), 501–520.

Pickering, J.F. (1983) The causes and consequences of abandoned mergers. *Journal of Industrial Economics*, **31**(3), 267–281.

Sudarsanam, P.S., P. Holl and A. Salami (1996) Shareholder wealth gains in mergers: Effects of synergy and ownership structure. *Journal of Business Finance and Accounting*, **23**, 673–698.

20

ORGANIZATIONAL ISSUES AND STRUCTURES

CHAPTER OUTLINE

CHAPTER OBJECTIVES

This chapter aims to explore the organizational issues that influence the size of management costs, which might in some circumstances put a limit on the size of the firm. At the end of this chapter you should be able to:

◆ Explain the nature of the principal–agent relationships found in a firm.

◆ Outline and analyse agency theory and agency costs.

◆ Analyse the difficulties of relating effort to reward and devising appropriate incentive schemes.

◆ Distinguish between U and M-form structures and their advantages and disadvantages for small, large and diversified enterprises.

INTRODUCTION

A key characteristic of the modern firm, identified in Chapter 1, is the divorce between ownership and control. The implications of the distinction were then discussed in the context of corporate governance and the consequences for the performance of a firm of differences in the objectives of owners and managers. In this chapter we propose to further that discussion by examining the implications for management costs and limits to the size of the firm; this will be achieved by discussing:

- The principal–agent theory and agency costs.
- And the costs associated with different organizational structures.

PRINCIPAL–AGENT ANALYSIS

When the owners of a firm no longer manage the firm themselves, a problem arises about how they will be able to induce their appointed managers to pursue the owners' rather than the managers' interests. This relationship is described as one between a principal (the owner) and an agent (the manager). Similar relationships exist within the firm between the chief executive and senior management, between senior management and middle management and between management and workers. These situations between higher and lower levels in a hierarchy are termed agency relation-ships. They arise where principals engage an agent, ''to perform some service on their behalf which involves delegating some decision making authority to the agent'' (Jensen and Meckling 1976, p. 106). If the principal does not achieve full compliance with the set of objectives, then this failure generates agency costs. To minimize agency costs, principals are continually looking for solutions to the problem of more closely aligning the interests of the agent with those of the principal; these are generally to be found in creating incentive schemes and changes in organizational structures to limit the ability of agents to pursue their own rather than the principal's objectives.

The essential ingredients of any agency relationship is that:

- The principal hires an agent to carry out tasks.
- The principal compensates the agent for undertaking the activity.
- The principal cannot fully observe the actions or effort of the agent.
- The principal cannot fully measure output either in terms of quantity or, more particularly, quality.
- The principal receives the proceeds of the agent's activities and retains the surplus.

Jensen and Meckling (1976) developed the theory of the principal and agent. They analysed how agency costs arise by comparing a firm owned and controlled by an owner-manager with one where ownership is shared by the manager and outside shareholders. They suggested that the owner-manager of a firm will have a choice between maximizing the value of the firm or spending money on what Williamson

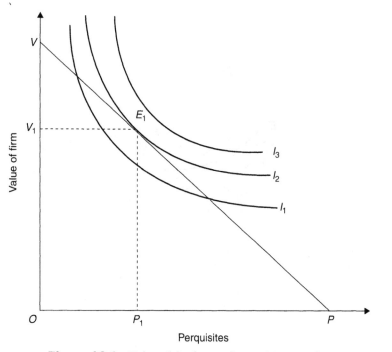

Figure 20.1 Value of the firm and perquisite spending

terms discretionary spending, or non-pecuniary benefits, or on on-the-job consumption. Such things might include spending on a luxury company car or an aeroplane, golf club membership and the time off to play. These expenditures add to the owner-manager's personal satisfaction and personal prestige but at the expense of the value of the firm. These extra costs imposed on the firm by unnecessary expenditure are termed agency costs.

Jensen and Meckling (1976) developed a simple model to explain the sources of agency costs. They assumed an owner-managed firm whose size is fixed. In Figure 20.1 we measure the present value of this firm on the vertical axis and the present value of perquisites on the horizontal axis. The line VP is drawn on the assumption that the total value of the firm (OV) can be traded for perquisites (OP), but that the sum of OV and OP is always constant. An owner-manager committed to maximizing the value of the firm would choose to be at V and spend nothing on perquisites. If the owner considers that perquisites add to his utility, then a position along the line VP would be chosen. Thus, the line VP acts in a similar way to a budget constraint. The owner-manager's preferences between V and P can be represented by a set of indifference curves I_1, I_2, I_3. The owner-manager maximizes utility at point E_1, where the indifference curve (I_2) is tangential to the frontier (VP). At E_1 the value of the firm is OV_1, the value of perquisites is OP_1 (where OP_1 is equal to VV_1) and the marginal utility gained from perquisites is equal to the marginal utility foregone by losing a unit of wealth.

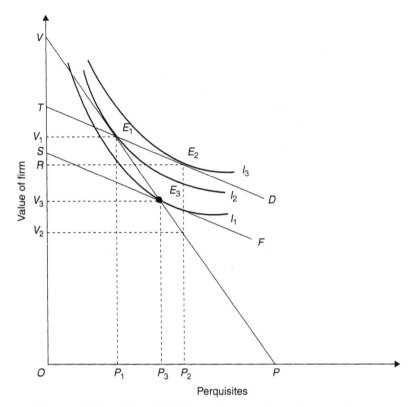

Figure 20.2 Value of the firm and perquisites and external owners

If the owner decides to sell 60% of the company to outside shareholders, then the owner is left with a 40% stake and managerial control, while the outside shareholders hold 60% of the value of the firm. If the outside shareholders pay 60% of the value of the firm (OV_1) for their stake, then they do so on the assumption that the manager continues to receive OP_1 in non-pecuniary benefits and that the future value of the firm will continue to be OV_1. However, in the new situation the manager might be expected to reconsider the level of spending on perquisites. If the manager-controller now spends an additional £100 on perquisites, then the present value of the firm is reduced by £100, while the personal wealth of the manager is reduced by only £40 and that of outside shareholders by £60. Therefore, the manager has an additional incentive to spend more on perquisites because an extra £1 of non-pecuniary benefits involves the loss of only 40 pence of wealth compared with 100 pence before the sale of the 60% stake to outside shareholders.

The choices now facing the manager can be illustrated using Figure 20.2. The relevant trade-off frontier is no longer VP but E_1E_2D, whose slope is a function of the proportion of the shares held by the manager. The slope of VP is -1 because each £1 spent on perquisites reduces the value of the firm to the owner-manager by £1. In the new situation each £1 spent on perquisites reduces the value of the firm to the manager by only 40 pence and to the outside owners by 60 pence. Hence, the slope of the value constraint (E_1E_2D) for the manager is given by the fact that the manager can trade £1 of perquisites for 40 pence of personal wealth, giving a slope of -0.4. With a given preference function the new equilibrium position is at E_2, where the indifference curve I_3 is tangential to the line E_1E_2D. If the manager increases expenditure on perquisites to OP_2, then the value of the firm is reduced to OV_2 – the loss to the manager is V_1R and to the outside owners it is RV_2.

This result assumes that the outside shareholders are willing to accept the reduction in the present value of the firm compared with the value when it was owner-controlled. If the outside shareholders had foreseen the action of the former owner-manager in increasing spending on perquisites, then they would have correctly identified the value of the firm after their share purchase and would have been prepared to pay only 60% of OV_2 rather than 60% of OV_1.

If the outside buyers had foreseen that the owner-manager would increase consumption of non-pecuniary benefits to OP_2, then they would have identified a point (E_3) lying on VP and the indifference curve of the owner-manager passing through it with a slope of E_1E_2. Restricting the owner-manager to E_3, means the value of the firm is now OV_3, which is greater than OV_2. Therefore, had the outside shareholders foreseen the actions of the owner-manager and been aware of his preference function, then they would have been willing to pay 60% of OV_3 rather than 60% of OV_1. The difference between OV_3 and OV_1 represents the reduction in the value of the firm as a result of the behaviour of the manager.

Principal–agent relationships

In the model discussed above the interests of the outside shareholders and the manager (or agent) do not perfectly coincide. They have different objectives in that the owners wish to maximize the present value of the firm, but the part-owner-manager wishes to maximize a function containing both wealth and perquisites. This type of analysis can be extended to many other relationships within the firm where the objectives of the principal and the agent are different. For example, the manager might expect the worker to work consistently and regularly all day. However, the worker might slack at certain times and pursue the personal goal of putting in the minimum effort for the reward offered. If the manager can observe the worker at all times, then slacking may not be an option for the worker. However, if the manager is monitoring a large group of workers, then the manager will only be able to monitor the individual worker some of the time. Thus, a manager cannot normally fully observe the effort put into a task by any individual.

The principal might find it equally difficult to observe and measure the output of an agent's effort. If the outcome of effort is not easily measured, then the principal may not be able to observe completely the link between effort and outcome. Thus, when the owners appoint a managing director to run a company on their behalf they can neither fully observe the mental and physical effort nor measure the relationship between this effort and the company's performance. This relationship depends not only on the efforts of the managing director but also on the efforts of others, market conditions and the state of the economy.

EFFORT, OUTCOMES AND REWARDS

A further problem may relate to how far an outcome is a function of the effort of the agent and how far is it dependent on factors outside his control. First, if effort and outcomes can be perfectly observed (i.e., there is perfect knowledge), then both the outcome (Q) and effort (E) can be fully observed. Thus, Q is a function of E, or $Q = f(E)$. The agent can be paid either on the basis of the observed effort or on the basis of the observed outcome.

Second, if we assume that the outcome (Q) is not just dependent on the effort of the agent but also on that of another factor, then the link between payment, effort and who shares the risks needs to be considered. For example, the sales of an ice cream salesman are a function of effort and the weather: a hot day will produce lots of sales, a cold wet day very few. Thus, we can say that outcome is a function of effort (E) and some other factor (S), so that we can write $Q = f(E, S)$. If effort is the same whatever the weather, what reward should the agent receive? The answer depends on who bears the risk of poor weather. If the agent receives the same reward irrespective of effort, then the risk of lower returns are met by the principal. However, if the agent's reward varies with sales but the principal's does not, then the agent bears the risk.

The indeterminate relationship between effort and outcome is illustrated in Table 20.1, where sales are a function of effort and the level of interest rates. Outcomes in the table are the result of two levels of effort and three levels of interest rates. Thus:

- If interest rates are high, then an increase in effort is assumed to have no impact on sales.
- If interest rates are at a medium level, then extra effort increases sales by £1,000.
- If interest rates are low, then extra effort increases sales by £2,000.

Thus, there is no clear relationship between effort and sales because of the influence of interest rates on sales. So, how should the agent be rewarded? There are a number of possible schemes. Let us say the agent is paid a flat fee of say £500:

- If interest rates are high, then the principal receives a surplus of £500 irrespective of the level of effort.

Table 20.1   Effort, sales and the state of the world

Effort	Sales (£) and state of the world		
	Low interest rates	Medium interest rates	High interest rates
Great (E_1)	5,000	3,000	1,000
Little (E_2)	3,000	2,000	1,000

Source Author

■ If interest rates fall to the medium level and the agent takes the easy effort option, then sales of £2,000 are generated and the principal now receives £1,500. If the agent were to choose the hard effort option, then the principal would receive an increased surplus of £2,500 while the agent still receives £500. In these circumstances the agent has no incentive to increase effort because he does not share in the higher revenue. To achieve higher sales the principal would have to induce the agent to exert more effort.

Let us say the agent is paid a flat fee of £1,000:

■ In a world of low interest rates the principal would have sales of either £3,000 or £5,000 depending on the level of effort of the agent. If the agent were paid a fixed fee of £1,000, then the principal would receive a residual income of £2,000 for low effort.
■ If interest rates rise to their medium level, then with the low effort outcome the principal's residual will fall to £500.
■ If interest rates rise to their high level, then with the same effort on the part of the agent the principal's net gain falls to zero.

It is not the fault of the agent that sales have fallen because the same effort is being made. The variation in sales is entirely the result of the other factor, the level of interest rates. A fixed payment irrespective of circumstances to the agent means that the principal takes all the risks and the initial level of reward may depend on the circumstances prevailing when the contract is signed.

To overcome the shortcomings of the arrangements outlined above the principal might seek to relate the rewards more closely to the level of effort and the level of sales. The problem lies in devising an incentive scheme to encourage extra effort and to share the risks between the principal and agent in such a way that does not discourage effort.

The nature of the incentives offered to agents may be of a financial nature. Rewards may be closely linked to output as in piece rate systems, where reward is directly linked to each unit produced or sold. The agent might be paid a basic salary with bonuses varying with output. For example, a basic payment of £500 might be supplemented by an additional reward of, say, 20% of all sales above £1,000. Thus, if interest rates were low, then the agent would earn the sums shown in Table 20.2,

Table 20.2   Agent reward and the state of the world

Effort	Sales (£) and state of the world		
	Low interest rates	Medium interest rates	High interest rates
Hard (E_1)	1,300(0.26)	900(0.3)	500(0.5)
Easy (E_2)	900(0.3)	700(0.35)	500(0.5)

Note   Agent's reward $= £500 + 0.2$ (Actual sales minus £1,000)
Source   Author

rewards would vary with effort and risks would be shared. The numbers in parenthesis in Table 20.2 show the proportion of total revenue going to the agent.

Risk sharing: symmetric information

The principles involved in risk sharing and devising incentive schemes can be illustrated diagrammatically. If we initially assume symmetric information so that effort can be fully observed, then the compensation of the agent can be explained with the help of Figure 20.3. On the horizontal axis is measured the agent's effort and on the vertical axis the expected pay-off or rewards to the agent and principal. The curve OI represents one of the agent's indifference curves that plots the level of effort against income and shows the minimum reward he will accept to exert any level of effort and further shows that greater effort will only be offered if the reward offered increases.

The total pay-off from the effort of the agent is shown by the line MP, which is assumed to be linear. Combining these two functions shows that from the principal's point of view the optimal level of the agent's effort is OE_1 because the vertical distance between line MP and curve OI is at greatest at this point. With a total pay-off of OR_1 the principal would receive P_1W_1. The problem for the principal lies in devising a reward structure that ensures the agent will put in effort OE_1. To reach this point the principal has to choose a reward structure to ensure the agent inputs the optimal effort; this requires a payment of E_1W_1.

The principal could choose to offer a contract that only pays the agent for a

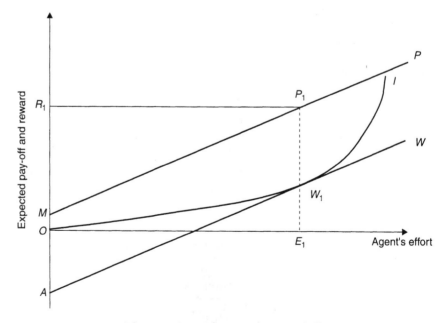

Figure 20.3   The agent's optimal effort

minimum OE_1 of effort (with no reward for any less or any greater effort). An alternative would be to offer the agent the reward structure represented by the line AW. To obtain the highest utility level achievable under this reward structure the agent would choose effort level OE_1 where the wage function is tangential to the indifference curve and receive payment of W_1E_1. Thus, because the principal can observe the exact effort of the agent he can select the appropriate reward for the agent to maximize the principal's return.

Asymmetric information

If the principal cannot observe the agent's level of effort, then we have a situation of asymmetric information. The principal could offer the agent a fixed wage; but, the agent then has no incentive to do a good job, because he can reduce effort and still receive the same reward. The exact opposite of the agent receiving a fixed payment is for the principal to receive a fixed payment (or rent) and for the agent to receive the residual and bear the risks attached. With this reward structure the agent has an incentive to make an extra effort; but, the principal who does not share in any surpluses may not have any incentive to maintain the quality of the resources supplied to the satisfaction of the agent.

The reward structures adopted will clearly depend on the attitudes of the two parties to bearing risk. In theory, either the principal or the agent can be risk-neutral, risk-averse or even risk-loving. If the principal and agent are risk-neutral, then neither has to be compensated for bearing risk; the principal will be happy to receive a fixed payment and provide maximum incentive to the agent.

Risk sharing

If we assume that the principal is risk-neutral because he has a portfolio of activities (e.g., shareholders) and the agent (e.g., a manager) is risk-averse because he has only one job, then the position can be analysed using Figure 20.4. In this the amount of risk borne by the agent is measured on the horizontal axis and the expected pay-off or reward is measured on the vertical axis. In the figure WI is the agent's indifference curve between risk and effort. A reward of OW must be paid to entice the agent to work. At this wage the agent bears no risk, the total pay-off is OE_3 and the principal receives WE_3. The function E_3P is the expected total pay-off as the degree of risk borne by the agent increases. To increase the expected potential pay-off the principal has to offer the agent an incentive contract to bear some of the risks involved. If the agent bears all the risks and the principal is paid a fixed rent, then with an expected pay-off of E_1 the principal would receive B_1T_1 and the agent R_1T_1. However, the principal maximizes his expected pay-off at point T_2 on the agent's indifference curve where the slope of the indifference curve is equal to the slope of line E_3P (or LM). At this point the agent bears some but not all of the risk, because R_2 is a less risky position than R_1. To get the agent to bear this level of risk the principal has to offer a payment of R_2T_2. (see Douma and Schreuder 2002, chap. 7 for further details).

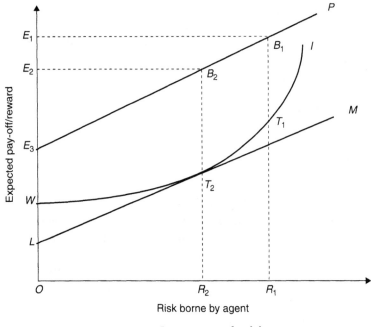

Figure 20.4   Incentives and risk bearing

This pattern of a risk-neutral principal and a risk-averse agent is to some extent mirrored in the relationship between shareholders and executives. The former can be regarded as risk-neutral as they hold diversified portfolios whereas executive managers are tied to the enterprise and failure may well result in them losing their positions. Thus, we would expect to find top managers being rewarded by performance-related schemes.

Reward schemes

To align the interests of owners and managers more closely it is suggested that managers should have equity stakes in a company and/or receive rewards more closely aligned to the performance of the firm. In practice, managerial reward schemes approved by the remuneration committees of companies appear to reward success but not penalize failure. Thus, the risks would appear to be borne by the owners rather than the managers. Such schemes have led to activism among institutional share-holders to curb what are seen as overgenerous incentive payments. Clearly, if performance is very poor, then shareholders might start to sell shares, the valuation ratio might fall and the company might become the subject of a takeover bid with the managers potentially losing their positions. However, assuming the results are not totally disastrous, then shareholders may find it difficult to act collectively because of their different objectives and the ease of selling shares.

Besides monetary incentives to compensate for extra effort, there may also be non-monetary factors at work, such as being part of a team where peer group pressure may bring out the best in everyone. Such a strategy is in the agent's interest because it may lead to: glowing references were he to apply for another job; getting promotion; and protecting his position if dismissals are considered. The management/owners might also encourage the workers to have an ownership stake in the company, either by encouraging them to buy shares or by introducing a share bonus scheme to encourage them to align their interests more closely with the company. That this is the case is illustrated by *The Guardian* newspaper's annual survey of directors of FTSE 100 companies paid more than a £1m in their company's latest financial year. In 2001 it found 141 such directors, 117 of whom received bonuses (83%), 86 received share options and 54 received payments to long-term investment plans (30 August 2001).

Case Study 20.1   Sliding-scale payments in coal mining

In many agreements both the agent and principal share the risks. In the franchising industry, for example, the owner of the franchise may share some of the risks of establishing a local outlet with the franchisee. In motor dealerships, salesmen are paid a low basic wage and a reward related to the number of cars sold. Thus, the salesman bears some of the risks with the principal; this is not a new issue. For example, in the coal industry, miners used to be rewarded for each tonne of coal mined, based on a sliding-scale agreement. The higher the market price the higher the reward and the lower the market price the lower the reward. Therefore, the miners shared in the owner's risks. The system in place in 1892 had a base price of 39.4 pence per tonne and for each rise or fall of 5 pence in the price of coal wages would rise or fall by 10% or 0.27 pence per ton. The base wage was approximately 7 pence per ton and the average miner earned approximately 75 pence per week. This system proved very contentious because both owners and workers felt they bore too many of the risks. The workers campaigned for a minimum wage and resented the wide fluctuations in wages, while the owners were keen to reduce the scale, particularly when prices were rising (Page Arnot, 1967).

Case Study 20.2   Managerial incentive schemes

Share or stock options awarded to managers are also used to improve performance. Share options give the manager the right to buy a given number of shares in the company at a predetermined price. For example, in year 1 an executive may be given the right to buy 100 shares in 3 years' time at a price of 50 pence. If the share price has increased to 120 pence when the option is exercised, the executive, ignoring trading costs, makes a profit of 70 pence per share.

Bruce and Buck (1997) surveyed a number of British and American studies and found share options to be an exception to the general tendency of finding no link between reward and performance. Oswald and Jahera (1991) found a positive relationship between managerial share ownership and performance. Using a sample of 645 US listed companies for the study period 1982–1987, they included managers and directors in their ownership data. Performance was measured by the difference between the risk-adjusted stock market return of the company and the sample as a whole. The relationship between size, ownership and performance was analysed using variance analysis and the results suggested that both size and ownership are statistically significant explanatory factors in determining firm performance, as measured by excess returns. The results support the hypothesis of a significant relationship between ownership and performance, even after controlling for size differences. The results showed higher excess returns for firms with higher levels of managerial ownership. This result implies that giving individuals a vested interest in the company is beneficial to the long-term performance of the business and, "support and strengthen earlier research which observed similar differences in the performance of manager controlled and owner-controlled firms" (p. 325).

Performance-related pay schemes for senior executives are controversial, and many individual examples receive extensive press coverage when large rewards appear to be correlated with declining performance. Conyon et al. (1995) identified a weak link between the remuneration of directors and the share price of the firm; this is not a surprising result, given the difficulty of measuring effort and the role of so many extraneous factors affecting overall firm performance. Like the coal miners whose wages were closely tied to price, managers are unlikely to want their salary too closely tied to the performance of the firm because rewards will rise and fall irrespective of effort. The generally accepted position is that the owners should bear the majority of risks, but it is possible to design a scheme where the owners bear none of the risks and the managers all of them.

The main advantage or, possibly, drawback of managerial share ownership or other incentive schemes is that managers may be tempted to adopt strategies and accounting policies that increase the value of the performance measure. For example, if share prices are the performance measure, then short-term profit maximization may be pursued, which may not be in the long-term interests of managers or shareholders. Movements in share prices are not just a function of the firm's performance but also of general economic changes and market sentiment.

ORGANIZATIONAL STRUCTURES

The general view of economics has been that only efficient organizations will survive in a competitive environment and, as a consequence, the organizational structure adopted by a firm does not matter. Chandler (1962) examined the historical development of successful enterprises and found major organizational innovations to be an important factor in allowing firms to grow. He identified a number of growth strategies and their impact on organizational structures. Growth generates inefficiencies in administrative structures and increases management costs: for example, an increase in the volume of output, product diversification, vertical integration and geographical expansion have each required firms to modify and innovate their organizational form to allow each growth strategy to be successful.

Chandler identified two major innovations in organizational form: unitary form (U-form) and divisional form (M-form) (Figure 20.5). The importance of organizational type for the theory of the firm was analysed by Williamson (1970). He argued that business behaviour is a function of market circumstances, internal efficiency, strategic decision processes and the internal compliance processes, with the last three

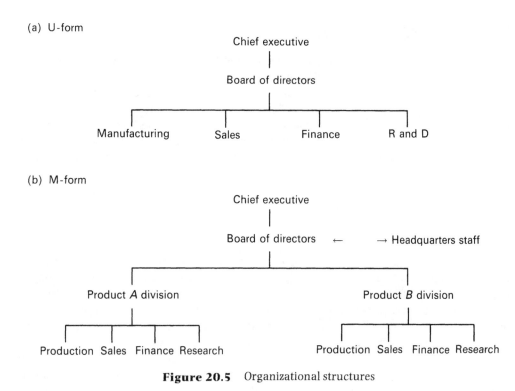

(a) U-form

(b) M-form

Figure 20.5 Organizational structures

depending on organizational form. Therefore, there is a need for organizational structure to be seen as an independent variable in explaining behaviour and constraining or expediting growth. He has also argued that, "the modern corporation is mainly to be understood as the product of a series of organisational innovations that have had the purpose of and effect of economising on transaction costs" (Williamson, 1985, p. 273).

The two organizational types compared and contrasted by Williamson were:

■ U-form: where the organizational structure is hierarchical, with a managing director and board at the top of a pyramidal structure. The firm is divided into functional areas covering such activities as sales, finance, production, R and D and personnel. These services are provided for all the product lines of the firm. A diagrammatic representation is found in Figure 20.5(a).

■ M-form: where the firm is divided into operating divisions or quasi-firms; these perform all the specialized functions for a single product and report to the chief executive. The divisions also transfer financial surpluses to headquarters which then controls the distribution to divisions to finance investments in the interests of the firm as a whole. Therefore, the M-form consists of a series of small (relative to the firm as a whole) U-form firms; this is illustrated in Figure 20.5(b).

U-FORM ORGANIZATIONS

The U-form firm emerged during the development of the American railways in the second half of the 19th century. The growth in size of the network together with the growth in traffic led to the creation of an administrative structure, the appointment of specialist managers, the development of internal accounting and control policies and to what is now termed the "unitary structure" of the firm; these incorporated "decentralized line and staff organization" giving managers the authority to carry out a particular function together with line authority to order subordinates to perform particular tasks.

Advantages

The growth of functional specialists provided the firm with more efficient performance through the effective division of labour: for example, employing marketing specialists improved the performance of that function and allowed the firm to increase its managerial capacity, so that it could expand. The growth of functional specialists also freed the chief executive from undertaking many of these duties and to give him more time to consider the strategic and entrepreneurial issues facing the firm.

The role of senior management is to manage the organization and implement its existing strategy. It does this by employing staff, signing contracts, ensuring production takes place and products are delivered. It also collects information to evaluate whether past decisions have been successful and to take appropriate action as a result. Another task is to communicate with staff and motivate them to work in the interests of the firm and fulfil the tasks allotted to them. Subordinates carry out many of these tasks. Finally, senior managers are responsible for determining and changing the strategy of the firm; this involves deciding the boundaries of the firm, the products to be added to or deleted from the existing portfolio, markets to be served and acquisitions or divestments to be made. The U-form firm is thought to carry out all these tasks effectively as long as the firm is a small or medium-sized single product enterprise. With growth and diversification the structure faces a number of problems.

Disadvantages

The unitary structure takes the form of a hierarchical or pyramid structure whereby the managing director gives orders to a functional director who gives directions to the next layer of management/workers down the line of control. Each level of the hierarchy will have its responsibilities for a particular aspect of a function and will report on its performance to the higher level that gave the orders.

Span of control   The number of levels of management required in a U-form firm is a function of the span of control of the manager and the number of operatives at the lowest level. With a span of control of 2, a workforce of 8 operatives would require 7 managers and a 4-tier organization. A doubling of the lowest level workforce to 16 would increase the number of supervisors to 15 and the number of tiers to 5. Increasing the span of control would clearly reduce the number of managers and tiers in an organization. With a span of control of 10, 1,000 workers could be supervised by 111 managers and the organization would have only 4 tiers. With a span of control of 2, the organization employing 1,024 operatives would require 11 tiers and 1,023 managers.

Increasing the span of control of supervisors or managers can therefore offset the rising costs of hierarchy; this is facilitated by the experiential learning of specialist managers and workers who will be able to undertake tasks more efficiently and with less supervision; this, together with organizational learning and reorganization, will increase the work capacity of all staff and hence the firm. However, as the number of operatives increases the U-firm will experience increasing layers in its organizational structure. At some point diminishing returns set in as the firm faces problems associated with the growing number of layers in the hierarchy (namely, control loss, information distortion and opportunistic behaviour).

Control loss is the cumulative reduction in management's overall ability to control the firm as it becomes larger; this is the result of increasing the number of levels in the pyramid for any given span of control. Those in the hierarchy who are employed to make decisions rely on those lower in the hierarchy to pass accurate information and data to them. However, information transferred between individuals is subject to distortion, accidental or deliberate, and to misinterpretation by the recipient, particularly when the information is summarized and interpreted for onward transmission to those higher in the hierarchy. Similar considerations apply to the transfer of orders from the top to the bottom of the organization. Directions from senior managers are interpreted by lower managers and converted into operational directions for those responsible for finally implementing decisions at the production level.

The transfer of information and directions through a hierarchy, therefore, leads to greater control loss the greater the number of layers. Such control losses limit the effectiveness of any hierarchy and of individual managers within it. To limit control loss there is a tendency for hierarchies to establish rules and procedures to guide every decision. While these work in a stable environment, the rules may be less relevant in an unstable one.

Control loss can be expressed as a function as follows:

$$C = 1 - F^{N-1}$$

where C = a measure of overall control loss, F = the fraction of information being passed accurately between layers in the hierarchy and N = the number of layers in the organizational structure. Thus, if:

- F is equal to 0.9 and n is equal to 3, then control loss is equal to 19%.
- F is equal to 0.9 and n is equal to 6, then control loss is equal to 41%.
- F is equal to 0.9 and n is equal to 12, then control loss is equal to 69%.

Thus, the fewer the number of levels in the organization and the higher the proportion of information accurately passed from one level to another the lower the control loss.

Increasing span of control One way of limiting the number of levels in the hierarchy as the organization grows is to increase the span of control. However, this means that a manager has less time to address any particular problem and to deal with individual staff, so that the outcome is likely to be poorer decision making and greater opportunities among staff to behave opportunistically.

Principal–agent analysis suggests that there is greater opportunity for opportunistic behaviour by agents if the principal becomes distant from the agent. The weaker the supervision the less effort will the agent be inclined to put into any task; this may be compounded where the agent possesses information or skills important to the business but not fully known or fully understood by their supervisors. Since their work is incompletely understood by their supervisors, information may be only partially and inaccurately transferred, so that senior managers find themselves making decisions with incomplete and possibly distorted information.

Crowding out Strategic Decision Making The board of directors may be made up of the senior operating officers for each of the functional areas together with the chief executive officer. Since the executive officers are primarily concerned with the efficient operation of their functional area, such boards are said to spend too little time on the wider strategic issues facing their enterprise. Each director may also behave opportunistically to favour his own department at the expense of others.

The function of the chief executive is to give the functional directors objectives and to co-ordinate their work. However, each functional executive may prosecute the interests of his particular group over those of others. The functions may cease to communicate with each other and pursue conflicting goals, making the work of the chief executive in pursuing the collective interests of the firm more difficult.

Self-interest and opportunistic behaviour A further result is that if resources are allocated to functional areas led by stronger and more powerful executives, then resources are misallocated. For example, if the importance of an executive is judged by the number of employees, then executives will try to increase the size of their part of the firm in terms of numbers employed. This problem is compounded by the difficulties faced in U-form firms in measuring the performance of individual functions. For example, if the firm increases sales of its product, which functional area is responsible for calculating an appropriate price? Is it marketing for selling, manufacturing for making a better product, or accounts? If the productivity of the functional areas cannot be measured, then the internal allocation of resources will follow political rather than efficiency criteria. These problems are further compounded if the firm produces a number of products because it is difficult to allocate costs to individual products.

Such opportunistic behaviour may be avoided at senior management level by the introduction of non-executive directors from outside the organization (see Chapter 1) and may be constrained by outside forces in the shape of competitors and shareholder preferences. If the administrative cost of a U-form structure becomes excessive, then the profits of the firm will decline and organizational structures re-examined. For example, the financial difficulties of the British Postal service in 2002, in the face of price controls and deregulation, led to a decision to reduce the number of administrative layers in the organization from 15 to 6 (*Financial Times*, 14 June 2002). The chairman attributed the problems partly to poor management and partly to excessive bureaucracy.

The simple U-form organization is considered appropriate for small and medium-sized firms since it generates efficiency from specialization of functions. It appears to be less efficient as size and complexity increase, particularly if the firm grows through product or market diversification; this is supported by empirical studies, which are considered in Case Study 20.3. However, there comes a point where the U-form structure begins to constrain the growth of a firm; this occurs when functional executives become overloaded and perform day-to-day operational tasks at the expense of appraisal and long-term strategy.

M-FORM ORGANIZATIONS

To overcome the organizational constraint on growth, firms experiment with new organizational forms. The essence of the M-form structure has already been described and can be observed in Figure 20.5(b).

Advantages

In this new structure the firm achieves economies of specialization at two levels: first, product specialization where each product produced by the firm becomes a separate division and, second, at the divisional level where use is made of functional specialist skills. Thus, the M-form combines both the benefits of a small-scale U-form organization at the division level and the economies of separation associated with each division producing a single product. The growth constraint preventing diversification is overcome by the firm being able to add new divisions for new products rather than having to reorganize the hierarchical structure.

Starting at the top of the enterprise, the chief executive is given time to make strategic decisions and to be responsible for the overall boundaries of the firm. Day-to-day operational decisions are the responsibility of the heads of divisions. The chief executive reports to and seeks advice from a board of directors (which does not have functional responsibilities), receives administrative and research support from the small number of headquarters staff, who also appraise the performance data supplied by divisions. The chief executive, freed from administrative duties, sets objectives for each division, gives orders to and receives reports from the head of each division. The chief executive also decides whether to add or delete divisions from the firm's portfolio of activities. The number of people reporting to the chief executive is a function of the number of divisions. Thus, in a 10-division firm the chief executive is responsible for the 10 heads of divisions. At this level the organizational structure is flat with a single tier of supervision of all divisions.

The head office of the M-form firm meets the administrative needs of the chief executive and the senior management team. It does not serve the interests of individual product divisions but the interests of the firm as a whole. Despite the small numbers of headquarters staff, the chief executive and senior management team appear to have few motives to behave opportunistically and distort the allocation of resources, though they might desire the number of staff and the functions of headquarters to increase in size.

A key feature of the M-form structure is that divisions remit financial surpluses to headquarters who in turn allocate resources to divisions on the basis of the greatest contribution to profitability. The operation of this internal capital market is the responsibility of headquarters. One of the criticisms levied against the U-form structure for a multi-product firm is that resources are retained by divisions and misallocated as senior divisional managers pursue their own goals. The external capital market does not correct this failure because the means of disciplining the managers of enterprises that have disappointing performance are weak. They consist essentially of investors selling shares, thereby reducing the firm's valuation ratio and takeover threats from other enterprises. The central management of the M-form firm can overcome these shortcomings by the superior information they have about the divisions, obtained by monitoring systems, checked by performance audits and backed by the ability to hire and fire managers.

The internal capital market means that divisions have no retained earnings and that they have to seek funding from headquarters for investment. Thus, providing headquarters stick to allocating investment according to expected returns, this will produce maximum benefits for the firm. The only way, it is argued, that the division can influence the allocation of resources is by putting forward-well-thought-out investment plans and not by using political influence. Ensuring that the investment proposals of divisions have a reasonable chance of making the predicted profits is the responsibility of headquarters staff. Their problem is that they do not necessarily have the skills that the divisions possess to question the underlying basis of the investment. In the long run, inflated returns that are not earned will reduce the credibility of the division's proposals. Thus, whether the internal capital market is superior may be debatable but clearly depends on the strict application of the resource allocation model and the commitment of headquarters staff to the overall objectives of the enterprise.

Individual divisions should be designed to be small enough to be organized as U-form enterprises and focused on a single or narrow range of products, so that functional specialization produces an efficient organizational structure. The division may also be able to fully exploit economies of scale, since a single product is being produced. However, economies of scope are not available unless the divisions trade with each other or there are central buying functions. These developments would be considered as corrupting the pure M-form structure and, therefore, limiting the benefits of the structure.

The M-form structure allows the performance of each division to be measured. If each division is responsible for a single product, then the performance of these can also be measured; this is an advantage over the U-form structure, where such comparisons are inherently difficult to make. In the M-form structure the performance of divisions can be compared and, depending on the objectives of the senior management and/or owners, resources can be withdrawn from or allocated to divisions; even whole divisions can be sold or closed down. If the cause of underperforming in divisions is attributed to their senior managers, then central management can act quickly to replace them.

Divisions can also be easily added with little or no impact on the other divisions. The M-form structure facilitates the growth of diversified enterprises because each division is in some senses an independent business. The limit to the number of divisions depends on the ability of central management to be able to control the information flows from individual divisions.

The advantages of the M-form structure lies in the control of divisions by a headquarters dedicated to improving the profitability of the firm as a whole. The M-form structure is said to limit opportunities for managerial discretion in divisions as the system permits greater central control of managerial slack, as headquarters are unlikely to sanction projects enhancing managerial utility at the expense of the firm as a whole. In addition, poorly performing divisions are easily identified and policy changes can be quickly made to restore performance.

Disadvantages

Whether M-form structures can deliver the benefits claimed depends on whether its purity is maintained. Over time, it can become corrupted if senior management and headquarters staff become involved in the day-to-day operations of divisions facing difficulties. Central management may not be as profit-oriented as the model postulates, and as a consequence there is less pressure on divisions to perform. In such circumstances, divisions may not have to compete for resources and may be allowed to retain some of their own funds. Also, if divisions grow, then they may face problems similar to those of growing U-form firms unless they can be subdivided to maintain the benefits of the divisional structure.

In addition, an M-form firm may move to an H-form, or holding company, structure as divisions try to assert their rights to retain their own profits. In this structure a holding company owns subsidiaries (or divisions); these can retain a separate legal identity and some or all of their financial surpluses. In such a structure the disciplinary control of central management over managerial discretion is significantly reduced. The H-form firm is sometimes viewed as an intermediate position between the U-form and the M-form.

Case Study 20.3   Organizational form – empirical studies

A number of empirical studies have been carried out in the UK and the USA to see whether M-form structures have been adopted by large firms and whether the performance of the firm is superior (Cable 1988, p. 30 summarized earlier studies). In what follows only the results of a number of UK studies are presented.

Steer and Cable (1978) found in 1970 that 71.5% of the top 100 UK enterprises had adopted M-form structures compared with 14.1% in 1950. Hill (1985) found from a survey of 144 companies in 1982 the proportion to be 61.1% and that there was evidence of a growing proportion of corrupted M-form structures either because they partially resembled holding companies or because they had divisions that were growing too complex.

Hill explored the relationship between organizational form and performance. He found that M-form firms had superior rates of return on capital and higher rates of profit than non-M-form organizations, providing a distinction is made between pure M-form firms and divisionalization (Hill, 1984, 1985a). He concluded that the pure M-form with its internal capital market produced greater profitability than mere divisionalization.

Hill (1988), using a sample of 156 large UK firms, investigated the relationship between control systems and performance and proposed that the control systems necessary to realize the economic benefits from related diversification are incompatible with the systems necessary to realize benefits from operating an internal capital market. This result supports the proposition that the M-form is better suited to companies engaged in unrelated diversification. He also found a negative relationship between M-form firms and profitability for the sample as a whole. However, for firms engaged in unrelated diversification there was a weak but positive relationship.

Ezzamel and Watson (1993) found that organizational form did not explain performance differences. They found that the length of time since adopting the present structure did allow firms to be differentiated; this applies to all structures and suggests than any organizational change leads to improved performance initially but the effect tails off. Such a conclusion was found by Dunsire et al. (1991) when studying various organizational changes in the public sector. They found that almost any change brought improved performance including agency status, nationalization and privatization.

In a more recent study, Weir (1995) investigated the incidence of M-form structures among medium and large-sized firms, excluding the top 250 largest firms, in the UK. He then used the data to see whether such structures led to superior profitability. The sample consisted of 68 large and 16 medium-sized firms, which were then classified by organizational structure. Of the large companies 13% were U-form, 66% were M-form and only 25% were pure M-form. Of the medium-sized companies 19% were U-form, 57% M-form and 13% were pure M-form.

The profitability of individual firms was measured relative to the performance of their industry group. They were then allocated to two groups: those earning above-average and those below-average profits. Irrespective of organizational structure the sample of medium-sized firms tended to have profits in excess of the industry average while large firms tended to perform less well than the industry average. For large firms the U-form structure was a poor performer with 75% earning below-average profits compared with 50% for medium-sized firms. All medium-sized firms operating pure M-form structures obtained above-average profitability but only 47% of large, pure M-form firms achieved above-average profitability. However, a majority of large firms classified as either transitional or corrupted M-form types achieved above-average performance.

Weir concluded that the claimed superiority of the M-form structure is not supported by the results. The failure of the M-form to achieve superior performance may be the result of:

■ Ineffective monitoring of divisional managers allowing discretionary behaviour to continue.
■ A failure to design rewards and incentive schemes for divisional managers to align their interests with those of the chief executive.
■ Staff at headquarters not being committed to pursuing profit maximization or implementing internal resource allocation rules that ensure efficient use of all financial surpluses.

Weir also explored the main criteria used in allocating funds internally. Pure M-form firms allocated resources to projects on the basis of the highest expected rates of return, while other structures allowed divisions to retain their own profits or allocate them to meet greatest needs.

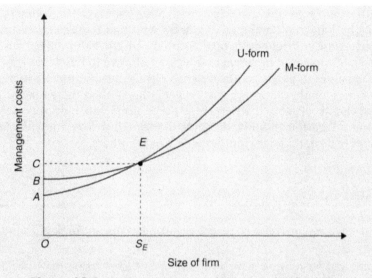

Figure 20.6 Management costs of U-form and M-form firms

Of those firms allocating resources to activities with the highest returns, 53% achieved above-average profits and 47% below-average profits. Of those achieving above-average returns, 26% were allocated by greatest profit (i.e., pure M-form), while 23% of under-performing firms also used greatest profit as the main criteria. Thus, Weir argued that the relationship between the internal resource allocation model and performance is complex and probably reflects inadequate investment appraisal within the enterprise.

Various studies suggest that the relationship between organizational form and performance can be tentatively summarized as in Figure 20.6. This figure measures firm size on the horizontal axis and management costs per unit of output on the vertical axis suggests that the U-form firm is appropriate for small firms while the M-form structure is appropriate for larger firms, where the notion of small and large is not specifically defined. However, particular structures may work for particular enterprises at any point in time.

LIMITS TO GROWTH AND SIZE OF THE FIRM

From time to time, commentators predict that economic activity will become concentrated in fewer and fewer large enterprises because of advances in production processes and the importance of economies of scale. The increasing size of the firm is further encouraged by diversification, the benefits of economies of scope and organizational innovations, such as the M-form structure.

Limits to the size and growth of the firm appear to arise from the increasing management costs of large organizations, their inability to apply their competences in all fields of human endeavour, changing production technology favouring small-scale production and consumer behaviour. All of these changes go together to favour smaller more specialist enterprises; this is reinforced by changes in consumer behaviour.

Galbraith (1967) in the *New Industrial State* envisaged consumers as totally malleable at the hands of dominant producers who had totally eroded the notion of consumer sovereignty. While firms take decisions on what to produce based on their understanding of consumer preferences, they do not have to buy what is on offer from dominant companies. If goods go unsold, then clearly the consumer prefers something else. If consumers want products that are differentiated, then there may be more room for small, efficiently organized enterprises. Large firms can hide the identity of the enterprise and sell various brands. However, if they fail to keep up with the changing characteristics of demand, opportunities will exist for others.

CHAPTER SUMMARY

In this chapter we explored the principal–agent relationship. In doing so we analysed:

- Organizational structures, which are important in determining the efficiency and effectiveness of the firm.
- The principal agent theory and the problem of aligning the interests of members of the firm with those of the organization as a whole. While incentives play their part, so does the organizational structure in encouraging commitment and efficient operation, thereby eliminating the tendency on the part of agents to behave opportunistically.
- Changes in organizational structures, which limit the growth in management costs and facilitate the growth of the firm.
- Limits to the size of the firm, which are related to economies of scale in production, the ability of the firm to meet the needs of its customers and the organizational structure needed to manage a growing enterprise.
- U-form, M-form and H-form structures.

REVIEW QUESTIONS

1 What do you understand by the term "agency theory"?
2 What is the source of the agency problem?
3 How might owners attempt to alleviate agency problems among senior managers?
4 If effort and outcomes cannot be clearly measured what problems are created for incentive schemes?
5 Identify the main characteristics of a U-form firm. What are its advantages and disadvantages? How does a U-form structure limit the growth in size of the firm?
6 Identify the main characteristics of a M-form firm. What are its advantages and disadvantages? How does an M-form structure allow the firm to increase its size?
7 Why do management costs increase as a U-form firm grows?
8 What impact does diversification have on the structure of the firm?
9 Does the empirical evidence support the superiority of the M-form over the U-form?
10 Evaluate the implications for performance of the M-form and the H-form firm.

REFERENCES AND FURTHER READING

Bartlett, C.A. and S. Ghoshal (1993) Beyond the M-form: Toward a managerial theory of the firm. *Strategic Management Journal*, **14**, 23–46.

Bruce, A. and T. Buck (1997) Executive reward and corporate governance. In: K. Keasey, S. Thompson and M. Wright (eds), *Corporate Governance*. Oxford University Press, Oxford, UK.

Cable, J.R. (1988) Organisational form and economic performance. In: S. Thompson and M. Wright (eds), *Internal Organisation, Efficiency and Profit*. Philip Allan, Oxford, UK.

Chandler, A.D. (1962) *Strategy and Structure: Chapters in the History of the Industrial Enterprise*. MIT Press, Cambridge, MA.

Conyon, M., P. Greff and S. Machin (1995) Taking care of business: Executive compensation in the UK. *Economic Journal*, **105**, 704–714.

Douma, S. and H. Schreuder (2002) *Economic Approaches to Organization* (3rd edn)., Prentice Hall, Englewood Cliffs, NJ.

Dunsire, A., K. Hartley and D. Parker (1991) Organisational status and performance: A summary of the findings. *Public Administration*, **69**, 21–40.

Ezzamel, M. and R. Watson (1993) Organisational form, ownership structure and corporate performance: A contextual empirical analysis of UK companies. *British Journal of Management*, **4**(3), 161–176.

Ferguson, P.R., G.J. Ferguson and R. Rothschild (1993) The organisation of firms: Efficiency, incentives and controls. *Business Economics* (Chapter 3). Macmillan, London.

Financial Times (2002) In the post. *Financial Times*, 14 June, p. 18.

Galbraith, J.K. (1967) *The New Industrial State*. Hamish Hamilton, London.

Guardian, The (2001) Rewarding the Boardroom. *The Guardian*, 30 August, p. 23.

Hill, C.W.L. (1984) Organisation of the firm: Efficiency, incentives and control. In: J.F. Pickering and T. Cockerill (eds), *Economic Management of the Firm*, Philip Allan, Oxford, UK.

Hill, C.W.L. (1985a) Internal organisation and enterprise performance. *Managerial and Decision Economics*, **6**, 210–216.

Hill, C.W.L. (1985b) Oliver Williamson and the M-form firm: A critical review. *Journal of Economic Issues*, **19**, 731–751.

Hill, C.W.L. (1988) Internal capital markets: Controls and financial performance in multi-divisional firms. *Journal of Industrial Economics*, **37**(1), 67–83.

Jensen, M. and W. Meckling (1976) Theory of the firm: Managerial ownership, agency costs, and ownership. *Journal of Financial Economics*, **3**, 305–360.

Keasey, K., S. Thompson and M. Wright (eds) (1997) *Corporate Governance*. Oxford University Press, Oxford, UK.

Oswald, S. and J.S. Jahera (1991) The influence of ownership on performance: An empirical study. *Strategic Management Journal*, **12**, 321–326.

Page Arnot, R. (1967) *South Wales Miners 1890–1914*. Allen & Unwin, London.

Steer, P. and J. Cable (1978) Internal organisation and profit: An empirical analysis of large UK companies. *Journal of Industrial Economics*, **27**, 13–30.

Thompson, R.S. (1981) Internal organisation and profit: A note: *Journal of Industrial Economics*, **30**, 201–211.

Thompson, S. and M. Wright (1988) *Internal Organisation, Efficiency and Profit*. Philip Allan, Oxford, UK.

Weir, C. (1995) Organisational structure and corporate performance: An analysis of medium and large UK firms. *Management Decision*, **33**(1), 24–32.

Williamson, O. (1970) *Corporate Control and Business Behaviour*. Prentice Hall, Englewood Cliffs, NJ.

Williamson, O.E. (1975) *Markets and Hierarchies: Analysis and anti-trust implications*. Free Press, New York.

21

THE GROWTH AND DEVELOPMENT OF THE FIRM: STAGECOACH GROUP PLC

CHAPTER OUTLINE

CHAPTER OBJECTIVES

This chapter aims to use the experience of Stagecoach in starting, growing and developing a business, to illustrate the themes explored in earlier chapters. At the end of this chapter you should be able to:

♦ Understand the economics of the bus industry including demand, costs and pricing.

♦ Outline the nature of the privatization process in the bus industry.

♦ Explain the reasons for the successful growth of the company.

♦ Outline the strategic moves made by the company.

♦ The balance between success and failure.

INTRODUCTION

Stagecoach was started in 1980 and grew in 20 years to be one of the largest bus companies, not just in the UK but in the world. It was founded by a brother and sister, Brian Souter and Ann Gloag, in their home town of Perth with a couple of second-hand buses that they used to run the first service from Dundee to London on 11 October 1980, two days after the deregulation of coach services (Sharkey and Gallagher 1995).

In 1980 the bus industry was heavily regulated and had experienced a long decline in demand. It did not appear to be an industry where significant opportunities existed for new, small businesses. However, this changed in the next 10 years as detailed regulation of entry and behaviour was replaced by a much more open regime, together with the privatization of national and local government-owned bus companies. The founders of Stagecoach made use of each of these changes to grow and develop the company, so that its success was described as a, "lesson in the application of private enterprise to the often hidebound world of public transport" (*Financial Times* 1993)

THE BUS INDUSTRY

The bus and coach industry can be divided into a number of sectors that include: regular, timetabled, short-distance services known as stage carriage services; regular, timetabled, long-distance, limited stop coach services; regular contract services and private hire services.

The Road Traffic Commissioners under the terms of the Road Traffic Act 1930 heavily regulated the first two of these activities. Licences were required before services could be provided and incumbents could object to a licence being awarded. Once granted, the Commissioners also controlled the frequency of service and fares, which could only be changed with permission. The result was that the majority of routes had a single operator, and even where there was more than one operator there was no price competition. The structure of routes and services responded only slowly to changing demand. Bus companies also continued to use large vehicles even where smaller ones might have been more appropriate.

Demand

The decline in passenger journeys began in the 1950s and has continued to the present day, because of the growth in car ownership and the substitution of private for public transport; this is demonstrated in Figure 21.1, which shows the decline in passenger journeys for the period 1973–1998. Nevertheless, buses are an important component of public transport. In 1999, 62% of public transport journeys were made by local bus (10 years earlier it was 69%), 9% by coach (8%) and 29% by rail (23%). The chart also shows the increase in the number of kilometres travelled by buses over the same period. This increase is explained by the use of smaller buses and more frequent services. For example, between 1986 and 1987 the proportion of bus stock represented by double-deckers fell from 35% to 24%, while single-deckers seating fewer than 35 passengers increased their share from 17% to 35%, with one-third of these seating fewer than 16 passengers.

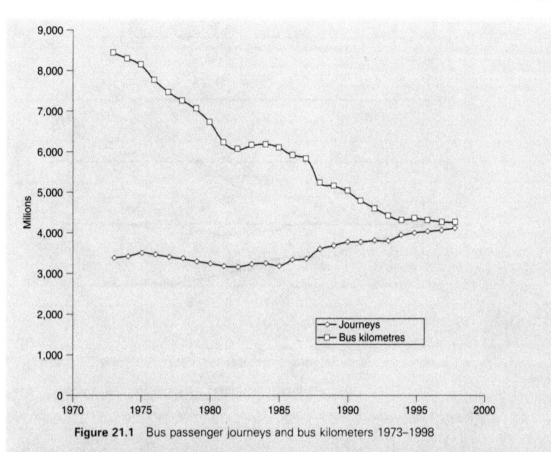

Figure 21.1 Bus passenger journeys and bus kilometers 1973–1998

The demand function for bus transport for local journeys is dependent on such variables as bus fares, the price of other forms of transport, income and the availability of substitutes, particularly cars. Other factors include the necessity of making the journey, the quality of the journey and the length of time it takes. The latter is related to the length of journey and the level of road congestion on the route.

The demand curve for local bus journeys on individual routes is seen to be very inelastic, particularly on routes where passengers have no alternative means of travel (such as the use of a car). Stubbs et al. (1980) report that the value of own price elasticity for local journeys generally varied between −0.21 and −0.61 (p. 23). Income elasticity is also negative, with the number of journeys made declining as income increases. Between 1996 and 1998 the poorest 20% of households made 99 bus journeys per person per year, while the richest 20% made only 35 bus journeys per person per year (DoT, 1999); this makes bus transport an inferior good (i.e., one where consumption declines with increasing income).

Estimating a demand function for buses

These relationships can be illustrated using UK published data from 1974 to 2000 (26 observations) to estimate a simple demand function for bus travel. The data were obtained from the Annual Abstracts of Transport Statistics (DoT 2002).

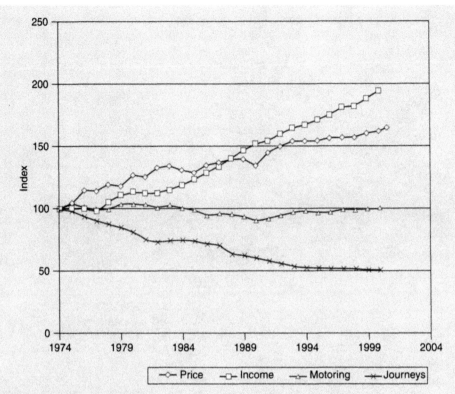

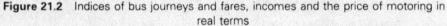

Figure 21.2   Indices of bus journeys and fares, incomes and the price of motoring in real terms

The function estimated was:

$$\log B = a \log F + b \log Y + c \log M$$

where Y = millions of bus journeys per annum, F = real bus fares, Y = real disposable income and M = real motoring costs. The reason this is in log form is to give direct estimates of the elasticities (as explained in Chapters 5 and 6). The estimated equation using least squares (with t-ratios in parentheses) is:

$$B = \underset{(15.6)}{5.903} - \underset{(-6.54)}{0.812F} - \underset{(-6.52)}{0.495Y} + \underset{(1.86)}{0.318M} \qquad R^2 = 0.985; F = 528.86$$

Own price elasticity and income elasticity are significant at the 5% level and have negative signs, while the price of motoring is significant at the 5% level but has a positive sign; these are all in line with expectations. The estimated own price elasticity for buses is −0.812, showing that it is inelastic but higher than the estimates suggested for individual routes. Income elasticity is −0.495, showing that as income increases so the number of bus journeys decreases. Finally, elasticity for the price of motoring is 0.318, showing that cars and buses are weak substitutes. Thus, a 1% rise in bus fares will reduce travel by 0.8%, a 1% increase in income will reduce bus travel by 0.5% and a 1% rise in the price of motoring will increase bus travel by 0.3%.

Production and costs

The production function of the bus industry includes the following capital and labour inputs:

■ Bus stock.
■ Terminal, garaging and maintenance facilities.
■ Platform staff (i.e., drivers and conductors).
■ Maintenance staff.
■ Supervisory and management staff.
■ Fuel.
■ Road use charges.

Output is bus kilometres. Each bus kilometre provides a number of bus seats per kilometre depending on the size of the bus, but can provide a much larger journey capacity depending on whether passengers travel for the whole route or only parts of a route. The potential trade-offs between labour and capital are complex because each bus requires one driver per journey irrespective of size, while larger buses may have conductors to save waiting time at bus stops. Maintenance and other staff vary and reductions are made as buses become more reliable and require less maintenance. Thus, in the 10 years following deregulation:

■ Output measured by number of bus kilometres increased by +23%.
■ The number of buses (not adjusted for size) increased by +9%.
■ The number of platform staff increased by +3%.
■ The number of maintenance staff declined by −35%.
■ The number of other staff declined by −39%.
■ The total number of staff declined by −12%.

The main costs incurred by bus operators are the purchase or hire of the vehicles (capital), labour costs, fuel maintenance and management. In the financial year 2000–2001, labour costs represented 47% of operating costs for Stagecoach as a whole. In the financial year 1969–1970 Hibbs (1975, p. 115) showed that drivers and conductors represented 47%, other staff 19.7%, fuel 7% and vehicles 15% of total costs for operators outside London. Therefore, controlling labour costs and making the most effective use of labour resources is crucial to the success of an individual company. For the industry as a whole, operating costs per vehicle kilometre (excluding depreciation) declined in real terms from 136 pence to 74 pence and from 145 pence to 87 pence (including depreciation), declines of 36% and 40%, respectively.

Early studies of cost functions in the bus industry found that in the short run average cost is a decreasing function of output over the whole of the observed output range and in the long run there was no evidence of economies of scale. Lee and Steedman (1970) examined the cost functions of local authority bus departments and found that the evidence supports the hypothesis of constant returns to scale. These conclusions were further supported by two studies by Ghosal (1970, 1972) using evidence from India and the USA. Hibbs (1975) pointed to the limitations of these studies because of difficulties of measuring output and the weakness of the data, arguing there must be considerable doubt about, "the conventional wisdom ... which seems to imply that a cautious expansion can wisely be undertaken, and that its profitable limits have not yet been reached" (pp. 123–124).

The implication of these studies – that there may be diseconomies of scale – does not accord with industry practice, which appears to support the notion that there are benefits from size in regular, timetabled bus services; this suggests that there may be advantages to firms operating larger fleets of buses, not from operating costs but from cost savings in covering for bus failure, maintenance and bus purchase. In addition, there may be managerial and financial advantages. Another advantage of size is the ability to offer a system of bus services or routes which allows passengers to make separate but linked journeys. These advantages generate economies of scope and greater revenue. Economies of scale arising from operating on a larger scale may therefore be of some relevance. If this is not the case, then the tendency to build large bus companies would have to be attributed to the managerial pursuit of growth purely for its own sake (see Hibbs 1975, chap. 9; DoTR 1984, para. 5.2).

Historically, the fare-stage part of the industry evolved into a number of holding companies, of which the largest were British Electric Traction and Thomas Tilling; these were able to combine the benefits of a large group with those of bus operation undertaken by local subsidiaries. The nationalized bus companies, but not municipal operators, maintained this pattern of operation, which has been repeated since deregulation by the creation of four large bus groups – namely, First Bus, Stagecoach, Arriva and National Express – which now control around 60% of the market.

Pricing

Under the old regulatory regime, the Traffic Commissioners controlled fares and approved a "fares table" for each route. In the new regulatory regime, bus companies are free to set their own prices, tempered only by the degree of competition and the willingness of passengers to pay the fares charged. Typically, the same bus fares apply throughout the day despite peak usage. They also have a fare structure that tends to taper with distance rather than charging a fixed rate per mile. Thus, bus fares are set to ensure that over the whole range of services offered the firm can either maximize revenue or achieve its desired profit margin. Individual bus trips cannot be expected necessarily to cover their variable costs because they are operating as part of a regular service. If the targets are not achieved, then the firm can change service frequencies or even drop routes to cut costs and raise usage on remaining services.

Typically, there is a relatively high charge for people making shorter journeys rather than longer ones. Thus, inner city users pay higher fares per mile into the city centre than do travellers living in the outer suburbs. If we assume bus travellers in inner areas are poorer than those in outer areas, then poorer passengers end up paying higher fares per mile than do richer passengers. Bus companies, unlike railway companies, tend not to use peak load pricing although the metropolitan passenger authorities did experiment in their areas, especially when services were provided by their own monopoly bus subsidiary. Another feature of the industry is the availability of weekly tickets offering unlimited travel, which encourages the use of buses at weekends, favours regular users and the use of the services of the issuing company.

The market structure also influences the nature of bus fares. Where a firm is the only operator on a route, it can experiment with fare structures: lower fares on routes or portions of routes where usage is low and higher fares where patronage is high. Where there is competition firms may have to match the fares of competitors or devise schemes to persuade customers to use their service rather than that of their rivals.

Table 21.1 summarizes the level of revenue earned and costs incurred per passenger in the local bus industry for 1999–2000. The rate of change for each indicator over the previous 10 years is also included. The table shows a decline in passenger journeys of

Table 21.1 Key indicators for the local bus industry in Great Britain 1999–2000

	Revenue costs[1]	10-year change (%)
Passenger journeys	£4,278m	−16
Fares paid by passengers	£2,270m	+3
Subsidies	£1,070m	−5
Total revenue	£3,340m	0
Average fares per passenger journey	£0.53	+23
Average subsidies per passenger journey	£0.25	+13
Total revenue per passenger journey	£0.78	+18
Operation costs[2] (per vehicle km)	£0.96	−25
Operation costs[2] (per passenger journey)	£0.56	−7

Notes [1]Revenue and costs are measured in 1999–2000 prices
[2]Operation costs include depreciation and allow for fuel duty rebate
Source Compiled by author using data extracted from *Annual Abstracts of Transport Statistics* (DoT 2001) and the Bus Facts website http://www.cpt-uk.org

16%, a fall in costs per passenger journey of 7%, an increase in fares per passenger journey of 20% and a decline in subsidies per journey by 5%. Overall, total revenue remained unchanged in real terms over the 10-year period.

The attractiveness of the bus industry

As was shown earlier, the bus industry has attractions in terms of its inelastic demand curve; this gives opportunities to make excess profits in the absence of competition, a characteristic that has led buses to be described as, "cash boxes on wheels with predictable revenue streams" (Davies 1994).

Although there is a general decline in terms of the numbers of journeys made, there are markets where the demand for bus journeys is increasing; this is a feature of urban areas where, for example, there are large numbers of students and individuals are encouraged not to use cars because parking in city centres is both difficult and expensive. In addition, entry into the bus market is relatively easy and inexpensive, because second-hand buses can be purchased and there appear to be no significant cost disadvantages in being small, added to which many large and long-established operators may have become inefficient and rivals can use price competition to weaken their profitability.

In 1980 when Stagecoach was founded, the bus industry did not look a promising industry to enter in terms of its profit potential: over 90% of journeys were made by state-owned bus companies and entry was regulated. At the time there was a general expectation of continued reduction in bus services where permitted, declining profitability and increasing government subsidies.

In declining industries the recommended strategy is to harvest and exit rather than enter. However, as Baden-Fuller and Stopford (1992) suggested, it is the company rather than the industry that is important in determining profitability. In any declining industry there may be significant opportunities for growth and expansion for an entrant willing to question the prevailing ethos and traditional ways of its incumbent enterprises. However, entry was not possible under the old regulatory regime in the industry.

In general terms the bus industry appeared in the early 1980s to be characterized by:

■ Declining demand.
■ Excess capacity.
■ High costs.
■ Inappropriately sized buses.
■ Falling quality of service.
■ Declining profitability.
■ Territorial companies with local monopoly power.
■ Managers who accepted regulation as a way of life.

This was supported by Hibbs (1989) who argued that, "the three decades after 1950 saw the bus and coach industry fall into a malaise that is well described by the aphorism that the biggest monopoly profit is a quiet life" (p. 167). The industry was therefore facing a crisis to which the answer was structural change; however, this was prevented and hindered by the old, rigid regulatory system. The need for change was also imperative because of government commitment to reduce subsidies to the industry in pursuit of cutting public spending.

The Conservative Government was elected in 1979 on a platform of reducing the role of government in the economy and was expected to consider changing the regulatory framework in the bus industry. In practice, it moved quickly to deregulate and remove barriers to competition in coach services (1980) and extended this to local bus services (1986). Thus, despite the gloomy economic outlook for the bus industry it was the expectation of a change in government policy creating new opportunities that was a major factor leading to the creation of Stagecoach.

GOVERNMENT POLICY CHANGES IN THE BUS INDUSTRY – CREATING OPPORTUNITIES

Deregulation of the bus industry took place in two stages. First, when long-distance services were deregulated by removing restrictions on entry, frequency and price (1980). The policy was deemed successful because new entry took place, fares fell and the number of passengers increased (see Davies 1984; Thompson and Whitfield 1995). National Express remained the dominant operator because it controlled entry to coach stations and operated a network of services that the large private entrant British Coachways could not replicate. However, individual companies were able to establish themselves on individual routes and to operate profitably.

Second, when local bus services outside London were deregulated and the privatization of state owned buses commenced (1986). The main features of the new regulatory regime were:

■ All operators required a licence subject to safety standards.
■ Licences for individual routes were no longer required.

- Any new route or service could be started, but 42 days' notice of entry was required. subsidies were to be awarded on a route basis by competitive tender.
- The industry became subject to competition law.

To facilitate the privatization of the National Bus Company and to encourage new entry and competition, the company was split into 73 subsidiaries and offered for sale to the highest bidders. No bidder was allowed to acquire more than three geographically dispersed divisions. The first subsidiary was sold in May 1986 and the last in April 1998. In total, 34 were initially sold to management, 5 to employee buyouts and the remainder to private companies, such as Stagecoach (Wright et al. 1994). Local authority buses were to become companies and eventually privatized piecemeal, while the Scottish Bus Group followed in 1991 and London Buses in 1994.

These policy initiatives generated both organizational and market changes, as well as creating opportunities for entrepreneurial activity for:

- Existing and new companies to compete on existing routes.
- Existing and new companies to start new routes.
- New or existing companies to purchase companies being privatized.

As a consequence of deregulation and privatization the industry became fragmented and ostensibly competitive. From it has emerged an industry in which four companies have become market leaders, while there are still large numbers of small companies offering regular services. The market leaders in order of bus fleet size are First Bus, Stagecoach, Arriva, National Express and Go-Ahead which between them have more than 60% of the market.

STAGECOACH START-UP

The founders

The founders of Stagecoach were Brian Souter and Ann Gloag. The latter had already established a small company hiring camper vans, while Souter was a chartered accountant. The new business was started in 1980 in response to changes coming to the industry.

There is no stereotype of the typical entrepreneur who goes on successfully both to create and build a successful enterprise. However, they were not only motivated by making money but also by a desire to build a company and take risks. Brian Souter is an unconventional figure in British business in that he does not wear business suits and ties. He is a committed Christian, a mature entrant to university and later qualified as a chartered accountant. He worked during his student days as a bus conductor in Glasgow. Coupling this first-hand knowledge of operating buses at the lowest level with a vision of developments in the bus industry, he was able to seize opportunities when they arose. Later, he was able to harness the support of people, from workers to city financiers, to support his long-term development plan. As the company grew, it needed to acquire a wider range of management skills; this was achieved by setting up individual subsidiaries and using the talents of existing middle managers, rather than senior managers who were too set in the ways of the old regulated industry. In short, the reasons for his entry into the bus industry were linked not only to the spotting of a business opportunity but also to his sister's involvement in the industry and the low costs of entry.

STAGECOACH: GROWTH AND DEVELOPMENT

Stage 1: first moves

The deregulation of long-distance services came into force on 9 October 1980. The founders of Stagecoach were ready to take advantage of this change. They decided that the market for intercity coaches was underdeveloped in Scotland and offered real opportunities for development. The Scottish Bus Group, a state-owned enterprise, was the monopoly supplier of the limited services that existed. The first service offered was from Dundee to London, twice per week, and was swiftly followed by other services from Aberdeen and Glasgow. They developed a distinctive pattern of service: offering refreshments on board and when new buses were acquired they included on-board toilets. Thus, Stagecoach developed a luxury image compared with the traditional, spartan nature of long-distance coach travel. These services became the mainstay of the company in its early years and were supplemented by a small number of local services.

The success of the venture is illustrated by the fact that after two years of operation its turnover had reached £1.3m, with a profit margin of 28%; this was achieved despite the fact that the Scottish Bus Group, having dismissed Stagecoach as an unimportant entrant, started to develop services in competition with them in 1992. The business flourished partly because of luck or good timing and partly because of the ability and hard work of the people running the company and the distinctive service it offered. The key was the readiness of the owner-managers to seize opportunities, to take on established enterprises and to take very limited rewards from the enterprise.

Stage 2: local deregulation and internal growth

To take advantage of the changes brought about by the 1985 Act deregulating local buses, Stagecoach made a major strategic decision and decided to move on three fronts. The major decision was to stay with buses, but to move from coaches to local bus services. In many ways this could be seen as diversification for, although buses and coaches serve similar purposes, the markets are very different: coach services tend to be seasonal with peak travel at holiday time and the distances travelled by coaches are much greater, creating servicing and logistical difficulties. Having decided to move into local services the question then was how?

Stagecoach decided to continue its policy of internal growth and to establish its own subsidiary and to do so in the market of their choice. The chosen routes were in Glasgow and the subsidiary was called Magicbus; this started to operate on D-day (deregulation day) – the 26 October 1986. The company decided to operate on three routes with innovative (or some would say traditional) types of services; these were provided by second-hand, ex-London Transport routemasters, using conductors (who had disappeared from other services). The intention was to create a significant impression and a speedier service. All of this provided a relatively low-risk form of entry into the local bus industry: that is, it was low cost and posed only a limited threat to the existing state-owned operators. The Glasgow market was attractive to many operators and as a result the city centre became flooded with buses causing significant congestion. The very competitive nature of the market resulting from new entry also led to price reductions, and what came to be known as "bus wars" erupted in many cities.

Stage 3: privatization and external growth

Another major decision was to bid to acquire subsidiaries of the National Bus Company (NBC) when they were put up for sale. The catalyst for the decision to change direction from mainly internal to mainly external growth was the privatization of NBC. The chosen method of privatization was to split the company into a large number of small units and to offer each for sale separately. These bite-size chunks of NBC were small enough to encourage bids from existing management and small companies. Buyers were allowed to acquire no more than three subsidiaries and not more than two operating in adjacent territories. Because of the confusion created by deregulation, the unglamorous image of the bus industry and the difficulty of valuing the companies, little interest was initially shown in the disposals that took place before deregulation day: the first 11 subsidiaries were sold without any contest to the existing management at low prices.

The first contested sale was the 12th subsidiary – Oxford City Buses. Stagecoach bid unsuccessfully and the management acquired the company. Stagecoach was eventually the successful bidder for Hampshire Bus, which it acquired for £2.2m in April 1987. This first major acquisition more than doubled the size of the company's bus fleet. Later in the same year, Cumberland Buses (£2.8m) and United Counties (£4.1m) were also purchased. As a result of these acquisitions, turnover increased from £4m in financial year 1986–1987 to £26.2m one year later, a fivefold increase. These were three widely scattered companies, distant from head office, which created significant managerial challenges for a small company. These were successfully solved, and the methodology developed prepared the way for further acquisitions, and their successful integration into Stagecoach.

From these acquisitions, the company was able to realize a substantial part of the bid price by selling town centre garages in Keswick, Workington and Southampton, as well as Southampton Bus, a part of Hampshire Bus. The profits made by these sales, which were higher than the book value of the assets, led to political criticism of asset stripping and profiteering: for example, the sale of Southampton Bus and the bus station raised £4.4m, twice the purchase price for the whole of Hampshire Bus.

Stage 4: the fallout from the privatization of NBC

In the four years between the privatization of National Bus and Scottish Bus, Stagecoach started to acquire former NBC subsidiaries that had been purchased by in-house management teams (supported by various start-up funds) who were keen to realize their investments when early opportunities arose. In 1988 and 1989, 10 such companies were purchased, and by the end of financial year 1989–1990 turnover had risen to almost £100m.

The next major phase of domestic expansion came with the purchase of two privatized Scottish Bus Company subsidiaries. Thereafter, bus companies were acquired regularly, to enable Stagecoach to become one of the UK's largest bus companies, with a market share of around 16–18%, and at the same time one of the world's largest bus companies. Between 1992 and 1996, 23 full and 2 partial acquisitions were completed in the UK.

Stage 5: diversification

The major decision to diversify away from buses came with the privatization of British Rail. In 1992, Stagecoach had started running a railway service from Aberdeen to London by negotiating the attachment of coaches to the night sleeper train; this did not prove successful. However, the privatization of British Rail gave it the opportunity to bid for licences to run passenger services.

Railway privatization, like that of NBC, split British Rail into a large number of subsidiaries. Stagecoach made many bids to acquire leases but it was only successful in acquiring South West Trains (1997) and the tiny Island Line on the Isle of Wight. A major change of direction from running passenger services came with the acquisition of one of the three rolling stock companies from the buyout management team in 1996 for £826m; this was by a significant margin the largest acquisition made by Stagecoach at that time, and, while railway-related, did not actually involve transporting passengers. Its other rail acquisition was a 49% stake in Virgin Rail acquired in 1998. Other transport-related acquisitions included Sheffield Tramways and Prestwich Airport.

Stage 6: international expansion

The first significant venture overseas came in 1989 with the acquisition of the BET bus subsidiary in Malawi for £800,000; this gave the company a fleet of 300 buses and a 51% stake, the government owning 49%, in United Transport Malawi. The venture was abandoned in 1997 following political changes and the deregulation of the market allowing unlicensed buses to operate. International expansion continued with the acquisition of public transport operators in Sweden, Portugal, New Zealand, Australia and Hong Kong, as well as a road toll company in mainland China.

In July 1999 the company made its biggest ever acquisition to date when it acquired Coach USA for £1.2bn; this made Stagecoach the second largest bus operator in North America with 12,000 employees, 6,500 buses and 3,000 taxicabs. An indication of the fragmented nature of the US bus and coach industry is that Coach USA market share was estimated to be 2%. The firm had grown rapidly as its founder Larry King acquired a collection of different types of bus operations, spread across 35 American states and Canada. It operated stage carriage commuter services in New York, coach chartering, tour operating, sightseeing and taxicabs. After its purchase by Stagecoach the new subsidiary continued to acquire small operators.

Stagecoach's 1999–2000 annual report said that, after an encouraging start: the business had not met expectations; opportunities existed to grow revenues and cut costs; restructuring was under way and significant economies were to be made by consolidation of facilities, rationalization of management and administration, and new maintenance and inventory systems. Operating margins, however, declined from 14.1% in the year following acquisition to 6% in 2001-2002. Stagecoach wrote down its investment by £376m in 2001 and £575m in 2002. As a result the company made its first annual pre-tax loss of £335m since its inception. Problems with the acquisition led to the replacement of management and the resignation of Stagecoach's managing director in July 2002.

Disposals

In line with the behaviour of companies that grow by acquisition, Stagecoach has both acquired and disposed of companies and assets. An early disposal was the sale of the company's long-distance coaches in 1989 to National Express for £1.6m; these formed 5% of the business at the time of the sale but had been 95% in 1985, before the major move into local services. Disposals have included Grey Coaches Canada (1992), Malawi Transport (1997), Swedebus (2000), Porterbrook (2000), Portugal Bus (2001), Prestwich Airport (2001) and the Hong Kong operations (2003). Coach USA is being substantially restructured and shrunk to concentrate on operations in the north-east and north central areas of the USA. Collectively, these accounted for approximately one-third of Stagecoach's turnover in 2002–2003. Stagecoach's aim was to concentrate on those elements that had predictable revenue streams. Its overseas bus interests have thus been reduced to those in New Zealand, where the company is the largest bus operator, and the USA.

Ownership finance and flotation

The initial start was financed from family savings, as was its expansion; this included a rich Canadian uncle who owned 40% of the enterprise. In 1983 the partnership was dissolved and a limited company formed with a significant guarantee (£400,000), again provided by their uncle. In 1986, institutional support was sought to enable the company to take advantage of the deregulation of the bus market. A total of £5m of preference shares were issued to double the capital base, and a bank facility of £50m was arranged. Seven major Scottish institutions supported the financial package.

The next major change in the financing of the company came with its flotation on 27 April 1993; this led to 21.8 million shares being placed with institutions and 11.7 million shares being offered to the public at 112p. The public offering was oversubscribed 6.9 times.

At the end of day 1 the share price closed at 124p, giving a first-day premium of 10%. At this time Brian Souter and Ann Gloag retained 55% of the shares; this fell to 28% when Porterbrook was purchased and the company restructured financially and then to 25% in 2002. Therefore, the firm is still owner or family-controlled (see discussion in Chapter 1).

Management philosophy

In its purchases of bus companies, Stagecoach's management team acted as a catalyst, "releasing energy which was buried there among the middle management" of the acquired company, having dispensed with the services of the incumbent senior managers (Wolmar 1998). To make the companies more efficient the following actions were taken:

- Simplifying management structures by having only four tiers: main board, board of the subsidiary, four-person team running the business and depot manager/bus driver.

- Adopting an M-form organizational structure, with a small head office employing 30 people.
- Handling finance centrally with loans being made to subsidiaries.
- Changing route patterns in line with current and potential market demand.
- Introducing a variety of bus sizes more suitable for existing and new services.
- Investing heavily in new buses and reaping the benefits of buying in bulk.
- Reducing maintenance costs on vehicles and cost of spares.
- Selling unwanted property to finance expansion.
- Agreeing productivity deals with the workforce.
- Raising profit margins to 15% on turnover, compared with 5% achieved by NBC.
- Pursuing organic growth through management efforts to improve fleet usage and quality of service.
- Engaging in aggressive competition against entrants into markets where Stagecoach was the dominant operator.

Stagecoach's philosophy in pursuing external growth was to acquire companies that were underperforming by its own standards (i.e., whose costs were higher and profit margins lower than the industry average). According to the MMC (1996) Stagecoach's costs were 20% below the industry average and its target profit margin was 15–18%.

Stagecoach has been described as company-run by manager shareholders. Brian Souter has been described by critics as ruthless and running an unprincipled, aggressively competitive company; others see him as an old-fashioned entrepreneur who is making the most of his resources and trying to outwit competitors to acquire market share and companies. Wolmar (1998a) argued that bus privatization and deregulation represented a once-and-for-all opportunity that was open to all entrepreneurs, but Souter was unique in fully perceiving the extent of the opportunities and willing to take the risks involved.

The aggressively competitive behaviour of the company brought it into conflict with the competition authorities. It was the subject of a record number of referrals to the Monopolies and Mergers Commission (MMC) who look into mergers and competition in local markets. The impact on the company was:

- To damage Stagecoach by giving it an aggressive, ruthless image.
- To prevent the acquisition of companies Stagecoach wished to purchase in its attempt to build territorial integrity.
- To limit profitability where behavioural controls were imposed.

Overall, the impact on the company's growth and profitability was limited since the company had already acquired areas of strength in parts of the country, but clearly its ability to exploit its dominant position was to some extent limited.

Boundaries

The firm has essentially seen its core competences as running fare-stage bus services, a policy it adopted for running rail services. The company stopped running long-distance services in the mid-1980s because of their cyclical nature and the problems of maintaining buses when they were a long way from the home base. However, Coach USA continued to run such services. It was a collection of diverse bus activities that included sightseeing in various US cities (New York being one), taxicabs and bus services. In the bus industry the company's policy is to own, operate and maintain its own fleet of vehicles; it does not hire them though the market. In the train industry, rolling stock and maintenance are hired through the market as a consequence of the UK privatization scheme that split the industry into track authorities, train operators, vehicle providers and maintenance firms. The company did own Porterbrook, a vehicle-leasing company, but decided it did not have the necessary competences or resources to operate it and disposed of it to Abbey National.

Stagecoach has stuck to its core competences in the bus industry and has extended them into other aspects of public transport, such as trams and light railways; these regular, short-distance services are seen as cash-generative and having growth potential, particularly where congestion is a problem and car use is limited by road charges or regulation.

This has also been recognized in the restructuring of Coach USA where seasonal and cyclical activities are being sold.

Growth

The company's main motivation in its early years was growth, initially by internal means but then growth became increasingly external. The growth of the company since 1984–1985 can be observed in Table 21.2 and Figure 21.3. Turnover grew steeply in the 1990s and peaked in financial year 1999–2000. As a consequence of disposals and problems at Coach USA, turnover actually declined in 2000–2001 and 2002–2003.

Table 21.2 Stagecoach's financial results

Financial year ending	Turnover (£m)	Profit before tax (£m)	Profit/Turnover (%)
1985	3.5	0.3	9.0
1986	3.3	0.4	14.2
1987	4.0	0.5	13.2
1988	26.2	5.0	19.2
1989	36.8	4.6	12.4
1990	98.4	8.0	8.1
1991	103.4	10.6	10.3
1992	140.7	15.7	11.1
1993	154.3	18.1	11.7
1994	191.0	23.2	12.1
1995	337.7	41.0	12.1
1996	501.2	55.8	11.3
1997	1,152.8	120.5	10.5
1998	1,381.5	155.7	11.3
1999	1,548.4	210.4	13.5
2000	2,179.1	255.3	11.7
2001	2,083.5	−335.2	−17.0
2002	2,111.4	42.0	1.9
2003	2,076.6	−500.2	−24.1

Source Compiled by author from annual reports, MMC reports and the Stagecoach website http://www.stagecoachholdings.com

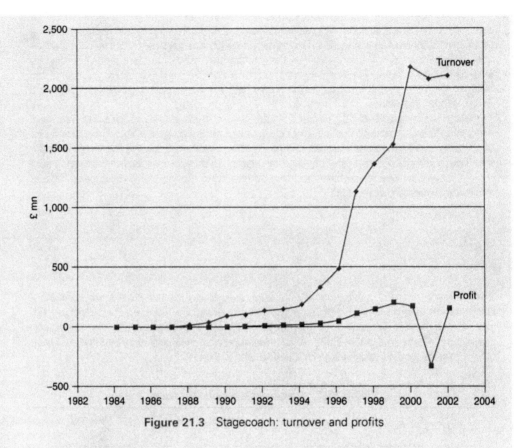

Figure 21.3   Stagecoach: turnover and profits

Management constraint

The Penrose (1959) view of management is that initially it facilitates growth as its capacity to manage grows. However, the capacity of management eventually becomes a constraint on growth as new managers have to be recruited and trained in the ways of the company. Stagecoach successfully coped with growth and adding new acquisitions up to 2000, which suggests that the management team coped with these changes. However, the acquisition of Coach USA and the difficulties faced in managing a large acquisition suggest that the company has hit a management constraint; this has been compounded by the loss of two chief executives. The re-emergence of Brian Souter as chief executive to sort out the problems of Coach USA raises the question of whether the company is still too dependent on its founder and whether a competent managerial team can be built without him. The operation of Coach USA proved too big a task for the existing management team, perhaps because it contained many of those elements of the bus business the company had avoided since 1986 (i.e., where its core competences did not apply).

Table 21.3   Directions of expansion

	Domestic, same industry	Domestic diversification	International, same industry	International diversification
Internal growth	Coaches Buses			
External growth acquisition	Buses	Rail operating Rail leasing Trams	Buses	Road tolls Rail Trams

Source   Author

Table 21.4   Stagecoach's results by division 2002–2003

	Turnover (£m)	Turnover growth (%)	Operating profit	Profit margin (%)	Employees	Vehicles
Buses						
UK	598.4	3.8	67.0	11.2	17,900	7,100
Overseas	183.3	−5.7	30.3	16.5	5,100	2,150
Coach USA	603.0	−11.7	14.0	2.3	10,600	12.600
Rail						
UK	413.6	2.7	38.2	9.2	5,250	1,150*
Virgin	276.1	5.7	7.2		3,600	1,030*

Note   * Data for 2001–2002
Source   Compiled by author using data from the annual reports for 2002 and 2003

STAGECOACH IN 2003

Stagecoach in 2003 is the result of the imagination of its founders, the seeking out of opportunities, the availability of finance, the employment of good managers who have made the best use of the company's assets with the exception of the setback of Coach USA. The pattern of development is summarized in Table 21.3; this shows expansion classified by internal and external expansion, on the one hand, and domestic and international change, on the other, in the same industry and new industries.

The main source of growth between 1986 and 2000 was through acquisition; this has created a company split into five main divisions. These divisions are summarized in Table 21.4, together with indicators of their relative size in financial year 2002–2003. The main divisions are now UK Buses, Overseas Buses, Coach USA, UK Rail and Virgin Trains (49% share).

CHAPTER SUMMARY

In this chapter we brought together a number of the aspects of business economics that we discussed in earlier chapters, in the context of the development of Stagecoach against the background of the UK and US bus industries. In doing this we analysed:

- Aspects of costs and demand, as well as the demand function for bus travel, confirming the industry to be a hostile environment in which to pursue a growth strategy, because of the negative income elasticity of demand and the absence of economies of scale.
- How the company survived many early difficulties to emerge as one of the largest bus companies in the world, in an essentially declining and fragmented industry.
- How the company's objectives to grow and achieve high profit margins were fulfilled from 1985 to 2000.
- How its performance has declined since 2000 and led to its first cut in dividend payment since flotation. As a consequence the share price has fallen from a peak of nearly 300p in 1998 to less than 20p in 2002. This decline is mainly attributed to the problems of Coach USA, and a slowdown in growth in the UK bus market has raised questions about the future of the company which will only be answered with the passage of time.

REVIEW QUESTIONS

1 Why might the bus industry be regarded as a hostile environment in which to start a new enterprise?
2 What factors might encourage a positive change in the income elasticity of demand for bus travel in the near future?
3 In what ways does Brian Souter appear to have the characteristics of a classical entrepreneur?
4 What types of pricing strategies might be used to encourage consumer loyalty in a competitive bus market?
5 Are economies of scale important in the bus industry?
6 What cost advantages have led to the emergence of large enterprises in the bus industry?
7 Why did the company see opportunities in a declining bus industry?
8 What are the main characteristics of the demand function for bus journeys?
9 What are the main characteristics of the supply side of the bus industry? What are the advantages for a multi-bus operator over a single-bus operator?
10 What factors account for Stagecoach's rapid growth?
11 What factors motivated Stagecoach to make acquisitions?
12 Why did the company successfully integrate acquisitions into the enterprise?
13 Has Stagecoach reached a barrier to its further growth?
14 Was the acquisition of Coach USA in pursuit of growth a major strategic error?

REFERENCES AND FURTHER READING

Baden-Fuller, C. and J. Stopford (1992) *Rejuvenating the Mature Business*, Routledge, London.

Beesley, M.E. (1990) Collusion and predation in the UK bus industry. *Journal of Transport Economics and Policy*, **24**(3), 295–310.

Buxton, J. (1993) Re-routed via the stock exchange: The proposed flotation of Stagecoach Holdings. *Financial Times*, 26 January, p. 21.

Davies, E. (1984) Express coaching since 1980: Liberalisation in practice. *Fiscal Studies*, **5**(1), 76–86.

Davies, S. (1994) Fleets of cash boxes on wheels. *Financial Times* (16, November, p. 22).

de Jong, G. and H. Gunn (2001) Recent evidence on car cost and time elasticities of travel demand in Europe. *Journal of Transport Economics and Policy*, **35**(2), 137–160.

DoT (1999) *Annual Abstracts of Transport Statistics* (Department of Transport). HMSO, London.

DoT (2001) *Annual Abstracts of Transport Statistics* (Department of Transport). HMSO, London.

DoT (2002) *Annual Abstracts of Transport Statistics* (Department of Transport). HMSO, London.

DoTR (1984) *Buses* (Department of Transport and the Regions Cmnd 9300). HMSO, London.

Ghosal, R.K. (1970) Economies of scale in bus transport: Some Indian experience. *Journal of Transport Economics and Policy*, **4**(1), 29–36.

Ghosal, R.K. (1972) Economies of scale in bus transport: Some US experience. *Journal of Transport Economics and Policy*, **6**(2), 151–153.

Hibbs, J. (1975) *The Bus and Coach Industry: Its economics and Organisation*. J.M. Dent, London.

Hibbs, J. (1989) Privatisation and competition in road passenger transport. In: Veljanovski (ed.), *Privatisation and Competition: A Market Prospectus* (Hobart Paperback No. 28). Institute of Economic Affairs, London.

Lee, N., and I. Steedman (1970) Economies of scale in bus transport: Some British municipal results. *Journal of Transport Economics and Policy*, **4**(1), 15–28.

Lorenz, A. (1997) Stagecoach broadens its gauge. *Management Today*, July, p. 28.

MMC (1996) *Chesterfield Transport* (Monopolies and Mergers Commission). HMSO, London.

Mulley, C. and M. Wright (1986) Buy-outs and the privatisation of National Bus. *Fiscal Studies*, **7**(3), 1–24.

Nash, C.A. (1993) British bus deregulation. *The Economic Journal*, **103**, 1042–1049.

Penrose, E.T. (1959) *The Theory of the Growth of the Firm*. Basil Blackwell, Oxford, UK.

Sharkey, G.M. and J.G. Gallagher (1995) Stagecoach Holdings plc. In: C. Clarke-Hill and K. Glaister (eds), *Case Studies in Strategic Management*. Pitman, London.

Stubbs, P., W.J. Tyson and M.Q. Dalvi (1980) Transport Economics. *Allen and Unwin*, London.

Economist, The (1998) Odd coupling (27 June, p. 58).

Thompson, D. and A. Whitfield (1995) Express coaching: Privatisation, incumbent advantage and the competitive process. In: M. Bishop, J. Kay and C. Meyer (eds), *The Regulatory Challenge*. Oxford University Press, Oxford, UK.

Wolmar, C. (1998a) On the road with Brian Souter. *Independent on Sunday*, 15 December, p. 27.

Wolmar, C. (1998b) *Stagecoach: A Classic Rags to Riches Tale from the Frontiers of Capitalism*. Orion Books, London

Wright, M., S. Thompson and K. Robie (1994) Management buy-outs and privatisation. In: M. Bishop, J. Kay and C. Meyer (eds), *Privatization and Economic Performance*. Oxford University Press, Oxford, UK.

PART **VI**

DECISION MAKING IN THE REGULATED AND PUBLIC SECTORS

22

DECISION MAKING IN REGULATED BUSINESSES

CHAPTER OUTLINE

CHAPTER OBJECTIVES

This chapter aims to examine government regulation of firms and markets. At the end of this chapter you should be able to:

◆ Explain why government regulation of monopolies is thought desirable.

◆ Identify the potential welfare gains and losses from restricting or promoting competition.

◆ Analyse the advantages and disadvantages of regulatory rules.

◆ Identify the main institutions and concerns of competiton policy in the EU and the UK, as well as their policy instruments.

INTRODUCTION

One of the roles of government in a market economy is to regulate private sector enterprises, ensuring that the unbridled pursuit of profit does not lead to a serious misallocation of resources and to outcomes that are unfair to consumers. Government regulation of business is all-pervasive in that there are rules governing the establishment of limited liability companies and rules about publishing annual reports and accounts which apply to all enterprises. In addition, there are specific regulations that apply to monopolistic enterprises, in general, and to specific enterprises, in particular. In this chapter we will:

- Explain the meaning and nature of regulation.
- Elucidate and critically analyse the arguments for regulation.
- Outline the advantages and disadvantages of various instruments for regulating utilities and natural monopolies.
- Explain the case for regulating specific anti-competitive practices associated with dominant firms.
- Outline the competition policies of the EU and UK.

WHAT IS REGULATION?

Regulation is the placing of constraints on the firm's behaviour by government in the public interest. It can be broadly divided into economic regulation concerned with monopolistic tendencies and socio-economic regulation concerned with achieving social goals, such as safer products, consumer protection, health and safety and environmental protection.

The first type of economic regulation is applied in specific industries and concerned with entry, price and output decisions. Its objective is to provide a substitute for competition and to ensure a quasi-competitive outcome in terms of price and output. Such a policy assumes that the outcomes of perfect competition, where prices are equal to long-run marginal cost, are an appropriate guide to judging the shortcomings of monopoly and for setting prices.

The second type of economic regulation is concerned with preventing competitive market structures from being undermined and, thus, with maintaining and even promoting competition. This policy is also concerned with preventing the abuse of dominant positions and discouraging anti-competitive behaviour in industry, in general.

Instruments of regulation

Governments have a range of instruments they can use to control and regulate business. The main instruments include:

- The setting of standards and licensing activities that may be applied by law or voluntarily by business.
- The control of pricing and investment.
- The holding of competitions or auctions for the right to supply a service to government specification.

These instruments have been used to deal with a number of problems including:

- Control of entry to ensure only reputable or financially sound enterprises supply a particular product or service (e.g., cinemas and banks).
- Setting of prices for certain activities, such as taxi fares and telephone calls.
- Control of rates of return on capital to limit profit making in such activities as the supply of water.
- Setting of standards to guarantee the quality and safety of such goods as electrical appliances.
- Regulation of the way certain products are sold, such as "cooling off" periods for buyers of insurance when they can withdraw from the contract.

Why regulation?

Regulation is intended to produce an outcome superior to the one that would prevail if the market were left to its own devices. The welfare losses associated with imperfectly competitive markets can be illustrated by making use of the efficiency guideline that price should be set equal to marginal cost. This rule is observed in a perfectly competitive market and maximizes the welfare of a community in terms of **consumer surplus** and **producer surplus**.

This can be illustrated by reference to Figure 22.1. In part (a) the firm faces a market price of OP_C, and chooses output OQ_C. To produce this output the firm will employ the optimal quantities of labour and capital to minimize cost. In Figure 22.1(b) the position for the market or industry as a whole is shown. The optimal output at market price P_C for the industry is OC_I. This output delivers net social benefits equal to the area ABC. This social surplus is made up of consumer and producer surplus. Consumer surplus is the difference between the demand curve, which shows the total sum of money consumers are prepared to pay, and the price they actually pay for each unit; this is equal to the area ABP_C. Producer surplus is the difference between the marginal cost curve, which is the cost of producing each unit of output, and the price the producer receives; this is equal to the area P_CBC. These concepts can be used to show the welfare losses incurred if price is not equal to marginal cost.

In earlier chapters we showed: that a monopolist maximizes profit where marginal revenue equals marginal cost, that the monopoly price will be greater than the competitive price and that monopoly output will be less than competitive output. Such a position is illustrated in Figure 22.2. In this diagram the competitive price is OP_C and the monopoly price is OP_M. Under competition, the sum of social surplus is equal to the area ABC, where consumer surplus is area ABP_C and producer surplus is area P_CBC. If the industry is monopolized and has the same demand and cost curves, then

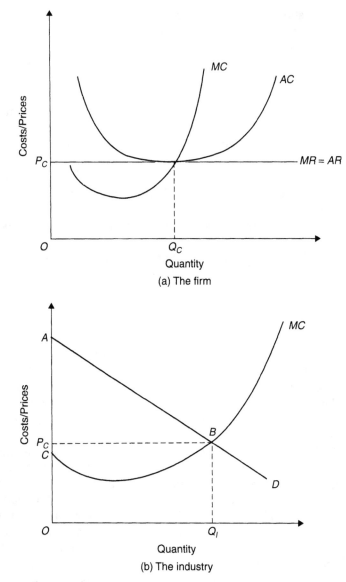

Figure 22.1 Economic welfare and perfect competition

social surplus is reduced to the area *AKLC*. This new position generates a net welfare loss of *KBL*. Under monopoly the social surplus *AKLC* is now distributed in favour of the producer. Producer surplus is now equal to area $P_M KLC$, which compared with $P_C BC$ is a net gain of $P_M KJP_C$, less the area *JBL*. With the loss of area $P_M KJP_C$, which becomes producer surplus, consumer surplus is now AKP_M and *KBJ* becomes the lost surplus, or the **deadweight loss** to consumers.

As has been shown, the arguments for regulation are based on the losses of social surplus, arising from the misallocation of resources in non-competitive markets.

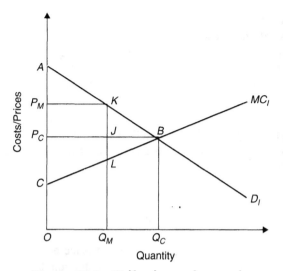

Figure 22.2 Welfare losses of monopoly

Besides higher prices and lower output, a government might also be concerned with the distribution of gains and losses that might be considered politically unacceptable. In this case the government may act to correct the unfair distribution.

Another argument for regulation is the consequences of destructive competition. Competition is deemed to be excessive when it leads to excess capacity, unreliable service to consumers and the failure of companies when prices fail to cover costs. In the UK, unregulated bus transport in the 1920s led to excessive supply, competition that was dangerous for passengers, unreliable service provision and the failure of firms. The more established firms wished to see the "pirates" or entrants running without timetables removed from the industry, so that a more reliable service was offered to passengers and their profits protected. The government responded to the demand of the bus lobby by introducing a regulatory system that required all operators to be licensed and that controlled both entry and fares.

Another explanation for the existence of regulation is that it is demanded by business and supplied by government. Firms like those in the 1920s' bus industry demand a regulated environment because it guarantees a "fair" price, limits entry, keeps unfair competition in check and provides "easy" profits. Governments supply regulation in response to political pressure from producer and consumer groups because it is seen as providing a better outcome than unbridled competition.

REGULATORY TOOLS FOR PROMOTING THE PUBLIC INTEREST

Regulators of monopolies are concerned with the behaviour of the following economic variables:

- Costs and their minimization.
- Demand – its level and growth.
- Investment requirements to maintain or expand capacity.
- Price–cost relationship to prevent excessive profits being made.
- "Fair" level of profit to ensure the company can remain in business and finance expansion.

Essentially, the regulator has to decide whether there is a need to control price or profit by setting levels for either that do not threaten the financial viability of the firm or the disruption of supply.

Marginal cost pricing in decreasing cost industries

The recommended rule for regulators (i.e., setting price equal to marginal cost) faces practical difficulties in industries that are characterized by declining average and marginal costs for the expected level of demand. The difficulty is that the firm is unable to cover its costs and, therefore, makes losses.

This problem is illustrated in Figure 22.3. With costs and revenues measured on the vertical axis and quantity produced on the horizontal axis, the average cost curve of the minimum-sized plant for the industry is presumed to be U-shaped, but the market demand curve is in the decreasing portion of the cost curve. Thus, there is only room for one firm if production is to be efficient.

If the facility is operated by a profit-maximizing enterprise, then it would charge the profit-maximizing price OP_π and produce quantity OQ_π. At this price the firm makes profits of $P_\pi FGH$. If the regulator orders the firm to set a price equal to marginal cost,

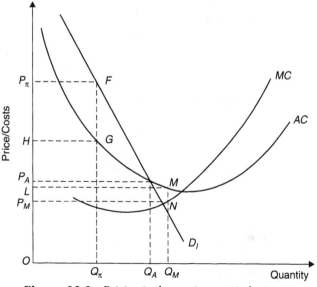

Figure 22.3 Pricing in decreasing cost industries

then the price will be OP_M and quantity OQ_M. However, charging the marginal cost price means that fixed costs are not recovered and the enterprise makes a loss of P_MLMN. The problem for the regulator and government is how to cover the losses if prices are set equal to marginal cost; this can be achieved by paying the firm a subsidy or, so that the firm remains financially viable, allowing it to use average cost pricing, two-part pricing or price discrimination.

Subsidies   If the government wishes to subsidize the firm, then it will have to do so from its general budget, which means every taxpayer would have to subsidize the enterprise whether they were consumers or not. In the case of utilities, such as water and electricity, every taxpayer is probably also a consumer. It may also be politically difficult for the government to offer subsidies where there is no general agreement on the social worth of the product or service being produced.

Average cost pricing   If the regulator sets a price of OP_A, then the firm would produce an output of OQ_A and would cover its costs, thus avoiding the subsidy problem. This solution also increases output and lowers prices (compared with the profit-maximizing position) and avoids subsidies. Thus, it is a popular solution to the regulatory problem, but does mean a less than optimal output is produced.

Two-part tariff   Another solution to the problem is to allow the firm to make an entry charge to recover fixed costs and then charge a price equal to marginal cost to cover variable costs; this allows consumers to buy OQ_M (the optimal quantity), but between them they must also pay to cover losses, or fixed costs $LMNP_M$, assuming that the fixed or entry charge does not deter the consumer from buying the marginal cost output.

Price discrimination   Another solution is to allow the firm to charge different prices to different groups of consumers, so that total revenue covers total cost. Consumers are distinguished by differences in their elasticities of demand, with those with inelastic demands paying higher prices than those with elastic demands. The set of prices that minimizes losses of consumer surplus while allowing the firm to cover its costs are termed "Ramsay prices".

In Figure 22.4 there are demand curves for two groups of consumers, which intersect at the level of marginal cost. Thus, both the X and Y groups of consumers pay the same price OP_M and consume the same quantity OQ_M if the marginal cost price is set. If the regulator allows the firm to charge the average cost price OP_A to cover costs, consumer group Y will reduce demand to OQ_1 and lose consumer surplus ABG, while consumer group X will reduce demand to OQ_3 and lose consumer surplus EFG. If different prices are charged to the separate groups with the aim of covering costs, then the optimum prices are OP_X and OP_Y. Consumer group X loses consumer surplus of HKG and group Y loses consumer surplus of JKG. The consumer surplus loss with differentiated Ramsay prices and the same reduction in consumption is $HKG + JKG$, which is less than the loss associated with average cost pricing of $ABG + EFG$.

Profit regulation

Another method of regulation is to restrict the profits a firm can earn by limiting earnings to a certain rate of return on capital [ROK]. The firm can set any price or

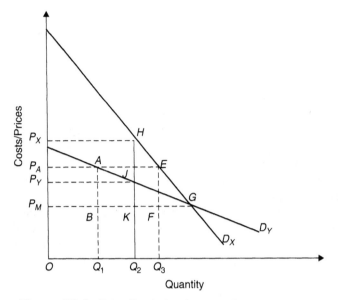

Figure 22.4 Price discrimination covering average costs

prices it chooses, providing its profits do not exceed the regulatory rate of return. In cost-plus pricing terms the firm should cover its variable costs and make sufficient profit to cover the costs of capital and make a profit.

The rate of return on capital set by the regulator has to be a "fair" one, not too high to be "unfair" to consumers nor too low to be "unfair" to the firm. It is also expected to be in line with the risk/return conditions in more competitive parts of the economy. Other factors to be considered are the cost of capital and the ability of the firm to attract capital to replace depreciated assets and to invest in additional capacity to meet any growth in demand. If the regulator fails to ensure the viability of the firm, then consumers could be faced with rationing of supplies.

Rate of return on capital regulation has been used widely in the USA, and business behaviour in response to the constraint has been widely documented. Firms tend to employ excessive quantities of capital and let costs increase because this will set off a regulatory review of the profit constraint and the prices charged. If the regulator sets a maximum allowable rate of profit π_R, which gives the firm profits of $\pi_R K$ (i.e., the rate of return multiplied by the capital base), then this sum covers payments to capital rK and the remainder is the firm's pure profit. If the capital base is £1,000, the allowed rate of return is 12% and the cost of capital 10%, then the maximum allowed regulatory profits are £120 because the profits required to meet capital costs are £100, leaving a pure profit of £20, or 2% on capital. If the firm adds an additional £100 of capital it is allowed to earn another £12 of regulatory profit, or £2 of pure profit.

In Figure 22.5 the profit function of the firm is plotted in relation to capital employed. The pure profit constraint facing the firm in absolute terms is represented by the line $(\pi - r)K$. An unregulated profit-maximizing firm would employ OK_1 units of capital and be allowed to earn profits of $K_1 B$, rather than the $K_1 A$ the regulated firm is

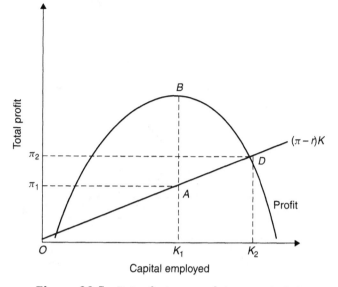

Figure 22.5 Rate of return regulatory constraint

allowed to earn. However, if the regulated firm increases its capital employed it can increase its absolute level of profits. If it increases it to the point where the allowed regulatory profits are equal to the profits given by the profit function, then it can increase its absolute profit from $O\pi_1$ to $O\pi_2$. Thus, the firm employs capital of OK_2, rather than OK_1; this effect of employing too much capital is termed the Averch–Johnson effect (1962).

Incentive schemes

To overcome the problems and difficulties associated with setting theoretically desirable prices and the shortcomings of rate of return on capital regulation, economists have sought to devise schemes that over a period of time will move prices toward average cost and create incentives for firms to be efficient. A theoretical scheme was suggested by Vogelsang and Finsinger (1979) and a practical one by Littlechild (1983).

The Vogelsang–Finsinger mechanism can be explained with the aid of Figure 22.6, where quantity is measured on the horizontal axis and price and costs on the vertical axis. The monopolist has a downward-sloping average cost curve AC_1 and in period 1 charges price OP_1, supplies OQ_1 and makes a profit of P_1BGP_2. In period 2 the regulator enforces a rule that the firm sets a price for period 2 equal to the average cost of production incurred in period 1. Thus, the firm charges OP_2, supplies OQ_2 and makes profits of P_2CEP_3 in period 2. The process is repeated in periods 3 and 4, by which time the price OP_4 in the figure will be close to being equal to average cost (Q_4N) and few supernormal profits will be earned. As a result of this step-by-step process, supernormal profits are eroded and consumer surplus increased with the fall

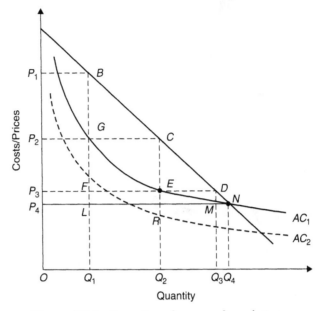

Figure 22.6   Incentive schemes and regulation

in price and profit.

The mechanism also creates an incentive for the firm to reduce average costs below cost curve AC_1 to prevent the eradication of supernormal profits. If the firm is inefficient, then becoming more efficient will reduce average costs. If the firm is producing at the minimum cost level, then the firm will have to innovate and improve productivity. If cost levels can be reduced to AC_2 in period 2, then the firm will increase its profits, given the price set for that period. However, in period 3 the price will be lower because the actual costs incurred in period 2 would be Q_2R, which would then become the price level in period 3.

Rate capping

In the 1980s when a number of utilities were privatized in the UK, it was decided to regulate them to prevent the exploitation of consumers and encourage efficiency. To avoid the problems identified with **rate of return regulation** a modified Vogelsang–Finsinger mechanism was proposed by Littlechild (1983) which became known as $RPI - X$.

The basic approach accepts the prices current at the time of privatization and, then, allows subsequent changes to be determined by a formula that includes unavoidable cost increases and potential cost savings. The first element is represented by changes in the retail price index (RPI) and the efficiency gains by (X). The allowed maximum price change is determined by the formula $RPI - X$. If RPI changes by 5% and the X factor is set at 3%, then in period 2 the regulated firm would be allowed to increase prices by up to 2%. In real terms the price charged is lower in each successive period, thereby forcing the firm in successive periods to lower its unit costs if profits are to be maintained. The formula is set for a period of 3 to 5 years and is changed after discussion between the regulator and the regulated enterprise. The value put on X is crucial to the working of the scheme, as the higher its value the greater the pressure put on the firm to be efficient.

Once its price cap has been set the firm can choose efficient production methods that reflect the relative prices of labour and capital. There are no distortions to factor price ratios to bias production in favour of capital or labour-intensive methods. The firm is allowed to keep any profits it makes in any given regulatory period and has an incentive to be as efficient as possible. In the negotiations for setting the next price cap, previous profits influence the outcome.

The advantages of the $RPI - X$ formula include:

■ Overcoming the measurement and informational difficulties of other schemes.
■ Providing incentives to keep costs to a minimum.
■ Making the return to shareholders a variable that puts pressure on managers to operate efficiently.
■ Implementing the scheme is inexpensive, since the RPI is a regularly measured economic indicator.
■ Transparency of the price formula.

The disadvantages are that:

■ Shareholders may receive an unfair share of the rewards.
■ Customers have to wait for a subsequent review period before prices fall.
■ Judgements still have to be made about "fair" profit levels and rates of return on capital.

The system in the UK envisaged regulation of privatized utilities being a temporary problem because another duty of the regulator is to foster competition; this was achieved by isolating the competitive elements of an industry from **natural monopoly** ones and encouraging competition. Progress has been made in formerly monopolistic sectors, such as gas, electricity and telephones, to give consumers a choice of supplier.

Case Study 22.1   Regulating BT

British Telecom (BT) was the first monopoly industry to be privatized. It was immediately subject to price cap regulation as shown in Table 22.1: column 1 shows the change in the retail price index, column 2 shows the X factor and column 3 the allowed price increase in the year. The initial level of X was set at 3%, which then increased to 6.25% and has stood at 4.5% since 1997.

In most years the actual increase in the basket of prices was less than the maximum, but in one or two years increases were slightly higher because of the cumulative effects of allowed price rises. Overall, if the allowed price changes had all been implemented the

Table 22.1   BT regulatory formula and price changes

Year to August	Change in retail price index (%)	X factor (%)	Allowed price change (%)	Telephone price index	Retail price index	Rate of return on capital
1984				100	100.0	16.7
1985	7	−3	4	103.7	107.0	18.3
1986	2.5	−3	−0.5	103.4	109.7	19.3
1987	4.2	−3	1.2	103.4	114.3	21.2
1988	4.6	−3	1.6	103.4	119.5	22.1
1989	8.3	−4.5	3.8	107	129.5	21.8
1990	9.8	−4.5	5.3	112.7	142.1	22.5
1991	5.8	−6.25	−0.45	111.9	150.4	22.4
1992	3.9	−6.25	−2.35	111.3	156.3	21.0
1993	1.2	−7.5	−6.3	103.6	158.1	13.6
1994	2.6	−7.5	−4.9	95.9	162.2	17.1
1995	3.5	−7.5	−4	94.2	167.9	15.6
1996	2.1	−7.5	−5.4	89.6	171.4	18.3
1997	2.9	−4.5	−1.6	88.2	176.4	18.9
1998	3.7	4.5	−0.8	87.6	182.9	19.5
1999	1.4	4.5	−3.1	84.8	185.5	19.2
2000	3.3	4.5	−1.2	83.7	191.6	18.2
2001	1.9	4.5	−2.6	81.5	195.3	14.9
2002	2.3	2.3	0.0	82.6	199.8	6.6

Source   Compiled by author using data from annual reports of BT and predecessor corporations

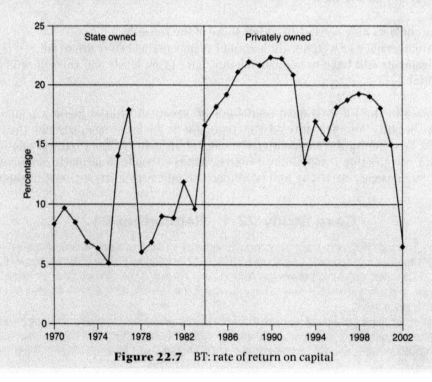

Figure 22.7   BT: rate of return on capital

telephone price index shown in column 4 would have stood at 83.3 in 2001, whereas it actually stood at 81.5. From the beginning the result has been declining prices in real terms and latterly in absolute terms. The changes in cost and efficiency levels are partly due to more efficient working methods and advances in telephone technology. Their adoption and implementation might be attributed to the incentive effects of the regulatory regime.

The impact on profitability is plotted in Figure 22.7, where the rate of return on capital is plotted from 1970 to 2000. The average rate of return is higher in the privatized period than in the state-owned period. Following privatization the rate of return increased, dropped in the recession of the early 1990s and was between 15% and 20% in the late 1990s. Thus, despite declining real prices in the regulated part of the business, BT managed to achieve rates of return in excess of 20% initially and in excess of 15% in the later years; this is partly explained by the growth in regulated business, growth in unregulated activity and the reduction in unit costs.

COMPETITION POLICY

Concerns of competition policy

Competition policy is concerned with preventing the abuse of a dominant position, collusive and anti-competitive practices and protecting market structures by policing mergers to prevent the emergence of dominant enterprises. A dominant firm is one with a significant market share which can influence the market price and maintain prices above competitive levels.

The adverse effects of dominance are analysed by identifying the welfare gains and losses. If the dominant firm's position is unassailable, then the approach developed earlier in this chapter is appropriate. However, if the dominant firm's position is likely to be challenged by existing or new firms, then the measurement of gains and losses should include the expected gains from dynamic change.

In Figure 22.8, a move from monopoly to competition is compared. Initially, the dominant firm is operating on cost curve CMC_M, and charging price OP_M. The net social benefits are indicated by the area $AKMC$. If the industry becomes competitive as the result of a new entry and the cost curve remains the same, then net welfare increases to the area ABC; and if competition brings efficiency improvements and shifts the cost curve to RMC_C, then welfare will increase to area ALR. Thus, promoting competition might be expected to bring lower prices and an increase in social welfare. However, an individual firm will seek short-term dominance by product and cost improvements. Such dominant positions may be held for only a short time and may not be of concern to the regulator. If a dominant position is persistent and rivals cannot find ways to undermine it, then such a situation should be of greater interest to a regulator.

ANTI-COMPETITIVE BEHAVIOUR, OR WHAT FIRMS CANNOT DO

Besides a general ability to raise prices above competitive levels, dominant firms have an ability to practice price discrimination (i.e., to charge different prices for the same

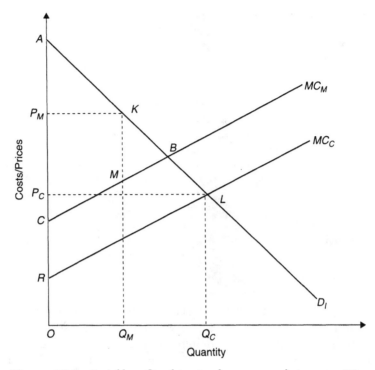

Figure 22.8 Social benefits of moving from monopoly to competition

good); this was discussed in Chapter 9. In a competitive market there is a general expectation that one price will prevail for undifferentiated goods and, where products are differentiated, those of a similar quality will have similar prices. Thus, the concern to competition regulators is whether the same products are sold at different prices to different buyers for reasons unrelated to cost: for example, the European Commission has investigated the variation in car prices between member states in Europe.

Another concern is where a dominant firm sets its price below the full cost of supply. Such a practice is common in retailing where firms use "loss-leaders" to encourage customers into their stores. When setting a price below cost is used as a weapon to bankrupt other competitors, then it is described as predatory pricing. It is the intention and the length of time a price is held below costs that makes for a situation of predatory pricing. For example, in the bus wars in Darlington, the effect of Stagecoach running services free of charge was to force into bankruptcy the incumbent Darlington Bus; this led to the withdrawal of a takeover bid and left Stagecoach in control of the local market (MMC 1995).

A variant of price discrimination is where a dominant firm offers selected customers discounts related to quantity purchased rather than to cost; this leaves smaller buyers at a competitive disadvantage. Such practices may be related to cost differences, but where they are not available to all firms in similar positions they may be regarded as anti-competitive. Similar practices occur where discounts are tied to buying a full range of products from a company or where buyers are forced to buy another product at the same time. This practice, known as bundling, has been used by Microsoft among others. The company was investigated by the US competition authorities for offering a web browser with its Windows operating system at no extra cost, making life difficult for Netscape whose major product was adversely affected. Microsoft was eventually found to have behaved anti-competitively after a series of appeals in 2001.

Another problem that can arise in the relationship between sellers and buyers involves restrictions on who can buy or distribute the product; these are known as vertical restraints. While a sweet shop offers for sale chocolate bars made by different firms, motor car showrooms only offer cars made by a single firm. Motor cars are said to be different because selling and maintaining them requires specialist knowledge. This practice limits competition between competing outlets and may lead to higher prices.

The pursuit of strategies that make it more difficult for potential rivals to enter a market is another example of anti-competitive behaviour. Incumbent dominant firms may deter entry by the use of limit prices, spending excessively on advertising and maintaining excess capacity to allow retaliatory threats to be seen as realistic.

Dominant firms may collude with their smaller competitors to ensure that activity within the industry is co-ordinated in the interests of the producers. Such practices include agreements to fix prices, to share markets, to limit or control capacity and to take part illegally in collusive tendering (see Chapter 9). Less formal agreements may take the form of price leadership, where price changes are co-ordinated to prevent price competition taking place.

Mergers

There are two types of mergers which may limit competition and give merging firms more market power: first, the horizontal merger where a direct competitor is purchased and market share is gained; and, second, where suppliers or sales outlets are acquired to limit the access of competitors to raw materials or market outlets. Both types of mergers may generate efficiency savings.

METHODOLOGY OF COMPETITION POLICY

Competition policy regards certain practices as illegal and others potentially undesirable. Thus, collusive behaviour is illegal, but holding a dominant market position is not. However, if the firm is suspected of abusing its position, then it will be investigated by the competition authorities who will then decide whether the firm is behaving wrongly. However, Case-by-case investigation can lead to inconsistent conclusions, making decision making difficult for managers because they may not be clear as to what is or is not allowed.

Defining the relevant market

Another important aspect of competition policy is the definition of the market. Whether the market is defined widely or narrowly, it clearly influences the measured market shares, for it is these that determine whether the firm has a dominant position. Markets are normally defined in terms of substitution. On the demand side, **cross elasticity** can be estimated to draw a market boundary. On the supply side, a similar concept can be used to try to measure whether an increase in supply would be forthcoming from adjacent industries if prices were to increase.

COMPETITION POLICY IN THE EU

Firms operating in the EU are subject to competition regulation at two levels: European and national. Where jurisdiction lies may sometimes be problematic, but it is normally with the Commission unless returned to national authorities. The source of EU competition policy is the Treaty of Rome: Article 81 (formerly 85) prohibits concerted or collusive agreements between firms; Article 82 (formerly 86) prohibits the abuse of a dominant position; and Regulation 4064/89, which came into force in 1990, prohibits mergers that strengthen or create a dominant position. The policy is designed to prevent restrictions or distortions to competition that are incompatible with the single market and liable to affect trade between member states adversely.

The Commissioner for Competition implements policy and the process is administered by the Commission, which undertakes investigations and makes decisions. Firms adversely affected by decisions can appeal to the Court of First Instance. After an investigation the Commission can come to a number of conclusions. It can either find no harm in the practice or merger investigated, decide to engage in discussions to see whether the firm can modify a practice or merger proposal to make it acceptable to the Commission or it can find against the firm and prohibit the practice or merger. The Commission also has the power to levy fines on firms failing to keep the rules or breaking the prohibitions: for example, operating a cartel or failing to notify the Commission of a merger that falls within the guidelines.

Article 81 prohibits all collusive agreements between firms which may affect trade between member states and whose aim is to prevent, restrict or distort competition. The Commission has to be notified of such agreements, though in practice many are operated secretly, obliging the authorities to seek out operational cartels. The Commission can decide that a collusive agreement that provides benefits in the form of cost savings and lower prices and covers less than 5% of a competitive market can be granted exemption. Automatically exempt are agreements between parent companies and subsidiaries and research and development co-operation between firms.

Group or block exemptions are granted to vertical arrangements that benefit consumers, such as exclusive distribution. One such exemption has been granted to the motor car industry to operate exclusive dealerships. The current exemption ended in 2002 and has been replaced by a new regime that will facilitate greater competition between dealers and the purchase of cars in other countries.

The Commission takes a harsh view of cartels and firms found to have participated in a cartel can be fined up to 10% of their turnover: for example, eight companies were fined a total of €855.22m in 2001 for participating in eight distinct, secret, market-sharing and price-fixing cartels that were involved in the production of vitamins (see Case Study 9.1). Firms found guilty by the Commission can appeal to the courts: for example, in the wood pulp cartel case of 1984, firms were found guilty but were cleared after appeal by the European Court of Justice in 1993.

An example of an abuse of a dominant position was the offer by British Airways of fidelity discounts that were not related to efficiency savings to agents selling tickets. Following a complaint by Virgin, the Commission prohibited BA from offering a system of loyalty incentives based on the volume of tickets sold by travel agents in the UK. The Commission found that the system infringed Article 82, because the rebates were based not on cost savings but on loyalty. Loyalty discounts are disallowed because they prevent smaller competitors from gaining market access. The Commission imposed a fine of €6.8m for a serious abuse of a dominant position over a period of 7 years.

Merger regulations

The Commission first started regulating mergers inside the EC in 1990. It is the organization that decides whether a merger creates or strengthens a dominant position, thereby reducing effective competition in the common market. A firm proposing a merger has to inform the Commission if the two parties have a worldwide turnover of more than €5bn or an EU turnover in excess of €250m; in addition, both firms must have less than two-thirds of their EU turnover within a member state. The firms are then required to complete a detailed questionnaire, the information provided being used to decide whether a dominant position has been created; this is in contrast to the USA, where the test is whether the merger is likely to appreciably lessen competition.

Among the factors considered by the Commission in reaching a decision are:

- The market position of the firms concerned.
- Their economic and financial power.
- The opportunities available to suppliers and users.
- Access to suppliers or markets.
- Supply and demand trends for the relevant goods or services.
- Legal and other barriers to market entry.
- The state of technical and economic progress.

At the end of the initial investigation, which takes up to 4 weeks, the Commission has to decide whether to approve the merger or send it for further investigation, which takes up to 4 months. At each stage, approval of the merger can be given subject to commitments by the firms concerned. Table 22.2 shows 335 mergers referred to the Commission in 2001. In phase I a total of 312 were approved including 13 after commitments. In phase II there were 20 investigations. Of these 5 were approved, 10 were approved with commitments and 5 mergers were rejected as being incompatible

Table 22.2 EU merger cases

Event	1999	2000	2001	Total (1990–2001)
Notifications	292	345	335	1,908
Cases withdrawn	12	14	128	77
Phase I				
Outside scope of regulation	1	1	1	53
Compatible	236	293	299	1,574
Compatible with commitments	19	28	13	86
Referral to member states	4	6	7	34
Total phase I decisions	*260*	*328*	*320*	*1,747*
Phase II				
Compatible	0	3	5	20
Compatible with commitments	8	12	10	57
Prohibited	1	2	5	18
Other	1	0	0	3
Total phase II decisions	*10*	*17*	*20*	*98*
Fines	4	1	0	6

Source Compiled by author using data extracted from European Commission Merger Statistics http://europe.eu.int/comm/competition/mergers/cases/stats.html

with the policy. These latter decisions increased the number of rejected mergers from 13 in the previous 10 years to 18 in total. Rejected mergers included that between Airtours and First Choice.

Another element in the policy is the approval of mergers subject to the disposal of certain assets, which lowers the potential level of dominance: for example, Nestlé's bid for Perrier in 1992 was approved by the Commission on condition that Nestlé sell certain of Perrier's brands. Nestlé sold Perrier's second largest brand Volvic to BSN, France's largest food group, creating a situation where surprisingly the two companies controlled more than two-thirds of the market.

Case Study 22.2 Airtours and First Choice – a rejected merger

One of the 18 mergers rejected by the Commission was that between two British package tour companies – Airtours and First Choice. It was rejected because the merger would create a market structure in which the major players would collectively have a dominant position, with consequent adverse effects on prices and other forms of competition. The merger would create a firm with a 32% market share and leave only two other major competitors of similar size and degree of vertical integration. As a result the three remaining large firms would control more than 80% of the market and have a collective ability to distort competition.

Airtours appealed to the Court of First Instance because the Commission decision was not based on the creation of a dominant position, the test in the regulation, but collective dominance. The Court did not reject the notion of collective dominance, but did not accept it would have the direct effect of enabling the merged firm and its competitors to adopt common policies to impede competition. To prove collective dominance the Commission would have to show that each member of the oligopoly knew how the others would behave (e.g., when setting price); there must be no incentive for a firm to depart from common policies, and a new entrant would not alter the co-ordination of the market.

Strengths and weaknesses

Merger regulation is a relatively speedy process, with the great majority of cases being decided within 1 month and the remainder in 4 months. Because a single body is responsible for notification, investigation and decision making, it becomes possible for firms to be well informed about its potential response to any given merger. The Commission's weaknesses include a lack of transparency in investigation, a lack of clarity in decision making and its role as judge and jury. The Commission, it is argued, has sweeping powers without significant external accountability, so that there is a lack of checks and balances. Appeals against Commission decisions can take a long time, though a "fast track" appeals procedure has been adopted for mergers to meet these outcomes.

Another point of criticism is the test of dominance (i.e., whether a merger strengthens or creates a dominant position). An alternative test is that used in the USA which examines whether there will be a substantial lessening of competition in the market after the merger. The latter test, it is claimed, is more flexible and could be used to block mergers that currently are approved. In practice, the difference between the two tests is to some extent semantic because they are not mutually exclusive tests. A change in the criteria would wipe out 11 years of precedent and create greater uncertainty for companies.

Another issue is the increasingly international nature of mergers and business operations; this creates conflicts between the EU and the USA. For example, mergers involving two US companies may well come within EU jurisdiction because of the potential company's market share; this generates parallel investigations that can lead to different decisions and disputes over sovereignty and precedence. A company may also have to make multiple notifications to numerous competition authorities of its intentions. A review of merger policy has taken place and proposals for reform were made, but have not yet been implemented (Papaionnou et al. 2002).

UK COMPETITION POLICY

The UK system of competition policy has developed piecemeal since the first legislation in 1948. It developed separate policies to deal with restrictive practices, dominant firms, anti-competitive practices and mergers. In 1998 a new Competition Act was passed by Parliament which recast the policy on restrictive practices and anti-competitive practices so that they fell into line with Articles 81 and 82 of the Treaty of

Rome. The objective was to overcome the limitations of previous legislation, to attack collusive practices and create a more competitive economy. Other aspects of policy, such as monopoly and merger policy, remained unchanged and are still based on the Fair Trading Act 1973.

The competition authorities in the UK comprise:

- The Office of Fair Trading (OFT) is a quasi-autonomous body that polices the state of markets, enforces and investigates cases arising under the 1998 legislation. It has to be informed of qualifying mergers and does the initial investigation.
- The Secretary of State for Trade and Industry, who acts on advice from the Director General of the OFT and receives reports from the Competition Commission. He also decides which recommendations from the Competition Commission should be implemented.
- The Competition Commission is an independent body appointed by the Secretary of State for Trade and Industry and investigates cases referred to it by the OFT and other regulators. It acts as an appeals body for decisions made by the OFT and the various utility regulators.

The Competition Act 1998 prohibits not only anti-competitive agreements that affect trade but also the abuse of dominant market positions that have the object or effect of preventing, restricting or distorting competition. Such practices are to be judged by whether they have an appreciable effect on competition rather than by the form or structure they take.

Companies can be fined up to 10% of turnover for not complying with the law, and participation in a cartel is now a criminal offence with punishment by imprisonment. Appeals under the new system can be made to the Competition Commission Appeals Panel.

In 2001 the OFT imposed its first fines. Napp Pharmaceuticals were fined £3.21m for supplying the cancer relief drug MST to hospitals at a 90% discount compared with charges in the retail market where GP prescriptions are processed. Aberdeen Journals were fined £1.3m for trying to drive a competitor out of business. The first fines for operating a cartel were imposed on Arriva and First Bus for co-ordinating their presence on routes in Leeds and Wakefield. The fines were reduced under the leniency provision for co-operation. In the case of the Link cash machine network it concluded that the co-operative arrangements between a large number of banks brought the consumer benefits that exceeded the possible anti-competitive effects (OFT 2002).

Mergers that involve worldwide assets of £70m or a potential market share of 25% must be notified to the Office of Fair Trading, which makes an initial judgement and recommends to the Secretary of State whether the case should be referred to the Competition Commission. The minister has the power not to refer a case and to refer against the advice of the OFT. The investigation by the Competition Commission then decides whether the merger is for or against the public interest, the impact of which on competition is one such aspect. Of the 356 mergers notified to the OFT in 2001 (OFT 2002):

- 200 qualified for further investigation;
- 10 cases were referred to the Competition Commission;

- 4 cases were found not to be against the public interest and were allowed to proceed;
- 2 cases were declared to be against the public interest;
- 4 cases were abandoned because the proposed merger was abandoned.

Case Study 22.3 Interbrew and the UK's competition regulators

In May 2000, Interbrew – a Belgian brewer – proposed buying Whitbread's brewing interests in the UK. The proposal was approved by the OFT and a decision made not to refer it to the Competition Commission because:

- The market share of the new brewer would increase by only 1%.
- It would only be the third largest brewer in the market.
- And it would break the ownership relationship between brewing and Whitbread's tied pubs and other outlets.

Later in the same year, Interbrew decided to acquire the worldwide brewing interests of Bass, the UK's largest brewer. The case was referred to the UK authorities by the EC. After consideration by the OFT it was referred to the Competition Commission. Following an investigation it decided that the merger would act against the public interest because the merger would:

- Make Interbrew the largest brewer, in the UK, with an overall market share of between 33 and 38%.
- Strengthen Interbrew's portfolio of leading brands.
- Create a duopoly between Interbrew and Scottish & Newcastle which would raise prices and lead to an increased emphasis on non-price competition, thereby raising barriers to entry and expansion by competing brands.

The Competition Commission considered various structural remedies but decided that no pattern of divestment would remedy the adverse effects of the merger and that Interbrew should divest itself of Bass's UK interests.

Interbrew then appealed to the High Court for a judicial review. It argued that the order to sell Bass's British operations was disproportionate. The High Court ruled that the Commission had failed to give Interbrew a fair chance to discuss alternatives to the Commission's chosen solution for dealing with feared market dominance and ordered the competition authorities to reconsider their decision.

The OFT put forward four possible remedies, and Interbrew accepted that it should dispose of Carling, which included the UK's largest selling brand of beer, together with the Caffrey's and Worthington brands. The market share of the businesses to be sold was estimated at 18%, second to Scottish & Newcastle. Eventually, consent was given for the sale of Bass in January 2002 to Adolph Coors, the third largest brewer in the USA.

CHAPTER SUMMARY

In this chapter we have examined the methods used by government to regulate dominant firms. In doing this we analysed:

■ How regulation by government can prevent firms from pursuing policies they otherwise would have done.

■ The need for regulation to stop firms acting collectively to co-ordinate markets by limiting competition and, thereby adding to their own profitability.

■ Two types of policy: the first type is aimed at regulating natural monopolies and utilities (which in recent experience in the UK followed privatization); this remains an ongoing problem unless competitive markets are developed. The second type is aimed at dominant firms, in general, and is designed to ensure that competitive forces are not undermined by firms with market power or by firms trying to create market power by acquisitions. Both sets of policies restrict the strategic choices that a firm can make.

REVIEW QUESTIONS

1 Why might the government seek to regulate utilities?
2 Compare and contrast the welfare gains and losses between monopoly and competition.
3 What problems does pursuing marginal cost pricing create in a monopoly where there are increasing returns to scale?
4 What methods might a regulator use to ensure a utility breaks even but does least damage to economic welfare?
5 Explain rate of return regulation. What are its advantages and disadvantages?
6 Explain price capping regulation. What are its main advantages and disadvantages?
7 What behavioural practices might a dominant firm adopt in pursuit of profit maximization which might be unacceptable to the competition regulators?
8 What are the main tests used by European competition authorities to decide whether a cartel, anti-competitive practice or merger is a good or a bad thing?
9 Using the EC's (or Competition Commission's) website select specific case studies of a cartel, an anti-competitive practice and a merger. Critically examine the reasons the Commission came to its conclusion.
10 Explain the methodology of competition policy and why outcomes are uncertain. Are there ways to reduce the degree of uncertainty that firms find unsettling?

REFERENCES AND FURTHER READINGS

Averch, H. and L. Johnson (1962) Behaviour of the firm under regulatory constraint. *American Economic Review*, **52**, 1052–1069.

Littlechild, S. (1983) *Regulation of British Telecommunications Profitability*. HMSO, London.

Markou, E. and C. Waddams Price (1997) *Effects of UK Utility Reform: Source and Distribution*. Institute of Public Policy Research, London.

MMC (1995) *The Supply of Bus services in north east England* (Monopolies and Mergers Commission Cmnd 2933). HMSO, London.

OFT (2002) *Annual Report 2001*(Office of Fair Trading Cmnd 773). HMSO, London.

Papaionnou, A., U. Diez, S. Ryan and D. Sjoblom (2002) Green paper on the review of the merger regulation. *Competition Policy Newsletter*, **1**, February, 65–68.

Train, K.E. (1991) *Optimal Regulation: The Economic Theory of Natural Monopoly*. MIT Press, Cambridge, MA.

Viscusi, W.K., J.M Vernon and J.E. Harrington (1995) *Economics of Regulation and Antitrust* (2nd edn). MIT Press, Cambridge, MA.

Vogelsang, I. and J. Finsinger (1979) A regulatory adjustment process for optimal pricing by multi-product firms. *Bell Journal of Economics*, **10**, 157–171.

Websites

European Commission Competition: http:// www.europa.eu.int/comm/competition
Competition Commission: http://www. competition-commission.org.uk
Office of Fair Trading: http://www.oft.gov.uk

PUBLIC SECTOR PRODUCTION

CHAPTER OUTLINE

CHAPTER OBJECTIVES

This chapter aims to explore the reasons governments establish state-owned production units. At the end of this chapter you should be able to:

◆ Define and explain the main causes of market failure.

◆ Explain the distinction between private and social costs and benefits.

◆ Outline the concepts of excludability and rivalry and their implications for production.

◆ Identify and explain the factors that influence the choice between public and private ownership of production.

◆ Outline and explain the shortcomings of public enterprise.

INTRODUCTION

A common feature of most economies is that some activities are undertaken not by private profit-seeking enterprises but by state-owned organizations, voluntary organizations and mutually owned organizations, whose prime objective is the service of the community or its members. In the UK these three types of organizations undertake a range of activities that is sometimes in competition with private operators. The main purpose of this chapter is to explore why public sector or government-controlled organizations are preferred by society to undertake certain activities. The reasons are to be found in the concept of market failure, the failures of specific private companies and the preference of society for alternative ways of organizing production. This chapter will examine:

- Aspects of market failure.
- Arguments for public sector production.
- Factors influencing the comparative performance of public and private organizations.

WHY PUBLIC SECTOR PRODUCTION?

In a market economy there is no single reason some activity should be conducted by a public sector rather than a privately owned profit-seeking organization. Generally, the decision to undertake an activity in the public sector is made because of the failures of the existing structure and the perceived benefit of change. Thus, the National Health Service was established in 1948 as much because of the failings of the previous system to meet the health needs of the vast majority of the population as of the Labour Government's commitment to public ownership. Thus, a whole list of factors relating to market and organizational failure may be relevant in influencing any change from public to private or private to public ownership. Many of these arguments come under the general heading of market failure. We will examine these first.

EXTERNALITIES

Externalities arise when benefits and costs are not wholly received by the intended consumer or fully incurred by the producer undertaking production. External benefits arise when a producer provides an unpaid-for benefit to another producer or consumer. For example, constructing a reservoir to provide water may also provide benefits to individuals in the form of flood prevention or to tourists admiring the dam and using the water for pleasure. External costs arise when the producer imposes costs on others who then receive no compensation. For example, electricity generated using coal also produces smoke and other pollutants, such as acid rain, which create costs

Table 23.1 Classifying externalities

Imposer of externality	Recipient of externality	
	Consumer benefits	Producer benefits
Consumer	Positive Negative	Positive Negative
Producer	Positive Negative	Positive Negative

Source Author

for other producers or consumers. Acid rain produced by electricity generators in the UK is delivered free of charge to Scandinavian countries by the prevailing westerly winds where it pollutes many lakes and has adverse effects on the environment.

Theoretically, externalities can be imposed by either a consumer or a producer and be received by either a consumer or producer. There are four possible relationships, and these are shown in Table 23.1. Producer–producer and producer–consumer are the two of these that have most impact on the functioning of markets. They can each generate a negative or positive consequence.

Externalities and markets

A distinction can be made between private and social costs, on the one hand, and between private and social benefits, on the other, the difference being external costs or external benefits. Thus, the social costs of an activity are equal to private costs plus external costs and the social benefits of an activity are equal to private benefits plus external benefits.

These differences are illustrated in Figure 23.1, where ED_P and FD_S are private and social benefits and GMC_P and HMC_S are private and social marginal costs. If just private costs and benefits are considered in production and consumption decisions, then, as can be observed in Figure 23.1(a), the quantity produced when demand is equal to private marginal cost is OQ_1 and the price charged is OP_1. At this output the marginal social costs are Q_1C_S which are greater than the private costs of Q_1C_P. The market price does not reflect the external costs C_PC_S and fails to transmit the correct information to the consumer about the costs and benefits attached to this good or service. The market will overproduce goods where social costs exceed private costs. If social costs were reflected in the market price, then the quantity OQ_2 would be produced and a charge of OP_2 imposed on the consumer. This charge covers private costs KQ_2 and external costs KL. The difficulty is finding a way of reflecting external costs in the price menu facing consumers.

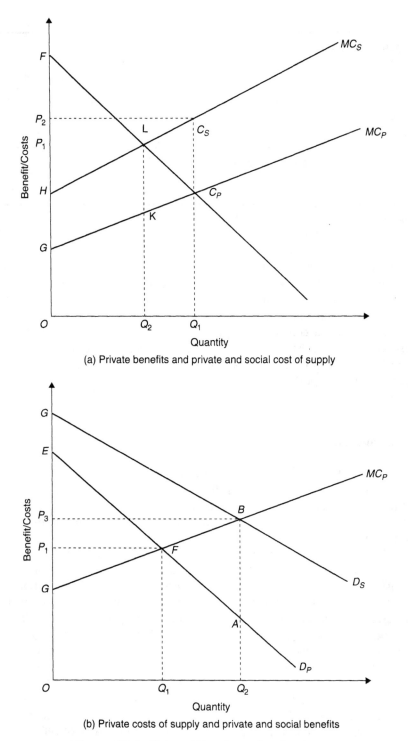

(a) Private benefits and private and social cost of supply

(b) Private costs of supply and private and social benefits

Figure 23.1 Externalities: demand and cost curves

In Figure 23.1(b), social benefits and private costs are considered, with no externalities in production. In this case, society would wish to see output OQ_2 produced, where marginal social benefits are equal to marginal private costs. However, if left to the market, then only OQ_1 is supplied, where marginal private benefits are equal to marginal private costs. If the desired output of OQ_2 were to be supplied, then the firm would require compensation of Q_3B. On the basis of their private benefits, consumers would only contribute Q_2A, leaving the sum AB to be met either by additional contributions from beneficiaries or by government subsidy. Again the difficulty lies in measuring the social benefit and devising a method of compensating the producer.

The market in the presence of externalities will misallocate resources. Where social costs exceed private costs the market overproduces and where social benefits exceed private benefits it underproduces. If externalities are significant, then the role of government may be to encourage socially desirable production by subsidizing an activity and to discourage socially undesirable activities by taxing or regulating them. The greater the proportion of social benefits generated by a given product the greater the compensation the private producer would require to produce the socially desired output. If a government does not wish to compensate or subsidize a private producer, then it might consider public rather than private production. However, if no price is charged for the publicly provided output, then the government has to have another mechanism other than ability to pay to allocate a quantity of the good to each citizen.

In practice, goods will provide varying quantities of private and social benefits. At one extreme will be goods that provide 100% private benefits, and at the other there will be those that provide 100% social benefits. In-between these extremes, goods will provide varying proportions of private and social benefits; this is illustrated in Figure 23.2, where the vertical axis measures the proportion of private and external benefits

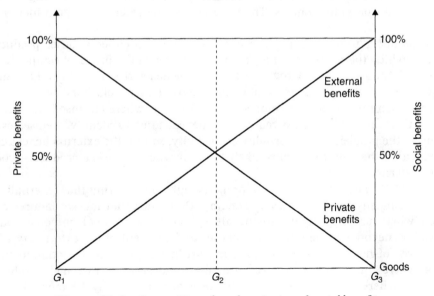

Figure 23.2 Composition of goods: private and social benefits

provided by products and on the horizontal axis are different types of goods. Thus, for good 1 all the benefits are private, for good 2 the benefits are 50% private and 50% external and for good 3 the benefits are 100% external with no private benefits whatsoever. In a market economy the majority of products are presumed to provide wholly private benefits and any element of external benefits can be safely ignored, but there are others where the social element cannot be ignored.

Property rights and externalities

If a negative **externality** is imposed on a third party but the activity is incorporated within the organization, then the externality is said to be internalized. For example, an external cost arising from coal mining is subsidence and damage to properties. If a coal producer takes into ownership the properties affected by their operations, then the costs of protecting the property become part of the costs of producing coal. Alternatively, if the coal producer agrees to compensate those whose property is damaged, then again the producer is aware of the external costs imposed by mining. However, if the producer does not accept liability or is not required by law to compensate, then the producer ignores these costs in producing coal. In these circumstances the externality is uncompensated and ignored. Therefore, externalities are a problem when property rights cannot be exercised. If the recipient of a negative externality has no right to compensation, then the externality goes uncompensated unless the originator volunteers to compensate the loser. If the recipient has a right to compensation, then property rights can be exercised. An alternative strategy to paying compensation is for the producer to stop the externality occurring: for example, by stopping pollution entering the air or water courses. The generator of the externality again incurs these costs.

If a producer provides a positive external benefit to either another producer or consumer which the recipient values with no enforcement of property rights, then the producer is unable to collect revenue from the beneficiaries and the welfare gain is received free. If the producer is able to receive either voluntary or compulsory payments, then the producer is compensated. However, where an unsolicited benefit is received there appear to be no reasons for beneficiaries to identify themselves. One solution to the problem is to internalize the activity, so that the external benefit can be utilized within the firm; this is most likely to occur where there is a producer–producer positive externality.

Coase (1960) explored the role of property rights in ensuring that externalities do not go uncompensated in a market economy. He argued that market failures can be avoided where property rights are tightly specified. An optimal outcome could be achieved by negotiation between the imposer and recipient of the externality as long as the costs of negotiation and contracting are not significant. Negotiation may be simpler where the numbers involved are small and becomes extremely problematic and costly where numbers are large, because agreement may be more difficult to reach.

Merit and bad goods

Participation in the market by consumers is a function of individual preferences and income. If the community believes that society is underconsuming or overconsuming certain goods because of their mix of social/private benefits and costs, then government may try to rectify this position. Such goods are termed **merit goods** if there are substantial social benefits associated with consumption and **bad goods** (or bads) if there are substantial social costs; for example, education and health care may be considered to be merit goods whereas cigarettes are considered to be a bad good.

Government action to correct underconsumption or overconsumption can take a number of forms. Government may try to change consumer preferences by:

- Propaganda, extolling the virtue or harm of the activity.
- Subsidize merit good to reduce the price.
- Tax bad goods to increase the price.
- Provide a general income grant to encourage consumption.
- Override individual preferences by making available vouchers that can only be spent on a particular merit good.
- Override individual preferences by making consumption compulsory for merit goods or illegal for bad goods.

CHARACTERISTICS OF GOODS: EXCLUDABILITY AND RIVALRY

Markets deal best with what are called **private goods**; these are goods characterized by the ability of the producer to exclude those who cannot pay from consuming, where consumption by one person deprives anyone else from consuming and the consumption benefits are wholly private (i.e., confined to the person purchasing the good). These two characteristics are known as "excludability" and "rivalry" and allow goods to be classified by their presence or absence; this leads to four categories of goods, which are illustrated in Table 23.2.

Private goods are both excludable and rival in consumption. If a consumer does not buy the good, then he cannot consume it. Consumption of one unit means it is not available for anyone else to consume. These goods are usually produced by the private sector and priced in the usual way.

Mixed or common goods are goods where exclusion is not possible since all potential users have the right to consume, but consumption by one individual reduces the

Table 23.2 Goods classified by excludability and rivalry

	Rivalry in consumption	Non-rivalry in consumption
Excludable	Private goods	Mixed or toll goods
Non-excludable	Mixed or Common goods	Public goods

Source Author

amount available for others. Typical examples of such situations are common land, public beaches and fisheries. Everyone has the right to catch fish, but doing so deprives others of catching the same fish. Overfishing leads to a reduction in fish stocks, but it is in no one's interest to stop fishing unless ownership rights are declared and limits put on fishing and depleting stocks. These goods can be: produced by the private sector and financed by user charges; supplied by the public sector at a price; or financed by taxation. The main problem is to prevent overuse where price cannot be used.

Mixed or toll goods are goods that are non-rival in consumption until they become crowded or congested, but exclusion is feasible. When underutilized, exclusion may not be desirable. However, when they become congested, exclusion becomes highly desirable: for example, roads and swimming pools with few cars and swimmers have plenty of space for everyone; this implies that additional consumers can use the facility at zero marginal cost. At some point the road and the pool start to become congested and it becomes desirable to prevent further users gaining access. Where entry charges are made these goods are known as "toll goods".

Swimming pools usually charge for entry or are run as clubs, while the majority of roads are generally free of charge, because of the difficulties of imposing and collecting tolls. Where there is limited access toll roads are utilized. Electronic developments are now making road charges feasible, particularly in congested cities, and a number of experiments are being undertaken. These goods can be produced privately or publicly and either sold at a price or be available at no charge.

Pure public goods are goods that are non-excludable and non-rival in consumption; this means that consumption by one individual does not reduce the amount available for another and that consumers cannot be excluded. Thus, individuals cannot be prevented from consuming if they choose to do so whether they have made a contribution toward the cost of supply or not; this is called the **free rider** problem. Examples of such goods include national defence, public health, street lighting and lighthouses. Lighthouses provide ships with a warning of dangerous rocks. The warning is available to all: warning one ship does not reduce the availability of the warning to other ships. In practice, it is difficult both to exclude any passing ship from benefiting and to collect a toll from it for its use of the lighthouse. In the UK, lighthouse charges or dues are levied but only on ships docking in the UK (see Coase 1974). Thus, public goods have significant exclusion costs and are either produced by the public sector or the private sector using contracts.

Demand and supply of public goods

The market will not provide a sufficient quantity of public goods if consumers can obtain the non-excludable benefits of public goods without paying for them. It is thus difficult to determine the appropriate quantity of a public good to supply. The problem is illustrated in Figure 23.3.

Assume that a society consists of two individuals, A and B, and that consumers are willing to reveal their willingness to pay for a public good. Since consumption by one individual does not reduce the quantity available to another, instead of adding

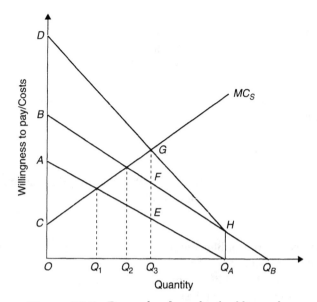

Figure 23.3 Demand and supply of public goods

demand curves horizontally they are summed vertically to see whether total willingness to pay justifies the provision of the service. The individual demand curves AQ_A and BQ_B are added vertically to give total willingness to pay and a community demand curve of $DGHQ_B$. Thus, the total willingness to pay is the area under this curve (namely, $ODHQ_B$). With a given marginal social cost curve of CMC_S the optimal quantity to be supplied is OQ_3. If only A's preferences were revealed, then only OQ_1 would be supplied. The free riding individual B could also consume this quantity. However, B may prefer a higher level of production and might be persuaded to reveal his preferences to help finance a higher level of provision. If B's preferences were revealed and A was the free rider, then A would be content with the provision of OQ_2 and would have no motivation to cease free riding.

PROVISION OF GOODS BY THE PUBLIC AND PRIVATE SECTOR

If consumers are unwilling to reveal their preferences or cannot be easily excluded from benefiting, then it is difficult to ensure that sufficient quantity is supplied. If revenue cannot be directly collected from consumers, then private producers will not supply unless they are motivated by philanthropic considerations. The community, in the shape of government or voluntary groups, have to act either to pay a private producer or to organize production themselves. In order to explain which option is chosen, it is necessary to explore why public production might be preferred to private production.

The options available to a government can be outlined by reference to Table 23.3. Assuming there are two options in terms of production (namely, public or private) and

Table 23.3   Classifying production

	Supplied at a price	Supplied "free" or state-financed
Public production	A	B
Private production	C	D

Source Author

two options in terms of pricing (namely, charging a price or making the service available free), then we can identify four options:

A   Goods produced by the public sector, but sold at a price normally set to recover variable and fixed costs.

B   Goods produced by the public sector, but supplied "free" or at a nominal charge – costs are met from the public purse.

C   Goods produced in the private sector, but sold at a price normally set to recover costs and make a profit.

D   Goods produced in the private sector, but supplied "free" or at a nominal charge – costs are met from the public purse.

In a market economy, goods are normally privately produced and sold at a price (box C) and will only be found in other categories as the consequence of social or political decisions; these will differ between countries, depending on political attitudes to markets and the success or failure of previous institutional structures. In any category, there could be a mixture of public, merit and private goods. For example, cigarettes are usually sold at a price but have been produced by state tobacco monopolies in countries, such as Italy and France, and by the private sector in the UK and the USA. In the UK, cigarettes are treated as a "bad" good, are heavily taxed and carry warnings against consumption. School education and health are provided "free" at the point of consumption in the UK alongside a market sector, while in other countries charges are levied whether provision is public or private. Motorway roads are tolled in France but "free" in the UK and Germany.

A product may not remain in the same box for all time. Products may move as a result of:

■   Nationalization: moving the production of goods from the private to the public sector.

■   Privatization: moving the production of goods from the public to the private sector.

■   Marketization: by charging for goods and services previously available "free".

■   Non-marketization: by making goods (previously charged for) available without charge.

ARGUMENTS FOR PUBLIC PRODUCTION

Production of goods by organizations and agencies owned and controlled by the state may be preferred for a host of reasons. In the inter-war and post-war years, governments throughout Europe generally increased their control of the economy through nationalization, because of the failures of the market economy and disadvantages of private ownership. However, since 1980 the same countries have reduced the level of state control though policies of privatization and deregulation, because of the advantages of the market economy and the failure of state ownership and production.

Inadequate private supply

A major argument for public production is that neither the volume of production nor its quality meets the requirements of society when production is left to the private sector. For example, in the 19th century the failure of the education system to meet society's needs of a more literate and skilled workforce led the British State to establish a state-owned and state-financed education system, designed to ensure every child should receive a minimum of education. Qualified teachers were gradually employed and inspectors sent to schools to ensure standards were acceptable. Similar considerations have applied to defence matters. When the supply of munitions was found to be deficient, the state established ordnance plants to meet the needs of the armed forces. Another reason for failure to supply may be related to the size and riskiness of a particular project. If private firms are unwilling to meet the risks, then they might seek government loans, subsidies and/or loan guarantees. In these circumstances a government may wish to see the whole community share the risks and may undertake the project under direct public control.

Asymmetric and imperfect information

Market supply can also turn out to be inadequate when producers and consumers have incomplete information available to them when making decisions, especially when the accuracy of such information varies. Where one party to a transaction has information that is not available to the other party, then situations of asymmetric information arise; this can lead to situations of adverse selection and moral hazard where the parties to an agreement are making the decision on the basis of different information. For example, the usual argument in the health insurance market is that prices are bid up if the insurer does not know the risks associated with any particular individual, leaving only the sick seeking insurance that they cannot afford. The result is that many people will be left uninsured. Thus, the alternative is seen as state provision of health insurance and health services. The latter is particularly motivated by a desire to make health care available to all individuals irrespective of their ability to pay. For example, between 1996 and 2001 the number of people buying health insurance in the UK fell by 17% because of a 59% increase in premiums. The large increase in premiums was attributed to the increasing cost of claims; many of those insured were becoming elderly and making more expensive claims. Those who cannot afford the higher premiums tend to be the elderly and the newly retired. Thus, when people become increasingly in need of health care they find that they can no longer afford the cover they expected and are forced to leave the private sector and become dependent on the state (Papworth, 2000).

Decreasing cost industries

Another argument used to justify public ownership is the presence of a decreasing cost function. If demand cannot justify more than one economic or sustainable organization, then efficiency requires a monopoly supplier. A monopoly supplier will exploit consumers by raising prices and restricting output and may have no interests in investing in the growth of capacity, despite the desire of the state to see growth in supply capacity. While the state may favour regulation of monopolies, it may also favour ownership because it then has influence not only on price but also objectives, management style, investment and growth. A typical example of an industry where public ownership is a dominant form is electricity. Electricity distribution is a natural monopoly and seen as important for economic development. Consequently, state ownership is seen as the preferred ownership structure in many but not all countries.

Social preference and ideology

Active periods of nationalization have been associated with the election of socialist governments in many countries. Socialists have believed that public ownership of key sectors of the economy is superior to private ownership and necessary not only to achieve increases in economic welfare but also to enable benefits to be more fairly distributed in a more egalitarian state. Public ownership was also thought necessary to help plan the economy, so that decisions about industry could be made to meet social and political objectives, thus avoiding being dictated to by the market. In practice, the commitment to public ownership has been dropped by many left-of-centre political parties in favour of greater regulation and other measures, to correct for market failures and to achieve other social objectives.

Sovereignty and ownership

An issue that has led to public production is concern over foreign ownership of sectors that the state might consider important for its efficient running and survival; these are often related to defence and infrastructure, but might also relate to other aspects of society, such as cultural institutions and the media. A government might prefer public ownership to foreign ownership of aerospace manufacturing, shipbuilding, airlines, shipping and armament manufacture, so preventing the termination of supply at inappropriate times. Such concerns do not always lead to public ownership but, instead, to restrictions on foreign ownership of certain industries, such as broadcasting and airlines.

Enterprise and managerial failure

In practice, many decisions to pursue public ownership are a response to a particular problem rather than to an ideological commitment. Public ownership has been used to rescue bankrupt companies, to solve industrial relations problems, to replace management, to prevent foreign ownership or to start enterprises when the private sector appears unwilling to take the initiative. Thus, companies in the UK have been taken into public ownership to maintain employment and presence in sectors thought to be important to the economy.

In practice, public ownership might be preferred in situations where:

■ The government is paying for or subsidizing provision.
■ The government is the major customer of a firm.
■ Politicians feel responsible to voters for industrial failure and consequent unemployment.
■ Democratic control is thought to be more important than the pursuit of private profit (e.g., the police or the armed forces).
■ Society prefers public to private production for reasons related to quality and safety, which are seen as incompatible with the pursuit of profit.

ORGANIZATIONAL ISSUES

Public sector organizations are similar in many ways to private organizations. They are both established to perform a service or produce a good and have to employ individuals and capital, combining them into productive teams. Public sector organizations have similar tasks to perform as carried out in private sector organizations. For example, bus services are provided by both private or public sector organizations. Services, such as social worker advice and assistance, can likewise be provided by the public sector, voluntary or even private organizations. In this section we will examine factors that help to explain the differences in structure and behaviour of public sector organizations from private sector profit-seeking organizations.

Organizational structures

Public sector organizations are different because they are owned and directed by the state to serve purposes determined by government and the wider community. The choice of organizational structure can be between government departments, independent agencies and independent public corporations. Some of the factors influencing that choice include:

- *Ownership*: public activities are normally wholly owned by the state; but, in some instances, ownership may be shared with private owners. In these cases, the state has a choice of being a passive partner (British Petroleum from the First World War until 1990) or an active partner controlling objectives and the appointment of managers.
- *Function*: this can vary from offering advice to ministers, to fighting wars and crime, to providing personal social services, to health care, to bus services. Each activity is different and will require a different organizational structure.
- *Objectives*: the type of structure established will depend on the objectives or purposes of the organization. One pursuing mainly social objectives will require a different structure from one trying to produce electricity as efficiently as possible and pursuing quasi-commercial goals. Organizations of the latter type are also expected to be enterprises and to be innovative.
- *Output*: these can vary from the intangible to the tangible and from private to public goods.
- *Consumer charges*: these can range from services that are received as entitlement at no direct costs to goods that are paid for at a quasi-commercial price.
- *Finance of organization*: this can range from government grants to sales revenue and retention of profit or to a mixture of both. In addition, some public bodies may have the right to raise loans (or debt capital) in commercial markets. They do not normally have access to equity markets.
- *Market*: public organizations may operate as monopoly suppliers, but could also be in competition with either other public or private suppliers.
- *Operational control*: public organizations are established by political decisions and are subject to political direction. Some organizations are subject to detailed political control and decision making, while others operate at arm's length and have a significant degree of management control.
- *Performance measurement*: precise performance targets may be appropriate in some activities but not in others. Again the choice of organization structure might reflect the method.

Depending on the particular task the government wishes to carry out, then a particular organizational structure will be selected. Thus, a government or local authority department might be appropriate for social services whereas a public enterprise might be appropriate for electricity or railways, though Indian Railways are still organized as a government department with the Minister of Railways directly answerable to parliament. Generally, developments in the public sector have been to create a divorce between political and managerial control and to make organizations financially self-supporting.

PUBLIC ENTERPRISE

Historically, the concept of the public enterprise in the UK was one where politicians set the long-term objectives and management were responsible for day-to-day decisions. The aim was to combine the notion of publicness with the concept of enterprise to serve the public interest. The concept of publicness implies serving the interests of the community as a whole rather than the private interests of the owners of capital. The government sets objectives that are fulfilled by managers who have no ownership stake and are presumed to serve the public interest. In addition, the organization is accountable to government and to society through democratic control, rather than to shareholders.

The concept of enterprise implies that managers can take judgemental decisions and incur risks in their decisions about how to produce and how to innovate. Thus, managers do not just have powers to implement existing production plans, but are allowed to change production to meet changes in demand, to introduce new products, to implement cost-saving production techniques and to undertake investments to ensure future production of the goods and services produced.

The critical issue is whether the two concepts can be efficiently synthesized. Politicians are unwilling to leave day-to-day decisions with political consequences to managers. There is always an incentive to intervene to prevent closure of production facilities or to stop prices increasing, if political advantage is expected. Politicians are unlikely to be concerned with long-term objectives because the time horizons of the electoral cycle are much shorter than the time frames required for investment decisions.

The board of a public enterprise is appointed by government ministers to run the company. The board then appoints the senior managers. Neither the boards nor the senior managers have the freedom to make the full range of "enterprise" decisions that are required of a private company. They are not allowed to diversify, make takeover bids or even set prices, because the politicians are always in the background. Thus, difficult decisions may be delayed and avoided for the sake of a reasonably quiet life. It is also difficult for politicians as owners to ensure management perform as efficiently as they might, were they to interfere in day-to-day decisions and change the objectives. Managers can always argue that without interference they would have achieved the set objectives. Alternatively, politicians can leave it to the managers and blame all unpalatable consequences on managerial shortcomings. However, at the end of the day the politicians have to answer for the consequences to the electorate. As a consequence the synthesis between "public" and "enterprise" is criticized as an inefficient compromise compared with private enterprise. Some aspects of the critique of the public sector organization compared with a private enterprise will now be examined.

PROPERTY RIGHTS APPROACH

A major difference between public sector and private sector organizations is the nature of ownership. In the former the owners are the community or voting citizens, whereas in the latter they are shareholders. Typically, the former will be a much larger group than the latter and, in practice, will look to the elected politicians to set objectives and to civil servants or audit agencies to measure performance. The citizen owners of the public enterprise are unable to exercise any ownership rights except via the ballot box, which is a somewhat indirect method.

In private sector organizations the owners or shareholders are able to use their ownership rights to influence the management. Shareholders can do this by selling their shares. If the number of sellers exceed the number of buyers, then the share price will fall, either causing the company's management to rethink their policies or making them vulnerable to a takeover bid because of the fall in the company's valuation ratio.

A second difference in ownership rights is that the owners of private firms are risk takers. If the company's performance declines so much that the company becomes bankrupt, then the shareholders see the value of their investment disappear and they become last in the line of creditors. Public sector agencies and enterprises generally cannot go bankrupt, though governments can change the management and limit financial aid if they so wish.

A third difference between public and private firms is that senior managers in private firms have ownership stakes in the enterprise. In large enterprises with a large and diverse body of shareholders, senior managers tend to have insignificant ownership stakes. Nevertheless, in order to ensure they align their interests with those of the shareholders they are given ownership rights as part of their remuneration package. Thus, property rights theory argues that public enterprises will be less efficient than private sector enterprises because of the lack of external pressure on managers to operate efficiently. If managers of the public enterprise are successful in running their enterprise efficiently, then they are personally unable to benefit (in the same way as private managers) from seeing their ownership stake increase in value.

INCENTIVES AND MONITORING

Managers in large private sector and public sector organizations are assumed to have a degree of managerial discretion. Thus, managers are presumed to maximize their own utility functions at the expense of owners, though the owners can offer managers incentives to limit the effects; in a successful firm, managers will have a large degree of independence as long as owners are content with the returns.

In the public sector, it is argued that senior managers have weak incentives to improve performance and face weak monitoring. Public sector managers will also be risk-averse because omissions are less easily recognized than major mistakes that lead to embarrassment for politicians and demands from voters for action. Thus, innovative activities and riskier investments are less likely to be undertaken by public enterprises unless they have political approval.

Another factor favouring public sector managers is that politicians tend to set imprecise objectives and to change them in midstream if it is in their political interest to do so. Failures to reach targets can be easily blamed on political interference,

Table 23.4 Sources of inefficiency in public enterprises

Indicator	Sources	Consequences
Internal inefficiency or low productivity	Low target rate of return Excessive rewards for input suppliers	Uses too many resources
Prices too low	Political control of price levels Low target rate of return Monopoly power not used	Excessive consumption Excessive use of resources Excessive investment
Inefficient price structures	Prices do not reflect marginal cost	Wrong output mix Excessive demand at peak
Overproduction	Prices too low	Excessive use of resources
Overinvestment	Low cost of capital Low risks	Investment diverted from more economic uses
Low profitability or losses	Prices are below costs	Lack of resources to invest and incentives to be efficient

Source Based on Shepherd (1982, p. 30)

preventing targets being achieved. However, politicians can overcome these problems by setting hard budget constraints and forcing managers to live within their budgets without any bailing out. However, their willingness to stick to hard budget constraints is always in doubt if the political consequences are serious.

Inefficiencies of public sector organizations

Public sector organizations, in a similar way to private enterprises, have had a whole range of criticisms levelled against them, generally leading to accusations of inefficient operation. Among these are that managers pursue power, status and maximization of budgets, are risk-averse and have little interest in minimizing the cost of supply. The workforce is highly unionized, wages are above free market levels and do not reward individual performance. The result is that public enterprises are assumed to be inefficient, charge prices that are low relative to costs, employ inefficient price structures and make little or no profit. These consequences are summarized in Table 23.4 and have been subject to some empirical investigation to see whether private enterprise is generally more efficient than public enterprise.

PUBLIC ENTERPRISE VERSUS PRIVATE ENTERPRISE PERFORMANCE COMPARED

The comparative performance of public and private enterprises has been investigated and produced inconclusive results. The results obtained are very much a function of performance at a particular point in time and the indicators used to measure performance, given the differing objectives of public and private enterprises. Typical indicators have included profitability, productivity and unit cost.

Millward (1982) in a major survey of the evidence concluded that there appeared to be no general ground for believing that managerial efficiency was lower in public firms. Vickers and Yarrow (1988) suggested, "that privately owned firms tend, on average, to be more internally efficient when competition in product markets is effective. ... However, when market power is significant, and particularly when company behaviour is subject to detailed regulation, there is little empirical justification for a general presumption in favour of either type of ownership, and case-by-case evaluation of the various trade-offs is therefore in order" (p. 40). Kay and Thompson (1985) also concluded: "Privatisation will tend to improve performance in a company only if supported by liberalisation; and if the two conflict, liberalisation is ideally to be preferred" (p. 25).

In the UK, comparative studies have been limited because public sector and private sector activity do not overlap. Pryke (1982) examined comparative performance in airlines and cross-channel ferries where there was public/private competition. He also looked at sales of gas and electricity appliances and examined productivity, profitability and output. He concluded that private firms tend to be more profitable and to exhibit greater internal efficiency than their public sector rivals.

Boardman and Vining (1989) surveying the empirical literature suggested that the literature provides only weak support for the superior performance of private enterprise. They argued that all the studies have been of natural monopolies and regulated monopolies and none has been set in competitive environments. They attempted to do this using the Fortune 500 of non-US industrial companies for 1983; these include 409 private companies, 23 mixed enterprises and 57 public corporations. They used a wide variety of statistics and found, for example, that for rate of return on equity private companies earned 4.3%, public enterprises −10% and mixed enterprises −14%. Their statistical tests showed that private companies were significantly more profitable than the other types and that mixed enterprises were less successful than state-owned enterprises.

Studies by Parker and Martin (1995) of privatized enterprises also failed to find improvements in performance in every case. In a number of cases they found significant improvements in performance came in the period before privatization; this was because the public enterprise needed to improve its performance to help its saleability to private owners. This suggests that privatization in the UK had the support of public sector managers and that, with the right objectives, the performance of public and private enterprise might be similar.

The overall conclusion from these studies is that the performance of an organization is as much a function of the competitive environment it operates in as its ownership status. Nevertheless, the general perception that public enterprises are less efficient than private sector enterprises has led to privatization and the introduction of competition in many sectors throughout the world.

Case Study 23.1   The postal service

Historically, the postal service has been seen as a public sector activity. Postal services worldwide have been organized either as government departments or as public corporations. However, in the 1990s a number of post offices were wholly or partially privatized, most notably in Holland, Germany and New Zealand. In the UK the Post Office was converted to a private company to give it greater commercial freedom, with the government owning all the shares.

The postal system has been a monopoly and operates a universal system in which letters of a particular weight are delivered throughout the country at the same price irrespective of the costs of collecting, transporting and delivering any single letter. When taken as a whole such large, integrated systems to collect and deliver mail can provide an efficient means of doing so. However, it would be perfectly possible to isolate certain postal flows (e.g., between large urban areas) and charge lower prices than the current universal charge. The consequences of competition would be to lower prices on profitable routes and increase prices on less profitable routes.

Because the postal system exists to do the same thing every day irrespective of how many letters are delivered the system's efficiency and profitability is very closely related to the volume of mail. In a well-organized and managed operation it is only when volume exceeds the capacity of the system that problems arise in meeting delivery deadlines. However, if the workforce becomes discontented, if there are insufficient staff and if capital equipment does not work, then delivery targets may not be met.

The postal system in the UK was initially in the public sector because of the need for the government to communicate with its citizens. It has also been said that it made it easier for government agents to intercept and read mail to ensure the safety of the monarch, government and state. The system has been in public ownership because of:

■ The need to cross-subsidize and to guarantee delivery to every household in the country.
■ The system has been best operated as a monopoly.
■ The system has generally been profitable because of its ability to raise postal charges from time to time.
■ Citizens like the universal system, but become dissatisfied when delays occur in mail delivery.

The industry is not a natural monopoly but a legal one, judged to deliver significant social benefits efficiently. However, that view has been questioned as a result of competition from the privatized Dutch and partially privatized German postal systems. With the loss of revenue because of substitute products, rising unit costs and growing difficulties in meeting delivery deadlines in London and other large cities, the Post Office has come to be viewed as bureaucratic and inefficient. It is also seen as not being innovative in seeking efficiency, with managers being more concerned to protect their own positions and departments.

Government policy has been to give the UK Post Office greater commercial freedom and at the same time remove its monopoly (i.e., to allow competition), while regulating the prices that can be charged. Thus, currently:

■ The Post Office is a private company that is state-owned.
■ The universal postal system still operates.
■ The price at which the postal monopoly is effective has been lowered.
■ The industry is now regulated by OfCom whose remit is for postal prices to increase by less than the rate of inflation.

- Licences are being issued to private firms to compete with the Post Office in collecting and delivering commercial mail and in bulk delivery.
- The closure of socially unnecessary local post offices

The government hopes the result will be a more efficient postal service with commercial freedom to compete with its continental rivals; this may mean higher prices and cuts in services. However, if the universal system of delivery is threatened, particularly in rural areas, then the voters may become dissatisfied and wish to see the system operate as a public monopoly even if it requires subsidies from a reluctant government.

CHAPTER SUMMARY

In this chapter we examined factors that influence the decision about whether some goods and services should be produced by government-owned organizations or not. In doing this we analysed:

- The main arguments that relate to areas of the economy where private enterprise fails to meet the expectations of society.
- The economic reasons that determine whether an activity should take place in public or private ownership. We found none. However, there are a number of economic factors that help shape the decision about whether to use public or private production including the nature of the good, externalities, monopoly and the consequences for income distribution.

In theory, there would appear to be no activities that could not be carried out by the private sector if the electorate and government choose to finance production and organize allocation that way.

REVIEW QUESTIONS

1 What do you understand by the term "market failure"? What are the main causes?
2 Explain the concept of externalities. What are the sources of social benefits and social costs? Why do markets misallocate resources in the presence of externalities?
3 Explain the concepts of excludability and rivalry in consumption and explain how they can be used to define private, public and merit goods.
4 What problems does the concept of "free riding" create for public sector organization?
5 What are the main economic arguments for certain goods and services to be produced in the public sector?
6 What factors determine whether a product or service produced by a public sector organization should be available "free" or at a cost-related price?
7 Why should public sector enterprises be less efficient than private sector enterprises?

8 Why are clearly specified property rights important in determining the performance of a public enterprise?

9 Is it possible to reconcile the concepts of "public" and "enterprise" in a single organization?

10 Explain why economists suggest that a bureaucrat's utility function can be summed into one that maximizes his budget. What are the implications or the size of the organization?

11 What objectives should a government set for a public enterprise selling a product or service with external benefits or costs and one selling a product where there are no externalities?

REFERENCES AND FURTHER READINGS

Boardman, A.F. and A.R. Vining (1989) Ownership and performance in competitive environments. *Journal of Law and Economics*, **32**, 1–33.

Caves, D. and Christiansen (1980) The relative efficiency of public and private enterprises in a competitive enterprise: The case of Canadian Railways. *Journal of Political Economy*, **88**, 958–986.

Coase, R.H. (1960) The problem of social cost. *Journal of Law and Economics*, **3**, 1–44.

Coase, R.H. (1974) The lighthouse in economics. *Journal of Law and Economics*, **17**, 357–376.

DTI (1999) *Post Office Reform: A World Class Service for the 21st Century* (Department of Trade and Industry Cmnd 4340). HMSO, London.

Duff, L. (1997) The economics of market failure. *The Economics of Governments and Markets* (Chapter 2). Longman, Harlow, UK.

Estrin, S. and D. de Meza (1990) The postal monopoly: A case study. *The Economic Review*, January, 2–7.

Kay, J. and D.J. Thompson (1985) Privatisation: A policy in search of a rationale? *Economic Journal*, **96**(1), 18–32.

Jones, T.T. and T.A.C. Cockerill (1985) Public sector enterprises. In: J.F. Pickering and T.A.C. Cockerill (eds), *Economic Analysis of the Firm*. Philip Allan, Oxford, UK.

Martin, S. and D. Parker (1997) *The Impact of Privatisation: Ownership and Corporate Performance*. Routledge, London.

Millward, R. (1982) The comparative performance of public and private enterprise. In: E. Roll (ed.) *The Mixed Economy*. Macmillan, London.

Millward, R., D. Parker, M. Sumner and N. Topham (1983) *Public Sector Economics*. Longman, London.

Millward, R. and D. Parker (1983) Public and private enterprise: Comparative behaviour and relative efficiency. In: R. Millward, D. Parker, M. Sumner and N. Topham (eds), *Public Sector Economics*. Longman, London.

Papworth, J. (2000) Take more care of yourself: Medical insurance and health cash plans. *The Guardian*, 5 August, p. 6.

Parker, D. and S. Martin (1995) The impact of privatisation on labour and total factor productivity. *Scottish Journal of Political Economy*, **42**(2), 201–220.

Pryke, R. (1981) *The Nationalised Industries: Policies and Performance since 1968*. Martin Robertson, Oxford, UK.

Shepherd, W.G. (1982) Public enterprises: Purposes and performance. In: W.T. Stanbury and F. Thompson (eds,) *Managing Public Enterprises*. Praeger, New York.

Stanbury, W.T. and F. Thompson (1982) *Managing Public Enterprises*. Praeger, New York.

Vickers, J. and G. Yarrow (1988) *Privatization: An Economic Analysis*. MIT Press, Cambridge, MA.

QUASI-MARKETS AND THE NON-MARKET PUBLIC SECTOR

CHAPTER OUTLINE

CHAPTER OBJECTIVES

This Chapter aims to examine decision making in the public sector where prices are not used to limit demand. At the end of this chapter you should be able to:

◆ Explain the difficulties for decision makers that arise from the absence of prices.

◆ Identify the shortcomings of public sector organizations and their operation in the interests of their employees and their failure to meet the needs of users.

◆ Explain the difficulties of measuring consumer preferences using collective decision-making processes.

◆ Outline the advantages and disadvantages of using of the exit, voice, loyalty framework to design quasi-markets.

◆ Explain the advantages and disadvantages of quasi-markets.

INTRODUCTION

The goods and services the public sector produces can be divided into two categories:

■ Those goods and services produced by public enterprises and sold at a price intended to cover costs.
■ And those goods and services produced by public agencies that are supplied to consumers either "free" or at nominal charges not intended to cover costs.

In this chapter we will examine the problems associated with the second category where price is not used and monopoly supply is the normal mode of production; this covers goods and services that produce significant social and private benefits. In the UK such activities include health care, education, personal social services, the police and the armed services.

The chapter will examine:

■ Decision making without prices.
■ Collective decision making and voting.
■ Consumer difficulties with public supply.
■ Quasi-markets.

DECISION MAKING IN THE ABSENCE OF PRICES

The managers of public enterprises that are financed by a direct grant by local or central government have no prices to guide them to find out what consumers expect of them or to measure the revenue products of the factors of production employed. With no market, consumers have no simple mechanism to express their preferences for particular goods and services or their satisfaction with what is actually supplied. Without knowledge of consumer preferences and demand functions the government may impose on the agencies simple supply and quality targets. The state education system has to provide "free" school education to all children between the age of 5 and 16. To add quality to quantity performance, schools must teach the national curriculum and targets are set, such as a certain proportion of pupils being able to read or the passing of examinations. Such targets tend to distort the allocation of resources, because fulfilling the targets becomes more important than fulfilling the true preferences of the ultimate consumers.

SUPPLY: ECONOMIC ANALYSIS OF BUREAUCRACY

Government organizations whose tasks are to provide un-priced goods and services are funded by government grants and tend to operate as monopoly suppliers. They tend to be organized as part of local or central government with politicians ultimately in control of setting objectives and assessing performance. Such organizational forms are part of the state bureaucracy and described as bureaucratic, which is taken to mean inefficient. The reasons are to be found in the objectives of senior bureaucrats, the monopoly relationship with government, excessive layers in the organization, narrowly compartmentalized jobs, the absence of consumer preferences and financial discipline.

There are several meanings of the term "bureaucracy" including its use as a term of abuse for any inefficient organization. A bureaucracy is a formal organization, characterized by a complex administrative hierarchy, specialization of skills and tasks and strongly prescribed limits on individual discretion captured in a set of rules (Jackson 1985, p. 5). Weber (1947) viewed bureaucracy as an "ideal" organization that maximizes the use of rational decision making and avoids inconsistent, unfair, biased and arbitrary decisions.

Despite this view of bureaucracy as an "ideal" managerial system, it has been criticized for a number of reasons:

- The rules become ends in themselves, resulting in goal displacement.
- The formal structure of bureaucracy ignores the informal structure within an organization and the conflict between the two.
- There is a conflict between those who have authority by position in the bureaucracy and those who have authority by technical competence.
- Bureaucracy, rather than being the servant of democracy and government, becomes the controller of what can be done.

The economic view of government servants is not to be seen as serving the public interest but as managers of private firms maximizing their own utility function; this might include power, prestige, income, security, loyalty and a desire to serve the public interest. Niskanen (1971) argued that all these variables in the utility function are a positive function of the size of the budget. Politicians set the budget so that the problem is one of bilateral monopoly where the size of the allocated budget is a function of the relative strength and bargaining power of the two parties.

A public sector agency can be viewed as a non-profit-making monopoly supplier providing a set of services to the government (and ultimately to citizen consumers) in return for an annual budget. The agency also holds information not available to those determining the budget and buying the services. The buyer, or budget setter, may know little of the supplier's cost functions or of alternative sources of supply. Niskanen's model is similar to that of Williamson's in that managers of private firms and public sector agencies have the discretion to allocate resources to activities that increase their personal utility.

Determination of the budget can be analysed in terms of the marginal benefit and marginal cost curves illustrated in Figure 24.1. In the diagram the marginal benefits of the agency's work are shown by the marginal benefit curve (MB); this is the demand curve for the agency's output (it is assumed the benefits decline with increasing size or output). The marginal cost of supply is represented by the marginal cost curve (MC) which is assumed to increase with size. If the buyer were trying to

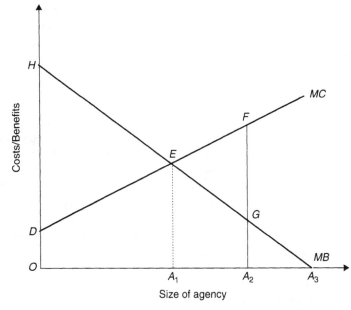

Figure 24.1   Economics of bureaucracy

equate marginal benefits with marginal cost, the equilibrium size of the agency would be at OA_1. However, the agency will be able to push the budget to the point where total benefits are equal to total costs (i.e., to agency size OA_2, where $ODFA_2$ is equal to $OHGA_2$). If the budget is pushed to OA_3 where marginal benefits from the activity are zero, then total cost would exceed total benefit. The agency is able to push the budget to OA_2 because it has information not available to the purchasing body about the relationship between inputs and outputs. The cost function might also be inflated because of X-inefficiency in the agency.

DEMAND: MERIT AND PUBLIC GOODS

Traditionally, the economist has assumed that the "consumer is king". This assertion applies to private goods where the consumer expresses his own preferences in the market and buys from those producers who best meet his preferences and offer value for money. If the consumer makes a mistaken decision and the good does not provide the expected benefit, then the consumer can be described as a dissatisfied one and need not purchase that producer's product again. Thus, in a conventional market the consumer is able to influence the behaviour of suppliers by taking his custom elsewhere.

Merit goods provide private and public benefits, and the government may take the view that consumers will not purchase sufficient units of the good or service if left to express their own preferences. To ensure the consumer consumes the "right" quantity the government may override the preferences of individuals and try to ensure they consume more that they would have in a private market. The way in which this might be done is to make the service available "free of charge" and leave the choice of how much to consume to the individual or to compel individuals to consume.

However, the government has to decide how much to supply whichever method is used, given that consumer preferences and willingness to buy will not determine the outcome. Likewise, goods that are characterized by an inability to exclude people from consuming them generate similar problems because it is not in the interests of individuals to reveal their preferences, leaving the government to decide the level of supply.

COLLECTIVE DECISION MAKING

If society does not trust the market to determine the quantity demanded and supplied of a merit or public good, then alternative decision-making mechanisms have to be utilized to determine the level of output. The government may seek to find consumer preferences through collective decision methods; this generally means making use of the political system and decisions being made by politicians elected by the community. Alternatively, people coming together on a voluntary basis and making voluntary contributions could determine the level of supply. However, the problem of **free riders** remains (i.e., individuals who can use the supply without paying, unless compelled to do so).

Voting systems

In the absence of markets, society can express its preferences through community voting. One way in which collective decisions might be made is by holding referenda or public meetings (in small communities) to determine the level of supply. Another way is to utilize the institutions of a representative democracy rather than community votes. For example, although Switzerland is a parliamentary democracy it also allows a referendum on any proposed law or policy to be held if 50,000 citizens request it and initiates legislation if 100,000 citizens sign a petition.

Direct voting

If a community wishes to decide whether to install public lighting in its streets, then a simple vote might be held to decide the outcome. However, before doing so the community has to decide the rules. Besides deciding who is eligible to vote it is also necessary to decide whether a simple majority of those voting will be sufficient to determine the outcome or whether a more substantial majority should be required. For example, it might be specified that all decisions have to be unanimous or that 75% of those voting must be in favour before a proposition is accepted. Since the whole

Table 24.1   Voter preferences for three levels of expenditure

Voter	Preference set 1	Voter	Preference set 2
A	$L > M > H$	A	$L > M > H$
B	$H > M > L$	B	$M > L > H$
C	$M > H > L$	C	$L > H > M$

Voting outcome	Voting outcome
M versus H: M wins 2 : 1	H versus M: H wins
M versus L: M wins 2 : 1	M versus L: M wins
Therefore, $H > L$ (this is confirmed in vote)	Therefore, $H > L$ (but a majority also votes)
H versus L: H wins 2 : 1	H versus L: L wins
M is first preference	Outcome indeterminate

Source Author

community will pay to implement such decisions there should, it is argued, be a significant and not just a bare majority in favour.

Simple questions put to the vote do not allow individuals to express their preferences fully or their total willingness to pay: one individual may be very keen on public lighting while others are less keen; some will favour a large number of high-quality lights whereas others will favour a minimalist system. To achieve a greater expression of preferences a whole range of options would have to be considered and voted on; this creates problems for voting systems.

Let us assume that there are three voting members of a community and three alternative levels of expenditure. The preferences of the three voters (A, B and C) between three levels of expenditure (namely, high H, medium M, and low L) are set out in Table 24.1. The decision rule is that the community will undertake the option approved by a simple majority.

In preference set 1, each individual is assumed to have an ordered preference set (i.e., not preferring two options like high and low spending to the medium level). Thus, individual A prefers the lowest level of spending to the medium and higher levels, individual B prefers a high level of spending to medium and low levels and individual C prefers a medium level to high or low spending.

The objective is to determine the community's choice of spending level by voting between pairs of options until one is clearly preferred. If medium versus high spending is voted on first, then medium spending wins by two votes to one. If medium versus low spending is voted on next, then medium defeats low by two votes to one. Thus, medium has defeated the other two options and is chosen. If a third vote were taken between the remaining pair, then high defeats low by two votes to one. Thus, the community's preference order is medium, high and low levels of spending.

In preference set 2, one individual (C) prefers the extremes (i.e., both low and high options are preferred to the medium one). If medium versus high spending is voted on first, then high spending wins by two votes to one. If medium versus low spending is voted on next, then medium defeats low by two votes to one. Thus, we should be able to infer that the group would prefer high to low spending. However, if a vote were held between high and low spending, then the result would favour low spending. Thus, in this case voting produces an inconsistent set of preferences for the community and the outcome would depend on the order in which the votes are taken: if high versus low were voted first, low would win; if medium versus low followed, then medium would be the preferred outcome. See Brown and Jackson (1990) for a more extensive discussion of Arrow's impossibility theorem, which is beyond the scope of this book.

Representative democracy

In democratic countries the political system operates by selecting representatives of parties, rather than having direct votes to determine programme outcomes. Downs (1957) explored the economic consequences of democracy and found that it poorly reflected the preferences of society as a whole and tended to favour producer groups.

The model assumes that the citizen-voters of a community choose elected representatives whose spending plans and political programmes they most approve of or are most closely aligned to their preferences. Therefore, citizens vote for politicians who will bring them the greatest level of utility. Political parties exist to bring together politicians who offer the community policies that they believe will win them office. Politicians are vote maximizers and are therefore motivated to win office. They have to put forward policies they believe will win approval from a majority of the voters.

If the defining issue between two political parties is the level of public spending, then a distribution map of voter intentions could be constructed as in Figure 24.2. In Figure 24.2(a) the voters are evenly distributed around the medium level of public spending, whereas in Figure 24.2(b) voters are distributed in a skewed way around a modal level of public spending, which that is higher than in Figure 24.2(a).

Let us assume that there are two political parties, one favouring lower public spending and the other higher public spending. To win a majority for its candidate, the low spending party has to increase its spending plans until its policies reflect the preferences of a majority of voters. To win a majority the high spending party has to reduce its spending plans until it too has the support of a majority of voters. Thus, the key to winning a majority is the attitude of the median voters: Figure 24.2(a) shows the winning party must satisfy those voters who favour public spending of OS_A and Figure 24.2(b) shows they must satisfy those that favour spending OS_B. Thus, for either party to achieve a minimum majority it must win the vote of the median voter (i.e., the middle voter) in the distribution. As a consequence, Downs argues, parties wishing to win office in a two party system will strive to meet the preferences of the median voter and all other voters will see their preferences only partially fulfilled. For other voters public spending is either too high or too low. Downs further argues that failure to appeal to the middle ground in a two-party system will mean exclusion from office. Thus, if the party that favours higher spending offers a spending level of S_B in Figure 24.2(a), then it will fail to win a majority, while in Figure 24.2(b) it would win a majority. Thus, the voting system is an extremely crude method of determining the level of supply of public and merit goods.

Downs also argues that such a system will tend to favour producer or supplier groups rather than consumer groups (e.g., farmers and defence suppliers rather than

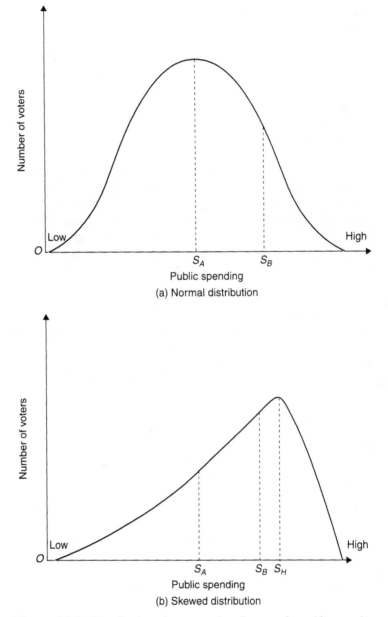

Figure 24.2 Distribution of voters and preferences for public spending

consumers of food). This outcome is explained by the degree of expected net gain or loss of individual voters. The average voter gains or loses little by marginal changes in the supply of public or merit goods. A small number of voters stand to lose or gain significantly from policy shifts. Therefore, they are strongly motivated to influence the political outcome in their favour and to convince politicians and voters of the worthiness of their cause. They may have significant resources to spend on forming pressure groups, supporting political parties and propagating their viewpoint. Large groups in which individual gains are small will be unable to attract mass resources to form pressure groups to influence the outcome. The average voter is also poorly informed and can be influenced by the information made available by special interest groups. Thus, there is a general tendency to oversupply special interest groups and to undersupply general interest public and merit goods.

This marketplace model of politics has been subject to much criticism. Some argue that the pursuit of personal utility is a naive specification for both voters and politicians. Both are motivated by wider concerns about what is good for the community and in the public interest. Politicians do not know the precise preferences of voters and cannot identify the median voter. In addition, some politicians base their policies on principles and ideology, seeing their role as winning voters to their cause rather than modifying their policies in favour of the median voter. Thus, a campaigning party may be able to shift the distribution of voters in their favour rather than moving to the current preferences of the median voter. Figure 24.2 shows a party favouring high public spending might shift the distribution of voters from that shown in Figure 24.2(a) to that shown in Figure 24.2(b).

The undersupply of public goods may also result if voters favour tax cuts, lower public spending and private benefits over higher taxes, higher public spending and the greater supply of public and merit goods. This problem was identified by Galbraith (1958) in his book *The Affluent Society*, in which he argued that there was a growing disparity in the supply of private and public goods, on the one hand, and a contrast between private affluence and public squalor, on the other.

EXIT, VOICE, LOYALTY

Hirschman (1970) argued that there are more direct ways that citizen-consumers can influence the supply of public and merit goods than by participating in the political voting process. This framework he termed "exit, voice and loyalty": the forces at work in conventional markets. In the markets for private goods, consumers influence the decisions made by suppliers by:

- Exiting (i.e., ceasing to consume a particular firm's product, so that the quantity purchased declines).
- Loyalty (i.e., by continuing to consume a particular firm's product they express their continued satisfaction and loyalty to the good).
- Voice (i.e., by making complaints to the producers about shortcomings in the quality of their products or delivery failure). However, in markets the ultimate sanction of exit is available.

Hirschman (1970), writing in the context of the USA, argued that citizen-voters had similar options available to them as private consumers. Since many public and merit goods are supplied by local political entities a satisfied citizen-consumer remains a loyal resident, while dissatisfied ones can move to another area or voice their discontent. The ability to leave one authority for another does however depend on the ability to meet the transaction costs of the exit decision.

In the UK, parents seeking the best state education for their children seek out the best schools and try to live in their catchment areas. The alternative to moving house may be to purchase private education. Those citizens unable to exit have to remain and accept the quality of service offered, complain to the supply agency or use their vote to bring political change. While the exit–voice–loyalty framework has a basic logic and can work for local services, it is difficult to see it applying at the national level. Discontent with the defence policies of the state cannot easily be avoided by moving to another country because there are many barriers preventing the mobility of people between countries.

CONSUMER DIFFICULTIES WITH PUBLIC SUPPLY

If goods and services are provided "free" at the point of consumption, then there will always be a tendency for demand to exceed supply. In addition, the marginal cost of supply will exceed the marginal benefits after a certain level of supply, so that the budget to meet the unconstrained demand would be significantly greater than the community would be willing to provide. Thus, to bring demand into line with supply, various rationing criteria have to be used; these include limiting service, so that each individual is entitled to the same amount per time period (e.g., individuals may have an entitlement to visit their doctor twice per year). However, some people will not use their entitlement, while others will want more visits. An alternative is to make visits to the doctor only available to those who pass a sickness test. While this will not work for initial visits to a general practitioner it can work for referral to hospitals where the doctor decides who needs further treatment. Therefore, rationing has to be based on some characteristic of the individual, such as age, health, disability and lack of income.

Another cause of consumer dissatisfaction with public services arises where the service does not meet the consumer's expectations. Thus, consumers become discontented and may seek to complain to the supplier organization or to their political representative. In addition, some consumers may be dissatisfied because they may not be fully aware of services available to them.

It has been argued that public sector agencies have no interest in making the availability of their services known to potential and eligible consumers because more users would put even more pressure on their limited resources; this is partly a failure of the political system to fund adequate budgets in line with the preferences of citizens to consume these services and partly the inadequacy of the management of the organization in effectively using its budget. An agency may have no incentive to meet the demands placed on it or to make the most effective use of its resources. The agency may be encouraged in such behaviour by the requirement to demonstrate to its political masters the need for a larger budget.

Politicians may view the problem of lack of supply as the result of the inefficient use of resources by the agency. The suppliers of funds may view the agency as inefficient, disinterested in its clients or customers and more interested in pursuing the self-interest of its managers and employees. To bring about more efficient operation, changed work practices and better use of facilities, the politicians or budget suppliers have a number of options. First, they can use budgetary pressure to force the managers to bring about more efficient operations. Second, politicians can attempt to get efficiency improvements with a given budget by setting targets, with penalties if they are not met. The ultimate penalty would be a change of management, in much the same way as a falling share price brings change in private enterprises. Third, politicians can seek solutions through changing the structures and organizations responsible for the service within the public sector. Such measures might include the use of competitive bidding to find the public (or possibly private) supplier who will meet the requirements for the service at minimum cost. Failure to win a contract might result in the agency ceasing to exist. In addition, the privatization of the agency could also be considered (see Young 1977).

Increasing consumer pressures

From the consumer viewpoint, organizational failure means a lack of responsiveness to consumer needs and the delivery of a low-quality but expensive service, which is controlled by professionals who believe they know best what the consumer wants and when they can have it. To get away from the approach where the supplier knows best to one where consumers can influence the nature of supply, several approaches (short of private markets) have been suggested.

First, service standards can be established so that consumers know what to expect from their supplier. Periodic, evaluative information about the supplier can then be published to show whether targets have or have not been met. This information can also be published in league tables so that the relative performance of agencies can be compared. Such standards and the use of league tables may change the behaviour of the supplier organization and help the consumer to make informed choices, but only if they are able to change suppliers. Where consumers are unable to exit or switch to a different supplier, they are left knowing they receive lower quality services than available elsewhere, but can only use the voice option to bring change. Knowing you attend the worst school, university or hospital does little to help consumer satisfaction if you cannot switch to a superior supplier. However, the targets and standards set may not be very meaningful and may undermine the delivery of services not included in the targets.

Second, it might be possible to increase the availability of voice channels to ensure closer links between consumers and producers, giving the producer a clearer under-standing of what the consumer wants from a public service; this is usually achieved by establishing consumer councils of one kind or another. Their effectiveness depends on the people appointed or elected to them and in the confidence the citizen-consumer has in them to influence managers to bring about improvements in service.

Third, it might also be possible to create structures that enable consumers to move from one public sector supplier to another, thereby creating more consumer pressure on the producer. Increasing the diversity of supply may be an option for some services, but will be a function of the size of the community and the efficient size of supply units. In large cities it may be possible to have competing suppliers but not in rural or less sparsely populated areas.

Fourth, it might be possible to decentralize political decision making, facilitating the movement of citizen-consumers between jurisdictions; this enables different budgetary authorities and supply agencies to use different production and organizational structures and methods, rather than have a unified structure throughout the country.

Fifth, it might be possible to make greater use of market-type mechanisms, such as competition between suppliers, and redistribute purchasing power toward citizen-consumers, so that they have greater influence over the producer. Such solutions are termed "quasi", or "internal", markets. We will examine them next.

THEORY OF QUASI, OR INTERNAL, MARKETS

Quasi-markets are mechanisms to help improve managerial decision making and organizational efficiency in the public sector. They are markets because they break down a single monopolistic supplier into competitive units and resources that follow consumer use of the service. They are described as "quasi" because, despite trying to generate market-like contracts between suppliers and customers, there are significant differences.

On the supply side there are multiple providers, but these are not necessarily financially independent, with profit and loss accounts, nor do they set out to maximize profit. Although it is anticipated that suppliers will be state-owned, they could be run by voluntary organizations, or even be privately owned: for example, each hospital or school can become an independent supplier in a quasi-market for health or education.

On the demand side, although the aim is to shift some market power toward consumers, it does not necessarily provide them with monetary purchasing power. In practice, although money transfers follow the consumer, decisions as to where the money is to be spent may be made by the individual or by an intermediary. Alternatively, consumers may be given purchasing power in the form of vouchers that can be spent, for example, on health or education. A school voucher might be worth £2,000 to be spent only at registered schools. If the entry price were greater than the value of the voucher, then consumers would have to find the difference from their own resources, thereby disadvantaging pupils from poorer homes. The alternative is to fix the price, but use other means to ration places at popular schools.

Thus, in a quasi-market, multiple suppliers compete for contracts to supply goods and services to individuals or groups of consumers who have some kind of purchasing power limited by the state. Buyers have to live with a budget constraint, while suppliers have to get revenue or budget transfers from buyer groups to finance their operations (Le Grand and Bartlett 1993, p. 10). Therefore, for quasi-markets to deliver an improved service, there must be real competition between suppliers; each buyer must have a choice between alternative suppliers and suppliers must be allowed to fail or leave the market.

For organizations that have never previously costed individual services there are real initial difficulties in establishing cost-based prices that will guide consumer choice. The setting of such prices requires the establishment of an accounting system that will collect the necessary information and the establishment of criteria to allocate fixed costs. In a market, unsuccessful suppliers who cannot earn sufficient revenue to cover costs leave the market, but in the public sector it may be politically difficult to close a local hospital or school despite it being unable to live within its budget. However, resources do not necessarily leave the market for they can be acquired and utilized by other more efficient suppliers. If this is not an option, then failing suppliers may well be subsidized, weakening the effectiveness of the quasi-market.

Contracts between a purchaser group and a hospital, for example, may be based on a price per service actually provided, and buyers may be able to select from a price list. The total revenue earned by the supplier will then be a function of price and the number of services provided. If individual consumers are responsible for payment, then this system will probably evolve toward a more competitive structure. Where the demand for services is a collective one, contracts may be less strongly detailed and merely promise to supply all the specified services for a given period of time. Thus, a contract will not specify the number of appendicitis operations to be carried out in one year but that all patients having that problem will be treated.

Another important element in the functioning of markets and contracts is the availability of information. Although a buyer might have signed a contract with a hospital, how does he know that the supplier has provided the quality of services specified in the contract and that all the promised resources have been used; this is a problem of information asymmetry and moral hazard. In addition, there may also be problems of adverse selection where suppliers have information not available to the buyers. To overcome such problems all suppliers have to provide standard information in the same form to all buyers. Whether the published information is what buyers require to make more informed decisions is another matter.

In a planned system the costs of using the market are avoided. If buyers and sellers agree to do business by contract, then monitoring and transaction costs will be incurred. Suppliers incur transaction costs as they try to generate cost information to set prices; this may require the employment of cost accountants and managerial staff not previously needed. More managers may be needed to ensure that staff undertake the tasks assigned to them and that services are kept within budget. Buyers have to search for information and ensure that the contract delivers all the services purchased. Clearly, there are transaction costs that have to be incurred if quasi-markets are to work, just as there are similar costs incurred in a planning system to ensure a balance between demand and supply.

Expected benefits and alternatives

Quasi-markets are expected to maximize output from given resources, deliver efficient production and minimize the costs of a given volume and quality of service. Simple, low costs may mean a cheap and low-quality service that does not deliver the quality of service expected by the consumers. Likewise, simple, high costs may also fail to deliver the quantity and quality of service required. Costs may be high because too many resources are employed and are utilized inefficiently. A quasi-market is expected to deliver productive efficiency because only efficient suppliers survive in a market environment.

Quasi-markets are also expected to deliver greater responsiveness to consumer needs and to be fair to all consumers. One of the problems of medical care is that some people have more illnesses than others, and in education some children have learning disabilities and all have different abilities. Thus, some consumers are going to be more costly to care for or to educate than others. If this means that the more expensive consumers are pushed to the back of the queue in favour of low-cost customers, then in the social context that would be deemed to be unfair. This effect will be accentuated if all consumers are allocated a given notional cash sum to spend on health or education; this would be unfair to those making more frequent use of the service and/or in need of expensive care, obliging them to top up their voucher from their own resources. If the system moves from meeting all needs to only meeting funded consumption, then some individuals will not get the care the old system delivered.

The alternative to a quasi-market is to move toward a free market in which consumers make their own provision for consuming merit goods. On the demand side, particularly in the area of health, individuals purchase insurance because of the uncertainty of illness, but experience in countries that use such a system suggests that there are individuals who cannot afford or choose not to afford health insurance and individuals who because of their health problems are uninsurable.

For other merit goods, it is perfectly possible to charge for consumption and to exclude those unable to pay. The question then becomes one of whether exclusion of some consumers deprives the community of significant social benefits and of the consequences for those individuals excluded. Consider, for example, whether there should be charges for entering museums. In the UK there has been a debate about whether national museums that had imposed charges in the 1980s should be available free. The decision was taken in 2001 that entry should be free because they provide significant benefits to those excluded and to the community in general. However, many museums continue to charge for entry.

However, museums are a key component of the leisure and tourism industry as well as of the education industry. Some museums are privately owned and primarily intend to entertain and inform, whereas others are research institutions whose primary purpose is to collect, preserve and display artefacts of the past, to educate and to inform current generations. The latter type of museum provides social benefits and receives government funding whereas the former depends on entry fees and voluntary donations.

The ability of an agency to maximize its budget may be limited if the government alters its position from a monopolist to a competitor supplier and contests are held to win the right to supply. The problem with contests is that there are costs in organizing them and there may be no other supplier with the necessary skills other than the existing agency. Another alternative is to alter payment systems to reward success and to tie the interests of the managers to those of the government.

Case Study 24.1 Health reform: the quasi-market approach

The National Health Service (NHS) was established in the UK in 1948. It was created as part of the Ministry of Health and block-funded by the central government, though notionally a proportion of national insurance payments were termed health contributions. It was both a planning and delivery organization, intended to provide appropriate health care to every citizen "free" at point of use. In practice, it was not possible to meet all health care needs as people's expectations of the service increased as a result of rising prosperity and longer lifespans. Instead, health care was rationed, not by ability to pay but primarily on the basis of medical need and in part by where the individual lived. In 1998–1999, spending on the NHS was £49bn, or 6% of GDP, with the service employing nearly 1 million people; this was equivalent to £790 per person or £1,895 per family. The government now intends to increase the rate of growth of health spending until it is equivalent to the European average.

Although centrally controlled and bureaucratic, the NHS relies on the dedication and professionalism of medical and other staff to meet the urgent needs of patients immediately and less urgent needs more slowly. However, it offers few positive incentives to staff to do a better job for patients and, probably, has some disincentives that discourage staff at all levels of giving of their best. The system was placed under tight financial constraints in the 1980s and 1990s because of government commitment to restrain and control public spending. At the same time, demands on the service were increasing at a rate higher than resources, leading to a deterioration in the quality of the service, as measured by waiting lists.

These were the problems the Conservative Government of 1979 decided to solve, not by privatizing health care and introducing a free market, but by introducing an internal market, or quasi-market (DoH 1989). The objective was to achieve greater efficiency, cost-effectiveness and more patient care from a given budget. By devolving decision making to local units and breaking down the hierarchical structure of the NHS, it was believed it would be possible to increase patient choice and make suppliers more responsive to patient needs. The changes included:

- Delegation of decision making to make the NHS responsive to patient needs.
- Creation of NHS hospital trusts with greater managerial discretion.
- Funding to follow patients.
- Reduction of waiting times and improvement in the quality of service.
- General practitioners able to have own budgets.
- Reduction in size of managerial bodies.
- Management by committee.
- Reform on "business lines".
- Audit of medical practices to ensure quality and value for money.

In this new market structure, purchasers were not individual patients but district health authorities or general practitioner fundholders. The former received an annual cash allocation based on population and the social characteristics of their population. They made "contracts" with providers in the public sector. The latter were to be allowed to opt to have their own budgets. They were funded on a per capita basis to purchase hospital services for patients and provide a wide range of their own services. The per capita funding did not recognize that patients' health needs vary with their age and their social circumstances. As a result, there was concern that those patients who cost a fundholder more than the annual grant would be refused care and forced to move to a less financially concerned general practitioner or even go without care.

The suppliers in the new market were to be mini-businesses that would have to cover their costs from contracts with purchasers. The main suppliers were to be self-governing trusts outside of district health authority control. The self-governing trusts would be independent businesses run by boards of directors. They would own their own assets, have a capital structure and be expected to cover costs including a 6% return on assets employed.

The link between buyers and sellers would be contractual. Under the old system, patients were automatically referred to their local hospital, unless a doctor chose to send them to see a particular consultant or to attend a specialized hospital. Contracts can take many forms but in the new market there were two main types: block contracts that relate funding to a level of capacity or availability of services and cost and volume contracts that specify a baseline level of activity beyond which funding is on a cost per case basis. These contracts tend to be incomplete because they are not fully specified (e.g., individual services are neither costed nor priced). Incomplete contracts can lead both to disputes between the two parties about the meaning of the contract and whether its terms have been fulfilled and to opportunistic behaviour by the supplier. Contentment with the contract depends on both sides being fully informed and the buyer being assured and informed that the purchased services are being delivered.

In time it was expected that suppliers would begin to understand and identify their cost functions and that prices for individual services would be developed, so that competition between suppliers would be based on price, not just on location or reputation. Ellwood (1996), after studying pricing and costing in the West Midlands, concluded that cost-based pricing had failed to provide the appropriate signals to purchasers in the first five years of the internal market. Prices neither accurately reflected resources employed nor enabled valid price comparisons to be made. Services tended to be heterogeneous, and there were high transaction costs associated with compiling costs and prices; this resulted in purchasers favouring block-style contracts. In addition, although there were a large number of suppliers throughout the country, in practice there were very few suppliers for purchasers to negotiate with unless patients were prepared to travel greater distances for hospital treatment.

A change of government ended the internal market experiment, although the purchaser–supplier divide was maintained and developed. The hospital trusts survived, though many merged to make them more economic in terms of size and cost-effective delivery. The demand side was returned to district health authorities with GP fundholders being abolished. The trusts were further changed with the creation of primary care trusts, which now commission health care rather than make contracts. The effect of the change was to reduce the number of commissioning bodies from 1,300 to 500.

Whether the internal market met the expectations of its originators is doubtful. It led to considerable transaction and management costs in setting up the new system, which were not offset by greater efficiency in producing services. The National Audit Office estimated that administration in all its guises accounted for 6% of NHS spending before the reforms and 10.5% after (The Economist, 23 March 1996). Ellwood (1996) concluded that, "there is little direct evidence which establishes definitively that efficiency has improved, although indirect evidence suggests that the market conditions are being put in place which provide the potential for efficiency gains in the future" and further that, "the emerging NHS market does not resemble the model espoused on the introduction of the internal market, that is, purchasers observing the prices charged by several providers for a particular product and selecting the lowest price provider as the one the with whom the purchaser will agree a contract'' (p. 300).

The main criticism of the system is that it undermined the founding principles of the NHS of universal care, based on need and not ability to pay. When cash is placed before health care needs the NHS ceases to be a social service or provider of merit good and becomes a private or market good. Those who believed private markets do not work were happy for the quasi-market experiment to fail, whereas supporters argued that the trial was curtailed too soon and that choice and ability to pay was never devolved to the patient, but retained by professionals. The impact of the quasi-market experiment was minimal because of the retention of central government control and because the experiment was based on an inadequate understanding of professional and managerial motivation.

CHAPTER SUMMARY

In this chapter we examined decision making in public sector organizations where prices are not used to ration consumption. In doing this we analysed:

- Collective decision-making procedures and found them to be imperfect ways for consumer-voters to express their preferences.
- The notion that public sector organizations serve producer rather than consumer interests.
- Proposals to utilize quasi-market procedures to increase the importance of the consumer in decision making.
- The alternative of a free market with independent buyers and private suppliers, but this solution has not had the support of the electorate.
- The reform of the health service to meet the rising expectations of consumers and users, which is an ongoing debate that sits at the very centre of the political agenda.

REVIEW QUESTIONS

1 What difficulties do consumers face in influencing the level and quality of the supply of merit and public goods?
2 Why do communities choose not to sell merit goods and public goods at a price to consumers?
3 What are the shortcomings of referenda in determining the quality and level of supply of merit and public goods?
4 Appraise critically the assumption of voters and politicians seeking to maximize their utility in the political marketplace.
5 Why does representative democracy fail to identify citizen-consumer preferences?
6 Why does representative democracy favour producer groups rather than consumers?
7 Appraise critically the exit–voice–loyalty approach of consumers putting pressure on public agencies to improve the supply of public and merit goods.

8 What problems does a grant-funded agency face when its consumers do not pay for its services?
9 Explain the principles of quasi-markets. Evaluate their success or failure in the NHS.
10 Find out how the quasi-market works in higher education. Would it be more efficient for each university and college to set a fee for each separate course which more closely reflected the costs of supply?

REFERENCES AND FURTHER READING

Brown, C. and P.M. Jackson (1990) *Public Sector Economics* (4th edn). Blackwell, Oxford, UK.

Chalkley, M. and J.M. Malcomson (1996) Competition in NHS quasi-markets. *Oxford Review of Economic Policy*, **12**(4), 89–99.

DoH (1989) *Working for Patients* (Department of Health Cm 555). HMSO, London.

DoH (1997) *A Modern and Dependable NHS for the Next Century* (Department of Health). HMSO, London.

Downs, A. (1957) *Economic Theory of Democracy*. Harper & Row, New York.

Duff, L. (1997) *The Economics of Government and Markets*. Longman, Harlow, UK.

Economist, The (23 March 1996) GP fundholding: Too little change, p. 50.

Ellwood, S. (1996) Pricing services in the UK NHS. *Financial Accountability and Management*, **12**(4), 281–301.

Ferlie, E. (1992) The creation and evolution of quasi-markets in the public sector: A problem for strategic management. *Strategic Management Journal*, **13**, 79–97.

Galbraith, J.K. (1958) *The Affluent Society*. Hamish Hamilton, London.

Hirschman, A.O. (1970) *Exit, Voice and Loyalty*. Harvard University Press, Cambridge, MA.

Jackson, P.M. (1982) *The Political Economy of Bureaucracy*. Philip Allan, Deddington, Oxford, UK.

Le Grand, J. (1991) Quasi markets and social policy. *Economic Journal*, **101**, 1256–1267.

Le Grand, J. and W. Bartlett (1993) *Quasi-Markets and Social Policy*. Macmillan, London.

Niskanen, W.A. (1971) *Bureaucracy: Servant or Master*. Institute of Economic Affairs, London.

Robinson, R. (1995) Are the NHS reforms working? *Economic Review*, November.

Tulloch, G. (1976) *The Vote Motive*. Institute of Economic Affairs, London.

Wanless, D. (2002) *Securing Our Future Health: Taking a Long Term View*. HM Treasury, London.

Weber, M. (1947) *The Theory of Economic and Social Organization*. Free Press, New York.

Young, D.R (1977) Consumer problems in the public sector. *Journal of Consumer Policy*, **1**(3), 205–225.

COST–BENEFIT ANALYSIS

CHAPTER OUTLINE

CHAPTER OBJECTIVES

This chapter aims to examine investment appraisal in the public sector and the difficulties involved in measuring social costs and benefits where there are no prices. At the end of this chapter you should be able to:

◆ Elucidate the differences between public and private investment.

◆ Identify the components of a cost–benefit analysis.

◆ Explain the ways in which social costs and benefits are estimated.

◆ Outline the difficulties and shortcomings of measuring social costs and benefits.

◆ Explain the different approaches to measuring a discount rate.

◆ Outline and explain the difficulties encountered in undertaking cost–benefit analysis.

INTRODUCTION

Investment appraisal in the public sector is in principle no different to that in the private sector. In that sense the analysis in Chapter 12 of the methods of investment appraisal in the private sector is equally relevant in the public sector. The differences arise with respect to the measurement of benefits and costs and the appropriate discount rate to use. Therefore, in this chapter cost–benefit analysis will be explored as a scheme of appraisal and measurement appropriate to the public sector and for firms concerned with the wider social impact of their investment decisions. Cost–benefit analysis is not just confined to investment decisions, it can be used to measure the impact, for example, of legislative changes. Therefore, it is a method of looking at the wider social impact of decisions, looking at the social and not just the private impact of expenditure. The difference lies in the approach to measurement and the benefits and costs to be measured.

PUBLIC AND PRIVATE INVESTMENT

The differences between private and public investment appraisal are shown in Table 25.1. The private firm only considers private revenues and costs, which are measured using market prices and accounting costs. Cost–benefit analysis measures social benefits and costs, using shadow prices that represent social value and social opportunity costs. The discount rate is the cost of capital for the private firm but the social rate of discount for a public organization. The importance of the technique lies in the need to appraise the use of public funds for investment to ensure that resources are being effectively used. Given the emphasis on measuring wider social benefits, it is important to clearly identify the costs and benefits that are to be counted. In a similar manner to private investment appraisal, cost–benefit analysis tries to measure in monetary terms as many of the social benefits and costs as possible; this allows the

Table 25.1 Comparison of public and private investment

Private investment		Public Investment	
Concept	Measure	Concept	Measure
Revenue	Market prices	Benefits	Social + Shadow prices
Expenditure	Accounting costs	Costs	Social opportunity costs
Discount rate	Cost of capital to firm or shareholder	Discount rate	Social discount rate
Test of viability	Accept if financial surplus or if NPV is positive	Test of viability	Accept if there is a social surplus or if NPV is positive

Source Author

addition of dated benefits and costs and the use of discounting procedures to obtain a net present value for all projects. The objective for a private firm is to maximize the net present value of profits or net cash flow, while the public sector will wish to maximize the net present value of net social benefits because it wishes to increase the economic welfare of society as a whole.

THEORETICAL FOUNDATIONS OF COST–BENEFIT ANALYSIS

Welfare criteria

The theory of cost–benefit analysis is based on welfare economics. Underlying welfare economics is a series of value judgements that are believed to be widely acceptable by society and the notion of compensation tests. Government activity in the economy is based on a belief that the actions it takes are for the benefit of society as a whole. Society is seen as a collective entity. However, society actually consists of individuals, and government policy changes may benefit some individuals, but impose losses on others. The widely acceptable value judgements in welfare economics are that individuals are the best judges of their own welfare, and that in evaluating the consequences of policy decisions all individuals should be counted. It is also assumed that individuals evaluate their gains or losses independently of what happens to any other individual. In evaluating a net change, it is assumed that if one person is made better off and no one is worse off, then the economic welfare of society is presumed to have increased. Such a situation where everyone gains is rare; the more usual situation is where some people gain and some lose. The problem is how to compare the gains of some against the losses of others; this can be done by the use of compensation tests.

Compensation tests are a means by which gains and losses can be compared and the net benefits of a project identified. The rule is that if the gainers from a project could compensate the losers for their losses and still be better off, then society can be judged to be better off and the project should proceed. For example, if the gainers value their benefits from a project to be worth £100,000 and the losers value their losses at £80,000, then the gainers could pay the loser £80,000 (i.e., compensate them for their losses) and still be £20,000 better off. The net benefit to society is, therefore, £20,000.

Distribution of benefits and costs

The government may not only be concerned with the net benefits but also with who gains and loses. For example, if the gainers are the rich and the losers the poor, then the government may wish to weight benefits and losses to the poorer members of the community more heavily than those to its wealthier members. The theoretical justification for doing this is that the marginal utility of money and of income varies with the quantity of money held or level of income a person receives. Thus, £1 to a poor person produces significantly more benefit or utility than a similar £1 to a rich person. In cost–benefit analysis, benefits are not normally measured in terms of utility but in terms of money; this implies that the marginal utility of money is constant, so that every £1 of benefit has the same value to society whoever receives it.

Willingness to pay

Cost–benefit analysis attempts to measure the total costs and benefits in monetary terms. To convert them into money, use is made of willingness to pay and willingness to be compensated curves, or demand and supply curves. In Figure 25.1 the demand curve shows the utility individuals receive from consuming a product translated into a willingness to pay for any given unit. The area under the demand curve *ADO* is the total willingness to pay for the quantity *OD* of the good or service. The supply curve *CBS* represents the marginal cost of supply, and the area *OCSD* is the total cost of supplying the quantity *OD*. The equilibrium output is *OQ* where the supply and demand curves intersect. At this output, total willingness to pay is equal to *OABQ* and the cost of supply is *OCBQ*. The difference between the two is area *ABC*; this comprises consumer surplus (the area above the price line and below the willingness to pay curve *ABP*) and producer surplus (the area below the price line and above the cost curve *PBC*). These two areas represent the social surplus of producing *OQ* and measure net social benefits. Changes in net social surplus, assuming prices are unchanged, can be used as a measure of the net social benefit of projects.

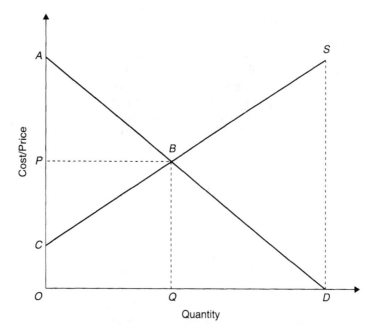

Figure 25.1   Consumer and producer surplus

WHICH BENEFITS AND COSTS?

Public sector investment projects are undertaken in the interests of the community as a whole, and generally involve social infrastructure, such as roads, railways, electricity networks and dams, which has significant social benefits for society. Cost–benefit analysis is thought to be an appropriate framework because many of the benefits and costs are social rather than private.

Direct benefits and costs

Cost–benefit analysis should include all gains and losses to all members of society that are the consequence of the project; these would include initially all the direct benefits and costs in much the same way as a private project. The building of a new motorway will have clear capital expenditures and maintenance costs. The resources used to build the motorway (or capital costs) can be easily identified because they will be hired or purchased to allow the process of construction to proceed. The direct benefits are also in principle easily identified in that they go to the users of the road. While users of the road may not pay, their benefits must be measured if a judgement is to be made about the value of the project.

Indirect benefits and costs

The construction of a new motorway may have an impact beyond the direct beneficiaries; these are the indirect benefits and costs. The new road may relieve congestion at some locations, creating benefits for other road users whose journeys may now be quicker than they previously were, while other road users suffer greater delays as new points of congestion are created. It may also reduce accidents on previously congested roads and save lives. The new motorway will also affect the pattern of business. Shops and petrol stations on the old routes will lose trade while new motorway service stations or businesses on new access roads will gain trade.

Technological spillovers

Public investment may create new opportunities for business and development. For example, the building of a new reservoir at Kielder Water in the forests of Northumbria has created new tourism and leisure opportunities using both the forest and water. The effect has been to create new businesses to meet the needs of the many visitors attracted to the area. Such knock-on effects are termed technological spillovers and are taken into account in a complete cost–benefit analysis because they add to the productive capacity of the community.

Technological spillovers are distinguished from pecuniary spillovers, which are not counted because they arise from changes in prices or a redistribution of activities, rather than from increases in production possibilities. An example of a pecuniary spillover is the increased activity of petrol stations on a new road which are offset by losses elsewhere because of the diversion of traffic. The distinction between technological and pecuniary spillovers is not a simple one to maintain in practice, because the indirect consequence of an investment may be both technological and pecuniary. Thus, motorway service centres deal not only with diverted traffic but also with newly generated traffic. They might also create new business opportunities in terms of catering, hotel rooms and retailing that previously were not required before the advent of motorway travel.

A major problem with measuring direct and more particularly indirect benefits is that of identifying all the individuals affected or getting them to identify themselves. Those affected significantly will identify themselves while those with less significant individual gains and losses might not, but in total these gains and/or losses might be very significant.

MEASURING BENEFITS AND COSTS

Market goods

Major distinctions in measuring costs and benefits are made between private and social benefits and costs, on the one hand, and between priced and non-priced benefits and costs, on the other. Market prices, even in the absence of externalities, are unlikely to reflect the social costs of resources used; this is because in imperfect markets there is a divergence between marginal cost and price. Valuing outputs or inputs at market prices would overstate the value of resources utilized. Even if prices reflect marginal costs, total revenue does not fully reflect the full benefits received; these are reflected in the total willingness to pay, which requires an estimation to be made of consumer surplus, which is then added to total revenue to obtain total benefits. To measure consumer surplus it is necessary to estimate the slope and position of the demand curve, which can be done by undertaking consumer surveys and estimating demand functions from past data (see Chapter 6).

Where market prices do not reflect marginal costs, it may be necessary to estimate shadow prices, which reflect the marginal opportunity costs of using the resources. For outputs, monopoly prices should be reduced to marginal cost, while for inputs, prices should reflect marginal productivity. Shadow prices may be obtained by using prices prevailing elsewhere. In agriculture, for example, it may be appropriate to use world market rather than internal market prices if the latter are distorted by subsidies and import restrictions. It may be also be feasible to use prices established in other sectors of the economy undertaking similar activities. The price of medical treatment in a competitive market might be used to value medical care provided by the public sector free to patients.

Benefits and costs should also be measured using prices prevailing in the base year, with no allowance for general price inflation being made. However, anticipated changes in relative prices should be allowed for, as they will change the quantities demanded. The case for building new roads is partly based on forecasts of long-run traffic growth. If major changes in the relative price of using motor vehicles are foreseen, either increasing or decreasing future road use, then they should be incorporated.

Externalities

Externalities arise where there are benefits or costs either received or imposed on other individuals. These benefits and costs are not priced, and alternative valuation procedures must be derived. The typical production externality involves producing unpriced disbenefits, in the form of pollution from factories and noise from traffic, which impose costs on their recipients. In Figure 25.2 it is assumed that there is a supply externality. The private supply curve is given by AS_P, and the supply curve incorporating private and social costs is given by CS_{P+S}. If private costs are considered by making use of demand curve GD, then OQ_P would be supplied at price OP_P, generating net benefits of GBA. If social costs are taken into account, then the optimal output would be OQ_S with price OP_S, generating net social benefits of GHC. If social costs are ignored, then the net social surplus GBA overestimates the net social benefits because social costs of $ACHB$ are ignored.

In Figure 25.3 it is assumed that there is a demand externality in the form of additional social benefits supplied indirectly. The private demand curve is ED_P, the social demand curve is FD_{P+S} and the supply curve is AS_P. If just private benefits are

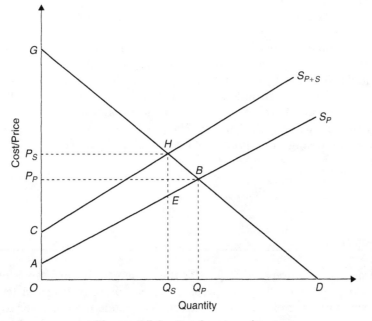

Figure 25.2 Supply externality

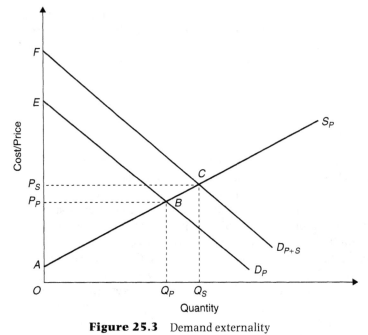

Figure 25.3   Demand externality

considered, then the agency would supply output OQ_P and sell at a price OP_P. If social benefits are taken into account, then the optimal output would be OQ_S with price OP_S being charged. If social benefits are ignored, then the net social surplus is the area EBA. If social benefits are counted, then the net social benefits is the area FCA. Thus, by ignoring social benefits, society would have foregone benefits equal to the area $FCBE$.

Measuring unpriced social or external benefits and costs is fraught with difficulty. The theoretical position is that these should reflect the subjective values put on them by individuals. If they are external costs, then their value should be equal to the amount of compensation an individual would accept for their lost utility. If they are social benefits, then their value should reflect the amount an individual is prepared to pay rather than go without the benefits. The problems of applying this principle can be illustrated by discussing the valuation of time saved and lives saved by the construction of new roads.

THE VALUE OF TIME

Users of transport are prepared to pay for the movement of themselves or their goods between two points, and they are prepared to pay more to travel faster rather than slower. A small number of travellers between Britain and the USA used to be willing to pay a substantial premium to travel supersonic by Concorde rather than subsonic by jumbo jet, although part of the premium was for a higher quality of on-board service. Reducing journey times will motivate travellers to choose travel by rail rather than road and underground or tramway in congested cities. However, choice of transport mode is also influenced by other factors, such as convenience, price and time considerations. Decisions about using a particular transport mode involve a trade-off between money and time.

Time has no value of its own, but time spent doing one thing cannot be spent doing others. Thus, time saved in travelling could be used for working or for leisure. The value of time is the net utility gained by using time in one way rather than another. At the margin, work time and leisure time would have the same value to the individual. However, since an employer is prepared to pay workers a wage rate that is at least equal to their marginal product, work time can be valued at the wage plus an addition for the overhead costs involved in employing people. In practice, for estimation purposes, this becomes the average hourly wage rate plus the overhead mark-up.

The value of leisure time is more problematic. Questionnaires and surveys have been used to estimate the trade-off between time and money in the choice between alternative forms of transport. Travellers have been asked to provide details of their own choices, and from their revealed preferences statistical relationships have then been inferred. Beesley (1965) suggested the following method. Let T_R = the time of the rejected journey, T_A = the time of the accepted journey, C_A = the cost of the chosen means of travel, C_R = the rejected mode and V_A = the minimum value of time saved by choosing the faster option. If the chosen means of travel is a 15-minute rail journey in preference to a 75-minute bus journey, with a relative rail fare of 500p and a bus fare of 200p, then:

$$V_A = (C_A - C_R)/(T_R - T_A) = (500 - 200)/(75 - 15) = 300/60 = 5\text{p per minute}$$

Thus, a traveller would be valuing time at 5p per minute or £3.00 per hour.

Beesley's method can be further explained using Figure 25.4, where time savings between alternative means of travel, are plotted on one axis and differences in costs on the other. In his initial study, Beesley studied the travel choices of a group of civil servants with similar incomes travelling into London. Each person was asked to specify his chosen means of travel to work and the rejected alternative. The difference in travelling time and the difference in money cost between the preferred and alternative modes of transport were then calculated and plotted in a diagram (illustrated in Figure 25.4). Each point represents the combination of time and cost for two alternative means of transport. At point R an individual saves OV minutes of time which is worth OM of money. The value of a unit of time is OM/OV. At S an individual is willing to sacrifice time for money (i.e., make a longer journey at a lower price). Thus, the individual is prepared to spend OW additional time travelling to save WS. In the diagram there are a multitude of points (such as R and S) which show the net saving of time and the net saving of money of each individual by using his preferred transport mode.

A straight line passing through the origin is fitted to the data, so that the smallest number of observations lie to the south-west of the line. If all travellers attach a value to time saving, then each of their chosen points will lie on or to the north-east of this

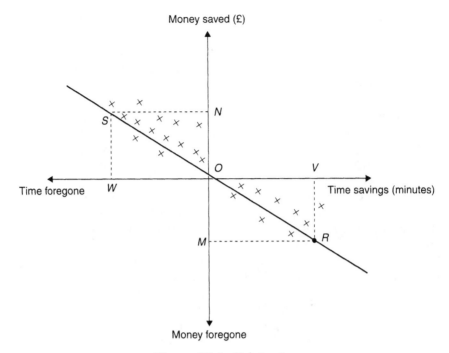

Figure 25.4 Valuing time

line. A point south-west of the line implies that the time savings achieved by using the preferred mode are not worth the monetary cost or that the money saved is not worth the extra travelling time. The slope of line *SOR* represents an estimate of the value of time saving to those included in the sample and others with similar characteristics.

Estimates using this procedure suggest that the value of leisure time is somewhere between 25and 40% of the wage rate. Lee and Dalvi (1969), using data collected in Manchester, found the average value of time savings for leisure time was about 30% of the gross hourly rate. Quarmby (1967) put the average value at between 21 and 25%. A problem with these studies is that every minute is given the same value irrespective of whether there is a minimum time loss before it has a meaningful economic effect. For example, does saving 3 minutes on a journey of 30 minutes have the same value as 60 minutes on a journey of 10 hours?

Estimates derived by the Department of Transport for the average value of time are presented in Table 25.2; this shows the average value of working time to be 1,157p and non-working or leisure time to be 374p, or 32% of the value of working time. A comprehensive review of studies that have valued travel time is to be found in Wardman (1998).

THE VALUE OF LIFE

Some public sector investments (such as roads or railway signalling) may prevent accidents and as a consequence save lives. A number of approaches have been

Table 25.2 The average value of time
(pence per hour at 1998 prices)

Working time	Resource cost per hour (pence)
Car driver	1,744
PSV driver	668
Train driver	1,498
Rail passenger	2,517
Cyclist	1,198
Walker	2,401
Average (all workers)	*1,157*
Non-working time	*374*

Source Compiled by author using data extracted from DETR (2000)

followed, but none is entirely satisfactory from a theoretical point of view where the emphasis should be on the individual's own valuation.

First, there is the human capital approach, which takes a person's lifetime earnings profile and calculates the present capital value that would produce that income stream; this is taken to be the economic value of life in terms of an individual's contribution to output. Using this approach, individuals with higher earnings are more highly valued compared with those with lower earnings and those not working in the market sector, who have no value at all. Younger workers with a full lifetime of work and earnings to come are more valuable than older workers with little time to retirement.

Second, there is the risk reduction approach, which asks individuals the amount of money they are prepared to pay to avoid death (or noise or pollution) or to have their life saved. Individuals are asked about the consequences of a small increase in the chance of them dying and how much compensation would be needed for them to accept the extra risk, or alternatively how much they would be prepared to pay to avoid the consequences (Sugden and Williams 1978, pp. 172–174).

Monetary values can be attributed as follows. Suppose a group of 100,000 individuals are prepared to pay £10 for a safety improvement that will reduce their individual risk of death by 1 in 100,000; this would mean that one person in the group would avoid premature death as a result of an accident. If the group between them would have been willing to pay £1m (100,000 times £10) to prevent one death, then this becomes the value of life. The approach does not value the lives of particular individuals, but that of the group collectively, to bring a small reduction in the risk of one of the group dying; this has been done in practice by either asking respondents or by inferring it from observing individual behaviour. For example, Jones-Lee (1976) asked a sample of people questions relating to their willingness to pay for improvements in safety while travelling. The answers implied a value to the respondents themselves of about £1.6m in 1982. The answers also implied that £0.5 should be added to pay for other people's safety. A second approach is to examine the relative earnings of people in riskier jobs where accidents and death are more likely. For accidents at work the premium is 20–25% where the risk of dying is 1 per 1,000 workers per year and

2–2.5% where the risk is 1 in 10,000. For average earnings of £9,000 the value of life is put by Marin (1988) at between £1.8m and £2.25m.

Case Study 25.1 Train protection systems and the saving of lives

In the UK there has been a continuing debate about the fitting of ATP (automatic train protection) systems to trains. Following the Clapham rail crash of 1988 in which 35 people died, British Rail started studying the potential use of APT to protect trains passing through danger signals. After every major railway accident the debate about whether that particular accident might or might not have been prevented by a warning system is reopened and promises made to fit such devices.

The main cause of deaths on the railway network are trespassers who constituted 63% between 1997 and 2000, while train accidents account for 4.2%, of which 2% might have been prevented if ATP had been installed (Glover 2001, p. 32). Between 1967 and 2000 there were 77 accidents involving trains which resulted in fatalities: of these, 36 involved one death (46.8%), 14 two deaths (18.1%) and 5 more than 10 victims (6.5%), accounting for 138 of the 308 deaths. Accidents involving more than 10 deaths are listed in Table 25.3, but only one of these (Ladbroke Grove) would have been prevented had ATP been fitted (Evans 2001). Overall, there were 31 accidents that resulted in 115 deaths that could have been prevented between 1967 and 2000 had ATP been fitted: on average, 3.83 lives per accident and 3.38 lives per year could have been prevented (see Table 25.4).

ATP is designed to prevent drivers passing through red signals; these are known as SPADS (signals passed at danger). AWS (automatic warning system) has been installed since 1957. Despite the fact it was developed for mechanical signalling and gives the driver an audible warning, or caution, which he has to acknowledge if a danger signal is passed, more sophisticated electronic signalling requires more sophisticated warning systems.

Following the Clapham crash, British Rail started fitting ATP systems on a trial basis. A review in 1994 showed that expectations had not been fulfilled because there were difficulties in fitting the systems to old trains. The net cost of installing ATP throughout the network was estimated to be £14.6m per death avoided; this compared with the Ministry of Transport's estimate of a death in road traffic accidents in 1992 to be £715,000 and British

Table 25.3 Major railway accidents (1967–2000)

Date	Accident	ATP-preventable	Deaths
1967	Hither Green	No	49
1973	West Ealing	No	10
1984	Polmont	No	13
1988	Clapham Junction	No	35
1999	Ladbroke Grove	Yes	31
	Subtotal		*138*
	Others		*170*

Source Based on data in Evans (2001)

Table 25.4 Mean number of accidents and fatalities (1967–2000)

	ATP-preventable	Other causes	Total
Number of accidents	30	47	77
Fatalities	115	193	308
Fatalities per accident			
Mean	3.83	4.11	4.00
Accidents per year	*0.88*	*1.38*	*2.26*
Fatalities per year	*3.38*	*5.67*	*9.05*

Source   Calculations by author based on data in Evans (2001)

Rail's proposed safety scheme where the value of a life saved was in the range of £1–2m. Thus, the benefits did not appear to justify the costs of installing ATP. It was decided not to fit ATP to the entire network and, instead, to carry out research on new systems with trials starting in 1997 (Ford 1994).

The Southall rail crash in September 1997 resulted in the deaths of seven passengers which could have been prevented if ATP had been fitted. Thames Trains, in a subsequent investigation, estimated that the cost of preventing a fatality would be £7.75m; this again was in excess of the typical value attributed to a life. So, it was decided not to install ATP, but a cheaper, less sophisticated system, known as the TPWS (train protection and warning system), instead.

In November 1999 there was a crash at Ladbroke Grove, on the same main line as the Southall crash two years earlier. This time a Thames diesel multiple unit (DMU) train went through a stop signal and into the path of an intercity hight-speed train (HST), resulting in 31 deaths: 24 on the DMU and 7 on the HST; this was an accident that might have been avoided had the ATP system been installed. The decision of the company not to install ATP was found to be reasonable by the official inquiry. The passage of the train through the danger signal was noted by the signalling centre, which sent a radio message to the driver to stop after he failed to stop within the agreed run-over. If the DMU had been fitted with ATP, then the train would have stopped automatically and the accident possibly avoided.

In 1999, railway regulations were passed requiring ATP to be fitted to all trains by the end of 2003; this is seen as an interim measure to stop trains passing through danger signals at speeds of up to 75 miles per hour. This time cost–benefit calculations were not allowed to influence the decision. The reason may be an increasing number of signals passed at danger, the potential of a major death toll when the lighter DMUs crash into heavier, locomotive-hauled trains and the perception of the public and politicians that the railways had become less safe: one accident killing 31 people has a greater impact than 31 individual deaths. Railway passengers expect railways to be much safer than travel by road, where individual drivers are willing to accept risks that they find unacceptable on a railway system where they pay to travel. The cost of saving a life on rail may be high compared with common valuations, but the government felt this was a necessary step to maintain public confidence in the privatized railway.

THE CHOICE OF DISCOUNT RATE

There are two relevant notions of the discount rate which might be appropriate in cost–benefit analysis. The first is the social time preference rate, which is the rate at which people wish to set aside current consumption to invest in resources to ensure future consumption. In other words, it is the rate at which an individual or a society prefers consuming now compared with waiting. Individuals are known to have high rates of time preference and usually prefer consumption now to waiting to consume in the future. However, society should be concerned more with the welfare of future generations than with individuals. Consequently, the social time preference rate would be lower than the private time preference rate, suggesting that society should consume less now and invest more. The social time preference rate determines the proportion of current output a society should set aside for investment and is not directly concerned with choices between individual projects.

The second concept is the social opportunity cost rate which reflects rates of return in other sectors of the economy; essentially, this is the government's cost of borrowing since it reflects the willingness of the private sector to lend money to the government. Government borrowing is considered to be less risky than private sector borrowing and is sometimes described as being risk-free. If government uses a significantly lower rate of discount than the private sector, then there will be overinvestment in public sector projects compared with private sector investment. Therefore, the opportunity cost rate tends to be the one preferred.

Case Study 25.2   Measuring the social benefits of a railway: the Cambrian Coast Line

Cost–benefit analysis has been used to study railway closures and investment. Railways are presumed to deliver significant social benefits beyond those to railway travellers, railway workers and revenue to railway companies. They keep passengers and freight off congested roads, reduce journey times and accidents and can be a significant force in economic development in areas with poor road connections to the national network. An example of a railway closure study, the first carried out by the British Government, was that for the Cambrian Coast Railway. It demonstrates the difficulty of deciding what to include and how to measure the benefits and costs.

In 1968, British Rail (BR) proposed the closure of the railway line that runs from Dovey Junction to Pwllheli, along Cardigan Bay. The line provides travel connections to Aberystwyth, Birmingham and London. The proposed closure came after the major rationalization of lines following the Beeching Report (1963). The Department of Transport proposed that a cost–benefit analysis should be undertaken to test the arguments that while the line was a loss maker to BR it provided significant social benefits to the community.

Cost–benefit analysis attempts to take into account all relevant social and private costs and benefits arising from a particular decision. The direct net social benefits arising from the closure of the railway are given by the loss of benefits to rail passengers, the cost of providing a replacement bus service and the cost of retaining the rail service. In addition, there are the wider social benefits to be accounted for.

To assist in the estimation of the costs and benefits a series of surveys were carried

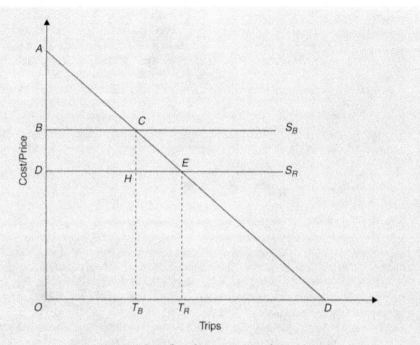

Figure 25.5 Benefits of preventing railway closures

out to estimate the numbers of passengers using the line. In addition, passengers and freight users were interviewed, using a structured questionnaire, and asked about journey times and what they would do if the railway service were withdrawn. In addition, opinions were sought from local authorities and other bodies in the region. In this way, it was hoped to elicit information to allow the calculation of relevant price elasticities of demand for rail services, the value of time and other social costs and benefits.

With a given demand curve AD for trips (shown in Figure 25.5) and known monetary prices and other user costs for rail and bus travel, the consequences of the withdrawal of the service can be identified. OD = the rail fare (and the bus fare), and OT_R = the number of trips made when the railway is operating. When the railway is withdrawn the traveller has the option of either using the replacement bus service or not travelling. The total user cost of using the replacement bus service is assumed to be OB, greater than that of using the train, because of the additional time involved and the lower level of comfort offered by the bus. Thus, where the user cost of bus travel is OB, the number of trips made is OT_B. Therefore, the number of bus trips is smaller than the number of railway trips, with $T_B T_R$ trips not being made.

When the railway is running, passengers make OT_R trips and pay $ODET_R$ in fares, leaving ADE of consumer surplus. The relevant welfare gains and losses that need to be measured, following the railway closure, can be identified as follows, with the outcome shown in column 2 of Table 25.3:

■ *Passengers not travelling* The loss of consumer surplus is the triangle CHE, which is the difference between the demand curve and the price line for the $T_B T_R$ trips not taken (benefit 2). These passengers also save the fares they previously paid to the railway, which is shown by the area HET_RT_B (benefit 3); this was treated by the study team as money remaining with passengers to be spent on other goods and was not included (i.e., it was not counted as revenue offsetting the costs included).

■ *Passengers continuing to travel by bus* They incur additional user costs of *BCHD* which is also the loss of consumer surplus to the railway traveller (benefit 1); this at a minimum is the additional time spent travelling by bus multiplied by the value of time.

■ *Other benefits* These include the costs of not providing an alternative bus service (benefit 6), the costs of road improvements required to meet additional road use (benefit 4) and the additional road accidents caused by additional traffic, none of which was included in the Ministry of Transport study (benefit 5).

The costs of running the railway are the savings that would be made if the railway did not operate. These include:

■ *Railway avoidable costs* The costs saved by not continuing to operate the railway, such as operating costs, rationalization expenditure and new rolling stock not purchased (cost 1). Annual operating costs were estimated to be £240,000. In addition, it was assumed that the existing stock would need replacing at a cost of £350,000. After allowing for rationalization charges and the ongoing costs of protecting sea defences, the estimated net present value over a 10-year period of railway avoidable costs was £1,768,000 (cost 1).

■ *Social cost savings* Some of the resources used in running the railway are no longer used. For example, workers become unemployed and their wages no longer represent their opportunity cost if the alternative to work is unemployment (cost 2). Thus, actual wage costs incurred are reduced to reflect the period of time workers might be unemployed.

The benefits and costs estimated by the Ministry of Transport study are shown in column 1 of Table 25.5, giving a negative net present value of −£695,500. Therefore, the study recommended closure of the line.

Richards (1972) questioned both the methodology and the calculation of benefits and costs. The main criticisms of the initial study was that the analysis was static, did not allow for growth in traffic and incomes and that there was no sensitivity analysis to test the robustness of the result to changes in key values. In addition, no consideration was given to income distribution issues or wider social benefits, such as the importance of rail to tourism or the greater reliability of rail transport in adverse weather conditions.

With the assistance of a new passenger survey in 1971, Richards identified passenger growth and recalculated benefits and costs using what he termed "optimistic and pessimistic outcomes".

The new passenger survey showed increasing passenger use of the line. Therefore, it was proposed that growth of 8% would be assumed for the optimistic estimate compared with no growth for the pessimistic model. Then, the value of time was increased to reflect increasing real incomes. Thus, in the pessimistic model the initial value of 15p per hour was increased by 3% per annum while for the optimistic model the value was 21p per hour, also increasing at 3% per annum. The estimated benefits combining the higher traffic flows and higher time values are shown in columns 3 and 4 of Table 25.5. The revenue loss to the railway company was included as were the costs of avoiding road accidents and roadworks. The costs of operating the railway were also revised in the light of new working methods.

The overall effect of these changes was to show that the net social benefits of the railway line were positive, even on the pessimistic assumptions. Therefore, the conclusion

Table 25.5 Social benefits of retaining the Cambrian Coast Railway for 10 years discounted at 8% (£ thousands)

Benefits of retention	MOT study (column 1)	Richard's study Pessimistic (column 2)	Richard's study Optimistic (column 3)
1 Additional travel time			
Adults	37	61	127
Children	—	2	3
2 Loss of benefit to rail passengers not travelling	38	39	161
3 Resource cost of revenue of public transport operators	—	235	415
4 Road costs avoided	50	90	134
5 Costs of road accidents	—	109	180
6 Additional cost of replacement bus service	413.5	497	538
Total benefit	*538.5*	*1,033*	*1,558*
Costs of retention			
1 Railway avoidable costs	−1,768	−1,343	−1,164
2 Less social costs	534	684	617
Total costs	*−1,234*	*−659*	*−547*
Net costs of retention	*−695.5*	*374*	*1,011*

Source   Compiled by author from data in MOT (1968) and Richards (1972)

was that subsidizing and continuing to operate the line contributed positive net social benefits. The closure of the line was initially postponed because of the 1970 general election and was eventually rescinded. As a result, the line never closed, eventually got new rolling stock and continues to operate to this day.

CONSISTENCY OF APPROACH

If cost–benefit analysis is to be used in evaluating public sector decisions, then it is important that a consistent set of investment guidelines is used for all decisions. However, this is not always the case. For example, in the UK different procedures are used to evaluate the social benefits of road and rail (and light rail) investment. The difference can be explained by examining Table 25.6, which shows the returns on a proposed light rail system in Manchester, known as the Metrolink, which is now fully operational.

The benefits in an appraisal of a road scheme include total benefits to users of the new road (time and operating cost savings), congestion relief to users of other roads, accident cost savings and environmental benefits (not valued but included in the

Table 25.6 Comparison of Manchester Metrolink benefits and costs
(£m – discounted 30-year totals)

(1) Analysis as a road scheme		(2) Analysis as a railway scheme	
Capital cost	87.00	Capital cost	87.00
BR capital cost avoided	−41.44		
Bus capital cost avoided	−1.80		
Net capital cost	43.76	Capital cost	87.00
Operating cost savings	8.06	BR capital expenditure saved	41.44
User benefits from time saving	58.46	Tendered bus services reduced	1.31
Revenue from ex-car users	12.19	PTA* contribution to BR avoided	36.98
Congestion reduction	6.00	Congestion savings	6.00
Accident cost savings	3.00	Accident cost savings	2.00
Total savings	97.71	Total savings	87.73
Total benefits	53.95	Total benefits	0.73

Source Ford (1994)
*   Passenger Transport Authority

appraisal framework). The railway procedure includes as benefits the proportion of user benefits captured in fares, congestion relief to road users (including bus passengers), accident cost savings (but not as generous as for roads) and environmental benefits (the same as for a road scheme). As a road scheme the results show total benefits to be £53.95m and as a railway scheme the benefits are much more marginal at £0.73m.

CHAPTER SUMMARY

In this chapter we examined investment appraisal in the public sector and the problems associated with measuring social costs and benefits. In doing this we analysed: the choice of discount rate.

- The complexity and difficulty of making acceptable measurement. This has meant that cost–benefit analysis has largely fallen into disuse in the UK. Nevertheless, cost–benefit judgements are still being made without formal analysis being undertaken.
- Public spending on investment to ensure environmental and safety benefits are justified on the basis of the wider social benefits. However, little formal quantitative analysis is undertaken in this area and critics can easily argue that the supposed benefits have been overestimated and that such spending is unnecessary.

REVIEW QUESTIONS

Exercise

Try to identify a recent public sector investment decision where the social benefits and costs were ignored. Identify the nature of the benefits and costs not included and whether the decision might have been different if they had been included.

Discussion questions

1 Distinguish between commercial investment appraisal and cost–benefit analysis.
2 In what ways does investment appraisal in the private sector differ from the public sector?
3 Which benefits/costs should be included in a cost–benefit analysis?
4 What is the social value of a benefit compared with actual amount paid for a purchase?
5 What is an externality? How might they be valued?
6 Why do public and private valuation of costs and benefits differ?
7 What problems are there with using market prices to value social benefits?
8 What are shadow prices? How might they be measured?
9 How might a shadow price for time savings and deaths avoided be determined?
10 What are the differences between the appropriate discount rate for a private and a public investment?
11 How might the social costs of large lorries be evaluated?
12 What factors might be considered in making the case for replacing a railway level crossing with a bridge?

REFERENCES AND FURTHER READING

Armitage, A. (1980) *Lorries, People and the Environment* (Report of an inquiry). HMSO, London.

Beeching Report (1963) *The Reshaping of British Railways* (British Railways Board). HMSO, London.

Beesley, M.E. (1965) The value of time spent travelling: Some new evidence. *Economica*, **32**, 174–185.

Beesley, M.E. and M.Q. Dalvi (1974) Spatial equilibrium and journey to work. *Journal of Transport Economics and Policy*, **8**, 197–222.

Brent, R.J. (1996) Applied Cost Benefit Analysis. Edward Elgar, Cheltenham, UK.

Button, K.J. and P.J. Barker (1975) Cambrian Coast Railway Line. *Case Studies in Cost–Benefit Analysis* (Chapter 2). Heinemann, London.

Dearden, S. (1990) Road freight transport: Social cost and market efficiency. *The Royal Bank of Scotland Review*, **168**, December, 28–42.

DETR (2000) Transport economics note No. 10. Available at: **http://www.dft.gov.uk**

Evans, A.W. (2001) Fatal main-line train accidents. *Modern Railways*, March, **58**, 23–27.

Ford, R. (1994) ATP unaffordable – official. *Modern Railways*, September, 522–523.

Foster, C.D. (2001) Michael Beesley and cost benefit analysis. *Journal of Transport Economics and Policy*, **35**(1), 3–30.

Glover, J. (2001) Traffic growth and automatic train protection(Report of talk given by Sir David Davies). *Modern Railways*, August, **58**, 31–33.

Jones-Lee, M. (1976) *The Value of Life: An Economic Analysis*. Martin Robertson, Oxford, UK.

Lee, N. and M.Q. Dalvi (1969) Variations in the value of travel time. *Manchester School*, **37**, 213–236.

Marin, A. (1988) The cost of avoiding death: Nuclear power regulation and spending on safety. *Royal Bank of Scotland Review*, **157**, 21–36.

Mishan, E.J. (1971) Loss of life and limb. *Cost–Benefit Analysis* (Chapter 22). George Allen & Unwin, London.

MOT (1968) *Cambrian Coast Line* (Ministry of Transport). HMSO, London.

Nash, C. (1992) Appraisal of railway projects. *Project Appraisal*, **7**(4), 211–218.

Pearce, D.W. and C.A. Nash (1981) *The Social Appraisal of Projects: A Text in Cost–Benefit Analysis*. Macmillan, London.

Quarmby, D.A. (1967) Choice of travel mode for the journey to work: Some findings. *Journal of Transport Economics and Policy*, **1**, 1–42.

Richards, K. (1972) The economics of the Cambrian Coast line. *Journal of Transport Economics and Policy*, **16**(3), 308–320.

Stubbs, P.C., W.J. Tyson and M.Q. Dalvi (1989) *Transport Economics*. George Allen & Unwin, London.

Sugden, R. and A. Williams (1978) *The Principles of Practical Cost–Benefit Analysis*. Oxford University Press, Oxford, UK.

Tyson, W. (1992) Appraisal of bus and light railway projects. *Project Appraisal*, **7**(4), 205–210.

Wardman, M. (1998) The value of travel time: A review of British Evidence. *Journal of Transport Economics and Policy*, **32**(3), 285–316.

Willis, K. (1991) The priceless countryside: The recreational benefits of environmental goods. *The Royal Bank of Scotland Review*, No. 172, 38–48.

GLOSSARY

Advertising Expenditure by the firm informing consumers of the availability and characteristics of the product. Advertisements contain information and can also be persuasive in nature to encourage more consumers to purchase the product.

Advertising elasticity of demand The responsiveness of demand to an increase or decrease in advertising expenditure.

Adverse selection A phenomenon whereby an increase in the insurance premium increases the overall riskiness of the pool of individuals who buy an insurance policy.

Advertising elasticity The percentage change in quantity demanded of a product divided by the percentage change in advertising the product, all other factors remaining unchanged.

Arc price elasticity of demand The average elasticity over a range of a demand curve.

Asset specificity The extent to which a resource is specific to its current use and has little or no alternative function.

Asymmetric information A situation where all decision makers or parties to an agreement do not have the same information.

Autocorrelation The lack of independence between sequential error terms within a model.

Average fixed cost Total fixed cost per unit of output.

Average product of labour The average amount of output per unit of labour.

Average revenue Total revenue divided by output.

Average total cost Total costs divided by output.

Average variable cost Total variable costs divided by output.

Bad goods Goods consumed where social costs of consumption exceed the private benefits.

Barometric price leadership A type of price leadership where price changes are initiated by a non-dominant firm in a market on the basis of current trends in the market.

Behavioural theory (of the firm) A theory developed to explain the interactions of the decision-making parties within an organization. Behavioural theories take into account the preferences and conflicting goals of the different groups within the firm and assume the firm will aim at satisfactory rather than maximum outcome.

Bertrand oligopoly A model of oligopoly that uses price as the strategic variable. In deciding its price a firm conjectures that its rivals will hold their prices constant.

Beta coefficient A measure of the variability of a firm's stock market price against the market as a whole.

Bounded rationality The limit to an individual ability to assimilate and process information due to constraints on knowledge, foresight, skill and time.

Budget line The set of bundles of goods that the consumer may purchase when all available income is spent.

Capital asset pricing model This relates the expected return of an asset to its risk.

Capital-deepening technical progress Where technical progress leads to a greater reduction in the employment of capital relative to labour.

Capital–labour ratio The ratio of the quantity of capital to the quantity of labour used in a production process.

Capital-saving technical process Technological progress that causes the marginal product of labour to increase compared with the marginal product of capital.

Cartel An agreement between a group of firms in a market or industry to control output so as to set monopoly prices.

Characteristics approach This analyses consumer behaviour when products are decomposed into their component characteristics.

Cobb–Douglas production function A production function, where $Q = AL^aK^b$, where Q = the quantity of output, L = labour, K = capital and a, b = positive constants.

Common good A resource, such as the sea or common land, that anyone can use.

Complementary product A product bought in combination with others. An increase in the price of good X will lead to a reduction in the demand for good X and the complementary good Y, other things being equal.

Conglomerate merger A merger involving firms not operating in the same market or linked in the production chain.

Constant return to scale A proportionate increase in all input quantities results in the same percentage increase in output.

Consumer surplus A monetary measure of the net benefits a consumer receives from consuming a given quantity of a good. It is the difference between the demand curve and the price line.

Control The ability to determine the objectives of the firm and appoint senior executives.

Co-operatives An organization owned by members and operated in their interest.

Core competence A key activity, process or system possessed by a firm which gives it a competitive advantage over its competitors.

Corporate governance   The ways in which companies are governed. The rules and guidelines concerning the appointment of senior executives.

Correlation coefficient   A statistical measure of the degree of association between two variables. The coefficient ranges from 1 to -1 indicating, respectively, a perfect linear relationship or a perfect inverse relationship. A coefficient of zero indicates no relationship.

Cost of capital   The opportunity cost to a firm of acquiring funds to undertake an investment. Used in discounting cash flows to choose between different projects.

Cournot Model   A model of oligopoly where the interdependent variable is output. In deciding on its output a firm conjectures that all competitors will hold output constant.

Cross elasticity of demand   The percentage change in the quantity of X divided by the percentage change in the price of Y. A positive relationship indicates goods are substitutes and a negative relationship that they are complements.

Cross-sectional data   Data collected for the same period of time which is split into certain groupings, based on income, age, etc.

Deadweight loss   The difference between the net economic benefit that would arise if the market were perfectly competitive and the net economic benefit attained at the monopoly equilibrium.

Decision tree   A graphical representation of the decision-making process. A decision tree illustrates the possibilities that the decision maker assesses when making a decision.

Decreasing return to scale   A situation where the proportionate increase in output is less than the increase in resources used.

Differentiated products   A product that substitutes for another, but is also different in significant ways, including characteristics, packaging and branding.

Diminishing marginal rate of substitution   If a consumer moves along a convex indifference curve, then he exhibits a diminishing marginal rate of substitution of x for y as more y is consumed.

Diseconomy of scale   This occurs when long-run average total costs increase faster than the increment in output.

Diversification   A strategy whereby a firm adds a new activity to its existing portfolio which is unrelated to its existing production.

Divorce between ownership and control   A situation where the managers setting objectives and making decisions are not the owners of the firm.

Dominant-firm price leadership A model of oligopoly price setting where the largest firm sets the market price and all other firms, who have no market power, follow the leader's decision.

Duopoly A market in which there are just two firms.

Durable good A goods, such as an automobile or an aeroplane, which provides valuable services over many years.

Economy of scale This occurs when long-run average total costs decrease as output is increased.

Economy of scope This occurs when the total cost of producing given quantities of two goods in the same firm is less than the total cost of producing those quantities in two single-product firms.

Engineering approach A method by which production engineers can assess the shape of the long-run average total cost curve.

Expected value The weighted average outcome of a project, given the different probabilities or likelihoods attached to a range of outcomes.

Experience good A good whose qualities can only be identified by the consumer through usage after buying the good.

Explicit costs A cost that involves a direct monetary outlay.

Externality A situation in which the market fails to reflect all the economic costs and/or benefits resulting from a particular operation.

First-degree price discrimination A situation where a firm sells each unit of output at a different price and converts all consumer surplus into profit.

Fixed cost A cost that does not vary as output changes.

Free rider An individual who benefits from the actions of others without payment.

Game theory A methodology for studying how interdependent decision makers make choices using appropriate strategies and pay-offs.

Horizontal merger The coming together under single ownership of two firms serving the same market (i.e., firms that compete with each other).

Identification problem A difficulty encountered in trying to identify the market demand curve and other variables from quantity–price observations.

Implicit cost A cost that does not involve outlays of cash.

Income effect The change in the amount of a good that a consumer can buy as purchasing power changes, holding all prices constant.

Income elasticity of demand A measure of the rate of percentage change of quantity demanded with respect to the percentage change in income, all other factors remaining unchanged.

Increasing return to scale   This occurs when the proportionate increase in output is greater than the proportionate increase in resources used.

Indifference curve   A line connecting a set of bundles of goods that yield the same level of satisfaction (or utility) to the consumer when consumed.

Indifference map   A set of indifference curves that give increased satisfaction as the consumers move to new curves to the right of existing ones.

Informative advertising   Advertisements that inform consumers with factual information about the product, price and availability.

Innovation   The process of developing an invention so that it can be used in production and sold to others.

Insider system   A system of corporate governance where the major shareholders are members of the executive board.

Internal rate of return   The discount rate on a project which makes the net cash flows of a project equal to zero.

Invention   The output resulting from an idea developed by an individual or group.

Isocost line   The set of combinations of labour and capital that yield the same total cost to the firm.

Isoquant   A line joining combinations of factors that yield the same output.

Labour-deepening technical progress   Where technical progress raises the marginal productivity relative to labour productivity.

Labour-saving technical progress   Where technical progress leads to a greater reduction in the employment of labour relative to capital.

Learning curve   The relationship between unit costs and cumulative output (also called the experience curve).

Linear demand curve   A straight line demand curve with the equation of $Q = a - bP$.

Long run   The period of time that is long enough for the firm to vary the quantities of all of its inputs.

Long-run average cost curve   The way average costs behave when all the factors of production are variable.

Management cost   The cost incurred by the firm in managing its activities.

Managerial theory of the firm   A theory that recognizes the divorce between ownership and control and stresses that managerial rather than owner goals are maximized.

Marginal cost   The change in total cost as output is changed by one unit.

Marginal utility of money   The marginal utility gained by an individual when receiving an additional unit of money in the form of income or wealth.

Marginal product of capital The increase in total output from employing an additional unit of capital.

Marginal product of labour The increase in total output from employing an additional unit of labour.

Marginal rate of substitution The rate at which a consumer will give up one good to get more of another.

Marginal rate of technical substitution The rate at which the quantity of capital can be substituted for labour as a firm moves along an isoquant.

Market demand curve A curve that shows the quantity of goods that consumers are willing to buy at different prices.

Market power A supplier or buyer has market power if it raises the price above the competitive level.

Mark-up pricing A pricing strategy where the market price is determined by adding a percentage addition to the direct cost (or average variable cost) of the product.

Maxi-max decision criterion A risk-seeking decision criterion. The decision maker chooses the best possible outcome for a project.

Maxi-min decision criterion A risk-averse decision criterion. The best of the worst possible outcomes for a project is chosen.

Merit good A good that is non-rival in consumption and excludable, but has a mixture of private and social benefits, so that government encourages consumption by subsidizing the price.

Mini-max regret decision criterion A risk-averse decision criterions. It measures the regret associated with making the wrong decision should a better outcome for a project occur.

Minimum efficient scale The point on the long-run average total cost curve where costs are minimized.

Monopolistic competition A market where firms compete by differentiating their products. The seller becomes a price maker rather than a price taker.

Monopoly A situation where one seller serves a market and, consequently, has power to set its price or output.

Moral hazard A phenomenon whereby an insured party exercises less care than he would in the absence of insurance.

Multi-collinearity The interrelationships between independent variables within an estimated model.

Mutual organization An enterprise owned by its members and operated in their interests.

Nash equilibrium   A situation in which each player chooses a strategy that gets him the highest pay-off, given the strategies chosen by the other players in the game.

Natural monopoly   A market in which, for any relevant level of industry output, the total cost incurred by a single firm is less than the combined total cost of two or more firms.

Net present value   The value of an investment project where future returns are discounted by the cost of capital of a firm or government discount rate.

Neutral technical progress   Where technical progress leads to the same proportionate reduction in the employment of labour and capital.

Normal profit   The profit a firm must make to make it worthwhile to stay in a market. In neoclassical economics a normal profit is included in the total costs of the firm.

Oligopoly   A market in which there are a few sellers, who are not only interdependent but must also consider their rivals' responses to any price change.

Opportunism   A situation where one party to a transaction or contract is able to take advantage of the other.

Ownership   The shareholders of a firm or the owners of a resource. Ownership gives the right to receive any residual income.

Payback period   The period of time required for the returns of a project to exactly equal the initial outlay.

Penetration price   The price of a new product set deliberately low to enable the firm to win a significant market share.

Perfect competition   A market structure with a large number of small suppliers, producing a homogeneous product, which cannot influence the market price.

Perfect information/knowledge   A situation where decision makers have complete knowledge of all information relevant to the decision about to be taken. All outcomes are known with certainty.

Persuasive advertising   Advertising designed to encourage consumers to purchase a product they otherwise would not have done.

Predatory pricing   Setting the price of a product below average variable costs.

Price discrimination   The practice of charging consumers different prices for the same good or service.

Price elasticity of demand   A measure of the responsiveness of the quantity demanded to a change in price.

Price elasticity of supply   A measure of the rate of the responsiveness of the quantity supplied with respect to a change in price.

Price fixing   A process by which firms within a market or industry agree the prices at which to sell their products.

Price leadership   A practice in a market where price is fixed by a recognized leader firm. All other firms set the same price.

Piece rigidity   An outcome in oligopolistic markets where prices do not automatically change in response to changes in supply or demand.

Price taker   A seller or a buyer that takes the price of the product as given when making an output or purchase decision.

Prisoner's dilemma   A game in which there is a conflict between the collective interest of all of the players in the game and the self-interest of individual players. Players would be better off colluding.

Private good   A good where the benefits of consumption are confined to the person consuming it.

Privatization   A process where the ownership of an organization switches from the public to the private sector.

Profit   A residual that is the difference between total revenue and total cost.

Producer surplus   A monetary measure of the benefit that producers derive from producing a good at a particular price. It is the area between the supply curve and the market price.

Product differentiation   Product differentiation occurs when two or more similar products possess attributes that, in the minds of consumers, makes them imperfect substitutes for each other.

Production function   A mathematical equation that shows the maximum quantity of output the firm can produce given the quantities of inputs that it might employ.

Profit maximization   An assumed objective of the owner-managed firm. To maximize profits a firm sets marginal cost equal to marginal revenue. In perfect competition, price is also equal to marginal cost. In a monopoly, price is greater than marginal cost.

Property rights   The exclusive control over the use of an asset or resource.

Public good   A good demanded collectively because consumption by one consumer does not reduce the quantity available to another and consumers cannot be excluded from benefiting, even if they make no financial contribution.

Rate of return regulation   A method of regulating natural monopolies or utilities where the firm's return on capital is restricted.

Reaction function   This shows the best response an oligopolistic firm can make, given it knows the likely reaction of its rivals.

Regression analysis   Statistical technique used to estimate a relationship between dependent and independent variables.

Return to scale   The concept that tells us by how much output will increase when all inputs are increased by a given percentage amount.

Risk   Where the probabilities of a range of outcomes for a project are known from previous experience.

Risk-averse   A decision maker who prefers a sure outcome to a risky outcome unless the rate of return is increased.

Risk-loving   A decision maker who prefers riskier returns to less riskier outcomes.

Risk-neutral   A decision maker who is indifferent to risk when comparing expected returns.

Risk premium   The payment necessary to make a risk-averse person indifferent between a riskless return and a riskier one.

Satisficing   An alternative to a maximizing policy, where the individual or organization attempts to satisfy the needs or requirements of different stakeholders.

Search good   A good whose qualities can be judged before purchasing.

Second-degree price discrimination   A seller engages in this by offering consumers quantity discounts.

Shareholder   The owner of a company's equity. Ownership gives the rights to vote, to receive dividend payments and to bear limited risk if the company goes bankrupt.

Short-run average cost curve   The average costs of production where one factor of production is fixed.

Skimming price   A price strategy of setting a high price initially for the product to "skim the cream off the market" before subsequently reducing the price.

Standard deviation   The square root of the variance of a distribution of risky outcomes.

Symmetric information   A situation where all decision makers or parties to an agreement have the same information.

Subjective likelihood   A probability that reflects the subjective expected outcomes of a decision maker.

Sunk cost   A cost that has already been incurred, cannot be recovered and is not relevant to current decisions.

Synergy   A situation where two or more activities undertaken together produces greater benefits. Often described as $2 + 2 = 5$.

Technically efficient   The set of outcomes where the firm is producing as much output as it can, given the amount of labour and capital employed.

Technical progress   A change in the production process enables a firm to achieve more output from a given combination of inputs or, equivalently, the same amount of output from fewer inputs.

Third-degree price discrimination   A seller practices this by charging different prices to different groups of consumer groups in a market separated by their elasticity of demand.

Time series data   Data collected over a period of time for a given variable (e.g., output).

Total cost function   A mathematical relationship that shows how total costs vary with the factors that influence total costs, including the quantity of output and the prices of inputs.

Total fixed cost   The cost of fixed inputs that do not vary with output.

Total revenue   Selling price times the quantity of products sold.

Total variable cost   The sum of expenditure on variable inputs, such as labour and materials.

Variance   A measure of the riskiness of a set of pay-offs with probabilities attached. It is the expected value of the squared deviations between the possible outcomes and the expected value of the pay-offs.

Vertical merger   A merger between two firms operating at different stages of the production process.

Transaction cost   The cost of using the market, such as discovering prices and making and enforcing contracts.

Uncertainty   Where there is no relevant previous experience and the expected pay-offs have subjective probabilities attached.

Variable cost   A cost that varies as output changes.

Vertical integration   Where a firm owns and/or controls activities either backward or forward from its position in the production chain.

INDEX